Sidonius
Letters Book 5, Part 1

Edinburgh Studies in Later Latin Literature

Series Editors
Gavin Kelly and Aaron Pelttari, University of Edinburgh

Ground-breaking scholarship on Latin literature from the later Roman and post-Roman world

Edinburgh Studies in Later Latin Literature offers a forum for new scholarship on important and sometimes neglected works. The later Roman and post-Roman world, between the second and seventh century, saw the creation of major texts and critical developments in writing. Texts of all kinds are treated here with careful attention to their various historical contexts.

Volumes include scholarly monographs and editions with commentaries. Modern critical and theoretical methods together provide new interpretations of the surviving Latin literature; these approaches include textual history, transmission, philology in the broad sense, and reception studies. This series provides access to our best understanding of what survives in the written record and makes modern interpretations of later Latin literature more widely available.

Editorial Advisory Board
Therese Fuhrer, University of Munich
Lucy Grig, University of Edinburgh
Isabella Gualandri, University of Milan
Philip Hardie, University of Cambridge
Calum Maciver, University of Edinburgh
Justin Stover, University of Edinburgh

Books available
Judith Hindermann, *Sidonius Apollinaris' Letters, Book 2: Text, Translation and Commentary*
Giulia Marolla, *Sidonius: Letters Book 5, Part 1. Text, Translation and Commentary*

https://edinburghuniversitypress.com/series-edinburgh-studies-in-later-latin-literature

SIDONIUS
LETTERS BOOK 5, PART 1

TEXT, TRANSLATION AND COMMENTARY

Giulia Marolla

EDINBURGH
University Press

Edinburgh University Press is one of the leading university presses in the UK. We publish academic books and journals in our selected subject areas across the humanities and social sciences, combining cutting-edge scholarship with high editorial and production values to produce academic works of lasting importance. For more information visit our website: edinburghuniversitypress.com

© Giulia Marolla 2023, 2024

Cover picture: Vatican City, Biblioteca Apostolica Vaticana, Urb. lat. 1515, f. 3v.
© Biblioteca Apostolica Vaticana, all rights reserved.

Edinburgh University Press Ltd
13 Infirmary Street
Edinburgh EH1 1LT

First published in hardback by Edinburgh University Press 2023

Typeset in Bembo
by R. J. Footring Ltd, Derby, and
printed and bound by CPI Group (UK) Ltd
Croydon, CR0 4YY

A CIP record for this book is available from the British Library

ISBN 978 1 3995 1077 6 (hardback)
ISBN 978 1 3995 1078 3 (paperback)
ISBN 978 1 3995 1079 0 (webready PDF)
ISBN 978 1 3995 1080 6 (epub)

The right of Giulia Marolla to be identified as the author of this work has been asserted in accordance with the Copyright, Designs and Patents Act 1988, and the Copyright and Related Rights Regulations 2003 (SI No. 2498).

CONTENTS

Lists of Figures	x
Acknowledgements	xi
List of Abbreviations	xii
General Introduction	1
Letters as autobiography?	2
The arrangement of the Letters	7
Themes and structure of Book 5	8
A life in autumn	9
Diversity of themes and letter lengths within Book 5	11
Categorisation of the letters by genre	13
Principles of arrangement	16
Manuscript tradition	18
The new stemma	18
The α branch and the *editio princeps*	21
An introduction to Letters 5.1–5.10	24
Prosopography	24
Dating	25
Sidonius' models: Pliny the Younger and Symmachus	27
Sidonius' language	28
Rare words	30
Neologisms	31
Most problematic readings	31
Prose rhythm	32
Letters 5.1–5.10. Text, Translation and Commentary	
Letter 1	43
Content	43
The addressee Petronius	43
The letter bearer Vindicius	45
Genre: an accompanying note and a *commendaticia*	45

CONTENTS

The opening letter	49
The letters Petronius reads and the new ones he has been gifted	51
Dating elements	53
SIDONIUS PETRONIO SUO SALUTEM	54
SIDONIUS TO HIS FRIEND PETRONIUS	55
Commentary	56
Letter 2	64
Content	64
The addressee Nymphidius	64
Sidonius and Mamertus Claudianus	65
Genre: a letter on literary matters	65
In the middle of a dispute	67
Nine arts: traces of Varro?	70
The merits of the *De statu animae*	73
The dedication of the *De statu animae*	77
Dating elements	79
SIDONIUS NYMPHIDIO SUO SALUTEM	82
SIDONIUS TO HIS DEAR NYMPHIDIUS	83
Commentary	84
Letter 3	93
Content	93
The addressee Apollinaris	93
Genre: the epistolary silence in Sidonius and its models	94
Beyond the model: traces of a rift with Apollinaris?	97
Internal evidence of uneasiness	100
External evidence	101
A valetudinarian letter	102
A topos within the topos?	102
Dating elements	105
SIDONIUS APOLLINARI SUO SALUTEM	108
SIDONIUS TO HIS DEAR APOLLINARIS	109
Commentary	110
Letter 4	123
Content	123
The addressee Simplicius: an identification problem	123
An alternative theory on Simplicius' identity	127

CONTENTS

Genre	129
Dating elements	130
SIDONIUS SIMPLICIO SUO SALUTEM	132
SIDONIUS TO HIS DEAR SIMPLICIUS	133
Commentary	134

Letter 5	142
Content	142
Genre: a letter of *admonitio*	142
The addressee Syagrius	144
Sidonius and the legislative activity of the Burgundians and Visigoths	145
Barbarisms	149
De barbarismis: Quintilian, Consentius and Sidonius	150
Dating elements	152
SIDONIUS SYAGRIO SUO SALUTEM	154
SIDONIUS TO HIS DEAR SYAGRIUS	155
Commentary	156

Letter 6	168
Content	168
The addressee Apollinaris	168
Genre	168
A rift is bridged	170
Context	170
The ambiguity in the mentions of Chilperic	171
The itinerary	173
Traces of an editing phase?	173
Dating elements	174
Seasonal reference	174
SIDONIUS APOLLINARI SUO SALUTEM	176
SIDONIUS TO HIS DEAR APOLLINARIS	177
Commentary	178

Letter 7	188
Content	188
The addressee Thaumastus	188
The models: Cicero, Tacitus, Juvenal and Apuleius	189
The features of informants	191

vii

CONTENTS

A display piece	193
The *tetrarcha*: Chilperic I or Chilperic II?	194
The Burgundian queen	199
The features of the rulers in *Ep.* 5.7	201
Dating elements	202
SIDONIUS THAUMASTO SUO SALUTEM	204
SIDONIUS TO HIS DEAR THAUMASTUS	205
Commentary	208
Letter 8	242
Content	242
The addressee Secundinus	242
Genre	243
Satire or *uersus populares*?	244
Sidonius' mentions of 'satire'	246
The Arles satire and the satires of Secundinus	247
Ablabius and the couplet against Constantine	251
Dating elements	252
SIDONIUS SECUNDINO SUO SALUTEM	256
SIDONIUS TO HIS DEAR SECUNDINUS	257
Commentary	258
Letter 9	272
Content	272
The addressee Aquilinus	272
Genre: a declaration of friendship	272
Historical context: emperors, generals and usurpers	275
Dating elements	278
SIDONIUS AQUILINO SUO SALUTEM	280
SIDONIUS TO HIS DEAR AQUILINUS	281
Commentary	282
Letter 10	295
Content	295
The addressee Sapaudus	295
Genre: literary matters and praise of intellectuals	296
Mamertus Claudianus' letter to Sapaudus	297
The theme of pretended literary decay	299
Dating elements	301

CONTENTS

SIDONIUS SAPAUDO SUO SALUTEM   304
SIDONIUS TO HIS DEAR SAPAUDUS   305
  Commentary   306

Appendix: Corrections to the Apparatus of Lütjohann and Loyen   322

Bibliography   327

Index Locorum   342
Index Nominum Antiquorum   360

FIGURES

Figures

1	Map of Sidonius' Gaul, c. 380–c. 480	xiv
2	Dolveck's stemma, simplified	19
3	Maple wood lyre, fragmented. Sutton Hoo, ship-burial mound	165
4	Genealogical tree of the Burgundian 'royal family'	196

Acknowledgements

Since the first day we discussed a PhD project on Book 5 in his office, back in 2016, Gavin Kelly has been vital to this research and I have incurred more debts to his wisdom and generosity than I can ever say. I should like to offer equally warm thanks to Stefania Santelia, who introduced me to late Latin literature and has been a constant and most precious interlocutor for a decade. My heartfelt thanks to Luciano Canfora, Silvia Condorelli, Roy Gibson, Aaron Pelttari and Joop van Waarden, who offered valuable reactions, suggestions and corrections. The book was also substantially improved by the comments of the anonymous readers who thoughtfully reviewed the manuscript. I profited from the generosity of Justin Favrod and Danuta Shanzer, who sent me their works during the gloomy months of national lockdown, and I thank with special warmth Roberta Berardi and Luisa Fizzarotti for their formidable bibliographical help. I am grateful to the Scuola Superiore di Studi Storici of the Università della Repubblica di San Marino for funding my work, to the scientific committee and staff in San Marino for taking care of my development as a scholar, to the staff at Biblioteca di Scienze dell'Antichità at the Università di Bari Aldo Moro, where I conducted most of the research, and to the ever-welcoming colleagues at the University of Edinburgh, where I spent the very first and last phases of writing. I would also like to thank the Institut de recherche et d'histoire des textes for allowing me access to a digital reproduction of CP 347 which belongs to a private collection and is not accessible to the public. I would like to offer additional thanks to the Press Committee of Edinburgh University Press, to Rachel Bridgewater, Ralph Footring, Carol Macdonald and the editorial staff of the Press who guided me during the publication process.

To my loving family: without your constant encouragement and support this book would never have been written.

ABBREVIATIONS

For full names of ancient authors and works see the Index locorum.

CIL   Mommsen, T., et al. (eds), *Corpus Inscriptionum Latinarum*, Berlin, 1863–.

CE   *Codex Euricianus.*

cett.   *ceteri codices* (all other manuscripts collated).

CLE   Bücheler, F. (ed.), *Carmina Latina Epigraphica*, editio stereotypa, Amsterdam, 1964 (Leipzig, 1897).

CSEL   Corpus Scriptorum Ecclesiasticorum Latinorum.

CTh   *Codex Theodosianus.*

DNP   *Der neue Pauly: Enzyklopädie der Antike*, H. Cancik and H. Schneider (eds), Stuttgart, 1996–2003.

IRHT   Institut de recherche et d'histoire des textes, Paris.

L&S   Lewis, C. T. and Short, C., *A Latin Dictionary*, Oxford, 1879.

LLT   *Library of Latin Texts Series A.*

MGH   Monumenta Germaniae Historica.

OCD   Hornblower, S., Spawforth, A. and Eidinow, E. (eds), *The Oxford Classical Dictionary* (4th edition), Oxford, 2012.

OLD   Glare, A. P., et al., *Oxford Latin Dictionary* (2nd edition), Oxford, 2012.

PCBE 4   Pietri, L. and Heijmans, M. (eds), *Prosopographie Chrétienne du Bas-Empire: 4 La Gaule Chrétienne (314–614)*, Paris, 2013.

PIR[1]   Kebbs, E., Dessau, H. and von Rohden, P. (eds), *Prosopographia Imperii Romani*, Berlin, 1897–8.

PIR[2]   Groag, E., Stein, A., et al. (eds), *Prosopographia Imperii Romani*, ed. altera, Berlin, 1933–2015.

PL   *Patrologia Latina.*

PLRE 1 and 2 Jones, A. H. M., Martindale, J. R. and Morris, J. (eds), *The Prosopography of the Later Roman Empire*, vol. I, *A.D. 260–395* (Cambridge, 1971); Martindale, J. R. (ed.),

LIST OF ABBREVIATIONS

	The Prosopography of the Later Roman Empire, vol. II, *A.D. 395–527* (Cambridge, 1980).
RE	Pauly, A. F., Wissowa, G., et al. (eds), *Paulys Real-Encyclopädie der classischen Altertumswissenschaft*, Stuttgart, 1893–1980.
TLL	Vollmer, F., et al. (eds), *Thesaurus Linguae Latinae*, Leipzig, 1900–.

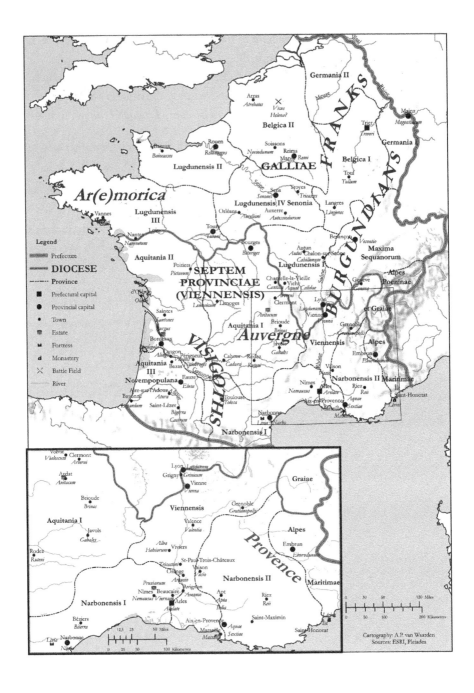

Figure 1. Map of Sidonius' Gaul, c. 380–c. 480. © Pieter van Waarden, all rights reserved.

General Introduction

Over the last fifty years there has been an ever-increasing scholarly interest in C. Sollius Apollinaris Sidonius' *Letters*.[1] Commentaries on single books of the letter collection have been issued since Helga Köhler published the commentary on Book 1 in 1995, followed by David Amherdt on Book 4, Filomena Giannotti on Book 3, Johannes van Waarden on Book 7 and Judith Hindermann on Book 2.[2] Commentaries on other Sidonian letter books are also being undertaken at the time of writing (2022): Willum Westenholz on Book 6, Marco Onorato on Book 8 and Silvia Condorelli on Book 9. Thus, this volume (the first of two volumes on Book 5, covering letters 1–10, with a second to cover letters 11–21) falls within a broader intellectual programme of providing the fundamental tool of a commentary for the complete *Letters* of Sidonius.[3]

---

1. Although claiming there is an 'explosion of studies' in a field happens to be an academic cliché, Kelly 2021a has demonstrated through statistical data that, as far as Sidonius is concerned, there really has been a surge of scholarly interest in the last decades, in particular in Italian scholarship from the 1990s, followed by increased scholarly production in French and English since 2010. For the *Letters*, landmarks include Isabella Gualandri's groundbreaking *Furtiva Lectio* (1979); Jill Harries' *Sidonius Apollinaris and the Fall of Rome* (1994) and Mathisen's numerous contributions on Sidonian prosopography (I will refer for brevity to his 'A Prosopography of Sidonius', which brings together many of his previous arguments – see Mathisen 2020). A most useful and complete account of Sidonian scholarship from the *editio princeps* to this day is in Furbetta 2020 (fifteenth to nineteenth centuries) and Condorelli 2020b (twentieth to twenty-first centuries).
2. Amherdt 2001; Giannotti 2016; van Waarden 2010 and 2016; Hindermann 2022.
3. The Sidonius Apollinaris for the Twenty-First Century project and the scholarly debate it fostered helped to make the gap in commentaries on Sidonius apparent, and some of the commentaries to appear are formally part of it. The need for Sidonian commentaries has been articulated in van Waarden's introductory remarks to *New Approaches to Sidonius Apollinaris* (2013, 3–11), where he also argues in favour of the publication of a comprehensive commentary on Sidonius' works. At the time of writing, Green (2022) published his English translation of and commentary on the *Carmina*, and an Italian translation and commentary is in preparation – see Santelia forthcoming.

This volume, with its projected sequel, is the first commentary on Book 5 to be published.[4] My study seeks to pursue a holistic approach, combining philological, historical and literary angles. For this reason, I provide readers with a freshly edited text, having collated the letters in the highest manuscripts of Franz Dolveck's *stemma codicum*.[5]

Letters as autobiography?

As an aristocrat, an office-holder, a poet and later bishop of Clermont in the period when Roman government was replaced by kingdoms under the Romans' former 'barbarian' allies, Sidonius (c. 430 – 479 or after) gives us vivid eyewitness testimony to both high politics and ordinary life. In Michael Kulikowski's words, 'Sidonius was born into a world that had ceased to exist at the time of his death'.[6] His artful letters are often the only source for the events described, and Book 5 provides readers with crucial insight on the transition to post-imperial Gaul. It testifies to the shift in relations between the (former) centre and peripheries, and to how the old categories are not applicable to the new local powers. Burgundians and Visigoths are the creators of a new system, which Sidonius finds hard to conceptualise, and is therefore even harder for scholars to conceptualise.

The events in Sidonius' life in relation to an ever-evolving political and social milieu, and to the turmoil of the last days of Roman rule in Gaul, are thoroughly analysed and contextualised in the comprehensive *Edinburgh Companion to Sidonius Apollinaris*. In light of the depth and breadth of information on Sidonius, his family and his time provided by the *Companion,* it seems superfluous to linger on details concerning his life in this volume. Therefore, this section will provide the reader with some biographical coordinates, useful for navigating the events mentioned in Book 5; however, for detailed information concerning the author and his time throughout the text, the reader will be redirected to chapters of the *Companion.*

---

4. Unpublished works on Book 5 include Giulietti's doctoral thesis on letters 1–13 (2014) at the University of Macerata, as well as a Master thesis (2003) by Becchi at the University of Siena (which has proved hard to locate).

5. I am thankful for having had access to Dolveck 2020 before its publication in *The Edinburgh Companion to Sidonius Apollinaris.*

6. Kulikowski 2020, 197. For the complexity of these years see also Delaplace 2015; Mratschek 2020, 214–36.

GENERAL INTRODUCTION

First, a necessary caveat: the information we have on Sidonius is purely autobiographical, as has been repeatedly pointed out, by Harries, Hanaghan, and van Waarden among others.[7] The partiality and fragmentary nature of the information Sidonius carefully chooses to enclose in his collection is an obstacle that cannot be overcome, and one has to acknowledge the limitedness of having Sidonius as the sole witness of most of the autobiographical events he mentions in his artful letter collection and specifically in Book 5.[8] Books 1–7 are believed to have been edited by Sidonius for publication in 477, soon after his return from exile, and it is impossible to state to what extent letters were modified, edulcorated or even created for the sake of publication.[9] As will be seen in more detail in the section on dating below, although a broad chronological progression can be detected in the first three books, Sidonius' letters are not arranged in chronological order, in accordance with epistolographical trends and with Pliny's programmatic assertion in his *Ep.* 1.1.1 *collegi non seruato temporis ordine.*[10]

In order to help the less experienced reader of Sidonius approaching the autobiographical mentions in Book 5, I list here the most relevant events in his life in relation to the letters of the book.

429–32 Sidonius was born in Lyon on 5 November, though in which year is uncertain.

452–5 Sidonius married Papianilla, daughter of Eparchius Avitus. *Ep.* 5.16 is addressed to Papianilla (it is the only letter to a woman in the collection) but it provides readers with scant information concerning her as it is entirely focused on her brother (see below).

455 Sidonius' father-in-law Eparchius Avitus became emperor with the support of the Visigothic king Theoderic II, praised for his Romanness and as a model of *ciuilitas.*[11] Theoderic has been

---

7. Harries 1994,1; Hanaghan 2019, 18–20; van Waarden 2020a, 13.

8. As is argued by Gibson and Morello 2012, 13, although letter collections cannot be equated with autobiography, 'clearly they possess autobiographical potential', which should be scrutinised.

9. For the date of publication see e.g. Harries 1994, 8; van Waarden 2020a, 26; for the impossibility of determining with any certainty the extent of letter adaptation or even creation for the collection see Kelly 2020, 181–5. In this book I signal passages which appear to have been supplemented with details for the sake of the readers and letters which could have been created for the collection: see e.g. the introduction to *Ep.* 5.7.

10. Gibson 2012, 68–70; Gibson 2020, 378 n. 39. Loyen's edition is generally followed in the present volume for Sidonius quotations.

11. On Theoderic II see Gualandri 2000, 107–18; Fascione 2019a, 53–62.

3

suggested as a likely candidate for the identification of the hunting *rex* of Secundinus' panegyrics mentioned in *Ep.* 5.8.

456 Sidonius recited the Panegyric for the consulship of Avitus in Rome (*Carm.* 7). Avitus, however, was defeated by Ricimer and is believed either to have been killed or to have been forced into a bishopric and to have died soon after.

458 Sidonius recited the Panegyric of Majorian (*Carm.* 5).

461 Majorian was murdered. Around this time Sidonius was baptised by Faustus of Riez, who is commonly believed to have been the author of the anonymous letter *Quaeris me*, refuted by Mamertus Claudianus in his *De statu animae*. For further context and for the dispute between the two see *Ep.* 5.2.

466–7 Euric murdered his brother Theoderic II and thus became king of the Visigoths. Sidonius presents him on various occasions as the embodiment of otherness and the negation of the good qualities of the former monarch.[12] In 467, at the head of a Gallic delegation, Sidonius informed emperor Anthemius of Euric's predatory attitude.

468 A prosperous year for Sidonius: he recited the Panegyric of Anthemius (*Carm.* 2) and was named *patricius* and *praefectus urbi*.

468–9 The 'Arvandus affair' took place. Sidonius informed Arvandus, the twice *praefectus praetorio Galliarum* (464–8),[13] of the accusations that a Gallic delegation comprising the author's relatives and friends was bringing against him, aiming at his impeachment. Arvandus, who was accused of collusion with the Visigoths, underestimated the seriousness of the charge and acted defiantly when questioned.[14] Sidonius, who at the time was *praefectus urbi* and therefore a judicial authority, did not attend the trial in Rome but neither did he explain his absence from the city. In 469, in the aftermath of the Arvandus affair, it seems likely Sidonius had been shunned by close friends and family members, as can be surmised from *Epp.* 5.3

---

12. On Euric as a *lupus* see Fo 1999, 21–2; for his being the antithesis of Theoderic see Gualandri 2000, 118–29, and Fascione 2019a, 62–3.

13. After the year 395 the system of prefects was stabilised, as is shown in the *Notitia Dignitatum*: the four prefectures of the Gauls, Italy, Illyricum, and the East were each entrusted to a praetorian prefect, who was the highest judicial, financial, and tax authority. See Jones 1964, I, 370; Porena 2007, and (for the East) Laniado 2018.

14. In *Ep.* 1.7 Sidonius describes the trial and admits he had alerted his friend Arvandus; on Arvandus see *PLRE* II, 157–8; Mathisen 2020, 82; Harries 1994, 159–66; see also the introductions to *Epp.* 5.3 and 5.4 in the present volume.

GENERAL INTRODUCTION

and 5.4, in which the author complains of being ignored by his relatives.

469   Sidonius probably published Book 1 of the *Letters*.

469–70   Sidonius' election as bishop of Clermont-Ferrand is dated to this time. Loyen believed the election could be dated as late as 471,[15] but an earlier date (469–70) is likelier. The possibility that his accession to the bishopric should be seen as a removal from political life when he was in disfavour for his implicit support of Arvandus deserves serious consideration.[16]

471–4   Every summer, Euric's Visigoths besieged Clermont. Sidonius led the resistance with the help of Burgundian troops and of his brother-in-law Ecdicius. As is argued by Delaplace, Sidonius started being closer to the Burgundians by virtue of their support against the Visigothic threat.[17] *Ep.* 5.12 to Calminius is written during one of the seasonal sieges.

473   Sidonius introduced *Rogationes* in Clermont. In *Ep.* 5.14 Sidonius explains that bishop Mamertus (the elder brother of Mamertus Claudianus)[18] is the *inuentor* of these public celebrations, which were being held at the time he was writing to the addressee, Aper.

474   Julius Nepos became emperor. In both *Epp.* 5.6.2 and 5.7.1, concerning rumours of his relative Apollinaris having encountered disfavour at the Burgundian court, he is vaguely mentioned as 'the new *princeps*'.[19] Presumably in 474 the emperor granted to Ecdicius, Sidonius' brother-in-law, the rank of patrician, and this appointment is enthusiastically welcomed by Sidonius in *Ep.* 5.16 to Papianilla. It seems worthy of mention, however, that in this laudatory self-representation of his extended family, the figure of Ecdicius overshadows that of the emperor, whose only acknowledged merit seems to be that of having granted him the rank of patrician, which had been repeatedly promised by the previous emperor, Anthemius.

475   Julius Nepos surrendered Auvergne to Euric in exchange for Provence and Sidonius was exiled to Livia.

---

15. Loyen 1970a, xv.

16. See van Waarden 2020a, 23. For the political significance of the bishopric in the fifth century see Consolino 1979, 89–91.

17. Delaplace 2015, 249.

18. See Mathisen 2020, 106.

19. A useful dating element for both letters – see comments ad loc.

476–7	Sidonius was pardoned, helped by Leo of Narbonne, who had a key role at Euric's court, being the writer of the king's speeches and probably his legislator.[20]
477	Sidonius is generally believed to have published Books 1–7 of the *Letters* in (or very close to) this year. It is the only certain *terminus ante quem* for those letters that lack dating elements and for which Loyen's chronology proves to be unsustainable or arbitrary. At separate points after 477, Books 8 and 9 were published.
479/ 480s	Death of Sidonius. The only two manuscripts containing Sidonius' epitaph have different readings when it comes to the date of his death.[21] The Madrid manuscript, known as codex *C* (*Matritensis* 9448) reads 21 August *Zenone imperatore*, 'under the reign of Zeno', an indication which leads to the inference that 491 is a *terminus ante quem* for the death of Sidonius. On the other hand, the epitaph in the IRHT manuscript (collection privée 347) reads 21 August *Zenone consule*, which leads scholars to date Sidonius' death to Zeno's consulship in 479. Valuable observations are being made by scholars in support of the reliability of both manuscript sources. The 479 date is rejected by scholars who consider *Ep.* 9.12 as evidence that Sidonius was still alive in 482; in this letter, the author states he has been poetically silent for three Olympiads.[22] Loyen dates the interruption of poetical production evoked in the letter to his becoming a man of the cloth (between 469 and 470) and therefore dates the composition of *Ep.* 9.12 to either 481 or 482.[23] Accepting Sidonius was still alive in 482, therefore, would not be coherent with the subscription of the IRHT manuscript; however, Kelly recently suggested an alternative:[24] the death date of 21 August 479 could be authentic should one consider that Sidonius' poetical silence started from his last major verse composition, namely the Panegyric of Anthemius, dated to 1 January 468.

---

20. See introduction to *Ep.* 5.5 and my comments in Marolla 2021a, 64–8 on Sidonius' changed attitude towards the Visigothic king.

21. For the *status quaestionis* see Mathisen 2020, 61–4. Two fragments of this epitaph were found in 1991 in Clermont-Ferrand (see Prévot 1993); although the discovery confirmed the authenticity of the transmitted text, the preserved fragments do not include the subscription concerning the date of his death.

22. *Ep.* 9.12.1–2 *ab exordio religiosae professionis … postquam in silentio decurri tres olympiadas.*

23. Loyen 1970a, xxiii; Loyen 1970b, 219. Similarly, Köhler 1995, 8.

24. Kelly 2020, 189.

GENERAL INTRODUCTION

The arrangement of the Letters

Being the editor of his own letter collection, Sidonius *chose* to structure it in nine books. The obvious model was the senatorial tradition of epistolary writing, and mainly the letters of Pliny the Younger and Symmachus, of which Sidonius intended to be a continuator.[25] And yet, structuring a letter collection in books was not the norm by the time Sidonius was publishing his correspondence. Not being characteristic of the collections which were chronologically closer to him, the book division was an artistic choice.

In terms of materiality, the book as a compositional unit was no longer necessary in the age of the codex, as is apparent when thinking of the great letter collections of Jerome, Paulinus of Nola and Augustine. These epistolary corpora were not originally divided into books and, as Gibson put it, 'there exists no late antique canonical edition or ordering of their correspondence'.[26] Jerome was keen to have his letters circulate early on, either independently or in thematical dossiers. There is evidence that he chose to have some of his pre-393 correspondence circulating as separate collections (mainly his *Epistularum ad diversos liber unus*; *Ad Marcellam epistularum liber unus* and his exchanges with Damasus), but a late antique or medieval archetype of his complete correspondence did not exist.[27] Paulinus is believed not to have kept copies of his own letters, and, in light of the probable lack of a single archetype for the manuscripts, the collection and publication of his letters are likely to have been posthumous.[28] As for Augustine, the manuscripts of his over 300 extant letters reflect traditions which diverge considerably from each other in terms of the order and number of letters transmitted.[29]

Unlike the collections of his immediate predecessors, Sidonius' *Letters* are not the product of arbitrariness, nor of the editorial criteria of others. Careful selection and arrangement of letters in books are the product of

---

25. As Sidonius declares programmatically in *Ep.* 1.1.1, on which more below.

26. Gibson 2012, 77. For Ambrose's not being a model for Sidonius, see Gibson 2020, 389 n. 85.

27. For further details see Cain 2009, 13–19, 68–71, 223–7. One could also mention his *Ep.* 123 on monogamy as a post-393 example. Jerome says the letter (*libellus*) will circulate as a treatise by the name of his addressee, Geruchia (*Ep.* 123.17), and urges her to read similar letters (*Epp.* 54 and 79) he has already written on the same topic together with the famous letter 22, which he calls *liber*. See Marolla 2017, 127–8.

28. Conybeare 2000, 13–15.

29. In 1981, Divjak published a substantial group of unknown letters (1*–29*) he found in two manuscripts, Marseille 209 and Par. lat. 16861. See Divjak 1981, ix–x; xiii–xiv.

well-pondered authorial design, which should not be overlooked when reading single letters of the collection.

Themes and structure of Book 5

Book 5 can be considered as a middle book in many respects other than its position in the collection, and looking at the *Letters* as a whole allows one to perceive its transitional nature. Book 1 notably centres around Rome and Sidonius' political influence, and while in Book 2 'Gallic aristocracy at leisure' could be considered the dominant theme,[30] in Book 3 Sidonius 'the bishop' is actively engaged in defending Clermont from Euric's siege and the author traces a portrait of himself as a leader of heroic stature.[31] Book 4 shows a complexity and variety of themes closer to those of Book 5,[32] whereas Book 6 is known as 'the book of the bishopric' since its letters are exclusively addressed to bishops. Letters to fellow bishops are similarly found in blocks in Books 7 (*Epp.* 1–11), 8 (*Epp.* 13–15) and 9 (*Epp.* 2–11). Moreover, the second half of Book 7 comprises letters dedicated to spiritual themes,[33] while both Book 8 and the second half of Book 9 stand out for the *carmina* studiously incorporated in the epistles.[34]

Compared with the Books 6 and 7,[35] Book 5 stands out for its peculiar features, since the author's representation of his literary persona touches upon different aspects of his life, and one can distinguish Sidonius the influential politician, the cultivated reader, the poet and the relative, while Sidonius the bishop mostly remains in the background. There are only passing mentions of the bishopric, such as the brief description of his feelings concerning

---

30. On *otium* in Book 2 see Hindermann 2022, viii–xii.
31. Mirroring Pliny's assumption of the consulship in his Book 3 – see Gibson 2012, 69. On the themes of the first three books being 'career, leisure and crisis' see Hindermann 2022, xi.
32. As argued by Gibson 2020, 378, the following broad topics can be identified in Book 4: 'politics and contemporary realities; literary matters; the courtesies and events of friendship, including praise of *amici*; and religious and ecclesiastical matters'. As will be argued in the section on the categorisation of the letters, the same themes are also distinctive of Book 5.
33. Letters 7.12–18 are significantly called 'the ascetic letters' by van Waarden 2016.
34. Sidonius claims to have written Book 8 at Petronius' request, by emptying his *scrinia* looking for additional letters to publish. For the dedication to Petronius also of Book 5, see the introduction to *Ep.* 5.1.
35. Books 1–7 are believed by most scholars to have been published together in 477; for this date see Kelly 2020, 180.

GENERAL INTRODUCTION

his appointment in *Ep.* 5.3, or, in *Ep.* 5.14, the invitation to preside over Rogations in Clermont, which, however, appears to be an excuse to ask the addressee, Aper, to visit, rather than a request of a spiritual nature. Hence, the bishopric does not appear to play a crucial role in the narrative of events in Book 5 and, unlike the blocks mentioned above, no letter is sent to a fellow bishop.

Unlike the straightforward complaints in Books 7–9,[36] Sidonius does not explicitly mention the deal struck between the emperor Julius Nepos and the Visigothic king Euric in 475, nor his exile in the aftermath of that truce. And yet, this does not necessarily entail that contemporary events are not mentioned in Book 5: quite the opposite. Sidonius may not be as explicit about the political situation or his personal disappointment as he appears to be in later books, but a close reading reveals that convoluted expressions and careful language conceal unease, for instance in mentioning his new bishopric (*Ep.* 5.3); in defining the role the Burgundians have in Lyon (*Epp.* 5.6–5.7), and in the affected *reticentia* of *Ep.* 5.12 to Calminius. In this letter, the besieged Sidonius states he cannot openly speak about the Visigoths and that the *necessitas silentii*, dictated by fear that letters may be intercepted, is no doubt familiar to the addressee.[37]

Entering the field of speculation, one may conjecture either that Sidonius was not 'ready to speak his mind' about contemporary events, as Gibson suggests,[38] or that in Book 5 he did not envisage including material that was to be discussed in later books, but no firm conclusion can be reached given the heterogeneous nature of this book, which will be discussed in the following pages.

A life in autumn

One narratological observation deserves to be made about the 'mood' of the book and its position in the narrative arc of the collection (this follows up on an acute suggestion by Joop van Waarden): both explicit discussion and passing mentions of time in Book 5 all concern autumn. The seasonal references start with the image of himself as a tree, scattering words in place of

---

36. According to Gibson (2020, 378) Books 7–9 'include the darkest and hardest political material of the collection'.
37. *Ep.* 5.12.1.
38. Gibson 2013a, 210.

leaves in *Ep.* 5.3.3. This autumnal image conveys the mood of Sidonius the newly elected bishop and his feeling of unworthiness when he thinks of the pastoral guidance which is expected of him. This is the least explicit seasonal reference in the book; however, its detection may be useful to interpret the more explicit ones. *Ep.* 5.6.1 starts with the seasonal indication that the letter recounts the events that happened at the beginning of autumn (*cum aestas decessit autumno*). Although fleeting, the mention (*Ep.* 5.13.1) of the fallen leaves, which the diligent Evantius has had removed to facilitate the passage of Seronatus, hints at the same seasonal frame; while in *Ep.* 5.17.4 the heat of the night is said to resemble that of summer days, despite it being early autumn (*etsi iam primo frigore tamen autumnalis Aurorae detepescebat*).

Hanaghan has highlighted the importance of the seasonal references in Sidonius' letter collection. As he rightly points out, 'a clear sense of the progression of time is conveyed to the reader through Book 2, from the early summer of *Ep.* 2.2 through to the late autumn of *Ep.* 2.14'.[39] The same sense of the passing of time is detected by Hanaghan in Book 3, where Constantius' winter journey to Clermont (*Ep.* 3.2) is followed by Ecdicius' brave defence of Clermont in the summer (*Ep.* 3.3).

And yet, the impression conveyed by Book 5, which comprises letters from very different times and places, is that events are set in a protracted autumn. There is no signalled seasonal change which may hint at time progression, not even in *Epp.* 5.6 and 5.7, which concern the same episode and in which it is clear that some time must have passed between their composition.

One may venture to suggest this is a way to mirror Sidonius' mood at the time he put the book together: his perception that the summer days of his younger adulthood are almost behind him and that he is entering the autumn of his life.[40] The idea that he is now approaching old age is

---

39. See Hanaghan 2019, 73.
40. On Sidonius' perception of ageing see van Waarden 2018, 191–6; Hanaghan 2019, 181–2. Note how, similarly, Cicero, in *Cato* 19 (71), makes old age equivalent to autumn. The parallelism age/seasons is traditionally attributed to Pythagoreanism, although it is usually winter that is linked to senescence: in Ov. *Met.* 15.199–214 Pythagoras himself compares human ageing to the passing of the seasons (see in particular v. 212 *senilis hiems*); see also Diog. Laert. 8.1.10, and for further parallels see Powell 1988, 243. Winter stands for old age also in, for example, *AP* 5.258 and 10.100 (on which see Albiani 1995, 317 and 325). One cannot fail to mention Horace's Ode 4.7 for reflection on the endless cycle of seasons compared to the inevitability of human mortality, on which see Thomas 2011, 174–84. On Horace being one of Sidonius' favourite poets, see Stoehr-Monjou 2013; Pelttari 2016; Mratschek 2017.

GENERAL INTRODUCTION

expressed explicitly in *Ep.* 5.9.4, where the author tells the addressee that they are *in annis iam senectutis initia pulsantibus*. After all, Book 5 is the last book of the initial collection of Books 1–7 to comprise letters from both before and after his election to bishop: a time of political and social transition which can be compared to the passage from summer to autumn (as the image of the tree in *Ep.* 5.3 seems to suggest). As stated above, this can be considered as a transitional book, for many reasons other than its place in the collection, and the seasonal setting may be listed as further evidence of its unique nature. The seasonal progression would also be coherent with the context of the last letter of the collection, since *Ep.* 9.16 is set in winter and the symbolic function the wintry conditions described by Sidonius have in the last letters of Book 9 are well known to scholars.[41]

Diversity of themes and letter lengths within Book 5

As Gibson suggests, ancient categorisations of epistolary writing can be applied to Sidonius' letters with interesting results, since he was versed in the same rhetorical studies from which these systems of classifications were created.[42] The themes of letters in Book 5 can be fruitfully compared to the twenty-one types in Pseudo-Demetrius' Τύποι Ἐπιστολικοί.[43] Although, as

---

41. See Hanaghan 2019, 180–4; Kelly 2020, 189.
42. Gibson 2020, 383.
43. The twenty-one types listed by the Pseudo-Demetrius *Praef.* are the following: (i) friendly, (ii) commendatory, (iii) blaming, (iv) reproachful, (v) consoling, (vi) censorious, (vii) admonishing, (viii) threatening, (ix) vituperative, (x) praising, (xi) advisory, (xii) supplicatory, (xiii) inquiring, (xiv) responding, (xv) allegorical, (xvi) accounting, (xvii) accusing, (xviii) apologetic, (xix) congratulatory, (xx) ironic, (xxi) thankful (translated by Malherbe 1988, 31). A later classification is that by Ps.-Libanius listed in Ἐπιστολιμαῖοι Χαρακτῆρες 4: (i) advice; (ii) blame; (iii) request; (iv) recommendation; (v) irony; (vi) thanks; (vii) friendship; (viii) entreaty; (ix) threat; (x) denial; (xi) command; (xii) repentance; (xiii) reproach; (xiv) sympathy; (xv) conciliation; (xvi) congratulation; (xvii) contempt; (xviii) counter-accusation; (xix) reply; (xx) provocation; (xxi) consolation; (xxii) insult; (xxiii) news; (xxiv) indignation; (xxv) representation; (xxvi) praise; (xxvii) instruction; (xxviii) refutation; (xxix) slander; (xxx) reproof; (xxxi) enquiry; (xxxii) encouragement; (xxxiii) consultation; (xxxiv) declaration; (xxxv) mockery; (xxxvi) jesting ; (xxxvii) coded communication; (xxxviii) suggestion; (xxxix) grief; (xl) love; (xli) mixed type. For this passage see Trapp 2003, 191 and 323–6. For these two manuals of letter writing see the edition by Malosse 2004. A useful anthology of ancient epistolary theorists is also in Malherbe 1988, 30–41; a comparative study is in Fögen 2018, 49–55.

11

is argued later, a single letter could be ascribed to more than one category, it seems useful to employ classifications which were probably familiar to Sidonius.[44] The theorisation of these types outlined by Paolo Cugusi (1983) in his *Evoluzione e forme dell'epistolografia latina* proved useful in conducting a comparative study between Sidonius and his predecessors, mainly his declared models in *Ep.* 1.1.1, Pliny the Younger and Symmachus. When approaching the commentary on Book 5, it seemed sensible to take this programmatic assertion into account, to try to understand whether and in what way the Plinian and Symmachan imprint is detectable in the book.[45]

Therefore, once ascribed to a genre, letters are here compared to those of Pliny and Symmachus in which the same themes occur. To this end, the lack of a comprehensive study concerning Symmachus' *Letters* has been an undeniable obstacle, but nonetheless a pervasive presence of this author in the topics as well as in the language of Book 5 has been detected. This approach led to satisfactory results: it seems appropriate to correct Hanaghan's recent scepticism concerning the influence of Symmachus on Sidonius.[46] In *Epp.* 5.1–5.10 Symmachus is a model of genre and expression, even more than Pliny.

Only in macroscopic terms – of the length of letters and of the organisation of the book – does Pliny surpass Symmachus as a model. Gibson's general remarks concerning the variety of length of the letters within Sidonius' books being a form of emulation of Pliny also apply to Book 5.[47] Like Pliny, and unlike Symmachus – whose letters are notably succinct – Sidonius includes within Book 5 short salutations, longer letters and even particularly long letters (such as *Epp.* 5.7 and 5.17). To this diversity in

---

44. Fernández López 1994 structured her study on the letters of Sidonius by dividing them according to their function: metalinguistic, phatic, expressive, impressive, and declarative/poetic (with twenty-five subdivisions). However, as argued by van Waarden 2010, 37, this classification 'is all-encompassing to the detriment of clarity'; Gibson 2020, 384 is of the same opinion.

45. The presence of the Plinian model in Sidonius' epistolary collection has been discussed at length by Roy Gibson – e.g. Gibson 2011; Gibson 2013a; Gibson 2013b.

46. Hanaghan 2019, 16: 'It is unclear how influential a model Symmachus was, if at all; "following Symmachus' *rotunditas*" could in its narrowest sense simply mean publishing a single volume of letters. Occasional connections between Symmachus and Sidonius may be considered more usefully a product of their broad generic compatibility than the more deep and meaningful textual relationship that Sidonius develops between his epistles and Pliny's'. Fascione 2020 argued in favour of the identification of Symmachus as a model in Sidonius' perception and depiction of otherness; for Symmachus' presence in Book 8 see also Fascione 2019b.

47. Gibson 2020, 375.

GENERAL INTRODUCTION

length corresponds a variety of themes and addressees, like in Pliny,[48] while Symmachus' Books 1–7 are organised by addressee.[49]

Categorisation of the letters by genre

The following categorisation (summarised in Table 1) shows how varied the themes of Book 5 are. Most of Sidonius' letters can be ascribed to more than one genre.[50]

Table 1. Genres of the letters in Book 5

Letter	Genre	Addressee
5.1	Commendation	Petronius
5.2	Direct request/literary matters	Nymphidius
5.3	Epistolary silence/valetudinarian	Apollinaris (relative)
5.4	Epistolary silence	Simplicius (relative)
5.5	*Epistula symbuleutica*	Syagrius
5.6	*Epistula symbuleutica*	Apollinaris (relative)
5.7	Vituperative	Thaumastus (relative)
5.8	Literary matters/epistolary silence	Secundinus
5.9	Declaration of friendship (and family history)	Aquilinus
5.10	Literary matters	Sapaudus
5.11	Declaration of friendship	Potentinus
5.12	Epistolary silence (his own)	Calminius
5.13	Vituperative	Pannychius
5.14	Invitation	Aper
5.15	Commendation	Ruricius
5.16	Informative	Papianilla (his wife)
5.17	*Lettera d'arte*	Eriphius
5.18	Declaration of friendship	Attalus
5.19	Legal issue	Pudens
5.20	*Epistula symbuleutica*	Pastor
5.21	Direct request	Sacerdos and Iustinus

48. See Gibson 2020, 378.

49. For this criterion of arrangement of Symmachus' letters, for the diversity of Symm. Books 8–10, and for what this implies concerning a later publication, see Kelly 2013, 264–7; Kelly 2015, 199–201.

50. As argued by Gibson 2020, 378 the same difficulty applies to all the collection: single letters could be placed in more than one thematic grouping. Pliny, in contrast, more often than not tried to confine himself to a single theme in each letter.

13

Commendation (*Epp.* 5.1; 5.15)

The collection is opened under the sign of Symmachus with a *commendaticia* (unusual at the beginning of a book). *Epp.* 5.1 and 5.15 are close to Symmachus' commendation letters in terms of length, style and status of the *commendatus*, being considerably different from Pliny's detached commendations for imperial high offices.

Declaration of friendship (*Epp.* 5.9; 5.11; 5.18)

Praise of the addressee, the intention of strengthening ties of friendship and the possibility that those ties may grant future favours are all elements that can be gathered from these letters, which do not give information to the addressees but can be considered as a way to reconnect and re-establish Sidonius' network of contacts. Incidentally, these letters provide the reader with a comprehensive view of the extent of Sidonius' influence, or, rather, of his intended self-presentation as an influential aristocrat. Declarations of friendship can often be read in Symmachus' collection.

Direct request (*Epp.* 5.2; 5.21)

Although *Ep.* 5.2 can also be ascribed to the genre of literary matters, this letter (like *Ep.* 5.21) ends on a pragmatic note. Sidonius demands the return of his copy of Mamertus Claudianus' *De statu animae*, while in *Ep.* 5.21 he brazenly claims for himself the *carmina* of Victorius, being his 'successor by profession', as the addressees are by birth.

Epistolary silence (of others in *Epp.* 5.3; 5.4; 5.8; his own in 5.12)

Much has been said in the commentary on epistolary silence and in particular on the pervasive presence – both thematic and linguistic – of Symmachus as model. Complaining about being ignored by the addressee or asking for forgiveness for one's own failure to write were standard forms of interaction.

Informative (*Ep.* 5.16)

For obvious reasons informative letters are the most common type of private letter, as argued by Cugusi.[51] And yet, in Book 5, the informative content is often subsidiary to other defining elements, with the exception of *Ep.* 5.16. This letter, addressed to his wife, Papianilla, is also the only letter addressed to a woman in Sidonius' letter collection, and yet it does not concern her directly as much as her brother, Ecdicius. Including this informative letter

---

51. Cugusi 1983, 106.

GENERAL INTRODUCTION

in the collection may have the purpose of highlighting the news that his brother-in-law had received patrician dignity.

Invitation (*Ep.* 5.14)
Letters of invitations are very common in letter writing. In *Ep.* 5.14 Sidonius invites Aper to attend *Rogations* in Clermont, though he does not spare his friend some wry comments on his being at leisure.

Legal (*Ep.* 5.19)
Though in some letters there are references to justice (*Ep.* 5.7) – or to minor legal issues like inheritance in *Ep.* 5.21 – *Ep.* 5.19 is the only letter of the book entirely dedicated to a crime and distinguishes itself as a legal letter. The son of Pudens' wet-nurse had seduced the daughter of Sidonius' wet-nurse, hence the author discusses reparations.

Lettera d'arte (*Ep.* 5.17)
Cugusi's definition of *lettera d'arte* as a text aimed at *delectare* rather than *docere* and which avails itself of numerous rhetorical devices seems apt to describe this letter.[52] *Ep.* 5.17 shows unity of content and the aim of informing the reader is overshadowed by the entertaining features of the writing. It is a type of letter favoured by Pliny the Younger.

Literary matters (*Epp.* 5.2; 5.8; 5.10)
As the introduction to *Ep.* 5.2 explains at length, letters on literary matters had been common in epistolary collections since the Late Republic. Both Pliny and Symmachus are wont to praise literary works of friends in their letter collections. While in Sidon. *Ep.* 5.2 the object of praise is not the addressee but Mamertus Claudianus, in *Epp.* 5.8 and 5.10 it is the addressee, Secundinus and Sapaudus respectively, who is praised for his literary prowess.

Symbuleuticae (*Epp.* 5.5; 5.6; 5.20)
Sidonius' *symbuleuticae* are very different from those of Pliny the Younger:[53] the latter usually wrote advisory letters to friends who were about to assume an imperial office, while Sidonius' unsolicited advice usually concerns personal matters. The author admonishes Syagrius to stop speaking Burgundian in *Ep.* 5.5, he exhorts his relative Apollinaris to inform him about

---

52. Cugusi 1983, 127.
53. See the introduction to *Ep.* 5.5.

his troubled situation (so that Sidonius may be of service) in *Ep.* 5.6, and in *Ep.* 5.20 he calls upon Pastor not to miss another city council meeting, since it is clear he is avoiding his peers in order not to receive another assignment as ambassador.

Valetudinarian (*Ep.* 5.3)
In addition to epistolatory silence, *Ep.* 5.3 is also ascribable to the genre of valetudinarian letters, given that Sidonius, unprompted, informs the addressee about his health. This is a type of letter often found in Symmachus' letter collection and, before him, in Fronto's.[54]

Vituperative (*Ep.* 5.7; 5.13)
The informants of *Ep.* 5.7 and Seronatus of *Ep.* 5.13 are the object of personal attacks in letters addressed to others. *Epp.* 5.7 and 5.13 could also be ascribed to the broader category of *lettere d'arte* for the sophistication of language and for the undeniable intent to entertain. And yet, highly polemical content, masterful belittlement of enemies through rhetorical devices including absurd images, abusive language and uncommon expressions reminiscent of the ferocity of archaic comedy are the dominant features of these two letters.

Principles of arrangement

At first glance, the most distinctive feature of Book 5 seems to be *uarietas*, in accordance with Pliny's abundant theorisation of variety as a leading principle in the arrangement of a letter collection. Pliny argued in favour of variety in style, length and content of letters, so that the reader would not have given up reading a letter collection. According to Pliny, even if single letters do not meet the taste of the reader, the author can be confident that the book as a whole is likely to be appreciated because of its *uarietas*.[55] Therefore, even if a book may comprise letters on the same topic, they should not be addressed to the same person,[56] and this is the case, in Sidonius' Book 5, with *Epp.* 3 and 4 as well as *Epp.* 6 and 7.

---

54. Over eighty of the extant letters that Fronto exchanged with Marcus Aurelius revolve around the narrative of sickness and health, and notably Book 5 of Fronto's *Ad M. Caesarem* is dominated by the theme. See Freisenbruch 2007, 236 and *passim*.
55. As is explained by Pliny in *Ep.* 2.5.8, when he pictures the letter collection as a sumptuous dinner: each of the guests will abstain from a certain number of dishes, but in the end they will all praise the dinner in its entirety.
56. On Pliny's *uarietas* see Gibson and Morello 2012, 244–7.

GENERAL INTRODUCTION

Apart from *uarietas*, one may wonder what principles of arrangement guided the author and whether they are detectable. Looking at the book in its entirety,[57] and leaving aside the prefatory *Ep.* 5.1, which is added as a dedicatory note accompanying the book, the straightforward requests with which Sidonius opens and ends Book 5 stand out: letters 5.2 and 5.21 oddly concern a direct and outspoken claim on literary works of others. In *Ep.* 5.2 Sidonius seeks to regain possession of his own copy of Mamertus Claudianus' *De statu animae*; while in *Ep.* 5.21 he claims the right to inherit the autograph works of a deceased friend. Both letters are characterised by a bluntness which is unmatched in the rest of the book and the underlying reason why Sidonius decided to begin and end a book with direct requests may elude us. However, if one looks past the outer appearance of these letters, the self-representation of himself as an authority when it comes to literature, being the possessor of a prestigious book (which had been dedicated to him by the author) and the legitimate 'literary heir' of Victorius' poems, may provide the reader with a possible answer. Authorial self-representation as a literary authority is also one of the main themes of the book, as can be argued when reading Sidonius' unprompted opinion on contemporary literature in *Epp.* 5.8 and 5.10. Hence, it may not be an unfair speculation that at a time when Sidonius is not publishing poetry, he is seeking to establish himself as a literary authority, by fostering intellectual debate over contemporary literature. It can be argued, therefore, that in a 'transitional book', Sidonius pictures himself in a transitional role, that of a leading figure in literary matters, since he is not openly a poet as he used to be, and not fully immersed in the role of bishop, as he will be in Book 6.

Moreover, as will be explained in the following section, the thematic block which stands out the most is constituted by letters 5.3–5.4 and 5.6–5.7, which all revolve around Sidonius' relatives. In particular, *Ep.* 5.7 decisively closes the block with a superabundant invective against the slanderers of his relative Apollinaris: the only addressee who receives two letters in the book (*Epp.* 5.3 and 5.6). One last group is that of letters which circulated independently among Sidonius' circle of friends. To this group can be ascribed the two vituperative letters, 5.7 and 5.13, as well as the *lettera d'arte* 5.17 – which appear to be excuses to flaunt Sidonius' literary prowess – and the same conclusion can be reached concerning *Ep.* 5.10, since Mamertus Claudianus' *Ep.* 2 appears to be a point-by-point answer to this letter.[58]

---

57. See Table 1, p. 13.
58. See introductions to *Epp.* 5.7 and 5.10.

17

Manuscript tradition

The new stemma

Sidonius is transmitted in over 100 witnesses. Setting aside florilegia and excerpts, Franz Dolveck recently created a new census with seventy-seven manuscripts of Sidonius' works,[59] and traced them back to a single archetype.[60] The stemma presented in Figure 2 simplifies Dolveck's stemma by removing hyparchetypes (not transmitted but reconstructed by him) and by taking into account only manuscripts containing the *Letters*. The stemma reproduces the higher manuscripts which Dolveck identifies, as well as lower ones which had been collated in the previous editions by Lütjohann, Mohr and Loyen, who considered them to be valuable witnesses.

The relevance of Dolveck's stemma lies in its bipartite structure, in light of which, if a reading in α agrees with *P* (or *PL*) one should have the reading of the archetype. For this reason, the reading *mellis* in *Ep.* 5.8, for example, was preferred to *fellis*, and in *Ep.* 5.9 *tenore* was preferred to the *facilior* reading *tempore*. Moreover, unusual spellings peculiar to *L* which had been chosen especially by Loyen out of respect for its antiquity have been reconsidered.[61]

Following Dolveck's stemma, I collated Book 5 in *C, L, M, P, Vat 1661* and *Leip*. I then checked single *lectiones* in *A, S, N, F* and *T*, given that *A* and *S* are placed high in the stemma by Dolveck, as high as the more ancient *C* (the first manuscript listed by Lütjohann), while *F* is chosen by Lütjohann for the *constitutio textus*,[62] and *N* is chosen by Loyen as the second-best witness.[63]

---

59. Dolveck 2020, 508–42.
60. Which is called *Ur-Archetyp* by Dolveck in the new census to avoid confusion; on its features see Dolveck 2020, 482–4.
61. *L* is dated between 814 and 830 in Dolveck 2020, 522; see the new census in Dolveck 2020, 508–42.
62. I can confirm the poor quality of the text in *F* hypothesised by Dolveck, as well as its belonging (for the *Letters*) to the same sub-branch as *Leip*. Even within the 'English family' (which is a valuable witness for the *Poems* rather than for the *Letters*) this manuscript is at the bottom of the stemma.
63. In his introduction on the manuscript tradition, Loyen 1970a, li states he believes that when the *lectio* in *N ante correctionem* 's'accorde avec celle de *L* nous avons toutes les chances de nous trouver en présence du texte authentique'. However, the collation of Book 5 in *N* did not result in useful evidence, and Dolveck's assertion can be validated.

GENERAL INTRODUCTION

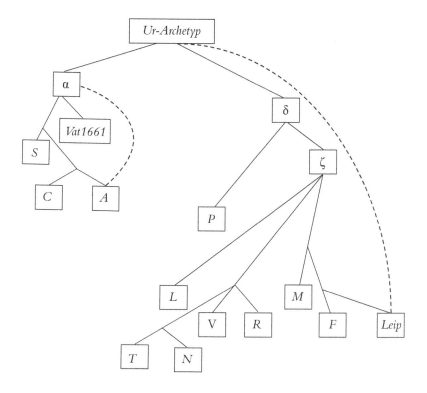

Figure 2. Dolveck's stemma, simplified

Table 2. α *branch*

A	Vatican City, Bibl. Vat., Vat. lat. 3421 (s. XI)
C	Madrid, BNE, 9448 (s. XI²)
S	Formerly Schøyen collection, now Paris, IRHT, collection privée, 347 (s. XII²)
Vat1661	Vatican City, Bibl. Vat., Vat. lat. 1661 (s. XII^{ex}/XIII^{in})

Table 3. δ *branch*

F	Paris, BNF, Par. lat. 9551 (s. XIII$^{1/4}$)
L	Oxford, Bodl. Libr., Laud. lat. 104 + Erlangen, UB, 2112/7 (s. IX¹)
Leip	Leipzig, UB, Rep. I 48 (s. XII or XIII$^{1/4}$)
M	Florence, BML, S. Marco 554 (s. XI²)
N	Paris, BNF, Par. lat. 18584 (s. X)
P	Paris, BNF, Par. lat. 2781 (s. X^{ex})
R	Reims, BM, 413 (s. IX$^{2/4}$)
T	Florence, BML, Plut. 45.23 (A s. XII, B s. XI)
V	Vatican City, Bibl. Vat., Vat. lat. 1783 (s. X-XI^{in})

SIDONIUS: LETTERS BOOK 5, PART 1

Listed below are links to the digital reproductions (where available) of the manuscripts I collated with indication of the *folia* in which Book 5 is attested.

α *branch*

A	<https://digi.vatlib.it/view/MSS_Vat.lat.3421> ff. 44v–53r.
C	<http://bdh-rd.bne.es/viewer.vm?id=0000105585&page=51> ff. 49r–57v.
S	private reproduction ff. 38r–45v.
Vat1661	<https://digi.vatlib.it/view/MSS_Vat.lat.1661> ff. 33v–39r.

δ *branch*

F	<https://gallica.bnf.fr/ark:/12148/btv1b10720833t/f28.item> ff. 23v–28r.
L	<https://bibliotheca-laureshamensis-digital.de/view/bodleian_mslaudlat104/0126> ff. 58v–69r.
Leip	private reproduction, ff. 39r–46v.
M	<http://mss.bmlonline.it/s.aspx?Id=AWOS41MkI1A4r7GxMdlG&c=S.%20Marco%20554#/oro/135> ff. 64r–76v.
N	<https://gallica.bnf.fr/ark:/12148/btv1b10720875c/f67.item.r=18584> ff. 61v–73r.
P	<https://gallica.bnf.fr/ark:/12148/btv1b10720839h/f56.item> ff. 52v–62r.
T	<http://mss.bmlonline.it/s.aspx?Id=AWOIfcHPI1A4r7GxMIZA&c=Sidonii%20Epistolae#/book> ff. 33v–37r.

The quality of the transmitted text is high overall, and for that reason the printed apparatus is negative and comprises only the most problematic readings. Readers can turn to the apparatus of Lütjohann (the only positive apparatus) for full details, though for some corrections see the appendix to the present volume.[64]

---

64. The apparatus in the editions by Mohr, Anderson, and Loyen is negative and heavily dependent on Lütjohann's collation. Note, however, that Lütjohann's apparatus is not consistently positive, a thing which led Loyen into some bad errors. See Furbetta 2020, 562–3 and Condorelli 2020b, 566–7 for a list of editions of Sidonius' text and for their features.

GENERAL INTRODUCTION

Dolveck's recent assessment provides much clarity about the relationship between the manuscripts, and it is worth listing the implications, if he is right.

First, if one takes into account the new stemma, most of the manuscripts standardly listed by Loyen (*FLMNT*) come from a single sub-branch, all deriving from hyparchetype ζ. This would make the readings of *P* and especially *C* more important, given that they come from two different hyparchetypes: δ and α.

The α branch and the editio princeps

The collation of Book 5 confirms that *Vat1661*, *A*, *C* and *S* belong to the same branch, as is argued by Dolveck. Here are listed, by way of example, some peculiar features of the α branch in the entirety of Book 5, which confirm Dolveck's classification:

Ep. 5.5.2   *ACSVat1661* have *de hilario uetere nouus flacco*, though *ilario* in *A* and *ylario* (with a y *littera incerta*) in *S*. *Flacco* is a reading of this family. *L* has *faccho*, while *falco* is attested (with different spellings) in *MP*.

Ep. 5.8.2   the word *coniugem* is missing from *ACSVat1661*.

Ep. 5.9.2   *tenore* appears in *ACSVat1661* (and also *P*) while *tempore* is attested in *LM* (note that *M* has *tempore*, but *tenore* is added by *M¹ super lineam*).

Ep. 5.10.1   the word *bene* is added in *ACSVat1661* (but also *M¹ super lineam* and *P¹ super lineam*).

Ep. 5.10.1   *etiam* is omitted in *ACSVat1661* (present in *LMP*).

Ep. 5.14.2   *sed* appears in *ACSVat1661* instead of *quod* (*LMP*).

Ep. 5.14.3   *dum* in *AC⁶⁵SVat1661* instead of *quando* (*L*) or *quod* (*MP*).

Ep. 5.16.1   *quaestor* is missing from both *C* and *Vat1661* but occurs in *AS*.

Ep. 5.16.1   *attigit* is given in *ACSVat1661* instead of *tetigit* (*LMP*).

Ep. 5.16.3   *quoque* is added in the text (*bona soror quoque optima es*) in *ACSVat1661* but not in *LMP*.

Ep. 5.17.4   *conductorium* appears in *ACSVat1661* instead of *conditorium* (*LMP*).

---

65. In *C* Lütjohann reads *dum*, as I do, while Loyen reads *cum*.

SIDONIUS: LETTERS BOOK 5, PART 1

According to Dolveck, *C* is not the best representative of its family, unlike *Vat1661* and *A* (after correction).[66] He argues that *C* was preferred by the editors because for a time it was the only witness of Sidonius' epitaph.[67] However, for Book 5, *Vat1661* has almost no readings that are different from *C*. The only different *lectiones* which may be worth taking into account are *reuerentia* instead of *uerecundia* (*AC*) in *Ep.* 5.4.1 and *fulloni* instead of *ortuloni* (*AC*) in *Ep.* 5.14.2.[68] Both these alternative readings are plausible in terms of meaning, and yet *uerecundia* and *hortuloni* are unanimously attested in the manuscript tradition, although with different spellings.[69]

Moreover, in *Vat1661* there are more than ten missing words in Book 5, far more than in *C* and *A*. There are also eight instances in which words or syntagmata are in a different order from the rest of the manuscript tradition, and on various occasions I registered solecisms and words in the wrong cases. The overall quality of *Vat1661*, therefore, is poorer than that of *C*. The collation of Book 5 confirms that *A* was corrected against a higher manuscript, possibly α itself, as is argued by Dolveck (see stemma). Therefore, although it is possible to confirm the relation between *A*, *C*, *S* and *Vat1661*, and thus to validate Dolveck's reconstruction of an α branch, there is no reason to prefer the *recentior Vat1661* to *C*, since both have readings which do not appear to be representative of the family. And yet, as Dolveck argues, *A*, *post correctionem*, is the best witness of the branch, and it seems sensible to suggest that an editor should try to ascertain which were the readings of α by collating all the manuscripts of this branch. The *concordia codicum* of the branch would give the reading of the hyparchetype, and if the tradition appears to be split, given the overall high quality of the text, it will tend to be clear which of the manuscripts of the branch has a mistake. It seems therefore that the sensible choice for an editor would be to use α to indicate the consensus of the branch.[70]

Furthermore, Dolveck suggests that the 1474 *editio princeps* by Ketelaer and de Leempt 'is derived from a manuscript of the *Vat1661* type' and argues that the model is *Vat1661* itself.[71] Having compared the collation of *Vat1661* and the text in the Ketelaer and de Leempt edition, I can confirm

---

66. Dolveck 2020, 503.
67. Dolveck 2020, 504 n. 65.
68. *Ortuloni* in *ACS*.
69. See below for *hortuloni/ortuloni/ortolano*.
70. On *C* (s. XI²) see Dolveck 2020, 518 n. 25; on *Vat1661* (s. XII^ex/XIII^in), see Dolveck 2020, 533 n. 69.
71. Dolveck 2020, 500.

GENERAL INTRODUCTION

that, as far as Book 5 is concerned, Dolveck's theory that the *editio* derives from a manuscript of the α family commands assent, since peculiar *lectiones* of the α family are found in it. However, apart from minor similarities in orthography between *Vat1661* and the *editio*, the only *lectio* which occurs in both this manuscript and the *editio princeps* is *Ep.* 5.2.1 *architectoria*, attested in the variant *architectorica* in both *A* and *C*. On the other hand, as stated above, *Vat1661* often inverts and omits single words (much more than *A* or *C*).[72]

Vat1661 also has different *lectiones* from those in the Ketelaer and de Leempt edition, such as:

- the already mentioned *Ep.* 5.4.1 *reuerentia* (not attested in *AC*) instead of *uerecundia*;
- *Ep.* 5.5.2 *flacco* (like *AC*) instead of *falco*;
- *Ep.* 5.12.1 *in hoc saeculo* (not attested in *AC*) instead of *in hoc solum*;
- *Ep.* 5.16.1 *attigit* (not attested in *AC*) instead of *tetegit*;
- *Ep.* 5.20.1 *legionis* (attested in *A*, but not in *C*) instead of *legationis*.

Ultimately, it does not seem likely that *Vat1661* itself was the source of the *editio princeps*, and if it was, it would have to have been collated against other manuscripts with great attention, and corrected in many instances. Furthermore, an explanation was already needed as to why and how the Flemish *editio princeps* would be modelled on a manuscript which was already in Rome at the time.[73] It seems likely that Ketelaer and de Leempt used as their primary exemplar a now lost manuscript of the α branch, perhaps a sibling of *Vat1661*.

---

72. For instance, the following omissions pose a challenge to Dolveck's suggestion that *Vat1661* is the source of the *editio princeps*, since none of these words is missing in it: *Ep.* 5.2.2 *liber* f. 34r l. 10; *Ep.* 5.3.3 *cui* f. 34r l. 2; *Ep.* 5.5.1 *quippe* f. 34v l. 5; *Ep.* 5.7.5 *confestim* f. 35r l. 9; *Ep.* 5.8.2 *coniugem* f. 35v l. 16; *Ep.* 5.11.3 *uitae* f. 36r l. 23; *Ep.* 5.12.1 *lacrimis* f. 36r l. 36; *Ep.* 5.16.1 *quaestor* f. 37r l. 35; *Ep.* 5.17.10 *tenebat* f. 38r l. 14. Conjunctions or monosyllabic words are not included in this list.
73. Since it was bought under pope Nicholas V (†1455). For details on the manuscript see Manfredi 1994, 445 and Dolveck 2020, 533.

SIDONIUS: LETTERS BOOK 5, PART 1

An introduction to Letters 5.1–5.10

Prosopography

Family plays a fundamental role in the unfolding of Book 5, to the point that, in the first half of the book, letters sent to family and friends are balanced in equal measure.[74] It seems possible to suggest that this is a book in which Sidonius is interested in drawing an articulate picture of his family relationships, even when there might have been animosity between his relatives and him, as can be surmised from *Epp.* 5.3 and 5.4. It seems likely that, after some time, these tensions subsided, since Sidonius triumphantly mentions his intervention in favour of his relative Apollinaris at the Burgundian court (*Epp.* 5.6 and 5.7). Self-representation concerns not only contemporary events involving his family members, but also family history, and *Ep.* 5.9 constitutes a unique document in this respect, since Sidonius relates that both his grandfather and his father had sided with Gallic usurpers. One could also ascribe to this group letter 5.16 to his wife Papianilla (in the second half of the book), since it answers the same need for representation, this time of his wife's side of the family, being focused on the career of Sidonius' brother-in-law, Ecdicius.

The first half of the book also provides the reader with a picture of some of Sidonius' aristocratic peers, who share his literary interests: the book is dedicated to Petronius, who keeps re-reading Sidonius' letters (*Ep.* 5.1.1), while *Ep.* 5.2 to Nymphidius is an excuse to praise Mamertus Claudianus' *De statu animae*, which Sidonius had lent to the addressee. Praise of a friend's literary works is also found in *Ep.* 5.8 to Secundinus (a poet known only thanks to Sidonius' *Letters*), while *Ep.* 5.5 to the noble Syagrius and *Ep.* 5.10 to the well-connected Sapaudus are further testimony that Sidonius' network of contacts comprises the most prominent members of the Gallic elite. As Mratschek puts it, the main criteria for Sidonius' selection of addressees 'were political utility and literary repute'.[75]

The survey of the addressees and of the other people mentioned in these letters has been conducted with a cautious approach towards prosopographical tools. For scholars of Late Antiquity, instruments such as the *Prosopography of the Later Roman Empire* and the *Prosopographie chrétienne du Bas-Empire* are fundamental sources of reference, and it would be unthinkable to start

---

74. Concentration on family is a feature of Symmachus' Books 1, 6, and 7.
75. Mratschek 2017, 311; see also Gibson 2020, 381.

24

GENERAL INTRODUCTION

research on any individual without consulting them.[76] In countless places these prosopographies represent an advance on previous knowledge. And yet, these useful tools, because of the comprehensiveness of their coverage, can hardly be expected to reflect all the possible nuances of interpretation. It is not uncommon that questions that are still open to interpretation or oversights in editions end up being part of prosopography and are then eventually accepted as facts, creating widespread conventional narratives.[77]

The overview of the sources concerning addressees and historical characters mentioned in *Epp.* 5.1–10 led to two major conclusions. The first concerns Sidonius' family history and the identity of Simplicius. As will be argued in the introductions to *Epp.* 5.3 and 5.4, a theory concerning his identity has been treated, thanks to incautious acceptance of the prosopographical reconstruction, as an undisputed fact. The second major prosopographical argument revises the standard view on the Burgundian Chilperic and his wife, mentioned in *Epp.* 5.6 and 5.7: the exegesis of the text will prove that assumptions on Burgundian history have been made on the basis of a false interpretation of the term *tetrarcha*,[78] and that Chilperic's wife has wrongly been identified with Caretena.

Dating

Like most surviving literary letter collections, Sidonius' does not come with dates and the letters often lack internal indications of dating, which appear to have been consciously blurred or removed by the author.[79] This choice has the effect of creating a narration that is, if not atemporal, at least chronologically vague, and of making many of the letters seem essayistic and exemplary, as is the case in particular of *Epp.* 5.2, 5.5, 5.7, 5.8 and 5.10.

---

76. Mathisen's 2020 prosopography of Sidonius' people was also a useful tool for this research.

77. A case of this sort was recently uncovered by Gavin Kelly, who proved that a man called Victor, who was supposedly named in *Carm.* 1.25 and had his own entry in *PLRE*, was a false reading in place of the word *doctor* in part of the manuscript tradition. See Kelly 2018.

78. *Ep.* 5.7.1.

79. Cicero is an exception to the rule of not including authorial datelines. As Gibson 2012, 61 puts it: 'around one third of his surviving correspondence gives the co-ordinates of composition, dispatch or receipt of a letter, with reference to place and/or date (usually day and month, rarely year)'.

It is known that the arrangement of Sidonius' letters does not follow a chronological order and, in light of the meagre evidence provided by most letters, a cautious approach to dating has been preferred in this commentary. Each letter is introduced by an overview of scholarship concerning possible dates, which are often considerably different. Dates *ad annum* suggested by Loyen – many of which are revealed to have no foundation (and yet were canonised through prosopography) – have frequently been reconsidered and a broader chronological arc is suggested here.

Hanaghan has an even more pessimistic approach to dating: he believes the *Letters* are all, to some extent, fictional, because they were edited for publication.[80] There may be fictional letters in the book and *Ep.* 5.7 seems like a good candidate, since it appears to have been conceived as a pamphlet which circulated independently rather than as a letter sent to Thaumastus. As Kelly has pointed out,[81] potential rewriting or revision for publication in the collection in 477 must be taken into account: what we have is what Sidonius chooses to publish and one is led to think that dating elements may have been deliberately blurred. A *uigilax lector*, to use Sidonius' words,[82] should also be wary when faced with other elements, which seem to be added in the published collection for the reader's sake, rather than being redundant information for the addressee. And yet, even though dating *ad annum* is most times impossible, a broader internal chronology can be achieved, since there are elements which may point to specific periods in Sidonius' life.

Take, for instance, internal elements useful for dating *Epp.* 5.3–5.8.[83] The trial of Arvandus, the aftermath of which is said to have pained the author,[84] is a potential *terminus post quem* for the epistolary silence of his family mentioned in *Epp.* 5.3 and 5.4. Sidonius had warned Arvandus that legal action was being brought against him, and in doing so had annoyed his own friends and family.[85] Moreover, the favourable political attitude towards the Burgundians, who helped Sidonius in defending Clermont from repeated Visigothic sieges, determines a notable change in how Sidonius refers to

---

[80] Hanaghan 2019, 14.

[81] Kelly 2020, 181.

[82] *Ep.* 5.2.1.

[83] Discussed in detail in the introductory section to each letter.

[84] *Ep.* 1.7.1.

[85] A thing which, according to Harries 1994, 12–15, may have led to his becoming a bishop under some duress. See also Delaplace 2015, 244. For this trial see the introductions to *Epp.* 5.3 and 5.4.

GENERAL INTRODUCTION

them in Book 5. Mathisen dated *Epp.* 5.5–5.8 all around 474.[86] And yet, in *Ep.* 5.5 the Burgundians are ridiculed and their image is filtered through the lenses of conventional misobarbaric topoi. In contrast, in *Epp.* 5.6 and 5.7 (dated between 474 and 475) the careful way of referring to them as benevolent *patroni* is evidence that Sidonius is more cautious and his anti-Burgundian attitude is considerably tempered by their help in defending Clermont from the Visigoths. Meanwhile, in *Ep.* 5.8, the reference to them as tyrannical leads me to date the letter before 5.6 and 5.7, since it can be ascribed to Sidonius' openly anti-Burgundian phase, like *Ep.* 5.5.

Sidonius' models: Pliny the Younger and Symmachus

Roy Gibson has argued that Sidonius directly imitates Pliny 'at best intermittently' in the middle books of his letter collection.[87] In light of the evidence provided by the commentary on letters 1–10 of this book, it seems that Gibson's suggestion can be partially sustained. The evidence gathered from *Epp.* 5.1–5.10 leads one to infer that distinctively Plinian reminiscences are more rarefied and less conspicuous than in previous books, but concern both epistolary themes and the use of Plinian expressions. One may mention, among the terms and expressions drawn from Pliny, the praise of *nouitas* in literary works of friends in Sidon. *Ep.* 5.2.2; *amaritudo* as a result of an offence in *Ep.* 5.4.2; and the markedly Plinian beginning of both *Ep.* 5.5 and *Ep.* 5.10.

Moreover, what emerges with clarity in the first half of the book is that the presence of Symmachus' influence in these letters, linguistically as well as thematically, is more pervasive than has previously been argued. Language often amplifies the reminiscence of the Symmachan model. That is the case, for instance, with the use of the verb *insinuo* to introduce a *commendatus* in *Ep.* 5.1 and with the numerous expressions pertaining to epistolary silence which occur in the first half of the book. In *Ep.* 5.3.1 the mention of the *talio silentii* (the retorting silence inflicted on the misbehaved addressee), the direct address *quod tacetis*, the contrasting *garrulitas* of the ignored sender (*Epp.* 5.3.1 and 5.4.1) and the *offensio* for not having received a *salutatio*

---

86. Mathisen 2013a, 245.

87. While in Books 1–3 and 7–9 Sidonius is wont to prove that he is an attentive reader of Pliny, Gibson argues that 'parallels begin to contract in Book 5 and dwindle towards zero in the Book of the Bishops (Book 6)'. See Gibson 2013b, 340 and 350.

debita (*Ep.* 5.4.1) are all themes and expressions attested often in Symmachus' complaints about epistolary silence. As the commentary explains, it is as if Sidonius concentrates in the space of two letters a repertoire of locutions Symmachus employed to convey frustration for being ignored. Reminiscent of Symmachus are also, for instance, the expression *familiaris pagina* (*Ep.* 5.6.2), which indicates a need for discretion in communication, as well as the expression *eloquii libertas* (*Ep.* 5.8.2), both of which are known to have previous occurrences exclusively in Symmachus. While the idea of the hereditary nature of friendship in *Ep.* 5.9 calls to mind both Pliny and Symmachus, the letter begins with the distinctly Symmachan syntagma *in meo aere duco.*

Other authors with whom Sidonius notably engages include Cicero, Quintilian, Tacitus, Juvenal, Apuleius, Ausonius, Ambrose and Jerome. When they are not simply a source for Sidonius but constitute a clear thematic or stylistic model, their presence is highlighted in the introductory section of each letter, together with that of Pliny and Symmachus.[88]

Sidonius' language

One does not need to have read much Sidonius to know how ornate and studiously ambiguous his prose can be. Gualandri has pointed out that this is a matter of taste as much as of elitism: his writings are designed to be read by a highly educated elite, entertained by this ambiguity and linguistic vivacity, who would have understood and enjoyed innuendos concealed in convoluted prose.[89] And yet, Sidonius' sophisticated images and obscure language are not only representative of the literary taste of his inner circle, but also of his time, being consistent with the aesthetic of late antique poetry and literary prose.[90] Furthermore, as Gualandri states, 'not every member of Sidonius' public, however learned, would have found him easy to follow',[91]

---

88. See e.g. *Epp.* 5.3, 5.5, and 5.7.
89. Moreover, for Sidonius challenging his friends to a sort of competition, testing if they could recognise the intertexts woven in his works, see Gualandri 1979, 85; see also La Penna 1995, 33–4.
90. See, for instance, Roberts 1989 on the late antique 'jewelled style'; and, on the poetical technique and lexicon of Sidonian poetry, see Onorato 2016.
91. Gualandri 2020, 282.

GENERAL INTRODUCTION

as is testified by the letter that Ruricius of Limoges writes to Sidonius' son, mentioning the 'obscurity' of his father's words.[92]

Sidonius aims to surprise the reader through unconventional lexical choices, unprecedented images and unattested *iuncturae*. What we have is but a glimpse of the literary Latin tradition Sidonius had at his disposal and therefore caution is required when claiming novelty of expression and linguistic paternity, and yet, what can be said with certainty is that Sidonius likes to experiment and chooses numerous expressions which are not known in other surviving texts. They had at least to be rare at the time and reflect how studiously complex his letters can be.

On many occasions Sidonius adopts varied forms of more common expressions: in *Epp.* 5.1–5.10 unattested (or distinctively Sidonian) *iuncturae* and syntagmata are so numerous that a list proves useful in visualising the taste for affectedness which characterises his prose:

Ep. 5.1   5.1.1 *uoluptuosa patientia*; 5.1.1 *ingenii fautor*; 5.1.2 *leuitica dignitas*; 5.1.3 *bipertita condicio*.

Ep. 5.2   5.2.1 *sectata philosophia*.

Ep. 5.3   5.3.1 *impudens alloquium*; 5.3.1 *tempus hostilitatis*; 5.3.2 *impietatis opinio*.

Ep. 5.4   5.4.1 *pagina garriens*.

Ep. 5.5   5.5.1 *per uirilem successionem*; 5.5.1 *immane narratu est*; 5.5.2 *scholae liberales*; 5.5.2 *pueritia imbuta*; 5.5.2 *desudata opulentia*; 5.5.2 *uaricosus Arpinas*.

Ep. 5.6   5.6.1 *reuerenda familiaritas*; 5.6.1 *recens caelibatus*; 5.6.1 *turbo barbaricus*; 5.6.1 *militaris improbitas*; 5.6.2 *relatus uenenatus*; 5.6.2 *explorata iracundia*.

Ep. 5.7   5.7.1 *clementiores barbari*; 5.7.6 *uirosa faex*.

Ep. 5.8   5.8.2 *piperata facundia*; 5.8.2 *fulmen ingenii*; 5.8.3 *improborum probra*; 5.8.3 *praeconia bonorum*.

Ep. 5.9   5.9.1 *laudabilis familiaritas*; 5.9.2 *sub uno contubernio*; 5.9.2 *compensatio*.

---

92. Ruric. *Ep.* 2.26 *Sollium enim nostrum domnum patremque communem, quem transcribendum sublimitati uestrae dedisse me dixeram, legendum recepi. Cuius lectio, sicut mihi antiquum restaurat affectum, ita prae obscuritate dictorum non accendit ingenium.* Either one thinks that Apollinaris had one of his father's works copied for Ruricius, as is argued by Mathisen (1999, 184), or that it was Ruricius who had a work of Sidonius copied for Apollinaris, as recently argued by Vessey (2019, 146–7). The difficulty of the text calls for a *recensio*, since Ruricius is confident that Apollinaris is the only one who can uncover the deeper meaning of some obscure passages of his father's works.

29

fraterna; 5.9.3 *antiquata dilectio*; 5.9.3 *similis familiaritas*; 5.9.3 *hereditaria praerogatiua*; 5.9.3 *multifaria opportunitas*; 5.9.4 *in annis iam senectutis initia pulsantibus*; 5.9.4 *praedicabilis proauus*.

Ep. 5.10   5.10.2 *iungere subolem*; 5.10.2 *scientiae obtentus*; 5.10.4 *Latia eruditio*; 5.10.4 *fastidium excitare*.

Rare words

Archaisms play an important role in the language of Sidonius' *Letters*: playing with rare words or employing refined expressions with an unattested meaning is one of the ways in which Sidonius represents his belonging to a restricted circle of intellectuals.[93] A number of archaisms in *Epp.* 5.1–5.10 are peculiar to archaic comedy, especially Plautus, and allow Sidonius to colour his language with realism, or at least vividness.[94] It seems likely that, together with his peers, he may have drawn many of these archaisms from Apuleius' works.[95] It is not uncommon to find archaisms or colloquial expressions in Plautus which resurface in Apuleius and then in Sidonius: that seems to be the case with the noun *pessulus* (*Ep.* 5.4.1); with the adjectives *robiginosus* (5.7.5) and *aequiperabilis* (5.10.3); and with the expression *diu quidem est* (5.8.1). The direct influence this author had on Sidonius is also discernible when one encounters the Apuleian coinage *machinatus* in Sidon. *Ep.* 5.6.2.

Furthermore, the use of some rare words is shared by Sidonius and his friend Mamertus Claudianus, and one can suggest that these were discussed by that literary circle and that the occurrence of an unusual term in either of their works was then mirrored by the other. See, for instance, the commentary ad loc. concerning the word *repondero*, attested only in Claudianus and in Sidon. *Ep.* 5.1.1; the expression *naeuus suspicionis*, attested only in Claudianus' *De statu animae* and in Sidon. *Ep.* 5.3.2; the use of *quispiam* (*Ep.* 5.6.2) favoured by both Sidonius and Claudianus in numerous contexts; and the internal echoes between Sidon. *Ep.* 5.10 and Claudianus' *Ep.* 2.

---

93. See for instance the commentary on *Ep.* 5.6.2 *quorumpiam*, especially on the use of the archaicising *quispiam* in Sidonius and Mamertus Claudianus.

94. One may wonder whether these words are demotic and had a separate life in *sermo cottidianus* and by using them Sidonius aims to flavour his language with realism; or, on the other hand, if they are indeed literary archaisms answering a taste for rare expressions.

95. For Sidonius' use of archaisms see Wolff 2020, 400; the same conclusions are reached with regard to Mamertus Claudianus by Alimonti 1975.

GENERAL INTRODUCTION

Neologisms

Sidonius' language is ever evolving and aims to surprise the cultivated reader through the use of new words. The message implied is that Latin is alive, and, for that reason, experimentalism is encouraged and is tangible proof of one's linguistic prowess. Besides, as Horace himself stated in *Ars poetica* 58–9, *licuit semperque licebit / signatum praesente nota producere nomen*, 'coining a word stamped with the mark of the time has always been legitimate and always will be'.[96]

The hapax legomena in letters 1–10 are sophisticated and it could be argued that the new coinages are all aimed at conveying realism. *Dulcare* (5.4.2) expresses the wish that Simplicius' haughty sons would 'sweeten' Sidonius' contempt; *indolatilis* (5.5.3), already detected by Gualandri,[97] serves the purpose of defining, with a single word, the stiffness and rigidness of barbarians; *castorinatus* (5.7.4) is a telling detail which allows the reader to picture the opulent look of enriched informants clad in beaver fur; while *tyrannopolitanus* (5.8.3) is an amusing quip that Sidonius' peers would have immediately associated with the people of Lyon.[98]

Most problematic readings

The most problematic readings in editions have been reconsidered as a result of the collation of the text, of the commentary, and of further reflection on prose rhythm (discussed in the next section). The following are the most relevant results.

In *Ep.* 5.3.4, having decided to leave *Atticas leges* in the text, I suggest a possible explanation for the expression. Sidonius loves periphrasis and often refers to people and objects without mentioning them directly. This kind of reference can be ascribed to what La Penna defined as Sidonius' keenness to supply riddles for the reader to solve.[99]

In *Ep.* 5.4.2 the reading *si* was conjectured for reasons of internal coherence.

---

96. On Sidonius' fondness for Horace's *Ars poetica*, see Pelttari 2016.
97. Gualandri 1979, 175–6.
98. See the commentary ad loc. for its contemporary occurrence in a law.
99. La Penna 1995, 11.

31

In *Ep.* 5.5.2 an overview of all the readings of *falco . . . halario* in the main families and in all the editions to this day led me to reach conclusions concerning this *crux*.

In *Ep.* 5.6.1 prose rhythm supports the retention of the reading *reuerenda familiaritas* unanimously transmitted in manuscripts, and allows one to reject the suggestions of editors.

In light of the stemma, in *Ep.* 5.8.2 I chose the reading *mellis* in place of *fellis*, printed in modern editions, and, in *Ep.* 5.8.3, *tyrannopolitanorum* in place of *tyrannopolitarum*.

In *Ep.* 5.9.2 instead of *commemorabantur*, transmitted in all the manuscript tradition, and of *commerebantur*, suggested by Anderson, I tentatively proposed, but did not put in the text, a new conjectural reading, *commorabantur*. In the same passage, instead of *tempore* (chosen by editors), I put in the text *tenore*, which is both stemmatically demanded and a *lectio difficilior*.

Prose rhythm

In classical prose rhythm, sentence or clause endings are regulated by syllabic quantity, while the medieval clausulae are accentual and, depending on the accent and number of syllables, one may identify various types of cursus, such as:

cursus planus ó~~ ó~
cursus tardus ó~~ ó~~
cursus velox ó~~~~ ó~
cursus trispondaicus ó~~~ ó~

For late antique authors, scholars refer to *cursus mixtus*: a combination of metrical and accentual sentence endings. Oberhelman and Hall theorised a system to detect the presence of *cursus mixtus* in any late antique text,[100] but having applied the system to a sample of Sidonius' *Letters*, van Waarden has recently reached the conclusion that 'there is no evidence of statistically convincing patterns in sentence endings, whether metrical or accentual (nor obviously therefore of *cursus mixtus*)' and adds that, given the author's poetic background, a lack of rhythmical discipline seems unlikely.[101]

---

100. See in particular Oberhelman and Hall 1984; Oberhelman 1988a; Oberhelman 1988b.
101. Van Waarden and Kelly 2020, 465. Van Waarden points out that in the speech at Bourges
   (*Ep.* 7.9), Sidonius rigorously applies the *cursus mixtus* technique.

GENERAL INTRODUCTION

In the same contribution Kelly has demonstrated that, although letters are not consistently clausulated, Sidonius' approach to clausulation 'is more metrical than it is accentual'.[102] Given that the approach based on *cursus mixtus* does not seem consistently useful when analysing Sidonius' *Letters*,[103] in this commentary Sidonius' use of metrical clausulation and its aesthetic function are highlighted whenever relevant. Sometimes Sidonius appears to favour lavish language and polysyllabic endings more than rhythm; and yet, even though clausulation may not be the main reason behind his lexical choices, it is often a tool subsidiary to punctuation, as can be surmised in particular when analysing the rhythm in Sidonius' enumerations.[104]

The rhythms favoured by Sidonius are listed in Table 4.

Table 4. Rhythms favoured by Sidonius

Cretic spondee	— ˘ — — x
Double cretic	— ˘ — — ˘ x
Cretic tribrach	— ˘ — ˘ ˘ x
Cretic ditrochee	— ˘ — — ˘ — x
Paeon I spondee	— ˘ ˘ ˘ — x
Paeon IV spondee	˘ ˘ ˘ — — x

To this list should also be added three clausulae which appear to be favoured by Sidonius. Two are highlighted by Kelly: the cretic iamb and the dactyl iamb.

The cretic iamb (— ˘ — ˘ x), incidentally, is the first clausula to appear in Book 5: *Ep.* 5.1.1 *e-pistulis meis*; and occurs, in the same letter, in 5.1.2 *neces-sarium meum* (being the first clausula of the second paragraph) and in 5.1.3 *per-sona gratiam*.[105]

The dactyl iamb (— ˘ ˘ ˘ x) is a rhythm which occurs often in *Epp.* 5.1–5.10. It occurs three times in the first letter alone: in 5.1.2 *pro-uincia fuit*; 5.1.2 *praemia putes* and 5.1.3 *suc-cedere parat*.[106]

---

102. Van Waarden and Kelly 2020, 471.

103. As is suggested in van Waarden and Kelly 2020, 467.

104. See also *Ep.* 5.7.2, which is rhythmically analysed as a telling sample by Kelly in van Waarden and Kelly 2020, 472–3.

105. See e.g. its occurrence in *Ep.* 5.2.2 *quicquid illud est*; 5.10.1 *optime facit* and *litteris honor* (see below for other occurrences in *Ep.* 5.10).

106. See also, by way of example, the occurrence of this clausula in *Ep.* 5.2.2 *fallere decet* and *reddere paras*; *Ep.* 5.8.3 *-talia manent*; *Ep.* 5.9.1 *tu quoque putas*; and see below for its occurrence in *Ep.* 5.10.

As Kelly has pointed out, both the cretic iamb and the dactyl iamb allow Sidonius to achieve *cursus planus* (ó~~ ó~) while avoiding the heroic clausula of hexameter endings, a rhythm he disliked.

Moreover, given the large number of **choriamb spondee** ($\overline{}\,\breve{}\,\breve{}\,\overline{}\;\overline{}{}^x$), I would propose adding it to Sidonius' favourite rhythms. See its occurrence, for instance, in *Epp.* 5.1.3 *aut ineat litem* and in the one-word *clausulae*, such as 5.4.1 *dissimularetur*, 5.5.1 *degenerauerunt*, 5.6.1 *afficiebatur* and 5.10.3 *gratificatusque*.

It can be argued that, in *Epp.* 5.1–5.10, the artificial and studied *ordo uerborum* often appears to answer the predilection for the author's favoured rhythms at the end of a clause and thus provides further evidence for Kelly's argument that Sidonius' approach to clausulation is more metrical than it is accentual.

However, this predilection is not systematic, as in the rest of the collection. Some letters have little clausulation, as is exemplified by *Ep.* 5.2, which lacks rhythmical clausulae in the section concerning the praise of Mamertus Claudianus, where one would expect a close attention to rhythm when Sidonius lists the disciplines which are said to inhabit Claudianus' literary work. Moreover, *Ep.* 5.3 is in particular worthy of mention, given its bipartite nature: while in § 1 and § 4 clausulation is not regular, § 2 and § 3 are consistently clausulated. In this case, the heightened attention to rhythm coincides with the most important sections of the letter, concerning the direct address to Apollinaris about his epistolary silence and the following carefully constructed passage on the 'weight' of the new appointment as bishop of Clermont. It is also noteworthy that the following *Ep.* 5.4, on epistolary silence, is entirely clausulated. Thus, Sidonius appears to have written these short complaints with an extra care which is likely to have been appreciated by his addressees.

It can also be argued that the final sections of the letters in particular are often (as a general trend) those showing a less consistent use of *clausulae*. The following is a survey of Sidonius' use of clausulation in the first half of Book 5. Comments on prose rhythm, when relevant, are made in the commentary.

Letter 1

Ep. 5.1 appears to be consistently clausulated with few exceptions, and, as argued above, its first clausula is a cretic iamb, one of the rhythms Sidonius shows a preference for; furthermore, unlike most letters of the book, the last paragraph appears to be consistently clausulated. Also worthy of mention

GENERAL INTRODUCTION

is Sidonius' predilection for repeating a rhythm in sequence, as is testified by the occurrence of three double cretics in § 2 at *nuper indeptus est*; *accommodatissimum*; and *iusseras non uacans*.

Letter 2

As argued above, the letter does not show consistent striving for metrical clausulae. The lack of systematic attention to rhythm is somewhat unexpected, given its studied appearance, the occurrence of rare words, of unattested *iuncturae*, and the enumeration of *artes*. Note that, however, as customary even in the less clausulated letters, both paragraphs of *Ep.* 5.2 are opened by clausulae: § 1 by a paeon IV spondee (*uolu-minibus inlustrem*) and § 2 by a sequence of two one-word cretic spondees (*excitatusque* and *transferendamque*). Also worthy of mention is the unusual higher clausulation of the last paragraph, and in particular of the last lines of the letter, as is argued in the commentary.

Letter 3

Ep. 5.3, like *Ep.* 5.2, shows only moderate attention to metrical clausulation, but nonetheless some features deserve mention. Each paragraph shows clausulation at the beginning: § 1 a cretic spondee at *tali-one frenari*; § 2 a cretic ditrochee at *supprimas actiones*; § 3 a double cretic with prodelision at *uos ualetis bene est*; §4 a cretic spondee at *restat orate*. Note, however, the consistent presence of clausulae at the end of § 2 and throughout § 3, the only paragraph showing consistent attention to rhythm. It seems worthy of attention that the latter is the section concerning the appointment as bishop. Sidonius thus appears to have lavished extra care, also from a rhythmical point of view, to the section dedicated to his self-representation.[107]

Letter 4

Unlike *Ep.* 5.3, this short letter is entirely clausulated; hence Sidonius appears to have devoted especial care to its composition. Note in particular that the letter is opened and ends with a double cretic clausula at *scripta qui miseram* and at *dul-care non desinant*. The letter shows a variety of Sidonius' favourite rhythms, including the $\overline{}\smile\smile\overline{}\ \overline{}{}^{\times}$ clausula (choriamb spondee) at § 1 *dissimularentur* and § 2 *inuidiam uerti*.

---

107. See commenary ad loc. for the detection of the clausulae of the paragraph.

35

SIDONIUS: LETTERS BOOK 5, PART 1

Letter 5

Although this letter is not entirely clausulated, attention to prose rhythm is high. It has been argued before that Sidonius enjoys repeating metrical clausulae, as is testified in this letter by two consecutive cretic ditrochees at *legibus disserendis* and *tri-chordibus temperandis*. The presence of a more consistent metrical clausulation helps the reader to navigate the first paragraph, which is characterised by a complex hypotactic structure. It is also useful in order to divide the enumerations in the third paragraph, which appear to have been coupled (as often in Sidonius). See, as exemplary of how clausulation helps reading the text, the following rhythms of § 1: the initial double cretic at *consulis pronepos*;[108] the dactyl cretic at *subicien-dam minus attinet*; the paeon I spondee at *semine poetae*; the cretic spondee at *uerba testantur*; the cretic iamb at *ne parum quidem*; the one-word clausula *degenerauerunt* creating one of Sidonius' favourite rhythms $-\smile\smile\:-\:-$ × (choriamb spondee); the cretic spondee with prodelision at *immane narratu est*; and the paeon I spondee at *facilitate rapuisse*. As stated above, the consecutive repetition of a rhythm is often found in Sidonius' *Letters*, and in this letter there are also consecutive couples of rhythms. In § 1 two cretic spondees at *garrien-ti forem claudis* and *pessulum opponis* (the latter with elision) are followed by two double cretics, *in-uitus indulgeo* and *esse denuntio*. Note also the two cretic ditrochees in § 2, at *su-perbiam filiorum* and *diligi sentientes*.

Letter 6

In its metrical clausulae as well as in other verbal effects, this is a carefully composed letter. As the commentary further explains, the three cretic spondees in § 1 are in particular worthy of mention and metrical clausulation comes to the translator's aid in this passage. The first paragraph also ends with two cretic tribrachs, at *turbo barbaricus* and at *concin-naret improbitas*.

Letter 7

Ep. 5.7 is not consistently clausulated, and some sections show more attention to rhythm than others. As is stated by Kelly,[109] in some passages, especially those characterised by long enumerations, metrical clausulae help to detect what appears to be an internal natural grouping.

Let us consider the opening paragraph as an example (Table 5): although attention to clausulation is high, one can note how enumerations are not

---

108. Scanned with a long *pro*, in accordance with Sidon. *Carm.* 11.133.
109. Van Waarden and Kelly 2020, 472–3.

GENERAL INTRODUCTION

entirely clausulated but divided into pairs, as is visible in case of the four blocks of compounds of *fero*.

The same happens in § 2 (see commentary ad loc.) and in § 3, where for instance the list of eight names of negative exempla is divided into two

Table 5. Clausulation in *Ep.* 5.7.1

Indagauimus tandem,	cretic spondee
amicitias criminarentur,	one-word cretic spondee
non fefellere uestigia.	double cretic
Hi nimirum sunt,	− − − − −
ut idem coram positus audisti,	paeon IV spondee
inter clementiores barbaros Gallia gemit.	dactyl iamb
Hi sunt, quos timent etiam qui timentur.	anapaest ditrochee
peculiariter prouincia manet,	dactyl iamb
inferre calumnias	− ᴗ ᴗ − ᴗ x (dactyl cretic)
deferre personas,	cretic spondee
afferre minas,	− − ᴗ ᴗ x
auferre substantias.	double cretic

Table 6. Clausulation in *Ep.* 5.7.3

tunicatis otia,	ᴗ ᴗ − − − ᴗ x (spondee cretic?)
stipendia paludatis,	paeon IV spondee
uiatica ueredariis,	paeon IV cretic
mercatoribus nundinas,	double cretic
munuscula legatis,	− ᴗ ᴗ − − x (choriamb spondee)
portoria quadruplatoribus,	double cretic
praedia prouincialibus,	cretic iamb
flamonia municipibus,	dactyl iamb
arcariis pondera,	double cretic
mensuras allectis,	− − − − x
salaria tabulariis,	− ᴗ ᴗ ᴗ ᴗ − ᴗ x (not a regular clausula, though *cursus octosyllabicus*)
dispositiones numerariis,	− ᴗ ᴗ − ᴗ x (dactyl cretic)
praetorianis sportulas,	− ᴗ − − − ᴗ x (spondee cretic?)
ciuitatibus indutias	− ᴗ ᴗ − − ᴗ x (choriamb cretic?)
uectigalia publicanis,	dactyl ditrochee
reuerentiam clericis,	double cretic

groups by metrical clausulae at *Massa Marcellus* (cretic spondee) and *Li-cinius et Pallas* (paeon IV spondee).

It is also worth analysing the enumeration of goods which are the object of the informers' envy in § 3, a section which is clausulated (Table 6), although not consistently, and that includes some of the metrical clausulae which are infrequent in Sidonius.[110]

Letter 8

Albeit not entirely clausulated, this letter distinguishes itself for the over-abundant presence of metrical clausulae. The detection of clausulation, often within the cola, helps navigating the – sometimes highly artificial – *ordo uerborum*. Take for instance the presence of two consecutive cretic spondee clausulae at § 1 *praedicantesque* and at *lectitabamus*. Subsidiary to punctuation within the clause in this paragraph is also the cretic spondee at *siue perfossae* followed by the double cretic at *regiis ictibus*. Moreover, it seems rhythm influences the *ordo uerborum* in particular in the last sentence of § 3, where the double cretic at *improborum probra* is followed by a paeon I spondee at *-conia bonorum*.

Letter 9

This letter is rigorously clausulated, a fact which, together with its subject matter of family history, provides further evidence for the supposition that it is to be intended as a display piece for the collection. Since clausulation often is subsidiary to punctuation it is consistently signalled throughout the commentary.

Letter 10

Ep. 5.10 proves to be useful to visualise Sidonius' predilection for his favourite endings. The first part of the letter, which concerns the praise of Sapaudus, Pragmatius and Priscus Valerianus, is characterised by lexical display, and the studied attention to detail emerges also in the careful choice of rhythmical clausulae. Note that clausulation is less consistent in the second half of the letter, a feature that, as argued above, is common to letters 1–10. Moreover, note Sidonius' predilection for patterns: he tends to use the same rhythm in consecutive clauses (see Table 7).[111]

---

110. See the statistics presented by van Waarden and Kelly 2020, 474–5.
111. See the sequence of two paeon IV spondee and two paeon I spondee in *Ep.* 5.10.2.

GENERAL INTRODUCTION

Table 7. Clausulation in *Ep.* 5.10

1.	*Si quid omnino Pragmatius illustris,*[112]	paeon IV spondee
	hoc inter reliquas animi uirtutes optime facit,	cretic iamb
	quod amore studiorum te singulariter amat,	dactyl iamb
	in quo solo uel maxume animum aduertit ueteris peritiae diligentiaeque resedisse uestigia.	double cretic
	Equidem non iniuria tibi fautor est;	double cretic/dactyl cretic
	nam debetur ab eo percopiosus litteris honor.	cretic iamb
2.	*Hunc olim perorantem et rhetorica sedilia plausibili oratione frangentem*	cretic spondee
	soter eloquens ultro in familiam patriciam adsciuit,	paeon IV spondee (with elision)
	licet illi ad hoc,	—
	ut sileam de genere uel censu,	paeon IV spondee
	aetas, uenustas, pudor patrocinarentur.	cretic spondee
	Sed, ut comperi,	—
	erubescebat iam etiam tunc uir serius	˘ ˘ — — — — ˘ x
	et formae dote placuisse,	paeon I spondee
	quippe cui merito ingenii suffecisset adamari.	paeon I spondee
	Et uere optimus quisque morum praestantius pulchritudine placet;	dactyl iamb
	porro autem praeteruolantia corporis decoramenta currentis aeui profectu defectuque labascunt.	dactyl spondee
	Hunc quoque manente sententia	double cretic
	Galliis post praefectus Priscus Valerianus	paeon I spondee
	consiliis suis tribunalibusque sociauit,	paeon I spondee
	iudicium antiquum perseuerantissime tenens,	cretic iamb
	ut cui scientiae obtentu iunxerat subolem,	cretic tribrach
	iungeret et dignitatem.	— ˘ ˘ — — ˘ — x
3.	*Tua uero tam clara, tam spectabilis dictio est,*	double cretic (with prodelision)
	ut illi diuisio Palaemonis,	— ˘ ˘ ˘ — ˘ x
	grauitas Gallionis,	anapaest ditrochee
	abundantia Delphidii,	˘ — — ˘ ˘ — ˘ ˘ x
	Agroecii disciplina,	cretic ditrochee
	fortitudo Alcimi,	double cretic with elision
	Adelphii teneritudo,	paeon I spondee
	rigor Magni,	—
	dulcedo Victorii	double cretic

Table continues over

---

112. Note how Sidonius starts with an internal clausula, a cretic spondee at *si quid omnino*.

39

non modo non superiora sed uix aequiperabilia   paeon I spondee
    scribant.
Sane ne uidear tibi sub hoc quasi hyperbolico rhetorum $-\smile\smile\ -\ -$ x
    catalogo blanditus quippiam gratificatusque,
solam tibi acrimoniam Quintiliani pompamque   tribrach ditrochee
    Palladii comparari non ambigo sed potius adquiesco.

4.   *Quapropter si quis post uos Latiae fauet eruditioni,* $\smile\smile\ -\smile\ -\smile\ -$x
    huic amicitiae gratias agit   cretic iamb
    et sodalitati uestrae, $\smile\ -\smile\ --\ -$x
    si quid hominis habet, $-\smile\ \smile\smile\ \smile$x
    tertius optat adhiberi.   paeon I spondee
    Quamquam, quod est grauius,   cretic tribrach
    non sit satis ambitus iste fastidium uobis excitaturus,   cretic spondee
    quia pauci studia nunc honorant,   tribrach ditrochee
    simul et naturali uitio fixum est radicatumque pectori-   paeon IV spondee
    bus humanis,
    ut qui non intellegunt artes non mirentur artifices.   cretic tribrach
    Vale.

LETTERS 5.1–5.10

TEXT, TRANSLATION AND COMMENTARY

Letter 1

Content

The letter is structured in three distinct sections, coinciding with the modern paragraph divisions:

§ 1 salutation and praise of Petronius;
§ 2 introduction of the bearer Vindicius, apology and a gift for Petronius;
§ 3 commendation of Vindicius and explanation of his legal problem.

The addressee Petronius

As can be seen in the apparatus, the manuscript tradition diverges on the name of the addressee: Petronius in Dolveck's δ branch, Petreius in his α branch.[1] The latter name has never been taken into serious consideration before, although Petreius is the addressee of another letter in the collection, *Ep.* 4.11, where it is to Petreius, the nephew of Mamertus Claudianus, that Sidonius addresses the heartfelt eulogy at the news of Claudianus' passing.[2] Still, the commonly printed name Petronius is much likelier to be correct. First of all, this is not the only letter sent to Petronius to be included in the collection, since he is also the addressee of *Ep.* 2.5 and of *Ep.* 8.1.[3] In both *Ep.* 2.5 and *Ep.* 5.1 Sidonius writes to Petronius seeking legal advice on behalf of his friends, Petronius being a renowned lawyer who had been sent in 469 to Rome, alongside Tonantius Ferreolus and Thaumastus (*Ep.* 1.7.4), to press charges against Arvandus, accused of treason for urging the

---

1. A confusion possibly originating from the superlinear abbreviation *Petrōius*.
2. Claudianus was his *auunculus* (*Ep.* 4.11.1); apart from this, we know nothing of Petreius. See Heinzelmann 1982, 668; Mathisen 2020, 113.
3. On Petronius see *PLRE* 2, s.v. Petronius 5, 863–4, *PCBE* 4, s.v. Petronius 3, 1475–6; Mathisen 2020, 113; Hindermann 2022, 199–200.

Visigothic king Euric to turn on the emperor Anthemius, to attack the Bretons north of the Loire and to divide Gaul with the Burgundians.[4]

Ep. 5.1 and *Ep.* 8.1 have a similar structure: in both letters Sidonius praises Petronius' noble-mindedness and selflessness in enhancing his literary fame, and subsequently recalls the addressee's eagerness and strong desire to read more of his works.[5] This similarity of structure and content points in the direction of Petronius, who would be a good candidate for the dedication of Book 5 also in terms of internal coherence of the Book. As will be explained in the introduction to *Ep.* 5.3, Sidonius' decision to warn Arvandus of the charges against him seems to have caused tensions with close friends and family members involved in the prosecution. The first half of the Book bears traces of Sidonius' attempts to resume contact with his relatives (Apollinaris, Thaumastus and Simplicius), who refuse to answer his letters. The dedication of Book 5 to Petronius, one of the three Gallic prosecutors of Arvandus, may be a way to bridge this ongoing rift: Sidonius is putting his name in a prominent and honorific first position in a book whose first half appears to be devoted to Sidonius' social reintegration.

Twice in *Ep.* 8.16 to Constantius, Sidonius calls Petronius *inlustris uir*, a title which allows one to suggest that at the time he has power (a present office) or prestige for having held power before (a past office).[6] Petronius' whereabouts are not known, but the Rhône region has been suggested by Mathisen[7] and Arles more specifically in *PCBE* 4. Though the latter suggestion is not accompanied by an explanation, Arles was the base of the praetorian prefecture,[8] and it is legitimate to wonder if Petronius might have been holding an office there, or if he might have been a lawyer serving at the prefecture.

---

4. See *Ep.* 1.7.5 and *PLRE* 2 s.v. Arvandus, 157; for the trial of Arvandus see also introductions to *Epp.* 5.3 and 5.4.

5. *Ep.* 8.1.1 *hinc est quod etiam scrinia Aruerna petis euentilari.*

6. During the fifth century, *illustres* were members of senatorial rank with privileges, fiscal and jurisdictional, higher than *spectabiles* and *clarissimi.* For instance, *spectabiles* of curial origin had to perform their civic duties in person, while *illustres* did so by proxy. See Jones 1964, II, 529; Jones 1964, III n. 16, as well as the commentary on *Ep.* 5.10.1 *Pragmatius illustris* for further context.

7. Mathisen 2013a, 245.

8. The prefecture had been transferred from Trier to Arles. While according to Chastagnol 1973 the move took place in 407, Palanque 1934 and 1973 argues for c. 395; see also Mathisen 2013b, 283–5 in support of this earlier date and for the *status quaestionis.*

LETTER 1

The letter bearer Vindicius

Vindicius might be a close friend or a relative of Sidonius.[9] *Ep.* 5.1 concerns him personally and not simply as a bearer, since Vindicius is sent to Petronius for legal advice: he considers himself legally entitled to a paternal cousin's inheritance and intends to take possession of it or to take his case to court. In the view of most scholars, Sidonius' interest in personally recommending Vindicius indicates this man was a deacon in the Auvergne diocese.[10]

He is also mentioned as a bearer at the beginning of Sidon. *Ep.* 7.4, a letter addressed to Fonteius, bishop of Vaison.[11] At the end of the same letter (7.4.4), a *gerulus* (letter-carrier) is commended by Sidonius to Fonteius, with a request that the latter help him with a problem he incurred while in Vaison; however, the identification of the second bearer in this last section with Vindicius is uncertain and debated.[12] As pointed out by van Waarden,[13] both *Epp.* 5.1 and 7.4 are introduced by the praise of the addressee and then followed by a direct request, expressed by the verb *commendo*, as was common in *commendaticiae*.

Genre: an accompanying note and a *commendaticia*

The text adheres to a seemingly conventional way of addressing someone who is sent literary works, by pretending that what is sent is less valuable than what was expected. Possible models for this letter are detectable in Pliny and Symmachus; Pliny, for instance, starts a letter to Paternus by saying:

> *Tu fortasse orationem, ut soles, et flagitas et exspectas; at ego quasi ex aliqua peregrina delicataque merce lusus meos tibi prodo.* (Plin. *Ep.* 4.14.1)

> Perhaps, as usual, you demand and anticipate a speech from me, but I am bringing to you, as from some exotic and alluring stock, my trifles.[14]

Furthermore, Symmachus' letter to Protadius begins very similarly:

---

9. See *PCBE* 4, s.v. Vindicius, 1985.
10. Anderson 1965, 170 n. 1; Loyen 1970a, 255; Bellès 1998, 94 n. 3.
11. See van Waarden 2010, 223–4.
12. *Ep.* 7.4.4 *praeterea commendo gerulum litterarum, cui istic, id est in Vasionensi oppido, quiddam necessitatis exortum sanari uestrae auctoritatis reuerentiaeque pondere potest.*
13. Van Waarden 2010, 240.
14. Unless stated otherwise, translations are mine.

45

Delectaris epistulis meis. Credo! Hinc est quod eas et saepe et ardenter efflagitas. Sed non statim mereor desidis notam, si nequeo tui amoris in me auaritiae satisfacere. (Symm. *Ep.* 4.33.1)

You enjoy my letters. I should think so! That is why you demand them often and zealously. But right now I do not deserve a reprimand for inactivity if I cannot satisfy the greediness of the affection you have for me.

Sidonius is certainly not new to this kind of formalism, as it is retrievable, as a topos, in various Sidonian passages.[15] For instance, in *Carm.* 9.9–11, the author says that he put together his *nugae temerariae* in a *libellus* because Felix 'ordered it', thus exposing him to the harsh judgement and jealousy of others.[16] Sidonius, then, pretends modesty when he warns Felix that *mandatis famulor, sed ante testor / lector quas patieris hic salebras (Carm.* 9.14–15).[17]

A similar *incipit* is also in *Ep.* 1.1, where Constantius is said to have been insistently asking Sidonius (and to have eventually persuaded him) to collect the letters in a volume. A further similar *incipit* is also in Sidon. *Ep.* 7.9, a letter to bishop Perpetuus concerning the episcopal election in Bourges of the year 470.[18]

Desiderio spiritalium lectionum . . . etiam illa, quae maxume tuarum scilicet aurium minime digna sunt occupare censuram, noscere cupis; siquidem iniungis, ut orationem, quam uideor ad plebem Biturigis in ecclesia sermocinatus, tibi dirigam; cui non rhetorica partitio, non oratoriae machinae, non grammaticales figurae congruentem decorem disciplinamque suppeditauerunt. (Sidon. *Ep.* 7.9.1)

In your longing for spiritual readings . . . you wish to become acquainted even with those works which are manifestly quite unworthy to be evaluated by ears such as yours; for you ask me to send you the oration which I am deemed to have delivered to the people of Bourges in the church. But it did not have an ounce of the suitable grace and expertise brought by rhetorical partition, oratorical artifices, and grammatical figures.

---

15. As stated by Loyen 1943, 99: 'cette modestie feinte n'a qu'un but, c'est de provoquer chez l'interlocuteur la *caritas*, qui s'emploie alors avec générosité'.
16. For a detailed analysis of the poem, see Franca Ela Consolino's groundbreaking article 'Codice retorico e manierismo stilistico nella poetica di Sidonio Apollinare' (1974). Consolino 1974, 430 detects the influence of Pliny in Sidonius' ostentatiously modest attitude; on *Carm.* 9 being both a letter and a dedication see Consolino 2020, 348–52; for the influence of Ausonius see also Santelia 2021 *passim*.
17. 'I obey your commands. But first, I declare to you, reader, what jolts you will have to suffer here.'
18. See commentary by van Waarden 2010, 416–20.

Sidonius once more affirms he is sending the works as gifts in response to the persistent requests of the addressee, depicted, as customary, as an eager bibliomaniac and enthusiastic reader of Sidonius' works.[19]

The similarities between the two passages by Pliny and Symmachus and Sidon. *Ep.* 5.1.1 and *Ep.* 7.9.1 lead one to presume that Sidonius deployed a habitual literary device when sending his writings as a gift introduced by a letter. It should also be noted, however, that as in Plin. *Ep.* 4.14 and Symm. *Ep.* 4.33, in Sidon. *Ep.* 7.9.1 the salutations are followed by a text of the author (Sidonius' speech for the election of the bishop of Bourges, which is enclosed with the letter);[20] while in *Ep.* 5.1, within the note accompanying his gifts is concealed a commendation letter for the bearer, to the point that *Ep.* 5.1 is ascribable to the genre of *litterae commendaticiae.*

According to the standard composition schemes of commendation letters it would seem that the *commendaticia* starts from the second paragraph.[21] The first and second paragraphs, in fact, not only show a conspicuous difference in terms of content but also in an abrupt change of style. While §1 is focused on the praise of the addressee, Petronius, and is characterised by a hypotactic and circumlocutory wording, § 2 immediately mentions the *commendatus*, Vindicius, and gets to the heart of the matter in a more sober and plain style. Such difference raises the suspicion that the original text may have undergone changes for publication.[22] Certainly, a book of letters could not have begun with the usual direct request (*commendo tibi . . .*)[23] and

---

19. In relation to the practice of sending his works to *sodales*, the *propempticon* of Sidon. *Carm.* 24 also comes to mind, with its detailed description of all the estates and friends his book of poetry will visit, even though Petronius is not listed among the friends who will receive the *libellus* on its way to the library of consul Magnus. On *Carm.* 24 see Santelia 2002a; Consolino 2020, 352–5.

20. For this letter being ascribable to *genus deliberatiuum* and *demonstratiuum*, see van Waarden 2010, 436.

21. As theorised by Cugusi 1983, 113, *litterae commendationis* were divided into the following parts: presentation of the person recommended; commendation introduced by the formula *commendo/commendatum habeas*; praise and connection with the commended; request for favour; expressions of gratitude and salutations.

22. See Cugusi's similar remarks (1983, 214–15) when arguing that the absence of contingent details in Pliny's letters is the result of re-elaboration of the epistles as originally sent, which entailed the removal of details in view of publication. As is argued in the General Introduction to the present volume, it is my opinion that the same can be said for Sidonius' correspondence.

23. Although Sidonius does begin other commendation letters (e.g. *Ep.* 6.10) with the immediate presentation of the commended.

it is possible that Sidonius had reshaped the first paragraph at a later stage, to start the book with a fitting homage to Petronius.

Commendation letters are one of the most common means of social interaction from classical to late antique epistolography. Being in a position to recommend someone entailed power and influence, as well as good social connections: a commendation probably benefited the *commendator* as much as the *commendatus*,[24] since it allowed the writer to keep alive social interactions, and gave an excuse to write to acquaintances, to wield power and to test one's authority. For instance, a quarter of the 902 letters of Symmachus' corpus are commendation letters, and in the first two books alone there are more than sixty *litterae commendaticiae*.[25]

Furthermore, *Ep.* 5.1 answers the criterion of 'triangulation of friendship' in commendation letters described by Roger Rees: invoking the relationship between the sender and the addressee, as well as reminding the former's liking of the person who needed commendation, allowed a sort of extension of obligations of the addressee toward the *commendatus*.[26] A recognition of Sidonian commendations in his letters reveals that on most occasions the author introduces someone looking for legal assistance,[27] while commendations for job posts are less numerous,[28] as are those requesting mediation or counsel for other private issues, most often concerning the bearer.[29]

In terms of content, there is a significant difference between Sidonian and Plinian *commendaticiae*, since the latter are mainly written as commendations for office, that is, concerning promotions of young officials.[30]

---

24. Roda 1996, 229 and 238. Both Cugusi 1983, 112 and Rees 2007, 152 suggest that in Cicero's Book 13 of the *Ad Familiares* the large number of *litterae commendaticiae* (dating to two specific years) are a trace of his revision of the corpus for publication and of his ambitions. Rees also highlights that, conversely, in Pliny's letters such commendations are more uniformly distributed across the corpus, being 'regular and consistent reminders of Pliny's influence as a patron across a broad chronological stretch', a consideration which seems fitting also in relation to the presence of these letters in Sidonius' corpus.

25. A was highlighted by Cugusi 1983, 113 n. 353bis and extensively by Roda 1996, 225 (but the first version of that contribution dates to 1986) and Marcone 1988, 145. Books 8 and 9 of Symmachus' correspondence have the largest number of *commendaticiae* – see Furbetta 2015b, 348–9.

26. Rees 2007, 156–7. He takes as examples letters from Cicero, Pliny and Fronto.

27. As in *Epp.* 2.5, 2.7, 3.5, 3.9, 3.10, 4.6, 5.1, 6.2, 6.3, 6.4, 6.5, 6.9, 6.11, 7.4, 7.10.

28. *Ep.* 5.15, 6.8, 6.10, 9.10.

29. *Epp.* 2.4, 4.7, 4.24, 8.13, 9.6. Book 6 of Sidonius' correspondence is the one with the largest number of *litterae commendaticiae*.

30. This is typical of Ciceronian correspondence as well as Plinian, see Fernández López 1994, 135–6.

One might wonder if this difference is ascribable to the political role and influence of Pliny being considerably greater than Sidonius'; those requiring commendations from the latter had more trivial and everyday needs (it also seems legitimate to assume that there were fewer available offices when Sidonius was writing). Another difference from Pliny's commendations resides in the fact that Sidonius' *commendaticiae* seem concise and only briefly outline the connection of the bearer to the author,[31] as Sidonius himself says in *Ep.* 8.13.4 *is efficacissime quemque commendat, qui meras causas iustae commendationis aperuerit.*

These elements lead one to hypothesise that Symmachus may have been a model for the Sidonian *commendaticiae* rather than Pliny, together with the observation that Symmachus' (and Sidonius') commendation letters are not only considerably more laconic but also less impersonal than Pliny's.[32] Marcone has argued that Sidonius' interest in the letters of Symmachus is confined to style, while the Plinian model is the only one followed 'structurally speaking'.[33] Whether or not this assertion is shareable as a general assumption, a case could be made that such letters are reminiscent of those of Symmachus not only in terms of tone but also in their overall structure; lastly, a further element worthy of consideration is that, unlike Pliny, who never begins a book with a commendation letter, *litterae commendaticiae* open Books 2 and 9 of the letters of Symmachus, as happens in Book 5 of Sidonius.

The opening letter

The choice to begin Book 5 with a similar letter is puzzling, since it diverges from all the prefatory letters of the other Sidonian books in terms of thematic consistency, content and length. The oddity of the choice is evident when these three elements are compared across all nine prefatory letters: *Ep.* 5.1 stands alone in these terms. This letter is the only one that has two themes; it is also the only one which includes a commendation – hence its style is more direct and less refined in the commendatory section – and, lastly,

---

31. In the section known as *probatio* the sender usually guaranteed that he knew the *commendatus* personally. See Fedeli 1998, 38; Furbetta 2015b, 348.

32. For the difference between Pliny's and Symmachus' letters and for the latter's shorter and more concise commendation letters see Marcone 1988, 146; Kelly 2013, 264–5; Kelly 2015, 197.

33. Marcone 1988, 150.

it is considerably shorter than all the other prefatory epistles in Sidonius, including *Ep.* 8.1, also sent to Petronius. It should be noted, incidentally, that *Ep.* 8.1 answers the need to justify the expansion of the collection with further letters: it has therefore all the features of a programmatic text, including, for instance, spiteful remarks on detractors.[34]

As stated above, starting a book with a *commendaticia* had a precedent in Symmachus' *Epp.* 2.1 and 9.1, and this may have been an incentive for Sidonius to start his own book similarly. However, unlike Sidon. *Ep.* 5.1, Symmachus' *Ep.* 2.1 immediately reveals its nature as a commendation letter by introducing the *commendatus* at the very beginning (*Ep.* 2.1.1 *Hic ille est Paralius.* . .). In contrast, the structure of Symm. *Ep.* 9.1 is similar to that of Sidon. *Ep.* 5.1, since a short introduction, complimentary of the addressee, is followed by the commendation, which, as usual in Symmachus, is concise, like that in Sidon. *Ep.* 5.1. This may lead to the conclusion that Sidon. *Ep.* 5.1 is a homage to the style of Symmachus, and yet two clarifications seem necessary. Firstly, Symmachus' Book 9 is openly a book with numerous *commendaticiae*,[35] while Sidonius' Book 5 is not. Secondly, in his commentary on Symmachus' Book 9, Roda asserts that the book circulated later than the first part of the collection and infers that Symmachus' Books 8, 9 and 10 were not known to Sidonius when he issued his epistolary collection. Roda was led to this conclusion by the analysis of Geisler's *loci similes* concerning Sidonius' letters and Symmachus' Books 8–10; according to the scholar, when it comes to the last three books of Symmachus' collection, the similarities concern usual expressions. Therefore, Roda suggests Symmachus' Books 8–10 were not published before Sidonius completed his letter collection.[36]

Only a comprehensive commentary of Sidonius' books may prove Roda right or wrong on this point. The intertextual connections listed by Geisler are often merely suggestions, and some are more valuable than others; that is why it does not seem safe to reject a priori the idea that Symm. *Ep.* 9.1 may have been exemplary for Sidonius.

---

34. See comments on the transitional nature of Book 5 in the General Introduction to the present volume.
35. The header of two (lost) manuscripts of Symmachus significantly describes the content of the book: Π (*Divionensis*) '*continens commendatitias*' and Γ (*Giphaniensis*) '*continens commendaticias*'. See Callu 2002, 2. However, Roda 1996, 228 urges caution regarding these *inscriptiones* and highlights the fact that of the 153 letters in the book only 36 are *commendaticiae*. See also Roda 1981, 72–3.
36. Roda 1981, 76.

LETTER 1

If Symm. *Ep.* 9.1 was a model for the position, structure and length of this letter, certainly Sidonius' choice to put it in this position is innovative in terms of the structural cohesion of his own collection, to the point that it could be surmised he may be experimenting with an unusual *incipit*. What makes this letter innovative, being the first of the book, is not its commendatory content *tout court*, as much as the fact it is a clever letter that seems a literary homage to an addressee who had already received Sidonian works, and only later reveals its disguised nature as a *commendaticia*.

The letters Petronius reads and the new ones he has been gifted

The element which seems to be most useful for the dating is the opening reference to the correspondent Petronius portrayed in the act of (re)reading Sidonius' *epistulae*. It might be possible that these letters, as Harries emphasises,[37] are simply ones sent to Petronius; however, the context and the importance of the addressee, who had a keen interest in Sidonius' writings, would suggest otherwise.

Conversely, this would seem an indication that, at the time this letter was written, the 'publication' of previous letters had already occurred, at least in the sense that those texts circulated, and that Petronius had his own copy of some of them.[38] It seems impossible, though, to detect which letters Petronius would have had available to read. For instance, Sidonius might be referring only to Book 1, or to Books 1 and 2, which, according to Loyen[39] (the former) and Harries (the latter), enjoyed an early circulation, before or right after Sidonius was appointed as bishop in 469; but he might also be alluding to Books 1–3 or only to Book 3,[40] according to the various theories concerning the possible private circulation of single books of the letters. An alternative option worthy of mention is that Sidonius is referring to a proto-collection of letters which does not coincide with the published books. As is argued in the General Introduction, it is also evident that some letters of Book 5 circulated individually, for example *Epp.* 5.7 and 5.10. Unfortunately, this is an issue destined to remain unsolved with the information we have.

---

37. Harries 1994, 9.
38. As Mathisen points out, it is extremely difficult to define 'private circulation', because it likely entailed selection and textual revision just like a formal publication. See Mathisen 2013a, 224 n. 12, who is here criticising Harries 1994, 4.
39. Loyen 1970a, xlviii–xlix.
40. See e.g. Anderson 1965, 101 n. 2; though the latter option seems unlikely.

Furthermore, in *Ep.* 5.1 Sidonius makes amends for not sending Petronius what he had asked of him, vaguely referring to something written on his *pugillares*. Although the conventionality of this *incipit* has already been discussed,[41] it would seem plausible that Petronius had asked Sidonius for more letters because he had already received Sidonian epistles he had enjoyed, and since it was to be at Petronius' request that he published Book 8. However, in *Ep.* 5.1.2 Sidonius declares that he sends Petronius only *neniae* instead of what is expected of him:

> I entrusted him instead with some trifles as a little present; albeit your virtue is such that you always prize my letters as mighty rewards.

The words *quamquam, quae tua sanctitas, semper grandia litteras nostras praemia putes* leave no doubt to what the *neniae* are: letters, even if not particularly refined, to entertain the friend waiting for something *more*. Petronius was probably expecting to read Sidonius' poetry and had to settle for some letters with an accompanying note. Even though Sidonius formally renounced writing poetry, he certainly continued to write verses on various occasions, as is attested by the presence in his books of letters of various *carmina*, written at that time, and not before the bishopric.[42]

This passage would seem almost deliberately non-specific and, if it is impossible to guess with some degree of certainty the content of the writing-tablets mentioned, the passage at least confirms there was an exchange of literary works between the two, prior to the dedication of Book 8 to Petronius.

---

41. For the modesty topos in Sidonius see Consolino 1974, 430–2.
42. One could mention, by way of example, the presence, in Books 8 and 9 of the letters, of poetry composed at that time and not before. In *Ep.* 8.9 Sidonius encloses in his letter to Lampridius verses he 'composed in the midst of mental tribulation' given his present situation of exile (*Ep.* 8.9.4 *ineptias istas, quas inter animi supplicia conscripsimus*); in *Ep.* 9.13, even though he asserts he has been busily engaged in writing prose more than poetry, Sidonius writes Asclepiads at Tonantius' request, so that the friend might declaim at a banquet. Moreover, in *Ep.* 9.15.1 he explicitly says he writes at Gelasius' request in the unfamiliar iambic senarius (*metrum infrequentatum*). It is also important to stress that the subsequent letter to Firminus attests that those verses sent to Gelasius circulated. In fact, since Firminus enjoyed reading them, Sidonius sends Sapphic stanzas to him in *Ep.* 9.16.3 *quia tibi nuper ad Gelasium uirum sat benignissimum missos iambicos placuisse pronuntias, per hos te quoque Mytilenaei oppidi uernulas munerabor* ('since you relate that you have enjoyed the iambic verses that not long ago I sent to the most kind Gelasius, I will reward you too with these, natives of the city of Mytilene'). On Sidonius' iambic senarii and Sapphic stanzas, see Condorelli 2020a, 455–7 and 459–61.

LETTER 1

Dating elements

According to Loyen, *Ep.* 5.1 was written between the end of 470 and the early months of 471, at what he thought was the beginning of Sidonius' episcopate.[43] He infers this from the use of the expression *post opem Christi* and from the mention (as letter-bearer) of the deacon Vindicius, whom Loyen believes to be a member of the Church of Auvergne.[44] As a matter of fact, that these elements alone might lead one to choose such a specific date for the letter is, at the very least, debatable.[45] However, Sidonius' appointment as bishop might well be the terminus *post quem* for the epistle, if we consider that it was common practice for deacons like Vindicius to deal with similar assignments from their superiors and for Sidonius, once he had become a bishop, to ask clergymen to be letter-bearers, as van Waarden points out.[46] That is also why Mathisen's suggestion to date the letter between 470 and 475, a broad range of years after his appointment, seems a more cautious and sensible choice. This letter is also dated to 478 in *PLRE* without specific explanation;[47] and yet there is no ground to sustain this dating, since Books 1–7 are generally believed to have been published as a single volume in 477.[48] This is one of the numerous letters for which one can only indicate a range of years, or that it was written presumably after the start of the bishopric, that is, after 469.

---

43. Loyen 1970a, 173 and 255. See also *PCBE* 4 s.v. Petronius 3, 1475–6; Bellès 1998, 88 is of the same opinion.
44. See also *PCBE* 4 s.v. Vindicius, 1985.
45. For Loyen's 'questionable habit' of using Christian expressions to date the letters, see Kelly 2020, 180.
46. Van Waarden 2010, 223–4. On the other hand, Amherdt 2001, 172 provides a list of clergymen who were letter bearers for Sidonius and asserts that, in comparison with Paulinus of Nola, Sidonius entrusted fewer letters to members of the clergy.
47. *PLRE* 2, s.v. Petronius 5, 863.
48. As is argued in Harries 1994, 9, followed by Mratschek 2017, 312, Hanaghan 2019, 170–4 and Kelly 2020, 185–9. Kelly also summarises previous theories concerning the publication of the collection.

SIDONIUS PETRONIO SUO SALUTEM

1. Audio quod lectitandis epistulis meis uoluptuosam patientiam inpendas. Magnum hoc est et litterarum uiro conuenientissimum, cum studiis ipse maxumis polleas, ea in aliis etiam minima complecti. Sed ex hoc ipso consummatissima tibi gloria reponderatur; nam satis eminet meritis ingenii proprii qui fuerit fautor alieni.

2. Commendo Vindicium necessarium meum, uirum religiosum et leuiticae dignitati, quam nuper indeptus est, accommodatissimum. Cui meis e pugillaribus transferre quae iusseras non uacans, proquam prouincia fuit, hic uobis aliquid neniarum munusculi uice detuli; quamquam, quae tua sanctitas, semper grandia litteras nostras praemia putes.

3. Interea necessitatem praefati portitoris insinuo, quem traxit isto negotii oborti bipertita condicio. Siquidem hac definitione perrexit, ut aut ineat litem aut adeat hereditatem. Nam patrueli paterno caelibi intestatoque defuncto per agnationis praerogatiuam succedere parat, nisi tamen coeptis factiosa uis obuiet. Contra quas tamen cunctas difficultates solus post opem Christi supplici tuo sufficis, cuius confido quod, si meruerit persona gratiam, consequetur causa uictoriam. Vale.

PETRONIO δ : PETREIO α
§ 2 cui *codd.* : qui *Gustafsson*
proquam *Gustafsson* : perquam *codd.*
prouincia α (prouintia *C*) *LMP* : prouinciam *Lütjohann*
detuli *Mohr* : detulit *codd.*

LETTER 1

SIDONIUS TO HIS FRIEND PETRONIUS

1. I hear that you devote a pleasurable endurance to repeatedly reading my letters. This is noble of you, most appropriate for a learned man, since you yourself are highly esteemed for most important literary works, and yet you embrace even the insignificant writings of others. But because of this, you are rewarded with the highest praise; for certainly he who is the patron of other people's genius quite distinguishes himself for the merits of his own.

2. I commend to your care my friend Vindicius: he is a pious man, and absolutely fit for the rank of deacon which he recently attained. Since I did not have time to transcribe for him what you had asked from my writing-tablets, as was my duty, I entrusted him instead with some trifles as a little present; albeit your virtue is such that you always prize my letters as mighty rewards.

3. Meanwhile, I convey the difficult situation experienced by the aforesaid bearer, who is drawn here by the twofold condition of a matter that has arisen, since he firmly upholds this resolution: either to go to trial or to take possession of his inheritance. In fact, by virtue of the prerogative of paternal consanguinity, he intends to succeed to his cousin on his father's side, who died unmarried and intestate, unless perhaps a violent faction opposes his purpose. Only you, after Christ's help, have the ability to deal with all these difficulties for this suppliant of yours, and I am sure his case will attain victory, should his character win your favour. Farewell.

Commentary

§ 1

Audio quod: The choice to begin Book 5 with such an informal expression seems to convey a sense of familiarity and ease in approaching the reading of the text. It is a construction which Sidonius employs more often than that of the accusative + infinitive (which for instance we find in the opening lines of *Ep.* 2.14.1 *audio . . . respondere uindemiam*). It also indicates that the relationship between the author and the addressee is friendly, since *audio quod* gives way to the recount of the hearsay – particularly flattering for Sidonius – that Petronius enjoyed reading his works repeatedly. This syntagma is variously attested in contexts of intended informality and direct address to the interlocutor, and the expression also conveys surprise about what is 'heard'. In Pliny the Younger's *Panegyricus* 65.1.4–5 (*quod ego nunc primum audio, nunc primum disco*) the panegyrist is surprised to hear that Trajan wishes to be subject to laws like any other Roman. Compare the opening sections of Aug. *Ep.* 179.1 to bishop John (*Pelagium . . . quem audio quod multum diligis*), and Aug. *Ep.* 217.1 to Vitalis, written after Augustine heard of his recent assertions close to Pelagianism; on this letter see Teske 2005, 52. The phrase appears three times in Sidonius' corpus: in *Ep.* 1.11, when describing the tense atmosphere looming over him at court, Sidonius has emperor Majorian wittily say to him (*Ep.* 1.11.13) '*audio, comes Sidoni, quod satiram scribas*'. In this case as well, the expression refers to hearsay and relates the surprise of the emperor, who, however, shows magnanimity and seems amused. The occurrence of the expression in *Ep.* 5.5.3 reflects the same mixture of surprise and amusement (see the commentary ad loc.) as is the case in this letter to Petronius. All three occurrences in Sidonius fit the discussion in the section *cum enuntiatione hypotactica* in *TLL* 2.1273 s.v. *audio* 59–75 (by Sinko).

lectitandis epistulis meis: the use of the frequentative *lectito* enhances the keen interest Petronius seems to have in reading Sidonius' writings. Since the first occurrences in Cicero, both in treatises and in *Letters* (e.g. Cic. *Brut.* 121; Cic. *Att.* 12.18.1), the term is widely attested in Latin texts, with an uncommonly large number of occurrences in the *Letters* of Pliny the Younger (an acknowledged model of Sidonius), where the verb is usually employed to enhance Pliny's or the addressee's interest in literature. See in particular the description of the library in Pliny's villa at Laurentum (Plin. *Ep.* 2.17.8), where an *armarium* contained 'books that were not to be read, but to be read many times' (*quod non legendos libros sed lectitandos capit*), and the index of Pliny the Elder's works sent in Plin. *Ep.* 3.5.1 to Baebius Macer, who 'frequently reads' (*lectitas*) his uncle's literary works. See also the similar praises of the eagerness to read of Calpurnia Hispulla's niece in Plin. *Ep.* 4.19.2, and of Pomponius Bassus in Plin. *Ep.* 4.23.1. In *Symm. Ep.* 7.18.3 Symmachus recounts that Attalus himself disclosed to him that he enjoys reading texts in Latin and Greek (*lectitasse autem te in multo otio utriusque linguae auctores, ipse index fuisti*). Note how Plin. *Epp.* 3.5 and 4.23 and Symm. *Ep.* 7.18 are all, like Sidon. *Ep.* 5.1, contexts in which the author reports something he heard, either from friends or from the addressee himself. The verb occurs often in Jerome and Augustine and is notably attested in Mamertus Claudianus' *Anim. praef.* p. 20 *en legisti, eruditissime uirorum, quod lectitabis*, when the author reminds Sidonius of his responsibility and role in the publishing process (see the introduction to *Ep.* 5.2 for further context). In *Anim.* 1.1, p. 24 (*chartulam . . . studiose lectitabant*) Claudianus polemically refers to how studiously his friends were reading Faustus' letter, to which the treatise constitutes a response. In most of the Sidonian occurrences, as in Pliny and Symmachus, the verb indicates the habit of frequently reading canonical literature: in the prose epilogue of Sidon. *Carm.* 22.6 it refers to Statius' *Siluae*; in *Ep.* 2.9.4, as a guest, Sidonius has at his disposal manuscripts of two pairs of authors he wishes to *lectitare* (Augustine and Varro for prose, Horace and Prudentius for poetry); in *Ep.* 2.10 the author wishes Hesperius' thirst for reading to be without limit. The same can be said for contemporary writings, either those of his friends (see Secundinus' verses in *Ep.* 5.8.1 and, in *Ep.* 9.9.8, Faustus' works, which Sidonius literally snatches from the bearer in order to read, re-read and excerpt them); or his own works eagerly read by others, as in *Ep.* 5.1.1 and in *Ep.* 9.11.6, when Lupus is said to have been jealously keeping a book by Sidonius so that he can re-read it at leisure. Only in *Ep.* 4.9.3 does the verb refer to Holy Scriptures and designates the frequent reading and chanting of Psalms. Lastly, it can be argued that *lectito* is used simply for variation from *legere* only in *Ep.* 7.18.3 (see van Waaden 2016, 266) and in *Ep.* 8.6.1. See *TLL* 7.2.1090 s.v. *lectito* 28 (by Beikircher); *L&S* s.v.

uoluptuosam patientiam: This elegant *iunctura* has its first occurrence in this letter and is not attested in later literature. The adjective *uoluptuosus* is post-Augustan and first appears in Plin. *Ep.* 3.19.2. Sidonius employs it often (e.g. in *Ep.* 1.5.1 to refer to a friend who enjoys reading his writings) while *tempus* is said to be *uoluptuosissimum* in Sidon. *Ep.* 2.9.1. See Geisler 1887, 365.

litterarum uiro: In *Ep.* 1.78.1 Symmachus defines Hesperius as *unus . . . ex summatibus litterarum uiris*, whom he wishes could appreciate his speech. In *Ep.* 7.14.1 the expression concerns Sidonius and his *sodales*. These two *loci similes* are listed in Geisler 1887, 365.

conuenientissimum: The first occurrence of this superlative is in the technical notations of Vitruvius 3.1.3; it then has the largest number of occurrences in Pliny the Younger and in Augustine (though in the latter the majority of occurrences concern the adverbial form *conuenientissime*). Pliny employs the superlative always in a context of praise of Trajan and in passages of artificial and studied tone: Plin. *Ep.* 3.18.1 concerns his decision to write the *Panegyricus*; *Epp.* 10.3a.2 and 10.41.1 are both addressed to the emperor; and lastly it occurs in the *Panegyricus* itself (87.1). Not only does Sidonius employ the superlative often in his works, but in the first part of this letter the overall presence of superlatives is overabundant, conveying a sense of artificiality and formalism reminiscent of Pliny's context.

magnum . . . maxumis . . . minima: The contraposition highlights Petronius' magnanimity and generosity, but it is also a display of false modesty on Sidonius' part. Note that the panache of the passage is heightened by rhythm: a double cretic at *maxumis polleas* and a paeon IV spondee at *minima complecti*.

consummatissima . . . gloria: The superlative is previously attested in Plin. *Ep.* 2.7.6 (referring to a *iuuenis*) and it also occurs other three times in Sidonius (*Epp.* 4.17.3, 7.2.1, 8.15.1), where it always concerns men (*uiri* and *pontifices*); therefore, the occurrence in *Ep.* 5.1 in *iunctura* with *gloria* is unique. Van Waarden 2010, 139 has pointed out that the superlative may be a southern Gallic usage since its only other attestation is in Cassian. *Conl.* 3.19.16 (*consummatissimo uiro similis*), at the beginning of the fifth century; see also *TLL* s.v. *consummo* 4.604.72 (by Elsperger) and, for Pliny's use, see Whitton 2013, 135.

reponderatur: The only known attestations of the verb *repondero*, which means 'to repay', are in Mamertus Claudianus and in other two passages of Sidonius' *Letters*; hence, the verb is ascribable to an extremely narrow geographic and chronological milieu. When ending the third book of the *De statu animae*, Claudianus polemically asserts that he has 'only repaid falsity with truth' (3.18 *solam tibi pro falsitate ueritatem haud pari uicissitudine reponderaui*); the Sidonian occurrences are in *Ep.* 1.4.3 (for which see Köhler 1995, 183) and in *Ep.* 9.11.8. For Sidonius being in possession of his own copy of Mamertus Claudianus' work see *Ep.* 5.2.

ingenii . . . fautor: The *iunctura* is Sidonian; however, note that Pliny ends *Ep.* 6.23.5 by stressing the importance of a patron (*fautor etiam commendatorque*) because 'even the most talented minds need guidance'. See also *TLL* 6.1.389 s.v. *fautor* 72 (by Hofmann).

§ 2

Commendo Vindicium necessarium meum: This is a common way of introducing the *commendatus* and constitutes the first element that allows one to define the letter as an *epistula commendaticia* (see the introduction also for Vindicius' identity). *Necessarius* could indicate friends, family members, or those who were close to someone through ties of obligation. For Vindicius, the latter seems fitting – see *TLL* 9.3.353 s.v. *necessarius* 11 (by Reineke and Rocchi).

leuiticae dignitati: The *iunctura* is Sidonian, and indicates that Vindicius was a deacon. A similar expression is used with regard to another letter bearer at the beginning of Sidon. *Ep.* 6.10.1 *gerulum litterarum leuitici ordinis honestat officium* ('the bearer of this letter holds with dignity the office of deacon').

quam nuper indeptus est, accommodatissimum: The redundant superlative is not often attested in Latin literature and mostly refers, rather than to people, to inanimate objects, as in Plin. *Ep.* 5.19.7 (a commendation letter for his freedman Zosimus, sent to a farm to enjoy fresh air and milk, *accommodatissimum* to his precarious health), with the sole exceptions of Cic. *Att.* 9.11A.3 (who defines himself as the most appropriate mediator between Caesar and Pompey) and of this Sidonian passage. As is explained in the General Introduction (in the section on prose rhythm), Sidonius employs the same rhythm in three consecutive clausulae: *nuper indeptus est*; *ac-commodatissimum* and the following *iusseras non uacans* are all double cretics.

Cui . . . detuli: Sidonius argues it was his duty (*prouincia*) to send what had been asked of him. With the meaning of 'social duty' the noun has occurrences since Plautus (e.g. *Capt.* 156; *Pseud.* 148); cf. Symm. *Ep.* 1.1.6 *tibi . . . optionis huius delego prouinciam*, Mam. Claud. *Anim.* 3.15, p. 184 *plusculum respondere mihi prouincia fuit* and the ironic occurrence in Sidon. *Ep.* 5.7.1. See *TLL* 10.2.2339 s.v. *prouincia* 47–68 (by Kruse). As can be surmised from the various conjectures listed in the apparatus, this passage has proved particularly problematic, to the point that Lütjohann has a *crux* in the body of the text. It is worth mentioning, in light of the collation, that *prouintia* is a mistake peculiar to *C*, and is not (as in Lütjohann's apparatus) in *P*. I chose what appears to be the least interventionist approach, by accepting only Gustafsson's conjecture *proquam,* instead of *perquam*, and *detuli* conjectured by Mohr (in place of *detulit* in *codd.*), a choice already made by both Anderson and Loyen. Anderson 1965, 171 n. 2, however, expressed doubts about *proquam*, and yet, palaeographically, the abbreviations of *per* and *pro* could easily be confused with each other. Warmington (in Anderson 1965, 171 n. 2) suggests 'qui . . . perquam praecinctus (*vel etiam* procinctus) fuit *aut* fui'. Therefore he accepts *qui* (Gustafsson's conjecture), leaves in the text *perquam* (*codd.*) and conjectures *praecinctus* (or *procinctus*) in place of the archetypal reading *prouincia*. Warmington thus suggests the following translation: 'Vindicius who, not having any time – he has been in a very great hurry – to copy from my tablets the writing which you had asked for, has here brought to you some doggerel as a humble gift'. And yet, it seems puzzling that Vindicius, who is known to be a letter bearer, should also be the one who copied the texts he is about to deliver. Sidonius had professional copyists at his disposal, as can be surmised when reading the detailed description of the skills of the *bybliopola* in *Ep.* 5.15, but the possibility that a letter bearer would be the same person as the copyist to whom Sidonius would entrust the transcription of what appears to be valuable and unpublished works does not seem compelling.

meis e pugillaribus transferre: The writing surface, either wooden or made of parchment, would probably serve as a personal notebook from which his writings were copied. See *TLL* 10.2.2534 s.v. *pugillaris* 11 (by Cipriani). For the use of *pugillares* see, for instance, Reynolds and Wilson 2013, 34–5 and 249. This noun is employed *stricto sensu* also in Sidon. *Ep.* 4.12.4 (on which see Amherdt 2001, 320) and in *Ep.* 5.17.10, though in the less frequently attested singular form. The word *pugillator* to indicate a letter bearer in *Ep.* 9.14.4 does not seem to match other uses of *pugillares* with the specific metonymical meaning of letters.

LETTER 1

quae iusseras: This reference suggests there had been exchanges of letters and a previous request of copies of Sidonius' works which had not been met.

aliquid neniarum munusculi uice detuli: The noun *nenia* does not simply refer to the composition of *epitaphia* (as in Sidon. *Epp.* 2.8.2, 4.11.6 and 7.17.1) but is here used as a pretended *diminutio* of the value of the works (epistles) he is sending along with this dedicatory letter. This also happens in *Ep.* 1.9.7 (*conlata uestris mea carmina . . . epitaphistarum neniis comparabuntur*), when Sidonius cleverly defines his works as similar to the *neniae* written by the composers of epitaphs in comparison to Heronius' hexameters; and also in the sense of 'trivialities' in *Ep.* 7.18.4 *his licebit neniis auocere*. On this last passage, see van Waarden 2016, 270. On Sidonius' systematic pretended denigration of his own works, defined as *nugae*, *quisquiliae* or *neniae*, see Loyen 1943, 99.

litteras nostras: As stated in the introduction to this letter, this *iunctura* reveals what the *neniae* consist of. See also van Waarden 2016, 270, who suggests *nenia* in *Ep.* 5.1.2 may indicate a 'small collection of letters'.

§ 3

necessitatem . . . portitoris insinuo: This start straightforwardly introduces the commendation, as was common practice. The verb *insinuo* was usually employed to express the act of making something or someone known as, for instance, in Plin. *Pan.* 62.2; see *TLL* 7.1.1915 s.v. *insinuo* 20–4 (by Hugenschmidt). Note the frequent use of the verb by Symmachus, specifically in the opening lines of commendation letters: Symm. *Epp.* 1.40 (*amicum meum promptus commendator insinuo*), 2.80, 9.10.1, 9.32 and 9.59. Sidonius variously employs the verb in other *commendaticiae* at the very beginning of the letters, thus in compliance with Symmachus' model. That is the case, for instance, with the commendation of the secretary in *Ep.* 5.15.1 *bybliopolam . . . insinuo*; with *Ep.* 7.4.1, in which 'Sidonius plunges *in medias res*', to quote van Waarden 2010, 220; and with *Ep.* 7.11.2 *portitorem nostri sermonis, insinuo*. In the last case, although the verb follows salutations of courtesy, it is the first element of the section of mere commendation, as in *Ep.* 5.1. Compare also *Ep.* 1.10.1 *eum tibi sodalem ueterem mihi insinuas*, in which it is Sidonius who receives a *commendaticia*. For this last occurrence, see Geisler 1887, 365. Although the syntagma *insinu** + *portitor** is not attested in earlier

61

literature, it occurs in a similar commendation by Sidonius' contemporary Faustus of Riez, *Ep.* 12, p. 219 (ed. Engelbrecht 1891) *portitorem sanctum presbyterum . . . insinuo.*

bipertita condicio: The *iunctura*, not known to occur previously, is also attested in Sidonius' philosophical dissertation to Philagrius of *Ep.* 7.14.8, where the human mind is said to be 'characterised by a bipartite condition' (van Waarden 2016, 153). Sidonius has a predilection for the adjective *bipertitus*, attested seven times in the *Letters*, notably in another passage of Book 5, when describing the two factions – one demanding the ball, the other boardgames – in the bizarre narrative of *Ep.* 5.17.6 *bipertitis . . . acclamationibus*. See also *TLL* 2.2002 s.v. *bipertitus* 67–9 (by Ihm). Like the previous *porti-toris insinuo, biper-tita condicio* also creates a cretic tribrach.

hac definitione perrexit: *Definitio* is attested with the rare meaning of 'resolution' exclusively in Christian contexts, for instance in Aug. *Serm.* 139.2 (*stabili definitione seruare*); see *TLL* 5.1.352 s.v. *definitio* 53–61 (by Bögel).

ut aut ineat litem aut adeat hereditatem: In the broader sense of engaging in a debate see Mar. Victorin. *Defin.* l. 6 *qui inituri sunt eam litem*; see also *TLL* 7.1.1297 s.v. *ineo* 38 (by Rehm), in which Victorinus' attestation is listed among those concerning hostilities. In Sidonius the syntagma *ineat litem* has a specific juridical meaning and its choice seems fitting for the purpose of the effective contraposition between *ineo* and *adeo*, as a way of ending the sentence efficaciously. *Adire hereditatem* is a syntagma attested more often and has its first occurrence in Cic. *Off.* 3.93. For the purpose of this commentary it seems useful to signal its two occurrences in Plin. *Epp.* 2.4.1 and 10.75.2, in contexts both pertaining to contingent situations, although not in commendations as in Sidonius (Pliny writes *Ep.* 2.4 as a creditor and *Ep.* 10.75 is an official letter to Trajan). For obvious reasons, this expression occurs most often in juridical texts, mainly in Gaius and Ulpian; the only occurrence in later Latin that precedes Sidonius is in Ambrose *Off.* 3.11.70 (ed. Davidson 2001).

per agnationis praerogatiuam: This syntagma, not attested before Sidonius, is used to indicate that the bearer's demands are legitimised by his right to succession by *agnatio*, that is, by virtue of paternal consanguinity. On *agnatio* as a fundamental concept at the basis of the right of intestate inheritance in Roman law and indicating the relationship between those descending from the paterfamilias in a purely male line see Kaser 1955, 58–9; *DNP* s.v. *agnatio*, 345 by Manthe; see also *TLL* 1.1349.46 (by Vollmer), which lists this Sidonian occurrence along with numerous juridical attestations, one of which, though later than Sidonius', appropriately summarises the concept because of its compendious nature, being a synthesis of previous Roman legislation: *Lex Romana Burgundionum,* 10.9 *sciendum tamen est, agnatos etiam longiori gradu positos cognatis proximioribus anteferri. Agnati enim sunt per uirilem sexum uenientes, cognati, qui per feminas ueniunt.* It would seem probable that those who may strongly oppose the succession by Vindicius could have been *cognati* instead of *agnati.* By virtue of *agnatio*, since Vindicius' cousin had died unmarried and intestate, as Sidonius remarks to present his case, he should have 'prerogative of inheritance' and therefore he should rightfully succeed.

factiosa uis: This is the only time this *iunctura* (which creates a double cretic at *facti-osa uis obuiet*) is known to occur. This studied adjective is employed by Sidonius also in *Ep.* 1.11.8 (when describing a *turba*), although, as is pointed out in *TLL* 6.1.138 s.v. *factiosus* 46–8 (by Wulff), in *Ep.* 1.11 it has the meaning of 'tumultuous' while the occurrence in *Ep.* 3.10.2 (*potentes factiososque*), in *Ep.* 5.1.3 and that of the adverb in *Ep.* 4.24.4 express the idea of *dolus*, deceit.

solus post opem Christi . . . consequetur causa uictoriam: That is quite a compliment to the addressee, in whose ability to solve the matter Sidonius puts his absolute trust, should Petronius find the *commendatus* to his liking. All the occurrences in Sidonius of *post opem Christi* and of similar expressions (e.g. *sub ope Christi*; *praeuio Christo*; *praesule deo*) are listed by Amherdt 2001, 79, who stresses how these interjections are interferences of *sermo cottidianus* in the author's prose, as was common practice: 'il est de bon ton de mêler à la lettre des expressions du langage parlé' says Amherdt 2001, 46. On the Sidonian use see also van Waarden 2010, 88. For the expression *post opem dei* (and *similia*) as part of epistolary *topica* since Cicero and for its presence in Symmachus see Cugusi 1983, 82. Considering the nature of said expressions as familiar and standard, it does not seem fruitful to linger on their usage on Sidonius' part in other passages of this book, for which the reader can refer to this note. Lastly, *difficultates* and the following *post opem Christi* create a sequence of two cretic spondee *clausulae.*

LETTER 2

Content

The witty note to Nymphidius asking him to return Sidonius' copy of the *De statu animae* is an excuse to praise Mamertus Claudianus' treatise, the commendation of which constitutes the focus of the the opening lines of the letter.

The addressee Nymphidius

The grace and splendid eloquence that Sidonius employs to praise Claudianus are suddenly followed by witty comments on Nymphidius' inability to keep his word, and by an ironic ending reminiscent of epigrammatic models. With its amicable address, the text conveys the impression that Sidonius and the addressee share a familiar code, and are on good terms; this assumption would explain the ending of the epistle, where Sidonius portrays Nymphidius as someone who is more reluctant to part with the parchment than with its content. Sidonius' wry remarks on the book not having found its way home should therefore be interpreted as overtly playful.

The information concerning Nymphidius detectable from the letter is scarce; however, there is nothing to contradict the possibility that he is the same Nymphidius mentioned in *Carm.* 15.200, grandfather of Araneola or Polemius and portrayed in the act of ratifying their contract of marriage in 461 or 462, other than the fact that he would have been quite old at the time of the letter, if a grandchild had been married over a decade before.[1]

---

1. For the identification with Nymphidius of *Carm.* 15 see Stroheker 1948, 196 n. 264, *PLRE* 2, s.v. Nymphidius 1, 789 and *PCBE* 4 s.v. Nymphidius, 1384. This possibility is rejected by Loyen 1960, 191 n. 27.

LETTER 2

Sidonius and Mamertus Claudianus

By contrast, the friendship between Mamertus Claudianus and Sidonius is well attested. For instance, in a letter included in Sidonius' epistolary collection, Claudianus defines himself as an intimate and close friend of Sidonius (*Ep.* 4.2.4 *egomet specialis atque intumus*).[2] In this letter Claudianus reproaches his friend for his silence: he had sent his *De statu animae*, dedicated to him, but although Sidonius has been corresponding with others, he is yet to comment on his work. The requested answer ensues in the Sidonian corpus: *Ep.* 4.3, in which the author apologises for the lateness of his response and thanks Claudianus for having dedicated his literary work to him.

The epistolary collection of Sidonius also bears witness to Claudianus' epitaph, written by Sidonius in *Ep.* 4.11, a letter sent to Claudianus' nephew Petreius. This is an example of elegant and emphatic writing, in which the author effectively portrays Claudianus as an enlightened philosopher, who hosted his disciples at his home with the purpose of discussion and sharing his wisdom with them.[3]

> *Deus bone, quid erat illud, quotiens ad eum sola consultationis gratia conueniebamus! Quam ille omnibus statim totum non dubitans, non fastidiens aperiebat, uoluptuosissimum reputans, si forte oborta quarumpiam quaestionum insolubilitate labyrinthica scientiae suae thesauri euentilarentur.* (Sidon. *Ep.* 4.11.2)

Good Lord! How delightful it was whenever we gathered at his place just for the sake of discussion! How he would explain all to everyone, without hesitation or disdain, since he considered it most pleasurable to winnow the treasures of his knowledge if, by chance, the labyrinthine insolubility of any dispute had arisen.

Genre: a letter on literary matters

The letter can be ascribed to the genre of 'epistles on literary matters' according to Cugusi's categorisation: a type of letter common in epistolary collections since the Late Republic. As Cugusi points out,[4] these letters

---

2. For extensive information on Mamertus Claudianus see *PCBE* 4, s.v. Mamertus Claudianus 1, 481; Mathisen 1982, 378.
3. For the rigour and patience showed by Claudianus in the discussions with his students and for the influence these lectures had on Sidonius, being a sort of an extension of his previous formal schooling, see Harries 1994, 107.
4. Cugusi 1983, 110.

usually reported the authors' opinions on literary works of others, and illustrious predecessors of the Sidonian letter include, for instance, Cicero commenting on Lucretius (*Q. fr.* 2.10 (9)), on Calvus (*Fam.* 15.21.4) and on Brutus (*Att.* 15.1A.2), as well as Seneca's judgements on Papirius Fabianus and Maecenas (*Epp.* 100 and 114).

Similar letters can also be found in Pliny's collection, notably those in which the author commented on the artistry of Pompeius Saturninus (*Ep.* 1.16), Silius Italicus (*Ep.* 3.7) and Martial (*Ep.* 3.21). Pliny's literary remarks mostly pertain to contemporary authors,[5] suggesting a certain amount of audacity, as noted by Cova.[6] In fact, what is said only in passing by Cicero becomes a feature in Pliny, who writes for posterity and therefore aims to give a picture of his literary time. To this list of more renowned authors, it is also possible to add Pliny's encouragement and councils to his friend Caninius, who was at the time composing a history of the Dacian War. After having warned the addressee of the dangers he may incur, Pliny firmly asks Caninius to send him the first part of the work 'as soon as it is finished or even before that' (Plin. *Ep.* 8.4).

Symmachus praises contemporary literature as well, for instance in *Ep.* 1.14, a heartfelt eulogy of *Mosella* sent to its author, Ausonius. In the letter Symmachus complains because Ausonius had not sent him his work.

> *Volitat tuus Mosella per manus sinusque multorum diuinis a te uersibus consecratus, sed tantum nostra ora praelabitur. Cur me istius libelli, quaeso, exortem esse uoluisti?* (Symm. *Ep.* 1.14.2)

> Hallowed by you in immortal verses, your Moselle flies about through the hands and pockets of many, but it glides past me. Why, I beseech you, did you want me to be deprived of your little book?

When Symmachus commends contemporaries, he seems to do so by directly writing to the addressee of his literary merits, instead of praising a third

---

5. For instance, Pliny stresses the importance of praising Saturninus because he is a contemporary, so that him still being alive shall not be of detriment to the fame of his works: *Ep.* 1.16.8 *neque enim debet operibus eius obesse quod uiuit*. On the other hand, the eulogies of Silius Italicus and Martial can be defined as epitaphs, written upon hearing of the death of the two authors.

6. As stressed by Cova 1966, 65, Pliny's interest in the present is coherent with his intention to be a promoter of culture: 'l'attenzione di Plinio è rivolta solo al presente, anzi al presente attivo, in coerenza con il suo proposito di giovare al ben fare, al suo ruolo di promotore della cultura'.

LETTER 2

party. By way of example, that is the case of Symmachus' recognition of Naucellius' value in Book 3.[7] Not only does Symmachus praise the friend's *opusculum* he had gifted him[8] and lauds his pages as *Tulliano segmentatae auro*,[9] but the relationship between the two can be considered as exemplary for Sidonius' appraisal of Mamertus Claudianus and for the features of their friendly exchanges. In both cases, the letters are eloquent in terms of mutual esteem and cooperation, which is testified by the personal intervention of Symmachus and Sidonius in the improvement of the friends' works. The former, in fact, affirms he amended the order of Naucellius' *eglogae* in the codex the addressee had sent him,[10] while the *Praefatio* of the *De statu animae* states Sidonius had a role in the publication of the treatise, as is argued in the following pages of this introduction. Sidonius, therefore, is legitimately following in the footsteps of his models when he writes this display piece, singing the praises of the contemporary author – and good friend of his – Mamertus Claudianus.

As far as lending books is concerned, as Pellizzari points out,[11] it would seem that Ammianus' taunts of senatorial libraries being 'sealed like tombs' (Amm. 14.6.18 *bibliothecis sepulchrorum ritu in perpetuum clausis*) does not match the intense activity of book loans to allow the making of personal copies testified by Symmachus, who, for instance, lends his newly acquired copy of Pliny the Elder's *Naturalis Historia* to Ausonius in *Ep.* 1.24 and gives a copy of Livy as a *munus* to Valerianus in *Ep.* 9.13.[12] Sidonius is, therefore, a continuator of this intellectual tradition.

In the middle of a dispute

It has already been pointed out by Fernández López, and subsequently by Amherdt, that there are exact connections between Sidon. *Ep.* 4.3 and

---

7. In particular *Epp.* 3.11, 3.12, 3.13, 3.14 and 3.15.
8. *Ep.* 3.11.3. The book was a translation of a Greek text, possibly *excerpta* of Aristotle's Πολιτεῖαι, as in Callu 1975 *passim*; Pellizzari 1998, 88; more recently, Van Hoof and Van Nuffelen 2020, 72 argued it was a work on Roman history.
9. Symm. *Ep.* 3.12.2.
10. Symm. *Ep.* 3.11.4 *carminum tuorum codicem reportandum puero tradidi, et quia eglogarum confusus ordo est, quem descripsimus, simul misi.* On Symmachus' role in the emendation of his friend's writings see Pellizzari 1998, 91.
11. Pellizzari 1998, 88.
12. An activity which of course had a precedent in Pliny, as in the previously mentioned *Ep.* 8.4.

Ep. 5.2 in the praise of Mamertus Claudianus' ability to master all the disciplines.[13]

Table 8 lists the matching occurrences, as outlined by Fernández López, to give a useful idea of the recurring subjects mentioned and of the similar phrasing in the two letters.[14]

Table 8. Matching occurrences in *Epp.* 5.2 and 4.3

Ep. 5.2	*Ep.* 4.3
grammatica diuidit	*diuidit ut Socrates*
oratoria declamat	*ut Aeschines . . . Demosthenes . . . Hortensius . . . Tullius*
arithmetica numerat	*cum Chrysippo numeros*
geometrica metitur	*cum Euclide mensuras*
musica ponderat	*cum Zeto pondera*
dialectica disputat	*nemo ... quae uoluit affirmare sic ualuit*
astrologia praenoscit	*cum Euphrate horoscopium – cum Atlante sidera*
architectonica struit	*cum Vitruuio perpendiculum . . . instruit ut Hieronymus, destruit ut Lactantius, adstruit ut Augustinus*
metrica modulatur	*cum Orpheo plectrum*

In *Ep.* 4.3, not only is the praise longer and more articulate than in *Ep.* 5.2, but there is also a direct comparison between Mamertus Claudianus and a long list of personalities that embody the disciplines they mastered. In *Ep.* 5.2, possibly the need to laud the work more than its author entails a shift to a less specific sphere of comparisons, even though the fields of knowledge mentioned remain the same.

And yet, it should be emphasised how Sidonius, even in the longer and more detailed praise in *Ep.* 4.3, never delves deeper and does not express any opinion on the philosophical content of the treatise. In *Ep.* 4.3.4, he points out that, from time to time, the rich, well-argued and tight argument of Claudianus is interspersed with *tempestiua dulcedo*, so that the reader's attention, exhausted by the thorough philosophical analysis, can rest through pleasant digressions, 'as if a harbour appears in the distance while travelling by open sea'.[15]

---

13. Fernández López 1994, 76; Amherdt 2001, 111.
14. For an extensive study of the parallels between the two letters see the following commentary.
15. Sidon. *Ep.* 4.3.4 *ut lectoris intentionem per euentilata disciplinarum philosophiae membra lassatam repente uoluptuosis excessibus quasi quibusdam pelagi sui portibus foueat?*

The impression this specific passage conveys, together with the overall lack of technicalities on Sidonius' part, is that Sidonius was not really interested in – or, rather, comfortable with – arguing over the detailed philosophical questions dealt with in Claudianus' *De statu animae*.[16] To quote Harries 1994, 109: 'although well-read in the Bible, Sidonius was not an original thinker, and he knew it. Acquaintance with the theological subtleties of Faustus and Claudianus may have convinced him of his unsuitability as a creative theological disputant; while capable of following others, he could not advance the subject himself.'

What is more, the fact Sidonius was also on friendly terms with Faustus of Riez,[17] to whom is ascribed the authorship of the letter *Quaeris me* – the content of which is refuted by Claudianus in *De statu animae* – put Sidonius in an uncomfortable position, to the point that it is likely he did not appreciate the violent tone of its attack on Faustus.[18] It does not seem fortuitous, in conclusion, that Sidonius passed his judgement on the *De statu animae* only after some time and at the explicit request of and after rebuke by Claudianus.[19]

One last piece of information gives a better idea of the troublesome situation Sidonius found himself in, being a friend of both disputants. As highlighted by Pricoco, the praise of Faustus seems a response to the accusations against him made by Claudianus, and the words of praise he dedicates to the two friends are very similar.[20] Both in fact are said to have the merit of

---

16. On the scant interest in philosophy and theology showed by Sidonius, see Bonjour and Solignac 1990, col. 817; Prévot 1997, 223; Santelia 2012, 16. On the other hand, on Sidonius' pastoral and liturgical competence, see Harries 1994, 108: 'because of his preoccupation with style, and his unwillingness to commit himself on doctrinal matters, Sidonius has seemed to some theologically naïve. Such an assessment, however, is incomplete and unfair. Although not a profound exponent of Christian doctrine, Sidonius' reading in the Bible, even as a layman, was extensive.' See also van Waarden 2011, 99 and 106.

17. Sidonius dedicates to Faustus *Carm.* 16 and *Epp.* 9.3 and 9.9, which testify sincere affection and esteem for the addressee. On the relationship between the two, see Santelia 2012, 42–5.

18. At the beginning of his treatise, Claudianus is particularly offensive and the core of his argument is that his opponent is philosophically ignorant and that his views are childish. See Pricoco 1965a, 116 and 121, and also Harries 1994, 109.

19. Claudianus and Sidonius were conscious of the author's identity according to Engelbrecht 1891, xx; of the same opinion is Pricoco 1965a, 115–6. For a detailed analysis of Claudianus' polemical response to Faustus, point by point, see Di Marco 1995.

20. Pricoco 1965a, 121–3.

having brought philosophy into Christianity,[21] and – though the following elements of comparison do not specifically concern Sidon. *Ep.* 5.2, but *Epp.* 4.3 and 4.11 on Claudianus and *Ep.* 9.9 on Faustus – both are said to have followed Plato without giving in to the exteriority entailed in the canonical image of a philosopher (beard and clothes), both employ syllogisms to solve the most difficult questions, and both have defended Christianity from the attacks of its opposers.[22]

Although *Ep.* 9.9 was probably written long after the letters to Claudianus, it constitutes an undeniable gesture of reconciliation and puts Sidonius in a position of neutrality by praising the two in a similar way and not acknowledging the superiority of one over the other.[23]

Nine arts: traces of Varro?

Notably, Loyen believes that in *Ep.* 5.2 Sidonius added architecture and metrics to the traditional liberal arts to get to the number nine, so that it would reflect the number of the Muses.[24] However, the fact that the same disciplines are also mentioned in Sidon. *Ep.* 4.3 might suggest that it was natural for Sidonius to consider the two subjects liberal arts, as if they were canonical.

It is peculiar that one of the few things known of Varro's *Disciplinarum libri* is that this work had nine sections, and it is commonly believed that apart from the seven arts which would become canonical, especially with Martianus Capella, at least one section was dedicated by Varro to architecture (as in Sidonius), while the last book is believed to have been on medicine.[25] Varro's subjects would therefore have been the following: three

---

21. Cf. *Epp.* 4.11.1 (*salua religione philosopharetur*) and 5.2.1 (*peritissimus Christianorum philosophus*) with *Ep.* 9.9.12 (*philosophiam . . . quae . . . mystico amplexu iam defaecata tecum membra coniunxit*). On the meaning of *philosophari,* with relation to Christian doctrine and not in contrast with paganism, see Consolino 1979, 99.
22. For the complete list of parallels between Sidon. *Epp.* 4.3, 4.11 and 9.3, see Pricoco 1965a, 121–2; for Sidonius' re-use of the captive woman in Deut. 21.11–13 as an allegory of Lady Philosophy 'taken by Faustus as his spiritual bride and life companion' see Vessey 2019, 141.
23. Vessey 2019, 142: 'Sidonius was creating a pair of contrasting but broadly compatible verbal autotypes or models of the Christian intellectual as one whose performance would challenge comparison with the "classics" of ancient Graeco-Roman culture'.
24. Loyen 1970a, 175.
25. For a detailed comparative study see Cristante 2008, 53.

literary arts (grammar, dialectic, rhetoric); four 'exact' disciplines (arithmetic, geometry, astronomy, architecture); and two technical arts (music and possibly medicine).[26] If, as Hadot demonstrated,[27] the medieval canon of seven arts did not derive from the Hellenistic tradition but was directly linked to Neoplatonism, one might wonder if Sidonius' list of nine arts was influenced by a more ancient vision of liberal arts that dated back to Varro.

In the three categories mentioned (literary, exact and technical), *Ep.* 5.2 matches Varro's subjects with the sole exception of medicine, which is replaced by *metrica* in Sidonius' letter. On the other hand, the direct influence Varro might have had on *De statu animae* is debated, and d'Alessandro, for instance, believes the author did not depend directly on Varro but rather on Augustine, who served as an intermediary source, to the point that Claudianus' testimony on Varro should be considered, according to the scholar, as 'a mosaic of Augustinian reminiscences'.[28] In fact, as d'Alessandro and Gasti – more recently – highlighted, Mamertus Claudianus' renowned quotation of Cicero's praise of Varro as *doctissimus* and *peritissimus* (Mam. Claud. *Anim.* 2.8, p. 130) is actually modelled on Aug. *Ciu.* 6.2 *'homine', inquit, 'omnium facile acutissimo et sine ulla dubitatione doctissimo'*, where Cicero says that Varro is 'the shrewdest and the most learned of all men'.

> *Marcus Varro, sui saeculi peritissimus et teste Tullio omnium sine dubitatione doctissimus, quid in musicis, quid <in arithmeticis>, quid in geometricis, quid in philosophomenon libris divina quadam disputatione contendit, nisi ut a uisibilibus ad inuisibilia, a localibus ad inlocalia, a corporeis ad incorporea miris aeternae artis modis abstrahat animum . . . ?* (Mam. Claud. *Anim.* 2.8, p. 130)

---

26. Capella's *De nuptiis* did not include medicine and architecture and had the following internal structure: grammar, dialectic, rhetoric, geometry, arithmetic, astronomy and, lastly, music, proceeding from the most concrete to the abstract disciplines; see Scarpa 1988, 6; Cristante 2008, 53. For an extensive analysis of the supposed influence Varro had on Martianus Capella, see Ritschl 1877, 352–402; and, in contrast with his view see Schievenin 1998, 478–93, who reaches the conclusion (p. 492) that Capella referred to Varro only through indirect tradition.
27. Hadot 1984, 156 contested Ritschl's belief that the seven arts already existed in the Hellenistic period and that the education of wealthy Greeks and Romans was founded on those seven arts.
28. d'Alessandro 1997, 368. For parallels and previous bibliography, see also Santelia 2016, 436; Gasti 2017, 308–10. While for instance Dahlmann 1935, 1258 and Solignac 1958, 122 n. 26 believed that Mamertus Claudianus' *De statu animae* is strictly connected to Varro's *Disciplinarum libri*, Hadot 1984, 187–90 is convinced that Claudianus did not have a direct knowledge of Varro's work but derived his knowledge from schoolbooks instead.

Marcus Varro was the most knowledgeable man of his age and, as Cicero attests, beyond doubt the most learned of all men, what does he strive to do, with a sort of godlike argument, in the books of music, of arithmetic, of geometry and of philosophising, other than to abstract the soul, through the astonishing variety of his deathless art, from things visible to invisible, from things that belong in space to things which do not, from the corporeal to the incorporeal . . .

Furthermore, it might also be useful to consider Mamertus Claudianus' list of arts – including philosophy[29] – that we can read in his letter to Sapaudus. If compared to the testimonies presented above, the uniqueness of the following passage lies in the polemical tone of Claudianus, who here laments the decay of Romanness, a decay which concerned various aspects of what made a Roman such, starting with the Latin language.[30]

> *Video enim os Romanum non modo neglegentiae, sed pudori esse Romanis, grammaticam uti quandam barbaram barbarismi et soloecismi pugno et calce propelli, dialecticen tamquam Amazonem stricto decertaturam gladio formidari, rhetoricam ac si[31] grandem dominam in angusto non recipi, musicen uero et geometricam atque arithmeticam tres quasi furias despui, posthinc philosophiam [atque] uti quoddam ominosum bestiale numerari.* (Mam. Claud. *Ep.* 2, p. 204)

In fact, I see Roman Eloquence being an object not only of neglect but considered as a source of shame for Romans, I see Grammar being pushed away, as any barbaric one would be, with the kick and fist of barbarism and of solecism, I see Dialectic being dreaded as an Amazon who, having unsheathed her sword, is about to fight, I see Rhetoric like a distinguished lady who is not welcome in a humble place; moreover, I see Music, Geometry and Arithmetic being spurned as the three Furies, and after these, Philosophy, treated as something beastly and ominous.[32]

It is not the purpose of this work to delve into the much-discussed and thorny problem of Claudianus' direct or indirect knowledge of Varro;[33] however, a more complete picture might be traced by adding a further element for reflection, which does not seem to have been highlighted

---

29. A thing that seems particularly fitting in light of the interests of the author.
30. See introduction to *Ep.* 5.10 for literary decay as a cliché.
31. *Acsi* in the edition was here presented as two words.
32. The only modern edition of the *De statu animae* is that of Engelbrecht 1885 (CSEL 11) and no translation of the text in any language has yet been published.
33. Varro is also mentioned for instance in Mam. Claud. *Ep.* 2, p. 206 among a canon of authors who should be read to improve one's style.

LETTER 2

before, and which can give an indication of the shared elitism and exquisite taste for literary games of the aristocratic circle of which he and Sidonius were members. In *Ep.* 5.2 Sidonius depicts Claudianus as *peritissimus philoso-phus* and *primus eruditorum*, in a way that is not only reminiscent of the two passages by Augustine and Claudianus himself mentioned above, but also of Quintilian's description of Varro.

> *Alterum illud etiam prius saturae genus . . . condidit Terentius Varro, uir Romanorum eruditissimus. Plurimos hic libros et doctissimos conposuit, peritissimus linguae Latinae et omnis antiquitatis et rerum Graecarum nostrarumque.* (Quint. *Inst.* 10.1.95–6)

> Previously that other type of satire too ... was founded by Terentius Varro, the most learned of all Romans. He wrote numerous very learned books, and was extremely knowledgeable about Latin language, about all antiquity and about both Greek and our history.

Sidonius' homage to Claudianus, therefore, is carried out through laudatory words which were once used to describe Varro. The point is that even if Augustine did constitute an intermediary source for the *De statu animae*, it seems sensible to assert that, in fifth-century Gaul, among that circle of *sodales*, Varro was considered to be a model for encyclopaedic studies, whether or not he was known directly.[34] It is easy to imagine that, by the time Claudianus issued his work, the themes of education, *artes liberales* – and possibly the same passages concerning Varro mentioned above – were discussed at length in that literary circle. In the conventional literary game that entailed concealing clever allusions and quotations in reciprocal pleas-antries, Sidonius' praise of his friend Claudianus, comparing him to none other than Varro, was perfectly in line with the taste of the time and of that specific group of intellectuals.[35]

The merits of the *De statu animae*

It should be emphasised that, as Santelia infers,[36] apart from the clear cor-respondences between *Ep.* 5.2 and 4.3, the disciplines mastered by the

---

34. Similar conclusions are reached by Santelia 2016, 436. Analysing *Anim.* 2.8, p. 130, the scholar draws attention to the evidence that *artes liberales* were probably an object of reflection and genuine debate in the intellectual milieu shared by the two.

35. In addition to this, Claudianus himself in *Anim.* 2.7, p. 127 praised Plato with similar words, calling him *princeps philosophus* and *maximus inter philosophos uir*.

36. Santelia 2003–2005, 7 n. 22.

73

deceased Mamertus Claudianus in the Sidonian epitaph (*Ep.* 4.11.6) are also evocative of the *Musae* and of the arts mentioned in *Ep.* 5.2.1. In the epitaph he is called *orator, dialecticus, poeta, / tractator, geometra, musicusque,* hence versed in the most renowned fields of knowledge that are listed in *Ep.* 5.2, after Sidonius defines him as *peritissimus philosophus* and *primus eruditorum.* It is clear then, that when Sidonius speaks of Claudianus, he has in mind a very specific and recurring image of savant capable of excelling in all the fields of knowledge.

However, only a closer look at the *De statu animae* can reveal whether those of Sidonius are just standardised pleasantries or whether his laudatory words match actual passages of Claudianus' work.[37] The following recognition is aimed at proving Sidonius' comments do not simply answer a topos but have in mind specific sections of his friend's work. Let us start by looking at the outline of the *De statu animae* provided in the *praefatio* dedicated to Sidonius, where Claudianus describes the content of each of the three books.

> *(Primus liber) abhinc itidem ad erudiendum in ea quae sunt obscuriora lectorem quippiam ex geometricis et arithmeticis atque etiam ex dialecticis et nonnullis . . . philosophomenon regulis . . . praelibauit.* (Mam. Claud. *Anim. praef.*, p. 19)

Hence, in the same way, in order to instruct the reader on some rather obscure passages, Book 1 examines some things taken from geometricians and arithmeticians as well as some from the dialecticians, and many from the principles of philosophers.

Claudianus then introduces Book 2 by saying:

> *Secundus post principium de mensura, numero et pondere non otiose et uti autumo non infructuose dissertat.* (Mam. Claud. *Anim. praef.*, p. 20)

Book 2, after the preface, deals with measure, number and weight in a way that is not ineffectual nor, I think, fruitless.

As stated here in the prefatory section, Claudianus does follow a multidisciplinary approach throughout the books in order to provide foundations and

---

37. It is striking how a work which was appreciated in the Middle Ages is so understudied nowadays. An example of how the *De statu animae* kept being read is, for instance, the quotation of two passages (*Anim.* 1.17 and 1.18) in the twelfth-century biography of the visionary Alpaïs of Cudot (ed. Stein 1995, 217). On Claudianus as a source of Cartesius and on his reception through to the nineteenth century, see Micaelli 2014, 206 n. 71.

sustain his assertions concerning the nature of the soul, and, in particular, the most technical disciplines play a crucial role in his argumentative process.

For instance, astrology is the first that comes into play, when, in *Anim.* 1.12–13, Claudianus contests Faustus' letter on the corporeality of angels and of stars, intertwining notions of astrology with the authority of Jerome (which Faustus himself had misinterpreted, in Claudianus' opinion) and of Paul.[38] And, symmetrically, astrology is also part of the dissertation in Book 3, where Claudianus argues that the sun, the moon and the stars are to be considered as bodies without a soul (*Anim.* 3.15, p. 184 *sicuti enim sol corpus est et saxum quodlibet longe disparile huic perinde tamen corpus est, sic equidem omnigenum natura uitarum incorporea scilicet omnis est*).

Arithmetic and geometry have a major role, starting in *Anim.* 1.15, where Claudianus affirms that what can be said with certainty for corporeal things in terms of addition, collocation in space or dimensions does not apply to the Trinity.[39] Furthermore, in *Anim.* 1.25, Claudianus is masterful in resorting to concrete examples taken from geometry, arithmetic and, lastly, dialectic in order to enlighten the reader with concrete examples (*ad erudiendum lectorem in ea quae obscura sunt*) and with the final aim of reaching the conclusion that one should not seek something that is 'not in place', like the soul, through something 'in place', that is, corporeality.[40]

His approach is that of a teacher, as testified by the following passage, which introduces the description of how to draw a triangle so that his example can be widely understood.

> *Nam qui uel aliquid eruditus est, credo, nouerit in geometrica disciplina quid sit punctum quidue linea, sed quia inter eos, qui ista dignabuntur legere, potest esse qui nesciat, de hoc ipso paululum dissertando quaeramus.* (Mam. Claud. *Anim.* 1.25, p. 88)

> Certainly I trust that he who is learned, even a little, will know what a point is in the discipline of geometry, and what a line is, but since among those who will deign to read these things there may be someone who does not know, let us examine the subject, discussing it briefly.

---

38. For the relationship between Claudianus and patristic texts, Augustine in particular, see Micaelli 2014, 193–5 and 197–200.

39. See *Anim.* 1.15, pp. 59–60.

40. Claudianus contentiously calls his adversary a 'new geometrist' (*Anim.* 2.3, p. 108), certainly a taunt, given the negative meaning the word *nouus* has also in Sidonius (see the insistent repetition of the word in Sidon. *Ep.* 5.5).

Claudianus also looks the part of a *grammaticus* in *Anim.* 2.3, where, for the efficacy of his explanation, he intertwines quotations from the Old and New Testaments (Mt. 7.3; Lc. 6.4; Prov. 6.6; Mt. 24.20) with Vergilian verses (*Aen.* 11.381; *Georg.* 4.83; *Aen.* 4.402–3), explaining the Vergilian passages through the Scriptural ones and vice versa. The author then uses them to his own advantage, in order to persuade the reader of the truth of his assertion, and he does so in an oratorical way, which, incidentally, seems reminiscent of the argumentative style of Jerome.[41]

As far as oratory is concerned, the very Ciceronian definitions of oratory and eloquence (*de Orat.* 1.5.17 and 1.6.20) are cited by Claudianus (*Anim.* 2.7) in the conclusion of a minutely erudite passage, in which are quoted Philolaus' *On Rhythms and Measures*,[42] Archytas of Tarentum, Hippo of Metapontum and Plato (to whom he then dedicates a long consecutive section of the work).

Apart from reference to Philolaus' work on rhythms and measures, music is also mentioned, although briefly, in *Anim.* 2.12, p. 149, where it is strictly referred to astrology and, mainly, to stars, which *distinctis numerose choris et musicis interuallis aetherem pingunt* ('rhythmically[43] decorate the aether with different dances and musical intervals'). The same also happens in *Anim.* 1.22, a particularly interesting passage which gives an overall idea of the conception of knowledge Claudianus had, that is, of it being the entirety of things stored in one's memory that, at some point, are going to be retrieved and reconsidered. This includes every colour, smell, sound, thing tasted or touched, but it is also applicable to disciplines, and knowledge of such subjects is interconnected, according to him.

> *In hac mihi reposita quodam modo sunt et grammatica, cum de dialecticis dissero, et rhetorica, cum de geometricis, et astrologica, cum de musicis, et hae simul omnes, cum de arithmeticis.* (Mam. Claud. *Anim.*1.22, p. 81)

> Somehow, in my memory, grammar is stored when I discourse on logic, rhetoric when on geometry, astrology when on music and all of these things together when I discourse on arithmetic.

---

41. Sidonius himself compares the friend's ability in instruction to that of Jerome in Sidon. *Ep.* 4.3.7 *instruit ut Hieronymus, destruit ut Lactantius, adstruit ut Augustinus.*
42. The authenticity of Philolaus' fragment has been debated. As Huffman 1993, 411 points out, the title is unattested elsewhere and it is possible Claudianus consulted a collection of Philolaus' writings which included spurious works.
43. It is my opinion that *numerose* here specifically refers to rhythm and musical harmony.

LETTER 2

Moreover, if Claudianus does not openly speak of *metrica*, it is neverthe-less possible to gather what Sidonius means in *Ep.* 5.2.1, by comparing the passage to the mention (*Ep.* 4.3.8) of his friend's mastery of metrics shown in a (not preserved) hymn. Although this praise does not concern the *De statu animae* specifically, it is useful in understanding how Sidonius sees Claudianus as perfectly comfortable in giving his text an ornate style, respecting, at any rate, the nature of the feet, of syllables, and the limiting space of the verses.[44]

> *Ita tibi facile factu est minutis trochaeis minutioribusque pyrrichiis non solum molossicas anapaesticasque ternarias sed epitritorum etiam paeonumque quaternatas superuenire iuncturas.* (Sidon. *Ep.* 4.3.8)

> It is so easy for you to surpass, with your short trochees and even shorter pyrrhics, not only the trisyllabic juxtaposition of molossi and anapaests, but also the quadrisyllabic juxtaposition of epitrites and paeons.

Though architecture does not seem to have an exact or at least clear match in Claudianus' text, it is not the first time Sidonius associates Claudianus with this discipline, since in *Ep.* 4.3.5 he pictures his friend as willing to hold the *perpendiculum*, the plumb line for measurements, alongside the master, Vitruvius.

The dedication of the *De statu animae*

As stated before, the fondness for the *De statu animae* displayed by Sidonius is also comprehensible in light of the fact that the treatise had been dedicated to him. In his *praefatio,* the author informs the reader that it was Sidonius who had solicited the edition of the treatise,[45] and it was therefore him that should have passed judgment on the work and on the letter *Quaeris me,* to which Claudianus contentiously responded.[46]

> *En legisti, eruditissime uirorum, quod lectitabis: tu modo faxis uti memineris non absque cura tui prodi oportere, quod publicari iubes. Neque ego de negotii pondere, sed de actionis leuitate dubitauerim. Proinde consilium tuum adserito et defensitato: quoniam, si in his secus aliquid, ego conscriptionis periclitabor, sed tu editionis. Vale et uige bonis uiribus, ueteris reparator eloquentiae.* (Mam. Claud. *Anim. praef.*, p. 20)

---

44. See Amherdt 2001, 154.
45. Mam. Claud. *Anim. praef.*, pp. 18–20.
46. On Claudianus' *praefatio* see Santelia 2003–2005, 9–11.

Behold, most learned of men, you have leafed through what you are going to read thoroughly; see to it that you remember that it is not without care for you that what you ask to be published is fittingly revealed to you. Nor would I question the weight of the deed, but its lightness instead; hence, defend and support what you yourself planned! For in this endeavour I will face judgement for the composition, but you will be held responsible for the publication. Be well and in good health, you renovator of ancient eloquence.

Furthermore, it does not seem to have been stressed by scholars that Sidonius is mentioned not only in the *praefatio*, but also in the introductory section of the *epilogus* of the *De statu animae*, in which is expressed, once more, Claudianus' wish for him to emend his work in a phase which would seem to precede its broader circulation. Claudianus also points out that part of the material he is sending Sidonius has already been sent to his friend not long before, a thing that would suggest there had been an ongoing discussion on the subject and that Sidonius was involved in the writing process when the work was still in a pre-publication phase.

> *Si non haec quae ad te scribo, uenerande uir, discutienda et emendanda transmitterem, rite potuit uideri superfluum et elatum docere uelle, quem sciam nosse, et ex paupertatis inopia dare dragmam ei, qui multa scientiarum abundat talenta. Hinc accidit quod libellorum a me transmissorum editio, quos philosophicae artis subtilissima disputatione disposui, me fecit cautum atque sollicitum, ut eorundem intellegentiam iudicio non committerem meo, sed ad potioris peritiam destinarem. Et non tantum ea, quae nunc ex eorum lectione percepi, uerum etiam quae unde iam pridem memoriae reseruanda mandaui iudicio tuo probanda transmisi.* (Mam. Claud. *Anim. epilog.*, p. 191)

Were it not that I was handing over these things that I am writing to you, venerable man, for discussion and correction, it could rightly seem pointless and haughty of me to want to teach a man whom I know has knowledge, and from my poor store to gift a drachma to him who is overflowing with talents of erudition. Hence it happens that the publication of the booklets sent off, arranged by me with the most accurate discussion of the art of philosophy, made me wary and anxious, since I was not entrusting their discernment to my own judgement, but I was directing them to the expertise of a better-qualified man; and it is not just those things that I have now understood from reading them, but also those things which I had already entrusted to memory, that I have sent for your approval.

It should be noted, however, that it was probably conventional to address friends to whom the work was dedicated, entrusting them with its revision, as if the dedication itself would grant a certain degree of quality of the work. Sidonius himself, in the dedication of Book 1 to Constantius (*Ep.* 1.1.3), writes that he is sending him his letters not simply *recensendas*, but *defaecadas*

LETTER 2

et limandas, thus entrusting, in the literary fiction of the prefatory letter, the quality of the collection to his judgement and counsel.[47]

If this is how the publication process worked (sending the writing to a friend, who edited it and passed it on), at least ideally, there is no way to know if Claudianus is describing a real exchange or if the passage is written for the sake of formalism, as literary fiction. In his monograph on Latin prose prefaces, Tore Janson dedicates enlightening pages to the theme of 'assistance' in prefatory texts in Classical and Late Antiquity.[48] As highlighted by Janson, the theme of asking for 'help with corrections' and of leaving the decision on publication to the recipient is variously attested in Cicero, Pliny and Statius;[49] it becomes common practice 'among specialist writers of the second and third centuries', such as Balbus and Solinus, and is popular in fifth-century late antique prefatory texts.[50] Sidon *Ep.* 1.1 and Mam. Claud. *Anim. praef.*, p. 20 are listed by Janson as examples of such popularity, to which one may add Sidon. *Ep.* 2.8.2, where Sidonius asks Desideratus' opinion on the quality of his poem for Filimatia: should he approve, he will enclose it in his collection of poems.[51] Therefore, instead of there being one copy sent only to Sidonius waiting for his comments – not immediately bestowed, as testified in *Ep.* 4.2 – it seems possible that a small number of copies already circulated among Claudianus' *sodales*, and that the manuscript later lent to Nymphidius may have been the dedication copy.

Dating elements

Considering that the *De statu animae* was written between 468 and 470,[52] it can be inferred that 470 legitimately constitutes the *terminus post quem* for

---

47. Compare this with Sidonius' dedication of Book 9 to Firminus, who has the duty of protecting the work and defending the author after the book circulates (*Ep.* 9.1.3), as well as with the similar requests to Felix in *Carm.* 9.329–31. See Condorelli 2015, 495–6; Hernández Lobato 2010a, 115–17.

48. Janson 1964, 141–9.

49. Janson 1964, 106.

50. Janson 1964, 141–2.

51. See Hindermann 2022, 234. To this list could also be added the direct address to the *uiri optimi* (the friends asked to pass judgement on his verses) by Luxorius in *Anth. Lat.* 19 R (6 SB); for a detailed analysis of this *praefatio*, see Cristante 2005–2006, 235–60. Compare also Avitus of Vienne's *Ep.* 43, in which Apollinaris (Sidonius' son) is expected to give his opinion on a poem; see Shanzer and Wood 2002, 340–2.

52. As is argued by van Waarden 2020a, 15 n. 14, the mention of Sidonius as *praefectorius patricius* (*Anim. praef.*, p. 18) indicates a date between 468 (when Sidonius was appointed

the writing of the letter. One could also be more cautious and consider the start of Sidonius' bishopric as a *terminus post quem*, since Claudianus addresses the *De statu animae* to *Sidonio patricio*, while he addresses his letter to Sidonius (Sidon. *Ep.* 4.2) to *Sidonio papa*, hence, already bishop.[53] It seems sensible therefore, considering the dating element in *Ep.* 4.2, to date *Ep.* 5.2 after his ordination. Loyen, in his chronology,[54] considers 471 as a probable date[55] and adds that *Ep.* 5.2 was written not long after *Ep.* 4.3. However, there is no element in the text which would indicate a specific year; therefore, Mathisen's more cautious attitude to the text and his suggestion to date it to a time frame of five years, between 470 and 475, seems commendable.[56]

One may wonder whether *Ep.* 5.2 was written after the death of Claudianus. As stated above, the letter does not provide any lead, apart from the mention of the *De statu animae*, and we are therefore entering the field of speculation. And yet, one cannot exclude the possibility that the text was written immediately after the death of his friend. If Claudianus' death is dated to 471, as Amherdt suggests,[57] then, taking into account Mathisen's time span (470–5), the possibility that Claudianus was already dead by the time Sidonius writes *Ep.* 5.2 must be taken seriously. Although it is known that the order of the letters in their published form is not strictly chronological, *Ep.* 4.11.6, the epitaph of Claudianus, and the description, at the end of the letter, of Sidonius' grief, far from his friend's grave,[58] would have drawn a line between what was published before and after Claudianus' death. In conclusion, in terms of internal coherence, it would seem odd to find a letter in praise of Claudianus, written when Claudianus was still alive, in a book which follows that containing his epitaph, but this is inevitably a speculative assertion since there are no further elements which could corroborate this hypothesis.

---

 praefectus urbi and, presumably, attained the rank of *patricius*) and 469/70 (when he was elected bishop).

53. Mamertus Claudianus' letter to Sidonius is mentioned above in this introduction.
54. Loyen 1970a, 255.
55. Bellès is of the same opinion.
56. Mathisen 2013a, 245.
57. Amherdt 2001, 280.
58. *Ep.* 4.11.7 *lacrimis habenas anima parturiente laxaui fecique ad epitaphium quod alii fecerunt ad sepulchrum.*

SIDONIUS NYMPHIDIO SUO SALUTEM

1. Librum de statu animae tribus uoluminibus inlustrem Mamertus Claudianus peritissimus Christianorum philosophus et quorumlibet primus eruditorum totis sectatae philosophiae membris, artibus partibusque comere et excolere curauit, nouem quas uocant Musas disciplinas aperiens esse, non feminas. Namque in paginis eius uigilax lector inueniet ueriora nomina Camenarum, quae propriam de se sibi pariunt nuncupationem. Illic enim et grammatica diuidit et oratoria declamat et arithmetica numerat et geometrica metitur et musica ponderat et dialectica disputat et astrologia praenoscit et architectonica struit et metrica modulatur.

2. Huius lectionis nouitate laetatus excitatusque maturitate raptim recensendam transferendamque, ut uideras, petisti, ut petieras, impetrasti sub sponsione citae redhibitionis. Nec me falli nec te fallere decet. Tempus est commodata restitui, quia liber ipse, si placuit, debuit exhibere satietatem, si displicuit, debuit mouere fastidium. Tu autem, quicquid illud est, fidem tuam celeriter absolue, ne si repetitum libellum serius reddere paras, membranas potius uidearis amare quam litteras. Vale

NYMPHIDIO *L edd.* : NIMPHIDIO α *MNPTRV* : MENPHIDIO *F*
§ 1 sectatae *codd.* : *an* secretae? *Lütjohann*

LETTER 2

SIDONIUS TO HIS DEAR NYMPHIDIUS

1. Mamertus Claudianus, the most competent philosopher among Christians and the first among all learned men, took care to adorn and refine his treatise *De statu animae*, distinguished for its three volumes, through all the elements, arts and parts of the philosophy that he follows; disclosing that those nine that are named Muses are sciences, not women. For indeed, in his pages, the attentive reader will find the truer names of the *Camenae*, who themselves produce their own appropriate appellation. In this treatise, in fact, it is grammar itself that divides into classes, it is oratory that declaims, arithmetic that counts, geometry that measures, music that appraises, dialectic that debates, astrology that foreknows, architecture that constructs and metre that modulates the rhythm.

2. Delighted with the novelty of this reading, stirred by its maturity, as soon as you realised this, you asked to review and copy it out hurriedly, and as soon as you asked, you had your request granted, with the pledge that you would return it quickly. It is not proper for me to be misled nor for you to mislead. It is time that what was borrowed is returned, because if the book itself was pleasing, it will have provided satiety, and if it was displeasing, it will have caused disgust by now. However, whatever the case, you should keep your word and be quick. Otherwise, if you intend to return at a later time the book that has already been claimed, you would find yourself seeming more attached to parchments than to their content. Farewell.

Commentary

§ 1

Librum . . . inlustrem: The only previous occurrence of this *iunctura* is in Tacitus *Dial.* 12.6, in which, however, *liber* refers to published speeches of Asinius Pollio and Messalla and not to 'books', as highlighted by Mayer 2001, 127. The uniqueness of the *iunctura* emphasises the already strong presence of *librum* as an opening word; the *liber* Sidonius refers to, in fact, will be the protagonist of the letter. The presence of a *paeon* IV spondee clausula at *-minibus inlustrem* suggests consideration of the words *uoluminibus* and *inlustrem* as being closely connected, and leads to the translation 'distinguished for its three volumes' instead of 'distinguished treatise in three volumes'. Anderson 1965, 173 here translates 'embellish the three volumes of his notable work' and Loyen 1970a, 175 'son livre remarquable en trois volumes'.

peritissimus Christianorum philosophus . . . primus eruditorum: It has already been pointed out in the introduction that this passage derives from Cicero's description of Varro, quoted in Augustine *Ciu.* 6.2 and in Mam. Claud. *Anim.* 2.8, p. 130, and that it also resembles the praise of Varro in Quint. *Inst.* 10.1.95–6. The only previous occurrence of the superlative *peritissimus* referred to the word *philosophus* is found in Aulus Gellius, who calls Theophrastus *philosophorum peritissimus* (Gell. 16.15.1). The image of Claudianus as a philosopher in service of (and in accordance with) Christian religion also occurs in Sidon. *Ep.* 4.11.1 *salua religione philosopharetur*; the same image is used to praise Claudianus' opponent, Faustus of Riez, in Sidon. *Ep.* 9.9.12 *philosophiam . . . quae mystico amplexu iam defaecata tecum membra coniunxit*. On this, see Pricoco 1965a, 121.

sectatae philosophiae: This is the only known occurrence of the syntagma *sectata philosophia*; while the expression *philosophiae sectator*, which indicates a disciple of a certain philosophical doctrine or, more generally, a 'student of philosophy' (*OLD* s.v. *sectator*, 1895), has more attestations, with occurrences in Gellius (e.g. Gell. 1.2.3 *adulescens philosophiae sectator, disciplinae . . . stoicae*). Moreover, *philosophi sectatores* are mentioned in Hier. *In Eccles.* 1.1 and in Aug. *Ciu.* 8.3; lastly, a *sectator philosophiae* is also mentioned in Macr. *Sat.* 7.1.8. In his edition, Lütjohann 1887, 79 writes '*an secretae?*' in the apparatus; however, as noted by Anderson 1965, 172, and Loyen 1970a,

LETTER 2

175, there is no reason to discard the reading, since it would not be the first time Sidonius employs this verb in the *Letters*. It occurs, in fact, in Sidon. *Ep.* 6.1.4 (*sectandae nobis humilitatis*), *Ep.* 7.2.5 (*pudicitiam . . . sectari*) and *Ep.* 7.9.9 (*sectatae anachoreseos*). For the specific philosophical meaning of the verb see *OLD* s.v. *sector*, 1896; moreover, van Waarden 2010, 465 points out how Sidonius usually employs the verb to express a repeated and intense way of pursuing a goal.

comere et excolere curauit: The syntagma is not known to occur elsewhere, and the same can be said for the verbs *comere* and *excolere*, which highlight the quality of Claudianus' writing and of his much refined style.

Musas disciplinas . . . non feminas: This is the first time such a phrase is attested.

uigilax lector inueniet: Let us first analyse the single elements composing this syntagma before considering it as a unity. The word *uigilax* is not common and has few attestations throughout Latin literature. Its first occurrences are in Prop. 4.7.15, where it describes staying awake all night; on this see Fedeli et al. 2015, 933. *Curae* are said to be *uigilaces* in Ov. *Met.* 2.779 *nec fruitur somno uigilacibus excita curis* (in both the Teubner edition by Anderson 1993 and the Oxford edition by Tarrant 2004 the *lectio uigilacibus* is preferred to *uigilatibus* and *uigilantibus*). As pointed out in *OLD* s.v. *uigilax*, 2272 (in which, however, the occurrence in Ovid is not mentioned), the word also occurs in Columella 7.9.10, being one of the qualities of a *custos porcorum*, and of birds in 8.2.11. Another occurrence, which has not been previously highlighted, is in Ausonius' *Ephemeris* 1.2 *iam strepit nidis uigilax hirundo*, where it describes a very awake and noisy swallow (see Green 1991, 246–7); it also occurs in Gaius *Dig.* 21.1.18, where it refers to the qualities and consequent value of slaves. In Sidon. *Ep.* 5.2, however, it is the reader who, if *uigilax*, will be rewarded by finding all the liberal arts in Mamertus Claudianus' text. Similar appeals to the reader's attention are in Augustine (though the word *uigilax* specifically is never attested in these contexts): see Aug. *Doct. christ.* 2.48 and 3.109 *ibi uigilare debet lectoris intentio* as well as Aug. *C. Iul.* 4.90.21–2 *lectorem igitur adhortor, ut conflictum nostrum uigilanter inspiciat*. It seems safe to say that Sidonius is drawing upon the text of *De statu animae* itself when he mentions its *uigilax lector*, since Claudianus, when nearing the peak of his argumentation, asks the reader to be *uigilax* and *uigilans*, 'watchful and alert', in *Anim.* 3.11, p. 173 *uigilacem*

85

uigilantemque simul quaero lectorem. If it is not possible to prove with certainty that Sidonius was alluding to this passage, the unusualness of the word and its only occurrence in *iunctura* with *lector* in Claudianus would at least prove it was a phrase Sidonius had found congenial and to his liking. It seems no coincidence, in fact, that Sidonius also employed the word *uigilax* when praising Lampridius, described in *Ep.* 8.11.6 as *in bucolica uigilax, parcus, carminabundus.* As stated above, however, it is also relevant to consider the expression as a whole. The syntagma *lector inueniet* became a commonplace in Late Antiquity, mainly from the fourth century onwards, and was used in both Christian and secular texts, as thoroughly argued by Pelttari 2017. In Macrobius (e.g. *Sat.* 1.16.30 *diligens lector inueniet*) the phrase always 'references a source or directs the reader to a specific passage under discussion' (Pelttari 2017, 217), while Sidonius appeals to what Pelttari, when describing the process in previous authors' productions, generally calls 'the reader's active discovery' (219). In the texts of the Fathers (e.g. Hier. *Ep.* 20.2 and Aug. *Trin.* 14.7), the expression is used as a brief note in order not to delve deeper in an explanation and to leave the search for exact matches or for broader contexts to readers, so that they can form their own ideas about a thorny problem; in contrast, the syntagma in Sidon. *Ep.* 5.2 introduces a list of qualities of the work and a description of what the reader can expect to find in it.

ueriora nomina Camenarum: *Camenae* seems to be employed simply as a synonym of *Musae* for *uariatio*. For the theme of men of letters being acquainted with the *Camenae*, see Symm. *Ep.* 1.20.1 to Ausonius, in which *Camenae* stand for literature (as highlighted by Salzman and Roberts 2011, 57); see also the praise of Protadius' literary ability in Symm. *Ep.* 4.18.1 *uos amici Camenarum flores ructatis Heliconis*, in which they stand for poetry. On this passage of Symmachus, see Callu 1972, 219 and Marcone 1987, 57.

grammatica . . . modulatur: As highlighted by Fernández López 1994, 76 and Amherdt 2001, 111, the list of *artes* mirrors the personalities listed in Sidon. *Ep.* 4.3 as embodiments of the disciplines they excelled at, while the novelty of *Ep.* 5.2 resides in the personification of the disciplines mentioned (see the introduction to this letter). Gualandri 1979, 147 mentions the list of *Ep.* 5.2 as proof that Sidonius did not read Greek and that he used nouns of Greek origin only to flaunt his knowledge in technical discussions. On Sidonius' habit of using Graecisms in blocks and in enumerations, as in this passage, see Foscarini, who is sceptical about Sidonius' first-hand knowledge

LETTER 2

of literary works in Greek (Foscarini 2019, 347 and 356–7). The issue of Sidonius' knowledge of Greek is a thorny one; his direct knowledge is favoured by Pricoco 1965b, 71–98. For the *status quaestionis*, see John 2021, 862–3. Every *ars* is followed by a verb which defines its meaning and purpose and, as Gualandri 1979, 77 n. 10 observes, the same 'gusto definitorio', taste for definition, is in Sidon. *Ep.* 4.1.2 (in which every literary genre mentioned to praise Probus is followed by its defining characteristic) and in Sidon. *Ep.* 8.11.6, where the account of the versatility of Lampridius, which may seem to be a description of his style, is again a list of genres followed by their definition.

grammatica diuidit: *Diuisiones* are the main feature of grammar, a thing that is immediately clear when one reads the first words of Donatus' *Ars Minor*: *partes orationis quot sunt? Octo. Quae? Nomen, pronomen . . .* Kaster 1988, 18–19 argues that the passage refers to grammar serving the purpose of dividing the cultured from the uncultured, creating a linguistic *limes* between what is Roman and what is extraneous to Romanness. Although this interpretation is not strictly based on the original meaning of the passage, it is in line with Sidonius' way of thinking. Moreover, in *Ep.* 4.3.6 Sidonius says Mamertus Claudianus *diuidit ut Socrates*, an expression interpreted by Amherdt 2001, 142 as an allusion to Socrates' endeavour to obtain universal definitions and to lead men through the maieutic art.

oratoria declamat: The oratory skills of Claudianus are also exemplified through a long list of famous orators in Sidon. *Ep.* 4.3.6 *ut Aeschines blanditur . . . persuadet ut Tullius.* The list includes the names of rivals, such as Aeschines and Demosthenes, Hortensius and Cicero; on this passage see Amherdt 2001, 143–9.

arithmetica numerat: Compare *Ep.* 4.3.5 (*cum Chrysippo numeros*), in which Sidonius pictures Claudianus as not refusing to discuss numbers with the Greek philosopher and mathematician Chrysippus if the chance presented itself. See Amherdt 2001, 139.

geometrica metitur: In Sidon. *Ep.* 4.3.5 the allusion to geometry is carried out through the mention of Euclid immediately after that of Chrysippus, as also happens in the praise of Faustus in *Ep.* 9.9.14; see Amherdt 2001, 139. Note that in *Ep.* 4.3.5 Sidonius also compares Claudianus to Archimedes holding a *radius,* the instrument used to measure figures traced on sand

(Amherdt 2001, 136) and that in *Ep.* 4.3.6 Pythagoras is also mentioned as the first name in a catalogue of philosophers.

musica ponderat: Claudianus is pictured as a peer of Orpheus in Sidon. *Ep.* 4.3.5 *non abnuit cum Orpheo plectrum.* Fernández López 1994, 76 compares the syntagma to *Ep.* 4.3.5 *cum Zeto pondera*, which refers to Claudianus not declining to weigh things with Zethus.

dialectica disputat: There is not an exact match for *ars dialectica* in Sidon. *Ep.* 4.3; however, Fernández López 1994, 76 compares this passage to *Ep.* 4.3.6 *nemo saeculo meo quae uoluit affirmare sic ualuit.*

astrologia praenoscit: Astrology is mentioned through three characters in Sidon. *Ep.* 4.3.5 *tenere non abnuit . . . cum Euphrate horoscopium . . . cum Thalete tempora, cum Atlante sidera.* Claudianus is in fact pictured there as an equal of the philosopher Euphrates of Tyre in holding a – possibly – astronomical instrument (the word *horoscopium* is not attested elsewhere, as notes Amherdt 2001, 136); as a peer of Thales of Miletus, founder of the discipline of astronomy; and, unexpectedly, also as an equal of a mythological character – Atlas, holding the weight of the celestial sphere.

architectonica struit: Sidonius alludes to architecture when, in *Ep.* 4.3.5, he pictures Claudianus as being on a par with Vitruvius in holding the *perpendiculum*, the plumb line widely used in the building trade to this day. The verb *struere* is also at the centre of a word game when Claudianus is compared to three Church Fathers in *Ep.* 4.3.7 *instruit ut Hieronymus, destruit ut Lactantius, adstruit ut Augustinus.* It would seem safe to assume that the use of the verb in both Sidonian letters when speaking of his friend – or at least the word game in *Ep.* 4.3 – may hint at *De statu animae*, since Claudianus himself, at the end of Book 3, says that he has written three volumes 'against a brief page' because it is more difficult to destroy falsehood than it is to create it: *Anim.* 3.17, p. 188 *sed non id negotii est fallaciam struere, quod destruere.*

metrica modulatur: While Fernández López 1994, 76 compares the reference to *metrica* to the mention of Orpheus holding the plectrum (which instead here was referred to music), the long section on the metrical qualities displayed by Claudianus, although referred to his hymn and not specifically to his philosophical treatise, cannot go unnoticed. Sidon. *Ep.* 4.3.8 *seruatis* *metrorum pedibus, pedum syllabis syllabarumque naturis* . . . pictures Claudianus as clever in respecting the meter and the spatial dimension of his short verse, while at the same time not renouncing an ornate style. See introduction to this letter and Condorelli 2020a, 441.

§ 2

nouitate laetatus excitatusque maturitate: As highlighted by Geisler 1887, 365, this passage is reminiscent of various Plinian passages. Cf. Plin. *Ep.* 2.19.7 *libro isti nouitas lenocinetur*, which concerns the reading of a Plinian speech. The addressee Cerialis, who asked to read it, may appreciate its novelty, despite the unconventionality of the writing. In Plin. *Ep.* 8.18.12 *aures hominum nouitate laetantur* is one of the closing remarks of the writer to Rufinus: the general assertion that 'hearing something new is always pleasurable' is a good excuse to encourage the addressee to write him a letter, should any occasion present itself. The *nouitas* of a writing is also mentioned positively by Pliny in *Ep.* 1.2.6, when he states his books already issued have now lost the *gratia nouitatis*, the glamour of being new, and the same expression is employed in Plin. *Ep.* 5.20.8. Moreover, in Plin. *Ep.* 3.13.2 *nouitas* is said to be the element which attracts most readers. Therefore, when Sidonius praises the work of Mamertus Claudianus for its novelty, it seems he has in mind a positive idea of *nouitas*, which he probably derived from Pliny the Younger and which, however, is in strong contrast with other assertions of Sidonius. The author, on various occasions (including here *Ep.* 5.5.3) strongly opposes what is *nouus* as something mediocre and destined, by nature, to be less than anything *uetus*. Claudianus also considers *nouitas* as something negative in *Anim.* 1.1, p. 24 (*et quia mortalium generi mos est, noui operis agnitione pellecti ad id percipiendum sedulo animo intenderant*)[59] when he describes his friends as particularly intent on reading Faustus' work because it is common 'for mortals' to be attracted by new works; moreover, when discrediting Faustus personally, he calls him *nouus geometra* (*Anim.* 2.3, p. 108) and *nouus academicus* (*Anim.* 3.3, p. 158). In Sidon. *Ep.* 5.2, the *nouitas* of writing can be seen as something positive also because the ambiguity of the noun is balanced by the mention of its *maturitas*, which is

---

59. This also seems to be an allusion to Pliny *Ep.* 3.13.2, mentioned above; however, in Pliny it does not express a polemical remark, whereas it is in Mamertus Claudianus.

an undoubtedly positive quality. Gualandri 1979, 78 n. 12 briefly mentions the existence of a formal antithesis between *nouitas* and *maturitas* in this phrase; however, the two elements are not necessarily in contrast as they are interpretable as complementary characteristics. In *TLL* 8.494 s.v. *maturitas* 74–5 (by Brandt), when in relation to a literary work, the noun has the specific meaning of *perfectio cum diligentia et moderatione*. To such a perfection Sidonius himself aspired, as can be deduced from his programmatic letter at the beginning of the collection, in which he states that he intends to follow the *uestigia* of Pliny's *disciplinam maturitatemque* (*Ep.* 1.1.1). See also the praise of the *maturitas* of Claudianus' writings in *Ep.* 4.3.4. For the occurrence of the verb *excitare* in this context, compare the occurrence, in relation to literary works of a friend, in Symm. *Ep.* 5.55, where Symmachus writes to Sallustius that the less he writes to him the more Symmachus is eager to read his letters (*cuius adpetentiam scriptorum tuorum raritas uehementius excitauit*). It seems paradigmatic of the attitude of members of this sort of literary circle that, when someone was made aware that a new work had been issued, he enthusiastically asked to read it and make his own copy of it.

raptim recensendam transferendamque: As soon as Nymphidius had known that Sidonius was in possession of the *De statu animae*, he had asked to revise Sidonius' exemplar and to have his own copy made. The only previous occurrence of these two verbs in the same context, concerning the practical activity of book copying, is in Augustine, *Cur. mort.* 3.5, 629 *quam propterea ex alio libro meo in istum transtuli, quia facilius hoc a me recenseri potuit.* On these two words in Sidonius see Santelia 2003–2005, 8 n. 25.

ut uideras, petisti, ut petieras . . . Nec me falli nec te fallere decet: The repeated polyptoton confers a rhythm to the phrase in a rhetorically effective way, which is favoured by Sidonius on various occasions in his most polemical passages (see e.g. the portraits of Seronatus in *Ep.* 2.1.2 *dissimulati furoris aperiri: aperte inuidet* and *Ep.* 5.13.3 *uincti trahuntur uincula trahentes*). Starting from this sentence there is a considerable difference, in terms of tone and content, between the first and second sections of the piece. Once the praise of Claudianus ends, the letter is suddenly straightforward, in a way that seems to testify that Sidonius and Nymphidius were close and he could display a tone of mocking reproach.

Tempus est commodata restitui: Sidonius appears to be rather technical, since he mentions the book loan as a *commodatum*, a noun that is specifically juridical; *Ep.* 5.2 is, for instance, the only occurrence in a non-juridical text signalled in *TLL* 3.1921 s.v. *commodatum* 34–43 (by Mertel) and one may wonder if the sudden technicality is to be ascribed, given the closing lines of the letter, to the usual Sidonian mixture of serious and openly comic elements which make his irony rarefied and subtle. Before analysing the meaning and models of the following culinary metaphor, note the attention to rhythm in this section, and in particular the two consecutive cretic tribrachs (*commo-data restitui* and *ipse si placuit*).

si placuit, debuit exhibere satietatem, si displicuit, debuit mouere fastidium: It is customary for Sidonius to employ the expression *placet . . . displicet*, and, in particular, as in this letter, it is found in closing remarks in *Ep.* 1.9.8 and in *Ep.* 5.17.11 (*si placet, edentes fouete; si displicet, delentes ignoscitote*). Other Sidonian occurrences are in *Epp.* 7.9.2 and 8.11.3 (in conclusion of the prose section preceding the *carmen* in the letter); as well as in poetry, specifically *Carm.* 18.2 and *Carm.* 22.3 (again at the end of the prose section which introduces the *Burgus Pontii Leontii carmen*). The use of the two forms in the same context is attested since Plautus and occurs in numerous authors (such as, for the largest number of occurrences, Cicero, Seneca, Ambrose and in particular Augustine, with more than 150 occurrences). Note in particular its presence in Plin. *Ep.* 3.13.5 (*adnota, quae putaueris corrigenda. Ita enim magis credam cetera tibi placere, si quaedam displicuisse cognouero*), a passage (in the closing remarks of the letter) that concerns proofreading. Moreover, in *Ep.* 5.2.2 Sidonius draws upon the image of food by referring to the concepts of satiety and disgust, *satietas* and *fastidium*, used here as symbols of alternative outcomes of the reception of the treatise. The addressee is supposed to be satiated if he enjoyed reading the text at length, or, should he have disliked its content, he is expected to be nauseated by the time Sidonius writes: either way, it is time he parted with what he borrowed. The image of 'literary indigestion' is employed metaphorically from Cicero on (e.g. *Mur.* 9.21, on which see Fantham 2013, 114). While there are no occurrences of the expression in Pliny the Younger, Symmachus employs it four times in his letters, and, in particular, in closing remarks in *Epp.* 4.63.2 and 9.28. But if the occurrences in Symmachus are similar to that in Sidon. *Ep.* 5.2 mainly for their position at the end of the text, the same dining metaphor, the presence of the two verbs (*placeo* and *displiceo*) and the hint at copying – should the reader find the letters to his liking – are all in Augustine *Ep.* 238.1, on which see Löhr 2016, 195. For a similar mention of *fastidium* in Sidon. *Ep.* 2.2.7, see Hindermann 2022, 116.

fidem tuam celeriter absolue: The imperative sanctions the change in tone as Sidonius prepares for a witty ending.

membranas potius . . . quam litteras: The conclusion of the letter is reminiscent of an epigrammatic *aprosdoketon*, a choice that is not unusual for Sidonius. See for instance, in Book 5 alone, the closing remarks of *Epp.* 5.5, 5.13 and 5.21. A similar image, though *a contrario*, is in Sidon. *Ep.* 4.3.3 *curae fuit causam potius implere quam paginam*, where Claudianus is pictured as being keen to say something meaningful rather than simply interested in 'filling the page'. As is argued in the General Introduction, the end of *Ep.* 5.2 is characterised by greater attention to rhythm and appears to be consistently clausulated, with a double cretic at *mo-uere fastidium*, a cretic iamb at *quicquid illud est* (which interestingly does not create a *cursus planus* as it does in most cases), a paeon IV spondee at *ce-leriter absolue*, a dactyl iamb at *reddere paras*, and a double cretic at *a-mare quam litteras*.

LETTER 3

Content

Sidonius reproaches Apollinaris for his silence and informs him of his precarious state of health due to a recent fever.

The addressee Apollinaris

Apollinaris was a relative of Sidonius – according to Mathisen's recent theory, his cousin,[1] brother of Thaumastus (the addressee of *Ep.* 5.7).[2] Apart from *Ep.* 5.3, Apollinaris received from Sidonius *Ep.* 4.6, a short note in which he expressed relief for Apollinaris' decision to put off his family's pilgrimage; and *Ep.* 5.6, for the content of which see the commentary ad loc. He also received *Epp.* 4.4 and 4.12, addressed jointly to Simplicius. While *Ep.* 4.4 has the features of a commendation letter,[3] *Ep.* 4.12 is a formal request to send Sidonius a second letter, since the initial copy was lost before delivery.[4] Apollinaris owned the estate of Vorocingus (near Nîmes), where Sidonius himself was a guest at some time between 462 and 464. In *Carm.* 24.52–74 Sidonius depicts a vivid image of the luxurious life Apollinaris led in his manor, fighting to protect his house from the summer heat, strolling around his magnificent gardens filled with blooming flowers and vineyards, whose splendour was reminiscent of the renowned gardens of the Indian king Porus.[5]

---

1. Contrary to the idea that he was his uncle, as in, for instance *PLRE* 2, 113–14 s.v. Apollinaris; *PCBE* 4, 161–3 s.v. Apollinaris 3. In *Ep.* 5.6.1 Sidonius says he is Thaumastus' brother.
2. For the uncertain kinship with Simplicius see the introduction to *Ep.* 5.4.
3. Amherdt 2001, 170.
4. Amherdt 2001, 306.
5. Vorocingus is also described in *Ep.* 2.9, along with Prusianum, the contiguous estate of Tonantius Ferreolus: the letter is an account of the exquisite hospitality Sidonius experienced there. See Santelia 2002a, 101–14, Green 2022, 277–8, and Hindermann 2022, 246–89.

After 469, Apollinaris left the region of Nîmes because of the attacks led by the Visigoths and moved to Vaison with Simplicius, as is attested in *Ep.* 7.4.4.[6] It was in Vaison that in 474 Apollinaris was charged with conspiracy against the Burgundian Chilperic I, in support of the emperor Julius Nepos. Informed of the precarious situation by Thaumastus, Sidonius wrote to Apollinaris (*Ep.* 5.6), reassuring him of his intention to intercede for him. The mission to the Burgundian court at Lyon turned out to be a success and, as Sidonius wrote in *Ep.* 5.7 to Thaumastus, Apollinaris was acquitted thanks to the mediation of Chilperic's anonymous Catholic wife.[7]

The proposal (in *PCBE* 4, 162) that, because of the presence of the term *uos*, *Ep.* 5.3 might be addressed also to Simplicius is not particularly convincing. Sidonius might be referring to both when employing the term *uos*, but it seems possible that *tu* and *uos* are simply alternatively employed to indicate a second person singular, as will be discussed in detail in this introduction. Sidonius would have probably mentioned Simplicius by name, were he writing to him as well, the way he did in *Epp.* 4.4 and 4.12, addressed explicitly to both.

Mathisen observes that not only do *Ep.* 5.3 (to Apollinaris) and *Ep.* 5.4 (to Simplicius) pertain to the same subject (their lack of correspondence to the author), but they also use similar wording, and therefore were likely written at the same time and archived together.[8] As highlighted in the commentary below, numerous expressions of *Ep.* 5.3 have clear correspondences with passages of *Ep.* 3.11 to Simplicius, in particular the last section, concerning epistolary silence (see the occurrence in *Ep.* 3.11.2 of *garrulitas*; *naeuo loquacitatis*; *alloquii impudentiam*).

Genre: the epistolary silence in Sidonius and its models

The first topos of letter writing found in *Ep.* 5.3 may be called 'epistolary silence': Apollinaris had not answered Sidonius' previous letter, which is not extant and supposedly concerned the news of his appointment as bishop of Clermont. The sender makes clear that he is bothered by the denial of an answer, a denial that has him worried in light of the perilous times they are living in.

---

6. See van Waarden 2010, 238.
7. *PCBE* 4, 163.
8. Mathisen 2013a, 244 n. 104; see also Mathisen 2014, 211.

LETTER 3

It is notoriously common for a letter writer to lament not having received news of the addressee.[9] Similar complaints are attested throughout epistolography and are directed both to close friends and relatives and to addressees with whom the author had a more formal relationship. Long epistolary silences are often accompanied by a display of anxiety on the sender's part, as testified, for example, in Plin. *Ep.* 1.11.1 *olim mihi nullas epistulas mittis*, a short message to Fabius Iustus entirely focused on the lack of correspondence and on Pliny's increasing feeling of preoccupation. The author says that even a simple *si uales bene est ego ualeo* – the way their grandfathers used to start their letters – would have sufficed.

A similar display of anxiety is in Plin. *Ep.* 3.17 to Servianus, another short letter dedicated to epistolary silence.

> *Rectene omnia, quod iam pridem epistulae tuae cessant? An omnia recte, sed occupatus es tu? An tu non occupatus, sed occasio scribendi uel rara uel nulla? Exime hunc mihi scrupulum, cui par esse non possum, exime autem uel data opera tabellario misso. Ego uiaticum, ego etiam praemium dabo, nuntiet modo quod opto. Ipse ualeo, si ualere est suspensum et anxium uiuere, exspectantem in horas timentemque pro capite amicissimo, quidquid accidere homini potest. Vale.* (Plin. *Ep.* 3.17)

> Is everything all right, since I have not received your letters for some time? Or everything is all right, but you are busy? Or you are not busy, but have little to no occasion to write? Relieve me of this anxiety, with which I cannot live, relieve me of it even by sending a messenger with this task. I will give him a provision for the journey, I will even give him a reward, if he only relates what I long for. As for me, I am doing well, if one can be well, when living in anxiety and uncertainty, hourly awaiting and in apprehension that anything that may befall men may have happened to a dearest friend. Farewell.

Gibson and Morello argue that, since this letter does not provide the reader with any specific information on the addressee, who is not previously mentioned in the letter collection, 'what Pliny offers here is, in fact, a concise template for any anxious letter ever written'.[10] It is also common to express (possibly pretended) bitterness and frustration at the lack of contact, as in Pliny's short letter to Paulinus, *Ep.* 2.2, where he says that he is 'deeply

---

9. On this topos, see Cugusi 1983, 76.
10. See Gibson and Morello 2012, 145 for Ovid's *Heroides* 1 as a model for Pliny's letter, recalling Penelope's speculations on Ulysses' fate, her trying to acquire news of him, and recounting her current situation.

95

angry' (*grauiter irascor*) because he has not received any correspondence for a long time and a similar anger can be placated only by 'numerous and lengthy letters' (*plurimas et longissimas*).[11]

Symmachus, for his part, reproaches silent addressees often, complaining that conventional rules of social interaction are not honoured by the defaulting correspondents. With Symmachus, however, encouraging the addressee to write back is even more of a customary practice and, as Cameron puts it, 'no one who studies the context in all these letters could be in any doubt that "silence" here means no more than delay in replying to the other's letter'. Cameron also states that in Symmachus' letters *silentium* should be interpreted as just a few days' silence, and not as a real interruption in communications.[12]

In particular, as highlighted in the commentary on *Ep.* 5.3, the mention of the *talio silentii*, a retorting silence with which the addressee is punished, shows a clear connection with numerous letters of Symmachus, who specifically uses the expression in contexts of epistolary silence. Suggestive of the model is also the presence in *Ep.* 5.3 of the direct address *quod tacetis*. Some of the numerous occurrences of similar addresses in Symmachus are listed in the commentary; see, by way of example, Symm. *Ep.* 3.82.1 *adhuc siles*. These direct remarks, bearing no trace of disguising finery, are distinctive of letters on epistolary silence,[13] and as highlighted by Cameron, Symmachus' *adhuc siles* is the exact translation of the Greek opening formula, attested earlier in Libanius *Ep.* 1129 ἔτι σιγᾷς; – 'Are you still silent?'[14]

An analysis of similar contexts from Symmachus' letter collection can clarify how customary it was for Symmachus (and therefore for his imitator) to express complaints about delayed answers. For instance, Ausonius is said to be too distracted by his good fortune to remember his duty as a correspondent in Symm. *Ep.* 1.13.1 *tibi, amice, scribendi obliuionem peperit res secunda* ('fortunate events made you forget to write, my friend'). In particular, Symmachus' Book 3 constitutes a useful repertoire of epistolary silence

---

11. The letter echoes various Catullan passages, starting with Catullus 85 in the *incipit*: Plin. *Ep.* 2.2.1 *irascor, nec liquet mihi an debeam, sed irascor*. For a detailed analysis of the various Catullan texts echoed in the letter, see Marchesi 2008, 89–96. See also Whitton 2013, 85–7.
12. Cameron 2015, 77–8.
13. As a prior example, though with a different formula, see Cicero's rebuke to his brother in *Q. fr.* 2.3.7 *a te post illam Ulbiensem epistulam nullas litteras accepi*.
14. A letter dated to 364, see Cameron 2015, 80. Libanius is unlikely to be an influence on Symmachus, but the two share this epistolary topos.

complaints: it contains a notably large number of similar appeals, and more than one directed to the same addressee. By way of example, in *Ep.* 3.18 Symmachus lists all the possible false excuses Gregorius might resort to in order to justify his silence,[15] and in *Ep.* 3.22 he again asks him to be more constant in writing. On three different occasions (*Epp.* 3.54, 3.56 and 3.60) Symmachus invites Richomeres, one of the most authoritative individuals at court, being Theodosius' *magister militum*, to write more often,[16] and, in doing so, the author follows a standardised way of writing *salutationes*, as highlighted by Pellizzari.[17] Through pungent remarks, in numerous passages (*Epp.* 3.81, 3.82, 3.83 and 3.86), Symmachus conveys puzzlement and irritation (e.g. *Ep.* 3.81.1 *suscensebam silentio tuo*) to Rufinus, whose silence contrasts with what is expected of him.

Irritation at epistolary silence is, for instance, the main element of Sidonius' following letter in Book 5: *Ep.* 5.4 to Simplicius. In particular, as highlighted in the commentary, Symm. *Ep.* 4.59 may have been exemplary for the composition of Sidon. *Ep.* 5.3 in light of the recurring themes, within the topic of 'silence', of *garrulitas* and *impudentia* of the sender in writing unrequitedly.

Beyond the model: traces of a rift with Apollinaris?

Since this topos of epistolary silence frequently occurs in Sidonius' declared models, it follows that it would have been natural for him to include similar expressions in his collection. And yet, despite its blatant echo of the Symmachan model, the silence with which Sidonius has been punished in *Epp.* 5.3 and 5.4 does not seem to be simply a customary 'few days' of delay in correspondence, as can often be said for Symmachus. The text of these letters testifies that the silence has been going on for quite some time, and it seems legitimate to infer that there has been a rift between Apollinaris,

---

15. He is probably *quaestor* of the palace at the time. Similar remarks are also in Symm. *Ep.* 3.4 to Iulianus Rusticus; see Pellizzari 1998, 106.

16. In particular, the ending of Symm. *Ep.* 1.15 to Ausonius – *cura ut ualeas et quia tibi facultas scribendi praesto est, adhibe uoluntatem* – and Symm. *Ep.* 3.54 *ego scribo, tu retices* are particularly emblematic of the laconic style of these rebukes.

17. Pellizzari 1998, 188: 'secondo un cliché collaudato, il contenuto s'incentra sulla volontà da parte dello scrivente di mantenere una solerte e assidua corrispondenza, alla quale tuttavia l'interlocutore tendeva abitualmente a sottrarsi'. For the other letters to this addressee see also Pellizzari 1998, 194; 198.

Simplicius and Sidonius, causing the interruption of epistolary exchanges. The stylistic fineries of the Symmachan echoes, creating a game of cross-references, may have the purpose of minimising the real extent of the rift, while still conveying the message that Sidonius is annoyed about this silent treatment. Concealing the irritation in clever Symmachan quotations on brief epistolary silence may also be a way to try to bridge the distance, in the hope of getting an answer from Apollinaris and Simplicius.

Similar appeals against epistolary silence are in Sidonius' letters to Magnus Felix (*Epp.* 3.4, 3.7 and 4.10) and to Felix's brother-in-law Polemius, who, for instance, is said to be *auarus in uerbis* (*Ep.* 4.14.2). In particular, as highlighted in the following commentary, *Ep.* 5.3 and *Ep.* 3.7 to Felix are also similar from a linguistic point of view: in both texts Sidonius chooses to present himself as a disturber, whose *garrulitas* is contrasted by the absolute silence of the addressee (cf. *Ep.* 5.3.1, and Felix's determination not to refrain *a continuandi silentii proposito* in *Ep.* 3.7.1); he recalls to both addressees their old ties of friendship (cf. the end of *Ep.* 5.3 and the appeal to *familiaritas antiqua* of *Ep.* 3.7.1); and points out that a further lack of answers would go against social rules (cf. the two questions of *Ep.* 5.3 with *Ep.* 3.7.1 *aut nescis quia garrulo non respondere conuicium est?*).[18]

Furthermore, the ending of another letter on epistolary silence to Felix, *Ep.* 3.4, is similar to the closing remarks in *Ep.* 5.3.3–4. Despite being punished by Felix 'for obscure offences', Sidonius still asks him to let him know if he is well (as in *Ep.* 5.3 *si uales . . .*) since they are living in evil times.[19]

> *Interea, si uel penes uos recta sunt, bene est. Neque enim huiusmodi pectore sumus, ut, licet apertis ipsi poenis propter criminum occulta plectamur, non agi prospere uel ubicumque uelimus. Nam certum est non minus uitiorum quam hostium esse captiuum, qui non etiam inter mala tempora bona uota seruauerit.* (Sidon. *Ep.* 3.4.2)

> Meanwhile, if all is well with you at least, that is good. We are not of such a mind that we do not wish others are doing prosperously wherever they may be, even though we are punished with evident penalties for obscure offences. It is certain that he who did not keep good wishes even during bad times is no less captive of his vices than he is of his enemies.

---

18. Cf. also the introduction to *Ep.* 5.4 and the commentary on *Ep.* 5.4.1 for further parallels.
19. On which see also the 'Dating elements' section in this introduction.

LETTER 3

As theorised by Harries, Sidonius' reiterated complaints here to Felix about silence, which on the surface may seem a 'not uncommon breach of etiquette', actually testify to years of voluntary interruption of communications on Felix's and Polemius' part,[20] as is confirmed by Sidonius' words in *Ep.* 4.10 to Felix, in which he laments being *annis multis insalutatus.* According to Harries, the reason behind this rift lies in Sidonius' support for Arvandus, the prefect of the Gaul brought to justice by the provincial council and whom Felix himself succeeded. Felix would have been prefect while Sidonius was in Rome trying to get a discharge for Arvandus, interfering with the counsel of many of his friends before leaving Rome. But Sidonius reveals that he actually did more than that. In *Ep.* 1.7 to Vincentius, which constitutes his version of the events, Sidonius declares that, together with Auxanius, he decided to inform Arvandus of the charge that was about to be brought against him by the three Gallic delegates, all close to Sidonius, Tonantius Ferreolus, Petronius, and a relative: Thaumastus.

> *Aruandi amicitias quoquo genere incursas inter ipsius aduersa uitare perfidum barbarum ignauum computabamus. Deferimus igitur nil tale metuenti totam perimachiam, quam summo artificio acres et flammei uiri occulere in tempus iudicii meditabantur.* (Sidon. *Ep.* 1.7.6)

> We believed it would have been dishonest, cruel and cowardly to disavow the friendship we had with Arvandus in such adverse times for him. So, to him who fears nothing, we immediately report the whole contrivance, which those subtle and fiery men intended, most craftily, to keep secret till trial.

Sidonius, therefore, challenged his own relatives and close friends, did not keep their secret and so spoilt the surprise effect they were seeking. It is no wonder, then, that he says that siding with Arvandus exposed him to general disfavour (*Ep.* 1.7.1 *nuper mihi inuidia conflata*).[21] His actions probably cost him the resentment of Felix and Polemius, and likely of the three delegates of the Gallic provincial council, who, eventually, forgave him, since they seem to be on friendly terms a few years later, as is testified by the letters in

---

20. On the rift between Sidonius, Felix and Polemius, see Harries 1994, 15–6 and 177–8; Harries 1996, 38.

21. Arvandus' downfall distresses Sidonius, who claims that *amari palam licet et capite damnatos* (*Ep.* 1.7.1) –'it is legitimate to love openly even those who are sentenced to death' – and later calls him *amicus* (*Ep.* 1.7.3). Therefore, he reclaims the rightness of his conduct, although he does not condone the actions of Arvandus and his arrogance, which in particular has proved to be incriminating.

99

Sidonius' collection.[22] Since the prosecutor Thaumastus can be identified with an uncle or a cousin,[23] it is legitimate to imagine that the disfavour encountered by Sidonius would have involved his family, since he actively opposed them by revealing their plans to Arvandus beforehand, even if that did not prevent the delegates from winning the case rapidly, with Arvandus being exiled in 469.[24]

The linguistic similarities between the letters sent to Felix, Polemius, Apollinaris and Simplicius on epistolary silence could be considered as further evidence that the reasons for this silence may be the same, and Sidonius may be looking for a reconciliation by appealing to the same concepts. Borrowing Harries' words: 'friends do not fail to greet each other for many years',[25] let alone close relatives, one may add.

This is only a theory, since, as often in Sidonius' letters, there are no other elements that would allow a clearer picture of the events. It seems likely, however, that Arvandus' trial may have been the cause of a momentary impasse and uncertainty in his family relationships that had resulted in a long interruption of communications since before his election to bishop.

Internal evidence of uneasiness

That Sidonius does not feel particularly comfortable in writing and is hesitant and cautious is testified by his choice of words. As recently pointed out by van Waarden, while other letters to family members – and even *Epp.* 4.6 and 5.6 to Apollinaris himself – belong to what he calls the '*ego-tu* category', a direct way of addressing the recipient, *Ep.* 5.3 stands out, being ascribable to the '*ego/nos-tu/uos*' category.[26] Expressions conveying unusual social distance for a letter to a relative (mainly the second person plural in numerous passages) are in fact intermittently mingled with terms expressing

---

22. He will write friendly letters to them: to Tonantius Ferreolus, *Ep.* 7.12, dated to 476/477 by Loyen 1970b, 65 and 215 n. 12 and by van Waarden 2016, 56; to Thaumastus, *Ep.* 5.7, dated to 474; and to Petronius, *Epp.* 5.1 (post 469) and 8.1 (dated to 479 by Loyen 1970b, 82 and Kaufmann 1995, 333. For the end of the rift see Harries 1994, 173.

23. Mathisen 2020, 123 believes him to be the elder Thaumastus.

24. For the date of the episode see Kelly 2020, 179. The accusers are also said to be extremely sly in Sidon. *Ep.* 1.7.11, where, knowing that Arvandus is extravagant and keen on dressing lavishly, they all appear in court in dark clothing, so that he would look bad in the eyes of the judges.

25. Harries 1994, 15.

26. Van Waarden 2020b, 426.

closeness, such as *frater*; this oscillating tone seems to testify that Sidonius does not know where he presently stands in relation to the addressee.[27]

The formal (plain underscore) and informal (wavy underscore) addresses are highlighted below in order to show how the forms are blended even in contiguous clauses. In particular, direct addresses are detectable in questions, as if the appeal to the interlocutor allows Sidonius to try to leave the formality behind.

> **5.3.1** *Par erat quidem garrulitatem nostram silentii uestri talione frenari. obsequium alloquii impudentis iteramus.*
>
> *Cuius improbitas . . . dinoscitur, quod tacetis.*
>
> *Ergone quid tempore hostilitatis ageretis, frater, nosse non merui? Dissimulastis trepido pro uobis amico uel securitatem prodere uel timorem?*
>
> **5.3.2** *Quid est aliud, si requirenti tuas supprimas actiones, quam suspicari eum, qui tui sollicitus existat . . .*
>
> *Namque, ut Crispus uester affirmat . . .*
>
> **5.3.3** *Interea si uel uos ualetis, bene est. Ego autem, infelicis conscientiae mole depressus, ui febrium nuper extremum salutis accessi . . .*
>
> *. . . tamquam sterilis arbor, cum non habeam opera pro pomis, spargo uerba pro foliis.*
>
> **5.3.4** *Quod restat, orate, . . . ab inferna propemodum sede remeauimus, ne, si in praeteritis criminibus manserimus, incipiat ad animae potius mortem pertinere quod uiuimus. Ecce quod agimus indicamus; ecce adhuc, quid agatis, inquirimus. Fit a nostra parte quod pium est, uos deinceps facite quod uidetur. Illud . . . credite incisum, nos sub ope Christi numquam admissuros amoris terminum, cuius studuimus fundare principium.*

External evidence

The silence must have gone on for quite some time, causing Sidonius' irritation to grow further. The following letter in the collection, *Ep.* 5.4 to Simplicius, bears traces of this extended hostility, and it seems possible that also Simplicius' sons were involved and were refusing to answer Sidonius. If Eulalia was the daughter of Simplicius, as has been suggested, since she was married to Probus, Magnus Felix's brother, the rift may have involved this side of the family as well.[28]

---

27. As argued by van Waarden 2020b, 418, the fluctuation of second person singulars and plurals in Sidonius is to be interpreted as 'an interplay of foreground and background, nearness and distance', which, according to van Waarden 2020b, 421, 'results in nuances of directness/indirectness, activity/passivity, responsibility/non-responsibility, or certainty/doubt'. See also van Waarden 2010, 49–52; van Waarden 2016, 45–7.

28. On the identity of Simplicius, see the introduction to *Ep.* 5.4.

In terms of internal coherence of the book, it seems reasonable to have letters on the reiterated epistolary silence of Apollinaris and Simplicius, followed, after the brief pause of one letter (which may also suggest that some time passed), by two letters (*Epp.* 5.6 and 5.7) in which it appears that, at least with part of the family, *concordia* had been restored in the interim.

A valetudinarian letter

In *Ep.* 5.3, directly linked to the first topos, is another recurring theme in epistolography: concern about the health of the addressee. [29] Cugusi points out that this topos is attested most frequently in 'humble contexts', as in numerous epistolary Greek and Latin papyri.[30] In Sidon. *Ep.* 5.3, the theme of anxiety over the health of Apollinaris is also an excuse to inform the addressee of his own health problems. Both features can be considered as distinctive of the genre of valetudinarian letters, in which Symmachus, once again, stands out for the number of occurrences. The complaints about his own poor health or that of others have been considered as one of the most commonly recurring themes in his letter collection, to the point that Symmachus has often been called a hypochondriac.[31] By way of example, Symmachus specifically mentions a violent fever weakening his strength in *Ep.* 3.38, as well as in *Ep.* 7.28, followed by an apology for the brevity of the letter, which is due to his ill-health.

A topos within the topos?

A violent fever, caused by the strain of travelling and by poisonous exhalations of air, is also mentioned by Sidonius in *Ep.* 1.5.8, the description of his journey from Lyon to Rome, where the illness is described in accordance

---

29. Widely attested in epistolography as testified, for example, in Cic. *Fam.* 16.14.1 (*tuis litteris nihilo sum factus certior quo modo te haberes*), or, closer to Sidonius, Symm. *Ep.* 3.86 to Rufinus, whose silence Symmachus justifies in light of his illness; however, a further lack of news would have him worried.
30. Cugusi 1983, 76–7.
31. As in McGeachy 1942, 110–11, who lists the letters Symmachus dedicates to this topic (thirty-seven on his own health and seventeen on that of others). See also Roda 1981, 213; Pellizzari 1998, 147. On the other hand, Cecconi 2002b, *passim* discards the possibility that the modern definition of hypochondriac may be applied to Symmachus.

LETTER 3

with canonical models;[32] however, the illness mentioned in *Ep.* 5.3 would seem to be of a different kind. The mention of Sidonius' fever, in fact, is entangled with that of his election as bishop, to the point that it is possible to wonder if the affliction is indeed physical or should be considered a crisis due to the *pondus* (*Ep.* 5.3.3) of the appointment.

Note that in *Ep.* 6.1 to his fellow bishop Lupus, Sidonius expresses a sense of unworthiness for his new role by employing a form of staged *recusatio* which is very similar to the one in *Ep.* 5.3.[33] Sidonius' doubts concerning his suitability for office seem in fact to be mirrored by the *erotēma* in *Ep.* 6.1.5.

> *Nam quis bene medelam aeger impertiat? Quis febriens arroganti tactu pulsum distinguat incolumem? Quis desertor scientiam rei militaris iure laudauerit? Quis esculentus abstemium competenter arguerit?*

> For how could a sick man impart a cure? How could one, ill of a fever, ever recognise a healthy pulse with his arrogant touch? How could a deserter justly praise military skill? How could the gluttonous suitably censure the abstemious?

Commenting on these letters, Harries affirms that 'the recollection of the transgressions of his past life weighed heavily on him and inhibited his intercessions for his people'.[34] She adds that, although Sidonius' self-abasement is exaggerated, there is something off in his words on the consecration, and reaches the conclusion that becoming bishop was not among his favoured options and that he may have become such 'under some duress'.[35]

In addition to what Harries says, it seems noticeable that in both letters the author's feeling of inadequacy is expressed through a comparison with the aridity and barrenness of nature. In *Ep.* 5.3.3 he represents himself as a tree incapable of bearing fruits and destined to scatter his leaves (his words) on the ground. When Sidonius writes to Lupus in *Ep.* 6.1.1, praising the bishop for his worthiness as a consoler of the sick and as a moral guide, he pictures himself, by contrast, as incapable of an adequate reply: *putris et fetida*

---

32. On which see Köhler 1995, 205.
33. Specifically, on the Sidonian typical *recusatio* of historiography and its models see Gualandri 1979, 29–33; Cugusi 1990. On the feeling of unworthiness expressed in both letters, see Harries 1994, 170. Similar expressions of unworthiness are also in Sidon *Ep.* 7.9.6, on which see van Waarden 2010, 451.
34. Harries 1994, 170.
35. Harries 1994, 172.

103

reatu terra, as 'putrid earth stinking with sin'. Since images of natural decay occur twice in passages concerning the new appointment as bishop, it is legitimate to wonder, as Harries does, if, through the seasonal comparison with the autumn tree, it is actually his feelings of downfall that are expressed, rather than a sense of inadequacy.

As shown in the commentary, when Sidonius in *Ep.* 5.3.3 says that he is compelled to teach before he can learn, he may be echoing Ambrose's reflections on his pastoral experience, and on being snatched from a life in tribunals into that of priesthood, forced to teach before he can learn.[36]

> *Ego enim raptus de tribunalibus atque administrationis infulis ad sacerdotium, docere uos coepi quod ipse non didici. Itaque factum est ut prius docere inciperem quam discere. Discendum igitur mihi simul et docendum est quoniam non uacauit ante discere.* (Ambr. *Off.* 1.1.4)

> I was snatched into the priesthood from a life spent at tribunals and amidst the paraphernalia of administrative office, and I began to teach you things I had not learnt myself. The result was that I started to teach before I had started to learn. With me, then, it is a matter of learning and teaching all at the same time, since no opportunity was given me to learn in advance.[37]

That of Ambrose was certainly one of the most renowned examples of a senator becoming a bishop, and Sidonius chooses to allude to that model and in particular to Ambrose's expression of humility in accepting the new role.

The image of himself as a tree, unable to bear fruit and scattering leaves to the ground, is also an echo of Augustine's interpretation (*Serm.* 89.1) of the episode of the fig tree in the gospel of Matthew (Mt. 21.12–19). In the gospel, Jesus, hungry, sees a fig tree which, however, bears only leaves and no fruit. When he then addresses the tree and says it will not bear fruit again, it withers at once. In *Serm.* 89.1 Augustine explains the episode as follows: the gospel terrifies the reader (*terruit nos*) and admonishes him not to have leaves without fruit (*ne folia habeamus et fructum non habeamus*), that is, words not matched by actions (*hoc autem breuiter exponitur: ne uerba adsint, et facta desint*). The tree, according to Augustine, represented the synagogue, criticised for its behaviour, since it had leaves but did not bear fruit. It

---

36. For further context and for a comparison with Ambr. *Paen.* 2.67, see the commentary below on § 3 *ante compulsus docere quam discere.*

37. Translation by Davidson 2001, 119.

seems possible, therefore, that, when alluding to his own pastoral mission, Sidonius defined his unworthiness by borrowing the image of the gospel and Augustine's interpretation.

Moreover, one may compare Sidonius' near-death experience in *Ep.* 5.3 to the famous passage describing the dream of the Judge in Jerome's *Ep.* 22.30. The episode takes place when Jerome is experiencing a violent fever and is almost on his deathbed. Jerome says that the fever had weakened him, to the point that he was skin and bone, his body had grown colder and preparations for his funeral had already been made.[38] It is known that the passage symbolises Jerome's feeling of unworthiness for his role, and the fictional internal conflict between being a Christian and avidly reading pagan texts.[39] Jerome's renowned passage could rightly be considered as a canonical representation of a crisis of conscience.

Therefore, even if Sidonius' fever was not fictional, he may have drawn upon the most renowned exemplum of unworthiness and inner conflict to describe what had happened to him. The same could be said for his allusions to Ambrose's and Augustine's passages; it is possible his feelings of inadequacy were real, but he still chose to express those feelings by echoing his models.

Dating elements

As Loyen points out, there are two elements which suggest a possible date for the letter. The first is that Sidonius refers to troubled times of hostility when he tells Apollinaris he would like to know how he is doing.[40] Loyen ascribes this to the defeat of emperor Anthemius' army at the hands of Euric on the left bank of the Rhone, near Arles (in 471);[41] the imperial army was led by the emperor's son Anthemiolus, who was killed with three of his generals. It is likely that the presence of the Burgundian troops had stopped

---

38. *Ep.* 22.30 *in media ferme quadragesima medullis infusa febris corpus inuasit exhaustum et sine ulla requie – quod dictu quoque incredibile sit – sic infelicia membra depasta est ut ossibus uix haererem. Interim parabantur exsequiae, et uitalis animae calor toto frigente iam corpore in solo tantum tepente pectusculo palpitabat, cum subito raptus in spiritu ad tribunal iudicis pertrahor.*

39. Diverging interpretations of the episode are e.g. Hagendahl 1958, 91 and 328; Adkin 1999, 162. For further bibliographical references on the subject see Marolla 2019, 91–5.

40. Loyen 1970a, 255.

41. See Harries 1994, 225.

Euric's advance,[42] but in any case the scale of the event was considerable, and Sidonius' apprehension would be understandable.

Second, and even more important, is the reference to his health issues, and specifically to a fever which would have weakened him considerably, immediately after he had received the appointment as bishop of Clermont. According to Loyen, these elements should allow the letter to be dated within a period spanning the end of 470 and the beginning of 471 (after the defeat of Anthemius' army) and, according to Mathisen, to 471.[43] However, as often happens when trying to date the letters, it is safe to say only that the ordination is the *terminus post quem* for the dramatic date of the letter.[44] Since the date of this appointment is itself debated, a time span starting from 469 should be considered a safer option.

As stated above, the letter may be closely related to letters sent to Magnus Felix, and the reasons for Felix's and Apollinaris' silence may be the same. In particular, in *Ep.* 3.4.1, before stressing how important it is to leave behind past recriminations *inter mala tempora*, Sidonius gives a description of the situation which is causing him to be *granditer anxius*: Clermont is surrounded by two enemies and has become the prey of both – it is regarded with suspicion by the Burgundians (though said to be its protectors) and is too close to the Visigoths (its invaders). It is safe to assume, therefore, that Sidonius is already a bishop when he writes this message to Felix, which Loyen dates to the end of 471 or 472,[45] Mathisen to 471–3.[46]

Although this is only a suggestion, the similar content and words used in the two letters may lead one to suggest that they could be dated to the same years: in both texts, silence is weighing on him, enquiries about the addressee's situation are made, and the binding laws of correspondence and old friendships are called to his aid. It seems legitimate, therefore, to suggest that the *tempus hostilitatis* of *Ep.* 5.3 and the *mala tempora* of *Ep.* 3.4 may be overlapping, and that a troubling political situation was a good excuse to write very similar letters, trying to bridge the distance at which Sidonius

---

42. Harries 1994, 225.
43. Mathisen 2013a, 245.
44. Mathisen 2013a, 239.
45. Loyen 1970a, 249; Kaufmann 1995, 306. On the date suggested see also Giannotti 2016, 159.
46. Mathisen 2013a, 239. The Visigothic aggressions in Auvergne, datable to between 471 and 475, are discussed in *Ep.* 3.4 and in numerous other passages of Book 3, as Kelly 2020, 179 points out.

had been put by both Magnus Felix and Apollinaris. One cannot exclude, however, that the thematic similarity could be the reason why Sidonius chooses a standardised repertoire of images and complaints.

SIDONIUS APOLLINARI SUO SALUTEM

1. Par erat quidem garrulitatem nostram silentii uestri talione frenari. Sed quoniam perfecta dilectio non tam debet recolere, quid officiorum soluat, quam meminisse, quid debeat, etiam nunc laxatis uerecundiae habenis obsequium alloquii impudentis iteramus. Cuius improbitas uel hinc maxime dinoscitur, quod tacetis. Ergone quid tempore hostilitatis ageretis, frater, nosse non merui? Dissimulastis trepido pro uobis amico uel securitatem prodere uel timorem?

2. Quid est aliud, si requirenti tuas supprimas actiones, quam suspicari eum, qui tui sollicitus existat, aut certe non gauisurum compertis prosperis aut tristem, si diuersa cesserint, non futurum? Facessat haec a bonis moribus impietatis opinio et a candore suo uera caritas naeuum tam miserae suspicionis eliminet. Namque, ut Crispus uester affirmat, idem uelle atque idem nolle, ea demum firma amicitia est.

3. Interea si uel uos ualetis, bene est. Ego autem, infelicis conscientiae mole depressus, ui febrium nuper extremum salutis accessi, utpote cui indignissimo tantae professionis pondus impactum est, qui miser, ante compulsus docere quam discere et ante praesumens bonum praedicare quam facere, tamquam sterilis arbor, cum non habeam opera pro pomis, spargo uerba pro foliis.

4. Quod restat, orate, ut operae pretium sit, quod ab inferna propemodum sede remeauimus, ne, si in praeteritis criminibus manserimus, incipiat ad animae potius mortem pertinere quod uiuimus. Ecce quod agimus indicamus; ecce adhuc, quid agatis, inquirimus. Fit a nostra parte quod pium est, uos deinceps facite quod uidetur. Illud sane uelut Atticas leges ita aeri credite incisum, nos sub ope Christi numquam admissuros amoris terminum, cuius studuimus fundare principium. Vale.

§ 2 supprimas *L edd.* : supprimis α (with *A post correctionem*) *MP*

§ 4 atticas *codd.* : antiquas *Gustafsson*
ita aeri *Geisler* : ita aere *codd.*: in aere *Lütjohann*

LETTER 3

SIDONIUS TO HIS DEAR APOLLINARIS

1. Now, it was right of you to curb my garrulousness with the retaliation of your silence. And yet, since a perfect affection should not think over which obligations it fulfils, as much as it should remember what it ought to fulfil, I am now still repeating the complaisance of impudently addressing you, giving free rein to my shamelessness. That this is bold of me is made abundantly clear by this fact: that you are silent. Well then, brother, didn't I deserve to know what you were doing at a time of hostility? Did you neglect to confide either your safety or your fears to a friend who was afraid for you?

2. If you conceal your deeds from someone who is enquiring about you, how is it different from being suspicious that he who shows himself concerned for you will not rejoice on learning good news, or will not be sad if the opposite occurs? May this ill opinion depart a good heart, and may true affection push away from its candour the stain of such a wretched suspicion. For, as your dear Sallust asserts: 'to desire the same thing and to shun the same thing, that, ultimately, is solid friendship'.

3. Meanwhile, I am pleased if you are in good health. For my part, overwhelmed by the burden of an unhappy conscience, I was not long ago close to death due to violent fevers; since the weight of such a high office has been thrust on me, most unworthy, miserable man, compelled to teach before I could learn, and presuming to preach good deeds before I did any. Just like a fruitless tree, since I do not have works in place of fruits, I scatter words in place of leaves.

4. For the time to come, pray that it is worthwhile that I returned almost from the underworld; so that, should I persist in committing past misdeeds, my survival would not rather lead to the death of my soul. Look, I disclose what I am doing, and look, I keep enquiring how you are. I am acting according to duty; in turn, you do as you please. Believe me, it is indeed engraved in bronze in the same way as the Attic laws that, with the assistance of Christ, I am never going to accept the end of a friendly relationship whose beginning I strove to establish. Farewell.

Commentary

§ 1

garrulitatem nostram: Sidonius is 'guilty' of verbosity, a thing that may justify Apollinaris' silence. The word has here the widely attested meaning of *uitium multa uel nimia loquentium* (*TLL* 6.2.1697 s.v. *garrulitas* 27–8 by Drexler), as in Plin. *Ep.* 9.10.2, where *garrulitas* is said to be the main feature of conversations happening *in uehiculo*. In the Sidonian context it does not seem to have a negative meaning of *uaniloquium, stultiloquium* as it does e.g. in Hier. *Ep.* 50.5.4. Compared with any other author, Sidonius employs this word very often and, as pointed out by van Waarden 2010, 191: 'it fits in with the self-depreciating mould in which this type of correspondence is cast (*urbanitas*)'. See on the same concept Amherdt 2001, 164 (commenting on the verb *garrire*). In particular, Sidonius refers it to his own epistolary 'babbling' in *Ep.* 3.7.1 (to Felix): *ego garrio, uos tacetis . . . Aut nescis quia garrulo non respondere conuicium est?* The similarity between these two letters may prove the silence was caused by Sidonius' siding with Arvandus – see the introduction to this letter and also here *passim*. Cf. *Ep.* 3.11.2, *Ep.* 5.4.1, the closing remarks of *Ep.* 7.2.10 and of *Ep.* 7.3.2 (*naturali garrulitate deblaterat*). See also *Ep.* 8.13.2 for *garrulitas* as opposed to *taciturnitas*, and *Ep.* 9.1.3, in which Sidonius' unrestrainable *garrulitas* is said to be responsible for the issuing of Book 9, which was being published *post denuntiatum terminum*. On *Ep.* 9.1.3 see Condorelli 2015, 494–5.

silentii uestri: The topos of epistolary silence recurs in the letter and is present from its beginning. For the models drawn on by Sidonius, and for the scheme *ego/nos-tu/uos*, unusual in letters to family and reflecting Sidonius' uneasiness in talking to Apollinaris, see the introduction.

talione frenari: Very similar, in terms of content and language, is Sidon. *Ep.* 9.1.4 *porro autem si me garrire compulso ipse reticere perseueraueris, te quoque silentii nostri talione ad uicem plecti non periniurium est* ('and yet, if, after forcing me to chatter, you yourself persevere in not answering, it is not very unjust if, in turn, you are punished with a retaliating silence from me'). It seems safe to assume that Symmachus may have been a model for the use of *talio* when complaining of epistolary silence, as shown by the following occurrences. If *talio* is usually mentioned in more formal juridical contexts (e.g. Cato *Hist.* 81; Sen. *Con.* 10.4.9; see *OLD* s.v. 2096)

LETTER 3

Symmachus seems to have been the first to employ the threat of the *talio silentii* in semi-serious letters: a retaliating silence from him is supposed to guarantee more frequent answers. That is the case of Symm. *Ep.* 1.65 (to his brother, Celsinus Titianus) *ne uos talione silentii mordeamus.* His slackness in answering testifies that he has no fear that Symmachus might 'bite back' with a retaliating silence. See *Ep.* 1.95.1 *talionem referre uitaui*, a warning to Syagrius that Symmachus avoided paying him back with silence (compare the similar Symm. *Ep.* 5.92), and Symm. *Ep.* 3.1 to Iulianus, where the *talio scribendi* is invoked as a retaliation for the brevity of the letters received. This tactic often proved to be unfruitful, as Symmachus states in *Ep.* 3.26 to Marinianus, who seems not to fear the repeated threats of *talio silentii*, knowing that Symmachus, eventually, will always write back (as also in Symm. *Ep.* 7.99). In *Ep.* 5.13, Symmachus spares the addressee what would have been an *aequum talio*, a fair punishment for his silence (cf. the Sidonian *par est*). Note, however, that in Sidon. *Ep.* 5.3 the 'fair' *talio silentii* is (in the fiction of the letter abiding by the commonplaces of the *urbanitas* mentioned above) a 'punishment' for his excessive verbosity. On this topos see Condorelli 2015, 498–9.

perfecta dilectio: Sidonius justifies his writing despite the silence of Apollinaris by appealing to this principle: when people are bound by true affection, as they are, one should not focus on what he has already done for the other as much as on what he can still do for him. It seems that, on a deeper level, the mention of the shared affection, betrayed by Apollinaris but not by the sender, would be a further element of benevolent reproach, in line with the standardised topical complaints of epistolary silence mentioned in the introduction to this letter. The *iunctura*, not attested before the famous passage in 1 Ioh. 4.18 *perfecta dilectio foras mittit timorem*, is often used by Church Fathers commenting on John's text, starting with Tertullian (e.g. *Scorp.* 12). See also the occurrence in Paul. Nol. *Ep.* 3.1 (ed. Hartel), together with the expression *uera caritas*, as in § 2.

laxatis uerecundiae habenis: While there is no other known occurrence of this syntagma, *laxare habenas* (*et similia*) is an expression often used with the metaphorical meaning (see *TLL* 6.3.2393 s.v. *habena* 40–79, by Bulhart) of giving free rein to one's desire, as in Aus. *Mos.* 389 *laxis . . . habenis*. In Sidon. *Ep.* 5.3, however, the syntagma specifically means to do something not particularly socially acceptable. See, with this meaning, Aug. *In Psalm.* 50.24 (*peruersa autem et falsa innocentia est, habenas laxare peccatis*), where 'free rein' is said to be wrongly given to one's sins and Aug. *Serm.* 20 (*ad peccandum*); a similar warning is also in Aug. *In Psalm.* 76.6 (*gaudiorum*). Certainly, the Sidonian context is different, there being no hint of moralism. The negativity of the author's *inuerecundia* is still part of his customary self-depreciation strategy. See also Sidon. *Carm.* 22.7 *non passim laxet habenas*, where Phoebus is reluctant to give free rein to poetry indiscriminately, and Sidon. *Ep.* 4.11.7: when writing Mamertus Claudianus' epitaph, Sidonius gave free rein to his tears.

obsequium alloquii impudentis iteramus: The topos of epistolary silence required the sender to keep on writing despite the lack of answers. *Alloquium* is attested since Horace and Ovid (see *TLL* s.v. 1.1692.60, by Vollmer) but, in particular, with transferred meaning, in epistles, to indicate 'letter exchanges' in Late Antiquity. Symmachus ends *Ep.* 1.5.2 hoping his father will be well and write more often (*date operam ualetudini et adloquio crebiori*); moreover, the expression does not only concern letters sent by Symmachus but also refers to letters he received, such as *Ep.* 2.49, and enjoyed, as with *Ep.* 2.73 (*religionis tuae uicissim pascor adloquiis*). See in particular the occurrence in *Ep.* 4.59 (*adloquii raritas*), where Symmachus discusses the epistolary silence of the addressee. This letter may have been a model for *Ep.* 5.3, since the self-presentation of the sender as a *flagitator* (an importunate asker), faith in the bond between the correspondents and reciprocal affection are certainly elements common to both texts. *Alloquium* is widely used with the meaning of 'correspondence' in other late antique letter collections, as in Ambr. *Ep.* 7.36.7 to Theodosius, as well as Jerome's *Epp.* 8.1 and 127.8 to Marcella (*mutuis solabamur adloquiis*). Cf. the occurrence in Sidon. *Ep.* 3.11.2 (see § 1 *garrulitatem nostram*), where the theme is the same – he is starting unsolicited correspondence; the *recursans alloquium* of *Ep.* 3.11.2 is matched by the *impudens alloquium* of *Ep.* 5.3 (*iunctura* not previously attested); the concept of *impudentia* itself is also in *Ep.* 3.11.2, as part of the apology for the possible inappropriateness of Sidonius' action of writing (*impudentia paginae praesentis*). Sidonius also mentions *alloquium* with the meaning of 'epistolary exchange' in *Ep.* 4.7.3, when he states that the vulgarity of messengers should not affect the chance of a more frequent conversation (*frequentioris alloquii*).

quod tacetis: Direct solicitation of an answer was the norm in letters complaining on epistolary silence, either to closer addressees, or in more formal contexts. The tone of these remarks is always semi-serious; for instance,

Symmachus often states that the silence of the addressee will not dissuade him from writing. See, e.g. the opening passages of Symm. *Ep.* 3.82.1 (*adhuc siles; sed loquacitas mea non cohibetur exemplo*) and Symm. *Ep.* 5.77 (*longum siles, sed ego talis exempli imitator esse non debeo*), akin to Symm. *Ep.* 9.36. Similarly, Sidonius' *garrulitas* is opposed to the silence of the addressee also in *Ep.* 3.7 *longum a litteris temperatis . . . ego garrio, uos tacetis*. For Felix's silence, for the similarities with *Ep.* 5.3 and for a similar occurrence in Greek epistolography, see the introduction.

Ergone . . . timorem? The two questions give emphasis to the pathetic tone the text is supposed to convey. The lack of news has worried Sidonius, because they are living in uncertain times. The expression *non merui* has the purpose of stressing (once again in accordance with standardised models) how frustrated Sidonius is at the silence. Cf. Symm. *Ep.* 8.50 *mutua scripta non merui*; in this short letter, Symmachus highlights his intention not to stop writing, as he does in many other contexts and as Sidonius himself does in *Ep.* 5.3.

frater: It is difficult to say with certainty what is the meaning of *frater* in this passage. The main obstacle is that the noun is employed various times by Sidonius in his letters and in different contexts, for instance, together with the word *domine,* in *Epp.* 2.13.8, 4.8.4 and 7.17.1. Loyen 1970a, 78 n. 56 believes that in the first context the term has the meaning of 'frère par la religion', as is most certainly also the case of *Ep.* 7.17.1; while Loyen thinks that, in *Ep.* 4.8.4, it has 'certainement le sens profane' of belonging to a literary brotherhood (Loyen 1970a, 129 n. 30). *Frater* may have either of these two meanings also in contexts in which it is referred to a third party, someone who is different from the addressee, as in *Ep.* 4.18.2 to Lucontius, where it designates Volusianus twice; *Ep.* 5.7.7 to Thaumastus, where it refers to Apollinaris and others (*fratres communes*); *Ep.* 5.17.6 to Eriphius, in reference to Domnicius (*frater meus*); *Ep.* 6.2.2, where it concerns Agrippinus; and *Ep.* 7.17.4, where it concerns Auxanius (in the last two cases, certainly 'religious brothers'). In other passages Sidonius specifies the element that makes someone, again someone different from the addressee, his 'brother': that is the case in *Ep.* 3.5.3, when Donidius is said to be *meus aetate frater,* 'his brother in age', and in *Ep.* 4.4.1, in which Faustinus is his *frater natalium parilitate*, his brother in that he is an exact contemporary. The *frater* of *Ep.* 5.3, therefore, stands out, being a direct address to the addressee instead of involving a third party, and not being defined by context in any way. If read in light of this survey, Mathisen's deduction that the noun indicates a *frater patruelis*, hence a cousin on his father's side, may be sustained (see Mathisen 2020, 59).

tempore hostilitatis: This is the first known occurrence of the expression *tempus hostilitatis*. The vague mention of a time of hostility has been interpreted as a dating element, specifically referred to the defeat of Anthemius' army at the hands of Euric in 471 (Loyen 1970a, 255; Harries 1994, 225). Compare the mention of ill times (*mala tempora*) in *Ep.* 3.4.2 on Magnus Felix's epistolary silence (see introduction and this commentary *passim*). For the possibility that *Epp.* 5.3 and 3.4 could be dated to the same year, see also the section 'Dating elements' in the introduction.

trepido pro uobis amico: The syntagma does not occur elsewhere, while the only previous occurrence of *trepidus amicus* is in Ov. *Met.* 13.69: a tirade against Ulysses, guilty of leaving Nestor behind out of cowardice; on which see Bömer 1982, 222. It would seem, therefore, that this is the first time the expression is employed to indicate a friend worried about somebody's fate.

§ 2

requirenti . . . futurum: The lack of news may be interpreted as Apollinaris' suspicion that Sidonius does not rejoice in hearing that he is doing well or that he is not concerned if he is not. Sidonius' fear that Apollinaris may think he does not care about him is also to be interpreted as a remark in line with the standardised reproaches for epistolary silence. Note that the reading of α*MP* is *supprimis*, while *supprimas* (only in *L*) is accepted by all editors; however, following Dolveck's theorisation, one should choose the former as the reading of the archetype. In terms of content, there is no strong reason to prefer one reading over the other: either is possible. While the type I conditional clause would give the text a sterner tone, being a sort of ultimatum, the subjunctive would confer a hypothetical nuance.

impietatis opinio: This *iunctura* does not occur elsewhere; however, the exaggerating tone it conveys is typical of letters on epistolary silence. Sidonius later stresses (§ 4) how *pius* his behaviour towards Apollinaris is, and that he expects the same courtesy from him.

114

uera caritas: The term *caritas* is widely attested with this meaning of '*amor, dilectio, affectus*' as a fundamental element at the basis of true friendship. As Pétré 1948, 32 puts it, unlike *amor, caritas* encompasses affection, esteem and respect. See e.g. the effective formulation of Cic. *Fin.* 2.83. On this see also *TLL* 3.460 s.v. *caritas* 37 (by Probst). In letter collections, the noun often occurs with this meaning, as in Symm. *Ep.* 4.42.1. Cf. also the occurrence of the *iunctura* in Paulinus of Nola's and Therasia's beginning of *Ep.* 3 (ed. Hartel) to Alypius, when the two praise the *uera caritas* and *perfecta dilectio* (on which see § 1) the addressee had shown towards them. Since both *iuncturae* also occur in Sidonius' letter, it is legitimate to wonder if the author had in mind Paulinus' and Therasia's text when writing to Apollinaris. It is noteworthy, anyway, that he adopts standard Christian vocabulary in what seems to be the first letter Sidonius, as a man of the cloth, sends to Apollinaris. More importantly, Sidonius, in a few lines, insists on the concept of a shared true friendship, a thing that is even more evident if these elements are put in sequence: *perfecta dilectio*, Apollinaris called *frater*, the definition of himself as a *trepidus amicus* and of their bond as *uera caritas*. Sidonius starts *Ep.* 3.1 to Avitus similarly, recalling the *multis uinculis caritatis*, 'the many chains of affection' which have bonded them since boyhood. Moreover, in *Ep.* 4.10.2 Sidonius tells Felix that, should he start writing to him like he used to (*si caritatis tuae morem pristino colloquiorum cursui reddis*) he would be *loquax* once again. Cf. also *Ep.* 7.4.4 *rogo, ut non habeat uestra caritas finem*, where Sidonius is not certain bishop Fonteius is intervening as a patron of Apollinaris and Simplicius and invokes his *caritas* towards them. On this passage see van Waarden 2010, 239.

naeuum tam miserae suspicionis: *Naeuum suspicionis* here clearly contrasts with the *candor*, the purity of the affection they have for each other. The only other known occurrence of the *iunctura* (already signalled by Geisler 1887, 365) is in Mam. Claud. *Anim.* 1.3, p. 35 *non caret naeuo suspicionis biceps ista prolocutio*. For Sidonius as a reader of this work, see comments on Sidon. *Ep.* 5.2. Cf. the occurrence of *naeuus* in Symm. *Ep.* 2.54 to Flavianus, in a similar context of epistolary silence. Urged to remedy the *neglecta familiaritas*, Symmachus blames Flavianus' messengers and concludes by saying that it would be disgraceful were he to have his name blemished for not upholding the obligations of friendship: *naeuum uiolatae religionis adtrahere* (for *religio* in Symmachus, see Cameron 2015, 72). Cf. also the 'mark of unrequired loquacity' in Sidon. *Ep.* 3.11.2 (*carebit sane nostrum naeuo loquacitatis officium*). Although in a different context, cf. Sidon. *Ep.* 8.11.4 *naeuo crudelitatis infecta*.

ut Crispus uester affirmat . . . firma amicitia est: It is common for Sidonius to mention authors in such an informal way – see for instance *Ep.* 3.6.2 *uestri Plotini* and *Ep.* 8.6.1 *uestri Arpinatis.* The quotation is from Catilina's speech in Sal. *Cat.* 20.4, and had become an aphorism, as is testified, for instance, by its occurrences in Donatus (*Commentum Terenti, Hecyra* 170), Jerome (who calls it *saecularis sententia* in *Ep.* 130.12) and Quoduultdeus (Pseudo-Augustine?) *De quattuor uirtutibus caritatis* 6. The aphorism conveyed the idea that a bond of friendship entails such an affinity that there is a common will friends share; see commentary on *Ep.* 5.9.4 *idem uelle, nolle* . . . For detailed information on the reception of Sallust's quotation see Tosi 2018, 1157–8 n. 1708.

§ 3

si uel uos ualetis, bene est: Widely attested in epistolary contexts, this formula, along with some variants (*si uales bene est* or *si uales bene est ego quidem ualeo*) was used as a standard formula of greeting after the *inscriptio* of a letter, hence was often in the abbreviated form. This sort of greeting, however, was probably in disuse by the time Sidonius writes, since Seneca (*Ep.* 15.1) mentions the formula *s.u.b.e.e.u.* as *mos antiquis fuit, usque ad meam seruatus aetatem.* As Cugusi 1983, 52–3 points out, Pliny also asserts that the formula was outdated by his time, and mentions it in *Ep.* 1.11 as *illud unde incipere priores solebant* (a letter on epistolary silence mentioned in the introduction to this letter). Symmachus employs it only once, in *Ep.* 4.28.4 *sufficiat aliquando celebrandae amicitiae: si uales, bene est.* This could be considered, therefore, as a fossil of epistolary conventions, a homage to letter writing, which, incidentally, does not occur in any other Sidonian letter. As is pointed out in the General Introduction, this is the only paragraph of *Ep.* 5.3 to be entirely clausulated, opened by a double cretic with prodelision at *uos ualetis bene est.*

infelicis conscientiae: This *iunctura* is previously attested in Quint. *Inst.* 6 *praef.* 10 and in Hier. *Ep.* 22.13. The occurrence in Quintilian refers to a profound state of melancholy the author was experiencing after the death of his son: Quint. *Inst.* 6 *praef.* 10 *non enim flosculos . . . sed iam . . . certos ac deformatos fructus ostenderat. Iuro per mala mea, per infelicem conscientiam . . .* The son, whose life ended beforehand, is represented as a tree which had already started not only blossoming but also bearing (well formed) fruit: *a contrario,*

LETTER 3

the tree metaphor is also employed by Sidonius in this paragraph, where he represents himself as an autumn tree scattering leaves. In Jerome's *Ep.* 22.13 the *iunctura* has the defined moralistic meaning of 'dirty conscience' and refers to widows whose 'miserable conscience' – stemming from the fact they are pregnant – is only 'masked by their deceptive clothes'. As far as the Sidonian passage is concerned, the *infelicitas* of his conscience may actually have the twofold meaning of unhappiness (more in line with the Quintilian passage) due to a feeling of unworthiness, or may refer to his actual unworthiness (in a more Hieronymian manner) because he has a 'dirty conscience', not feeling fit for the bishopric.

mole depressus: The expression, which occurs e.g. in *CTh.* 10.17.3 (*debitorum*) and 13.11.4 (*afanticorum*), and in Ambr. *In Luc.* 7.194 (about bodies being weightless after resurrection), in Sidonius indicates his feeling overwhelmed by the mental weight of his conscience. *Mole depressus* creates the first of a series of three cretic spondee clausulae.

ui febrium nuper extremum salutis accessi: Informing the addressee of one's own health was customary in valetudinarian letters. The same expression is in Symm. *Ep.* 1.48 *Paulina . . . extremum salutis accesserat*; and similar descriptions of violent fevers are in Symm. *Ep.* 3.38 and *Ep.* 7.28. As highlighted in the introduction, Sidonius mentions a fever also in *Ep.* 1.5.8, and says it was caused by the difficult journey (exhalations of unhealthy air). In *Ep.* 5.3.3 the author infers it was the stress of his appointment that had caused the violent fever. *Sa-lutis accessi* creates the second cretic spondee clausula in a row.

indignissimo tantae professionis pondus impactum est: The expression *pondus professionis* is previously attested exclusively in John Cassian, *Inst.* 4.33 (ed. Guy 1965), a passage concerning the importance of fully understanding what monastic life entails, in order to embrace it with proper knowledge of the weight of the *professio*. The noun in that passage means 'religious life', as here in Sidonius, who significatively also employs the same syntagma (*pondus professionis impactum est*) or variations of it in other letters. In *Ep.* 4.3.9 he says that his way of writing is changing in light of the *inpacta professio* (the bishopric); in *Ep.* 6.1.5 (*ora . . . quantum meas deprimat oneris impositi massa ceruices*) Sidonius recalls the weight of the appointment, which, again, is said to have been imposed, pressing on his shoulders (see the introduction and the commentary on *praedicare quam facere . . . sterilis arbor* below). The same thought is expressed by the author when speaking of his own appointment as arbitrator in his speech for the election of Bourges in *Ep.* 7.9.6 *professionis huiusce pondus impactum est*. As Harries 1994, 169–70 and van Waarden 2010, 451 rightly point out, there seems to be some degree of historical and psychological reality behind the customary theatricality surrounding these expressions of unworthiness. *Pondus impactum est* creates the third cretic spondee clausula in a row (this time with prodelision).

miser: Sidonius calls himself *miser* in relation to his role as bishop also in *Ep.* 6.1.5.

ante compulsus docere quam discere: Specular to this passage is the above-mentioned Sidon. *Ep.* 7.9.6. Van Waarden (2010, 453) has persuasively suggested a comparison with Ambr. *Off.* 1.1.4 *factum est ut prius docere inciperem quam discere* (on which, see introduction). As highlighted by Davidson 2001, 447–8, this expression has numerous attestations throughout Antiquity and Late Antiquity, to the point that it can be considered almost proverbial, in particular after the famous *sententia* in Sen. *Ep.* 7.8 *homines dum docent discunt*. By way of example, it occurs eight times in Jerome's letters. On this, see *TLL* 5.1.1331 s.v. *disco* 57–60 (by Gudeman) and Tosi 2018, 320 n. 454. Compare also Sidonius' passage with Ambr. *Paen.* 2.67 *non eram dignus uocari episcopus . . . et sum quidem minimus omnium episcoporum et infimus merito.* In conclusion, if – as Davidson 2001, 446 says, commenting on Ambrose's assertions – it was common practice in Late Antiquity to decline high office to show humility before accepting, it seems legitimate to infer that, though probably sincere, Sidonius is here, nonetheless, using a standard way of expressing unworthiness for new appointments by alluding to the best-known example of a senator becoming a bishop. For the possibility that showing unworthiness had become a fashion and for the reasons behind reluctance to accept, see Norton 2007, 192 and 199–201. Another clausula, *do-cere quam discere*, creates a double cretic.

praedicare quam facere, tamquam sterilis arbor . . . spargo uerba pro foliis: As discussed in the introduction to this letter, this is not the only time Sidonius expresses his feeling of unfitness for the role of bishop through images of natural decay. In particular, in *Ep.* 6.1.1, Sidonius defines himself as *putris et fetida reatu terra* in comparison with the holiness of bishop Lupus.

LETTER 3

As stated above (see the commentary on *infelicis conscientiae*) this passage can be compared to the opposite image used by Quintilian *Inst.* 6 *praef.* 10 of his son as a tree, which, despite its youth, was already bearing well formed fruit (*certos ac deformatos fructus*). However, Augustine *Serm.* 89.1, which discusses the episode of the fig tree in Mt. 21.12–19, may enlighten the meaning of Sidonius' words (as is explained in the introduction). The image should be referred to those who preach without acting accordingly (the synagogue, in the gospel), and it is easy to see how it would appeal to Sidonius' feelings of unworthiness, since he says he is compelled to teach before he can learn and set an example. The common expression *uentis uerba profundere* is used, since Lucretius 4.931, in a variety of contexts to express the futility of one's words. On this see Tosi 2018, 375 n. 538. The last lines of § 3 are all clausulated: with a cretic tribrach (*praedi-care quam facere*); followed by a paeon I spondee (*tam-quam sterilis arbor*); a paeon IV spondee (*opera pro pomis*) and lastly by another cretic tribrach (*uerba pro foliis*).

§ 4

Quod restat: This informal expression is variously attested in the Sidonian corpus (e.g. in *Epp.* 3.1.4, 3.2.4, 4.15.2, 9.3.6) to express a wish or a prayer.

ut operae pretium sit: Another informal sentence, attested for instance in Symm. *Ep.* 5.25 *ut operae sit pretium, quod in exactore mittendo litteris tuis et monitis satisfeci* (followed by *quod*, as in Sidonius); and in Augustine to Oceanus, who was deserving an answer – *Ep.* 180.5 *ut operae pretium sit tecum litteris conloqui*.

quod ab inferna propemodum sede remeauimus: This would suggest Sidonius' illness has been serious, or, at least, that is what he wants Apollinaris to believe; possibly, an exaggeration in relating the illness would grant him a reply to his letter. For the possibility that Sidonius may have in mind the description of the fever which preceded the dream of the Judge in Hier. *Ep.* 22.30 as an exemplum of a crisis of conscience, see introduction to this letter. *Inferna sedes* is a *iunctura* variously attested in Classical authors (e.g. Verg. *Aen.* 8.244; Ov. *Met.* 3.504) and is not common in Christian authors. For a bishop it would have been more appropriate, or at least customary, to use the substantive form *infernus* or *infernum* (often in neuter plural), as attested in *TLL* 7.1.1372. s.v. *infernus* 70 ff. (by Ehlers).

Ecce quod agimus indicamus; ecce adhuc, quid agatis, inquirimus: As is common in valetudinarian letters, the sender informs the addressee of how he is doing but he expects the same courtesy in return. See e.g. Cic. *Fam.* 16.14.1 *tuis litteris nihilo sum factus certior quomodo te haberes*; Symm. *Ep.* 1.10 to his father, since he has heard what he is doing (*quid rerum geramus, audistis*), to tell him in turn the good news about his health and activities (*facite uicissim uestrae salutis atque actuum prospera nouerimus*), so that he will spend his time in Campania 'without the resentment for his silence' (*sine offensa uestri silentii*). For the canonicity of Symmachus' anxiety about or relief over the health of correspondents, see Cameron 2015, 68.

Fit a nostra parte . . . facite quod uidetur: The lack of fineries is a standard feature of letters on epistolary silence; see the introduction. It is noticeable that Sidonius refers to the act of answering as doing *quod pium est*: there is a social duty to comply with, when exchanging letters with family and close friends. This is reminiscent of the similar insistence on the concept of *religio*, 'scrupulousness', in Symmachus' letters when referring to the duty to fulfil one's responsibility in epistolary exchanges with friends. For the 'code of conduct' entailing social *officia* and *munera* in Symmachus see Salzman and Roberts 2011, xlix–l.

uelut Atticas leges ita aeri credite incisum: Gustafsson 1882, 85 suggested changing the attested reading *Atticas* to *antiquas*, while, in Lütjohann 1887, 80, *ita aeri* is Geisler's conjecture for *ita aere* of codd. Supposing the reading *Atticas leges* is correct, one possible explanation is that Sidonius refers here to Solon's laws, although the nature of the materials of the *axones* and *kurbeis*, on which the laws were inscribed, is still a thorny and much discussed theme for historians. Although there have been some suggestions that Solon's laws could have been inscribed on metal, the majority of scholars believe they were written on wooden tablets, and later carved in stone; for a detailed and comprehensive analysis of different theories see Davis 2011, who reaches the conclusion that *axones* were made of wood and that *kurbeis* were *stelae*. And yet, there is one occurrence of the *iunctura Atticae leges* which may enlighten the meaning of the Sidonian passage. When narrating the events in 456–451 BC, Livy mentions *Atticae leges* which had been brought to Rome in order to serve as an example for the redaction of the Law of the Twelve Tables. Liv. 3.31 says that Roman delegates were sent to Athens with orders to copy the laws of Solon; in Liv 3.32 and 3.33 the envoys are said to have returned with Athenian laws and details of the arrangements made to start compiling a new code; and lastly in Liv. 3.34.7 the centuriate comitia met and adopted the Laws of the Ten Tables (the original number before two were added). The same episode is related, for instance, in Dionysius of Halicarnassus' *Antiquitates Romanae* 10.51.5 (the embassy was sent to Athens and to Greek cities in Italy), 10.53 (the return of ambassadors with Attic laws) and in 10.57.6, where he adds that the new corpus was engraved in bronze and set up in the Forum. On the sources of the episode see the studies by Poma 1984 and d'Ippolito 1998. Therefore, when Sidonius says that his affection for Apollinaris is immortal, engraved in bronze (*aeri . . . incisum*) like the Attic laws, it seems reasonable to assert that *Atticas* is a genuine reading and that it could mean the 'Law of the Twelve Tables'. It would not be unusual for Sidonius to use a circumlocutory expression to mention something widely known under a different name, hence to call the Twelve Tables *Atticae leges* because they were said to have been modelled on the Solonian corpus. When referring to an eternal corpus of laws, what better and most authoritative example than the Law of the Twelve Tables?

sub ope Christi: On this expression, see the commentary on *solus post opem Christi* in *Ep.* 5.1.3.

admissuros amoris terminum . . . fundare principium: *Amor* is to be intended as *caritas* (see comments above), that is, affection is a fundamental prerequisite for any genuine friendship. Is seems useful to compare the appeal to *amor* exhorting Claudius Claudianus to write despite the silence of Probinus in *Carm. min* 41.8, a letter on epistolary silence in elegiac couplets, which significantly begins with a direct request to the addressee: 41.1 *quem, precor, inter nos habitura silentia finem?* Loyen 1970a, 234 considers the occurrence of the terms *amicus* and *amor* in Sidon. *Ep.* 5.3 as a testimony to the true affection between him and Apollinaris. An appeal to the previous bond, which should be remembered by the defaulting addressee, is also in Sidon. *Ep.* 3.7.1 to Felix, in which Sidonius recalls their *antiqua familiaritas*. The letter to Felix has already been mentioned in this commentary for its tone and content mirrored by Sidon. *Ep.* 5.3. One last consideration: since the addressee was a relative, Sidonius' mention of having strived to *fundare amoris principium*, rather than mean 'his effort in starting a friendly relationship', could specifically refer to his effort in establishing and maintaining (in light of the troubled times) epistolary exchanges with the addressee.

Letter 4

Content

This letter is a complaint about epistolary silence addressed to Simplicius, who is exhorted to answer Sidonius and to convince his offspring to bridge the rift with the author.

The addressee Simplicius: an identification problem[1]

A pivotal role in defining the structure of the first part of Book 5 is played by the relationship between the author and Apollinaris, Thaumastus and Simplicius, three relatives to whom a group of letters is devoted (*Epp.* 5.3, 5.4, 5.6 and 5.7), and whose kinship with Sidonius needs discussion. The only certain information which can be gathered from these texts, and is unanimously accepted, is that Apollinaris and Thaumastus are brothers. By the majority of scholars they have been considered to be Sidonius' uncles;[2] however, Stevens, and more recently Mathisen, demonstrated that the evidence in the letters leads rather to the inference that they were Sidonius' cousins.[3]

---

1. For a detailed discussion and for Sidonius' family tree, see Marolla forthcoming a.
2. Starting with prosopographical tools. On Apollinaris: Stroheker 1948, 145; *PLRE* 2, 113–14; *PCBE* 4, 161–3; Kaufmann 1995, 278. On Simplicius: Stroheker 1948, 219; *PLRE* 2, 1015; *PCBE* 4, 1818; Kaufmann 1995, 348. On Thaumastus: Stroheker 1948, 223; *PLRE* 2, 1062; *PCBE* 4, 1867; Kaufmann 1995, 351. See also Amherdt 2001, 209 and 305.
3. Stevens 1933, 140; Mathisen 2020, 58–9 argues that *frater* in *Ep.* 5.3 may have the exact meaning of *frater patruelis*, hence of 'cousin', given Sidonius' description of Eulalia as *soror* in *Ep.* 4.1.1, by virtue of what he calls *patruelis, non germana fraternitas*. Eulalia's kinship will be further discussed in the following section in this introduction ('An alternative theory on Simplicius' identity'). See Amherdt 2001, 69 and also the new prosopographical entries in Mathisen 2020, 80–1 (on Apollinaris); 122 (on Simplicius); 123 (on Thaumastus). In support of the traditional theory that they were Sidonius' uncles see Giannotti 2021, 169–77.

In the entries dedicated to this addressee in prosopographical tools, Simplicius is said to be a brother to Apollinaris and Thaumastus, and thus also an uncle or cousin of Sidonius.[4] There is no element, however, which would allow one to state with any degree of certainty that Simplicius is these men's brother, and the following discussion is aimed at proving that this kinship is not demonstrable in light of the passages usually mentioned as evidence.

The letters addressed to Simplicius by Sidonius are the following:

Ep. 3.11   letter of congratulations on the marriage of his daughter;

Ep. 4.7   witty and playful commendation letter for its messenger, mocked by Sidonius for his *rusticitas*, which, through contrast, brightens Simplicius' *urbanitas*;

Ep. 5.4   complaint about his and his sons' epistolary silence;

Ep. 4.4   jointly with Apollinaris, a commendation letter for the bearer;

Ep. 4.12   jointly with Apollinaris, a request to resend a letter which had been lost in transit.

It should be noted that in both *Epp.* 4.4 and 4.12, Simplicius' name precedes that of Apollinaris in the heading and that this choice could be ascribable to an age difference between the two.[5] Note that also in *Ep.* 7.4.4, addressed to bishop Fonteius, Simplicius is mentioned before Apollinaris,[6] when the two are described as *uerissimi domini* of Sidonius' soul.[7] Simplicius, therefore, would have been either older than Apollinaris or more venerable in some way, hence deserving first mention. From this letter it can also be gathered that after the Visigoths attacked the region of Nîmes in 469, Simplicius

---

4. Note that this assumption is not in earlier studies; for instance, Semple 1930, 29–33 considered Simplicius a friend; Stevens 1933, 140 and 151 believed him to be a friend of Apollinaris and already stated that Apollinaris and Thaumastus were Sidonius' cousins; while in Anderson's edition (1965, 179) Simplicius is mentioned as a non-identifiable relative (Simplicius and Apollinaris are generally said to be Sidonius' kinsmen, in accordance with Semple 1930, 29–33).

5. As is pointed out by Kaufmann 1995, 348, who believes the order of the names is proof that Simplicius is Apollinaris' older brother and that Simplicius is younger than Thaumastus, although the second seems only a suggestion, as it is not supported by evidence.

6. For the intimate nuance of this expression, see van Waarden 2010, 237–8.

7. It has never been pointed out, to my knowledge, that even though the expression is undoubtedly intimate, Sidonius probably derives it from Symmachus, who calls Flavianus *pectoris mei dominus* in *Ep.* 3.86.2; the same expression occurs also in Symm. *Epp.* 7.104.2 and 8.29. See Pellizzari 1998, 237 for its Greek origin.

lived in close proximity – or more likely together with – Apollinaris, in Vaison.[8] The fact that Simplicius received two letters jointly with Apollinaris and that they fled and probably lived together are the only elements which would suggest they could be related, but Sidonius does not give any explicit information on the nature of this relationship.

However, both *PLRE* and *PCBE* cite passages as evidence of their kinship as brothers, widely accepted so far.[9] Let us start with *Ep.* 2.9, a letter to Donidius in which Sidonius describes the delights of his sojourn as a guest in the adjacent properties of Ferreolus and of Apollinaris. In *PLRE* 2 (s.v. Simplicius 8) the following passage is mentioned as proof of the fact that Simplicius is an uncle of Sidonius and brother of Apollinaris and Thaumastus.[10]

> *Igitur mane cotidiano partibus super hospite prima et grata contentio, quaenam potissimum anterius edulibus nostris culina fumaret; nec sane poterat ex aequo diuisioni lancem ponere uicissitudo, licet uni domui mecum, alteri cum meis uinculum foret propinquitatis, quia Ferreolo praefectorio uiro praeter necessitudinem sibi debitam dabat aetas et dignitas primi inuitatoris praerogatiuam.* (Sidon. *Ep.* 2.9.3)

> Every morning, then, a first pleasant dispute arose between the two sides over their guest, as to which of the kitchens would first smoke for our meals; nor was it possible to be impartial by alternation. Though one is my kinsman, the other has a family tie with my wife. Since, in addition to our relationship, Ferreolus is of prefectorian rank, his age and dignity gave him the right to be the first to invite me.

The passage testifies that Apollinaris is Sidonius' kinsman, and that Ferreolus is his wife's relative. The two are portrayed as engaging in a daily dispute over who should have the pleasure of Sidonius' company first, and the whole letter is but a long description of the leisurely activities they engage in to pass the time, between sumptuous banquets (*senatorium ad morem*), good reads, dense conversations and even the occasional post-prandial horse ride. And yet, in this passage, as in all the letter, Simplicius is never mentioned, and there is not even a passing reference to any of Apollinaris' brothers.

---

8. *Ep.* 7.4.4 specifically mentions the whereabouts of Fonteius, who visits Simplicius and Apollinaris and is said to be *istic, id est in Vasionensi oppido.* See Harries 1994, 33 and Mathisen 2020, 81 and 122.

9. *PLRE* 2, s.v. Simplicius 8, 1015; *PCBE* 4, s.v. Simplicius 8, 1818–19.

10. Also in Kaufmann 1995, 348.

Although Sidon. *Carm.* 24.89 (*hunc pronus prope patruum saluta*) concerns Thaumastus (mentioned at v. 85), *PLRE* 2 lists the passage as evidence that Simplicius is one of the three 'uncles'.[11] In this *carmen* Sidonius exhorts his *libellus* to visit all his closest friends and relatives: *Carm.* 24.84–9 *exin tende gradum Tribusque Villis / Thaumastum expete, quemlibet duorum: / quorum iunior est mihi sodalis / et collega simul graduque frater; / quod si fors senior tibi inuenitur, / hunc pronus prope patruum saluta.*[12] Loyen believes the two Thaumasti are father and son, hence uncle and first cousin of Sidonius,[13] and his view has become the one widely accepted.[14] As stated before, Mathisen maintained that the *senior* in the *carmen* is Thaumastus the elder, uncle of Sidonius, while the *iunior* is his son, Thaumastus the younger (brother to Apollinaris and cousin of Sidonius).[15] And yet, whatever kinship one reads into that passage, Simplicius is never mentioned in those verses nor in all the *carmen*.

Moreover, in *PCBE* 4, Simplicius is immediately identified as brother of Apollinaris and Thaumastus in light of the mention of *fratres communes* in the pamphlet against Burgundian informants that is *Ep.* 5.7.[16] In the same entry, by virtue of the same mention, Simplicius is said to have been accused of treason together with Apollinaris.[17] Firstly, as is argued in the commentary on *Ep.* 5.7, the word game between *fratres communes* and *communis patronus* should not go unnoticed.[18] In this case too, however, Simplicius is not

---

11. *PLRE* 2, s.v. Simplicius 8, 1015; also Kaufmann 1995, 348.

12. Anderson 1936, 325 believes the name Thaumastus entails a word game and translates the passage as follows: 'Thence wend your way at the Three Manors and visit Thaumastus – either of the two Wonders: the younger is my bosom-friend and also my colleague and in standing my brother; but if you chance to find the elder, bow low and salute him as almost my uncle'. On this passage see Green 2022, 279 n. 36.

13. 'Cousin germain' also in Loyen's translation of *Carm.* 24.87, Loyen I, 167; Loyen 1943, 74, as in *PLRE* 2, s.v. Thaumastus 1, 1062; *PCBE* 4 s.v. Thaumastus 1, 1867.

14. Loyen 1943, 75 n. 108.

15. Mathisen 2020, 58–9. As stated above, Mathisen believes *Ep.* 5.6 mentions the younger Thaumastus.

16. A letter previously mentioned in this context for the definition of Apollinaris as *germanus* of Thaumastus. See *PCBE* 4 s.v. Simplicius 8, 1818–19 and also *PCBE* 4 s.v. Apollinaris 3, 161. The 'common brothers' are identified with Simplicius and Apollinaris also by Mathisen 2020, 58 n. 197.

17. Also in *PCBE* 4 s.v. Apollinaris 3, 163; *PCBE* 4 s.v. Thaumastus 1, 1867. The reader may turn to the commentary on *Ep.* 5.7.7 for further context.

18. See commentary ad loc. Sidonius is here toying with the idea that a Burgundian is now 'protector of us all', while those involved are actual 'brothers to us' and the two juxtaposed expressions bear a notably different weight. If the sincerity of referring to friends as *fratres communes* is not questionable, one could not exclude the possibility that the idea of having a Burgundian as a common defender would have taken a humourless laugh out of the

mentioned in the passage nor anywhere in *Epp.* 5.6 and 5.7. The variety of meanings the word *frater* has in Sidonius has been discussed in the commentary on *Ep.* 5.3.1, and in *Ep.* 5.7 it would not seem to indicate specifically a number of cousins (*fratres patrueles*). The presence of the plural and of the adjective *communes* leads one to think Sidonius refers to a group of friends, one shared with Thaumastus and which included his cousin Apollinaris.

In *Ep.* 5.6 to Apollinaris there is only a vague reference to the possibility that the suspicion may concern those close to Apollinaris as well, but the secret contrivance is reported to be only his: *tuo machinatu.* Apart from the mention of Thaumastus, the only reference to others is found when Sidonius asks to be informed *si quid hinc tibi tuisque suspicionis incutitur* ('if any suspicion is thrown upon you and yours'), and in the subsequent *ne uobis . . . opportunitas pereat.* 'Yours', then, can be interpreted as either 'your family' or 'close friends', but there is no mention of Simplicius.

It is likely that the information on Simplicius in the prosopographies derives from Loyen's edition,[19] in which the kinship is said to be certain. And yet, the only evidence detectable from the letters is that Apollinaris and Simplicius lived together or close to each other, and that Sidonius addresses letters to both. One cannot exclude the possibility that he was Apollinaris' brother, but neither can one pretend that the texts we have demonstrate this kinship.

An alternative theory on Simplicius' identity

Let us consider an alternative theory concerning Simplicius' identity.[20] As stated above,[21] Magnus Felix, Apollinaris and Simplicius refused to answer

---

reader of this polemical writing, while at the same time being, to the inquisitive eyes of the informants, a pretended praise of the sovereigns. A problematic use of the adjective is also in *Ep.* 4.12 to Apollinaris and Simplicius, where Sidonius' son is called *filius communis.* The passage is translated very differently in Anderson 1965, 111, 'the son to all of us', and Loyen 1970a, 21, 'mon fils et moi nous méditons ensemble'. A peculiar view is taken by Hodgkin 1880, 340–1, who translates 'I, together with your son' and believes Sidonius was acting as preceptor of Simplicius' son; Amherdt does not comment this *iunctura.*

19. Loyen 1970a, 234: '*fratrum communium* désignant Apollinaris et Simplicius'.
20. Fernández López 1994, 64 n. 26 maintains that the Simplicius in *Ep.* 3.11 is the same as the bishop of Bourges (*PLRE* 2, s.v. Simplicius 9, 1015) mentioned in *Epp.* 7.8 and 7.9. According to van Waarden 2010, 392–3, a certain identification is impossible, due to lack of evidence. The same can be said for the mention of a Simplicus in *Ep.* 7.6.9. For the *status quaestionis*, see Giannotti 2016, 206; for further details Marolla forthcoming a.
21. See introduction to *Ep.* 5.3.

Sidonius' letters for some time and it seems likely that the reason for this silence is his involvement in Arvandus' trial.[22] The similarities between letters sent to Felix, Apollinaris and Simplicius include Sidonius' reiterated *garrulitas* contrasting with the firm refusal of an answer[23] and his pointing out how unfair it is that his course of action is pious, while Felix, Apollinaris, Simplicius and his sons are not showing to respect old bonds of friendship and kin, by not acting as one would expect them to.[24] Besides, as stated in the General Introduction, Pliny's *uarietas* entailed that there may have been two consecutive letters on the same subject, provided that they were addressed to different people, as is the case with *Epp* 5.3 and 5.4.

Sidonius states that Simplicius' silence is to be imputed to his sons (*Ep.* 5.4.2), who wronged the author (5.4.1 *reos meos*). His calling into question Simplicius' *patria auctoritas* after having tried to contact them without getting an answer for some time makes clear that this is a sort of ultimatum: resorting to the father may be a decisive way to end the rift, appealing to his authoritativeness.

It has been suggested that Eulalia, whose marriage to Probus (Magnus Felix's brother) is mentioned in *Carm.* 24.94–5 and in *Ep.* 4.1, could be Simplicius' unnamed daughter, whose marriage is praised in *Ep.* 3.11.[25] In this letter 'all the leaders of their land'[26] praise Simplicius' qualities as a *paterfamilias*, his daughter, and his choice of an excellent son-in-law. The mention of the highest nobility of Gaul and of Simplicius and his daughter's father-in-law as *parentes ambo uenerabiles* would be appropriate for a high-rank marriage like that of Eulalia to Probus. As stated above, in *Ep.* 4.1, Eulalia is said to be Sidonius' *soror patruelis*, so she is certainly his cousin.[27] The

---

22. Felix's silence lasted for years: see *Ep.* 4.10.1 *erumpo in salutationem licet seram, domine meus, annis ipse iam multis insalutatus.* Complaints about epistolary silence are also addressed to Felix in *Epp.* 3.4 and 3.7 and to Polemius in *Ep.* 4.14.

23. See commentary on *Ep.* 5.3.1 *garrulitatem nostram* and 5.4.1 *paginae garrienti.*

24. In *Ep.* 3.4.2 Sidonius tells Felix that he has been punished for obscure offences, while he has been acting piously; cf. also *Ep.* 5.3.4 *fit a nostra parte quod pium est*; and *Ep.* 5.4.2 *contractae apud nos offensae amaritudinem*, where he is the one offended.

25. *PLRE* 2 s.v. Eulalia, 418: 'her father was possibly Simplicius, who had an (unnamed) daughter of whose marriage Sidonius approved; Sid. Ap. *Ep.* 3.11.1–2'; see also *PLRE* 2, s.v. Probus 4, 910; *PLRE* 2, stemma 14, 1317; Kaufmann 1995, 348; Giannotti 2016, 206. Santelia 2002a, 124 suggests Eulalia is a telling name, alluding to the Greek verb λαλέω, to indicate female eloquence.

26. *Ep.* 3.11.1 *nostrates idemque summates uiri.*

27. In a passage already mentioned before, being a proof, according to Mathisen 2020, 59, that the use of *frater* in relation to Apollinaris should be considered an abbreviated form of *frater patruelis.*

LETTER 4

assumption that Eulalia is Simplicius' daughter would lead one to suggest that Simplicius is Sidonius' uncle on his father's side and not his cousin, as Apollinaris and Thaumastus probably are; he would therefore be uncle of Sidonius and of the younger Thaumastus and Apollinaris.

Should Eulalia be Simplicius' daughter, it would be possible that she and her husband Probus are the haughty *filii* who disrespect Sidonius by not answering him in *Ep.* 5.4. Sidonius would have wronged both his and Magnus Felix's family by siding with Arvandus, and a possible involvement of Probus in his brother's epistolary silence seems probable. The image of Simplicius *praestantissimus paterfamilias*,[28] whose educational skills are enhanced in *Ep.* 3.11, would be denied when, at the end of *Ep.* 5.4, Sidonius calls upon the same *patria auctoritas*, exhorting Simplicius to admonish his offspring, rectifying their misconduct, as if he had failed to raise them to be deferential. Simplicius' identity as an uncle of the younger Thaumastus, Apollinaris and Sidonius would also be coherent with the evidence that Apollinaris and Simplicius were close enough relatives to combine their households at a time of political turmoil.

Genre

The tone and content of this letter are very similar to those of *Ep.* 5.3 to Apollinaris: see the introduction to *Ep.* 5.3 for the topos of 'epistolary silence', for Sidonius' models and in particular for the reminiscences of Symmachus. As highlighted in the commentary, Symmachus is echoed numerous times in *Ep.* 5.4, in terms of both content and language. And yet, as stated in the introduction to *Ep.* 5.3, if the many Symmachan reminiscences constitute a repertoire upon which Sidonius draws abundantly, Sidonius' *Epp.* 5.3 and 5.4 differ from Symmachus' customary complaints about epistolary silence in that they seem to concern a real rift between him and the addressees.

Sidonius makes use of one of his declared models and resorts to expressions typical of Symmachus' complaints, such as his *garrire* compared to the addressee's silence, the lack of an answer causing *offensio*, the possibility of a retorting silence (see the Symmachan *talio silentii*), *superbia* as the main feature of someone who refuses to answer, and *adsiduitas* in writing

---

28. *Ep.* 3.11.1.

as causing *fastidium*. The author concentrates in a single context numerous themes and expressions of typical complaints about silence scattered across Symmachus' epistolary collection.

Dating elements

Loyen dates the letter to a period prior to the year 470, and vaguely suggests it was written in Aydat, Clermont or Lyon.[29] In his chronology, Loyen adds that the letter seems to be written shortly after *Ep.* 4.7, and that its humorous tone suggests it dates to before the episcopate.[30] Mathisen sees this letter as 'accompanying' *Ep.* 5.3 to Apollinaris, dates them to 471 (due to the reference to hostilities), and believes the two letters were written at the same time and archived together.[31] There is, however, no element in the text which would lead one to infer a specific date.

If the rift with Simplicius is to be connected with the one with Apollinaris (for which see the introduction to *Ep.* 5.3) Arvandus' trial in 469 may likely constitute a *terminus post quem*.

---

29. Loyen 1970a, 179; however, the indication is not very helpful since this is anywhere that Sidonius lived. Kaufmann 1995, 348 relies on Loyen's date suggestion.
30. Loyen 1970a, 255. As discussed in the General Introduction to the present volume, Loyen has a habit of dating letters on debatable grounds, and believes less 'serious letters' are to be dated before the bishopric.
31. Mathisen 2013a, 244.

SIDONIUS SIMPLICIO SUO SALUTEM

1. Quod non recepi scripta qui miseram, imputo amicitiae, sed deputo plus pudori. Nam, nisi praeter aequum autumo, ut salutatio mihi debita dissimularetur, non illud contumacia sed uerecundia fuit. At si ulterius paginae garrienti forem claudis, si pessulum opponis, quieti quidem tuae non inuitus indulgeo, sed non procul a te reos meos inuenturum me esse denuntio.

2. Nam totam silentii uestri inuidiam uerti non iniurium est ad superbiam filiorum, qui se diligi sentientes quoddam patiuntur de nostra sedulitate fastidium. Quos monere pro patria auctoritate debetis, ut contractae apud nos offensae amaritudinem politis affatibus dulcare non desinant. Vale.

§ 1 si pessulum *Marolla* : pessulum *codd.*
imputo *codd.* : non imputo *Loyen* : (M^1 *super lineam adnotat* culpo amicitiam)

§ 2 debetis : α (debemtis *Vat1661*) *MP* : debebitis *L*

LETTER 4

SIDONIUS TO HIS DEAR SIMPLICIUS

1. That I did not receive an answer to the writings I sent, I ascribe to a fault in friendship, but I do impute it more to reserve. For, unless I am not judging fairly, it was not out of arrogance that the greeting which was owed to me was ignored, but out of embarrassment. And yet, if you shut the door on my chatty page any further, if you lock it with a bolt, I at any rate will gladly have regard for your peace: but I declare that I will find my offenders not far from you.

2. In fact, it is not unjust to ascribe all the resentment of your silence to the haughtiness of your children, who, aware of being loved, have a certain aversion to my zeal. You shall, by virtue of paternal authority, admonish them so that they will not desist from sweetening, through refined epistles, the bitterness of the offence caused to me. Farewell.

Commentary

§ 1

Quod non recepi scripta qui miseram: For the theme of epistolary silence, and in particular for the underlying Symmachan model, see the introduction to *Ep.* 5.3. The word *scriptum* with the specific meaning of 'written communication' is variously attested; see e.g. Cic. *Att.* 9.10.10, where, mentioning a letter he received, Cicero affirms *his ego tuis scriptis me consolor*. Other occurrences are e.g. in Tac. *Ann.* 13.23, in Suet. *Cl.* 3.2 (as signalled in *OLD* s.v. *scriptum*, 1887), in Ammianus 31.12.8 and in numerous letters of Symmachus. See the opening line of Symm. *Ep.* 1.59 to Probus, who had urged him to write often; or the occurrence in Symm. *Ep.* 2.48.1, where *scripta reddita* is the letter the author receives from Flavianus. With this meaning, the term is also attested in Symmachus' letters on epistolary silence sent to Richomeres. In Symm. *Ep.* 3.54, even though Richomeres has not been answering, the certainty of their affection will be sufficient; then, when informed of Richomeres' precarious state of health, Symmachus begs him to send *scripta aut mandata* (*Ep.* 3.56). For Symmachan letters on Richomeres' silence, see Pellizzari 1998, 187; and, here, see the introduction to *Ep.* 5.3. In the similar context of Mamertus Claudianus' letter to Sidonius (Sidon. *Ep.* 4.2.2 *saepenumero scriptis uestris alii inpertiuntur*), the term occurs when Claudianus reproaches his friend for writing to others, unworthy of his letters, but not to him. Moreover, in his closing remarks (*Ep.* 4.2.4 *porro enim ambiguo caret tam te puniendum scripto meo, quam punior egomet silentio tuo*), Claudianus playfully asserts that Sidonius is punished because he has to read his letter, just as Claudianus is punished by having to endure his denial of an answer. With this meaning the noun also occurs in Sidonius' letter to Simplicius himself and Apollinaris, *Ep.* 4.12.4 *recurrite ad pugillares, replicate membranas et scripta rescribite*, urging them to rewrite a letter which had been lost in transit. An opposite exhortation is that of *Ep.* 9.3 to Faustus, in which Sidonius affirms that it would be wise not to correspond too often (*stilo frequentiori renuntiare*) since inquisitive searchers stop letter carriers, and, if they do not find anything incriminating, they believe information has been shared orally (*Ep.* 9.3.2 *quae non inueniuntur scripta mandata creduntur*). Among the occurrences of the syntagma *scripta mittere*, notable – also in terms of thematic recurrence – is Augustine's complaint about Jerome's epistolary silence in *Ep.* 71.1. After having sent two letters with no answer, Augustine wonders if Jerome did reply and his letters never reached him (*ea ipsa scripta, quae iam misisti, iterum mitte*), and, should he have no copies of what he had sent, he invites Jerome to 'dictate once more' (*rursus dicta, quod legam*). Similar entertaining complaints for Jerome's silence are also in Aug. *Ep.* 82.

imputo amicitiae, sed deputo plus pudori: Loyen here conjectures *non* before *imputo*; and yet, adding *non* would provide us with a possible *lectio facilior*. It can be argued that leaving the transmitted reading and not adding *non* would be a sensible choice, since not answering *is* a fault in friendship (and, as Sidonius states, he is growing impatient) but is, even more, the consequence of Simplicius finding himself in a difficult position, since his sons chose to ignore Sidonius. The juxtaposition of the two compound verbs is already attested in late Latin in two passages, both concerning doctrinal dissertations: Tert. *Herm.* 13 (*bona . . . deo deputabuntur, ut nec mala illi imputentur*) and Aug. *C. Iul.* 4.2, on Manicheans and Pelagians. As listed by Geisler 1887, 366, the verb *imputo*, followed by the dative with the meaning of 'blaming someone or something', is also attested in Plin. *Ep.* 6.20.20 *tibi . . . imputabis* (Tacitus should blame himself for asking Pliny for details if he finds them unworthy of a letter) and in Plin. *Ep.* 9.13, which answers Quadratus' request for a letter with details on the vindication of Helvidius, when there was already a speech Pliny had published on the matter. The letter Quadratus receives ends up being as long as the speech itself, but it is not Pliny's fault: *Ep.* 9.13.26 *sed imputabis tibi, qui contentus libris non fuisti.* A similar use of the verb with the dative is in Sidon. *Ep.* 7.7.6 *ignoscite afflictis nec imputate maerentibus* ('forgive our embarrassment and do not blame our gloominess'). For what concerns the contrast between *amicitia* and *pudor*, compare Symm. *Ep.* 9.87: the addressee had openly praised Symmachus for his eloquence, a thing appropriate for their friendship (*amicitiae nostrae*), but not for his *pudor*, which prevents Symmachus from considering himself praiseworthy. The two words, however, are not known to occur in other complaints on epistolary silence.

nisi praeter aequum autumo: The syntagma *praeter aequum* has few attestations before Sidonius, namely in Plaut. *Bacch.* 418, Ter. *Hec.* 226, Cic. *Inu.* 1.19.27 and, notably, in the first letter of Symmachus' corpus, which is focused on the duty to write to his father, *Ep.* 1.1 *nam praeter aequum censet, qui inter dispares obsequium par requirit. Itaque uester sermo ex beneficio proficiscitur, noster ex debito* ('for he who seeks for equal deference among those who are unequal, in not assessing fairly. And so your discourse arises from generosity, mine from obligation'). Despite it not being a common expression, Sidonius employs it often in his letters (*Epp.* 4.3.1, 4.11.7, 7.2.9, 7.14.1 and 9.11.8) but with the less frequently attested meaning of *putare, suspicari*; see *TLL* 2.1606 s.v. *autumo* 78–9 (by Zimmermann). The verb is also attested with this meaning in *Anim. praef.*, p. 20, when Claudianus says the second book of the treatise *non otiose et uti autumo non infructuose dissertat*; cf. also his letter to Sidonius (Sidon. *Ep.* 4.2.4 *uti ego autumo*).

salutatio mihi debita: The syntagma has attestations only in late Latin letters, beginning with Symmachus and his contemporary Ambrose. Symmachus puts an end to his own epistolary silence by writing to Ausonius *Ep.* 1.35 (*debito te honore salutationis inpertio*), while, in *Ep.* 2.89, Symmachus tells Flavianus that, although he recently wrote to him, he can gladly 'double' the owed salutations (*debitam salutionem*); furthermore, in *Ep.* 7.72, Symmachus writes a laconic 'owed salutation' (*honorificentiam . . . debitae salutationis*) to his brothers as soon as he reaches Milan. In Ambr. *Ep. extra coll.* 3.2 to Theodosius, Ambrose says that, should someone think that idleness is the reason why he did not write before, he has to find an excuse to comply with his *debitum salutationis obsequium* ('due deference to greeting'). Similar syntagmata are also attested in Augustine's letters: a *debitum salutationis* is owed to Proba (Aug. *Ep.* 131); and the phrase *salutationem debitam reddo* occurs in Aug. *Ep.* 192.1 and *Ep.* 269. It is important to stress that, in all the occurrences mentioned, the expression is always referred to a duty of the sender to the addressee, while the Sidonian occurrence is the only case in which it is the sender who requires a *salutatio* 'owed' to him. Sidonius employs a canonical expression but overturns its usage, by inserting it in the opposite context of a complaint about epistolary silence. Stressing how the salutation is 'owed to him' reinforces the impression that Sidonius' complaint is serious and he is not simply writing in compliance with standard models of letter writing.

non illud contumacia sed uerecundia fuit: This passage is here translated in accordance with the suggestion in van Waarden 2010, 473 that the *uerecundia* has the specific meaning of 'embarrassment' and that *uerecundia* was a key concept in social intercourse. For this meaning see *OLD*, s.v. *uerecundia*, 2243: 'a sense of shame consequent on, or inhibiting, dishonourable or disgraceful conduct'. Other occurrences of the two substantives in the same context are not attested.

LETTER 4

paginae garrienti: For the numerous occurrences of *garrulitas* and *garrire* in Sidonius see the commentary on *garrulitatem nostram* in *Ep.* 5.3. In particular, on the verb *garrire* as a usual way of expressing Sidonius' self-deprecation, not to be taken too seriously, and as a customary expression of *urbanitas*, see Amherdt 2001, 164; van Waarden 2010, 191. Unlike the other occurrences, in *Ep.* 5.4 it is the *pagina* itself, the letter, which is personified and said to be verbose. A similar previous occurrence of this image is, for instance, in Hor. *Sat.* 1.10.41, where Fundanius is said to be the only living comedy writer capable of 'filling the volumes with chatter of everyday speech' (*garrire libellos*); see Brown 1993, 188. Moreover, Jerome says he intends to respond to Rufinus' accusations when the long-lost friend publishes those books *qui per angulos garriunt et furtiua accusatione me mordent* (Hier. *Adu. Rufin.* 1.4). See Lardet 1993, 31 and 121 for context and for the aggressiveness of Jerome's metaphor. One last occurrence of a personified work *garriens* is even closer chronologically and geographically: in *Anim.* 3.12, p. 176 (*qui interimunt animas garrientibus nugis*), Mamertus Claudianus argues against those who destroy souls with their 'verbose trifles'.

forem claudis, si pessulum opponis: *Si* was conjectured for reasons of internal coherence. The sentence that follows is clearly the apodosis; therefore, this is a second protasis and adding *si* makes it much clearer. The image of closing the door on someone is immediately reminiscent of παρακλαυσίθυρα sung by the *exclusus amator*, attested since Alcaeus (fr. 374 Voigt) and later becoming a conventional theme of Greek and Latin comedy and love elegy. It will be useful to mention, only by way of example, the cruel door in Prop 1.16.17–18; and the words against the guardian who closes the door and locks it with a hundred bolts in Ov. *Ars* 2.635–6. For the origins of the theme and its evolution in Latin literature see Fedeli 1980; 363–7 and 383. Note that, in Sidonius, it is the personified *pagina* to be left outside of Simplicius' locked door, as, still in elegiac poetry, Tibullus' words are cast out of the door in 2.6.12 (*excutiunt clausae fortia uerba fores*); and in Ov. *Am.* 2.1.17 the poet's ambitious project to write an epic poem is abruptly sabotaged by the mistress who closes the door, uninterested (*clausit amica fores*); on this passage, see McKeown 1998, 15. The choice of the word *pessulus* demands attention, since it is not known to occur frequently and is mostly attested in comedy e.g. the *adulescens* Phaedromus' address to bolts in Plaut. *Curc.* 147 and his following complaint directed at those *pessuli pessumi*, apparently asleep (Plaut. *Curc.* 153). Apuleius shows a preference for this noun, which has numerous occurrences in *Met.* (1.11, 1.14, 3.15, 4.18,

9.20); in later Latin, it is used with a figurative meaning after Jerome's translation of the *Canticum Canticorum* (5.6 *pessulum ostii mei aperui dilecto meo*), in Ps. Aug. *Serm.* 120.1 and in Aponius' *expositio* of the *Canticum* (8.8, 8.17); see *TLL* 10.1.1917 s.v. *pessulus* 47–51 (by Ley-Hutton). If compared to previous occurrences, Sidonius' choice to adapt the image to a context of epistolary silence between friends is indeed innovative. Note that *garrien-ti forem claudis* and *pessulum opponis* (with elision) create two consecutive cretic spondees.

quieti quidem tuae . . . indulgeo: It was legitimate, in case the addressee was determined not to answer, to imply that an equal vengeful silence might have ensued. Cf., for instance, Symmachus' benign threat of *talio silentii* in *Ep.* 1.65, and see the introduction to *Ep.* 5.3 as well as the commentary on *Ep.* 5.3.1 *talione frenari*. *In-uitus indulgeo* is the first of a couple of consecutive double cretics.

sed non procul a te reos meos inuenturum me esse denuntio: The passage states clearly that Simplicius is not directly responsible for the silence, but those who wronged Sidonius are to be found close to him. The occurrence of *reos* and *denuntio*, both terms pertaining to a juridical sphere, leads one to interpret this as a deliberately hyperbolic phrase. As usual, Sidonius is serious, up to a certain point. Similarly, serious and facetious phrases are intermingled in *Ep.* 1.11.4, in which Sidonius has Paeonius say *iniuriae communis iam reum inueni*, when he points an accusing finger at Sidonius, believing he is the author of the irreverent Satire of Arles. Note that *esse denuntio* is a second consecutive double cretic.

§ 2

Nam totam silentii uestri inuidiam uerti: For the theme of epistolary silence and its models, see the introduction to *Ep.* 5.3; and see the commentary on *Ep.* 5.3.1 *silentii uestri* and *talione frenari* as well as *quod tacetis*. See also the closing line of Symmachus' letter to Iulianus, *Ep.* 3.5.2 *inuidiam silentii diluisse*, where the author says he has the merit of having put their relationship back on track (*in uiam reduxi*) after mutual protracted epistolary silence (*nostri silentii diuturnitas*). For Symmachus' ceremonious attitude in bridging the distance between him and the addressee in this letter, see Pellizzari 1998, 75. For *uerto* meaning 'to attach blame to someone else' see *OLD* s.v. *uerto*, 2253.

LETTER 4

non iniurium est: This syntagma is not attested before Sidonius, who employs it also in *Ep.* 7.1.7, on which see van Waarden 2010, 124. It later occurs in Ennodius, *Dict.* 8.

ad superbiam filiorum: The fact that Sidonius here refers to *filii* constitutes evidence that Simplicius had more than one son or daughter (but for further reflection see the introduction to this letter). In Symm. *Ep.* 8.49, an apology for his epistolary silence, Symmachus ascribes his slowness in answering to a feeling of unworthiness with regard to Vitalis' style, and asserts that he then decided to write so that he may not seem to be acting arrogantly: *malui enim tibi stilo quam superbia displicere.* In a similar context, Sidonius begins *Ep.* 5.12.1 by asserting that the slowness of his correspondence with Calminius is not to be imputed to his *superbia* but to the 'violence of others'. There are two consecutive cretic ditrochee clausulae here, at *su-perbiam filiorum* and at *diligi sentientes.*

qui se diligi sentientes: The translation of this passage, 'aware of being loved', reflects the vagueness of the Latin. Note that Anderson 1965, 179 translates 'well aware of *my* affection for them', while Loyen 1970a, 179 opts for 'se sachant l'objet de *ton* affection'. Anderson's translation, however, seems more coherent, since Simplicius' children would choose not to answer, knowing that Sidonius' affection for them would remain unaltered.

quoddam patiuntur de nostra sedulitate fastidium: The mention of *sedulitas*, of Sidonius' being insistent, is an indication that the author intends to represent himself as someone who has been trying to re-establish the epistolary exchanges with Simplicius' family for some time. Borrowing Symmachus' words in *Ep.* 1.3.3 (although ascribable to a different context): *sedulitas enim, quae non compensatur, onerosa est.* The noun is variously attested with a positive meaning (see e.g. Cic. *Fam.* 8.11.2 and Hor. *Ep.* 1.7.8) and Symmachus, in *Ep.* 7.6, praises his son's *sedulitas animi*, for having sent him a letter. In Sidon. *Ep.* 5.4, the fact that Sidonius' *sedulitas* generates *fastidium* stresses the injustice of the epistolary silence with which he has been punished. For unappreciated *sedulitas*, see e.g. Cic. *Agr.* 2.12. As van Waarden 2010, 169 puts it (commenting on Sidon. *Ep.* 7.2.5), *sedulitas* expresses 'insistence in social intercourse, trying persistently to come into contact with someone'; cf. with this meaning Sidon. *Ep.* 9.4.1, an appeal to bishop Graecus to double their epistolary exchanges, since they are living in troubled times. Cf. also *Ep.* 5.3 to Apollinaris, in which Sidonius insistently remarks how his *pius* behaviour contrasts with the *impietas* of his addressee, who maintains his silence. For another occurrence of the uncommon syntagma *fastidium pati*, see Symm. *Ep.* 4.63. For the occurrence of *fastidium* in Sidonius, in particular in dining metaphors, see the commentary on *si placuit . . . fastidium* in *Ep.* 5.2.2. As van Waarden 2010, 547 points out, it is a commonplace to mention *fastidium* 'on account of a letter which is verbose, attention too much felt etc.' as Sidonius does in *Epp.* 1.7.3, 2.2.7 and 7.10.2. Cf. Symmachus' complaint to Maximilianus in *Ep.* 8.51, where the paucity of the addressee's letters (*raritas*) hints at his aversion to the assiduity of Symmachus' communications addressed to him (*adsiduitatem . . . tibi esse fastidio*).

Quos monere pro patria auctoritate debetis: Since the reading *debebitis* (chosen by Lütjohann, Anderson and Loyen) is attested exclusively in *L*, according to the relationship of the manuscripts theorised by Dolveck, one should discard it in favour of *debetis*, which is the consensus of α*P*. However, both readings are plausible since *debebitis* could have some attraction (being a more polite way of addressing Simplicius). Moreover, both would create clausulae: a cretic spondee at *-tate debetis* or a double cretic at *-tate debebitis*. In relation to the meaning of the passage, there is no element in the letter which may lead to the conclusion that the *filii* mentioned are not adults. Assuming they are adults, this phrase is certainly not flattering. The appeal to their father's authoritative voice to admonish them belittles their choice not to correspond with Sidonius. While the syntagma *monere pro patria auctoritate* is not known to occur elsewhere, the *iuncturae patria auctoritas* and in particular *auctoritas patris* are widely attested. See, by way of example, Cic. *Ver.* 2.2.97, where not even the *auctoritas patris* can sedate Stenius' anger; or Cic. *Cael.* 37, in which, after the tirade against Clodia, Cicero says he will turn to Caelius, calling upon *auctoritatem patriam seueritatemque*. For the occurrences of the *iunctura*, from Cicero to Jerome, see *TLL* 2.1214. 78–1215.7 s.v. *auctoritas* (by Münscher).

ut contractae . . . offensae amaritudinem: The only previous ocurrence of the syntagma *offensae amaritudo* (*et similia*) is in the Shepherd of Hermas, *Similitud.* 9.31. In epistolary contexts, a useful comparison for the figurative meaning of *amaritudo* in relation to an offence is Plin. *Ep.* 6.8.8 *attendas ne in bilem et amaritudinem uertat iniuria*. Among the numerous occurrences in Symmachus, *amaritudo* is the result of the enmity between Flavianus and Hephaestio (*Ep.* 2.18.1) and the figurative game is pushed even further when

Symmachus, determined to convince the two to reach a reconciliation in *Ep.* 2.18.2, mentions he intends to rely on Eusebius, who *iam poterit amara condire.* For the rift between the two, see Cecconi 2002a, 201. Compare also Symm. *Ep.* 5.92: Symmachus complains about the epistolary silence of Helpidius, who, however, happens to be in contact with Symmachus' son, and has expressed *amaritudo* towards Symmachus himself (cf. the commentary on *talione frenari* in Sidon. *Ep.* 5.3). *Amaritudo* also occurs to indicate the outcome of a rift and of subsequent hearsay in Symm. *Ep.* 7.100. In contrast, the *iunctura contracta offensa* is not common, and before Sidonius it occurs only in Cypr. *Idol.* 4 and in Arnobius (*Adu. Nat.* 7.7, 7.27), all concerning religious offences. The word *offensa* occurs often in Symmachus' letters on epistolary silence; see e.g. the closing remarks of *Ep.* 1.10, where it has the purpose of preventing the epistolary silence of the addressee. A similar context of offending silence (which could have caused a *talio silentii*) is also in Symm. *Ep.* 1.95. Furthermore, Symmachus says that a previous *offensio* for epistolary silence was overcome by the joy of receiving news in *Ep.* 3.81 *suscensebam silentio tuo; sed . . . uicit offensionem uoluptas.* On the other hand, it is Symmachus who decides to write to Naucellius *Ep.* 3.15 so that his silence would not be imitated by the addressee (*si tua offensio imitaretur tacentem*). On this letter and on the skirmish between the two see Pellizzari 1998, 98.

politis affatibus dulcare non desinant: Simplicius' *filii* may right this wrong by writing to Sidonius sweet conciliatory words. The verb *dulco* seems to be a Sidonian coinage, since it is not known to have occurrences before the praising verses in Sidon. *Carm.* 2.106 and this passage of *Ep.* 5.4; see *TLL* 5.1.2198 s.v. *dulco* 69–77 (by Lackenbacher). Contrasting *amaritudo* and *dulcedo* actually occur in numerous passages of Augustine, e.g. *Conf.* 13.23 *in dulcedinem gratiae tuae . . . in perpetua impietatis amaritudine* and *Contra Faust.* 9.2 *relicto iudaismo ex amaritudine transisse in dulcedinem*, as well as of Jerome, e.g. *Ep.* 78.3 *omnem amaritudinem uertens in dulcedinem ut Dei uocem . . . audiret.* Note how comfortable Sidonius is in favouring the use of imaginative language in connection with the sensory semantic field. In particular, he draws upon terms pertaining to the sense of taste with an extended meaning, as is the case of Secundinus' *piperata facundia* in *Ep.* 5.8.

LETTER 5

Content

Sidonius expresses amusement at the news that Syagrius, descendant of a consul and a learned man himself, is spending time among Burgundians, being a respected member at court. The letter ends with a final exhortation not to forget the Latin language.

Genre: a letter of *admonitio*

Ep. 5.5 can be ascribed to letters of *admonitio* (or *symbuleuticae*), a genre which, according to Cugusi, has its roots in late Republican treatises in form of letters, such as in Cicero's renowned letter to his brother (*Q. fr.* 1.1).[1]

Sherwin-White and Cugusi detect *symbuleuticae* also in Pliny's epistolary collection, where, however, the epistles have lost their nature of treatise and are notably short, and considerably different from previous models.[2] It is worthy of emphasis that, among the *admonitiones* the two scholars signal, Pliny's *Epp.* 8.24 and 9.5 could be compared with Sidonius' letter, which, like all of Pliny's letters of *admonitio*, is closed with an exhortative section. However, unlike Sidonius' letter to Syagrius, Pliny's letters have the purpose of reminding addressees of the duties of official posts, and are composed of general admonitions and exhortations to behave honourably while holding new offices.[3] It seems that the political function *symbuleuticae* traditionally had, and maintained (although with some formal changes) in Pliny, is

---

1. According to Shackleton Bailey 1980, 147, the length and style of *Q. fr.*1.1suggest it was intended for wider circulation. For the much-debated *Q. fr.*1.1 and *Commentariolum*, I refer to the *status quaestionis* in Prost 2017. Cugusi 1983, 122 and 185 also mentions the *Commentariolum petitionis* and Sal. *Epistulae ad Caesarem senem*, although with reservations about their authenticity.
2. Sherwin-White 1966, 2 and 42; Cugusi 1983, 222. See *Ep.* 5.6 for a complete list of Pliny's *admonitiones*.
3. The two other *admonitiones* mentioned by Cugusi are Pliny's *Epp.* 2.6.6 and 7.1.7, which, however, fall into the category of letters with the aim of *sub exemplo praemonere*, since a

LETTER 5

overturned by Sidonius. In *Ep.* 5.5 his unrequested advice does not concern imperial office-holding, but Syagrius' undefined office as trusted adviser at the Burgundian court. Therefore, if *Ep.* 5.5 is to be considered as an *admonitio*, Sidonius studiously chooses to adapt an old genre to new content.

Among the few letters of Book 5 which can be related to a Plinian model (considerably fewer than in other books) Roy Gibson mentions *Ep.* 5.5 as an echo of Pliny's *Ep.* 5.17.[4] While the comparison cannot be made from a formal point of view, a similarity by contrast can be detected in the two letters, and an overview of the Plinian context seems, therefore, necessary. In *Ep.* 5.17 to Vestricius Spurinna, a patron of young men of letters, Pliny recalls having attended a recital of Calpurnius Piso's 'flowing, delicate and smooth elegiac couplets' and having appreciated in particular his versatility in raising and lowering the tone while reading. The performer, therefore, is lauded for his ability to add attraction to the lines with his voice and his manners. Pliny adds that at the end of the recital he had encouraged the young Calpurnius Piso to continue studying and practising, teaching his descendants just like his ancestors had taught him. The contrast with what would be expected of Syagrius by virtue of his ancestry is evident, and Pliny's closing remarks strongly contrast with the neglect of Syagrius' inherited literary tradition. Sidonius starts out from where Pliny finishes, with an emphasis on the *nobilitas* of the addressee. Compare the mention of *statuas* at the beginning of Sidonius' *Ep.* 5.5.1 with *imagines*, the busts of the aristocratic ancestors which seem to tacitly approve of and encourage their descendants at the end of Pliny's *Ep.* 5.17.6.

One could also add that Pliny's description of the verses performed and of the performance itself expresses harmony, sinuosity of Latin: it is a praise of a language that is vibrant, that adapts to lower and higher tones, shifting from one genre to another. Instead, in Sidonius, Burgundians (and thus their language) are described as *indolatiles*, static, stiff and monotone like their three-stringed instruments. To sum up, their description is the negation of the praise of Latin language and culture found in Pliny's *Ep.* 5.17.

It seems legitimate to wonder if this letter circulated as a display piece (as seems to be plausible for instance for *Epp.* 5.7 and 5.10) prior to the publication of the book. The content is in fact suggestive of private circulation among the group of friends Sidonius and Syagrius share.

---

long *exemplum* in the letter is closed by a last paragraph of admonition. Sidonius' *Ep.* 5.5 cannot be ascribed to this category.

4. Gibson 2013b, 350 n. 35. I am grateful to Professor Gibson for his expert advice.

The addressee Syagrius

As Sidonius informs the reader in *Ep.* 5.5.1, Syagrius was great-grandson by male succession of Flavius Afranius Syagrius,[5] consul in 382 and poet, whose tomb was in Lyon.[6] Moreover, Syagrius was nephew of Tonantius Ferreolus,[7] whose wife, Papianilla, was related to Sidonius' wife of the same name.[8]

To Syagrius is also addressed *Ep.* 8.8, a stern reprimand over his life choices, since he dedicated his time to farming his estate of Taionnacus instead of pursuing consular ambitions.[9] Sirmond suggested the estate could be in Taionnus,[10] in the Aeduan territory and not far from Autun, both visible in the Tabula Peutingeriana.[11] In his *Index Locorum,* Mommsen[12] defined Taionnacus as possibly located in the territory of the Suessiones, and hence in Gallia Belgica, a most unlikely location for a Lyonais aristocrat.[13] Could it be that Mommsen was confusing this Syagrius with another well-known Syagrius, the 'king of the Romans', who was based in Soissons?[14]

---

5. *PLRE* 1, s.v. Syagrius 2, 862.
6. As Sidonius tells Eriphius in *Ep.* 5.17.4, recalling a crowded procession he took part in and the moments afterwards, when oppressed by the sultry atmosphere and by the dazzle of the torchlights, the crowd scattered and many lingered at consul Syagrius' grave.
7. In fact, Ferreolus was Flavius Afranius Syagrius' grandson, as attested in Sidon. *Ep.* 1.7.4 and in *Ep.* 7.12.1. The consul is also mentioned in *Carm.* 24 as Ferreolus' ancestor.
8. Tonantius Ferreolus' wife Papianilla is mentioned in *Carm.* 24.37, on which see Santelia 2002a, 89–90; according to Harries 1994, 34 n. 30 and Green 2022, 276 n. 15, Ferreolus' wife was sister or cousin of Avitus, father of Sidonius' wife Papianilla.
9. Though Mommsen (Lütjohann 1887, 436) did not believe the addressees were in fact the same person, and Mohr 1895, 389 in his *Index* listed them as father (Syagrius of *Ep.* 5.5) and son (Syagrius of *Ep.* 8.8). Note also that Sidon. *Ep.* 2.4 is addressed to Sagittarius in most of the δ branch but to Syagrius in all the α branch. See Kelly 2021c and Marolla forthcoming b.
10. In the Tabula Peutingeriana, next to Augustodonum (Autun), is indicated the presence of what is commonly identified with Telonno (Toulon-sur-Arroux), a toponym which might easily be read as Teionno or Taionno, both etymologically plausible. Sirmond 1614, *Notae* 144: TAIONNACUS] *vide an referri hunc possit Taionnus, quam Tabula itineraria in Aeduis locat, haud procul Augustoduno.* This opinion is shared by Kaufmann 1995, 349, who refers to Anderson's explanatory note on Sirmond (Anderson 1965, 436–7).
11. See also Talbert et al. 2000, *Telonnum* FRA, 18 B3. The second and third letters are now indistinct on the map. An interesting trace of the reading *Teionnum* is in d'Anville 1760, 639.
12. Mommsen in Lütjohann 1887, 446.
13. Whatmough 1970, 774 lists *Taionnacus* in the toponyms of Gallia Belgica, with the description 'near Soissons?'; however, it seems likely the presence of this location in his list might have been influenced by Mommsen's *Index*, since Sidonius is the only reference cited, and the expression used is very close to Mommsen's.
14. See *PLRE* 2 s.v. Syagrius 2, 1041–2.

On the contrary, Stroheker and Loyen generally located Taionnacus in Lugdunensis Prima.[15] Although Sirmond's suggestion seems more plausible, so far there is no further evidence to confirm his theory. A survey of possible different Gallic locations deriving from the name *Taionnacus* did not result in any satisfactory result.

Syagrius seems to be close to Sidonius: the presence of the verbs *memini* and then *habeo compertum* might indicate that at least the first part of Syagrius' schooling years was spent in close proximity with the author, probably in Lyon, as Sidonius remembers clearly that Syagrius attended schools of liberal arts and then he 'knows for a fact', probably informed by others, that Syagrius continued his studies of rhetoric. It can also be inferred that the two were on good terms and that they belonged to the same intellectual circle, since in § 3 Sidonius refers to 'how much laughter' Syagrius' philo-barbarism causes him 'and the others', thus referring to a shared group of friends.

In *Ep.* 8.8.1 Sidonius refers to Syagrius as *Gallicanae flos iuuentutis*, a description which led Loyen and *PCBE* 4[16] to surmise that he and Sidonius were classmates during their years as students of grammar. Note, however, that this kind of expression, variously attested in Livy, Cicero and Ambrose, as the commentary further explains, would be more fittingly addressed to someone younger, instead of an exact contemporary.

Sidonius and the legislative activity of the Burgundians and Visigoths

Ep. 5.5 playfully reports that Syagrius had a prominent role at the Burgundian court, being respected by the elders and consulted as an arbitrator. His description as a 'Solon of the Burgundians' has led some scholars to suggest Syagrius had a role in the interpretation of an established Burgundian legislative corpus.[17]

Although Sidonius is probably exaggerating here, it is worth making further observations on this mention and putting it into context, since an increasing Burgundian interest in defining customs and usages in the fixed form of a statute was soon to emerge with the creation of the *Lex*

---

15. Stroheker 1948, 221 n. 369; Loyen 1970a, 234 n. 7.

16. Loyen 1970a, 235 n. 8; *PCBE* 4 s.v. Syagrius 2, 1845.

17. As in Luiselli 1992, 602 and 606, who considers *Ep.* 5.5 as proof of the existence of a legislative corpus to be dated before the year 451, hence prior to the *Lex Burgundionum*.

Burgundionum, attributed controversially either – under the name of *Lex Gundobada* – to Gundobad[18] or to Gundobad's son, king Sigismund.[19] Although picturing Syagrius as the founder of the Burgundian law system would mean to indulge in Sidonius' ironic portrait of his friend, it seems possible he had an active role in a proto-legislative phase embedded in the Roman model, at a time when the Burgundians faced the difficulties of exercising control over a region which already had a strong legislative Roman tradition, as is testified by the subsequent coexistence of the *Lex Romana Burgundionum* and the *Lex Burgundionum* as complementary corpora.[20]

As Saitta says,[21] traces of this proto-legislative phase can be found in two passages of the *Lex Burgundionum*: in the *Praefatio* Gundobad refers to the legislative activity of his ancestors Gundioc and Chilperic I (*cum de parentum nostrisque constitutionibus . . . cogitemus*); as also in *Prima Const.* 8 *sicut a parentibus nostris statutum est.*

Furthermore, the role of Syagrius as an interpreter is considered by Frye to be an important testimony of an otherwise overlooked aspect of life at the Burgundian court, which apparently needed interpreters. For this reason, Frye ascribes the legislative evolution under Gundobad's reign to the king's knowledge of spoken and written Latin, which allowed him to overcome the technical difficulties of his predecessors. Unlike them, Gundobad did not need interpreters, and the issue of a legislative corpus allowed him to make an ideological statement, reinforcing his role as sovereign.[22]

It could be objected that Sidonius' reproach to his friend seems to lose its credibility if one reads in (what is generally believed to be) Sidonius' own funerary epitaph a testimony of the role Sidonius himself might have had at barbarian courts, consulted by Burgundians or Visigoths in the systematisation of their legislative corpus.[23]

---

18. As in Saitta 2006, 50. The scholar asserts that the *terminus post quem* for the development of a regular legislative activity is 443, and from that moment on the Burgundian sovereigns perceived the urgency and necessity of creating a compact legislative corpus (Saitta 2006, 82); see *PLRE* 2, s.v. Gundobadus 1, 524–5; *ODLA* s.v. Gundobad (by Raymond Van Dam and Simon Loseby); for some corrections, see the introductions to *Epp.* 5.6 and 5.7.
19. The second possibility is considered more accurate in *ODLA* s.v. *Lex Burgundionum* (*Liber Constitutionum, Lex Gundobada*) (by Thomas Faulkner).
20. See *ODLA* s.v. *Lex Romana Burgundionum* (by Thomas Faulkner); see also Frye 1990, 199–212 for a detailed overview of the constitutive phases of the corpus.
21. Saitta 2006, 83.
22. Frye 1990, 203 and 205.
23. As in Wood 2016, 6. The same remark is made by van Waarden, who suggests a collaboration with Euric (see <https://sidonapol.org/epitaph/>).

The epitaph (vv. 4–7) reads as follows:

rector militiae forique iudex
mundi inter tumidas quietus undas,
causarum moderans subinde motus
leges barbarico dedit furori.[24]

Military commander, judge in the forum,
quiet in the midst of the world's stormy waves
and then by moderating the turmoil of lawsuits,
he imposed laws on the barbarian fury.

Should the epitaph be Sidonius' and not that of his son Apollinaris, as Montzamir reasonably suggested,[25] a legitimate explanation of the passage may be that it is simply metaphorical, Sidonius being the restorer of order and calm in the 'stormy' water that is life under barbarian rulers.[26] And yet, the ambiguity of the passage instils doubt. *Dare leges*, right after the mention of Sidonius as the one 'moderating the turmoil of lawsuits', is an oddly specific expression, which is variously attested with the precise meaning of 'to legislate' in numerous passages.[27] In particular, Wood considers *dare leges* in the epitaph as proof 'of the involvement of Romans in Burgundian legislation before the days of Gundobad and Sigismund', and asserts that, at some point, Sidonius might have even worked alongside the addressee of *Ep.* 5.5, Syagrius.[28] This deduction is rather speculative, since we do not have elements to support the theory that there was cooperation between the two, and the tone of *Ep.* 5.5 would seem to discourage the pursuit of such a theory.

One may wonder, however, if it is possible that Sidonius attained a legislative role and if the mention of the role as judge in the epitaph (v. 4 *forique iudex*) could be referred not only to his duty as *praefectus urbi* in 468–9 or to the *episcopalis audientia* while being bishop of Clermont,[29] but also to a role he had later in life, when the situation had radically changed and, after besieging Clermont every summer from 471 to 474, the Visigothic king

---

24. *CLE* 1516. An analysis of the *carmen* and a comparison with Sidonius' *Ep.* 3.12.5 is in Cugusi 1985, 111–13.
25. Montzamir 2017, Marolla forthcoming b.
26. As in Mascoli 2004, 171. On the epitaph see also Prévot 1993, 228 and Condorelli 2013, 278; the latter highlights that the metaphor of the *tumidae undae* echoes Sidon. *Ep.* 9.16.3. See also Furbetta 2015a on a new witness.
27. Attestations of the occurrence of this expression with a legislative meaning are in the hundreds.
28. Wood 2016, 10.
29. As is suggested by Prévot 1993, 228.

Euric had been given the region of Auvergne by Julius Nepos, and Sidonius had been exiled for two years.[30] It may not be an unfair speculation that Sidonius dealt with some forms of negotiations with barbarians, since the *Codex Euricianus* did not envisage the official appointment of judges, and it prescribed the assignment of influential locals as arbiters in controversies.[31]

Inevitably, necessity changed Sidonius' tone towards Euric. Evidence for the overtly different attitude Sidonius later had towards cooperation with the Visigoths can be traced in *Ep.* 8.3, addressed to Leo of Narbonne, who, thanks to his influence as Euric's spokesman, had freed Sidonius from exile.

> *Sepone pauxillulum conclamatissimas declamationes, quas oris regii uice conficis, quibus ipse rex inclitus modo corda terrificat gentium transmarinarum, modo de superiore cum barbaris ad Vachalin trementibus foedus uictor innodat, modo per promotae limitem sortis ut populos sub armis, sic frenat arma sub legibus.* (*Ep.* 8.3.3)

> Put aside for a moment those much acclaimed declamations which you compose as spokesman of the king, and through which the famous king himself terrifies the hearts of nations who live across the sea, or, once he has won, from his commanding post, ties the trembling barbarians on the banks of the Waal into a treaty, or, through the extent of his enlarged domains,[32] just like he bridled people with arms, he now bridles arms with laws.

The explicit mention of laws being Euric's main weapon has been considered proof of the role Leo of Narbonne might have had in the composition of the Visigothic legislative corpus.[33]

The treatment reserved to Leo, author of Euric's speeches according to this letter, is in strong contrast with that reserved to Syagrius, not only because of their status and age, but mainly because of the circumstances. Over a time span of a few years, Sidonius' haughtiness against Burgundians shown in *Ep.* 5.5 subsided; he sided with them against Euric, and after his defeat and exile found himself in a precarious situation, one that left no space for sarcasm.[34] Sidonius was actually in debt to Leo and was in no

---

30. On his relationship with the Visigoths in this phase, see Gualandri 2000, 118–29.
31. As in, e.g., *CE* 282 and *CE* 289 (ed. D' Ors 2014); see Harries 2001, 39–51; Marolla 2021a, 67. On the mention of Visigothic laws in Sidon. *Ep.* 2.1.3, see Hindermann 2022, 76–7.
32. This phrase is as in Anderson 1965, 411.
33. *PLRE* 2, Leo 5, 662; Loyen 1970b, 197, 7. Jill Harries describes the presence of Syagrius and Leo of Narbonne at the Burgundian and Visigothic court as 'a symptom of the alteration in the Gothic and Burgundian ideas of themselves as a state' (Harries 1994, 61).
34. See the section 'Dating elements' below for the conclusions which can be reached in terms of dating.

position to tease him about his involvement at the Visigothic court; on the contrary, Leo's role even constituted a matter of praise.

Barbarisms

Ep. 5.5 has often been mentioned as an example of Sidonius' personal crusade against the linguistic contamination from barbarians. Sidonius' disdain for barbarian sounds is undeniable, and his definition of barbarian language as *euphonia gentis alienae* in this letter should undoubtedly be considered ironic.[35]

In the hyperbolic and bizarre picture depicted by the author, his friend not only translates letters in Latin for the Burgundians, but has learned their language so well that he has become paradoxically their mentor, so that the Burgundians are afraid to pronounce a mistake (*barbarismus*) in their own language in his presence.[36] In this case it would seem that the term has the broader meaning of *uitium*, instead of *barbarolexis* (the use of foreign expressions in Latin), though the latter is a meaning more common in Sidonius:[37] that is why this particular choice enhances the irony of the passage.

Among the Sidonian passages in which the term *barbarismus* occurs, its presence in *Ep.* 4.17.1 to Arbogast, is particularly noticeable. This letter, dated after Sidonius' appointment as bishop,[38] is antithetical to *Ep.* 5.5 in both tone and content, since the author praises Arbogast for his *caritas*, for his *uerecundia* and, especially, for his *urbanitas*. Arbogast's value resides in his ability to live among barbarians and yet not to contaminate with barbarisms his Latin eloquence, an ability expressed with the realistic image of Arbogast drinking water from the Mosella but literally belching (*ructas*) the water of the Tiber.[39]

It can be argued that, in Sidonius' view, what connotes someone as a barbarian is not his origin or his upbringing as much as his embracing of the entirety of conventions, habits and, mainly, language that would define him as such. When Sidonius wants to stigmatise this un-Roman behaviour,

---

35. Santelia 2019, 295.
36. An analysis of the passage is in Squillante 2009, 149.
37. For this specific categorisation see Condorelli 2001a, 102 and 108.
38. See Amherdt 2001, 378.
39. Although the verb *ructare* in Sidonius and in other Christian authors often means 'to utter while speaking', Amherdt 2001, 385–6 points out that in this case the verb should be interpreted as having its popular original meaning.

he draws upon the standardised figures and expressions which are part of what Fascione befittingly calls 'the rhetoric of barbarity': a repertoire of images denigrating various aspects of otherness, from food to clothing.[40] In Sidonius' view, Latin grammar in particular is the element which more than anything defines and determines a boundary between what is Roman or philo-Roman and the rest of the world, and it is easy to imagine him playing the part of the grammarian, as described by Kaster: as a *custos*, on a par with a military commander in charge of the defence of an imaginary linguistic *limes*.[41]

Ep. 5.5.1, according to Mathisen,[42] is proof of the new importance literature attained in fifth-century Gaul, as is with the following passage of *Ep.* 8.2.2: 'because the imperial ranks and offices now have been swept away, through which it was possible to distinguish each best man from the worst, from now on to know literature will be the only indication of nobility'.[43] Mathisen points out that while for Syagrius' ancestor the pairing of political and literary glory was still possible, and the former preceded the latter, as Sidonius wistfully recalls, for nobility, dedicating oneself to literary glory has become a substitute for a secular career, because the latter is now impossible.

De barbarismis: Quintilian, Consentius and Sidonius

There is a section of Quintilian's *Institutio Oratoria* (1.5), which, in some editions, goes under the name *De barbarismis*. After asserting that *barbarismum pluribus modis accipimus* (1.5.7) Quintilian lists three categories of barbarisms: the first is due to the contact with outer populations (specifically African or Spanish), which causes the entrance of foreign words in Latin language; the second is of a moral kind, specifically related to bad manners, as Quintilian says (1.5.9): *ut is, a quo insolenter quid aut minaciter aut crudeliter dictum sit, barbare locutus existimatur* ('when someone speaks insolently, or in a threatening or brutal manner, we believe he spoke as a barbarian'); and thirdly, Quintilian mentions a barbarism, quite popular among the common people, in adding or removing a letter or a syllable from a word, or putting another in the wrong position (1.5.10). Similar categories appear in Consentius'

---

40. See Fascione 2018, 37 and Egetenmeyr 2021, 153–6
41. Kaster 1988, 18–19.
42. Mathisen 1988, 52.
43. Translation in Mathisen 1988, 52.

De barbarismis et metaplasmis: for Quintilian's first category, see Cons. *DBM* 2.1–10, though Consentius emphasises that a word introduced in Latin from a foreign language is a case of *barbarolexis*, rather than a barbarism *stricto sensu*. Quintilian's second category of 'behavioural barbarism' is mentioned in Cons. *DBM* 17.21–18.7, while most of the treatise deals with the third category, briefly described in Cons. *DBM* 1.10–20.[44] The following recognition of the occurrences of *barbarismus* in Sidonius' letters is aimed at showing that they fall within the categories outlined in *Inst.* 1.5. With a show of grammatical mastery, Sidonius encompasses in his collection all the different meanings listed by Quintilian.

In *Ep.* 2.10.1 Sidonius encourages Hesperius to keep practising his literary skills, and adds, in a gloomy tone:

> *Tantum increbuit multitudo desidiosorum ut, nisi uel paucissimi quique meram linguae Latiaris proprietatem de triuialium barbarismorum robigine uindicaueritis, eam breui abolitam defleamus interemptamque.*

> To such extent did the number of the indolent increase that, unless you, so few, could rescue the rightness of the Latin language from the rust of vulgar barbarisms, we shall soon mourn its obliteration and disappearance.

Hence, in this context, barbarisms are words corrupting the Latin language, corroding (the image of rust is effective to this end) the purity of Latin. This use could probably fall within Quintilian's first category, if not the third. To the first category could also be ascribed *Ep.* 4.17.1 *sic barbarorum familiaris, quod tamen nescius barbarismorum*, the praise of Arbogast, who manages not to contaminate with barbarisms his Latin eloquence.[45]

Quintilian's second and more abstract category, of barbarisms as behavioural flaws, comes to mind when an exiled and unhappy Sidonius writes *Ep.* 9.3 to Faustus and explains that, given the circumstances, it is not possible for him to exchange lively correspondence, for it would seem a 'moral barbarism', a fundamentally wrong behaviour, discordant with the situation he finds himself in: *Ep.* 9.3.3 *porro autem quidam barbarismus est morum sermo iucundus et animus afflictus.*

The noun has the specific meaning of grammatical mistake, as in Quintilian's third category, in *Ep.* 9.11.6 *neque enim in his, quae tractaueris, ulla*

---

44. On the possible identification of Consentius with the addressee of Sidon *Carm.* 23, see Mari 2021, 2–10.

45. This passage shows a word game similar to that of *Ep.* 5.5, as already stated by Amherdt 2001, 386 – see previous section.

culpabitur aut distinctionum raritas aut frequentia barbarismorum, where Sidonius commends bishop Lupus. Having sent him his autograph writings, he is sure Lupus' copies will be free from errors of punctuation or grammar.

It could be inferred, therefore, that Sidonius' use of the various nuances of the term, like only the best teachers of grammar would do, according to Quint. *Inst.* 1.5.7, is not arbitrary but refers to a certain codification, which Sidonius probably derived from his years as a student of grammar. Moreover, Sidonius does not ascribe grammatical works to either Consentius, and yet the lack of evidence does not exclude either of them being the author of the *De barbarismis et metaplasmis,*[46] and – one may add – whoever the author was, Sidonius might have read the work or discussed it within his circle.

Dating elements

Sidonius writes two letters to Syagrius: *Epp.* 5.5 and 8.8, which are the only source of information concerning this addressee. Most scholars believe *Ep.* 8.8 was written before *Ep.* 5.5, but published later, thus being one of the letters Sidonius admits to having 'pulled out of a drawer' in order to publish Book 8 (see Table 9).[47] Therefore, the various hypotheses about the date of *Ep.* 5.5 tend to consider *Ep.* 8.8 as a *terminus post quem.*

Table 9. Suggested dates for *Epp.* 5.5 and 8.8

	Anderson	Loyen	PLRE 2	PCBE 4
Ep. 5.5	-	Before 469/470	Presumably after 474	Not long after 8.8
Ep. 8.8	-	c. 467	474	The 460s

While Anderson does not suggest a date for the letters, Loyen dates *Ep.* 8.8 to 467 and believes that *Ep.* 5.5 could not have been written after the years 469–70, and that, instead, it might have been sent many years prior to 469.[48] Loyen believes the letter is pre-ordination but beyond that he gives no firm grounds for his dates, although it is possible to relate his supposition

---

46. See Mari 2021, 8.
47. In the prefatory letter of the book, Sidonius says Petronius had asked him to *scrinia Aruerna . . . euentilari* (*Ep.* 8.1.1) with the aim of retrieving unpublished letters to gather in Book 8. Loyen 1970b, 216, for instance, believes *Ep.* 8.8 is one of those letters 'que Sidoine a retrouvées dans ses tiroirs'.
48. See Loyen 1970b, 101 and Loyen 1970a, 255.

to the tone of the writing, which probably led him to categorise the letter as written before the episcopate.

However, *PLRE* 2 (s.v. Syagrius 3, 1042) dates *Ep.* 8.8, later than the others, to the year 474 but does not date *Ep.* 5.5, while *PCBE* 4 (s.v. Syagrius 2, 1845) states that *Ep.* 8.8 was written in the 460s and suggests *Ep.* 5.5 should be dated to not long afterwards.

Such uncertainty is to be attributed to the usual difficulty in finding dating elements in the letter collection, a major obstacle which in this case is worsened by Sidonius' recovery of previous letters for the composition of Book 8.

Mathisen pointed out the arbitrariness of dating *Ep.* 5.5 to 469/70, a date accepted, apart from Loyen, also by Stroheker and Köhler.[49] Mathisen's reconstruction leads one to date the letter around 474 (as in *PLRE*), for two reasons: firstly, the reference to hearsay in the letter would suggest that Sidonius was already living in Clermont rather than Lyon at the time of writing; furthermore, Mathisen wonders whether this letter, along with *Ep.* 5.8 to Secundinus, was then associated with *Ep.* 5.6 to Apollinaris and *Ep.* 5.7 to Thaumastus because they were all written at the same time, whether they were put together at a later stage, when Sidonius was assembling Book 5, or they just merged in the book because they had been archived together. The latter possibility seems to be validated by the content of this group of four letters (*Epp.* 5.5–5.8) all concerning the Burgundians in some way; however, the continuity in subject matter does not necessarily entail that they had been written at the same time.[50] On the contrary, the mentions of Burgundians in these letters evidently concern different phases of Sidonius' life. As is argued in the General Introduction and in the introductions to the relevant letters, the anti-Burgundian remarks in *Epp.* 5.5 and 5.8 lead to the inference that these two letters pre-date *Epp.* 5.6 and 5.7, in which the mentions of Burgundian rulers are cryptic and awkward but non-hostile.

If dating *Ep.* 5.5 *ad annum* is impossible, in light of the marked anti-Burgundian content it seems sensible to consider the bishopric, hence 469, as a possible *terminus ante quem*. Once a bishop, Sidonius shows sympathy for the Burgundians in order to defend Clermont from Euric's incursions.[51]

---

49. Stroheker 1948, 221; Köhler 1995, 349. See Mathisen 2013a, 244: '*Ep.* 5.5, in which Sidonius' friend Syagrius of Lyon is described as the Solon of the Burgundians because of his knowledge of Burgundian law, usually is dated to 469 or 470, for no strong reason'.

50. See the similar conclusions reached in the section 'Dating elements' for *Ep.* 5.8.

51. Delaplace 2015, 249 argues that from the moment Sidonius becomes bishop of Clermont his political position shifts in favour of Burgundians.

SIDONIUS SYAGRIO SUO SALUTEM

1. Cum sis consulis pronepos idque per uirilem successionem (quamquam id ad causam subiciendam minus attinet), cum sis igitur e semine poetae, cui procul dubio statuas dederant litterae, si trabeae non dedissent (quod etiam nunc auctoris culta uersibus uerba testantur), a quo studia posterorum ne parum quidem, quippe in hac parte, degenerauerunt, immane narratu est, quantum stupeam sermonis te Germanici notitiam tanta facilitate rapuisse.

2. Atqui pueritiam tuam competenter scholis liberalibus memini imbutam et saepenumero acriter eloquenterque declamasse coram oratore satis habeo compertum. Atque haec cum ita sint, uelim dicas, unde subito hauserunt pectora tua euphoniam gentis alienae, ut modo mihi post ferulas lectionis Maronianae postque desudatam uaricosi Arpinatis opulentiam loquacitatemque quasi de halarione uetere nouus falco prorumpas?

3. Aestimari minime potest, quanto mihi ceterisque sit risui, quotiens audio, quod te praesente formidet linguae suae facere barbarus barbarismum. Adstupet tibi epistulas interpretanti curua Germanorum senectus et negotiis mutuis arbitrum te disceptatoremque desumit. Nouus Burgundionum Solon in legibus disserendis, nouus Amphion in citharis, sed trichordibus, temperandis, amaris, frequentaris, expeteris, oblectas, eligeris, adhiberis, decernis, audiris. Et quamquam aeque corporibus ac sensu rigidi sint indolatilesque, amplectuntur in te pariter et discunt sermonem patrium, cor Latinum.

4. Restat hoc unum, uir facetissime, ut nihilo segnius, uel cum uacabit, aliquid lectioni operis impendas custodiasque hoc, prout es elegantissimus, temperamentum, ut ista tibi lingua teneatur, ne ridearis, illa exerceatur, ut rideas. Vale.

---

§ 2 halarione *Marolla* : hilario α (ilario *A* : ylario *S*) *MP* : harilao *L* : halario *Savaron* : haliaeëto/haliaëto *Warmington* : auiario *Burke* : areola *Courcelle*
falco *MP* (falcho *P*) : faccho *L* : flacco α

LETTER 5

SIDONIUS TO HIS DEAR SYAGRIUS

1. Since you are the great-grandson of a consul, and you are such by male succession (although this is less pertinent in presenting my case); since therefore you are the descendant of a poet, whose literary works would without a doubt have granted him the dedication of statues, had the purple robes not done so (a thing attested, to this day, by the refined words in his verses), from whom the enthusiasm of posterity has not retreated even a little, especially in the field of poetry, there is no way to express how astounded I am to hear that you have so readily taken possession of a knowledge of the Germanic language.

2. And yet, I do remember that, in your boyhood, you were suitably instructed by schools of liberal studies, and I know for a fact that often you declaimed vehemently and eloquently before the eyes of the orator. That being the case, I would like you to tell me whence your mind suddenly drank in the euphony of a foreign people? And how is it possible that, after the beatings of our Vergil classes and the hard-earned opulence and garrulity of the varicose man of Arpinum, you take flight like a young falcon from an old eagle?

3. By no means can it be imagined how much laughter it causes me and the others, whenever I hear that in your presence a barbarian fears to pronounce a barbarism in his own language. The stooping elder among the Germans is amazed at you when you translate letters, and they chose you as judge and arbitrator in mutual affairs. A new Solon of the Burgundians in the disposition of laws, a new Amphion in tuning lyres, albeit three-stringed, you are loved, visited frequently, sought out, you amuse them, you are chosen, consulted, you take decisions, you are listened to. And though they are equally rough and unteachable in their bodies and in their feeling, they embrace in you and simultaneously learn their ancestral language and the Latin spirit.

4. Only one thing remains to be said, finest of men, that even when you have free time, you shall be devoted with equal dedication to reading literature and that you shall preserve this balance, just as you are most cultivated: that while retaining this language of ours you won't be laughed at, you should practise that one so that you can be the one to laugh. Farewell.

Commentary

§ 1

Cum sis: These words introduce a series of concessive clauses, laudatory of Syagrius' great-grandfather, at the end of which Sidonius affirms that, in light of the political and intellectual background of his family, Syagrius' interest and readiness in learning the Germanic idiom is all the more deplorable. The model for this passage may be the opening paragraph of Pliny's letter to Calpurnia Hispulla, Plin. *Ep.* 4.19.1 (*cum sis pietatis exemplum...*). Since Calpurnia is most dutiful and loves her niece as if she were her own, Pliny 'knows' that she will be glad to hear that her niece has proved worthy of her family. In Pliny the *cum* introduces a causal clause and does not have a concessive nuance; also, the main clause is not in contrast with the opening subordinate (as it is in Sidonius) but is a natural consequence of what is expressed in the opening line. The same rhetorical device with the opening concessive clause is employed by Sidonius in *Ep.* 6.1.3 to Lupus, but in that case the context is praise for Lupus, who, despite being in the 'front line of faith' for his renowned role as bishop, does not despise the 'last ones' and still continues his apostolic mission.

consulis pronepos: The consul mentioned is Flavius Afranius Syagrius, also a poet, according to this letter. There are two senators named Syagrius in 381 and in 382: according to *PLRE* 1 (s.v. Syagrius 2, 862) and Mathisen 2020, 122 the addressee's ancestor would have been *praefectus urbi Romae* in 381 and consul in 382; for a different interpretation see Porena 2019, *passim*. The addressee Syagrius is also said to be of patrician lineage in *Ep.* 8.8.1 and his ancestor is mentioned various times in Sidonius' letter collection. In *Ep.* 1.7.4 Sidonius says that the consul was also Tonantius Ferreolus' grandfather on his maternal side. Consul Syagrius' tomb was in Lyon, where Sidonius rests and sits in the shade with the *primi ciuium* after attending a crowded and stifling celebration in *Ep.* 5.17.4. This Syagrius is also believed to be the friend to whom Ausonius dedicates *Praef.* 2.1–2 ed. Green (*pectoris ut nostri sedem colis, alme Syagri, / communemque habitas alter ego Ausonium*), though a possible alternative identification with the consul of 381 is debated; see Green 1991, 238–9. Cf. the General Introduction for the metrical clausulae of this paragraph and how they help in translating it.

per uirilem successionem: The *iunctura* is not attested before Sidonius, whereas the formula *per uirilem sexum descendens* is attested in Ulp. *Reg.* 11.4. For Sidonius, pointing out that the kinship is by male succession has a twofold meaning. It should be a matter of pride for Syagrius and at the same time it is an aggravating circumstance. Being in some way a more entitled descendant of a consul than others (Tonantius Ferreolus was such by female succession – see *Ep.* 1.7.4), he is expected to behave accordingly.

ad causam subiciendam: The impression this first long and hypotactic paragraph conveys is that Sidonius draws on technical language to achieve his purpose of convincing Syagrius. The expression *subicere causam* is attested for instance in Cic. *Ver.* 2.5.146, where it means to 'make excuses' in somebody's (Verres' own) defence, while Sidonius is showing himself in the opposite act of presenting his case, as a lawyer would, to convince Syagrius. While in Quint. *Inst.* 1.6.38 the expression concerns an etymological remark meaning 'to explain the origin of words', the three occurrences in Augustine (*C. Faust.* 2.2; *In euang. Ioh.* 108.1; *C. Iul. op. imperf.* 2.108) all pertain to the act of explaining and do not reflect the quasi-judicial nuance the syntagma seems to have later in Sidonius.

trabeae: The purple robes are the symbol of the consulship which had granted Syagrius' ancestor a statue in his honour. Previous attestations of *trabea* as specifically indicating consulship are for instance in Claud. *In Ruf.* 1.248–9 (*ibat grandaeuus nato moriente superstes / post trabeas exul*) when he recalls the misdeeds of Rufinus against a man who, despite having been a consul, was exiled after the murder of his son; and in Symm. *Ep.* 9.112 (*te annalem trabeam meruisse*), the *incipit* of a congratulatory letter for the election of his friend.

immane narratu est: The syntagma seems to be attested here for the first time as a variant of the more common *immane dictu*, which occurs in Sidon. *Ep.* 1.1.2. Sidonius often employs the adjective *immanis* (there are seven occurrences exclusively in the *Letters*) but probably its unrefined nature did not make it suitable for the register of the *Carmina*; see also *TLL* 7.441 s.v. *immanis* 53 (by Labhardt).

sermonis . . . Germanici: The series of merits of the ancestor highlights by contrast the illicitness of the addressee's attitude, by opposing a perfectly Roman and honourable behaviour to Syagrius' philo-Germanism; the *sermo*

Germanicus is therefore a defining element of his non-Roman behaviour. The *iunctura* has a negative connotation since its first attestation in Suet. *Cal.* 47, a passage in which Caligula acted as director of a carnivalesque staging: lacking real Germans for his triumph, he recruited the tallest Gauls to play the part of German prisoners, had them grow and dye their hair red, *sermonem Germanicum addiscere et nomina barbarica ferre* ('learn the German tongue and pretend they had German names'). It is noteworthy that *sermo Germanicus* echoes the *germanica uerba* surrounding Sidonius in *Carm.* 12.4, when he ascribes the impossibility of composing an epithalamium for his friend Catullinus to the burdensome presence of indiscreet and malodorous Burgundians who besiege his kitchen during the several days' banquet with which king Gundioc celebrated his return to Lyon in 461; see Tschernjak 2003, 163; Santelia 2019, 297–8. As stated in the introduction to this letter, the common anti-Burgundian reference leads to the conclusion that *Ep.* 5.5 was written earlier than Mathisen suggested, before Sidonius sided with them to defend Clermont from the Visigoths.

rapuisse: Syagrius makes the new language his own swiftly and easily. The suddenness of his behaviour worsens his position in the eyes of Sidonius, though the tone of the writing is teasing. It seems important to stress how Syagrius is an active subject in the action of 'taking possession' of the new language: he does not succumb to it but it would seem he actively and convincedly learns it out of interest.

§ 2

pueritiam . . . imbutam: Similar attestations concerning education are in Suet. *Nero* 20.1 *inter ceteras disciplinas pueritiae tempore imbutus*; and in *HA Sept. Seu.* 1.4 *in prima pueritia, priusquam Latinis Graecisque litteris imbuer-etur*; however, in none of the occurrences is the *pueritia* itself defined as *imbuta*, hence this is a variant on the usual phrase. Cf. Sidon. *Ep.* 4.21.4 *te imbuendum liberalibus disciplinis*; and see the commentary on *Ep.* 5.9.4 *imbua-musque liberos*.

scholis liberalibus: The *iunctura*, a variation of the more common expression *scholae artium liberalium*, does not seem to be attested before Sidonius. One should, however, consider, as explained by John 2018, 26, that education

LETTER 5

was at this time more than ever a matter of status and pride.[52] Sidonius'
vision of the world was divided in two: those with Roman education (not
necessarily Romans by birth) and others. Sidonius in *Ep.* 4.17.2 reminds
Arbogast that *quanto antecellunt beluis homines, tanto anteferri rusticis institutos*
('education distinguishes cultivated men from peasants in the same way that
humans are different from beasts'). Once this distinction is clear, one can
fully understand how unconceivable it is for Sidonius that Syagrius neglects
the education and the annexed status which belongs to him not only by
birth right but also as an accomplishment for his years as a student. Gaul was
a praised centre of scholastic excellence at the beginning of the fifth century,
and in particular Mathisen 2005, 6–8 firmly refutes the entrenched opinion
that the quality of schools in Gaul abruptly declined after the settlement
of Visigoths in Aquitania in 418 and Burgundians in Sapaudia in 442. As
Mathisen 2005, 10–11 explains, the teaching of secular subjects continued
because barbarians needed educated persons to fill secular positions and this
is testified also by the number of teachers whose names are attested. On this
topic, John's appendix (2018, 243–54) with lists of the teachers, rhetors,
grammarians and students known from the mid-fourth century to late fifth
century is most valuable and proves to be useful as a tool to understand the
intellectual vivacity of the region at that time.

subito: Like the *rapuisse* at the end of the first section, Sidonius stresses
how this interest in studying a barbarian language was sudden, abrupt and
contrary to his upbringing and traditional education.

euphoniam gentis alienae: To the ears of any Roman-speaking man, the
sermo Germanicus had nothing of the *suauitas pronuntiationis* the term *euphonia*
implied, as in *TLL* 5.2.1074 s.v. *euphonia* 38 (by Kapp and Meyer). The
irony is emphasised by the definition of the *gens* as *aliena*, highlighting the
concept of otherness and non-Romanness of the Burgundians. On the representation of otherness in Sidonius see Egetenmeyr 2019.

post ferulas lectionis Maronianae: Vergil and Cicero are chosen as representative of canonical texts studied in school. The passage was translated
as 'the beatings of our Vergil classes'; however, one has to agree with
Condorelli's interpretation of the – otherwise ambiguous – mention of the

---

52. I am grateful to Alison John who allowed me to read her PhD dissertation before its
publication for the purpose of my research.

159

ferulae, as a symbol of the authoritative power of the teacher who physically hit negligent students. *Ferulae tristes* were defined by Martial (10.62.10) as the *sceptra pedagogorum* (see Condorelli 2001a, 105 n. 14) and Juvenal (1.15), in his programmatic *recusatio* of epic in favour of satire, evokes having received proper Roman education through the same image: *et nos ergo manum ferulae subduximus* ('I too, have withdrawn my hand from under the cane'). In Juvenal (7.210) even the mighty Achilles is afraid of the *uirga magistri*, and in his *Confessiones* (1.14) Augustine recalls the dread of the punishments and menaces of his teacher when he struggled to learn Greek; on the student-beating literary topos see Morton Braund 1996, 78 and Saller 1994, 148–9. Compare the similar mention of corporal punishment in Sidon. *Ep.* 2.10.1 (on which see Hindermann 2022, 296–7). Sidonius has the intent to show the difficulty in learning and acquiring the education which Syagrius then suddenly neglects, betraying years of hard study. The contraposition between what was acquired with sacrifice and the previous expressions of suddenness serves the purpose of showing Syagrius' choice as not well pondered and reckless.

desudatam uaricosi Arpinatis opulentiam loquacitatemque: Although the models mentioned are canonical, the way Sidonius mentions them is original and refined. The *iunctura desudata opulentia* is not otherwise attested; however, Apuleius had mentioned *opulentia* as the defining quality of Cicero's style in a list of authors who would have approved of Avitus' oration had they read it: *Apol.* 95.5 *ut in illa neque Cato grauitatem requirat . . . nec parsimoniam Sallustius nec opulentiam Cicero* (the style of this Apuleian passage is close to Sidonius' predilection for enumerations – see for instance the list of qualities of Claudianus' *De statu animae* in *Ep.* 5.2 but also lists in *Epp.* 5.7 and 5.8). Furthermore, Symmachus mentioned the *opulentia Tulliana* together with Maronian *proprietas* in *Ep.* 1.32.3. Note that *opulentia* and *loquacitas* express similar concepts and that Sidonius' prose is itself redundant and artificial in this passage.

uaricosi Arpinatis: This unusual definition of Cicero as *uaricosus* is attested also in Quintilian, Dio Cassius and Macrobius. Quint. *Inst.* 11.3.143 focuses on a refutation of the report by Plinius Secundus, according to whom Cicero used to wear a long toga *ad calceos*, touching his feet, to hide his varicose veins (*uelandorum uaricum gratia*). Quintilian discards this as a fantasy and ascribes this custom to a common practice among Greek orators which was again *à la mode* for many successors of Cicero. In fact, as Kroll 1963,

LETTER 5

324 n. 4 points out, the longer toga became the norm only a generation later, while the *exigua toga* was not used anymore. Another reference to the length of Cicero's toga as an expedient to completely 'cover up the ugliness of his legs' is in Dio Cassius 46.18.2 ἵνα τὰ αἴσχη τῶν σκελῶν συγκρύπτῃς, a passage centred on the derision of Cicero's *mollitia*, on which see notes to the *BL* edition by Bertrand (in Fromentin 2008, 162–3 n. 87–9). Again, Cicero is said to have had a problem with varicose veins in Macrobius' retelling of an irreverent exchange among him and Vatinius: when Cicero had boasted to have been borne in triumph on the shoulders of citizens after his return from exile, Vatinius had asked (Macr. *Sat.* 2.3.5) *unde ergo tibi uarices?* ('how then did you get those varicose veins?'). As Macrobius reports, this was one of many unpleasant comments the two had reciprocally exchanged, and Kaster 2011, 339 n. 32 suggests that 'the jibe perhaps alludes not just to the unsightliness of varicose veins but also to the belief that they caused impotence (Arist. *Problems* 4.20 878b–879a)', an interpretation that would considerably worsen the maliciousness of the comment. Apart from the anecdotic and entertaining nature of the matter, whether Sidonius is studiously echoing these sources, or is simply reporting widely known information, why does he define Cicero as 'varicose' in a context of Ciceronian praise? One possible answer may be related to the standing position of orators, varicose veins being one of the drawbacks of the job, as suggested for instance by Dalton 1915, 54 n. 1 and Anderson 1965, 181 n. 3, somehow praiseworthy to the eyes of Sidonius; however, it could be argued that in this passage Sidonius simply shows off his knowledge and finds an unconventional way of mentioning Cicero to adorn his writing and to impress the reader. Condorelli's interpretation of the passage seems the most compelling: Sidonius would have exploited the ambiguity of the expression, playing with the known fact that Cicero had varicose veins and referring at the same time to the challenge of studying his overabundant and bloated style (Condorelli 2001a, 106 n. 14). Note how Sidonius enjoys mentioning authors with the toponym of their birthplace (there are only four mentions of the name *Cicero* compared with eight occurrences of *Tullius* and eight of *Arpinas* in his corpus). One last notation concerns rhythm: see the usual choice of the -*que* in order to have a cretic spondee at *loquacitatemque*.

quasi de halarione uetere nouus falco prorumpas: While the reading *falco* has been chosen since Ketelaer and van Leempt's *editio princeps*, that of *hilario* (*harilao* in *L*) remains a *crux* in editions and various attempts at conjectures have been made by scholars. Savaron 1599, 310 conjectures *halario*, arguing that *halarius* is to be considered as the mightiest of eagles: 'Est autem Halarius avis, quae, ut Aquila inter reliquas volucres, sic illa inter aquilas principem locum obtinet, . . . et haec lectio sua non carebit elegantia, Syagrius enim ex Halario vetere, novus falco prorumpit, id est homine liberale et docto, indoctus et inliberalis'. Savaron substantiates his conjecture by quoting John of Salisbury's *Policraticus* 1.13 *aquila namque, sicut rex auium est (si non [h] alarionem excipias, quae forte aquilarum species potentissima est)*; cf. Migne 1855 and Keats-Rohan 1993. The image of Syagrius as a young hawk which parts from an old and mighty eagle seems coherent with the context, since the eagle would represent Romanness itself, from which Syagrius would be departing, being interested in barbarian culture and language. With the exception of Baret 1878, 332–3, who enclosed Savaron's conjecture in the body of the text, this reading has not been endorsed by scholars. My suggestion is that it should be reinstated – but in light of John of Salisbury's testimony in a third declension ablative *halarione* with *-ne* lost before *ue-* of *uetere*, rather than in the second declension ablative *halario*. One may be hesitant to conjecture a word not attested in Latin of Antiquity; nonetheless, there is a good case to be made for it, since John of Salisbury was a reader of Sidonius and it was at John's hand that the *Florilegium Gallicum*, comprising excerpts from Sidonius' letters, had been compiled for Thomas Becket. Thus, his passage may be considered as a unique testimony, serving as a gloss to Sidonius' *Ep.* 5.5.2. It could be suggested that John had found the word interesting (either in Sidonius or elsewhere) and had then used it in the *Policraticus*, but, since it was an unusual expression, he had enclosed an explanation of the noun in his text. On the presence of Sidonius in twelfth-century *florilegia* and in particular in John's *Florilegium Gallicum* see Chronopoulos 2020, 645; see also Hernández Lobato 2020, 669 on the *Policraticus* being 'peppered with borrowings from Sidonius' letters'. It could also be suggested that a trace of the reading survives in the ancient French noun *alerion* or *alérion*, meaning 'grande espêce d'aigle' according to Ménage's *Dictionnaire etymologique de la Langue Françoise* (1750, vol. I, s.v. Alérions, 32) and Godefroy's *Dictionnaire de l'ancienne langue française* (1881, vol. I, 218); for numerous examples of its occurrence in early modern texts in French see also Tobler and Lommatzsch 1955, 296–7. Its later use in French heraldry with the meaning of 'small eagle' baffled Du Cange (1883–1887, vol. I, col. 159b s.v. *alario*) when commenting on its occurrence in John of Salisbury's passage; see also Blaise 1975, s.v., 31. It is worth, however, listing other conjectures. In Anderson 1965, 182 *harilao* is left in the text, and in the apparatus Warmington relates

LETTER 5

that Anderson believed *harilao* meant 'nest of a bird of prey'; he then conjectures *haliaeëto* or *haliaëto* as 'sea eagle', while Burke conjectures *auiario*. Lastly, Loyen 1970a, 180 accepts Courcelle's conjecture *areola*, meaning 'from his old nest' and justifies the conjecture (Loyen 1970a, 235) by noting that *areola*, diminutive of *area*, is attested in Plin. *Ep.* 5.6.20.

§ 3

barbarus barbarismum: Sidonius describes a ludicrous scene, picturing barbarians as afraid of pronouncing mistakes in their own language in the presence of Syagrius. The term is employed by Sidonius with various meanings in *Epp.* 2.10, 4.17, 9.3 and 9.11; see the introduction to this letter for a detailed comparison between these occurrences and the meanings listed in Quint. *Inst.* 1.5. On barbarisms in Sidonius see Condorelli 2001a, 103. Cf. Mam. Claud. *Ep.* 2, p. 204 *grammaticam uti quandam barbaram barbarismi et soloecismi pugno et calce propelli*. The word game *barbaram … barbarismi* is similar to that of Sidon. *Epp.* 5.5 and 4.17, and is at the heart of a passionate defence of the purity of Latin dedicated to Sapaudus (the addressee of Sidon. *Ep.* 5.10). Gualandri 1979, 25 considers the recurrence of the theme as testimony that this Gallic literary circle shared the concern that Latin might have been contaminated beyond repair; for further comments and for an alternative interpretation see the introduction to *Ep.* 5.10.

curua Germanorum senectus: It is impossible to ascertain whether Sidonius refers to a specific political institution or generally to a traditional idea of elders as holders of knowledge and decisiveness. It is noteworthy, though, that in the later testimony that is the *Lex Burgundionum*, we find mentioned *comites* and *proceres* as the advisers with whose counsel the king issued the law code, aiming at *integritas* and *aequitas iudicandi* (*LB Prima Const.* 1.2). The *comites pagorum* and *comites ciuitatum* had individual autonomy in the territories they presided over; see for instance *LB Prima Const.* 5 and *Prima Const. in fine*. Saitta 2006, 74 considers the *comes* as the political figure who had the most authority after the king, having civil and military powers. Furthermore, *LB Prima Const.* 5 also mentions *obtimates* immediately before mentioning the members of the king's retinue, and, throughout the corpus, *obtimates* are said to have been involved in the issue of laws concerning inheritance and the use of the death penalty, as Wood 2016, 9 points out. Although it is impossible to ascertain whether Sidonius refers to a specific category, we do know that members of the higher ranks did have institutionalised roles at court.

arbitrum te disceptatoremque desumit: Among the earlier attestations of the hendiadys *arbiter–disceptator*, the following seems deserving of a closer analysis. See Cic. *Rep.* 5.3 *nec uero quisquam priuatus erat disceptator aut arbiter litis, sed omnia conficiebantur iudiciis regis* ('nor was any private citizen judge or arbitrator of a dispute, but all things were decided by the king's judgements'). He then adds that 'their Numa' had followed the example of Greek kings, taking upon himself the duty to deal with public affairs and administer justice. If read in light of the context and of the mention of the years spent studying the complex Ciceronian eloquence, these words convey the impression that Sidonius may be alluding to the passage of *De Re Publica*, availing himself of a shared code and of a rarefied and clever irony. Having spent many years making Cicero's style his own, Syagrius could be reminded that it is not the job of a private citizen to legislate in place of the king, let alone to have kingly powers in a foreign reign.

Nouus Burgundionum Solon in legibus disserendis: To Sidonius, what is *nouus* is often *deterior*, a concept already expressed in § 2. Despite the uncertain identification of the two elements as an eagle and a bird (or something else), what is *uetus* is represented as more authoritative and legitimate than the *nouus*, which expresses inexperience and a flawed variation of the perfection of the model. The *iunctura* here has a twofold purpose: it clearly has a comic effect, since the friend is compared to Solon, but at the same time it is evocative of the subtext that the new has a lesser value than the old. The bantering tone of the writing may lead one to agree with Mathisen 1993, 124, who suggests that Syagrius was not serving in any official capacity and that he was 'rather reorienting his legal practice in response to the needs of the times'. Mathisen also adds that this choice shows Syagrius' pragmatism and clear vision of the situation, having realised that the Burgundians 'were there to *stay* as the administrators of Gaul'. As much as Mathisen's argument is embraceable, as stated in the introduction to this letter, one cannot exclude *tout court* the possibility that Syagrius was involved, even just peripherally, in a proto-legislative phase. This is the first of a series of two cretic ditrochees.

nouus Amphion in citharis, sed trichordibus temperandis: Amphion, son of Zeus and Antiope, built the walls of Thebes by enchanting the stones with the sound of his lyre; the myth is notably attested in Hes. fr. 182 M-W and in Latin tradition, for instance in Prop. 3.2.5–6 and Stat. *Theb.* 4.356–60. Considering the previous reference to Solon, the mention of Amphion might refer to his building the city, hence to a Syagrius founder as well as to a lyre player. Two elements enhance the irony of the passage: the anaphoric repetition of the adjective *nouus* for the third time in the letter effectively reinforces the message that what is new has a lesser value than what is old; furthermore, the final *sed trichordibus* ('albeit three-stringed') is an even more effective *aprosdoketon*, with a variation of the scheme previously employed, since, before, *nouus . . . Solon* was not followed by any further pejorative element. The most evolved *citharae*, from the second century onwards, had up to eighteen strings (Luiselli Fadda 1988–1989, 224; Scoditti 2009, 117), hence it is easy to imagine the comic effect the image of Syagrius playing a three-stringed lyre had for Roman nobility, but it seems also that Sidonius exaggerates in belittling the instrument. Archaeological finds of Germanic *citharae* include instruments of no fewer than seven or six strings, such as the famous sixth/seventh-century Sutton Hoo lyre (Figure 3).

Figure 3. Maple wood lyre, fragmented. Sutton Hoo, ship-burial mound: 1. © The Trustees of the British Museum

Another problematic element in the passage is the use of the verb *temperare*. Luiselli Fadda 1988–1989, 225 believes, with good cause, that Loyen's translation (Loyen 1970a, 181, 'dans le jeu de la cithare') does not do justice to the term. *Temperare* in fact has a specific technical meaning, that is, 'to tune or to string', as in Ov. *Met.* 10.108 *qui citharam neruis . . . temperat* (*L&S* s.v. 1. A. 2). Anderson 1965, 183 n. 3 and Loyen 1970a, 181 n. 11 mention Plutarch, *De mus.* 18.2, to support the persuasive interpretation of the three strings as a pejorative element; note, however, that in the Plutarchian passage the three-stringed lyre is an element of the eulogy of Olympus, whose plain compositions for three-stringed lyres surpassed by far those composed for instruments with more strings. Note that *tri-chordibus, temperandis* creates a second consecutive cretic ditrochee.

amaris, frequentaris, expeteris, oblectas . . . decernis, audiris: As is argued in the General Introduction in the section on prose rhythm, the verbs are coupled through metrical clausulae, a thing most common in Sidonius' enumerations: a cretic spondee at *ama-ris frequentaris*, a paeon IV spondee at *ex-peteris oblectas* and another cretic spondee at *de-cernis audiris*.

rigidi sint indolatilesque: *Indolatilis* is a Sidonian hapax, recognised by Isabella Gualandri in her *Furtiva Lectio* (1979, 175–6), in which a realistic and effective explanation of the Sidonian context is provided by comparing Sidonius' image of barbaric *rigiditas* to the stiffness of a wooden puppet whose traits are only roughly outlined. Gualandri ascribes to the same sense of incompleteness and rigidity the explanation of *indolatilis* and suggests a comparison with Ammianus' description of the robust and stooped body of Huns in 31.2.2 *quales in commarginandis pontibus effigiati stipites dolantur incompte*, a passage which Gualandri 1979, 176 believes may have been a model also for Sidonius *Carm.* 2.243–69. On the Huns, described by Ammianus as 'prodigiously misshapen', see Kelly 2008, 14. The origin of the Sidonian term *indolatilis*, meaning *non dolatus, impolitus* (*TLL* 7.2.1219 s.v. *indolatilis* 72–4, by Rubenbauer), conveys an image of something which cannot be shaped. According to Sidonius, Burgundians cannot be 'shaped', either in body or in mind, and hence cannot become cultured.

discunt sermonem patrium, cor Latinum: Sidonius ends this section by saying that Syagrius teaches Burgundians their own language (*sermo patrius*) and yet he has hope that he may also instil in them the Roman wisdom. Squillante 2009, 149 interprets the passage as an encouragement to keep reading the texts he was educated with, and to share them with the barbarians, so that they could be 'educated to Roman emotions'.

§ 4

Restat . . . ut: Sidonius seems to be fond of this expression, as is testified by its numerous occurrences in his letters (*Epp.* 3.1.4, 3.2.4, 4.15.2, 4.24.7, 5.3.4, 5.15.2, 6.6.2, 8.16.5, 9.16.3).

uir facetissime: In this paragraph the addressee is praised with two superlatives, *facetissimus* and *elegantissimus*. Sidonius is fond of the expressions made of the word *uir* followed by a superlative and he uses this sort of *iuncturae* in all of the epistolary corpus. Compare, for instance, the similar occurrences in Book 5 alone: *Epp.* 5.1.1 *uir conuenientissimus*; 5.1.2 *uir accommodatissimus*; 5.9.1 *uir capacissimus*; 5.17.2 *uir amplissimus*.

ista tibi lingua teneatur, ne rideatis, illa exerceatur, ut rideas: The distance between Latin and Burgundian is expressed by the different demonstrative *ista/illa*, the latter expressing distance and, again, stressing the concept of 'otherness' implied throughout the letter. The same can be said for the alternative passive and active forms of the verb *ridearis/rideas*: Syagrius will not be laughed at if he keeps 'this language' and he can be the one to laugh, practising the barbaric language only to denigrate it, as is expected of him. The letter ends with a double cretic, *exerce-atur ut rideas*, the same clausula opening § 1.

167

LETTER 6

Content

Informed by Thaumastus that Apollinaris may be suspected of treason at the Burgundian court, after rumours of him siding with Julius Nepos, Sidonius offers to help.

The addressee Apollinaris

For Apollinaris, possibly cousin of Sidonius, see the introduction to *Ep.* 5.3. For his relationship with Thaumastus and Simplicius see the introduction to *Ep.* 5.4. Symmetrically, *Ep.* 5.6 to Apollinaris provides detailed information on Thaumastus, while *Ep.* 5.7 to Thaumastus exclusively concerns Apollinaris' situation.

Genre

The ending of *Ep.* 5.6 can reasonably lead one to ascribe the text to the genre of 'admonitions' (*epistulae symbuleuticae*), a category described for Pliny's letter collection by Sherwin-White (systematically) and mentioned by Cugusi.[1] For a different kind of letter of admonition, see the introduction to *Ep.* 5.5. In Pliny, the exhortative section is likewise usually at the end of the letter.

There are, however, substantial differences between this letter and Pliny's admonitions: for instance, the latter are mostly preceded by examples taken from his experience. Pliny enjoys advising *sub exemplo*, to the point that

---

1. In particular Sherwin-White 1966, 45 lists admonitions in all the books of Pliny' letters: Book 1 (*Epp.* 3, 9, 18, 23); Book 2 (*Ep.* 6); Book 4 (*Epp.* 3, 23, 24); Book 6 (*Epp.* 29, 34); Book 7 (*Epp.* 3, 9, 26, 28); Book 8 (*Epp.* 22, 24); Book 9 (*Epp.* 5, 6, 9, 12, 17, 21, 24, 29, 30). See also Cugusi 1983, 222.

the category of admonitions often overlaps with that of anecdotes.[2] Even though the themes of Pliny's admonitions are various, there is an underlying common core to them: they all concern mundane exhortations and are filled with pleasantries. Pliny's admonitions concern, for instance, friends exhorted to enjoy contemplative life (*Epp.* 1.3, 1.9) or to visit him (*Ep.* 7.3), lists of subjects worth studying (*Ep.* 7.9), instructions for new job posts (*Epp.* 8.24, 9.5) and friendly advice on ending a disagreement (*Ep.* 9.21). Unlike these admonitions, Sidonius' *Ep.* 5.6 concerns a worrisome threat, and it is reasonable to assume that, in addition to the direct involvement of the king,[3] his kinship with Apollinaris made Sidonius sincerely concerned.

The lack of a unitary systematic study of the entirety of Symmachus' epistolary collection is an obstacle when it comes to tracing a definite pattern in his epistolary admonitions and, consequently, in Sidonius' use of models. Similar concerns do not seem to be expressed in Symmachus' letters of admonition,[4] as much as in letters in which he mentions political intrigues, mainly those concerning his close friend Nicomachus Flavianus. That is the case, for instance, of *Ep.* 3.69 to Richomeres, whose entourage circulated unpleasant rumours about both Nicomachus Flavianus senior and junior.[5] Symmachus calls the plotters perverse (*scaeui*) and accuses them of cowardice, since they spread rumours only in Flavianus' *absentia*. Moreover, in *Ep.* 3.86.2, when Symmachus compliments Rufinus for his friendship with Flavianus – whom he calls *pectoris mei dominus*, just like Sidonius will say Simplicius and Apollinaris are *uerissimi domini animae meae* in *Ep.* 7.4.4 – he points out the new friendship is causing the envy of *inprobi* who may try

---

2. As is highlighted by Sherwin-White 1966, 44; see also Lilja 1969, 68–70.

3. Here and elsewhere the Burgundian Chilperic is termed 'king' for brevity, although, as the commentary further explains, Sidonius is extremely reluctant to call him that, and Chilperic's position may not have been that well defined at the time of the events described in the letter.

4. By way of example, in *Ep.* 2.25 Symmachus states he chooses to enclose, in a separate document, a list of warnings to Flavianus so that the letter itself would not be too verbose. In Symm. *Ep.* 9.129 the author gives fatherly advice (*ut parens moneo*) exhorting the addressee to end a rift with a common friend and to inform him, as a governor and friendly arbitrator, of his reasons. On this letter see Callu 2002, 132; Roda 1981, 291–2. Symmachus is often asked by his addressees to look into juridical trials, as is testified, by way of example, in *Epp.* 6.2 and 6.5.

5. Symmachus is not keen on lingering, detailed explanations of the accusations, and relies on subsidiary materials, as Pellizzari 1998, 208 points out, consisting of oral accounts and of attached *breuiaria*, so that the letter would not be too long, a thing contrary to the 'finalità filofrontetiche' which impeded detailed discussion of important matters.

to undermine their bond.[6] For similar content, one could also mention the ending of Symmachus' *Ep.* 4.15 to the newly elected consul Bauto (a Frank).[7] In *Ep.* 4.15.2, Symmachus says he has to defend himself from a *fraus aliena* aimed at undermining his relationship with Bauto.

A rift is bridged

If, as argued before, Sidonius' *Ep.* 5.3 to Apollinaris and *Ep.* 5.4 to Simplicius are to be related to the Arvandus affair, and could be considered as tangible proof that there has been a momentary rift in the family,[8] *Ep.* 5.6 to Apollinaris and *Ep.* 5.7 to Thaumastus would then testify that peace has later been restored, and, possibly, two-way epistolary contacts resumed. Otherwise, Sidonius would have likely complained about a protracted silence on Apollinaris' part, as he repeatedly does in *Ep.* 5.3. Sidonius' renewed ease in writing to Apollinaris is evident if one compares the consistency in the use of the second person singular in *Ep.* 5.6 and the more distant tone of *Ep.* 5.3, where Sidonius' blatant uneasiness is also expressed through the alternate use of the second person singular and plural.[9]

Context

Ep. 5.6 provides context for *Ep.* 5.7 and precedes it chronologically. In *Ep.* 5.6 Sidonius asks Apollinaris to confirm that the rumours reported by Thaumastus are true, and that Apollinaris is indeed suspected of betrayal. Should the information prove to be accurate, he is determined to offer his help.[10] The role that Sidonius might have in resolving matters figures prominently at the end of the letter, where the author stresses the importance of his presence at the Burgundian court and hints at his influence there. Some time must have passed between the writing of *Ep.* 5.6 and *Ep.* 5.7, at least enough time to let Sidonius solve the matter and change his

---

6. *Ep.* 3.86.2 *ne quid in tales amicos fascino liceat*; see the commentary in Pellizzari 1998, 237.

7. On Bauto, see *PLRE* 1, s.v. Bauto, 159.

8. See the introduction to *Ep.* 5.3.

9. For the use of second person singular and second person plural in *Ep.* 5.3 see there; on the subject, see also van Waarden 2020b.

10. In *Ep.* 5.7 Sidonius reports how, through his intervention and with the help of the Burgundian queen, Apollinaris' name was in fact rehabilitated.

way of addressing Chilperic, first as a *magister militum* in *Ep.* 5.6.2, then as *tetrarcha noster* in *Ep.* 5.7.1. One role does not necessarily exclude the other, and Chilperic could have retained his title and be at the same time *magister militum per Gallias* and Burgundian king, and yet, Sidonius' choice to call him *tetrarcha noster* only at a later time seems worthy of notice.[11]

The *laus* of Chilperic's wife in the subsequent letter (*Ep.* 5.7.7) is proof that, in *Ep.* 5.6.2, Sidonius might be directly referring to his influence over the queen, or likely over a member of the court close to her. The Burgundian court was based in Lyon, as can be surmised from Sidon. *Ep.* 5.7.7 *praesens potestas Lugdunensem Germaniam regit*; and from *Ep.* 6.12.3, when Sidonius refers to Chilperic and his spouse as the bishop of Lyon's king and queen.[12] Saitta considers Sidonius' mentions of the Burgundian king as settled in Lyon to be a dating element, and consequently ascribes the Burgundian settlement there to 'a few years before 474'.[13]

Furthermore, in *Ep.* 5.6 Sidonius does not know yet who are those who slandered Apollinaris, since he vaguely refers to either *turbo barbaricus* or *militaris improbitas* as possible offenders. The vagueness of these expressions appears deliberate, and suggests Sidonius does not know if the rumour was conceived by 'a savage throng' – a belittling way of referring to Burgundian civilians – or by 'military dishonesty'. The detailed portrait of the informants in *Ep.* 5.7, in contrast, testifies that Sidonius, once informed of the identity of those involved, chooses to target them as soon as Apollinaris' reputation is cleared.

The ambiguity in the mentions of Chilperic

As often in Sidonius, the tone of the letter is not immediately apprehended. There are, however, various elements, highlighted in the commentary, which, taken together, suggest that this letter is meant to be interception proof at the time of its composition, or at least slander proof for its publication in the letter collection. 'Careful choice of words' would be an effective

---

11. See the commentary ad loc. for the meaning of this expression and for the misconception created by its erroneous interpretation.
12. *Ep.* 6.12.3 to Patiens. See also *PLRE* 2, s.v. Chilpericus II, 286–7; Mathisen 2020, 87.
13. Saitta 2006, 28. There had been Burgundians in Lyon for a while beforehand, although in a less official capacity. For Lyon as 'main capital of the Burgundian kingdom' and first seat of Chilperic see Saitta 2006, 29, and before him Coville 1928, 164.

headline to summarise the content of this text – not only macroscopically, through the use of syntagmata which do not have previous occurrences, but also on a deeper, sub-textual, level.

As the commentary further explains, the request Sidonius makes that Apollinaris should answer him through private correspondence[14] hints at the need for discretion and at the urgency of the matter.[15] Carefully chosen and ostentatiously prudent also are the ways in which Sidonius mentions Chilperic and Julius Nepos. The first in fact is called *magister militum uictoriosissimus*, with the same superlative employed in epigraphical sources to praise victorious emperors.[16]

Sidonius, on the contrary, chooses not to name Chiperic's opponent, Julius Nepos, directly, and only a vague mention of the opposite faction under *a nouus princeps* is both in this letter and in *Ep.* 5.7.[17] And yet, although Sidonius employs a flattering and hyperbolic expression when referring to Chilperic as *uictoriosissimus*, the king's *iracundia* that Apollinaris may incur, as well as the already mentioned *turbo barbaricus* to indicate possible Burgundian spies, are typical ways of referring to the barbarians as irascible, deceitful and unreliable.[18] As the commentary on § 2 further explains, *iracundia* was not a desirable feature in a ruler, as exemplified by Ammianus Marcellinus' description of Valentinian's anger, which made him, by contrast, unworthy of comparison to his predecessor, Julian.[19]

The mention of another passage concerning Chilperic seems useful to form a clearer picture of Sidonius' opinion on the Burgundian king. In his *Ep.* 6.12 to Patiens, bishop of Lyon,[20] he says that the addressee's sobriety can rely on the support of the Burgundian king and queen, for very different reasons (*Ep.* 6.12.3 *ut constet indesinenter regem praesentem prandia tua, reginam laudare ieiunia*). Once again, as also in *Ep.* 5.7, the queen is depicted in a more favourable light, to the detriment of the king's image. She praises the bishop's fasting, while the king is said to be most interested in the banquets

---

14. *Familiares paginae* in *Ep.* 5.6.2 is a Symmachan *iunctura* (see the commentary below).
15. In particular, if the passage is compared to the mention of the inquisitive eyes of informers reading Sidonius' correspondence looking for incriminating evidence in *Ep.* 5.7.
16. As highlighted in the commentary on this passage.
17. Julius Nepos is, however, named and praised in the – very different – context of *Ep.* 5.16, for which see the commentary on § 2 below.
18. See Fascione 2019a, 75. Worthy of mention is also the *ira Gothorum* surrounding Sidonius in *Ep.* 3.4.1.
19. See the commentary there and Amm. 28.1.23; for the comparison between Julian and Valentinian see Kelly 2008, 308.
20. A letter mentioned above in relation to the Burgundian court being in Lyon.

the bishop hosts. In the eyes of Sidonius, Chilperic is therefore irascible *and* voracious, thus embodying a perfect combination of Roman clichés on barbarity. Borrowing Kulikowski's words: '[Chilperic] was not, of course, recognised outside the territories controlled by the Burgundians, though those Arverni who remained implacably opposed to Euric, Sidonius loudly amongst them, accepted the fiction of his legitimacy'.[21]

It is as if Sidonius, although being formally respectful in order to be apparently blameless, cannot restrain himself from saying that the Burgundians may be their new protectors but they are still barbarians 'to the core'. The words of warning to Ecdicius on the dangers entailed in being too close to Burgundian rulers seem to clarify in no uncertain terms Sidonius' real feelings on the sovereigns.

Actutum in patriam receptui canere festina et adsiduitatem tuam periculosae regum familiaritati celer exime, quorum consuetudinem spectatissimus quisque flammarum naturae bene comparat, quae sicut paululum a se remota inluminant, ita satis sibi admota comburunt. (Sidon. *Ep.* 3.3.9)

Hurry up and sound the retreat to your homeland and, quick, remove your constant presence from dangerous friendships with kings. Whoever is most experienced is right to compare their companionship to the nature of flames, which illuminate what is at a short distance the same way they burn what is put close enough to them.

The itinerary

Sidonius has left Clermont-Ferrand, visited Thaumastus in Vienne, and then presumably is already in Lyon when he writes to Apollinaris, because his being already at court is what allows him to intercede for him. The letter does not allow one to infer whether Apollinaris was in Vaison at the time.

Traces of an editing phase?

Ep. 5.6 is meant to inform Apollinaris, but some information is redundant: Apollinaris was certainly aware of his brother Thaumastus' recent widowhood. It would seem that this kind of detail is put in the text later,

---

21. Kulikowski 2020, 211.

adding a clarifying context for a broader audience's sake, rather than for the addressee's. This could be considered as evidence that the text was reshaped for publication, as most certainly was the case with *Ep.* 5.7, a pamphlet rather than a letter, presumably conceived and written for the purpose of wide circulation, and not as a private message.[22]

Dating elements

Apollinaris' accusations constitute a *terminus post quem* for dating both *Epp.* 5.6 and 5.7, which pertain to two phases: while *Ep.* 5.6 concerns an initial stage, when whisperings reached Thaumastus, *Ep.* 5.7 is to be dated immediately after Apollinaris' acquittal. Julius Nepos became emperor in June 474, and Vaison consequently sided with him, and so avoided inclusion within the Burgundian kingdom for a while. Therefore, *Ep.* 5.6 is to be dated to early autumn, as Sidonius informs us at the beginning of the letter (*Ep.* 5.6.1 *cum primum aestas decessit autumno*), of the year 474.[23]

Seasonal reference

Autumn is mentioned more than once by Sidonius as a season suitable for travel.[24] Its suitability is first connected to the interruption of hostilities by the Visigoths at the end of summer, as Sidonius himself states for instance at the beginning of this letter. As Heather effectively puts it: 'every summer, for four years (471–474) Visigothic would-be besiegers appeared outside the city of Clermont-Ferrand in the Auvergne without ever managing to force their way inside'.[25] In *Ep.* 3.3, Sidonius thoroughly recalls how bravely Ecdicius, with only a handful of men, faced the Visigoths besieging Clermont in the summer.[26] Then, in *Ep.* 3.7.4, he describes the gnawing

---

22. On the issue of Sidonius' letters being revised for publication see Kelly 2020, 181: 'the letters exist on a continuum between real documents and compositions for the collection'.
23. As in *PLRE* 2, s.v. Thaumastus 1, 1062; Thaumastus *PCBE* 4, s.v. Thaumastus 1, 1867.
24. See the General Introduction on the autumnal setting of the book. For seasons as large temporal units, creating a 'macro chronology' in Sidonius' letters, see Hanaghan 2019, 73.
25. Heather 2006, 416.
26. Hanaghan 2019, 73 interprets the mention of the *nox succincta* in *Ep.* 3.3.7 as a detail concerning the fact that in summer the night does not last long enough for the Visigoths

fear that gripped the besieged, even after the barbarians retreated to their winter quartiers, for there was a tacit consensus, among those still guarding their posts, that the threat was only being delayed and the Goths would return.[27] By contrast, the long and detailed description – in *Ep.* 3.2.3 – of all the difficulties encountered by Constantius when travelling from Lyon to Clermont in winter are a fitting example of the unsuitability of that season for travel.[28]

---

to bury their comrades' bodies and hide the actual number of losses inflicted by Ecdicius and his men before the sun rises. Loyen 1970a, 222 n. 10 instead dates the episode to spring, and Giannotti 2016, 152 highlights how the expression may also indicate a subjective sense of the passing of time for the hurried Visigoths.

27. Sidon. *Ep.* 3.7.4 *quia, etsi barbarus in hiberna concedat, mage differunt quam relinquant semel radicatam corda formidinem.* See Heather 2006, 416 and 419. See also Stevens' analysis of the siege of Clermont, still unsurpassed, in particular Stevens 1933, 148. For the siege of Clermont and the looming presence of Goths see also Sidon. *Ep.* 7.10.1 *et ego istic inter semiustas muri fragilis clausus angustias belli terrore contigui desiderio de uobis meo nequaquam satisfacere permittor.* Sidonius is confined behind the flimsiness of a 'half-burnt fragile wall', and the fear of a war which is too close (*belli terror contingui*) paralyzes him. On the context of this passage see van Waarden 2010, 533–4.

28. On the winter setting of the letter see Loyen 1970a, 248 n. 2 and Giannotti 2016, 122.

SIDONIUS APOLLINARI SUO SALUTEM

1. Cum primum aestas decessit autumno et Aruernorum timor potuit ali-
quantisper ratione temporis temperari, Viennam ueni, ubi Thaumastum,
germanum tuum, quem pro iure uel sanguinis uel aetatis reuerenda familiaritate complector, maestissimum inueni. Qui quamquam recenti caelibatu
granditer afficiebatur, pro te tamen parum minus anxius erat: timebat enim
uerebaturque, ne quam tibi calumniam turbo barbaricus aut militaris concinnaret improbitas.

2. Namque confirmat magistro militum Chilperico, uictoriosissimo uiro,
relatu uenenato quorumpiam sceleratorum fuisse secreto insusurratum tuo
praecipue machinatu oppidum Vasionense partibus noui principis applicari.
Si quid hinc tibi tuisque suspicionis incutitur, raptim doce recursu familiarium paginarum, ne uobis sollicitudinis aut praesentiae meae opportunitas
pereat. Curae mihi peculiariter erit, si quid tamen cauendum existimabis,
ut te faciat aut gratia impetrata securum aut explorata iracundia cautiorem.
Vale.

§ 1 reuerenda *codd* : reuerendo/reuerendae *Mohr*

LETTER 6

SIDONIUS TO HIS DEAR APOLLINARIS

1. As soon as summer gave place to autumn, and Clermont's fear could be mitigated for a while in light of the season, I reached Vienne, where I found your brother Thaumastus – whom I favour with respectful familiarity having regard both to kinship and to age – extremely unhappy. Although strongly affected by his recent widowhood, he was nevertheless no less worried for you: he was indeed afraid and apprehensive at what kind of false accusation the barbarian throng or military dishonesty might conjure up against you.

2. For he asserts that by the venomous account of some vicious men, it was secretly whispered in the ear of the – ever victorious – master of the soldiers Chilperic, that it was mainly because of your contrivance that the town of Vaison joined the side of the new emperor. Hence, if any suspicion is thrown upon you and yours, hurriedly inform me by answering with a private letter, so that the advantage you might get from my concern and my presence here is not squandered. It will be my special concern, in case you reckon that you need to watch out in any way, to ensure that you are untroubled once favour is obtained for you, or more cautious in case Chilperic's anger is ascertained. Farewell.

Commentary

§ 1

Cum primum aestas decessit autumno: As listed by Geisler 1887, 366, the same syntagma occurs in Symm. 2.6.2 *aestas prope decessit autumno*. Cf. also Symm. *Ep.* 4.54.3 (*nondum in hiemem praecipitat autumnus*), Symm. *Ep.* 4.58.1 (*nam decedebat autumnus*) and Symm. *Ep.* 5.97 (*mitigatis autumni aestibus*). A similar image is at the beginning of Sidon. *Ep.* 2.2.1 *iam uer decedit aestati* (on which see Hindermann 2022, 89) and in *Ep.* 5.17.4: the decription of the heat of what seemed like a summer night, even though it was 'growing cool with the first cold of the autumnal aurora'. In all the Sidonian passages (*Epp.* 2.2, 5.6 and 5.17) the seasonal reference provides the reader with context for the composition of the letters, a thing that creates, according to Hanaghan 2019, 73, a macro-chronology of Sidonius' letters, which usually lack dating elements (Kelly 2020, 179–85). Cf. Sidon. *Ep.* 8.9.1 *cum primum Burdigalam ueni*, where as soon as Sidonius reaches Bordeaux, a courier gives him a letter from Lampridius.

Aruernorum timor . . . ratione temporis temperari: Context is essential to understand the word game *ratione temporis temperari*, a figura etymologica with heavy alliteration. The fear experienced by the Arverni is mitigated by the seasonal change, i.e. by the temporary absence of the Visigoths. However, as stated in the introduction to this letter, the Arverni were fully aware that the retreat of the Visigoths, in order to winter elsewhere, was just an interruption of hostilities and that the end of winter would be followed by new incursions. For the threat being only delayed, cf. Sidon. *Ep.* 3.7.4. For the expression *ratio temporis*, see *Ep.* 3.13.10 (Giannotti 2016, 256) and for the occurrence of *ratio temporum* in *Ep.* 7.11.1, meaning 'circumstances of the time', see van Waarden 2010, 551. The Arverni are also mentioned at the beginning of a letter concerning Constantius' visit to Clermont during a truce: *Ep.* 3.2.1 *salutat populus Aruernus . . .* his presence within their half-demolished walls (*sanctum pedem semirutis moenibus intulisti*) soothed their worries for a while. See the mention of *Ep.* 3.2 in the introduction in connection with the difficulties encountered by Constantius, who travelled in winter, and Giannotti 2016, 122.

Viennam ueni: A word game characterised by heavy alliteration similar to that of the previous figura etymologica *temporis temperari*. As stated above,

LETTER 6

the end of summer (i.e. of hostilities) allows Sidonius to travel and to visit Thaumastus in Vienne.

Thaumastum, germanum tuum: As stated in the section 'Prosopography' in the General Introduction, the description of Thaumastus as *germanus* indicates that Apollinaris and he are brothers by blood (cf. *Ep.* 5.7.1 to Thaumastus himself). A useful comparison is that with Sidon. *Ep.* 4.1.1, in which Probus' wife is said to be tied to Sidonius by *patruelis, non germana fraternitas* – not a brotherly relationship but a cousinly one.

pro iure uel sanguinis uel aetatis reuerenda familiaritate complector: Sidonius respects Thaumastus by virtue of the *ius sanguinis*, the bond of blood they share, and of the *ius aetatis*, which likely indicates that Thaumastus was older than Sidonius and, as such, treated with 'respectful familiarity'; the diverging interpretation in Mathisen 2020, 59 was corrected in *Addenda et Corrigenda* online.[29] Sidonius often employs *uel . . . uel . . .* deprived of its disjunctive force and 'nearly as a synonym of *et . . . et*' (as in *L&S* s.v. *uel* 2a). For a similar use, see Sidon. *Ep.* 3.11.2 *uel sic electus gener uel educta sic filia*, in which the opinion good men hold of Simplicius is confirmed both by his laudable choice of son-in-law and by the upbringing of his daughter. This is the only known occurrence of the expression *reuerenda familiaritas*, a *iunctura* attested in all the manuscript tradition. The unusual *iunctura*, despite the *concordia codicum*, led Mohr 1895, 109 to conjecture 'an *reuerendo*, uel melius *reuerendae*?' The latter seems a most fitting conjecture: *reuerendae* would refer to *aetatis* instead of *familiaritate*, providing further evidence of Sidonius being younger than Thaumastus. Mohr's conjecture is mentioned in apparatus by Anderson 1965, 184 n. 2, and Loyen 1970a, 182. However, on the grounds of prose rhythm, the *lectio* transmitted would be a better choice, since a colon ending at *aetatis* would constitute a cretic spondee (one of Sidonius' favourite clausulae), while an alternative colon ending at *reuerendae* would be heroic clausula, a pattern Sidonius generally avoids, or else one must read on without a clausula after the long prepositional phrase. Incidentally, the cretic spondee would also be the first of a series of three, along with *familiari-tate complector* and *maes-tissimum inueni* (the latter with elision).

maestissimum inueni: Thaumastus is very aggrieved by both the death of his wife and the slanders involving his brother. The only previous occurrence

---

29. <https://sidonapol.org/companion-add-and-correct>.

of the syntagma is in the renowned episode of Lucretia, Liv. 1.58.6 *sedentem maestam . . . inueniunt*. The superlative form of this adjective has its first occurrence in *Aen.* 2.270, when a *maestissimus Hector* appears to Aeneas in a dream, and is thereafter rarely attested. Sidonius employs it also at the beginning of another letter concerning grief, *Ep.* 2.8.1 *maestissimus haec tibi nuntio*, when he informs Desideratus of Filimatia's death (see Hindermann 2022, 222).

recenti caelibatu granditer afficiebatur: The spelling out in detail of Thaumastus' recent widowhood seems to be redundant and written for the sake of the reader of the epistolary collection rather than for Apollinaris, who is certainly aware of his sister-in-law's passing and that this circumstance would be distressing for Thaumastus (see the introduction to this letter). Sidonius is always looking for unconventional ways of expressing conventional concepts, a thing that explains why the widowhood is mentioned through the *iunctura recens caelibatus*, and by using the syntagma *caelibatu afficiebatur*, both not known to occur elsewhere.

pro te tamen parum minus anxius erat: Expressions of distress and anxiety over friends are customary in Symmachus' letters, in which the adjective *anxius* is often attested, mainly in complaints about epistolary silence. See, by way of example, Symmachus' worries about Richomeres and his request to appease his *animus pro te anxius* in *Ep.* 3.56, by providing him with information on his health, if not with letters at least through messengers; see Pellizzari 1998, 194 for context. A different kind of anxiety – not for Felix, the addressee, but for his own situation – is that expressed by Sidonius in *Ep.* 3.4.1, when the letter-bearer brings Sidonius' letters *quas granditer anxius exaraui* ('which I have written in great anxiety'), since Sidonius is surrounded by the *ira* of the Goths and the *inuidia* of the Burgundians.

timebat enim uerebaturque: The insistence on Thaumastus' preoccupation hints at the seriousness of the situation and that Sidonius himself is sincerely worried. Wolff 2020, 409 mentions this passage as a useful example of Sidonius' predilection for verbal abundance and in particular for redundancy. Among the numerous previous occurrences of the two synonyms in the same context (e.g. Liv. 39.37.17 and Plin. *Ep.* 4.9.7), see in particular Aus. *Ep.* 22.30–1 (Green) *si prodi, Pauline, times nostraeque uereris / crimen amicitiae. Tanaquil tua nesciat istud*, a reproach to Paulinus of Nola for his silence and an appeal not to inform his wife in case he 'dreads the charge of Ausonius'

LETTER 6

friendship'. For the mention of Tanaquil, to whom Ausonius malevolently compared Paulinus' wife Therasia and to whom Sidonius will compare the Burgundian queen in the following letter, see the commentary on *Ep.* 5.7.7.

calumniam . . . concinnaret: This syntagma is rare and has only three attestations before Sidonius, a further element which proves, as stated above, that he carefully chooses his words even in a letter which would appear to have been written in the heat of the moment, or, at least, he does so for its publication. In Arnobius *Adu. Nat.* 5.1 the phrase *ne quis forte nos aestimet concinnare per calumnias crimina* introduces the quotation of a passage by Valerius Antias, mentioned in order to argue against pagan traditions. The occurrence in Rufinus' *Continuatio* of Eusebius' *Historia Ecclesiastica* (10.18) concerns a trial (Athanasius') in which the judges are said to be *aliquanti concinnatae calumniae conscii.* Lastly, Jerome states that Pelagius and his circle merely reproduce past calumnies: *In. Ier.* 4.1.3 *ueteres . . . calumnias concinnantes.*

turbo barbaricus aut militaris . . . improbitas: As stated in the introduction, Sidonius does not seem to know who slandered Apollinaris, since he vaguely refers to either a 'barbarian throng', hence Burgundian civilians, or 'military dishonesty' as the possible sources. This is one of the passages in which it seems impossible to decode with any degree of certainty the meaning of Sidonius' deliberately prudent language. One possible interpretation could be that Thaumastus himself did not have detailed information at the time he spoke with the author, and that Sidonius is first asking for a clearer picture of events so that he can be of service to Apollinaris. The *inuectiua* against informants of *Ep.* 5.7 testifies that Sidonius, once the situation had settled, was aware of the identity of the accusers. Once again, the choice of words is innovative: *turbo*, which literally indicates a 'whirlwind' and is here effectively used with a figurative meaning, expresses the confusion caused by this throng (as in *OLD* s.v. *turbo*, 2196). Although the *iunctura turbo barbaricus* does not have previous occurrences, one cannot look past the clear Ovidian matrix behind this expression. The similar *barbara turba* is often attested, for instance in Ovid *Pont.* 3.2.38, when even the *barbara turba* of Getae and Sarmatians is aware of the qualities of Ovid's addressees. In *Rem.* 594, Phyllis' death is said to be caused by her loneliness, since she used to wander with streaming hair, like the *barbara turba* of the Thracian Bacchae; and a similar meaning of 'savage throng' is in Juvenal's satire against the Egyptians, whom he calls *barbara turba* in 15.46. Other

181

occurrences of the expression concern a strictly military meaning which is not referable to Sidon. *Ep.* 5.6, such as *Tristia* 5.10.27–8, in which even inside of fortified garrisons 'the barbaric throng mixed with the Greeks strikes fear'. The image is also a belittling way to refer to crowds of enemy soldiers, e.g. in Cato's speech in Lucan 2.309–10, and in Caesar's harangue before battle (Lucan 7.272–3) not to fear undisciplined barbarian *turbae* (unable to bear not only the sound of Roman trumpets but also of their own clamour). With this belittling military meaning, Sidonius mentions a *turba* of Scythians of which Hormidac is a citizen (*ciuis* is undoubtedly used ironically) in *Carm.* 2.240–1 *ipsis quoque gentibus illic / barbara barbaricis* (they are 'barbarous even for barbarians'). Note also that the *iunctura militaris improbitas* is not known to occur before this passage; the only known previous occurrence of a similar expression is in Cic. *Att.* 6.4.1, in which *militum improbitas* is one of the reasons why it would be wise to leave Quintus with full authority in Cilicia. It seems legitimate to suggest that in Sidonius the expression may refer to those holding high military rank, who would profit from Apollinaris' downfall. The paragraph is closed by two cretic tribrachs, at *turbo barbaricus* and *concinnaret improbitas*.

§ 2

magistro militum Chilperico: In 473–4 Chilperic had become *magister utriusque militiae per Gallias* and *patricius*. It seems noticeable, as stated in the introduction, that Sidonius calls him *tetrarcha noster* only in the following letter, after some time has passed, which raises the question of whether, at the time he writes *Ep.* 5.6, he intentionally chooses to mention Chilperic's role only as *magister militum*. Chilperic may have become king in the period between *Epp.* 5.6 and 5.7, or, if he already was a king in *Ep.* 5.6, Sidonius may feel reluctant to name him as such, unlike in *Ep.* 5.7. See *PLRE* 2, s.v. Chilpericus II, 286–7; *ODLA* s.v. Chilperic II of Burgundy; and Mathisen 2020, 87 s.v. Chilpericus. The second paragraph, which is highly clausulated, is opened by a cretic ditrochee (*militum Chilperico*) followed by a dactyl iamb (*uictorio-sissimo uiro*) and by a cretic spondee (*insusurratum*).

uictoriosissimo uiro: The superlative form of the adjective is not attested frequently in Latin literature. It occurs only in late Latin, and apart from singular occurrences in minor authors of Sermons (Maximus Taurinensis and Petrus Chrysologus) and in Arnobius Junior (*Ad Greg.* 16, *Praedest.*

LETTER 6

3.13 and 26) it is attested in Augustine, who refers it to Constantine in *Ciu.* 5.25; to the martyr Cyprianus in *Contra Iulianum* 2.3.6 and 2.8.25; and to *spiritus* in *De cura pro mortuis gerenda* 6.8 (commenting on the latter passage, Rose 2013, 234 says that the expression is 'a characteristic expression in the theology of martyrdom'). And yet, if *uictoriosissimus* is not attested frequently, and only in Christian literature, it is however attested in numerous inscriptions. Research conducted by consulting an epigraphic database such as that of Clauss-Slaby[30] or Europeana Eagle Project[31] provides numerous examples. Superlatives are overabundant in introductory formulas praising emperors in late antique inscriptions, in line with an overall ceremonial trend and taste for panegyrical ornamentations of the time. Chastagnol 1988, 20 rightly observes that *ubique uictor* and *uictoriosissimus* are usually found in inscriptions celebrating the liberation of territories and military victories against usurpers or barbarians. He also gives some examples (Chastagnol 1988, 20 n. 55) of inscriptions qualifying an emperor as *uictoriosissimus* after military successes – such as Aurelianus in *CIL* VI 1112 once he restored the unity of the Empire in 274 – but one could also mention Aurelianus as *perpetuus uictoriosissimus* in *CIL* VIII 10205 (undated) and *super omnes principes uictoriosissimus* in *CIL* XI 3878 (dated between 271 and 275). Constantine is called *uictoriosissimus* after the battle of the Milvian Bridge in *CIL* VI 1145; *CIL* VIII 2241, 7008 and 7010; *CIL* X 7204. Honorius and Theodosius II are said to be *uictoriosissimi* after the death of Alaric and the retreat of the Goths in *CIL* VI 1718 (dated between 412 and 414). As the mentioned inscriptions abundantly exemplify, *uictoriosissimus* is an exclusively imperial epithet, and there are no occurrences of it designating a *magister utriusque militiae* or any other officer. Once again, the awkwardness of language reflects Sidonius' ostentatiously prudent attitude. A contemporary reader would have perceived that there was something awkward about a *magister utriusque militiae* being given a customary imperial epithet and praise which had once been bestowed on emperors while, in the same sentence, the actual emperor is mentioned as merely 'the new *princeps*'.

relatu uenenato: This *iunctura* does not have previous occurrences. Geisler 1887, 366 signals the similarity with *Ep.* 4.22.6, in which Sidonius compares critics to vipers waiting to bite, although his addressee, Leo, did

---

30. <http://www.manfredclauss.de/>.
31. <https://www.eagle-network.eu/>.

not give them any excuse to attack him *uenenato morsu*. Geisler also points to Symm. *Ep.* 1.31.2, in which the author asks Ausonius if he fears *aemuli uenena lectoris* ('the venoms of a jealous reader'). And yet, while Symm. *Ep.* 1.31.2 and Sidon. *Ep.* 4.22.6 show similarities, since they both concern 'venoms' of literary competitors, in Sidon. *Ep.* 5.6.2, *relatus uenenatus* is a venomous political slander, and does not concern a literary quarrel. The same concept appears in *Ep.* 5.7.6, where Chilperic is said to have been inevitably influenced against Apollinaris by his tendentious and malevolent intermediaries.

quorumpiam sceleratorum: Sidonius has a predilection for the use of *quispiam* (forty-two occurrences in his works, while *quidam* occurs ninety-four times). Van Waarden 2010, 146 points out that *quispiam* was probably already an archaism in old Latin, and to this consideration one may add that, unsurprisingly, *quispiam* has numerous occurrences in Mamertus Claudianus' *De statu animae*, a work characterised by a complex and archaising style. For the use of the word *sceleratus* in a context of political conspiracy see Sal. *Cat.* 52.36. Since the conspirators' actions had put the state in great danger, Cato recommends the death penalty for those who confessed or have been caught *in flagrante delicto*. Slanderers are said to be *saeui* in Symm. *Ep.* 3.69.1 to Richomeres, and *inprobi* in *Ep.* 3.86.2 to Rufinus – see the introduction to this letter.

secreto insusurratum: The syntagma does not have other occurrences. The alliteration of the sibilant consonant in *sceleratorum fuisse secreto insusurratum* cleverly calls to mind the sound one might make while whispering. At the same time, the sonority of these words, if related to the aforementioned 'venomous' report, vividly pictures informants as snakes, hissing in the ear of Chilperic. The action of whispering is indissolubly linked to the idea of insinuating allegations, as in Cic. *Ver.* 2.5.107, when Cleomenes, described as *familiarissimus* to Verres (*propter flagitiorum ac turpitudinum societatem*), sits by his side and whispers words in his ear 'as he is wont to do' (*ad aurem familiariter, ut solitus erat, insusurrare*). Note that, in *Ep.* 5.7.7, Sidonius explicitly refers to *In Verrem* by calling the slanderers *Cibyratae*. See *Ep.* 5.7.7 also for what had been whispered in Chilperic's ears and for the intervention of the queen: through the same gesture, that is, whispering in the ear of the king, she is able to undo what the slanderers had done and to literally 'clean' his ears, i.e. change his mind. As stated above, *insusurratum* creates a one-word cretic spondee.

LETTER 6

tuo praecipue machinatu: As pointed out in *TLL* 8.16 s.v. *machinatus* 82–3 (by Dietzfelbinger), before Sidonius there is only one known occurrence of the substantive, in Apul. *Apol.* 74 *me suo machinatu reum postulatum*. Rufinus is portrayed by Apuleius as the real accuser, whose *machinatus* dragged him to trial. There may be further elements linking this passage and Sidonius' account of Apollinaris' slanders (see the commentary on *Ep.* 5.7).

oppidum Vasionense: As van Waarden 2010, 242 points out, the use of the adjective instead of the genitive is idiomatic in Sidonius, and the same expression is attested in *Ep.* 7.4.4 (although it is suspected to be a gloss); compare also *Ep.* 1.8.2 *Caesenatis . . . oppidi*; *Ep.* 7.5.3 *oppidum Aruernum*; and *Ep.* 9.16.3 *Mytilenaei oppida*.

partibus noui principis applicari: Vaison had sided against Chilperic. As pointed out by Hanaghan 2019, 114–15, Sidonius does not explicitly refer to the identity of the new emperor, that is, Julius Nepos, neither here nor in *Ep.* 5.7. Only in *Ep.* 5.16.2 is Julius Nepos openly named as the one who appointed Papianilla's brother Ecdicius to the rank of *patricius*, and who therefore is a 'most excellent Augustus' (*sancte Iulius Nepos, armis pariter summus Augustus ac moribus*). The contrast with the passing mention of him as *nouus princeps* here is certainly striking, and should be related also to the mention of Chilperic as *uictoriosissimus magister militum* (see above). The possibility that the letter might be intercepted in transit or has to be slander proof for publication seems to play a crucial role in Sidonius' choice of words.

Si quid . . . suspicionis incutitur: Sidonius asks Apollinaris to inform him if he and others close to him are actually under suspicion. The words *tibi tuisque* have been interpreted as proof that Simplicius had been accused as well. As stated above, there is no element in *Epp.* 5.6 and 5.7 which would support this theory (on which see the introduction to *Ep.* 5.4).

recursu familiarium paginarum: This syntagma shows traces of the influence Symmachus' letters have over Sidonius, as signalled by Geisler 1887, 366. See e.g. Symm. *Ep.* 1.86 *recursus sermonis* and *Ep.* 6.39 *recursus adloquii* (a complaint about the addressees' epistolary silence). Note also that the *iunctura familiaris pagina* is previously attested exclusively in Symmachus. In *Ep.* 2.35.2 to Nicomachus Flavianus, Symmachus states that, unlike in the time of their ancestors (i.e. Cicero), state affairs are no longer a suitable topic for private correspondence (*familiares paginae*): as Cameron 2015, 104 effectively summarises, talk of politics is 'strictly off limits' for Symmachus, and so his remark is a subtle complaint about the lack of free speech (on the passage see also Cecconi 2002a, 264–5; Sogno 2017, 183). Symmachus demands *familiares paginae* of his friends in *Epp.* 5.70 and 8.26; and the expression describes his own answer to a request in *Ep.* 9.56. The *iunctura* does not occur elsewhere in Sidonius' letter collection. It seems reasonable to infer that, through the Symmachan reminiscence, Sidonius is also asking Apollinaris to be cautious by sending him 'private correspondence'. This detail, together with the mention of Chilperic as *uictoriosissimus* and the vague mention of Julius Nepos, would indicate *Ep.* 5.6 was written (or at least published) with the aim of being interception proof. The term *pagina* is used to indicate a letter already in Cic. *Att.* 6.2.3 and it frequently occurs in Symmachus' and in Sidonius' letter collections: e.g. Sidon. *Epp.* 1.2.1, 4.7.2, 4.8.1, 4.16.1, 5.4.1 (see commentary ad loc.), 5.12.1 and 7.2.2. See Amherdt 2001, 213–14; van Waarden 2010, 147 and Hindermann 2022, 114.

ne uobis sollicitudinis aut praesentiae meae opportunitas pereat: For comparison, see Sidon. *Ep.* 6.4.2, a *commendaticia* in which Leo's *auctoritas*, together with his physical presence (*opportunitas praesentiae tuae*), will be beneficial to his full comprehension of a legal problem involving the letter bearer.

Curae mihi peculiariter erit: The syntagma *curae mihi erit* has numerous attestations almost exclusively in epistolary contexts. See its occurrence with the superlative in Cic. Att. 6.2.2 *mihi erit maximae curae*, and also Q. *fr.* 2.13.2 *maximae uero mihi curae erit*. Cf. also Plin. *Ep.* 7.10.2 and Symm. *Epp.* 3.55.2 and 3.81.4.

cauendum existimabis: This syntagma is not known to occur elsewhere.

aut gratia impetrata securum aut explorata iracundia cautiorem: Sidonius suggests Apollinaris should profit from his presence at court. His intervention would allow the addressee to feel safer should he be back in Chilperic's graces, or more cautious should Chilperic's anger be confirmed. The *iunctura* *gratia impetrata* has only one previous occurrence, in Plin. *Ep.* 6.33.7 *non despero gratiam . . . impetraturam*, in which, however, it concerns the addressee's appreciation of a speech Pliny is sending him. Compare Symm. *Ep.* 5.58 *nec tamen impetrationis gratiam mihi uindico*, in which Symmachus states he does not intend to claim credit for an exemption obtained by Thalassus' son. Also, the second colon, *aut explorata iracundia cautiorem*, does not have occurrences before Sidonius, and the same can be said for the *iunctura explorata iracundia*. As stated in the introduction, *iracundia* is not a suitable feature for someone in a position of power. It seems useful to compare this passage to the occurrence of *iracundia* in Ammianus 28.1.23 *aegre imperatoris iracundiam tulit*, concerning Valentinian, described as furious upon hearing that the death penalty he requested for the author of an *inuectiua* (which depicted Valentinian as *auarus et truculentus*) has been commuted by the Senate into exile. As Kelly 2008, 308 points out, Valentinian's anger is one of the features (together with failed military expeditions and acts of cruelty) Ammianus emphasises in order to make clear that the emperor is inferior to his predecessor Julian. The comparison with Ammianus' negative portrait of Valentinian exemplifies that this kind of attitude is not suitable for a ruler, and that a similar mention can arguably be interpreted as criticism on Sidonius' part. Other occurrences of the term in Sidonius do not concern anyone in an official post as high as Chilperic's. Sidonius' own outburst is mentioned in *Ep.* 3.12.3, when the author recounts having punished on the spot grave diggers who desecrated his grandfather's burial ground in Lyon, and states that once he asked the bishop to forgive his *iracundia*, he received praises instead, since his rage was more than justified; see Giannotti 2016, 212 for context. Moreover, in Sidon. *Ep.* 8.11.4 *iracundia* is also listed as one of Lampridius' flaws.

LETTER 7

Content

A stream of fierce invective against the accusers of Apollinaris, whose name has just been cleared thanks to the intervention of the Burgundian queen.

The addressee Thaumastus

From *Ep.* 5.6 it can be gathered that Thaumastus lived in Vienne at the time Sidonius visited him, and had recently been widowed. Sidonius' remarks concerning his deference for him by virtue of his age could suggest Thaumastus was probably Apollinaris' older brother,[1] and older cousin of Sidonius.[2]

Mathisen mentions part of *Ep.* 5.6.1[3] as evidence that Thaumastus and Sidonius were cousins of the same age and that he is to be identified with the younger Thaumastus, son of the elder Thaumastus mentioned in *Carm.* 24.[4] As much as the possibility that Sidonius and Thaumastus were cousins commands more assent, the passage of *Ep.* 5.6.1, on the whole, hints at a difference in age between them. Thaumastus seems to be an older brother of Apollinaris, and older cousin of Sidonius, which wins him some extra deference on Sidonius' part: *pro iure uel sanguinis uel aetatis reuerenda familiaritate complector* (5.6.1).[5]

Moreover, a Thaumastus was one of the three delegates sent from Gaul with the purpose of impeaching Arvandus.[6] As Sidonius himself recalls

---

1. They are said to be *germani* in *Epp.* 5.6.1 and 5.7.1.
2. See the introduction to *Ep.* 5.4 for the kinship between Sidonius, Apollinaris, Thaumastus and Simplicius.
3. Taking the genitive with the wrong noun, Mathisen 2020, 59 quotes only part of the sentence *quem pro ... aetatis reuerenda familiaritate complector*, and thus translates 'by reverent familiarity of age'. See also Mathisen 2020, 123. This passage will be discussed in the following pages.
4. Mathisen 2020, 59 says 'he and Thaumastus were of the same generation'.
5. See commentary ad loc.
6. According to Mathisen 2020, 123, the prosecutor of Arvandus was the elder Thaumastus, father of the addressee of *Ep.* 5.7.

LETTER 7

in *Ep.* 1.7, along with Thaumastus there were the ex-prefect Tonantius Ferreolus and Petronius, addressee of the first letter of Book 5 (see the introduction to *Ep.* 5.1).[7] These same Thaumasti are also mentioned (in *Carm.* 24.84–9) at the estate at Tres Villae, probably Saint Mathieu de Tréviers.[8]

The models: Cicero, Tacitus, Juvenal and Apuleius

Various genres and allusions to a wide range of sources, from oratory to historiography, contribute to the creation of the architecture of this layered text. It will be useful to offer a comprehensive view of the most significant and recurring models.

Oratory provided Sidonius with a repertoire of invectives against informers, and, as Cicero states in his *de Orat.* 2.236–7, irony, if placed in the right hands, is a most powerful weapon. Making a witness unreliable through mockery allows the lawyer to project a positive image of the defendant,[9] and although *Ep.* 5.7 is not a piece of oratory, it avails itself of oratorical techniques. One may think for instance of the criticism of social background, thievishness, unusual clothing, behaviour and cowardice in this letter, which are all standard features of those subject to *uituperatio*.[10] By way of example, Cicero ridicules Piso for his grandfather's occupations and Gallic origin (*In Pis* fr. IX N), for wearing sandals (he is called *soleatus*) on occasions suitable for wearing *calcei* (*In Pis.* 6.13). Ridiculing informants has the undeniable effect of clearing Apollinaris, whose actions are never addressed or mentioned in the letter. The focus is entirely on the informants.

---

7. The three brought as evidence an incriminating letter which had been intercepted and which proved that Arvandus had incited Euric not to make peace with Anthemius 'the Greek emperor', but instead to divide Gaul between the Visigoths and Burgundians. On the Arvandus affair and on the possibility it determined a rift in Sidonius' family, see the introduction to *Ep.* 5.3.

8. Santelia 2002a, 25; for the passage, see the introduction to *Ep.* 5.4.

9. On Cicero's use of irony to discredit the adversary see for instance Fantham 2004, 191; Powell 2007, 10.

10. For the theorisation of a total of ten topoi of invective in Greek models see Süss 1910, 247–55. For their occurrence in Cicero's *In Pisonem* and for occurrences of the same images used against Cicero himself see Süss 1910, 259–60 and Nisbet 1961, 193–7. On Cicero's invectives see also Corbeill 2002, 200–1. See Cicero's mention of awkward clothing in Cic. *Vat.* 12.30, quoted in the commentary on § 4 *albati* . . .

In particular, it seems worth emphasising how much this text owes to Cicero's *In Verrem*. Sidonius alludes to *In Verrem* from the beginning (§ 1), when he describes his search for the truth as being like a hunt.[11] The informants' misdeeds throughout the letter are preceded by the same expression (*hi sunt* followed by the relative) that Cicero employs in a passage later quoted by Sidonius. Parallels with *In Verrem* are also detectable in the denigrating mention of *quadruplatores* (§ 3), in the incivility of informants as *Scythae* (§ 4), in their ability to prosper in *dubia tempora* (§ 5), in their being new tyrants like Phalaris (§ 6) and, of course, in their mention, recognised by scholars, as *Cibyratae* (§ 7), the two brothers Verres hired and of which Sidonius' informants are epigones. But Sidonius' mastery of models, as stated before, is layered, and it seems possible that he may also refer to a later tradition of portraying the Cibyratae as slanderers rather than thieves, as the commentary further explains.

Historiographical models are also embedded in the fabric of other sections of this letter, which is enriched by numerous and refined historical exempla. One may mention the 'catalogue of famous slanderers' Sidonius studiously creates in *Ep.* 5.7.3, which actually is a catalogue of nefarious men, since it comprises professional slanderers but also powerful *liberti*, not known to have been *delatores*. This section, as the commentary explains, seems in particular indebted to Tacitus's *Annales* and *Historiae*, as well as to Juvenal's *Satires*. As pointed out by Mratschek, Sidonius often remodels history in order to 'create identity from the past'.[12] By relating contemporary events to a mythical and historical imagery, Sidonius is able to create his own version of events and to mould the readers' opinion through the evocative mention of renowned exempla, positive and negative, which were part of a collective cultural heritage.

Moreover, the letter is, at its core, an invective, and the anaphoric repetition which characterises the first four paragraphs, apart from the already mentioned influence of Cicero, can be productively compared to Apuleius' harsh invective against his accuser Herennius Rufinus, who fabricated charges against the author.[13]

> *Hic est enim pueruli huius instigator, hic accusationis auctor, hic aduocatorum conductor, hic testium coemptor, hic totius calumniae fornacula, hic Aemiliani huius*

---

11. As already pointed out by Gualandri 1979, 132.
12. Mratschek 2020, 239–40.
13. As the commentary further explains, Apuleius is one of the authors Sidonius favours stylistically and linguistically; see also Wolff 2020, 400.

fax et flagellum, idque apud omnis intemperantissime gloriatur, me suo machinatu reum postulatum. Et sane habet in istis quod sibi plaudat. Est enim omnium litium depector, omnium falsorum commentator, omnium simulationum architectus, omnium malorum seminarium, nec non idem libidinum ganearumque locus, lustrum, lupanar. (Apul. *Apol.* 74.5–6)

For he is the one who incited this silly boy, he is the bringer of this accusation, he is the hirer of lawyers, he is the suborner of witnesses, he is the kindler of all this slander, he is the torch and scourge of Aemilianus here. And, in the presence of all, he brags most immoderately that it is through his contrivance that I have been brought to trial. He certainly has good grounds in this for self-congratulation. For he is the intermediary of every lawsuit, the contriver of every perjury, the architect of every pretence, the seedbed of every wickedness, and also the very home, the dive, the whorehouse of lust and gluttonous eating.

Commenting on Apuleius' passage, Hunink points out how the syntactic order, the repetitive style and the sound effects (in particular the alliteration of *f*, which is also in Sidonius' invective) 'turn the passage into an example of verbal magic'.[14] Hunink also highlights how the attack is constituted by a series of insults, by rare neologisms and by the piling up of metaphors which build the climax. One could similarly describe Sidonius' invective. That Apuleius' rant might have been a model for *Ep.* 5.7 is confirmed by the occurrence of Apuleius' neologism *machinatus* in the previous letter, to Apollinaris.[15] As pointed out by Wolff, for Sidonius, Apuleius is 'an essential model for language and style, even though he is never claimed as such'.[16]

The features of informants

The portrait of the slanderers who accused Apollinaris of treason is studiously crafted by evoking all sorts of images and paradoxical situations, in order to create an ever-lasting image of deceivers by trade, envious parasites, rapacious and greedy for money. They are socially placed among *parvenus*, unable to manage a new wealth amassed too rapidly, and, for that, unfitting in most contexts, disrespectful of ranks and social conventions.

---

14. Hunink 1997, 190.
15. Cf. *Ep.* 5.6.2.
16. Wolff 2020, 400.

In *Ep.* 5.7.4, informants are called *pelliti*, a word which is itself evocative of barbarity and echoes numerous literary depictions of *barbaries*, but Sidonius pushes the image even further, calling them, with a hapax, *castorinati*: clad in beaver fur. Their thefts, cheatings and extortions are said to contaminate every aspect of civilised society, from trials to festivities. And yet, these men remain anonymous throughout the letter and, as the commentary further explains, it is impossible to state with certainty if they are Romans or barbarians. The possibility they are Gallo-Romans in the orbit of the Burgundian court in Lyon, seems, however, worthy of further reflection, because Sidonius' denigration would involve describing them as completely barbarised and even worse than barbarians themselves.[17] As Kulikowski points out, if in the 430s most of provincials would have recognised only the emperor's authority: 'forty years later, by contrast, a meaningful majority of provincial elites could see themselves as Romans and yet actively prefer a Gothic or Burgundian king to the emperor. Sidonius lived through that momentous transformation in worldview, and he was never able to reconcile himself to it.'[18]

Throughout the letter the informants' already beastly features are subject to a metamorphosis: triggered by cupidity, they turn into a new chimera; but even this transformation is grotesque, and the image described by Sidonius is not scary as much as it is odd and ludicrous. The same can be said for Sidonius' portrait of Seronatus in *Ep.* 2.1 and in particular in *Ep.* 5.13, where this Gallo-Roman exactor of taxes, allied with Euric, is described through odd beastly images. In *Ep.* 5.13.1 Seronatus moves clumsily and with difficulty, like an enormous whale preceded by his entourage of *musculi*, and later turns into a snake (a recurring image also in *Ep.* 5.7), slithering to reach the victims he will bleed dry with taxes.[19] In *Ep.* 2.1.2, a long *accumulatio*, similar to that of *Ep.* 5.7, compares Seronatus to slaves, tyrants

---

17. Of this opinion is for instance Loyen 1963, 437, who is, however, influenced by the historical events close to him, and by the image of a 'German invader'. Loyen considers the Burgundian presence in Gaul in terms of Germanic conquest, and explicitly says he finds a possible Gallo-Roman collaborationism understandable in light of episodes of French collaborationism with Germany during the Second World War; see also Mathisen 1993, 74–6; Kelly 2016 (blogpost). As pointed out by Wolff 2018, 215–16, Loyen alludes to contemporary history by consciously using a Second World War vocabulary when he describes fifth-century Gaul.

18. Kulikowski 2020, 204.

19. A parallel with Seronatus, himself a delator, is also suggested by Furbetta 2014–2015a, 148. For the portrait of Seronatus as a new Catilina and for his inappropriate behaviour see Fascione 2016, 455–9, Egetenmeyr 2021, 158–9 and Hindermann 2022, 64–6 and 71–6.

LETTER 7

and barbarians; he is cruel and greedy – *et ridentibus conuocatis ructat inter ciues pugnas, inter barbaros litteras.* In light of the brutal and 'barbaric' portrait of Seronatus, who is even more despicable because he is a Gallo-Roman, it would not be any wonder if the same barbarian features would be attributed to Gallo-Roman informants in *Ep.* 5.7.

A display piece

When thinking of the genres combining to create the background of this text, so different from those of other letters (note the absence of Symmachus as a model), one cannot fail to take into account whom it was written for. It is unlikely that a text like this, with its carefully constructed game of allusions, intertexts and exempla, was only intended to be read in Thaumastus' home; it rather seems to be conceived as a display piece, at least in the version we read in the collection. One cannot discard the possibility that this text was adapted or even created for the publication of the collection in 477. The ever careful way of mentioning Burgundian rulers, never by name, always through ambiguous terms (*tetrarcha, patronus*) or by way of exempla, should be read in light of Sidonius' decision to publish this text.

Therefore, if it is impossible to state if or how much a hypothetical original letter was revised when it entered the collection, one should take into account that in 477 Sidonius consciously decides to publish a display piece that pictures Apollinaris as being on good terms with the Burgundian king and depicts Burgundians as protectors, after Clermont was ceded to the Visigoths.[20] Despite the huge amount of detail and the layered models Sidonius masters, he is extremely vague and imprecise when it comes to describing the informants, to the point that we cannot state with certainty if they were Gallo-Romans or barbarians. And yet, by focusing attention on them, Sidonius is able to create a specific narrative of the episode, because discrediting the informants entails minimising the problem Apollinaris had at court and labelling it as a mere misunderstanding. Perhaps this text was written for circulation before its publication, but, ultimately, the underlying political message of the letter Sidonius publishes is that, in 477, he is keen on showing his relative Apollinaris as being on good terms with the Burgundian rulers.

---

20. For the issues of dating the letters and of adaptations made in view of the publication see Kelly 2020, 181.

The *tetrarcha*: Chilperic I or Chilperic II?

Over the years it has been debated whether the Burgundian king mentioned in this letter is Chilperic I (the Elder) or his nephew, Chilperic II (the Younger).[21] In particular, the identification problem arises from scholarly speculation around the meaning of the expression *tetrarcha* in *Ep.* 5.7.1. If one interprets the word as meaning 'king subordinate to Rome', the term would apply to Chilperic I; those who consider the word as meaning 'one of four rulers' refer the term to Chilperic II, since he was one of four brothers. So far, the dearth of information concerning this phase of Burgundian politics has not allowed scholars to reach a unanimous conclusion, since it is impossible to compare the deliberately ambiguous term *tetrarcha* with any other contemporary source using the same expression.

And yet, as the commentary further explains, the word *tetrarcha* is never attested in ancient Latin sources with the contemporary meaning of 'one of four rulers', and Diocletian and his colleagues are never mentioned as such in ancient texts, despite them being the 'tetrarchs' *par excellence*.[22] Therefore, the modern and contemporary pervasive use of the word tetrarchy in connection to Diocletian's collegial division of power was wrongly applied to Sidonius' fifth-century text, a thing which subsequently led to the misconception that four Burgundian rulers shared the power, and, consequently, that Chilperic must have been Chilperic II, because the latter is known to have had three brothers. The etymological interpretation of *tetrarcha* in relation to Chilperic is actually already in Vignier's *Rerum Burgundionum Chronicon* (1575),[23] which is mentioned together with Gregory of Tours (on which more below) as a source by Savaron.[24] An overview of the *status*

---

21. Note, as stated above, that the Burgundian rulers are here mentioned as 'king' and 'queen' by convention, even though, at the time (474–5), they are not yet territorial monarchs, a situation mirrored also by Sidonius' awkwardness in referring to them.
22. According to Leadbetter 2009, 3–6 the word does not seem to have referred to Diocletian's division of imperial power before it appeared in Hermann Schiller's *Geschichte der römischen Kaiserzeit*. Leadbetter maintains its wider circulation is due to its use by Otto Seeck in the first volume of his *Geschichte des Untergangs der antiken Welt* (1897). However, the noun *tetrarchia* is used to refer to the division of power between emperors and Caesars already in Godefroy's commentary on the Theodosian Code (1665, vol. II, 240).
23. The *Chronicon* at p. 13 (sub anno 451) reads: 'Burgundicam ditionem in quatuor Tetrarchias divisisse volunt'.
24. Savaron 1609, 328: 'Chilpericum . . . proprie Tetrarcham appellat, quartam enim regni Burgundionum partem occupabat, quod ab excessu Gundicarij regnum Burgundionum in tetrarchias diuisum fuisset, Gregorij Epitom. ms. & Chron. Burgund. An. 451'. The noun *tetrarcha* is explained similarly by Sirmond 1652, *Notae*, 55.

LETTER 7

quaestionis seems necessary, also in light of the interpretation of the text in this commentary.

Identifying Chilperic I with the *magister militum* of *Ep.* 5.6 and with the ruler mentioned in *Ep.* 5.7 necessarily entails giving the word *tetrarcha* its original meaning: Sidonius chose an antiquated way of indicating a 'minor king under Roman protection'.[25] Furbetta is also of this opinion: she has pointed out that by the time Sidonius writes, the term *tetrarcha* has become archaic, and that in the past it was used to designate kings who, being tied to Rome by patronage, were actually subjects as *foederati*, hence still under Rome's orbit.[26] With this meaning the word has numerous attestations, for which see the commentary ad loc. Sidonius' preference for unconventional expressions would be a plausible reason for the choice of this word, uncommon at his time.[27] Moreover, Chilperic is said to be *tetrarcha noster*, and this meaning, downsizing if compared to that of *rex*, would be most suitable in light of the presence of the possessive adjective.

The idea that Chilperic I is the king mentioned in *Ep.* 5.7 is sustained by numerous scholars, especially Loyen,[28] Luiselli[29] and Saitta.[30] A detailed argument in favour of the identification with Chilperic I is provided by Justin Favrod in his monograph on the political history of the Burgundians,[31] followed by Kaiser's *Die Burgunder*.[32] The genealogical reconstruction in Figure 4 is based on this theory.

According to the reconstruction of Loyen, Favrod and Kaiser, Gundioc was the first king to settle in Sapaudia in 443, and his brother Chilperic I ruled with him at least starting from 456. Gundioc died between 463 and 472 and Chilperic I continued ruling till his death, in around 477.

---

25. As in *TLG* s.v. τετράρχης, 1782; *OLD* s.v. *tetrarches*, 2132. With this meaning see also *L&S* s.v. *tetrarches*, 'the title of a petty prince'.

26. Furbetta 2014–2015a, 148.

27. Of this opinion is also Favrod 1997, 152, who states that the etymological meaning of the word was soon surpassed by that of 'un roi client de Rome, même lorsqu'il était seul à la tête d'un pays. Nous pensons que c'est dans cette acception, la plus habituelle, que Sidoine utilise ce terme. Les arguments pour démontrer un règne d'Hilpéric le Jeune ne nous paraissent donc pas convaincants.' I would like to thank Justin Favrod for sending me his work privately at a time of national lockdown.

28. Loyen 1970a, 235 n. 13 and n. 14.

29. Luiselli 1992, 603.

30. Saitta 2006, 26–7.

31. For the identification of *tetrarcha* as Chilperic I (Hilpéric l'Ancien) see Favrod 1997, 148–54.

32. Kaiser 2004, 57 and 115–19. Of the same opinion is also Furbetta 2014–2015a, 145 n. 80.

195

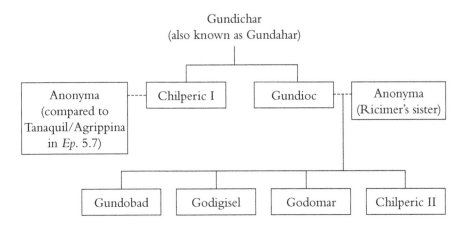

Figure 4. Genealogical tree of the Burgundian 'royal family'

Both Favrod and Kaiser point out that at the time of Chilperic I's death, two of Gundioc's four sons, Chilperic II and Godomar, had already died, so that Gundobad and Godigisel jointly succeeded their uncle Chilperic I.[33] This theory goes back to Jahn's monograph *Die Geschichte der Burgundionen und Burgundiens*,[34] in which Jahn states that the king mentioned by Sidonius is 'without a doubt' Chilperic I, in light of a passage of the *Lex Burgundionum* in which Gundobad names, after his father, his uncle as his immediate predecessor.

> *Si quos apud regiae memoriae auctores nostros, id est: Gibicam, Gundomarem, Gislaharium, Gundaharium, patrem quoque nostrum et patruum liberos liberasue fuisse constiterit, in eadem libertate permaneant.* (LB 3)

> If it is ascertained that any of them have been free men or free women in the days of our predecessors of royal memory, that is: Gibica, Gundomar, Gislahar, Gundahar, my father and my uncle, they may remain free.

It should be pointed out that, in the *Rerum Burgundionum Chronicon*, Vignier mentions this passage of *LB*, and admits that its existence is a hindrance to

---

33. Favrod 1997, 143–5 also points out that Chilperic I was the last Burgundian king who was also a *magister militum*, thus having the power once held by the provincial governor through a high military office.
34. Jahn's observations are still valuable: see Jahn 1874, 529.

the hypothesis that Chilperic ruled together with his brothers, because the names listed are explicitly said to be his predecessors, and not his contemporaries.[35]

On the contrary, according to (among others) Anderson, *PLRE, ODLA* and, most recently, Mathisen,[36] the king mentioned in *Ep.* 5.7.1 is to be identified with Chilperic II exclusively by virtue of the interpretation of *tetrarcha* as meaning that the king was one of four sovereigns 'all ruling at the same time', since Chilperic II had three brothers: Gundobad, Godigisel and Godomar.

Further evidence comes from the brief account of the succession to the Burgundian throne provided by Gregory of Tours in his *Historia Francorum*.

> *Fuit igitur et Gundeuechus rex Burgundionum . . . Huic fuerunt quattuor filii: Gundobadus, Godigisilus, Chilpericus et Godomarus. Igitur et Gundobadus Chilperichum fratrem suum interfecit gladio uxoremque eius, ligato ad collum lapide, aquis inmersit. Huius duas filias exilio condemnauit.*[37] (Greg. Tur. *Hist.* 2.28)

In this passage, Gregory of Tours does not mention Chilperic I. The four sons of king Gundioc are named and the first, Gundobad, is said to have brutally 'killed his brother Chilperic II with a sword, and drowned Chilperic's wife with a stone hung around her neck. He then sent his two daughters into exile.' There is no reference, however, to the four brothers all ruling together at any time, and the description provided by Gregory of Tours would not be in contrast with the first theory mentioned above, according to which Gundobad succeeded his uncle Chilperic I. The 'definitive nature' of prosopographical tools, mainly of *PLRE*, granted diffusion of this information, although this theory seems to rely entirely on the interpretation of the word *tetrarcha*.

Furthermore, there are also scholars, like Reydellet and Frye, who believe that the term *tetrarcha* should not be taken seriously.[38] In particular, Reydellet believes that *tetrarcha* is to be intended maliciously as a reference to the tetrarch Herod Antipas or simply as a way to mock Chilperic, and

---

35. Vignier 1575, 13.
36. Anderson 1965, 186 n. 2; *PLRE* 2, s.v. Chilpericus II; *ODLA* s.v. Chilperic II of Burgundy; Mathisen 2020, 87–8.
37. The text in Oldoni's edition was here emended: *ligatu ad collum lapidem* was changed in *ligato ad collum lapide.*
38. According to Frye 1990, 204, Sidonius 'regarded Chilperic's authority as something of a joke'.

that, to this purpose, Sidonius also recalls the series of tyrants that could have become more vicious because of calumniators.[39]

As highlighted in the introduction to *Ep.* 5.6, when it comes to Burgundian rulers, Sidonius' attitude is ambiguous and can only be described as ostentatiously cautious.[40] The awkwardness of referring to Chilperic with the archaic term *tetrarcha* is comparable to that of calling him *magister militum uictoriosissimus* in *Ep.* 5.6.2.[41] A careful reader would have likely perceived it was an unusual way of speaking, but it is difficult to interpret the image of the rulers as openly ironic; it may, rather, be considered as a portrait made of affectedly and studiously prudent language.

A prudent attitude towards the Burgundian rulers would also make sense if *Ep.* 5.7 was in fact originally conceived to be circulated as a pamphlet against informants, but it was also useful for the publication of the collection. Either way, it would not have been sensible to openly mock the same rulers who showed benevolence to Apollinaris, but of course this does not mean that Sidonius could not have been contemptuous privately.[42]

This interpretation may be supported by the similar conclusions reached by Alessandro Fo with regard to the real motive for Sidonius' laudatory references to the Visigoth king Euric in *Ep.* 8.9 to Lampridius. Fo highlights how Sidonius attacks Euric by means of a weft of ambiguous terms, encoded in such a way that only his educated peers would have been able to detect his allegorical tone:[43] the formal deference of the writing would be denied on a deeper level.[44] Even though *Epp.* 5.7 and 8.9 concern two very

---

39. Reydellet 1981, 92–3; see also Saitta 2006, 27. Herod Antipas is called tetrarch of Galilee in Flavius Josephus, *passim*, and also in Christian authors, e.g. Lact. *Inst.* 4.18.6 and Aug. *Cons. euang.* 2.43.91.
40. Furbetta 2014–2015a, 148: 'les comparaisons soulignent la bonté du roi et de son épouse mais introduisent aussi une distance prudente'.
41. An adjective reserved to emperors: see the commentary ad loc.
42. Compare *Ep.* 5.7 to Symmachus 'directly speaking to those who may intercept his correspondence' (Sogno 2006, 63) in *Ep.* 2.12 to Flavianus, which addresses the problem of epistolary espionage and theft of letters.
43. Fo 1999, 20 and 29.
44. Fo 1999, 34: 'L'incensamento tributato al re da Sidonio a livello esplicito si rovescia, grazie alla cornice, nel consueto disprezzo. E abbiamo allora un carme cortigiano di encomio e deferenza, ma confezionato in una struttura a sorpresa che di fatto ne smentisce e rinnega l'orientamento. Tale smentita corre su di un piano inattingibile ai barbari, precisamente anzi proprio sul piano che li separa dai colti romani sconfitti: e cioè il piano del patrimonio culturale.'

different moments in the life of Sidonius[45] and two different rulers (Burgundians and Visigoths), the author's ambiguity and polyvalence of expression seem worthy of comparison.

Even though Chilperic is a barbarian, and as such Sidonius may feel disdain (unspoken) for him, he cannot show overt animosity towards him because at this time Chilperic is an interlocutor, and an ally in protecting Clermont from the repeated incursions of the Visigoths.[46] As observed by Delaplace, already in the invective against Seronatus of *Ep.* 2.1.4 Sidonius seems oriented towards an alliance of the Auvergne aristocracy with the Burgundians when he states that under Ecdicius they are ready to 'renounce their fatherland', and therefore, while being averse to the Visigoths, who are, at this time, legitimate *foederati* of Rome (under both Anthemius and Julius Nepos) Sidonius 'secretly sided with Burgundians' even though he never explicitly says so in his letters.[47]

It seems also important to stress how archaeological findings suggest that Burgundians and Gallo-Romans interacted peacefully at this time, and that for instance the lack of distinctively Burgundian archaeological findings in Lyon can be considered as proof that Burgundian aristocrats were integrated and that even the installation of the Burgundian king in the *praetorium* of Lyon did not have 'structural' consequences, and appears to have been in continuity with the past.[48]

The Burgundian queen

Conflicting information is also found if one looks into the identity of the queen mentioned in this letter. In light of what was said above on the identity of the king, she has been identified either as the spouse of Chilperic I or

---

45. When Sidonius wrote *Ep.* 8.9 he was in exile, and his possessions had been confiscated after Auvergne was given to Euric in 475 in exchange for Provence.

46. As also pointed out by Furbetta 2014–2015a, 148. Sidonius' disdain for Burgundians is openly expressed on other occasions, for instance in *Carm.* 12, where Sidonius manifests deep uneasiness over their unbearable coarseness, on which see Santelia 2019, 296–8; Consolino 2020, 358; Green 2022, 193.

47. Delaplace 2015, 247–9.

48. For archaeological findings suggesting that Burgundians and Romans lived peacefully see e.g. Mercier and Mercier-Rolland 1974, 63; and in particular the monograph by Katalin Escher 2005, 80–9, whom I would like to thank for personally discussing the subject with me.

Chilperic II, and the former seems more probable in light of the meaning of the term *tetrarcha* and of the passage in *LB* 3. Moreover, it seems likely that the queen was Catholic, since in Sidon. *Ep.* 6.12.3 she is said to have praised bishop Patiens' fasts (while her husband enjoyed his feasts).[49]

By those who mention her as wife of Chilperic II (mainly *PLRE*, *ODLA* and, most recently, Mathisen)[50] the queen is said to be known as Caretena; however, this identification is not supported by evidence. In fact, it is arguable that Caretena was the wife of king Gundobad, who succeeded Chilperic I and is said to have killed his brother Chilperic II.[51] Caretena is known for having funded the construction of the basilica of Saint Michael in Lyon, in which she was buried in 506, aged fifty, as is stated in CIL XIII 2372.[52] Therefore, she would have been young (eighteen or nineteen years old) at the dramatic date of *Ep.* 5.7 (474–5). Moreover, there is one source, a passage of the *Vita sancti Marcelli*, which explicitly mentions Caretena as the wife of Gundobad, as pointed out by Dolbeau in the edition of the *uita*, and by Heinzelmann in his *Gallische Prosopographie*.[53] The queen is first named for having invited Marcellus to the inauguration of the basilica of Saint Michel d'Ainay.

> *Itaque dum regina Burgundionum nomine Carathena in honorem beati archangeli Michaelis basilicam miro opere fabricasset et ad dedicandum sanctissimum locum multorum inuitasset praesentiam sacerdotum.* . . (*Vita Marcelli* 9.1)

She is then asked to intercede with her husband to reduce taxes, and she is explicitly mentioned as king Gundobad's spouse (*principis compar, coniux*).

> . . . *nisi ut per christianam principis comparem ad aures Gundebaudi regis sancti uiri suggestio perueniret. Cumque durus eius animus ad praestandum beneficium minime precatu coniugis flecteretur, sanctus uir ad praesentiam eius ualedicturus adueniens.* . .
> (*Vita Marcelli* 9.1–2)

---

49. *Ep.* 6.12.3 *regem praesentem prandia tua, reginam laudare ieiunia.*
50. *PLRE* 2, 260 s.v. Caretena; *ODLA* s.v. Caretena; Mathisen 2020, 87 and 132.
51. See Gregory of Tours as discussed above.
52. = *CLE* 1365, reported also in *PLRE*, *ODLA* and Mathisen 2020. For a detailed analysis of the inscription see Kampers 2000. For context, and in particular for Caretena as Gundobad's spouse, see Kampers 2000, 10.
53. Dolbeau 1984, 124 n. 47. Heinzelmann 1982, 574 s.v. Carathena (Caretena) states in no uncertain terms that the entry in *PLRE* is wrong: 'die Notiz bei *PLRE* wurde korrigiert nach: 1.V. Marcelli . . . 2. *Epitaphium Caretenes*'. On this identification see also Oldoni 1981, 572 n. 121; Wood 1990, 60; Harries 1994, 232; Kaiser 2004, 159.

LETTER 7

Even though this passage gives evidence that the Caretena of the afore-mentioned inscription is not to be identified with the queen in *Ep.* 5.7, it is notable that, a few years apart, under different rulers, the *modus operandi* of Marcellus is analogous to that of Sidonius. They both reach for a Burgundian (Catholic) queen in order to intercede for them, and to approach the king with a request.[54] The image of both kings is also similar: Gundobad's *duritia* mirrors Chilperic's *iracundia* in Sidonius' *Ep.* 5.6. Gundobad, however, is even more unmerciful than his predecessor, since, unlike Chilperic, his *durus animus* is not persuaded by his spouse's prayers.

The features of the rulers in *Ep.* 5.7

The king and the queen (*Ep.* 5.7.7) are never named directly but through two historical royal couples, belonging to different times: Lucumo (Tarquinius Priscus) and Tanaquil; Germanicus and Agrippina the Elder. This choice, once again, is rather unusual.

The mention of the Burgundian kingdom as *Germania Lugdunensis* cannot go unnoticed, and neither can the reference to the Etruscan kings, foreign rulers of Romans, just like Chilperic and his queen. The change, though presented as a natural continuity with the past, is still a radical change, immediately perceivable also when considering the way Sidonius addresses Chilperic.

Unlike that of the queen, the portrait of Chilperic is unflattering, although subtly so. See for instance the long list of negative exempla (*Ep.* 5.7.6) of the most famous bad rulers, who could have become even worse had they been influenced by the same informers: the underlying message is that Chilperic may have been one of them. The image that emerges is that of a man who is prey to his cunning court; like Ammianus' Constantius, he is easily manipulated, and not only by nefarious informants but also by his spouse, who is able to change his mind. To this end, the mention of him as Lucumo is most evocative, since it indicates that the queen, as a new Tanaquil, has great influence over him. As stated above, Sidonius' ability in mastering the models allows him to allude to a specific version of the myth

---

54. As Kaiser 2004, 152 points out, while Gundobad, for instance, is known to have been an Arian, all Burgundian queens are known to have been Catholic, including the *anonyma* of *Ep.* 5.7 and Gundobad's wife, Caretena.

about the Etruscan kings, that is, Livy's portrait of Tanaquil as a sly and most capable politician, who leads Tarquinius on and personally oversees the succession.

If the comparison with Germanicus seems mostly tied to the word game with *Germania Lugdunensis*, so that 'a German Germanicus rules over Germany' (but as shown in the commentary there may be more to this mention) the couple is, as that of the Etruscan kings, well balanced, and the mention of Agrippina confirms an overall positive image of the Burgundian queen as a strong-willed and powerful leader.

Dating elements

The position of *Ep.* 5.7 in the book is strictly dependent on the fact that this letter is intended to be read right after *Ep.* 5.6, which provides context, and constitutes a *terminus post quem* for the events of *Ep.* 5.7. As stated in the introduction to *Ep.* 5.6, Julius Nepos became emperor in June 474, and the mention of him as a *nouus princeps* in *Ep.* 5.6.2, together with the seasonal reference to autumn at the very beginning of the letter, allow us to date the events of *Ep.* 5.6 to autumn 474.

In *Ep.* 5.7 Julius Nepos is still a *nouus princeps*, but there are no further dating elements which could lead to the inference of a dramatic date, apart from the insistent mention of the Burgundian king through images of regality, while in *Ep.* 5.6 he is called *magister militum*. Some time must have passed in order for Sidonius to gather information and intercede for Apollinaris, and one could consider a time span between the end of 474 and 475 as a possible dramatic date for the events. Loyen precisely dates the letter to October 474, although there is no evidence to ascertain how long it took Sidonius to exonerate Apollinaris.[55]

Also worthy of mention is Furbetta's suggestion that the date of composition of both *Epp.* 5.6 and 5.7 is probably chronologically close to that of the publication of Book 5.[56] This consideration leads to further reflection on the date of composition, and on that of revision of *Ep.* 5.7 for publication, as the dates do not necessarily coincide with the dramatic date of the letter. One cannot exclude, therefore, that the mention of the Burgundian

---

55. Loyen 1970a, 256.
56. Furbetta 2014–2015a, 147.

king as *patronus communis* and the recognition of his role in *Ep.* 5.7 are tied to the publication of Books 1–7 in 477, rather than to the dramatic date of 474–5. As stated above, it can be argued that Sidonius' sympathy for the Burgundians significantly grew over time, and with cause, since in 475 Clermont was ceded to the Visigoths.[57]

57. Delaplace 2015, 249–50.

SIDONIUS THAUMASTO SUO SALUTEM

1. Indagauimus tandem, qui apud tetrarcham nostrum germani tui et e diuerso partium noui principis amicitias criminarentur, si tamen fidam sodalium sagacitatem clandestina delatorum non fefellere uestigia. Hi nimirum sunt, ut idem coram positus audisti, quos se iamdudum perpeti inter clementiores barbaros Gallia gemit. Hi sunt, quos timent etiam qui timentur. Hi sunt, quos haec peculiariter prouincia manet, inferre calumnias, deferre personas, afferre minas, auferre substantias.

2. Hi sunt, quorum laudari audis in otio occupationes, in pace praedas, inter arma fugas, inter uina uictorias. Hi sunt qui causas morantur adhibiti, impediunt praetermissi, fastidiunt admoniti, obliuiscuntur locupletati. Hi sunt, qui emunt lites, uendunt intercessiones, deputant arbitros, iudicanda dictant, dictata conuellunt, attrahunt litigaturos, protrahunt audiendos, trahunt addictos, retrahunt transigentes. Hi sunt, quos si petas etiam nullo aduersante beneficium, piget promittere, pudet negare, paenitet praestitisse.

3. Hi sunt, quorum comparationi digitum tollerent Narcissus, Asiaticus, Massa, Marcellus, Carus, Parthenius, Licinius et Pallas. Hi sunt, qui inuident tunicatis otia, stipendia paludatis, uiatica ueredariis, mercatoribus nundinas, munuscula legatis, portoria quadruplatoribus, praedia prouincialibus, flamonia municipibus, arcariis pondera, mensuras allectis, salaria tabulariis, dispositiones numerariis, praetorianis sportulas, ciuitatibus indutias, uectigalia publicanis, reuerentiam clericis, originem nobilibus, consessum prioribus, congressum aequalibus, cinctis iura, discinctis priuilegia, scholas instituendis, mercedes instituentibus, litteras institutis.

§ 1 manet α *LMP* : meret *T*

§ 3 ueredariis α *MP* : ueraedariis *L*

LETTER 7

SIDONIUS TO HIS DEAR THAUMASTUS

1. At last, we hunted out the men who before our allied king denounced the friendly relationship between your brother and on the other hand the side of the new emperor's supporters – at least if the hidden tracks of the informers did not escape the trustworthy sense of smell of our companions. They are definitely, as you yourself have heard in person, those that Gaul laments having been forced to tolerate for some time among the milder barbarians. They are those who even the feared fear. They are those who have the particular assignment of bringing false accusations, of denouncing people, of posing threats, of confiscating possessions.

2. They are those whom you hear praised for their activity in leisure time, looting in periods of peace, flight in wartime, victories amidst wine. They are those who delay lawsuits once they are called as witness, those who hinder when left out, are haughty when admonished, forgetful once enriched. They are those who buy court cases, sell interventions, appoint judges, dictate verdicts, subvert orders, attract quarrelsome men, who delay those who are to be heard, who draw away those condemned and draw back those who are striking a deal. They are those who, if you ask a favour, even though nobody opposes, are reluctant to make promises, ashamed to refuse, and who repent of having made themselves available.

3. They are those in comparison with whom Narcissus, Asiaticus, Massa, Marcellus, Carus, Parthenius, Licinius and Pallas would admit defeat. They are those who envy those at leisure their idleness, soldiers their wages, messengers their rations, merchants their market days, letter-carriers their small presents, taxers their tolls, country-dwellers their estates, town-dwellers their offices as flamen, bankers their weights, collectors their measures, accountants their salaries, bookkeepers their dispositions, functionaries of the prefect's office their tips, cities their tax extensions, tax gatherers their imposts, clergymen their esteem, nobles their ancestry, superiors the right to a seat, equals their assemblies, officials their regulations, retired officials their privileges, students their schools, teachers their wages, learned men their education.

SIDONIUS: LETTERS BOOK 5, PART 1

4. Hi sunt, qui nouis opibus ebrii, ut et minima cognoscas, per utendi intemperantiam produnt imperitiam possidendi; nam libenter incedunt armati ad epulas, albati ad exsequias, pelliti ad ecclesias, pullati ad nuptias, castorinati ad laetanias. Nullum illis genus hominum, ordinum, temporum cordi est. In foro Scythae, in cubiculo uiperae, in conuiuio scurrae, in exactionibus Harpyiae, in conlocutionibus statuae, in quaestionibus bestiae, in tractatibus cocleae, in contractibus trapezitae; ad intellegendum saxei, ad iudicandum lignei, ad succensendum flammei, ad ignoscendum ferrei, ad amicitias pardi, ad facetias ursi, ad fallendum uulpes, ad superbiendum tauri, ad consumendum minotauri.

5. Spes firmas in rerum motibus habent, dubia tempora certius amant, et ignauia pariter conscientiaque trepidantes, cum sint in praetoriis leones, in castris lepores, timent foedera, ne discutiantur, bella, ne pugnent. Quorum si nares afflauerit uspiam robiginosi aura marsupii, confestim uidebis illic et oculos Argi et manus Briarei et Sphingarum ungues et periuria Laomedontis et Ulixis argutias et Sinonis fallacias et fidem Polymestoris et pietatem Pygmalionis adhiberi.

6. His moribus obruunt uirum non minus bonitate quam potestate praestantem. Sed quid faciat unus, undique uenenato uallatus interprete? Quid, inquam, faciat, cui natura cum bonis, uita cum malis est? Ad quorum consilia Phalaris cruentior, Mida cupidior, Ancus iactantior, Tarquinius superbior, Tiberius callidior, Gaius periculosior, Claudius socordior, Nero impurior, Galba auarior, Otho audacior, Vitellius sumptuosior, Domitianus truculentior, redderetur.

7. Sane, quod principaliter medetur afflictis, temperat Lucumonem nostrum Tanaquil sua et aures mariti uirosa susurronum faece completas opportunitate salsi sermonis eruderat. Cuius studio factum scire uos par est, nihil interim quieti fratrum communium apud animum communis patroni iuniorum Cibyratarum uenena nocuisse neque quicquam deo propitiante nocitura, si modo, quamdiu praesens potestas Lugdunensem Germaniam regit, nostrum suumque Germanicum praesens Agrippina moderetur. Vale.

---

§ 4 letanias α : lętanias *MP* : litanias *L*
succensendum α *MP* : suscensendum *L*

§ 7 factum *super lineam* M[1] : *omisit Sirmond* : <o> factum! *coniecit Warmington*

LETTER 7

4. They are those who, intoxicated by their new wealth (to make you aware even of the most trivial details), reveal their inexperience in its possession through immoderation in its usage. For instance, they willingly attend feasts armed, funerals clothed in white, churches clad in skins, weddings garbed in mourning, litanies clothed in beaver fur. They do not value any type of men, rank or occasion. They are Scythians in the forum, vipers in the bedroom, buffoons at banquets, Harpies in exaction, statues in conversation, beasts in disputes, snails in discussions, moneylenders in transactions; they are like stones to understand, like logs in pronouncing judgement, like fire in anger, like iron in forgiving, like leopards in friendships, like bears in witticisms, like foxes in deceits, like bulls in arrogance and like minotaurs in eating.

5. They have strong expectations from uprisings, they enjoy with most certainty uncertain times, being equally nervous from cowardice and from a bad conscience, since they are lions at court, hares in the encampment, fearful of treaties they might have to break and wars they might have to fight. If somewhere the scent of a rusty pouch blows to their nose, in that case you will see, at once, the eyes of Argus, the hands of Briareus, the claws of Sphinxes, the perjuries of Laomedon, the slyness of Ulysses, the deceits of Sinon, the trustworthiness of Polymestor and the loyalty of Pygmalion.

6. Through these behaviours they overwhelm a man who excels in kindness no less than in authority. And yet, what could a single man do, surrounded on all sides by venomous intermediaries? What, I say, could one do, one whose nature is to be in the company of honest men but life puts among evil ones? If exposed to these men's counsels, Phalaris would have become more blood-thirsty, Midas more greedy, Ancus more ambitious, Tarquinius more proud, Tiberius more cunning, Gaius more dangerous, Claudius more sluggish, Nero more vile, Galba more avaricious, Otho more reckless, Vitellius more lavish, Domitian more ferocious.

7. However, and this is of immediate comfort to those aggrieved, our Lucumo is tempered by his Tanaquil, and she cleanses the ears of her husband, filled with the poisonous trash of blabbermouths, through her timely and sharp conversation. It is right that you should know the outcome thanks to her support: that the poisons of these junior Cibyratae in the meantime have done no damage to the serenity of our common brothers in the mind of our common protector, and, God willing, not a thing will harm them, or at least as long as the present ruler governs Germania Lugdunensis and as long as the present Agrippina shall temper her, and our, Germanicus. Farewell.

Commentary

§ 1

Indagauimus tandem: This opening *in medias res* is unusual but most fitting if one reads *Ep.* 5.7 immediately after 5.6. It is as if the reader is waiting to know the developments of a situation already explained in the previous letter; therefore, the place *Ep.* 5.7 has in the collection creates meaning that would otherwise be absent. Sidonius immediately relates that he has 'hunted out' the slanderers: the verb *indagare* is in the strictest sense suggestive of hunting (*TLL* 7.1.1104 s.v. *indago* 63, by Nelz, *proprie de uenatione*), just like *sagacitas* in the following clause, as is highlighted by Gualandri 1979, 132. Compare the occurrence, with a similar meaning, in Cic. *Ver.* 2.2.135 *indagare et odorari solebat*, a description of Timarchides, Verres' *longa manus*, skilful at 'hunting out and smelling out whatever had happened in the province'. It is notable that also in Cicero's passage *indagare* and *odorari* evoke a hunting scene. The verb also occurs in Sidon. *Ep.* 6.4.2 (*seriem totius indagare uiolentiae*), when the author asks Lupus to meet the parties face to face in order to investigate a crime. In Sidon. *Ep.* 9.3.2 *secretum omne gerulorum peruigil explorator indagat*, it is the sender and the addressee Faustus who should be wary, because letter-bearers are searched, hence it would be wise not to exchange letters at all. A more pleasant context is that of *Ep.* 9.9.6, also addressed to Faustus. In this case it is Sidonius who, by chance, has come across Faustus' works, which had not been sent to him, and is uncertain whether to be glad he discovered the books (*uel quid indagasse me gaudeam*), or angry at Faustus for concealing them from him (*uel quid te celasse succenseam*). The first two words of *Ep.* 5.7 create a cretic spondee: see the General Introduction for the prose rhythm of this paragraph.

apud tetrarcham nostrum: Chilperic is never mentioned by name in this letter. In §7 he is also called *Lucumo noster, patronus communis* and *Germanicus noster*; compare also the previous mention of Chilperic as *magister militum uictoriosissimus* in *Ep.* 5.6.2. *Tetrarcha* is not known to occur elsewhere in *iunctura* with the possessive adjective; see the introduction to this letter for an overview of scholarly speculation on its meaning. As stated by Anderson 1965, 186 n. 2: 'in the imperial times of Rome, the word tetrarch meant a dependent prince; or a ruler of part only of a kingdom; or ruler of a very small territory'. The word usually concerned specifically eastern provinces:

it is attested with this meaning for instance in Cicero (e.g. *Dom.* 60; *Att.* 2.9.1; *Phil.* 11.31); in Caesar *Ciu.* 3.3.2 Deiotarus is called *tetrarches Gallograeciae*; in Lucan 7.226–8 tetrarchs, kings (*tetrarchae regesque*), tyrants and all those who wear purple are subdued to Rome's force. See also the tetrarchs of regions neighbouring Syria mentioned in Tac. *Ann.* 15.25, and Symm. *Rel.* 9.3 (*ut pro captiuis tetrarchis Indicae currum beluae praeuenirent*), a reference to the undeserved and spectacular triumphs of previous emperors, where, instead of defeated kings taken prisoner, elephants preceded the triumphator's chariot, on which see commentary by Vera 1981, 83 and 86. In Prudentius' *Cathemerinon* 6.69 the more frequently attested variant *tetrarches* is used to refer to Joseph holding a position of power at the Egyptian court, as in more ancient sources. It seems reasonable to assert that in this case as well the term did not indicate an – otherwise unattested – division of power between four Burgundian rulers, but instead was an elaborate and affected way to designate a minor king subject to Rome. Sidonius' preference for unusual words as well as his preference for ambiguous expressions (in both *Epp.* 5.6 and 5.7) are coherent with his choice to employ this noun. In light of the meaning of the word *tetrarcha*, in this commentary the ruler has been identified with Chilperic I rather than Chilperic II; for detailed bibliographical references see the introduction to *Ep.* 5.7.

germani tui: Thaumastus and Apollinaris are brothers by blood. By referring to Apollinaris as Thaumastus' *germanus*, Sidonius mirrors *Ep.* 5.6.1 *Thaumastum, germanum tuum*. See also the introduction to *Ep.* 5.3.

et e diuerso partium noui principis amicitias criminarentur: It has been pointed out by Mathisen 2013a, 243 (and also Mathisen 2014, 211) that the same wording occurs in *Ep.* 5.6.2 *partibus noui principis*. See the commentary on *Ep.* 5.6.2 for the meaning of this expression and Hanaghan 2019, 114–15 for Sidonius' reluctance to mention Julius Nepos by name. Mentioning a Burgundian as 'our *tetrarcha*' and Julius Nepos in both letters simply as 'the new emperor' feels surrealistic and is due to careful choice of language (see introduction). Moreover, the syntagma *criminor amicitias* is not known to occur elsewhere. This passage is mentioned in *TLL* 4.1198 s.v. *criminor* 63 (by Burger) as being among the occurrences of the verb with the accusative, though it should be pointed out that it could be moved there from section '3 a' to section '3 c: *aliquid apud aliquem*' in light of the presence of *apud tetrarcham nostrum* in this text.

si tamen fidam sodalium sagacitatem: Sidonius informs Thaumastus that he previously sent trustworthy friends on the hunt, in order to uncover the identity of the Burgundian informants. Gualandri 1979, 132 has pointed out how the term *sagacitas* specifically pertains to the semantic sphere of hunting and in particular to the sense of smell of hounds. For the *sagacitas canum* see e.g. Cic. *N.D.* 2.151 and 158; Sen. *Ben.* 2.29.1; Sen. *Ep.* 76.8; and the bucolic setting of Symm. *Ep.* 3.23. In *Ep.* 2.9.2 Sidonius benevolently calls himself a prey of *sagacissimi exploratores*, the cleverest scouts, sent out from Apollinaris and Ferreolus' estates to intercept him and be the first to invite him. The description of these scouts, setting out 'traps of kindness' even on the most impervious paths, is also reminiscent of a hunting scene, albeit a positive one. Sidonius' and his companions' search for evidence, on the tracks of the informers, is therefore vividly described as a hunting scene, and to the same figurative language is here related the verb *indagauimus* at the beginning of the letter. Sidonius often refers to his close friends with the term *sodales*, which also conveys the idea of fraternity, defining those who share a bond of affection and also intellectual ties (see e.g. comments in Amherdt 2001, 221 and for it being a 'technical word' see Santelia 2002a, 65). *Sodalis* occurs in Sidonius' *Letters* and in his *Carmina* as frequently as it does in Cicero, despite Sidonius' works being considerably shorter than Cicero's surviving works; it has more than thirty occurrences (e.g. Sidon. *Epp.* 1.5.2, 1.10.1, 3.13.10, 4.14.4, 5.11.1, 8.6.10 and, in particular *Carm.* 24.3–4, his *libellus* is being sent *ad sodales, / quorum nomina sedulus notaui*) while it rarely occurs in Pliny the Younger and Symmachus.

clandestina delatorum non fefellere uestigia: The informants are sly and covered their tracks, so that Sidonius hopes that his trusted 'hounds' were not misled. As is pointed out by Bellès 1998, 107, the mention of tracks (*uestigia*) is well suited to the idea of an underlying imagery of hunting. Although this syntagma is not known to occur elsewhere, cf. Ammianus 29.3.8 *ne uestigia quidem ulla delatorum reperta sunt criminum*. When describing the numerous atrocities attributable to Valentinian, the historian states that, despite the tortures inflicted, no traces of the reported crimes were found. The perfect in *-ere* seems to be favoured in order to create a double cretic clausula.

Hi nimirum sunt . . . quos: This phrase introduces a long negative portrait of informers, which covers most of the letter, from § 1 to § 5. This description is marked by the anaphorical repetition of *hi sunt* + relative, which

LETTER 7

imparts a pressing pace to the text, in a way Furbetta 2013, 35 effectively described as 'obsessive'. A similar syntagma is notably attested in Cic. *Ver.* 2.4.31, in the description of Verres' henchmen from Cibyra, a passage Sidonius explicitly refers to in § 7 (see commentary ad loc.). According to Loyen 1970a, 235, Sidonius avails himself of the declamatory style 'avec beaucoup de rhétorique et de mauvais goût'. Anaphorical repetitions are a common feature of declamatory speeches, as summarised, for instance, by the anonymous author of the *Rhetorica ad Herennium* (4.19), who considers anaphora (*repetitio*) praiseworthy in light of its *uenustas, grauitas* and *acrimonia*, elements which make it suitable *et ad ornandam et ad exaugendam orationem.* In Tac. *Ag.* 34 (*hi sunt, quos . . . clamore debellastis; hi ceterorum Britannorum fugacissimi . . .*) the anaphora *hi sunt* + relative occurs in Agricola's impassioned speech before battle, where it introduces deprecating remarks on some tribes of Britons, described as accustomed to fleeing, in a context of denigration somewhat analogous to that of Sidonius: having previously attacked a legion, they had been beaten 'by a shout'. Sidonius himself employs the same rhetorical device in a laudatory context in *Ep.* 7.7.2 to bishop Graecus; in that passage, however, the anaphora effectively marks the rhythm of a moving description of the Arverni's courage in withstanding the Goths' attacks. See van Waarden 2010, 352 on the marked increase in the use of the phrase *hi sunt qu** in later Latin; for the context of *Ep.* 7.7.2 see also Mratschek 2013, 263. Compare the similar convincing purpose of Augustine *In Psalm.* 71.5 *nimirum ergo hi sunt quos alius habet psalmus*, which, incidentally, is the only passage of another author known to include the adverb *nimirum* in the syntagma. Sidonius also employs the expression in *Ep.* 9.14.4 to Burgundio, with the sole purpose of providing a definition of palindromes (*hi nimirum sunt recurrentes, qui metro stante . . .*), on which see Condorelli 2020a, 451. A similar rhetorical device is in Apuleius *Apol.* 74.5–7, in a savage invective against Herennius Rufinus, accused of having personally hired advocates and bribed witnesses in order to 'light the fire' of the accusation against the author. For its being a model for Sidonius and for further context see the introduction; see also the commentary on *Ep.* 5.6.2 *tuo praecipue machinatu.*

ut idem coram positus audisti: This phrase, 'as you yourself have heard in person', indicates that Sidonius has confirmed what Thaumastus had heard from someone else, or that they had already discussed the same in person. The latter option has been suggested also by Anderson 1965, 187 n. 4, who, according to Warmington, proposed the readings 'heard from my lips' and 'heard on the spot'. The possibility that Sidonius and Thaumastus had already discussed what was about to be written seems worthy of further reflection, even though the obscurity of the expression is an obstacle which cannot be overcome. And yet, the detail of Thaumastus having already heard what Sidonius is about to lay out is useful to confirm that the text is more of a display piece, rather than a real source of information for Thaumastus. Note that the choice of the shortened form, *audisti*, answers the purpose of creating a paeon IV spondee clausula.

se iamdudum perpeti inter clementiores barbaros Gallia gemit: This passage is ambiguous and open to interpretation. It could either mean that the informants are barbarians, worse than their 'milder' fellow barbarians, or that they are Gallo-Romans, fiercer than the 'milder barbarians', i.e. the Burgundians. Calling Burgundians *clementiores barbari* – a *iunctura* which does not have previous attestations – seems an accurate representation of how Sidonius perceives their presence. The bishop relies on their support to defend Clermont, and at this moment they are an important political ally, but they still remain barbarians to him. Both Anderson and Warmington are inclined to interpret this as evidence that the slanderers were 'Gallo-Roman self seekers', considered to be worse than barbarians (Anderson 1965, 187 n. 5). Loyen 1970a, 235 is of the same opinion, as also Mathisen 1993, 74–5. The non-stop oscillation between tepid praises, exaggerated (and awkward) mentions of their rulers, and the bluntness of an expression like *clementiores barbari* make this ostentatiously ambiguous piece also studiously cautious.

Hi sunt, quos timent etiam qui timentur: The slanderers are said to be dangerous, to the point that even those who are usually feared, fear them. This image is coherent with the feral portrait of informants.

Hi sunt, quos haec peculiariter prouincia manet: *Manet* is the reading of α*LMP*, and is left in the text in accordance with the choice of previous editors. *Meret* is the reading of *T*, a mistake easily explainable on palaeographical grounds. Baret 1878, 325 mentions (adding: *ut opinor, recte*) the reading *moeret* attested in von der Woweren's edition (1598, 108); however, the meaning 'to lament or mourn' does not seem coherent with the context (Loyen wrongly lists *maeret* as Baret's own reading). *Manet* in § 1 is considered to have the meaning of *est* in *TLL* 10.2.2339 s.v. *prouincia* (*usu laxiore*) 66–7 (by Kruse). Therefore, it is translated here as 'have the particular assignment': it is as if 'the duty' of being treacherous falls on them. *Prouincia*

LETTER 7

defined an official duty (cf. the commentary on *Ep.* 5.1.2), but here, with a deliberately comic effect, it introduces a list or reprehensible behaviours. The word *prouincia* is attested humorously in numerous contexts in Latin (as attested in *OLD* s.v. *prouincia,* 1658), see e.g. Plautus *Capt.* 474, where buying provisions is said to have been a *parasitorum prouincia*; and Cic. *Cael.* 63, in which Cicero discredits witnesses who had taken upon themselves the *prouincia* of 'lurking in baths' (*ut in balneas contruderentur*), on which see Dyck 2013, 155.

inferre calumnias, deferre personas, afferre minas, auferre substantias: The series is characterised by the occurrence of four compounds of *fero* + four feminine first declension accusative plural nouns. It can be argued that the echoing sound effects created by this *accumulatio* mirror and amplify what is being said, effectively conveying the brutality of the actions mentioned. Sidonius' choice to exclusively use compounds of *fero* also results in the occurrence of unattested and rare expressions. In particular, before Sidonius, the syntagma *inferre calumnias* occurs only in Augustine's *Collatio cum Maximino 7 non decet in religione . . . calumniam inferre.* While the syntagma *deferre personas* is not known to occur elsewhere, *afferre minas* previously occurs in the very different context of Sen. *Nat.* 1.6.1. *Auferre substantias* is an uncommon expression (with less than ten known occurrences) and is exclusively attested in late Latin, e.g. Tert. *De carnis resurrectione* 62 and Rufin. *Orig. in Num.* 6.2. See the General Introduction, in the section on prose rhythm, for the metrical clausulae in this passage.

§ 2

Hi sunt, quorum laudari audis in otio occupationes: Being praised for one's *occupationes in otio* is an oxymoronic locution, introducing a series of antithetical contrapositions which concern the whole paragraph. An effective, although positive, example is Aug. *Ep.* 95.9, in which the author says he thought Paulinus of Nola would have been *in otio,* but he heard instead that he is busy with *occupationes incredibiles.* Geisler 1887, 366 suggests a comparison with Sidon. *Ep.* 1.5.11 *occupatissimam uacationem,* in which the author ironically says he intends to speak of the difficulties he encountered whenever 'the most busy holiday' of the whole city will be over. Geisler also suggests this expression be compared to Plin. *Ep.* 9.6.4 *dies . . . quos alii otiosissimis occupationibus perdunt,* a wry description of horse races, for

213

which Pliny does not share his fellow citizens' enthusiasm. See also Köhler 1995, 215. The context of *Ep.* 5.7.2, is not, strictly speaking, similar to the other contexts mentioned, and the tone is even more fiercely polemical. A different context is also that of Sidon. *Carm.* 23.484 *laudandam reor occupationem*, in which spending time with his friends is said to be a good way of passing time.

in pace praedas, inter arma fugas, inter uina uictorias: These syntagmata picture the informants as cowards, who are keen on looting in periods of peace, who flee the battlefield and can win only drinking competitions. As stated in the introduction to this letter, attacks concerning someone's cowardice were standard themes of invective. Similar is Sidonius' assertion in § 5 *cum sint in praetoriis leones, in castris lepores* (see commentary below).

Hi sunt qui causas morantur adhibiti: This is the first of a list of interferences in the judicial system carried out by the informants, who clearly have a position of power which allows them to be manipulative and to delay trials when called to testify. For *adhibiti* specifically meaning 'called in as witnesses' see *TLL* 1.642 s.v. *adhibeo* 79–82 (by Prinz); *OLD*, s.v. 45. For informants interfering with trials see the introduction to this letter.

impediunt praetermissi, fastidiunt admoniti: These expressions, not known to occur in other contexts, are a direct way of picturing the informants in absolute control of courtrooms.

obliuiscuntur locupletati: These men are also easily bribed, and paying them will make them 'forgetful' in favour of the briber.

Hi sunt, qui emunt lites . . . retrahunt transigentes: Kelly pointed out that even though the primary effect of this section of the letter comes from 'the dazzling lexical display', clausulation has an important role, since it helps to mark 'what seem to be the natural groupings of these short phrases' as if it is part of the punctuation (van Waarden and Kelly 2020, 473). In particular, Kelly (ibid.) highlights how there are regular clausulae at *deputant arbitros* (double cretic), *dictata conuellunt* (cretic spondee), *protrahunt audiendos* (cretic ditrochee) and *retrahunt transigentes* (cretic or anapaest ditrochee).

LETTER 7

Hi sunt, qui emunt lites: The informants are accused of buying court cases. The expression *emere lites* is not known to occur frequently in Latin, though it is, interestingly, attested in Plautus (and, what is more, preceded by *hi sunt qui*), in Milphio's address to deceitful lawyers who are wont to invent litigation, in Plaut. *Poen.* 587 *hi sunt qui, si nihil est quicum litigent, lites emunt.* On this passage, see Mendelsohn 1907, 106; of the same opinion is Moodie 2015, 139. A similar context is that of Cic. *Clu.* 36 (102) *Oppianicum iudici ad emendas sententias dedisse pecuniam.*

uendunt intercessiones: This expression is previously attested exclusively in Maximus of Turin *Sermo* 26.4 (in which, however, it concerns clerical appropriation of widows' properties); in Sidonius it depicts men as guilty of commodification of sentences.

deputant arbitros, iudicanda dictant, dictata conuellunt: These men dictate verdicts and at the same time subvert previous judgements; it is clear that courtrooms are under their control. Note that the passage is characterised by the polyptoton *dictant, dictata.*

attrahunt litigaturos . . . retrahunt transigentes: Symmetrically, Sidonius chooses to list four compounds of *traho*, as he did before with *fero* (see § 1), a rhetorical device which gives rhythm and instils a sense of anticipation for the list of misdeeds. When reading the series *attrahunt litigaturos, protrahunt audiendos, trahunt addictos, retrahunt transigentes*, the rolling sound produced by the rhotic and by the two dental consonants amplifies the meaning of the words. These syntagmata are not known to have previous occurrences, with the sole exception of *trahere addictos*, which occurs in – the very different context – of Prop. 3.11.2, a declaration of submission to the loved woman.

si petas etiam nullo aduersante beneficium: *Nullo aduersante* is not a common expression, and is previously attested notably in Tacitus *Ann.* 1.2.1, where it concerns Octavianus' unhindered accession to power.

piget promittere, pudet negare, paenitet praestitisse: The first and last syntagmata are Sidonian, while *pudet negare* has previous occurrences in Seneca rhetor *Contr.* 7.8.4 and Martial 4.12.1–2, two passages which, however, are not relatable to Sidonius' context, since they both concern

215

confessions of an erotic nature. Note that the tricolon is constituted by three impersonal verbs all beginning with the same letter.

§ 3

Hi sunt, quorum comparationi digitum tollerent: *Digitum tollere* was an effective way of registering bids during public auctions. With this meaning, the occurrence in Sidon. *Ep.* 5.7.3 is mentioned in *TLL* 5.1.1127 s.v. *digitus* 9 (by Rubenbauer) together with Cic. *Ver.* 2.1.141 *digitum tollit Iunius patruus* (on which see Mitchell 1986, 218) and Ambr. *Ep.* 2.7.17. And yet, although Sidonius' use of the expression is certainly metaphorical, in this letter it does not concern, strictly speaking, an auction (as in Cicero and Ambrose) as much as a competition of wickedness which the informants would easily win. For this reason, the passage has been translated in accordance with the definition provided by Anderson 1965, 189 n. 3, where lifting up a finger is considered as 'polite recognition of superiority or admission of defeat'. The same interpretation is mirrored by Loyen's translation (Loyen 1970a, 184): 's'avoueraient vaincus'.

Narcissus, Asiaticus, Massa, Marcellus, Carus, Parthenius, Licinius et Pallas: This is the first time Sidonius resorts to historical exempla in the letter (as he will do also in § 6 and § 7). It seems worthy of notice that the 'slanderers' Sidonius mentions all operate in a time span which goes from 31 BC to AD 96, from Augustus to Domitian: the same chronological span covered by the Roman bad rulers who constitute another list in § 6 and, in particular, Claudius, Nero, Vitellius and Domitian, for which see also the similar occurrences in the *Carmina* (in the commentary on § 6). It seems that when it comes to providing exempla, Sidonius has in mind this specific period of Roman history from which he is comfortable to draw negative images, probably in compliance with Tacitus, Suetonius and Ausonius (see the commentary on § 6). Mentioning this as simply a catalogue of 'powerful freedmen', as already in Sirmond's *Notae ad Sidonium* 1614, 92 ('Caesariani omnes liberti, prauo ingenio, delationumque infamia clari'), and later in Anderson 1965, 188 n. 2 and Loyen 1970a 236 n. 16, would be to over-simplify the complex and layered catalogue provided by Sidonius in this passage. As pointed out by Rivière 2002, 387, Sidonius is listing the names of personalities who can be called *delatores* with good reason (i.e. Massa, Marcellus and Carus) together with the names of freedmen who had a pivotal role in schemes and political plots. And yet, they all serve Sidonius' purpose well, because to him there is no difference between *delatores* in fiscal and political trials and powerful statesmen. The names mentioned as exempla of wickedness, attested as such already in satire (mainly Martial and Juvenal) and in historical accounts (Tacitus in particular), are consciously juxtaposed to create a negative ideal of nastiness, surpassed by the new *delatores* he has to deal with. On the use of historical exempla in Sidonius see the introduction to this letter and Mratschek 2020, 239–40. However, the plots and *delationes* of the characters mentioned were certainly much superior to the crimes of these contemporary informants, to the point that it is legitimate to suggest that Sidonius' *accumulatio*, filled with overabundant erudition, creates a feeling of awkwardness in the reader, who is aware that these informants (later described as gauche and graceless even in dressing) could *not* compete with their notorious predecessors. See also Rivière 2002, 389. The list of four names is divided in two by the cretic spondee clausula (at *Massa Marcellus*) and closed by the paeon IV spondee clausula (at *-cinius et Pallas*). See the General Introduction for the prose rhythm in this paragraph. **Narcissus**: An influential freedman holding the position *ab epistulis* under emperor Claudius (Suet. *Cl.* 28.1), Narcissus is known to have been personally involved in politics (Dio 60.19.2) and, in league with Messalina, to have removed powerful senators, before persuading Claudius to have Messalina killed, as can be surmised from Tac. *Ann.* 11.33–5; Sen. *Nat.* 4a. *praef.* 15; and, in particular on his role in Messalina's death, Tac. *Ann.* 11.37–8. As pointed out by Rutledge 2001, 31, Tacitus presents Narcissus' denunciation of Messalina as a *delatio*, in which not only did Narcissus play the role of *delator* but he also recruited others to play *delatores*, such as Calpurnia and Cleopatra (who testify before Claudius in Tac. *Ann.* 11.30). For his *delatio*, Narcissus was promptly rewarded after Messalina's death, as stated in Tac. *Ann.* 11.38; see also Juvenal 14.329–31. Lastly, in light of the mention of Narcissus in Sidonius' letter, it seems worthy of mention that, according to Dio Cassius 61.34.5 (Xiph. 146, 5–15 R. St.), Narcissus kept *libelli* of accusation which he later burned after Claudius' death; on this, see Millar 1967, 15. For further biographical information on Narcissus see *RE* s.v. Narcissus 1, by Stein; *DNP* s.v. Narcissus II 1, by W. Eck; and *OCD* s.v. Narcissus 2. **Asiaticus**: This freedman of Vitellius is said to have exercised great influence over him; see his unflattering description in Tac. *Hist.* 2.57 *foedum mancipium et malis artibus ambitiosum* ('a disgusting slave who sought power by wicked intrigues'). Tacitus also states that Asiaticus, among others, sought promotion not by integrity but by 'glutting

Vitellius' insatiable appetite' for *libidines* (*Hist.* 2.95). See *PIR²* A 1216. **Massa**: A renowned slanderer who operated under Vespasian and was of equestrian rank. Juvenal 1.35 *quem Massa timet* ('one whom even Massa fears'), seems to be echoed by Sidonius in § 1 *quos timent etiam qui timentur*. Massa is also mentioned as exemplum of rapacity in Martial 12.28.2; moreover, Tacitus *Hist.* 4.50 depicts him as *optimo cuique exitiosus* ('ruinous even to the best men'), and states his name is to reappear often among the causes of evils of the time. Massa was later accused of misconduct under Domitian, one of the prosecutors being Pliny the Younger, who mentions the trial in *Epp.* 3.4.4–6 and 6.29.8, and gives a detailed account to Tacitus in *Ep.* 7.33.4–8. For biographical details see prosopographical entries in *PIR²* B 26; Rutledge 2001, 202–4; Soldevila et al. 2019, 381. **Marcellus:** Titus Clodius Eprius Marcellus was a *homo nouus*, as malevolently remarked in Tac. *Dial.* 8.2–3, who made a fortune under Nero and was elevated to consulship in 62 AD. Tacitus relates that, four years later, Marcellus successfully prosecuted Thrasea Paetus for *maiestas*, receiving, as a reward, the considerable sum of five million sesterces (Tac. *Ann.* 16.33.2). The portrait Tacitus gives of Marcellus is that of a threatening man who addresses a violent speech against Thrasea Paetus (*Ann.* 16.28), as remarked by Rutledge 2001, 226, who also highlights how the adjectives employed by Tacitus to describe Marcellus (*Ann.* 16.29.1 *toruus ac minax*) call to mind the qualities of fierce animals. Feral depiction of informants is, as stated above (e.g. in the commentary on §1), one of the main features of Sidonius' invective in this letter. Together with the Thrasea Paetus case, Marcellus' involvement in 'wrecking the lives of many innocent persons', as stated in Tac. *Hist.* 4.7.3 *satis Marcello, quod Neronem in exitium tot innocentium impulerit*, would have made him a perfect candidate for a list of famous slanderers. See *PIR²* E 84 and Rutledge 2001, 225–8 for detailed prosopographical entries on Marcellus. **Carus**: Mentioned as a known *delator* in Martial 12.25.5 and in Juvenal 1.36 (immediately after the mention of Baebius Massa). In *Ep.* 7.19.5 Pliny says that, as prosecutor of Herennius Senecio in 93 AD, Mettius Carus harshly questioned Fannia, wife of Helvidius Priscus (and daughter of Thrasea Paetus), who confessed to having given her husband's *commentarii* to Senecio so that he could complete his *Life of Helvidius Priscus*. Moreover, Pliny (*Ep.* 7.27.14 *in scrinio eius datus a Caro de me libellus inuentus est*) relates that Carus had given Domitian a dossier against Pliny himself, which was found after Domitian's death. Pliny's threatening image of Carus *quaerens minaciter* (Plin. *Ep.* 7.19.5), and gathering accusations against him as well, matches Sidonius' description of the intimidating attitude of informants.

See prosopographical entries in *PIR*[2] M 562; Rutledge 2001, 245–6; Soldevilla et al. 2019, 115. **Parthenius**: An imperial slave, freed by Nero, Parthenius was *cubicularius* under Domitian. According to Dio Cassius 67.17.1, Parthenius was involved in Domitian's assassination, having removed the blade from a sword the emperor always had under his pillow so that he could not defend himself from Stephanus' attack. In his epigram 11.1, Martial warns his *liber*: it would remain unrolled (*ineuolutus*) should it visit Parthenius, too busy to take an interest in his trifles, since he 'does not read books, only *libelli*' (Mart. 11.1.5 *libros non legit ille, sed libellos*). As Kay 1985, 53 points out commenting on this epigram, the fact that less than three months after Domitian's death Martial addresses a poem to Parthenius incidentally testifies to how influential Parthenius still was. According to Eutrop. 8.1, together with Petronius Secundus, Parthenius also established Nerva as next emperor. See *PIR*[2] C 951a; Soldevilla et al. 2019, 450–2. **Licinius, Pallas**: The two are mentioned together for their proverbial wealth also in Juv. 1.108–9 *ego possideo plus / Pallante et Licinis?* Note that Juvenal's first satire has been previously cited for the mention of Massa (Juv. 1.35). **Licinius**: A freedman of Augustus (Suet. *Aug.* 67) not known to be a *delator* but mentioned for malversation as *procurator* of Gaul in Dio 54.21. He is mentioned for his wealth in Persius 2.36, again in Juvenal 14.306 – see above on Satire 14 for the occurrence of Narcissus' name – and also in Seneca *Epp.* 119.9 and 120.19. For Licinius see *PIR*[1] L 193; *PIR*[2] I 381; Soldevilla et al. 2019, 340. For the two mentions in Juvenal see Courtney 2013, 88 and 519. **Pallas**: Marcus Antonius Pallas was initially a slave of the emperor Claudius' mother, Antonia, who, according to Josephus *Ant. Iud.* 18.6.6 (182), entrusted him, 'the most faithful of her servants' (τῷ πιστοτάτῳ τῶν δούλων), to deliver the message of warning to Tiberius against Sejanus. Pallas later became a powerful freedman, and, as stated for Licinius, he is not known as a *delator*. As the above-mentioned passage of Juvenal 1.108–9 illustrates, Pallas was known to have amassed immense wealth while being *a rationibus* under Claudius. In Suet. *Cl.* 28.1 he is mentioned in this capacity (immediately after Narcissus – see above). See also Dio 61.3 for Pallas' later association with Agrippina. Tacitus and Pliny the Younger sternly comment on his having received *ornamenta praetoria* as a reward for having proposed a penalty on women who married slaves, and in particular for the senatorial decree inscribed on his tomb, which commemorated his frugality since he had refused a monetary reward the Senate offered him in that circumstance: Tac. *Ann.* 12.53; Plin. *Epp.* 7.29 and 8.6. On Pallas, see *PIR*[2] A 858; Oost 1958; *OCD* s.v. *Antonius Pallas*, by Syme.

Hi sunt, qui inuident tunicatis otia: As highlighted in Anderson's edition (1965, 189 n. 4) the word *tunicatus* entails that someone is wearing informal dress, as in Plin. *Ep.* 5.6.45, when Pliny says that in his home in Tuscany he never needs to wear a formal toga and he can spend his days enjoying peace and quiet. Moreover, as suggested by Geisler 1887, 366, a similar idea is expressed in Sidon. *Ep.* 2.14.2, where *tunicata quies* is an echo of Martial 10.51.6. In terms of content, *inuident*, the verb at the centre of the phrase introducing a long list of things which are subject to the envy of the informants, is peculiar to *barbaries* in Sidonius' works. Barbarians are often said to be envious of Gallo-Romans in Sidonius: in *Ep.* 3.1.4 Goths are described as *modo inuidiosi huius anguli etiam desolata proprietate potiantur*, so envious of his 'corner of land' that, just to make it their own, they would devastate it. *Inuidia* is ascribed specifically to the Burgundian allies in *Ep.* 3.4.1 (*nec propugnantum caremus inuidia*). Very similar is Sidonius' apology to Auspicius in *Ep.* 7.11.1 for his infrequent visits, which are to be imputed to the *periculum* constituted by his neighbours (the Goths) and to the *inuidia* of his *patroni* (the Burgundians). The informants' *inuidia*, therefore, may be interpreted as one of the many features through which their *barbaries* manifests itself. Note that Seronatus, whose negative portrait (in *Epp.* 2.1 and 5.13) has been rightly signalled by Furbetta 2014–2015a, 148 for its similarities with this description of informants (see the introduction), is said to *aperte inuidere* in *Ep.* 2.1.2, in a similar context of denigrating *accumulatio*.

stipendia paludatis: *Paludati* were soldiers who dressed in a military cloak, a *paludamentum*. This expression contrasts with the previous *tunicatis otia* and testifies that informants are envious of anything: they envy those who are at leisure for their idleness and at the same time they long for the wages of soldiers.

uiatica ueredariis: Anderson and Loyen adopt the otherwise unattested spelling *ueraedariis* out of respect for *L*, but the normal orthography of the other manuscripts should be respected. The syntagma does not occur elsewhere and the word *ueredarius* is rarely used. Attested only in late Latin since Firmicus Maternus *Math.* 3.11.18 and, significantly for Sidonius, in Symm. *Ep.* 7.14, it designates a messenger of the imperial post (see *OLD* s.v. 2243). The noun *uiaticum* also occurs in Sidon. *Epp.* 7.2.3 and 7.7.6, as pointed out by van Waarden 2010, 378.

munuscula legatis: The reference to the compensation (*munuscula*) leads

LETTER 7

one to think the term *legatus* may be here an alternative way of referring to a letter-carrier instead of an ambassador. Of the same opinion is Loyen 1970a, 184, who translates with 'courrier'. As pointed out by Amherdt 2001, 206, Wolff 2020, 404 and Hindermann 2022, 181–2, Sidonius uses a variety of terms to designate letter-bearers, including *baiulus* (*Epp.* 4.7.1 and 6.4.1), *gerulus* (*Epp.* 2.11.2, 6.10.1 and 8.13.3), *portitor* (*Epp.* 6.4.2 and 7.10.1), *pugillator* (*Ep.* 9.14.4) and *tabellarius* (*Epp.* 2.3.1 and 4.8.1). The syntagma, which is not known to occur elsewhere, gives evidence of a collateral aspect of letter writing, that is, compensating the letter-carrier. The role of letter-carriers went far beyond delivering mail, as it entailed, for instance, bringing gifts, waiting for responses and, in particular, conveying oral messages, which, for various reasons, not least interception, were not entrusted to written form. See, e.g. Augustine's definition of a *legatus* as 'a living letter' in *Ep.* 31.2. On the role of letter-carriers in late antique letter writing see Conybeare 2000, 33–40.

portoria quadruplatoribus: A *quadruplator* was a bringer of a criminal accusation, for which he was rewarded, as stated in *OLD* s.v. *quadruplator*. The term often occurs in contexts of denigration; in particular, it concerns Verres' freedman Timarchides, who had 'any professional and mercenary prosecutor in his power' in Cic. *Ver.* 2.2.135 *accusatorum et quadruplatorum quicquid erat, habebat in potestate.* And yet, although the Ciceronian echo is suggestive in light of the following mention of *In Verrem*, in Sidonius' letter the term appears in a list of legitimate activities. Therefore, this element, together with the presence of *portoria*, which indicates tolls, leads one to translate *quadruplator* as 'taxer', in accordance with *L&S* s.v. *quadruplator* 1. Anderson 1965, 191 has 'customs officers' and similarly Loyen 1970a, 184.

praedia prouincialibus, flamonia municipibus: Warmington reports a question he found in Anderson's annotations on this passage: 'does *prouincialibus* here mean country-dwellers?' (Anderson 1965, 190 n. 2). The word is translated as 'provincials' both in Anderson and Loyen; and yet, Anderson's note may be a lead worth pursuing, because the following syntagma, *flamonia municipibus*, provides further context. A contraposition between provincials and inhabitants of *municipia* would not make sense at this time, since imperial provinces were organised in *municipia*. It seems sensible therefore to accept Anderson's suggestion and to interpret the passage as meaning that the informants would envy those who live in the country for their estates and those who live in *municipia* – and likely provincial *municipia*,

221

we may add – for their *flamonia*. Sidonius' passage is mentioned in *TLL* 6.1.875 s.v. *flamonium* 71 (by Bickel) as an example of *flamonium municipale*. The mention of the honour of *flamen* in fifth-century Gaul is to be considered in relation to the social importance priesthoods still had, although in a desacralised form. The honour had lost its pagan associations, as testified, for instance, by the sixth-century Ammaedera (Haïdra) inscriptions (*CIL* VIII 10516 and 11528) which celebrate a *flamen perpetuus Christianus* in Vandal Africa. On *flamen Christianus* see De Rossi 1878, 33–6; Cabrol et al. 1923, s.v. Flamines Chrétiens 1643–51; Chastagnol and Duval 1974, 99; Di Bernardino 1998, 42.

arcariis pondera . . . uectigalia publicanis: This section of Sidonius' *accumulatio* concerns the informants' lust for money, which leads them to envy any source of wealth. Even in what may seem like an ordinary list of positions and rewards, Sidonius' choice of words is careful as always, and the uncommon expressions chosen enrich the verbosity of the passage. For instance, in late Latin *arcarius* specifically designates a money changer or a banker, as in *TLL* 2.438 s.v. *arcarius* 50–1 (by Klotz), which lists this passage among the rare occurrences of the noun, after *HA Alex*. 43.4; Symm. *Ep.* 1.68; and Vulg. *Esth*. 3.9. Moreover, in *TLL* 1.1666 s.v. *allego* 9 (by Vollmer) Sidon. *Ep.* 5.7.3 is the only literary source mentioned (amidst numerous epigraphic occurrences) of *allectus* as indicating a provincial honour. A *tabularius* was an accountant; although it is not known to occur often, this noun is attested in Apul. *Apol*. 78.6 (*tabulario Pontiani praesente*), a work already mentioned as one of the probable models of this letter (see the introduction); see also its occurrence in Amm. 28.1.5 and 15, and in Symm. *Ep.* 9.10. Although in a context of praise, Sidonius employs *tabularius* in the similar *accumulatio* of *Ep*. 4.11.5 *habens in eo consiliarium in iudiciis . . . tabularium in tributis*. *Numerarius* is a technical term meaning 'bookkeeper' and exclusively attested in late Latin. *Numerarii* are mentioned only in Ammianus 19.9.2; Symm. *Ep.* 9.50; twice in Augustine (*Lib. arb.* 2.11; *In Psalm*. 146.11); and in Sidon. *Epp*. 1.11.6 and 2.1.3.

praetorianis sportulas: Officials of the praetorian prefect are called *praetoriani* also in other late antique sources, such as Symm. *Ep.* 2.75 and *CTh*. 6.10.3; see *TLL* 10.2.1067 s.v. *praetorianus* 45–50 (by Schmitz). 'Praetorians', as translated by Anderson 1965, 191 and Loyen 1970a, 184, does not reflect the exact meaning of the passage. The *iunctura* is not known to occur elsewhere, but testifies to the common practice of giving 'additional tips' to officials, who were able to considerably increase their salaries; for this phenomenon see Jones 1964, vol. II, 1055–6 (who calls them *praefectiani*).

ciuitatibus indutias: For *indutiae* as meaning 'delay in paying taxes' in late Latin, see *TLL* 7.1.1279 s.v. *indutiae* 66–80 (by Gumpoltsberger); the noun occurs with this specific juridical meaning for instance in *CTh.* 11.1.34, and in Sidon. *Ep.* 4.24.2 and also 4.24.5, a letter in which Sidonius personally intercedes in favour of an insolvent man, on which see Amherdt 2001, 490.

uectigalia publicanis: On *uectigalia* as taxes specifically introduced by Constantine, as can be gathered by *CTh.* 4.13.1, see Jones 1964, vol. I, 430. Symmachus mentions *publicani* as collectors of *quinquagesimae uectigal* in *Ep.* 5.62, as pointed out by Jones 1964, vol. III, 105 n. 47.

reuerentiam clericis . . . discinctis priuilegia: The lust for benefits of an economic nature is followed by the informants' longing for prestige and power connected to status, a thing which indirectly testifies to their being *parvenus*. Worthy of mention is in particular the presence of *cincti* and *discincti*. The two terms are to be interpreted as meaning 'people in office' and 'retired officials', since the *cingulum* was indicative of office holding. In *TLL* 5.1.1316 s.v. *discinctus* 57–9 (by Gudeman) *discinctus* is considered to be a synonym of *priuatus*, deprived of any negative connotation, exclusively in this passage and in the similar context of Sidon. *Ep.* 1.9.4, where Avienus, when in office (*cinctus*), is said to be less influential than Basilius out of office (*discinctus*). The same word-game occurs in the description of Arvandus' sudden arrest in Sidon. *Ep.* 1.7.3 *prius cinctus custodia quam potestate discinctus*, translated by Anderson 1936, 369 as 'burdened by guards before he was disburdened of his office'; on this passage see Köhler 1995, 237.

scholas instituendis, mercedes instituentibus, litteras institutis: The list is closed by these three cola. The polyptoton *instituendis . . . instituentibus . . . institutis*, at first glance, catalyses the attention, to the point that the focus of this ending would seem to be a lust for intellectual superiority arising from schooling – a thing that would have elevated the social aspirations of the informants, had Sidonius not put right in the middle that they envy teachers 'their wages' (*mercedes*), reaffirming that, ultimately, their real interest lies in preying on wealth, and in the mere appearance of being learned for the social recognition it entails.

SIDONIUS: LETTERS BOOK 5, PART 1

§ 4

Hi sunt, qui: This beginning reminds the reader that the anaphorical section started in § 2 is still ongoing, and serves the purpose of introducing a new long enumeration within the macro-enumeration. Gualandri 1979, 63 n. 95 mentions the following passage as an example of Sidonius' predilection for asyndetic *accumulatio* together with *Epp.* 1.5.4, 1.9.2 and 4.1.2.

nouis opibus ebrii: In *TLL* 5.2.15 s.v. *ebrius* 7–17 (by Bannier), Sidonius' passage is listed among a few occurrences of the metaphorical use of *ebrietas*, starting with Horace's portrait of Cleopatra *fortunaque dulci ebria* in *Carm.* 1.37.11–12, a passage Geisler 1887, 366 already suggested should be compared with the occurrence in *Ep.* 5.7.4. Compare the similar occurrence in Symm. *Ep.* 1.8, although *ebrius* is there followed by an uncommon genitive (*multae luxuriae*). As suggested by Gualandri 1979, 123, it seems possible that the greater metaphoric use of *ebrietas* in biblical language may have influenced late Latin authors (e.g. Aug. *Conf.* 5.13, in which Manicheans are said to be *uanitatibus ebrii*) as well as Sidonius, who employs the term with this nuance also in *Carm.* 5.32, in which a spear is said to be *ebria caede uirum* ('drunk with the slaughter of men').

per utendi intemperantiam produnt imperitiam possidendi: This highly alliterated passage efficaciously summarises the content of the whole paragraph, constituted by a long list of examples of how the informants, with their looks and behaviours, appear socially awkward in any circumstance because of their inexperience in managing new wealth in conditions they are not accustomed to.

nam libenter incedunt armati ad epulas: *Incedere armati* immediately evokes a military context, see e.g. *Aen.* 9.308, where Nisus and Euryalus *protinus armati incedunt* passing over the city walls to reach Aeneas. In Sidonius' passage, *ad epulas* contrasts with any heroic expectation, and ridicules the informants for their inadequacy. All the references to inadequate ways of dressing are a common feature of invectives (see the introduction to this letter).

albati ad exsequias: The irony of this syntagma is manifest. Romans were accustomed to wearing dark clothes when in mourning, as is testified e.g. in Tibullus 3.2.17–18 (*ossa / incinctae nigra candida ueste legent*) and in Ov.

Met. 6.568 (*induiturque atras uestes*) when Procne changes into mourning clothes at the announcement of her sister's death (cf. also Ov. *Met.* 8.448; 778). Juvenal 10.244–5 mentions dark mourning clothes (*nigra ueste*) when discussing old age, which entails having to endure 'perpetual mourning'. One last example, taken from historiography, is in Tac. *Hist.* 3.67, where Vitellius, once informed of the defection of his soldiers, exits the palace clad in mourning clothes, *pullo amictu*, followed by his family *uelut in funebrem pompam*. A useful comparison for a similar unsuitability of clothing is Cicero's attack on Vatinius (*Vat.* 12.30), who attended a banquet in a *toga pulla*, and Cicero sarcastically wonders if he had ever seen anyone doing such a thing: *quo exemplo, quo more feceris*.

pelliti ad ecclesias: The word *pellitus* is undoubtedly evocative of barbarity, although it is impossible to ascertain if the informants are actual barbarians or Gallo-Romans described as barbarians. Here they are pictured while they go to church covered in fur, and the inappropriateness of a similar clothing would be equally effective for barbarians going to church in their traditional clothes, or for Gallo-Romans going to church dressed as barbarians. In light of the similar description of Seronatus, if they were Gallo-Romans, Sidonius would be here describing them as combining the worst barbarian features in order to make fun of them (see the introduction). The topos of 'barbarians in fur' is attested in particular after Ovid, who, for instance, describes the shores confining him as 'too exposed to the *pelliti* Coralli' in *Pont.* 4.8.83; *pelliti* are Getae at the beginning of *Pont.* 4.10.2; see also *Trist.* 5.10.32 (see the commentary on *Ep.* 5.6.1 *turbo barbaricus. . .*). There are various occurrences of the term *pelliti* referred to barbarians in poetry. In Claud. *Carm.* 5.78–84, Rufinus is accused of having mingled with the Visigoths, betraying his Roman *toga* for the *fuluae pelles* of barbarians (on which see Garuti 1979, 944). Claud. *Carm.* 8.466 (*metitur pellita iuuentus*) triumphantly describes Stilicho's expedition to Greece. In Claudian's *Bellum Geticum* the term concerns an entertaining description of the assembly summoned by Alaric, a paradoxical barbarian senate, made of 'long-haired *patres* in fur': *Carm.* 26.481–2 *crinigeri sedere patres, pellita Getarum / curia* (although Garuti 1979, 949 believes *pellitus* here has a merely descriptive function and is not to be intended as a specifically misobarbaric connotation). Paulinus of Nola, in *Carm.* 10.246 (ed. Hartel = 3 ed. Green Appendix B) *dignaque pellitis habitas deserta Bigerris?*, reminds Ausonius that even in Bordeaux Ausonius is not far from 'skin-clad Bigerri'. For this Ovidian reminiscence see Fielding 2017, 41–2. Rutilius Namatianus has in mind Ovid's and Claudian's image of 'barbarians in fur' when he describes Rome held captive, in *De reditu suo* 2.49, *satellitibus pellitis*; see Wolff 2007, 106 n. 263. Before Sidonius, the topos occurs also in prose, see e.g. Hier. *Ep.* 60.4, where the *pellitorum turba populorum* are barbarians converted to Christianity. Sidonius makes this topos his own, and employs it in relation to Theoderic I, called *pellitus princeps* in *Carm.* 7.219 – and *rex ferox* (7.222) – see also *pellitae . . . turmae* marching behind Roman trumpets in 7.349. Theoderic II is called *pellitus hospes* in *Carm.* 5.563 and in *Ep.* 1.2.4 his guard is defined (with an expression reminiscent of Rutilius) as a *pellitorum turba satellitum*. Furthermore, in *Ep.* 7.9.19 the term *pellitus* is opposed to *purpuratus* in order to express the contrast between Romanness and barbarity; for the context of this occurrence, see van Waarden 2010, 504–5; for some of the Sidonian occurrences of *pellitus* see Fascione 2018, 38 and Egetenmeyr 2021, 153–4. In light of this brief survey of occurrences, it is possible to state that in the previous authors mentioned, as in Sidonius, *pellitus* is an identifying feature of barbarians, and, as Köhler 1995, 140 put it, *pellitus* can be considered a synonym for 'barbarous' even outside the sphere of clothing. The latter is not the case with *Ep.* 5.7.4, since awkward clothing is the *fil rouge* of this section, but in light of Köhler's remark, and of the evidence presented, it feels safe to assume that the informants of *Ep.* 5.7 need not be barbarians but are studiously portrayed as barbarous.

pullati ad nuptias: As stated above, *pullae uestes* were worn by mourners (see commentary on § 4 *albati ad exsequias*). The word *pullatus* is not known to occur often; for its occurrence in contexts specifically pertaining funerals, see e.g. Juv. 3.213 and Amm. 29.2.13 (although there the term is a conjecture in place of the transmitted reading *polleati*); see *TLL* 10.2.2.2581 s.v. *pullatus* 55–65 (by Spoth).

castorinati: *Castorinatus* is a Sidonian hapax, through which Sidonius is able to create a suggestive and entertaining picture in the reader's mind. Compare this occurrence to Claudian's *Carm. min.* 10 *De birro castoreo*, a playful description of a particularly worn out (possibly second-hand) beaver overcoat, which thus retains 'only the name' of beaver fur. The quality of the *birrum* is betrayed by its price, since the owner did not pay much for it (*Carm. min.* 10.3–4 *quid sit, iam scire potestis: / si mihi nulla fides, credite uel pretio*). It could be surmised that beaver fur was usually much more expensive, and it then seems likely that Sidonius mentions beaver fur as a costly piece of clothing, since the *delatores* are said to be showing off their new opulence. On *Carm.*

LETTER 7

min. 10, see Ricci 2001, 59 and Charlet 2018, 112, who also points out that a luxury *copertorium* cost up to thirty-six *solidi*, but a military cloak only cost one. The previously mentioned pelts and the beaver fur seem *Realien* which malevolently refer to daily life and not simply to literary models. To the Burgundians, hunting was not a sport as much as a survival technique, as pointed out by Saitta 2006, 82–3 and 122–3, who analyses the importance hunting has in the *Lex Burgundionum* and the severity of punishment for the theft of hunting dogs or falcons (*LB* 97 and 98).

ad laetanias: Sidonius describes informants, clothed in beaver fur, while attending public prayers, *laetaniae* (or *litaniae*), a word which specifically concerns the *dies rogationum*, as in *TLL* 7.2.1502 s.v. *litania* 55–7 (by Meijer); for the institution of *Rogationes* see Sidon. *Ep.* 5.14. All the editors chose the spelling *litanias*, which is the reading of *L*. Both spellings have occurrences after Sidonius with the exception of one prior occurrence of *litania* (*CTh.* 16.5.30.2, AD 396). And yet, in light of Dolveck's stemma, one should consider *laetanias* as the reading of the archetype. This description is a variation of the previous *pelliti ad ecclesias* and, as stated above, if the informants are barbarians their attending public prayers would be odd (Burgundians being traditionally Arians); even if they were Gallo-Romans, the image would be equally ironic, since they legitimately attend public prayers but dressed as barbarians.

Nullum illis genus hominum, ordinum, temporum cordi est: The object of Sidonius' attack shifts from the inappropriateness of the informants' outfits to their behaviour, socially unacceptable in various places and social interactions, as listed below. Cf. the description of Seronatus' clumsy and inappropriate behaviour in *Ep.* 2.1.3, on which see Hindermann 2022, 66–77.

In foro Scythae: In the Classical world, Scythians were a recurring exemplum of barbarity, associated with ignorance, noise and dullness. For example, one may think of the entertaining character of the Scythian archer in Aristophanes' *Tesmophoriazusae*, who perfectly embodies this stereotype. Cicero refers to Scythians as barbarians *par excellence*: even *they* would be shaken by his words in Cic. *Ver.* 2.5.149–50 *si haec apud Scythas dicerem . . . tamen animos etiam barbarorum hominum permouerem*. Interestingly, in Cicero, Scythians, the embodiment of barbarity, are opposed to the *forum* as an emblem of civility and Romanness. In light of Cicero's passage, the irony of

227

Sidonius is even more blatant. See also king Theoderic II's mention of how Avitus' tutoring softened his *Scythicos . . . mores*, his Scythian ways, in *Carm.* 7.498. As pointed out in *OCD* s.v. Scythia (by Braund), Goths, Alans and Huns, located in Scythia after the third century, are often given the features of their Scythian predecessors and are regularly called 'Scythae'.

in cubiculo uiperae, in conuiuio scurrae: Sidonius transitions from public *forum* to household spaces, in particular the private *cubiculum* in which informants are represented as dangerous vipers, and the *conuiuium* in which their social awkwardness (their being buffoons) is evident. Cf. the list of Seronatus' wrongdoings in *Ep.* 2.1.3, on which see Hindermann 2022, 71–4. The image of informants as snakes is recurrent in Sidonius' account – see the commentary on *Ep.* 5.6.2 *relatu uenenato* and *Ep.* 5.7.7 *et aures mariti* . . . See also the description of Seronatus in *Ep.* 5.13.2 as 'a serpent barely slithering out of his den'.

in exactionibus Harpyiae: Once again, Sidonius refers to the rapacity of the informants, and the parallel with Harpies emphasises their swiftness in exaction. For effective comparison see Apollonius of Rhodes *Argon.* 2.187–93: a powerful description of Harpies harassing Phineus, snatching, even from his mouth, the food he tries to eat.

in conlocutionibus statuae: This description of informants as 'statues in conversation' calls to mind the *indolatiles* Burgundians in Sidon. *Ep.* 5.5.3, 'equally rough and unteachable in their bodies and in their feeling'. Together with the following parallel with beasts and snails, this seems further evidence that the informants are described through the topoi of barbarity.

in quaestionibus bestiae, in tractatibus cocleae: Bad temper and violent attitude were a typical feature of the canonical representation of barbarians: see the discussion of Chilperic's *iracundia* in the commentary on *Ep.* 5.6.2. For the mention of barbarians as not being particularly bright, see the commentary above. The comic effect created by the juxtaposition of the vehemence of beasts and the slowness of snails is particularly noteworthy.

in contractibus trapezitae: Gualandri 1979, 159 n. 53 lists *trapezita* among Sidonius' use of Graecisms pertaining to daily life. *Trapezita* (and its varant *tarpezita*) are often attested in Plautus (e.g. *Capt.* 193 and *Trin.* 425) and sporadically resurface in late Latin authors, as in Symmachus' *Relatio* 3.15. It

LETTER 7

is not uncommon for Sidonius to employ Greek calques attested in archaic comedy, as pointed out by Foscarini 2019, 353. *Trapezita* also occurs in Sidon. *Ep.* 1.7.8, when Arvandus, ignoring the warnings of the impending accusation, parades the Capitoline Terrace, and, while wandering about, scans *pretiosa trapezitarum inuolucra*.

ad intellegendum saxei, ad iudicandum lignei, ad succensendum flammei, ad ignoscendum ferrei: The reading *succensendum* is clearly that of the archetype, though modern editors have chosen the rarer spelling *suscensendum*, which is unique to *L*, presumably out of respect for its antiquity. In this section the description of informants is carried out through the peculiar sequence of gerunds followed by adjectives of material with identical endings. Geisler 1887, 366 compares the passage to Plin. *Ep.* 2.3.7 *saxeus ferreusque es*, while the whole section of comparisons does not seem to have previous attestations. These are all common images, which still concern the same key concepts discussed above: the barbarian or barbarised informants are dull, stiff and bad tempered. Moreover, their being stiff and 'wooden' calls to mind once more the *indolatiles* Burgundians of *Ep.* 5.5.3, a passage already mentioned for the comparison to statues in this paragraph.

ad amicitias pardi, ad facetias ursi, ad fallendum uulpes, ad superbiendum tauri, ad consumendum minotauri: The informants are then compared to a series of animals (leopards, bears, foxes and bulls) leading to an unexpected ending with the mention of their mythological minotaur-like hunger.

§ 5

dubia tempora certius amant: As the commentary on Cibyrates in § 7 explains, Cicero's *In Verrem* is one of the texts Sidonius often refers to in this letter, that is why the occurrence of the Ciceronian expression *dubia tempora* seems noteworthy, since it appears twice in *In Verrem*, first in Cic. *Ver.* 2.5.1, when Cicero anticipates Hortensius' defence, which is that Verres' status as a good commander would have constituted a reason not to condemn him in light of his past actions in 'uncertain times' for the state, in case those uncertainties were to be faced once more: *Ver.* 2.5.4 *sit fur . . . at est bonus imperator, at felix et ad dubia rei publicae tempora reseruandus*. It is in the same uncertainties that Sidonius' informants prosper, making the most of *dubia* *tempora*. Other occurrences of the *iunctura* are for instance in Cic. *Font.* 42; Horace *Carm.* 4.9.36; and in Seneca's Thyestes 605–6. For the problem of leadership through difficult times see also Ammianus 18.6.2; a similar thought is also in the laudatory and sententious Sidon. *Carm.* 7.550–1 *dubio sub tempore regnum / non regit ignauus.*

cum sint in praetoriis leones, in castris lepores: This proverb is widely attested in Greek and Latin literature in numerous variants. In Aristophanes' *Peace* 1189–90 ὄντες οἴκοι μὲν λέοντες, / ἐν μάχῃ δ᾽ ἀλώπεκες ('acting like lions at home but like foxes in battle') effectively opposes the less honourable behaviour of the fox to the 'brutal and uncompromising power of the lion' (Olson 1998, 295). A useful comparison, signalled by Olson 1998 and by Tosi 2018, 1091 n. 1618, is with the similar sayings in Plu. *Sull.* 41.2 (Σύγκρ. 3.2), Aelianus *Varia Historia* 13.9 and Arr. *Epict.* 4.5.37. Variants of this saying occur also in Latin texts, for instance in Petronius' *Satyricon* 44.14 *populus est domi leones foras uulpes*, and later in Tertullian, who, however opposes lions to the fleeting attitude of deers in *De corona militis* 1 *in pace leones et in proelio ceruos*. For the reception of this proverb through the Renaissance to modern languages see Tosi 2018, 1092 n. 1620.

timent foedera, ne discutiantur, bella, ne pugnent: This seems like a follow-up of the previous saying: the informants even fear *foedera* they might have to break and battles they might have to fight.

Quorum si nares afflauerit uspiam robiginosi aura marsupii: Ultimately, what moves the informants is always the promise of wealth. Gualandri 1979, 173 n. 98 rightly lists *robiginosus* among the numerous rarely attested words, originally pertaining to archaic comedy, Sidonius is keen on using. *Robiginosus* is known to have only four previous occurrences in Latin: in Plautus, *Stichus* 230 (referred to a *strigilis*); Martial 5.28.7 (metaphorically applied to *dentes*); Fronto *Ep.* 2.14 (a *gladium*); and Apul. *Soc.* 5 (a *telum* covered in blood). It then exclusively occurs in Sidonius, twice, in *Ep.* 1.6.4 (referred to *enses*) and in this passage. For Sidonius' preference for adjectives ending in *–osus*, which are 'a feature of colloquial diction', see Hindermann 2022, 166–7.

oculos Argi et manus Briarei et Sphingarum ungues: An entertaining tricolon of mythological exempla to represent the informants' greed. It is noteworthy that Sidonius skilfully plays on bodily images, as if the

LETTER 7

faint scent of money would physically transform the informants' features into those of mythological monsters, resulting in a whole new monstrous chimaera forged in the reader's mind. These beasts, with eyes all over their face, a hundred hands and sharp claws, are the same predators mentioned at the beginning of the letter, when Sidonius recalls having sent hounds 'to follow their tracks'. However, as stated in the introduction, these monsters are not so much scary as bizarre. **oculos Argi**: Argus πανόπτης ('all seeing'), guardian of Io in various versions of the myth, was (and still is in modern languages) of proverbial vigilance due to his number of eyes. See *DNP* s.v. Argos I 5 (by Graf). Previous Latin mentions of 'the eyes of Argus' are for instance in Plautus *Aul.* 555 *Argus . . . oculeus totus* and in Ovid *Am.* 3.4.19–20 *centum fronte oculos, centum ceruice gerebat / Argus*. Compare also *Met.* 1.625 and *Ars* 3.617–19, in which the woman is said to be able to elude any kind of vigilance, even if 'as many eyes as those of Argus' watched her. See also the similar passing reference in Jerome's *Ep.* 54.9 to Furia. **manus Briarei et Sphingarum ungues**: *Briareus* was one of the Hekatoncheires, the 'hundred-handed', who helped Zeus in the battle with the Titans (Hes. *Theog.* 626–8); see *DNP* s.v. Hekatoncheires (by Nünlist) and also *OCD* s.v. Hecatoncheires, 651. Compare Sil. 13.587–9 *sedet ostia Ditis / centenis suetus Briareus recludere palmis / et Sphinx, uirgineos rictus infecta cruore*, since in the same context is also mentioned a Sphinx, as in Sidonius. In Silius Italicus, Briareus is accustomed to open the gates of Pluto with his 'hundred hands'; moreover, Silius' description lingers on the mouth of the Sphinx, stained with blood, and this is the only previous occurrence of the syntagmata in the same context. Sidonius, for his part, effectively chooses lion claws as a symbol of the fierceness of the Sphinx, and, consequently, of the informants' predatory attitude. See also Oedipus' description of the Sphinx, impatiently moving rocks with its claw while waiting to disembowel him in Sen. *Oed.* 99–100. Note that Sidonius employs here the rarely attested first declension form, which occurs in the singular in Ovid (*Trist.* 4.7.17; *Ibis* 378) and in Aug. *Ciu.* 18.13, while the only known occurrences of the first declension plural *Sphingae* are in Ps. Quint. *Decl.* 12.26, Plin. *Nat.* 8.72 (though there presumably referred to an animal) and Aug. *Ciu.* 16.8.

et periuria Laomedontis et Ulixis argutias et Sinonis fallacias: The 'physical' transformation of the informants is followed by a behavioural metamorphosis, expressed through this second tricolon of mythological exempla. When the informants 'smell money', their awkward attitude, described in previous paragraphs, is substituted by calculated slyness and

231

cunning. **periuria Laomedontis**: The mythical king of Troy, known for his treachery, refused to compensate Poseidon and Apollo for their help in building the city walls, and later refused to give Hercules the compensation he promised him for saving his daughter, who would have been sacrificed to a sea monster to placate Poseidon; see *DNP* s.v. Laomedon (by Stoevesandt) for the various Greek sources concerning this myth. The *iunctura* seems Vergilian, and Geisler 1887, 366 rightly suggests a comparison with Verg. *Georg.* 1.502 *Laomedonteae periuria Troiae*, in which Romans are said to be paying for Laomedon's offences, and with the similar occurrence in *Aen.* 4.542, in which Laomedon's treacheries are extended to all Trojans. Laomedon is said to have been killed *ob periurium* in Lact. *Epit.* 7.2; *Laomedontea periuria* causing Priamus' ruin are also mentioned as negative pagan exemplum in Aug. *Ciu.* 3.2. **Ulixis argutias**: The *iunctura* is not known to have previous occurrences. By virtue of his deceptions, Ulysses is condemned in Greek tragedy, as exemplified by Hecuba's violent invective against him at the news she would have become his slave in Euripides *Tro.* 283–7, in which Ulysses is said to be vile and lawless, and most harmful because of his 'forked tongue' (v. 286 διπτύχῳ γλώσσᾳ), which decided the fate of Troy. Deprived of the Homeric heroism, Ulysses' name is always followed by derogatory adjectives in Verg. *Aen.* Book 2, where he is described as cruel (*durus* in *Aen.* 2.7), deceitful (*pellax* in *Aen.* 2.90), detestable (*dirus* in *Aen.* 2.762) and – significantly for the occurrence in Sidonius – Aeneas himself calls him a deviser of crimes (*scelerum inuentor* in *Aen.* 2.164). Sidonius refers specifically to this degraded image of Ulysses, whose *argutiae* are most deceitful and cause harm. On Vergil's devaluation of Ulysses and on his tragic models see Perutelli 2006, 35–41 and Ganiban 2009, 57–70. **et Sinonis fallacias**: As Perutelli 2006, 36 points out, in Aeneas' account of events of Verg. *Aen.* Book 2, Sinon is a *longa manus* of Ulysses, an extension of his cunning. In *Aen.* 2.57–198, Sinon gains the Trojans' trust by pretending he is harassed by Ulysses while in fact being his accomplice. It is Sinon, *dolis instructus* (*Aen.* 2.152), who persuades them to accept the horse 'with trickery and perjury' in *Aen.* 2.195 *insidiis periurique arte*.

et fidem Polymestoris et pietatem Pygmalionis adhiberi: The two last syntagmata of this accumulation of mythical exempla differ from the preceding ones by the introduction of two antiphrastic images. Both Polymestor and Pygmalion are known to have betrayed the sacredness of *fides* and *pietas* purely out of greediness. Attracted by Polydorus' wealth, the Thracian king Polymestor killed him, thus betraying his word given to

LETTER 7

Priamus, who had entrusted his son to his care (for the episode see Verg. *Aen.* 3.19–68 and Ov. *Met.* 13.429–38). Out of the same blinding lust for richness, Pygmalion violated familial *pietas* and killed his brother-in-law Sychaeus in Verg. *Aen.* 1.347–50. Through the mention of Polymestor and Pygmalion, the ending of this section of negative exempla is led back to the initial assertion: irrational thirst for prosperity is ultimately the only motive driving the informers.

§ 6

His moribus obruunt uirum non minus bonitate quam potestate praestantem: This section is opened by the mention of Chilperic, overwhelmed by the ever-pressing behaviour of the informants. To stress how the king himself is blameless, Sidonius employs a terminology which is specifically Christian, and attested in numerous contexts as referred to the perfection of God in his capacity of *pastor pastorum* (as in Aug. *Serm.* 138.4). *Bonitas* and *potestas* occur together exclusively as divine attributes in Ambr. *De Fide* 2.2, Paul. Nol. *Carm.* 20.226 (ed. Hartel) and in numerous other passages by Augustine, e.g. *Quant. Anim.* 28.55 and *Gen. ad litt.* 11.22.

Sed quid faciat unus, undique uenenato uallatus interprete? ... cui natura cum bonis, uita cum malis est? The description of Chilperic, surrounded on all sides, once again evokes the image of the informants as predators (see § 4 and § 5) circling their prey, the king, since he is the source of their new wealth. According to Sidonius, Chilperic would be misled, because the news he receives is subject to the dangerous *detorsio* of the informants. Sidonius remarks that he is virtuous (compare *bonus* with *bonitas* at the beginning of the paragraph) and the *mali* surrounding him filter the truth: a clarification which seems necessary in order to avoid open criticism of Chilperic. The word *uenenatus* is only one of the many references to these informants as snakes (see the commentary on *Ep.* 5.6.2 *secreto insusurratum*, *Ep.* 5.7.4 *in cubiculo uiperae . . .*, *Ep.* 5.7.7 *et aures mariti . . .*). While the *iunctura uenenatus interpres* is not known to occur elsewhere, the association of detractors with venomous snakes is attested for instance in Verg. *Georg.* 2.378–9, Hor. *Ep.* 1.14.38 and Symm. *Ep.* 1.31.2 *an uereris aemuli uenena lectoris, ne libellus tuus admorsu duri dentis uratur?* Here, Symmachus answers Ausonius' complaint about the unauthorised circulation of a work of his, affirming that 'once a work leaves its author it becomes public property', and wonders if Ausonius' concern is ascribable to 'the venomous teeth of his harsh critics'. For the context of Symmachus' letter see Salzman and Roberts 2011, 71–3. Moreover, as suggested by Geisler 1887, 366, a similar image occurs in Sidon. *Ep.* 4.22.6 *colubrinis . . . molaribus*, where the 'viper teeth' biting Sidonius are those of his detractors, while Leo is immune to their *uenenatus morsus.* On Sidonius' models for the use of the image of venom see Amherdt 2001, 471.

Ad quorum consilia Phalaris cruentior . . . Domitianus truculentior: A new *accumulatio* of negative historical exempla, this time arranged in chronological order. The monarchs, ranging from Phalaris, tyrant of Syracuse, to emperor Domitian, are all mentioned for their renowned flaws, which, according to Sidonius, would have been even worse (note the series of overabundant comparatives) had those rulers had similar advisers to those of Chilperic. And yet, the choice to mock Chilperic by comparing him to a tyrant (cf. the people of Lyon subject to the Burgundians called *tyranno-politani* in *Ep.* 5.8) and to kings and emperors notoriously criticised for their flaws cannot go unnoticed. Sidonius does not say that even the best rulers would have been negatively affected by the presence of those advisers, but that the worst of them would have been even worse, and this statement carries weight. Although such a comparison follows the mention of Chilperic's *bonitas*, one could arguably consider him as belonging to that group of devious monarchs; furthermore, this subtlety would be coherent with Sidonius' convoluted – but always careful – way of referring to the Burgundians in this phase. It is possible that the Roman catalogue of emperors may be modelled on Ausonius' *Caesares*, a work which was transmitted alongside Sidonius' works in all the branches of Sidonius' manuscript tradition (see Dolveck 2020, 484) and therefore was already in the archetype 'as we can reconstruct it' (a thing which should warn us of the possibility that it was Sidonius who collected the complete works, as pointed out by Kelly 2020, 177). Ausonius is not quoted verbatim in *Ep.* 5.7, but his work certainly constituted a useful catalogue, overtly modelled on Suetonius (Aus. *Caes.* 4–5), of the key moral features and flaws of the twelve Caesars (Aus. *Caes.* 1–93). In accordance with Ausonius' model, Sidonius leaves out Vespasian and Titus, who are praised in Aus. *Caes.* 15–16. It has already been pointed out that Sidonius is fond of *accumulatio*, and, as rightly suggested by Furbetta 2014–2015a, 150 n. 97, it is useful to compare the Roman rulers mentioned in this letter to the similar enumerations in Sidonius' Panegyric of Majorian (*Carm.* 5) and Panegyric of Avitus (*Carm.* 7), which also bear traces of the

LETTER 7

same Ausonian model. In *Carm.* 5.321–5 it is Africa that reminds Rome of her impious emperors, each through an image representative of his faults. A similar passage is that of *Carm.* 7.104–15, where Rome weeps for her fate and lists the emperors who wronged her most, associating each of them, as already in *Carm.* 5, with an image of decadence: Tiberius with Capri, Gaius with *caligae*, Claudius with censorship, Nero with his death (his only good action), Galba in connection to Piso, Otho with vanity, Vitellius with gluttony; each of them has contributed to leaving her *lassa* to the Flavian dynasty. And yet, if in both *Carmina* the negative models are opposed to the palingenetic ascent of Trajan and to the age of prosperity under his rule, in *Ep.* 5.7 there is not an equally positive perspective. As stated above, Chilperic is mocked as if he could be one of that lot, and he is certainly no Trajan. For the negative historical exempla in the *Carmina* see Guillaumin 2013, 98–9. **Phalaris cruentior**: Phalaris is not specifically mentioned as *cruentus* in previous texts, but is often called *crudelis* in Cicero, notably in *Ver.* 2.5.145, where Verres is presented as a new Sicilian tyrant. See the commentary on § 5 for the importance of *In Verrem* as a model. **Mida cupidior**: Midas is previously mentioned as a negative exemplum for his *cupiditas* in Aus. *Hered.* 14 (= 6.14 ed. Green). **Ancus iactantior**: In *Aen.* 6.815, with the same *iunctura*, the fourth king of Rome is described as he follows his predecessor Tullius Hostilius, already taking too much pleasure in popular favour. Sidonius' use of *iactantior* is here translated as 'more ambitious' in light of Horsfall's 2013, 556 suggestion that, in Vergil's passage, this translation is preferable to 'boastful, arrogant' of *OLD* s.v. *iactans*, 894. **Tarquinius superbior**: This easy word-game with the superlative of Tarquinius' *cognomen* is not previously attested. **Tiberius callidior**: Tiberius' craftiness (*calliditas*) is mentioned twice in Tac. *Ann.* 2.30.3 and 11.3.2. **Gaius periculosior**: There are no known occurrences of Caligula being called *periculosus*. **Claudius socordior**: In Tacitus' account of Claudius' poisoning (*Ann.* 12.67) the emperor's sluggishness (*socordia*) is, together with his excessive drinking of wine (*uinolentia*), the reason why the effect of the poisoned mushrooms was not immediately perceivable, a thing that alarmed Agrippina. According to Suetonius *Cl.* 3.2, when upbraiding someone for his *socordia*, Antonia would compare him to her *stultus* son Claudius. **Nero impurior**: In *HA Comm.* 19.2 Commodus is said to be *saeuior Domitiano, impurior Nerone.* The context of this occurrence is in particular deserving of attention, since these remarks are part of the loud *adclamationes* of Commodus' *damnatio memoriae* by the Senate, a passage which is said to be quoted from Marius Maximus in *Comm.* 18 (a divisive assertion for scholars – for the *status* *quaestionis* and different views on its truthfulness see Birley 1997; Paschoud 1999; Kulikowski 2007; Molinier-Arbo 2010). The style of this damning acclamation, the repetition of the invectives against Commodus – all the sections are closed by *unco trahatur* ('let him be dragged with a hook!') – the *accumulatio* of images of foulness is strongly reminiscent of Sidonius' context. Commodus, like Sidonius' informants, is never mentioned by name or as emperor, but instead is repeatedly called 'foe, murderer, gladiator' in *HA* (on which see Baldwin 1981, 140) and also in Cassius Dio 74.2. **Galba auarior**: The soldiers complain about Galba's avarice in Tac. *Hist.* 1.5; see also a similar mention in *Hist.* 1.38. **Otho audacior, Vitellius sumptuosior**: Cf. Tac. *Hist.* 2.31 *Otho luxu saeuitia audacia rei publicae exitiosior ducebatur.* According to Tacitus, 'due to his luxury, cruelty and daring' Otho was considered more dangerous than Vitellius, whose gluttony made him a danger only to himself. **Domitianus truculentior**: See, for comparison, in Plin. *Pan.* 52.7, the description of the statue of Domitian (*saeuissimi domini atrocissima effigies*) as an extension of his ferociousness, worshipped with as much bloodshed of sacrificial victims as the emperor himself was wont to shed the blood of humans.

§ 7

Sane . . . temperat Lucumonem nostrum Tanaquil sua: Only the queen's presence counters the negative actions of informants. By virtue of her influence over Chilperic, he did not turn into a worse tyrant, a thing of 'immediate comfort to those aggrieved', i.e. to Apollinaris. Sidonius chooses to call Chilperic *Lucumo noster*, 'our Lucumo', not mentioning the Burgundian rulers by name but through the parallel with Tarquinius Priscus and Tanaquil, another foreign royal couple. Compare *Lucumo noster* to *tetrarcha noster* (in § 1) and *communis patronus* and *Germanicus noster* (in this paragraph). This is not the first time Tanaquil is mentioned in the works of Sidonius. Tonantius Ferreolus' wife, Papianilla, is said to be even more virtuous than Tanaquil, embodying a perfect *uxor lanifica* of the Archaic age in *Carm.* 24.39, in accordance with the most ancient version of the myth, as in Paul. Fest. 85 L, Seneca's *De Matrimonio* fr. 79 and Plin. *Nat.* 8.194 (see Santelia 2002a, 91 and 94–5; Santini 2005, 205). One could argue that, in this letter, Sidonius rather draws upon Livy's literary portrait of Tanaquil as scheming, personally involved in politics, munificent with *consilia* both to Tarquinius (Liv. 1.34.7) and to Servius Tullius (Liv. 1.41.4). In Livy, Tanaquil's strong personality emerges in the two speeches she delivers, inspiring Servius with courage and the crowd with confidence, on which see Ogilvie 1965, 143 and 161, who calls her a *'femme fatale'*. On the controversial issue of Tacitus' portrait of Livia being modelled on Livy's Tanaquil, see Ogilvie 1965, 161–4 (in favour); and, on the *status quaestionis*, Bauman 1994, 177–88. Note how Sidonius' identification of the Burgundian queen with the Livian Tanaquil puts her in a positive light, making her the heroine in resolving the issue, and that, as stated by Favrod 1997, 247 n. 80 and Furbetta 2014–2015a, 147 n. 86, this role of intermediary with the king will be a feature of other Burgundian queens (see remarks on the *Vita sancti Marcelli* in the introduction). Similar positive mentions of Tanaquil after Livy are also the praises for her divinatory art in Sil. 13.818–20 and in Claud. *Carm. min.* 30.15–16 (on which see Consolino 1986, 77–8). Unlike Sidonius, negative mentions of Tanaquil appear for instance in Juvenal and in Ausonius, which Geisler 1887, 366 suggested be compared to § 7, possibly for the occurrence of the possessive adjective in both contexts. In the violent invective of Juv. 6.565–71 the woman, called *Tanaquil tua*, is said to have consulted an astrologist to predict the deaths of her mother, her husband, her sister, her uncles and her lover. Also Aus. *Ep.* 22.30–1 (Green) *Tanaquil tua*, the passing mention of Paulinus of Nola's wife Therasia as Tanaquil, is not flattering and is aimed at suggesting the friend is bent to her will (see also Mondin 1995, 247–8); eventually Paulinus responded to this jibe in *Carm.* 10.192 (ed. Hartel) *nec Tanaquil mihi, sed Lucretia coniunx* (for context see Trout 1999, 69–71 and Santini 2005, 206). When mentioning the Burgundian queen as Tanaquil, Sidonius lacks the polemical intent of Ausonius, and the queen is pictured as positively steering her husband.

et aures mariti uirosa susurronum faece completas: Another reference to the informants as venomous snakes (see commentary on *Ep.* 5.6.2, and here § 4 and § 6), whispering vile insinuations in Chilperic's ear. The substantive *susurro* is attested only in late Latin, since Cyprian's *Ad Quirinum* 3.110, with fewer than twenty occurrences, and notably in Jerome *Epp.* 11.4, 108.19 and 125.19. The *iunctura uirosa faex* is not previously attested, and in *L&S* (s.v. *uirosus*) this passage is the only one quoted for the metaphoric use of the adjective, translated as 'foul'. Compare Sidonius' occurrence with Symm. *Or.* 4.7, where Symmachus' disdain of the *libertina ac plebeia faex* is not that distant from Sidonius' classism in this letter. As noted by Gualandri 1979, 113 n. 24, similar in wording, but not as strong as the occurrence here in § 7, is Sidon. *Ep.* 3.13.11, where men whose tongues are soaked

SIDONIUS: LETTERS BOOK 5, PART 1

with *loquacis faece petulantiae* ('the filth of wanton blabber') are those with the dirtiest conscience. Gualandri 1979, 113 also points out that the occurrence in Sidonius of similar metaphors 'robuste e concrete' is ascribable to the influence of biblical language.

opportunitate salsi sermonis: The expression is very rarely attested, and apart from Sidonius it is known to occur exclusively in Firm. *Mat.* 8.7.1 and Ennod. *Ep.* 2.12.2; see Furbetta 2014–2015a, 149 n. 95. Sidonius employs it also to describe his conversations with his friends in *Ep.* 2.9.9 and in the series of exclamations expressing his enthusiasm for Constantius' visit to besieged Clermont in *Ep.* 3.2.1. Expressions relatable to the sense of taste are common in Sidonius, see e.g. the *piperata facundia* and the *salsa libertas* in the following *Ep.* 5.8.2 (see commentary ad loc.) and, similarly, the *mellea* and *piperata* epigrams in *Ep.* 8.11.7. For Sidonius' use of metaphorical expressions, see Wolff 2020, 403.

eruderat: Like the previous syntagma, the verb *erudero* is rarely attested since its first occurrence in Varro *Rust.* 2.2.7, where it concerns cleaning *solum*; it then occurs mostly with this literal meaning, also in Sidon. *Ep.* 5.13.1, where it concerns cleaning the roads by removing fallen leaves. In *TLL* 5.2.827 s.v. *erudero* 81 (by Kapp and Meyer) the only passages mentioned for the metaphorical use of the verb are by Sidonius and, later, by Ennodius (*Opusc.* 10.3). See also Sidon. *Ep.* 5.15.1, where a book has been *de superuacuis sententiis eruderatum*; and, notably, *Ep.* 7.6.3, where the spiritual *stercora* swept away with *rastra* ('hoes of prayer') definitely call to mind the *faex* cleaned out by the queen; see van Waarden 2010, 295.

Cuius studio factum scire uos par est: Sirmond gives no explanation for his removal of *factum*, nor does Warmington comment on his conjecture (in Anderson 1965, 194). *Factum* can be considered to be a noun, provided that a comma is added after *est*, and this punctuation is justifiable since *scire uos par est* is a cretic spondee clausula. The passage is translated as: 'it is right that you should know the outcome thanks to her support, that . . .' A similar use of the noun *factum* can be found in *Ep.* 3.12.5 *ut uitium non faciat in marmore lapidicida; quod factum . . . mihi magis quam quadratario liuidus lector adscribet*. Should one consider *factum* as a passive verb and supply *est* or *esse*, the passage could be translated as 'it is right that you should know that thanks to her support, it was achieved / it was decided that . . .'; however, one would normally expect *factum est/esse* to be followed by *ut* +

LETTER 7

subjunctive, as in Sidon. *Ep.* 7.9.3 *factum est, ut omnes non aspernanter audirent* and in *Carm.* 2.280–2 *factum est ut . . . terga daret.*

fratrum communium apud animum communis patroni: Much has been said in this commentary on the meaning of the expression *fratres communes*, and on Sidonius' conventional use of *frater* to indicate spiritual brotherhood. It has been argued that the possibility envisaged in *PCBE* 4 that this expression refers to the involvement of Simplicius is to be rejected (see the introduction to *Ep.* 5.4). Compare the mention of king Chilperic as *patronus* to that of the Burgundians as *patroni* in *Ep.* 7.11.1. The expression *communis patronus* is coherent with the previous *Lucumo noster* at the beginning of this paragraph, with *tetrarcha noster* at the beginning of the letter (§ 1) and, symmetrically, with *Germanicus noster* at the end of the letter.

iuniorum Cibyratarum uenena: The mention of the informants as *iuniores Cibyrates* is an explicit homage to *In Verrem*. The two brothers from Cibyra, Tlepolemus and Hiero, first appear in *Ver.* 2.4.30, when Cicero introduces them as suspected of having plundered the temple of Apollo in Cibyra and states that, as exiled for that crime, they were promptly hired by Verres, who availed himself of their skills as thieves and spies. While recounting their threats and thieveries, the two are described as bloodhounds in Cic. *Ver.* 2.4.31 (*canes uenaticos diceres*) and the same image occurs in *Ver.* 2.4.47. This portrait of the Cibyrates as hunting dogs, scenting and tracking anything that may have been of interest to them, and acquiring it by threats or promises, ruthlessly availing themselves of flattery as well as of extortion, makes them the perfect models and predecessors to their junior version Sidonius has just described. One thinks of the informants' monstrous metamorphosis in § 5, triggered only by some 'scent of money' blowing to their nose. If the reference to Cicero is known to scholars (see, e.g. the passing mentions in Furbetta 2014–2015a, 146 n. 84 and 149 n. 93 and in Wolff 2020, 400), further reflection is needed. One may wonder if the mention hides further criticism, because in Cicero the two are mere procurers for Verres, an extension of their master (they are 'his eyes' in *Ver.* 2.4.33). Chilperic, however, is merely influenced by the informants surrounding him – he is not an instigator like Verres. It has never been observed that the occurrence of the Cibyrates' image in Ammianus Marcellinus 15.3.3, and the whole of his description of slanderers 15.3.3–11, seems closer to their mention in Sidonius than the Ciceronian model itself. In Amm. 15.3.3, emperor Constantius is said to have 'opened his heart and made it accessible to many lurking men' (*insidiantibus multis*). Ammianus compares these informants to beasts that go hunting for rumours, 'tearing apart with feral bites' the highest officials. They are even worse than Ciceronian Cibyrates, whose only object of adulation was Verres, because they torment *membra rei publicae* (15.3.3). For Ammianus' use of exempla see Kelly 2008, 276. In Ammianus 15.3.4, one of the informants is called Catena for his ability to intertwine inextricable tangles of slander, making up an extraordinary number of baseless accusations. Moreover, in Amm. 15.3.5 Mercurius is compared to 'a dog that is covertly a biter' (*clam mordax canis*) since he listens to descriptions of dreams at banquets and *id uenenatis artibus coloratum in peius, patulis imperatoris auribus infundebat* ('having given to it a worse colour by his venomous skills, he poured it into the wide open ears of the emperor'), a passage strongly reminiscent of the *uenena* whispered in the ears of the Burgundian king (see Kelly 2008, 172 for 'Ammianus' fondness for casting the officials of Constantius in the language of Plautine comedy'). Reading this text in light of that of Ammianus may allow one to better understand Sidonius' invective, because Chilperic is not represented as a new Verres, and he is arguably more similar to Constantius, because, like him, he is *ad suspiciones . . . mollis et penetrabilis* in Amm. 15.3.9 ('weak and easily influenced by suspicions'). Note, however, that references to history following the Flavian dynasty do not occur often in Sidonius, although, in *Ep.* 5.8.2, Constantine's killing of his wife, Fausta, and his son, Crispus, is mentioned as a negative exemplum. And yet, if one cannot assume that Ammianus may have been a model for this section, since he is not a historian Sidonius mentions, and since no secure allusions have been identified, one may wonder if there was an otherwise unattested (rhetorical?) tradition, according to which Cibyratae had become emblematic of slander, rather than of theft.

praesens potestas: Chilperic's *potestas* is already mentioned in § 6 as that which makes him *praestans*. In this case the term specifically concerns his control over the region, and is relatable to the mention of Chilperic as *patronus*. The lexical choice of such a generic term seems to betray the usual Sidonian awkwardness when speaking of Burgundian rulers (see the commentary on *magistro militum* and on *uictoriosissimo* in *Ep.* 5.6.2). In such an unstable and unwonted situation, it is understandable that Sidonius is reluctant to call Chilperic's rule something other than a *patronatus*.

Lugdunensem Germaniam: An unattested and oxymoronic expression of 'poignant sarcasm' as Kulikowski fittingly puts it (2020, 236 n. 174). The

Gallic province of *Lugdunensis prima* is transformed into *Germania* because Burgundians rule over Lyon. Note also the further word game in the following mention of Chilperic as Germanicus.

nostrum suumque Germanicum praesens Agrippina moderetur: Cf. the possessive adjectives *Lucumo noster* and *Tanaquil sua* at the beginning of the paragraph. In this case, the choice of the historical couple Germanicus and Agrippina is dictated by the intention to play further on the previous *Germania Lugdunensis* through the speaking name of Germanicus. At the same time, however, Germanicus was known for his campaigns against Germans and, according to Tacitus' portrait, he was popular and loved by the people who favoured him, unlike Tiberius (*Ann.* 1.33). Apart from the obvious ethnic reason, Chilperic may be called Germanicus also for his support against the Goths, being therefore a new Germanicus fighting against Germans. The Sidonian allusion is, as usual when Burgundian rulers are involved, layered, and lends itself to different interpretations. Germanicus' wife, Agrippina the Elder, is portrayed by Tacitus *Ann.* 1.33 as of rather *indomitus animus*, which, however, she had channelled into a *bonus animus* out of devotion to Germanicus. Agrippina is also said to have followed Germanicus in his campaigns and to have been strong-willed, even acting as a general in a moment of crisis (*Ann.* 1.69). Agrippina's devotion to her husband (see also *Ann.* 2.75 and how she is praised as by the crowd as *decus patriae* in *Ann.* 3.4), together with her strong personality, make her a suitable alter ego for Sidonius' panegyrical portrait of the Burgundian queen. See the above commentary on *temperat Lucumonem* . . . and the introduction to *Ep.* 5.7 for the theme of Catholic Burgundian queens having a pivotal role as intermediaries with their hard and irascible husbands.

LETTER 8

Content

A letter in praise of Secundinus, described as author of hexameters, epithalamia and panegyrics. Sidonius' interest is most captivated by his phalaecian hendecasyllables, written against the people of Lyon and praised for their *piperata facundia*, their 'spiced eloquence'.

The addressee Secundinus

The informality of the author's way of addressing Secundinus in this letter testifies that the two are on good terms, as the commentary further explains.[1] Sidonius is the only source of information on Secundinus,[2] mentioned as a distinguished poet also in *Ep.* 2.10, where Sidonius tells Hesperius of the dedication of the Lyon cathedral, which featured three inscribed poems, one written by him, one by Constantius and one by Secundinus.[3]

> *Huius igitur aedis extimis rogatu praefati antistitis tumultuarium carmen inscripsi trochaeis triplicibus adhuc mihi iamque tibi perfamiliaribus. Namque ab hexametris eminentium poetarum Constantii et Secundini uicinantia altari basilicae latera clarescunt, quos in hanc paginam admitti nostra quam maxume uerecundia uetat, quam suas otiositates trepidanter edentem meliorum carminum comparatio premit.* (*Ep.* 2.10.3)

In this passage Constantius and Secundinus are called *eminentes poetae* and their respective inscriptions are said to be both in hexameters and located on either side of the altar, while Sidonius' is in 'triple trochees'

---

1. See e.g. the consistent use of the second person singular.
2. See *PLRE* 2 s.v. Secundinus 3, 985; Heinzelmann 1982 s.v. Secundinus 2, 690; *PCBE* 4, 1724; Mathisen 2020, 120.
3. Constantius is the same poet from Lyon to whom Sidonius dedicates the first eight books of the *Letters*. See *PLRE* 2, s.v. Constantius 10, 320; *PCBE* 4, s.v. Constantius 3, 521–2. On *Ep.* 2.10, see Onorato 2020, 86–90 and Hindermann 2022, 290–4 and 302–7.

(i.e. hendecasyllables) and on 'the outermost part of the church': the apse. Unfortunately, Sidonius chooses not to transmit the text of his colleagues' inscriptions, ascribing his reticence to the shame (*uerecundia uetat*) of having his 'unworthy text compared to such superior compositions'.[4]

Genre

The beginning of the letter ('it has been a long time since we . . . eagerly read the hexameters') immediately evokes the features of letters on epistolary silence, a standard way, in particular in Symmachus' collection, of writing to friends.[5] As stated before in this commentary, complaining about epistolary silence did not necessarily mean that the addressee had been reluctant to write, but rather was, most often, a polite way of claiming a friend's attention and of showing one's affection.

But this letter is also ascribable to the category of 'epistles on literary matters' theorised by Cugusi, a type of letter already mentioned in the introductory section to *Ep.* 5.2.[6] In particular, as the commentary further explains, the praise of the friend's works in *Ep.* 5.8 is very similar, in terms of content and language, to Pliny the Younger's *Epp.* 1.16.5, 4.3.4 and 6.21.5.[7] Moreover, Stoehr-Monjou believes that in *Ep.* 5.8 (as already in *Ep.* 4.22) Sidonius is alluding to Pliny's *Ep.* 5.8: his *recusatio* of historiography.[8] According to Stoehr-Monjou, Sidonius hints 'numerically' at his model, and in particular at Pliny's assertion that *historia quoquo modo scripta delectat*, even in the form of *sermunculi* and *fabellae*.[9] In compliance with this recognition of men's taste for anecdotes and small talk, Sidonius supposedly inserted the detail of Constantine's murders of Fausta and Crispus, also relating the

---

4. For this declaration of modesty and for Sidonius' choice not to copy Constantius' and Secundinus' verses see Santelia 2007, 306–7 and Condorelli 2008, 197. For Sidonius concealing his pride for gaining the most important place in the new church see Hernández Lobato 2010b, 298. For Sidonius' choice of the phalaecian hendecasyllable, in order for his poem to stand out, see Onorato 2020, 88.
5. See the introduction to *Ep.* 5.3 for detailed information on letters concerning epistolary silence in Symmachus and in Sidonius.
6. To which we refer here, in order to avoid repetition. See Cugusi 1983, 110.
7. *Ep.* 5.8 constitutes an exception; in fact, so far, the commentary on other letters of the book confirms Gibson's observation (2013b, 350) that Pliny's presence 'begins to contract in Sidonius' Book 5', in favour of a considerable presence of Symmachus, one may add.
8. Stoehr-Monjou 2012, 246.
9. Plin. *Ep.* 5.8.4.

SIDONIUS: LETTERS BOOK 5, PART 1

gruesome ways in which they were killed (contraposing a boiling bath to the chill of poison).[10]

It should be pointed out that the praise of Secundinus granted him his own spot in Sidonius' letter collection, and, actually, if it were not for Sidonius, we would not know of this author's existence. In particular, before Sidonius, his declared model, Symmachus, is keen to praise friends' works by addressing them directly, instead of writing to a third party.[11] It seems therefore useful, in order to provide context for the genre of this text, to compare Sidon. *Ep.* 5.8 to Symm. *Ep.* 1.14.2, where the praise of Ausonius' *Mosella* is also followed by affectionate criticism for not having received the work, unlike others.[12] A fruitful comparison is also that with Symmachus' letters to Naucellius (*Epp.* 3.11–13) containing praises of the addressee's works.

Satire or *uersus populares?*

In *Ep.* 5.8.3 Sidonius exhorts Secundinus to continue devoting himself to *facetis satirarum coloribus* and, in doing so, he makes explicit that the 'spiced and salty' verses he mentioned before are satires.[13] One should, however, reconsider Sidonius' use of the word, which does not match the features of the satirical genre as we know it. Secundinus' verses, which are undoubtedly of satirical content, seem closer to a modern idea of satire than to the genre as it was canonised in ancient literature in terms of both content and metre. Secundinus' verses are direct attacks on his fellow citizens, likely to have been *ad personam*, since their circulation is said to have been hindered by those attacked (*Ep.* 5.8.1). Moreover, Secundinus writes hendecasyllables, whereas satire was traditionally in hexameters.

Secundinus' verses are significantly compared to Ablabius' couplet in hendecasyllables against Constantine, a parallel which may give a clearer idea of what is being discussed in this passage: not satires *stricto sensu* but *uersus populares*. In his *Tra poesia e politica: le pasquinate nell'antica Roma*, Giovanni Cupaiuolo has outlined the tradition of what he calls 'political verses', mostly anonymous expressions of protest against politicians, renowned

---

10. Sidon. *Ep.* 5.8.2. See the commentary ad loc. for Sidonius' chronological inversion of the deaths.
11. As Sidonius does, for instance, in *Ep.* 5.2 when praising Mamertus' *De statu animae* to his addressee, Nymphidius.
12. See the introduction to *Ep.* 5.2 in the present volume
13. For further observations on Sidonius' mentions of 'satires' see Marolla 2021b, *passim*.

LETTER 8

aristocrats and emperors. These verses express a more visceral form of invective, reminiscent of the ὀνομαστὶ κωμῳδεῖν of Attic comedy, which, after Lucilius, was lost in Roman satire, in favour of a 'more philosophical and introspective critique'.[14] One could also take into account Seneca's *Apocolocyntosis*, Juvenal's satires, the unique attacks made by the emperor Julian on his predecessors in his *Caesares*,[15] or Ausonius' own *Caesares*, works comprising fierce attacks on emperors, but all dead ones. On the contrary, *uersus populares* are something different, a vibrant expression of discontentment when the politician or the emperor attacked is alive and bears with these forms of popular opinion.

When tracing a history of the genre, Cupaiuolo outlines how metrically various *uersus populares* are (from the most common trochaic septenarii, iambic senarii and elegiac distichs to the later and less attested hendecasyllables).[16] He also points out how emperors became the favourite object of these attacks, which started to be written more often by men of culture and officers expressing their dissent for specific political choices, rather than being an expression of generic popular discontent.[17] As the commentary explains, the distich against Tiberius, who is said to have turned the golden age into an iron age, is very similar to the anti-Constantinian couplet mentioned by Sidonius.[18] Suetonius mentions numerous distichs addressed to Tiberius, who, for instance, is said to be hated by his own mother,[19] and to enjoy 'drinking blood the way he used to drink wine'.[20] Galba is criticised for being too strict in a mocking verse which became very popular in the camp (*statim . . . per castra iactatum est*).[21] Nero is the object of numerous attacks in verse, also in Greek, as is testified by Suet. *Ner.* 39.2, for his liaison with

---

14. See Cupaiuolo 1993, 7–10.
15. Julian fiercely represents his predecessors, from Augustus, the 'chameleon', to Constantine, embraced by Luxury and guided by Debauchery to an all-forgiving Jesus in *Caes.* 335–6.
16. Cupaiuolo 1993, 138.
17. Cupaiuolo 1993, 63. Cupaiuolo 1993, 10 n. 8 lists numerous collections of *uersus populares* in *editions*, starting with Bernstein's *Versus ludicri in Romanorum Caesares priores olim compositi* (1810), Baehrens' *Fragmenta Poetarum Romanorum* (1886) and Morel's *Fragmenta Poetarum Latinorum* (1927), to which one can add the more recent edition by Blänsdorf 2011.
18. Suet. *Tib.* 59.1 *aurea mutasti Saturni saecula, Caesar / incolumi nam te ferrea semper erunt.*
19. Suet. *Tib.* 59.1 *asper et immitis, breuiter uis omnia dicam? / dispeream, si te mater amare potest.*
20. Suet. *Tib.* 59.1 *fastidit uinum, quia iam sitit iste cruorem / tam bibit hunc auide, quam bibit ante merum.* For all the distichs against Tiberius see Cupaiuolo 1993, 65–8.
21. Suet. *Gal.* 6.2 *disce miles militare: Galba est, non Gaetulicus.*

Poppaea, for the matricide and for the construction of the *Domus Aurea*.[22] Domitian[23] and Commodus,[24] among others, are also known to have been objects of similar anonymous verses.[25]

It seems important to highlight how these verses were 'published' by being engraved or placed in public places, so that even people randomly passing by could read and pass on the taunts. *Versus populares* were placed in symbolically significant spots. That is also the case of the distich against Constantine, which, in *Ep.* 5.8.2, is said to have been hung on the gates of the imperial palace. It seems likely that Secundinus' verses were published and circulated, since Sidonius says their diffusion was voluntarily hindered by those who had been criticised. Sidonius' letter, therefore, is a unique text, since it is the only witness of this anti-Constantinian invective in hendecasyllables, but also because it testifies that the genre was still alive in fifth-century Gaul.

Sidonius' mentions of 'satire'

An overview seems necessary to put Sidonius' testimony in context, since the reference to satire in *Ep.* 5.8 would otherwise mislead the reader. As stated above, Sidonius' use of the word 'satire' is actually closer to a contemporary idea of political slander and does not always refer to works in hexameters.[26] Sidonius' assertion of being admittedly keen on using hendecasyllables when writing a *lusus* in *Ep.* 9.15.1 – a thing Gelasius reproaches him for – should probably be referred to this extended use of the word *satira*. Hendecasyllable is mentioned as *perfamiliaris* to Sidonius in *Ep.* 2.10.3, and, as Condorelli effectively puts it, 'è metro caro a Sidonio, perché compatto e scorrevole (*rotundatus*)'.[27]

---

22. Cupaiuolo 1993, 70–3. See, for instance, the graffito which is said to have appeared in many places comparing Nero to other famous matricides, in Dio Cassius 62.16 Νέρων Ὀρέστης Ἀλκμέων μητροκτόνοι.
23. See e.g. Suet. *Dom.* 14.2, where a couplet in Greek is introduced by a remark on how easily these verses circulated: *sparsi libelli cum his uersibus erant*; see also Mart. *Spec.* 37 (33) *Flauia gens, quantum tibi tertius abstulit heres! / paene fuit tanti, non habuisse duos.*
24. Commodus is badly insulted in six pentameters transmitted by *HA* Lampr. *Diad.* 7.2–4, where they are said to have been translated from Greek.
25. See Cupaiuolo 1993, 77 and 81.
26. All references to satire, henceforth, take into account the wider meaning given to this word by Sidonius, as straightforward writings condemning contemporary politics.
27. Condorelli 2008, 196 n. 48. See also Sidonius' description of the metre in *Carm.* 23.25–8 *triplicis metrum trochaei / spondeo comitante dactyloque, / dulces hendecasyllabos, tuumque / blando*

The same background of *uersus populares* and their distinctive features outlined in the previous section – hendecasyllables (also), written to mock living politicians, known to have been widespread, publicly placed and tolerated even by the powerful rulers attacked – can also be referred to other explicit mentions of satire in Sidonius, who expresses his interest in the genre, which is praised with enthusiastic words on various occasions.[28]

In *Ep.* 5.17, the description of the writing Sidonius is asked to compose 'against someone who does not tolerate good days' seems to fall within the broader category of Sidonian satire.[29]

> *Da postulatae tu ueniam cantilenae. Illud autem ambo, quod maius est quodque me nuper in quendam dies bonos male ferentem parabolice seu figurate dictare iussistis quodque expeditum cras dirigetur, clam recensete; et, si placet, edentes fouete; si displicet, delentes ignoscitote.* (*Ep.* 5.17.11)

Please be indulgent with this silly song you asked. On the other hand, it is more important what both of you recently asked me to compose, either metaphorically or figuratively, against someone who does not tolerate good days, a thing that is ready and tomorrow will be on its way to you: go through it privately and, if you like it, divulge it by publishing it; if it does not satisfy you, destroy it and do forgive me.

The Arles satire and the satires of Secundinus

The satire mentioned in *Ep.* 1.11 circulated anonymously in Arles in 461, under the reign of Majorian, until Paeonius, the former *praefectus praetorio Galliarum* and one of those lampooned in the satire, formally accused Sidonius of being its author. The entertaining account of the events involves a peculiar scene in which the emperor personally addresses the issue with Sidonius at a banquet, telling him '*audio, comes Sidoni, quod satiram scribas*' and asking Sidonius to 'spare him, at least'.[30] After Sidonius' firm refutation and his request to openly challenge the accuser, the matter is resolved with

---

faenore Sollium ligasti. For a detailed argument on the features of Sidonian hendecasyllables, and on their occurrences in the corpus, see Condorelli 2020a, 440 and 453–5.

28. E.g. *mordacitas* in *Ep.* 5.8.2 – see the commentary ad loc. for further praises.

29. See the commentary on *Ep.* 5.8.2 for the occurrence of the adverb *figurate* in both contexts.

30. *Ep.* 1.11.13.

the emperor's request that Sidonius will compose verses on the spot against Paeonius.[31]

According to Loyen, Sidonius' praise of satire in Book 5 contrasts strongly with his firm denial, in *Ep.* 1.11, of being the author of the satire that circulated in Arles, since Sidonius oddly refers to the same topic in two antithetical ways.[32] Stoehr-Monjou believes this is part of a game of allusions, connected to the inner coherence of the corpus, with the praise of Theoderic II and the denial of being a satirist in Book 1 (*Epp.* 1.2 and 1.11) opposed to the critique of 'tyrannical Burgundians' and a praise of satire in Book 5 (*Ep.* 5.8).[33] Before discussing the matter of *Ep.* 1.11 at length, it should be emphasised that Secundinus' satire mentioned in *Ep.* 5.8 is not an attack on Burgundians, since their mention as tyrants is but incidental (as the commentary explains) and is a way of insulting the people of Lyon more than Burgundians. Sidonius states in no uncertain terms that the object of Secundinus' attacks is the misdeeds of 'their fellow citizens' of Lyon.[34]

One should also consider that *Ep.* 1.11 is a refutation of a specific text, not of a genre: in the letter there is no intrinsic criticism of the genre itself, and the allusion to satire as adequate for elderly writers – being too risky for younger ones – does not entail a negative judgement, given that Sidonius playfully implies he would himself be old enough were he to be the writer of such a text.[35] He feels the need to deny the paternity of *that* satire because of the political repercussions that might fall on its author, since the widespread whispers of having written that had already exposed him politically.[36]

It is worthy of note that the emperor shows no surprise and actual amusement at the news of Sidonius being a satirist, asking him, with a laugh, to be merciful to him.[37] His reaction would seem to hint that it was

---

31. For the Horatian model of the passage see Mazzoli 2005–2006, 178. Sidonius composes an elegiac distich on the spot.

32. Loyen 1970a, 255; see also Stoehr-Monjou 2012, 240.

33. Stoehr-Monjou 2012, 246.

34. Note that the description is reminiscent of that of the informants in the *Ep.* 5.7. In *Ep.* 5.8, people of Lyon are said to be greedy, swelling with richness and wrongdoings, and likely to be of immortal fame because of their misdeeds. As the commentary further explains, both attacks may actually be directed to people of Lyon.

35. *Ep.* 1.11.1.

36. See *Ep.* 1.11.2 *illud quod me sinistrae rumor ac fumus opinionis adflauit.* Paeonius unleashed against him, unaware of the entire matter, the hatred of a multitude of people of the worst kind (*Ep.* 1.11.7).

37. *Ep.* 1.11.13. Sidonius shows he is in friendly terms with Majorian; on the episode see also Hanaghan 2019, 110–12.

not that unusual for a satire to circulate at court, even though the whole narrative of the episode is highly stylised, if not fictional, and filled with such self-praise that Sidonius emerges as a character of heroic stature. But, nonetheless, this lenient attitude of the emperor matches the indulgence of his predecessors towards *uersus populares* discussed above.

Also worthy of mention is the fact that, in both *Epp.* 1.11 and 5.8, satirical verses are said to be publicly displayed in places which represent the essence of imperial power. Indeed, that was the distinctive feature of *uersus populares*, as stated previously. In *Ep.* 1.11.3, Sidonius' friend Catullinus is said to have read and laughed aloud at the content of the satire, adding that the poem deserved to be engraved in letters made of gold and to be publicly displayed at the Rostra or in the Capitol. Similarly, when praising Secundinus in *Ep.* 5.8.2, Sidonius mentions that the distich against Constantine, written by an absolutely central figure at his court, was affixed defiantly to the entrance of the imperial palace.

At the end of the episode in *Ep.* 1.11, Sidonius receives an official *placet* from the emperor to write satirical verses against his accuser, as is noted by Mazzoli, who, through the detection of the Horatian model of *Ep.* 1.11, pictures Sidonius as perfectly comfortable with satire, and reads the episode at Arles as the moment that for Sidonius programmatically sanctions the legitimacy of writing satires.[38] The episode is in fact at the end of Book 1, and, incidentally, Book 2 starts with a letter of harsh satirical content.[39]

Further evidence that these 'satirical' verses circulated under Majorian may be given by the content of the elegiac couplet attributed to Sidonius, or to his entourage,[40] transmitted (after Ovid's *Halieutica*) by Vindobonensis latinus 277 (58^r) and by its apograph Parisinus latinus 8071.[41]

---

38. Mazzoli 2005–2006, 178.

39. On the evolution of Sidonian satire, which goes beyond Horace, Mazzoli follows Blänsdorf 1993, 131, who perceives Sidonius as the precursor of medieval political and ecclesiastical satire. Mazzoli 2005–2006, 182 also mentions *Ep.* 4.18.6 to show how Sidonius appreciates the effectiveness and vehemence of satire: 'al tono blando usato nei confronti d'un amico da troppo tempo assente sostituisce alla fine la minaccia di ricorrere, se necessario, *uersibus quoque satirographis*, perché *efficacius, citius, ardentius natura mortalium culpat aliqua quam laudet*'.

40. Since Pithou 1590, 466, who reports that 'non sine ratione putet aliquis esse Sidonii'; similarly, Sirmond 1652, *Notae*, 118, and Lütjohann 1887, xxii. For the information concerning this finding and for the linguistic similarities between this distich and Sidon. *Carm.* 5 (153–4) and *Carm.* 13 (17–18) see Santelia 2005, 71–2. See also Dolveck 2020, 481 n. 12.

41. For Par. lat. 8071 apograph of Vindob. lat. 277, see Shackleton Bailey's edition (1982,

Ceruus, aper, coluber non cursu, dente ueneno
uitarunt ictus, Maioriane, tuos.
(*Anth. Lat.* 387 SB = 391 R)

The text, which could be translated as follows 'not even by running, biting or poison, did the stag, boar or snake escape your blows, Majorian', is unfortunately transmitted without any indication of context, but it can be interpreted as a jest: Majorian is said to be intimidating and effective in brutally annihilating his enemies.[42] Given this interpretation of the text, and in light of what was said above on *uersus populares*, van Waarden's suggestion to link this distich to the 'satirical' context of *Ep.* 1.11 is here welcome as further evidence that the genre was still popular.[43]

As the commentary on *Ep.* 5.8.3 explains, when Sidonius mentions satire he is keen on pointing out that, although he enjoys satirical compositions, one should write them only when one can count on the *securitas* of the right political protection. That is why he declares it would not be advisable for him to write history in *Ep.* 4.22.5: a truthful description of contemporary misdeeds would inevitably have him blend 'the shades and scents of satire',[44] causing him to encounter general disfavour. A similar assertion can also be found in *Carm.* 12.20–2 *sed iam Musa tacet tenetque habenas / paucis hendecasyllabis iocata, / ne quisquam satiram uel hos uocaret*. The Muse is pictured in the act of 'drawing rein' and of stopping Sidonius after a few hendecasyllables, 'lest anyone call also *these* verses a satire'. The addressee is the same Catullinus who read enthusiastically the Satire of Arles, to which it seems the *uel hos* ('these verses as well') refer. While pretending to write a *recusatio* of satire, Sidonius has just finished writing one, filled with misobarbaric comments on the appearance of the Burgundians.[45] By virtue of what was said above, *Carm.* 12 has, also metrically since it is in hendecasyllables and

---

vi). I can confirm from the digitisations that in both manuscripts the couplet is copied without any kind of distinguishing mark.

42. Of this opinion seems also Dolveck 2020, who mentions the distich as being 'against Majorian'.

43. Van Waarden 2020a, 17 n. 33: 'could it be associated with the satire that circulated in Arles, for which Sidonius was decried, in *Ep.* 1.11?'

44. *Ep.* 4.22.5 *color odorque satiricus admiscet.*

45. Smolak 2008, 49–50 ascribes the choice not to use hexameter in this *Carmen* to the need to avoid being openly satirical; on the allusion to *Ep.* 1.11 in *Carm.* 12 and on the simulated *recusatio* see also Condorelli 2008, 124–6; Santelia 2019, 301–2; Consolino 2020, 358; Mratschek 2020, 21–5.

LETTER 8

not in hexameters, the features of what Sidonius mentions as 'satire' also in
Ep. 5.8.[46]

The passages mentioned, in conclusion, lead to the inference that the
genre of *uersus populares* was alive in fifth-century southern Gaul. Although
rulers were traditionally lenient towards these expressions of dissent, not all
of them tolerated the jibes, as can be surmised by the issue of *CTh.* 9.34.1–
10, *De famosis libellis.* As noted by Köhler,[47] *De famosis libellis* constitutes a
factual background for the narrative of the Satire of Arles episode, and, one
could add, also for *Ep.* 5.8. The fact that a specific section of the *Codex*
condemned slanderers to severe punishments is proof that satirical writings
were perceived as a problem of some sort; for instance, pamphlets should
be burnt according to *CTh.* 9.34.10, an eastern law of 406.[48] Even in *Ep.*
1.11.13, although Majorian is portrayed as entertained and indulgent, when
Sidonius asks for the emperor's permission to write verses against Paeonius,
he adds that he is counting on Majorian's clemency and has no intention
of breaking the law: *oro ut indultu clementiae tuae praeter iuris iniuriam in ac-
cusatorem meum quae uolo scribam.*

Ablabius and the couplet against Constantine

Since Sidonius' *Ep.* 5.8 is the only source for the distich against Constantine,
portrayed as a new Nero, the letter has attracted the attention of leading
scholars in the field. Sidonius glosses the couplet, ascribing it to Ablabius,
Constantine's praetorian prefect from 329 to 337 and consul in 331. He also
says that the invective concerns the killings of Constantine's wife, Fausta,
and of his son, Crispus, both brutally murdered at the emperor's command.

Callu reads the distich as a testimony of the tensions that had risen at court
between 326 and 330, after the jewelled diadem entered the official portraits
of Constantine, since it was perceived as an expression of autocracy.[49] And
yet, Sidonius' (otherwise unattested) mention of Ablabius being covertly

---

46. For further thoughts on this see Marolla 2021b, 142–4.
47. Köhler 1995, 289–90. *CTh.* 9.34.9 orders the reporting of authors of slanderous letters.
48. *CTh.* 9.34.10, *Imppp. Arcadius, Honorius et Theodosius aaa. Anthemio praefecto praetorio et
patricio. Uniuersi, qui famosis libellis inimicis suis uelut uenenatum quoddam telum iniecerint, ii
etiam, qui famosam seriem scriptionis impudenti agnitam lectione non ilico discerpserint uel flammis
exusserint uel lectorem cognitum prodiderint, ultorem suis ceruicibus gladium reformident. dat. iiii
kal. mai. Constantinopoli Arcadio a. ui et Probo conss.* (28 April 406).
49. Callu 1995b, 502.

oppositional is puzzling. As summarised by Barnes, 'Sidonius can hardly be correct in attributing the distich to the praetorian prefect of Constantine'.[50]

A convincing explanation is provided by Chausson, who highlights that not only is Ablabius known to have been a member of Constantine's entourage, close to the emperor, but he is also known to have prospered in the years following the deaths of Crispus and Fausta, which took place in 326.[51] Chausson also recalls that Ablabius' career advanced in particular between 329 and 337, and therefore suggests that Sidonius (who also inverts the order of the killings) may have got the name of the emperor wrong, and therefore he – or his source – may have confused Constantine with Constantius. In light of his career, an eventual protest against Constantius in 337, after Constantine's death, would also be coherent with Sidonius' mention of Ablabius as consul, and with his subsequent disappearance from sources, possibly due to his being victim of Constantius' purges in the second half of 337.[52]

Barnes concludes that Sidonius may have depended on a fourth-century anti-Christian source, which compared the first Christian emperor to the first emperor who put Christians to death.[53] Harries does not mention Ablabius as the author of the distich, but believes it to be the work of an 'anonymous scribbler'.[54] In conclusion, it seems probable that either the author of the distich was not Ablabius, or, if it were him, it was likely addressed to Constantius and not to his father, Constantine.

Dating elements

There is no element in the letter which allows scholars to date it with any degree of certainty, and Table 10 shows some of the different dates suggested in editions and in prosopography.

Anderson is the only who believes the Burgundian 'tyrant' is to be identified with Gundobad, and therefore suggests a date later than any other scholar, that is, 477,[55] the likely year of the publication of the *Letters*. Kaufmann is probably influenced by the dates of *Epp.* 5.6 and 5.7 and,

---

50. Barnes 2011, 145.
51. Chausson 2002, 208–9.
52. See Chausson 2002, 209 n. 15 and 210.
53. Barnes 2011, 168.
54. Harries 2014, 206.
55. Anderson 1965, 198 n. 1.

LETTER 8

Table 10. The date of *Ep.* 5.8

Anderson	Loyen	*PLRE* II	Heinzelmann	*PCBE* 4	Blänsdorf	Kaufmann
477	467	–	467	460–9	465	474

therefore, suggests a contemporary dramatic date,[56] which, however, is not supported by evidence, as explained below. On the contrary, it will be argued that an earlier date, closer to the years suggested by Loyen,[57] Heinzelmann,[58] Blänsdorf[59] and *PCBE* 4[60] seems preferable, although it should be emphasised that any attempt at dating *ad annum* is not supported by evidence.

As stated above, our information on Secundinus comes exclusively from Sidonius. Schetter argues that 'the first chronological fixed point' concerning Secundinus is the dedication of Lyon cathedral,[61] which he dates to between 469 and 471.[62] Unfortunately, it seems that the dating of the cathedral depends entirely on the date given to *Ep.* 2.10, and, consequently, given to Sidonius' inscription (= *Carm.* 27) for the church mentioned in it; but there are no elements allowing one to date *Ep.* 2.10 *ad annum* either. Kelly recently argued that poems in the letters need not have been written after the publication of the *Carmina minora*,[63] and that it seems likely that the dramatic date of *Carm.* 27 may have pre-dated said publication, which should be dated to the 460s, rather than precisely to 469.

However, Loyen's observation that *Ep.* 5.8 should be dated to before the bishopric is worthy of further reflection, since Sidonius mentions the people of Lyon as *nostri tyrannopolitani*, a thing which, according to Loyen,

---

56. Kaufmann 1995, 346.
57. Loyen 1970a, 255 suggests dating *Ep.* 5.8 precisely to 467 for no strong reason and adds that the reference to 'our *tyrannopolitani*' leads to the inference that Sidonius still felt 'exclusivement Lyonnais', which means the letter should be dated to before the bishopric.
58. Heinzelmann 1982, 690.
59. Blänsdorf 1993, 127.
60. *PCBE* 4 s.v. Secundinus 1, 1724.
61. Sidonius does not explicitly refer to the name of the church in *Ep.* 2.10, though the suggestion that it may be the same church of Saint Justus described in *Ep.* 5.17 is appealing. See for instance the antiquarian study on the churches of Lyon by Meynis 1872, 2, followed by Tatu 1877, 46–67; of the same opinion is also Anderson 1936, 462.
62. In an article dedicated to Secundinus, Schetter 1964, 257–9; Loyen 1970a, 255 dates Secudinus' inscription to 469.
63. Kelly 2020, 177–8.

may indicate he still thinks of himself as Lyonnais.[64] Although this is only a suggestion, a comparison with *Ep.* 3.3 may support Loyen's point. When writing to Ecdicius, Sidonius, already a bishop, speaks of people of Clermont as *Aruerni mei* (*Ep.* 3.3.1) and, more significantly, he ends the letter mentioning them as *nostrates*, that is, their fellow countrymen (*Ep.* 3.3.9).

In favour of an *ante* 469 date, as the commentary further explains, it can be added that it seems likely that *Ep.* 5.8 pre-dated *Epp.* 5.6 and 5.7. The people of Lyon – the *tyrannopolitani* – are likely to be the same as the 'informants' attacked in *Ep.* 5.7 for their wrongdoings, from which they are said to have benefited economically in both letters. This mention could be a trace that the citizens of Lyon were already the object of attacks before the pamphlet that is *Ep.* 5.7, and the implicit mention of Burgundians as tyrants in *Ep.* 5.8 seems coherent with a hostile attitude Sidonius had towards Burgundians before they proved to be useful allies against the Visigoths attacking Clermont.[65] The more careful ways of referring to Burgundians in *Epp.* 5.6 and 5.7 (dated between 474 and 475) are indicative, if compared to the mention of *tyrannopolitani*, of a new, non-overtly hostile attitude on Sidonius' part.

A further indication of a date for *Ep.* 5.8 (at least a *terminus post quem*) could be given if one could identify the 'hunting ruler' celebrated by Secundinus.[66] Schetter[67] states that the observation that is decisive in this respect has been made by Savaron,[68] who suggested identifying the hunting *rex* with the Visigoth king Theoderic II, whose portrait is in Sidon. *Ep.* 1.2. In *Ep.* 1.2.5 Sidonius describes the hunting skills and habits of Theoderic II, lingering over trivial details and picturing what Gualandri fittingly calls 'a regal choreography' rather than a hunting scene.[69] Schetter's conclusion that the Gothic king likely enjoyed being portrayed as an able hunter, and that a subject such as that of the *perfossae regiis ictibus ferae* of *Ep.* 5.8.1 'must have been to his taste', is not demonstrable.[70] It can be argued, however,

---

64. Loyen 1970a, 255.
65. For his changed attitude, discussed in the introduction to *Ep.* 5.7, see Delaplace 2015, 249.
66. *Ep.* 5.8.1.
67. Schetter 1964, 257.
68. Savaron 1609, 339.
69. Note, in particular, the digression on the king's most adequate and virile way of having his bow handed to him in *Ep.* 1.2.5. On this passage see Gualandri 2000, 111–12.
70. Gualandri 1979, 69–70 analyses Sidonius' choice of picturing Theoderic's *ciuilitas* and calmness through daily activities such as going hunting or playing dice, and compares it to Pliny's *Panegyricus*.

LETTER 8

that Sidonius is keen on representing Theoderic II as Roman-friendly and literate,[71] in contrast to his predecessors, Theoderic I and Thorismund, and in particular to his uncultured successor, his brother Euric.[72] According to Sidonius, Theoderic II had received a classical education, and his tutor had been Eparchius Avitus, Sidonius' father-in-law — and, later, emperor, with the Goths' support.[73] In Sidon. *Carm.* 7.495–9, Theoderic II recalls being entrusted to Avitus for the teaching of Roman law and poetry, and learning lines by heart so that the knowledge of Vergil would 'soften his Scythian ways'.[74] Schetter believes that, in particular in light of this education, Theoderic II would have appreciated reading that his hunting skills were praised in hexameters.[75] It seems important to stress that Sidonius is interested in portraying an idealised model that contrasts antithetically with Euric's figure.[76] And yet, although one could be more cautious than Schetter, the suggestion that the hunting king may be Theoderic II remains an appealing one.

Although one may assume that Secundinus, like Sidonius himself, had written verses in praise of Theoderic II, it is impossible to state whether he had written them during Theoderic's reign (453–66)[77] or after his death. In light of the paucity of evidence, it seems only sensible to reach the conclusion that *Ep.* 5.8 was written before Sidonius' tenure of the bishopric, in the 460s.

---

71. See also *Carm.* 23.71, where Theoderic II is called *Romanae columen salusque gentis* ('pillar and salvation of the Roman race').

72. As Gualandri 1979, 67 remarks, even in the physical description, Euric is a negative model opposed to the positive figure of Theoderic II. See also Fascione 2019a, 64, who closely follows Gualandri's arguments and fittingly calls Euric the 'anti-Theoderic'.

73. On the nature of Avitus' allegiance with Theoderic II, see Delaplace 2015, 215–19; Kulikowski 2020, 207.

74. For another mention of Scythians as exemplary of *barbaries*, see the commentary on *Ep.* 5.7.4.

75. Schetter 1964, 258.

76. Mratschek 2020, 234.

77. Gillett 1999, 3 suggests dating Theoderic II's death and Euric's accession to 467.

SIDONIUS SECUNDINO SUO SALUTEM

1. Diu quidem est, quod te hexametris familiarius inseruientem stupentes praedicantesque lectitabamus. Erat siquidem materia iucunda, seu nuptiales tibi thalamorum faces siue perfossae regiis ictibus ferae describerentur. Sed triplicibus trochaeis nuper in metrum hendecasyllabum compaginatis nihil, ne tuo quidem iudicio, simile fecisti.

2. Deus bone, quid illic inesse mellis, leporis piperataeque facundiae minime tacitus inspexi! Nisi quod feruentis fulmen ingenii et eloquii salsa libertas plus personis forte quam causis impediebantur; ut mihi non figuratius Constantini domum uitamque uideatur uel pupugisse uersu gemello consul Ablabius uel momordisse disticho tali clam Palatinis foribus appenso:

> Saturni aurea saecla quis requirat?
> Sunt haec gemmea, sed Neroniana.

Quia scilicet praedictus Augustus isdem fere temporibus extinxerat coniugem Faustam calore balnei, filium Crispum frigore ueneni.

3. Tu tamen nihilo segnius operam saltim facetis satirarum coloribus intrepidus impende. Nam tua scripta nostrorum uitiis proficientibus tyrannopolitanorum locupletabuntur. Non enim tam mediocriter intumescunt quos nostra iudicia, saecula, loca fortunatos putant, ut de nominibus ipsorum quandoque reminiscendis sit posteritas laboratura: namque improborum probra aeque ut praeconia bonorum inmortalia manent. Vale.

---

§ 2 mellis α MPT^1 : fellis *LT*
Ablabius *Wilamowitz* : Ablauius *codd.*

§ 3 tiranno politanorum α (tyranno politanorum *A*) M^1 : tiranno polinorum *P* : tyrannopolitarum *LM*
saecula loca α *MPT* : seculi loca *L* : seculi culpa *Leo* : seculi loco *Warmington*

LETTER 8

SIDONIUS TO HIS DEAR SECUNDINUS

1. It has been a long time indeed since we, amazed and lauding you, eagerly read the hexameters to which you are wont to be devoted. For the topic was delightful, either when you represented nuptial torches or wild beasts stabbed by the royal strokes. But you have written nothing, not even in your own judgement, comparable to your recent triple trochees fashioned together into the hendecasyllabic metre.

2. Good God, I contemplated what pleasantness, wit and spiced eloquence was there and could absolutely not keep silent! Save only that the thunderbolt of a blazing intellect and the sharp freedom of speech were perhaps hindered by people rather than by subject matter. And so it seems to me that consul Ablabius did not puncture or bite the life and family of Constantine with a couplet more allusive in its innuendos, when a distich was secretly hung on the gates of the imperial palace, as follows:

> Who would miss the golden age of Saturn?
> This is an age of gems, though Neronian.

Because, of course, at almost the same time, the aforementioned Augustus had killed his wife Fausta through the heat of a bath, and his son Crispus through the chill of poison.

3. As for you, however: devote yourself to work, without slacking off and with undiminished zeal, at least on the witty shades of your satires. For your writings are to be enriched by the growing vices of our fellow citizens of Tyrannopolis. They are not so mildly swollen up, those that our judgements, times and place consider prosperous, that someday future generations will not strive to call to mind their names: in fact, shameful acts of wicked men last forever, just like the commendations of good ones. Farewell.

SIDONIUS: LETTERS BOOK 5, PART 1

Commentary

§ 1

Diu quidem est: This beginning is straightforward and immediately pictures Sidonius and Secundinus as *sodales*, with Sidonius eagerly reading the friend's works. Much has been said in this commentary (see the introductions to *Epp.* 5.3 and 5.4) on the genre of letters on epistolary silence as standard means of social interaction. The Symmachan model is in particular useful to understand the meaning of this text – a friendly exchange which, incidentally, also serves the purpose of praising Secundinus, giving him his own spot in the collection; on the genre of 'letters on literary matters' see the introduction to *Ep.* 5.2. For the informal locution *diu est quod*, attested in Plautus (*Amph.* 302), and which resurfaced in later Latin (e.g. Apul. *Met.* 1.24), see *TLL* 5.1559 s.v. *diu* 32–5 (by Hofmann). This expression also occurs at the beginning of Sidon. *Ep.* 7.6.1 *diuque est quod inuicem diligimus ex aequo*, where it concerns a declaration of long-standing friendship between Sidonius and the addressee.

quod te hexametris familiarius inseruientem stupentes praedicantesque lectitabamus: Sidonius is keen on describing the friend as comfortable with writing hexameters, and himself as expectantly waiting to read them. As Condorelli 2020a, 445 points out, in these first lines Sidonius 'ascribes to the epic metre a solemnity fitting for celebratory poetry', that is, epithalamia and panegyrics. Note that also Secundinus' inscription for the Lyon basilica was written in hexameters, as Sidonius states in *Ep.* 2.10.3. The overabundance of this syntagma (note the three consecutive present participles) has puzzled translators; in particular, the occurrence of *inseruire* referred to metre is unattested. The verb is here translated as 'to be devoted to'. Note that the section ends with two cretic spondee clausulae within and at the end of the colon at *praedicantesque* and *lectitabamus*. **familiarius**: Similarly, Sidonius describes hendecasyllables as *perfamiliares* to him in the already mentioned *Ep.* 2.10.3. **lectitabamus**: The frequentative *lectito* is specifically used to indicate the act of reading many times and with interest the literary productions of friends also in *Anim. praef.*, p. 20 (for this passage see the introduction to *Ep.* 5.2). The expression occurs with this meaning in numerous contexts, and Sidonius employs it often: see the commentary on *Ep.* 5.1.1 for a detailed analysis of the occurrences of the verb in previous authors and in Sidonius. The verb creates a cretic spondee at the end of the

258

LETTER 8

sentence, and thus it seems it may have been preferable for Sidonius also on the grounds of clausulation.

Erat siquidem materia iucunda: Pleasantness of subject is a fundamental feature of one's writings. Compare, albeit concerning a standard depreca-tio of the author's own work, Plin. *Nat. praef.* 12, on his work not being dedicated to events pleasurable to narrate (*iucunda dictu*) or to read, but, instead, to *sterilis materia*. A similar occurrence is, still in a standardised self-deprecatory introductory section, in Ausonius' *Parentalia praef.* (10 A Green): his little book is not dedicated to a cheerful subject nor is it attractive in title (*nec materia amoenum est nec appellatione iucundum*). Note the paeon IV spondee clausula subsidiary to punctuation at *ma-teria iucunda*.

seu nuptiales tibi thalamorum faces: Through the metonymical image of nuptial torches, Sidonius pictures Secundinus as author of epithalamia. The presence of the poeticism *thalamorum* seems overabundant.

siue perfossae regiis ictibus ferae describerentur: Secundinus also wrote celebratory poetry in hexameters. The mention of the hunting *rex* leads to the inference that Secundinus wrote a panegyric of a barbarian king. Following Savaron's suggestion, Schetter 1964, *passim*, compared this passage to Sidonius' own description of the hunting Theoderic II, and believed the same Gothic king had been praised by Secundinus. See the introduction for the dating evidence possibly deriving from this assumption. Of different opinion is Loyen 1970a, 236 n. 24, who believes the passage is to be referred to a Burgundian king. There is no further evidence, however, which would allow one to reach a definitive conclusion and the fact that Secundinus possibly was from Lyon does not mean he could not have written a panegyric for the Visigothic king. Rhythm is subsidiary to punctuation within the clause – see the cretic spondee at *siue perfossae* followed by the double cretic at *regiis ictibus*.

Sed triplicibus trochaeis nuper in metrum hendecasyllabum com-paginatis: This metre allows Secundinus to surpass his own praiseworthy compositions in hexameters, which have been mentioned previously. As Gualandri 1979, 150 points out, when Sidonius lists feet and meters he does so complacently, by using 'elliptic and allusive formulas'. The three trochees are the distinctive feature of the phalaecian hendecasyllable, as Sidonius states also in other passages. An even more detailed definition is that in

Carm. 23.25–7 *triplicis metrum trochaei / spondeo comitante dactyloque, / dulces hendecasyllabos*, where the author describes the structure of the hendecasyllable: a spondee followed by a dactyl and then by three trochees – on which see Semple 1930, 34–5 and Condorelli 2020a, 453–4. Cf. *Ep.* 2.10.3, where the author says he wrote for the Lyon basilica *trochaeis triplicibus adhuc mihi . . . perfamiliaribus*, on which see Hindermann 2022, 304–5. Condorelli 2020a, 454 mentions *Ep.* 5.8.1 as exemplary to understand the meaning of *rotundati hendecasyllabi* as opposed to *acuti elegi* in *Ep.* 8.4.2. As Condorelli explains, Sidonius ascribes to hendecasyllables fluidity and harmoniousness (features which made them fitting for *leuis* poetry) also in *Ep.* 8.11.5, where they are said to be *lubrici et enodes* ('gliding and smooth'), and in *Ep.* 9.13.2, where they are said to be *teretes* ('polished'). As noted by van Waarden 2016, 63, the late occurrence of *triplex* instead of *tres* with plural nouns 'was originally a poetical mannerism'; on Sidonius' preference for this adjective see Hindermann 2022, 124.

nihil, ne tuo quidem iudicio, simile fecisti: This kind of information, which seems to have been included for the sake of the reader, is useful to picture Secundinus' own judgement of his production. It constitutes further evidence that there is familiarity between the two, together with the consistent use of the second person singular throughout the letter (see the introduction). Note the paeon IV spondee clausula at *simile fecisti*.

§ 2

Deus bone: This is arguably one of Sidonius' favourite colloquial expressions to convey enthusiasm, modelled on spoken language, rather than an expression tied to a religious context, as stated also for *post opem Christi* and *similia* (see the commentary on *Ep.* 5.1.3). In this respect, it is notable that *deus bone*, which occurs in *Epp.* 1.9.1, 3.2.1, 4.1.2, 4.11.2, 4.12.1 and 7.13.2, does not occur in episcopal letters. Similar conclusions are reached by Köhler 1995, 267; by Amherdt 2001, 78, who fittingly points out how often the similar *di boni* is found in pagan authors (with numerous occurrences in Cicero, e.g. *Att.* 8.16.1 and *Phil.* 2.80); and by van Waarden 2016, 90. The latter also points out that, apart from the single occurrence in Sidonius' Book 7, all the others concern Books 1–5.

quid illic inesse . . . salsa libertas: The passage is strongly reminiscent of

LETTER 8

Pliny the Younger's affectionate praises of the literary prowess of friends. The same features are praised for instance in Plin. *Ep.* 1.16.5, where he describes the quality of Pompeius Saturninus' verses: *quantum illis leporis, dulcedinis, amaritudinis, amoris!* In *Ep.* 4.3.4 Pliny directly praises Arrius Antoninus with similar words: *quantum ibi humanitatis, uenustatis, quam dulcia illa, quam amantia, quam arguta, quam recta!* Compare Sidonius' passage also with the praises of Vergilius Romanus (author of comedies modelled on ancient comedy and destined to become exemplary) in Plin. *Ep.* 6.21.5 *non illi uis, non granditas, non subtilitas, non amaritudo, non dulcedo, non lepos defuit.*

mellis: In light of Dolveck's stemma, *mellis* is the reading of the archetype, given the agreement of α and *P* (this reading is adopted in Savaron 1609, 338), while *fellis* is a conjecture – or a slip – of the ancestor of *LT* (adopted in Lütjohann 1887, 83; Anderson 1965, 196; and Loyen 1970a, 187, out of respect for *L*). The word *mel* is commonly employed to praise the pleasantness of literary compositions (and often opposed to *fel*). *Mel* would be fitting given the following reference to *lepos*, making *piperata facundia* the only element flagging up, at the end of the section, the satirical content of the writing. Compare Sidonius' occurrence to Symm. *Ep.* 1.31.1 *oblita Tulliano melle festiuitas*, when Symmachus praises a letter Ausonius sent to him for its 'wittiness coated in Tullian honey'. Cf. also Sidon. *Ep.* 7.13.2 *abundat animi sale, cum consulitur, melle, cum consulit* ('he is plenty of salt when he is consulted, of honey when he is consulting'). When commenting on the passage, van Waarden 2010, 226; 2016, 91 points out how common this metaphor was in Late Antiquity, being effective in expressing how the 'inside' is supposed to be 'pithy, full of conceits', while the outside (i.e. expression) should be perceived as smooth and polished. See also Sidon. *Ep.* 4.16.1 *accepi . . . paginam uestram, quae plus mellis an salis habeat incertum est*, when Sidonius cannot say if Ruricius' page is 'more salty or honeyed', and *Ep.* 8.11.7, quoted below. And yet, the alternative occurrence of *fel* would be equally justifiable on the grounds of meaning and one could compare other occurrences of *fel* to indicate acrimony in literary compositions. In particular, Martial criticises epigrams lacking *sal* and *fel* (since no one reads them) in 7.25.3–4. The same image is used by Pliny in *Ep.* 3.21.1 *qui plurimum in scribendo et salis haberet et fellis* – the epitaph written at the news of Martial's death. Furbetta 2014–2015b, 110 remarks that Sidonius' use of *fel* may also be reminiscent of Ausonius' laudatory mentions of the writings of others as 'well balanced in bitterness': see Aus. *Prof.* 4.19, 15.2 and *Ep.* 11.5 (ed. Green). Geisler 1887, 366 compares this occurrence to

261

that in Sidon. *Ep.* 1.2, a letter already mentioned for the description of the hunting *rex*. In *Ep.* 1.2.9, comedians are present at banquets but they are not allowed to harass guests with the 'bitterness of their biting tongue' (*ita ut nullus conuiua mordacis linguae felle feriatur*).

leporis: *Lepos* occurs as a defining element of a literary work from Plautus, see e.g. 'the wit and fun' (*lepos ludusque*) characterising his comedy in *Asin.* 13. Among the occurrences of the word with this meaning (for which see *OLD* s.v. *lepos*, 1120) it seems useful to consider Apul. *Apol.* 94.6 *di boni, qua doctrina, quo lepore, qua uerborum amoenitate simul et iucunditate*. In this passage, Apuleius praises with enthusiastic words Lollianus Avitus' letter as a rhetorical masterpiece. Apart from the similar context of praise of a friend's writing, note also the occurrence of *di boni*, like in Sidonius. Apuleius' *Apologia* has been mentioned in the commentaries on *Epp.* 5.6 and 5.7; for Apuleius being an important linguistic and stylistic model for Sidonius see Wolff 2020, 400.

piperataeque facundiae: The adjective *piperatus* is representative of Sidonius' keenness to employ vivid language which often pertains to the semantic sphere of taste. The word is previously known to occur with a figurative meaning in Martial 8.59.4, where it is referred to a thief's hand, but with this specific meaning of 'spiced' literary composition, it has occurrences exclusively in Sidonius. The noun concerns Lampridius' epigrams and is part of a longer dining metaphor in *Ep.* 8.11.7 *non pauca piperata, mellea multa . . . omnia tamen salsa* ('a few spiced up and many honeyed, a seasoning of salt in all of them'). *Piperatus* appears in Wolff's list of words Sidonius employs with a metaphorical meaning, see Wolff 2020, 403 and *TLL* 10.1. 2189 s.v. *piperatus* 1–4 (by Spoth). Note the double cretic at *-taeque facundiae*.

minime tacitus inspexi: Note the paeon IV spondee clausula at *tacitus inspexi*.

feruentis fulmen ingenii: The *iunctura fulmen ingenii*, which is not known to have other occurrences, is listed in *TLL* 6.1.1528 s.v. *fulmen*, 41–3 (by Rubenbauer) together with Aug. *C. Iul. op. imperf.* 1.137, where Julian tells Augustine that he is speaking *contra fulmina rationis*. To this, one could also add Jerome's definition of Rufinus' unsustainable *fulmen eloquentiae* (*Adu. Rufin.* 3.6). Although Sidonius lacks the polemical intent of Jerome, in

Ep. 5.8 the image of the thunderbolt effectively represents the vitality and strength of Secundinus' wit. In contrast, the occurrence of *feruens ingenium* in Horace *Sat.* 1.10.62–3 (when he says that the genius of Cassius the Etruscan was more impetuous than a wild stream) gives the impression that when Sidonius praises the verses of satirical content of the friend, he does so with words reminiscent of the language of satire. It then occurs exclusively in Christian authors: in Arnobius Junior's *Praedest.* 1.16 it concerns presbyter Sabinianus, said to be *feruentissimus in ingenio*; see also (though in general remarks) Hier. *In Is.* 9.29.15 and Aug. *Doctr. Christ.* 4.3.4. Metrical clausulation gives rhythm to this section of compliments – note the cretic tribrach at *fulmen ingenii*.

et eloquii salsa libertas: The syntagma is not known to occur before Sidonius, and is similar to the previous *piperata facundia*. *Salsus/piperatus* occur also in *Ep.* 8.11.7 (quoted above). As stated before, Sidonius is keen on employing expressions pertaining to the sense of taste (see Wolff 2020, 403). For similar occurrences (concerning the writings of friends) see Sidon. *Epp.* 4.16.1 (quoted above) and 9.12.1, where the lexicon of taste creates a wider metaphor and Oresius' letter is described as *lucida, salsa* and *mellea* ('luminous, salty and honeyed'). Cf. also Sidon. *Epp.* 2.9.9, 3.2.1 and 5.7.7, where the Burgundian queen is said to have cleaned the ears of the king, full of slanders, through a *salsus sermo*. The *iunctura eloquii libertas* is attested only in Symmachus' praise of Valentinian I, said to be the restorer of *libertas forensis eloquii* in *Or.* 2.29, having untied the *uincla linguarum* of writers with his victories against the Alamanni (see Sogno 2006, 12 for the context of this panegyric). On *libertas* in Sidon. *Ep.* 2.1.4 and for other occurrences, see Hindermann 2022, 78. Note the cretic spondee at *salsa libertas*.

plus personis forte quam causis impediebantur: Secundinus' wit and freedom of speech 'were perhaps hindered by people rather than by subject matter'. The meaning of this sentence is rather obscure and has led to different translations. Anderson 1965, 197 translates it as 'tended to take less liberty with persons than with abuses', but this interpretation would not be coherent with the following comparison with Ablabius' personal attacks on Constantine; Loyen 1970a, 186 chooses a more literal translation, 'étaient peut-être plus entravées par les personnes que par le sujet'. *Causae* and *personae* are mentioned as the essence of Sidonius' letters in *Ep.* 1.1.1. As Köhler 1995, 103 points out, Sidonius here states that he aims at *uarietas*: the letter writer should adjust his style to the subject, to the persons involved and to the circumstances of his writing. In *Ep.* 7.18.4 *singulae causae singulis . . . epistulis*, Sidonius says that, generally, a subject is entirely discussed in one letter, and in *Ep.* 9.11.3 *uario causarum, temporum personarumque congestu*, he had written a book loaded 'with a variegated assemblage of subjects, circumstances and persons'. In light of these Sidonian occurrences, one could interpret this passage as testimony that Secundinus' writing had been somehow hindered, not because of subject matter (*causae*), but because of opposition from individuals, hence the circulation of these satirical verses had possibly been hampered by the people of Lyon, who were criticised in them.

ut mihi . . . uideatur: Note the familiarity conveyed by this expression. As stated above, the consistency in the use of first person singular and of second person singular indicate friendliness between the two.

non figuratius: The comparative of the adverb *figurate* is not known to have other occurrences in Latin. In *TLL* 6.1.746 s.v. *figurate*, 17 (by Bauer), Sidonius' passage is listed among those in which *figurate* means 'with obscure and cryptical language'. Note that Semple 1930, 35 compares *figuratius* to *uocabula figurata* of *Ep.* 8.11.3, where Sidonius makes explicit that he is about to use an encoded language in the following verses, so that the meaning of the *carmen* is not obscure to the reader. In light of this comparison, Semple translates the passage in *Ep.* 5.8.2 with 'innuendo no less remote in its al-lusiveness'. And yet, as the introduction further explains, a comparison with Sidon. *Ep.* 5.17.11 seems even more fitting, since the passage gives evidence that a *maius* work, written *parabolice seu figurate* ('either metaphorically or figuratively'), was promised by Sidonius: a 'satire'? See the introduction for further observations.

Constantini domum uitamque uideatur . . . consul Ablabius: According to Sidonius, Secundinus surpasses Ablabius, considered as a model in light of his personal attacks on Constantine's household and on the life he lives. This is the only time Sidonius explicitly mentions Constantine, since the reference in *Ep.* 5.9.1 to an 'inconstant Constantine', given the context, is to be referred to Constantine III. On Ablabius in *Ep.* 5.8 see the introduc-tion, the section below, and also Stoehr-Monjou 2012, 247–60 and Marolla 2021b, 134–6. Emperors who lived after the second century are not often mentioned as exemplary (positively or negatively) by Sidonius. As stated for *Ep.* 5.7.6, he is keen on employing standardised exempla drawn from a more remote past; hence this passage, together with the even broader references to political figures in *Ep.* 5.9 (generals, usurpers and emperors who lived between the fourth and fifth century) is distinctive of Book 5. Note that *-tamque uideatur* creates a paeon I spondee.

pupugisse . . . momordisse: The two verbs *pungo* and *mordeo* are known to occur together only in Cic. *Tusc.* 3.34.82, where philosophy is said to remove any affliction for the soul, also when *paupertas momordit* or *ignominia pupugit*. A similar metaphoric occurrence of *pungo* is in Sidon. *Ep.* 7.9.11, where *pungentes linguae* are said to harm good people. For this and previous occurrences of *pungo* as meaning 'stabbing with words' see van Waarden 2010, 474–5. The verb *mordeo*, which conveys an even stronger image, is employed metaphorically to indicate 'biting' remarks for instance in Hor. *Carm.* 4.3.16 *dente . . . mordeor inuido*; it also occurs in Juvenal (e.g. 9.10 *ioco mordente*); and notably in Symm. *Ep.* 5.44, where he admits that in a previous letter he 'has bitten' Neoterius. Symmachus is also keen on using this verb metaphorically, applying it to all sorts of contexts; see for instance the expressions threatening the *talio silentii* in Symm. *Epp.* 1.65, 3.1 and 5.92, for which see the introduction to Sidon. *Ep.* 5.3. Sidonius employs the verb metaphorically only in *Ep.* 9.13.4 and 5 (concerning *inuidia*); it is useful, however, to consider occurrences of the adjective *mordax* in his works, since they all concern 'satirical' contexts. See the previously mentioned *lingua mordax* of *Ep.* 1.2.9 (see the commentary above on *mellis*); in *Ep.* 1.11.2 the Satire of Arles is said to be *uersuum plena satiricorum mordacium*; in *Ep.* 8.11.6 *in materia . . . satirica sollicitus et mordax*, the versatility of rhetor Lampridius is exemplified by his mastery in adapting his style to the genre; see also *Carm.* 9.268, where Martial is said to be *mordax sine fine*, and *Carm.* 23.452 *mordacem . . . Flaccum*. It can be argued that *mordacitas*, as a defining element of satire, is for Sidonius a markedly positive feature, both in past and contemporary writers. Note that the double cretic at *consul Ablabius* is followed by a cretic spondee clausula at *uel momordisse*.

uersu gemello: The *iunctura* is not known to have occurrences before Sidonius and the interpretation of this expression seems twofold. It may be used for *uariatio*, to indicate that the verse is 'double', that is, a distich, and with this meaning the occurrence is mentioned in *TLL* 6.2.1735, s.v. *gemellus*, 63 (by Hey); Semple 1930, 35, however, suggests it should be translated as 'using a verse the twin of yours', that is, using the hendecasyllable.

consul Ablabius: Ablabius was praetorian prefect under Constantine from 329 to 337 and consul in 331. Constantine entrusted Constantius to his guidance, but after the emperor's death, Ablabius was dismissed and later executed, as testified in Eunapius *Vit. Soph.* 6.3.9–13 (Wright = 464); Hier. *Chron.* s.a. 338; and Zos. 2.40.3 In light of his biography, Chausson's suggestion that Sidonius (or his source) confused Constantius with his father, with regard to a possible rebellion of Ablabius, seems worthy of attention, together with the possibility that the distich may refer to Constantine but be wrongly attributed to Ablabius (see the introduction). In *RE* s.v. Ablabius 1, 103, Seeck already expressed doubts concerning the distich being Ablabius'. See also *PLRE* 1 s.v. Ablabius 4, 3–4; on Ablabius' career, apart from the previously mentioned Callu 1995b and Chausson 2002, see Porena 2014.

disticho tali clam Palatinis foribus appenso: Sidonius is the only source for this episode. Compare *foribus appenso* (which creates a paeon IV spondee clausula) to the mention of cloths hanging from the doors of Maximus' home in Sidon. *Ep.* 4.24.3 *Cilicum uela foribus appensa.*

Saturni aurea saecla quis requirat? / Sunt haec gemmea, sed Neroniana: Presenting contemporary history as a degraded version of the golden age of Saturn is a known cliché. In this distich, the illusion that contemporary history is *gemmea* is abruptly interrupted by *sed Neroniana*, an epigrammatic *fulmen in clausula*. As suggested by Cupaiuolo 1993, 84 and later by Stoehr-Monjou 2012, 243, it seems likely that this passage was modelled on the couplet written against Tiberius transmitted by Suetonius *Tib.* 59 *aurea mutasti Saturni saecula, Caesar / incolumi nam te ferrea semper erunt*. Similar negative suggestions are also in the *Historia Augusta*, when 'Lampridius', addressing Constantine, states he intends to trace a profile of Elagabalus' successors: *HA Elag.* 35.4–5 *Diocletianus, aurei parens saeculi, et Maximianus, ut uulgo dicitur, ferrei*. As Harries 2014, 206 points out, the distich mentioned in *Ep.* 5.8 can be compared to Lactantius' use of the image of the golden age of Saturn in the *Diuinae Institutiones*, to the indirect praise of Constantine through the blame of Diocletian's patron, Jupiter, whose parricide led to the end of the golden age, that is, of justice (Lact. *Inst.* 5.5.1–6 and 13). According to Lactantius (*Inst.* 5.8.6–9), only the restoration of moral order, that is, of monotheism, could bring a new golden age later described in Book 7 (*Inst.* 7.24.8–11); for the mentions of the golden age in the *Diuinae Institutiones*, see e.g. Swift 1968 and Lettieri 2013. Furthermore,

LETTER 8

Publilius Optatianus Porfyrius had praised Constantine as the restorer of the *aurea saecula* on many occasions. In particular, see the *uersus intexti*, with notable virtuosity, in Opt. *Carm.* 2.II (Roman numerals indicate their being acrostic) *aurea sic mundo disponas saecula toto*; *Carm.* 3.VI (*Camena*) *uersu consignans aurea saecla*; *Carm.* 10.V, *aurei saeculi restaurator*; and the similar praises of Constantine's golden age in Opt. *Carm.* 3.12, 3.18, 5.28, 7.24 and 19.32 (ed. Polara 2004). Therefore, Harries' 2014 suggestion that the author of the distich in *Ep.* 5.8 refers polemically precisely to this image of Constantine as a bringer of new prosperity seems worthy of appraisal.

Quia scilicet praedictus Augustus . . . frigore ueneni: These two deaths are connected in numerous sources and the role Constantine had in them is a *uexata quaestio*, discussed at length by scholars. Sidonius here inverts the chronological order of the killings: Crispus is known to have died before Fausta, and Stoehr-Monjou 2012, 256 has argued that the inverted order is aimed at creating a gradation of *saeuitia*, but ultimately it seems impossible to state whether Sidonius inverts the order consciously or not. Rhetorically, 'a hot bath, cold poison' is an easier order than 'cold poison, a hot bath', since coldness is not an inherent quality of poison and is not necessary to the description of what happened. Crispus' death had led to speculation concerning Fausta's role and responsibility in connection to it, and for instance the anonymous author of the *Epitome de Caesaribus* 41.11 (with a cautious *ut putant*) relates that *Fausta suggerente* Constantine ordered Crispus' killing. Barnes 2011, 146 argues that Crispus had not been murdered but sentenced to death, and executed after trial at Pola, a detail known only through the passing mention in Ammianus 14.11.20, who probably described Crispus' death in the lost books (Kelly 2008, 286). But Sidonius is certainly not the first to ascribe these deaths to Constantine, condemned as murders since Julian *Caes.* 336 a–b, Eutropius 10.6.3 (who relates these events to the emperor's *mutatio in peius*), Jerome *Chron.* s.a. 325–326 and Zosimus 2.29.2. The tradition on the killings later becomes twofold: Fausta is portrayed either as a victim resembling Nero's Octavia, or, in Christian sources, as a new Phaedra, who seduced Crispus, leading to his death. For a detailed overview of the sources concerning the episode and of scholarly speculation see Marasco 1993; Barnes 2011, 145–50; Stoehr-Monjou 2012, 255–60; Zecchini 2017. Note the specular construction in the description of the two deaths by Sidonius: the kinship (*coniugem/filium*) is followed by the name of the killed, by the ablative of means (the antithetical *calore/frigore*) and then by the genitive (*balnei/ueneni*). As Stoehr-Monjou 2012, 244 pointed out,

267

coniugem Faustam and *filium Crispum* also have the same rhythm, a cretic spondee.

coniugem Faustam calore balnei: Among the sources relating the episode, compare in particular the similar phrase in *Epitome de Caesaribus* 41.12 *uxorem suam Faustam in balneas ardentes coniectam interemit*. Also Zosimus 2.29.2 mentions the detail of the hot bath, and Barnes believes both texts depended on the anti-Christian Eunapius of Sardis. As suggested by Harries 2014, 206, the tradition on the death of Fausta in the bath is to be referred to the death of Octavia, similarly described in Tac. *Ann.* 14.64 *praeferuidi balnei uapore enecatur*. This allusion, together with the *saecla Neroniana* of the distich, leads to the inference that there was an anti-Constantinian propaganda which associated Constantine with Nero, and that Sidonius may draw this information from an anti-Christian source. On Fausta, see the detailed entry in *RE* s.v. Fausta 3, 2084–6 (by Seeck) and *PLRE* 1, 325–6.

filium Crispum frigore ueneni: Sidonius is the only author who relates that Crispus died from poisoning, as pointed out also by Woods 1998, 80 and Zecchini 2017, 127 n. 2. On Crispus see *RE* s.v. Crispus 9, 1722–24 (by Seeck) and *PLRE* 1 s.v. Crispus 4, 233.

§ 3

Tu tamen nihilo segnius operam . . . intrepidus impende: This beginning is particularly verbose and overabundant. The presence of *tamen* can be related to the previous mention of people who are said to have hindered Secundinus' satirical production in § 2 (*plus personis forte quam causis impediebantur*); Sidonius therefore exhorts the friend to keep writing despite the difficulties he might face. This long phrase is closed by a paeon IV spondee at *–trepidus impende*.

facetis satirarum coloribus: As stated in the introduction and in the commentary above, the denied authorship of the Satire of Arles does not imply Sidonius did not appreciate the genre. On the contrary, the mention of 'the witty shades' of Secundinus' satires provides further evidence that Sidonius enjoyed the vivacity of these verses. The syntagma is not known to have other occurrences, but the mention in Sidon. *Ep.* 4.22.5 of *color odorque satiricus* is worthy of analysis. According to Sidonius, writing contemporary

LETTER 8

history would not be advisable for a cleric, since it would be shameful to tell falsehoods, while speaking the truth on the infamous could be dangerous and lead to *maxuma offensa*, because, inevitably, the 'colour and scent of satire' would blend (*admiscet*) in such a work; see also the introduction to *Ep.* 5.8 for this passage.

Nam tua scripta . . . locupletabuntur: The vices of 'our' *tyrannopolitani* provide Secundinus with new appealing material for his satires. It is likely that 'the citizens of Tyrannopolis' are the same who are said to have hindered the circulation of the verses which made fun of them. This passage is not clausulated, but Sidonius effectively represents the overabundance of growing vices through a series of long words, as is highlighted by Wolff 2020, 411.

nostrorum . . . tyrannopolitanorum: *Tyrannopolitanus* is probably a Sidonian *hapax*, as signalled by Gualandri 1979, 162 n. 65 and later by Wolff 2020, 399. The spelling *tyrannopolitarum* is preferred to *tyrannopolitanorum* by modern editors, but the latter appears to be stemmatically demanded. Note, however, that the word occurs in a law by Glycerius and Leo dated to 473: ed. Haenel 1857, 260 n. 1226 *tyrannopolitas esse se malint*.[78] This occurrence might provide support to the reading *tyrannopolita* in place of *tyrannopolitanus*. Since there is no clear date for Sidonius' *Ep.* 5.8, it seems impossible to state with certainty which text predates the other, as Mathisen (2013a, 244 n. 101) does, suggesting a date of 474 for *Ep.* 5.8. And yet, as stated in the introduction, it seems probable that the letter should be dated earlier, and that any exact indication of date is not possible. Certainly, Sidon. *Ep.* 5.8.3 is the first literary context in which the word is known to occur. One could also add that Sidonius is wont to form new words from Greek, which have the advantage of making his text ambiguous, as is the case of *tyrannopolitani/ tyrannopolitae* (for Sidonius' use of Greek words see Onorato 2016, 287–306; Foscarini 2019). Moreover, the possessive adjective leads one to infer that the 'fellow citizens' mentioned are the citizens of Lyon, at the time supposedly 'ruled by a tyrant', hence by an unidentifiable Burgundian king (Loyen 1970a, 187 n. 27). This mention of Burgundians as tyrants seems problematic if read in light of the extremely careful and prudent mentions of the Burgundian king and of his spouse in *Ep.* 5.7. And yet, dating *Ep.* 5.8

---

78. Haenel's edition is old and in need of replacement; therefore, for accuracy purposes, I checked the reading in the digitisation of the source manuscript, *Vat. Reg.* 1997, 112ᵛ, available at <https://digi.vatlib.it/view/MSS_Reg.lat.1997>.

before what Delaplace 2015, 249 called Sidonius' 'siding with Burgundians' would also help by making the harshness of the expression less surprising. There is no reason to think that the dramatic date of *Ep.* 5.8 should be after that of *Epp.* 5.6 and 5.7 (474–5). Actually, as stated above, it seems possible that it should be dated to a few years before. Instead of interpreting this passage as evidence that Sidonius' attitude towards Burgundians was constantly wavering, as Fascione 2019a, 78 does, dating this letter before the Apollinaris incident would lead to the already discussed theory that Sidonius' hostility towards the Burgundians was tempered over time in light of their aid in defending Clermont from the Goths. Moreover, it seems that the term is an original way of insulting Lyonnaise citizens (for whom he has no sympathy, as will be clear in the following passage) as much as their barbarian ruler. It should also be pointed out that the tone of the passage is rather playful: Sidonius is making fun of his fellow citizens, and this passage does not have the features of an invective against barbarity (but for a different view, see Fascione 2019a, 77–9).

Non enim tam mediocriter intumescunt: The verb *intumesco* is attested metaphorically to indicate someone 'inflated with arrogance' in numerous contexts, as shown in *TLL* 7.2.100 s.v. *intumesco* 13–52 (by Mühmelt). This unflattering description of the people of Lyon actually calls to mind that of the informants in *Ep.* 5.7, likely to have been Gallo-Romans described as completely barbarised. Since the Burgundian court was based in Lyon, it seems highly possible that the mentions in *Ep.* 5.8 are to be referred to the same Gallo-Roman *parvenus* who are said to have profited from the Burgundian presence in *Ep.* 5.7. As argued above, *Ep.* 5.8 is likely to have preceded *Ep.* 5.7 chronologically: that would also explain the passing reference to people of Lyon as 'ruled by a tyrant', since the animosity of Sidonius towards Burgundians is toned down by the time he writes *Ep.* 5.7 (474–5). Note the dactyl ditrochee clausula at *-ocriter intumescunt*.

quos nostra iudicia, saecula, loca fortunatos putant: Loyen's conservative approach to this passage (*sacula, loca*) seems preferable, given the *consensus codicum* on *loca*. Leo's emendation, *saeculi culpa*, which could be translated as 'through a fault in this age', does not have any occurrences in manuscripts, albeit being fitting in terms of meaning. Warmington (Anderson 1965, 611) suggests *saeculi loco*, also unattested, and offers two possible translations: 'fortunate in a worldly degree' or 'fortunate by mere circumstance (or position, or rank)'. And yet, as Warmington himself points out, the plural *saecula* would be plausible in light of the *saecla* (*aurea*, *gemmea*, and *Neroniana*) mentioned above. A comprehensive view of the passage suggests that Sidonius here turns to his own time and place, by alluding to his previous words. In his time, unworthy men, criticised by Secundinus, are considered to be lucky by virtue of their fortunes, but Sidonius later explains their fame is destined to be immortal, albeit for the wrong reasons.

ut de nominibus ipsorum . . . namque improborum probra aeque ut praeconia bonorum inmortalia manent: These nefarious men are granted immortal fame for their wickedness. The letter, therefore, ends on a moralistic note: unfortunately, wicked men enjoy the same fame as good ones. The *iunctura improborum probra*, a *figura etymologica*, in not known to have previous occurrences, like the following *praeconia bonorum*. Moreover, the chiasmus genitive + nominative (*improborum probra*) followed by nominative + genitive (*praeconia bonorum*) may be favoured by Sidonius on the grounds of rhythm, since there is a double cretic at *improborum probra* and a paeon I spondee at *-conia bonorum*.

LETTER 9

Content

Sidonius argues that he and Aquilinus should bequeath their friendship to their children Apollinaris and Rusticus, given that this bond has already been shared by three generations: that of Sidonius' and Aquilinus' grandfathers, that of their fathers and, ultimately, by that of Sidonius and of the addressee.

The addressee Aquilinus

Aquilinus is a peer of Sidonius: the two are equal in age, they were both brought up in Lyon and they are said to have shared the same teacher (*Ep.* 5.9.3). This addressee is not otherwise known.

Genre: a declaration of friendship

Ep. 5.9 can be ascribed to the broad epistolary genre of declarations of friendship,[1] correspondence which aims to maintain or re-establish not only a tie of friendship with the addressee, but also the obligations and mutual support entailed in that friendship. The presence of this letter in the collection can be interpreted either as a way to reconnect with Aquilinus, who lived in Lyon, since Sidonius appears to be already in Clermont at the time of writing, or, more likely, as a portrayal of the friend and of their aristocratic ancestry that poses as a letter. Although Sidonius is a bishop, he speaks exclusively as an aristocrat.

First of all, comparisons with Pliny can be made with regard to specific themes which occur in *Ep.* 5.9, since, when Sidonius refers to long-lasting bonds, he draws inspiration from a standardised repertoire of arguments.

---

1. On this category see the General Introduction.

LETTER 9

For instance, it seems useful to compare it to two remarkably similar Plinian passages: *Epp.* 1.19 and 2.13. The first is a letter to Romatius Firmus, where the list of the many reasons by virtue of which Pliny and Firmus are friends (*contubernales*) introduces a funding offer on the author's part.[2]

> *Municeps tu meus et condiscipulus et ab ineunte aetate contubernalis, pater tuus et matri et auunculo meo, mihi etiam, quantum aetatis diuersitas passa est, familiaris: magnae et graues causae cur suscipere, augere dignitatem tuam debeam.* (Plin. *Ep.* 1.19.1)

> You are my fellow townsman, my schoolfellow and intimate friend since we were children. Your father was close to my mother, to my uncle and even to me insofar as the age difference allowed. Thus, the reasons why I should take you under my protection and further your position are major and substantial ones.

Romatius Firmus and Pliny are said to be fellow citizens, to have shared the same education and to have been close since they were children. Like Sidonius does in *Ep.* 5.9, family ties are called as witnesses to the appropriateness of the friendship; the bond, already formed by the previous generation – Romatius' father was a friend of Pliny's mother and uncle (and ultimately his friend too, despite the age difference) – makes it even more likely that the two of them are close.

'Reasons to be close' are also listed in *Ep.* 2.13 to Priscus, a *commendaticia* for Pliny's friend Voconius Romanus, in which sections 5–9 are dedicated to a flattering portrait of the *commendatus* and to an explanation of the old ties between them. In particular, the beginning of the commendatory section can be fruitfully compared to Sidonius' context, since Pliny mentions how close he and Voconius Romanus had been during their years of schooling, being 'inseparable either in the city of Rome or in the countryside, sharing both serious and playful matters'.[3]

> *Hunc ego, cum simul studeremus, arte familiariterque dilexi; ille meus in urbe, ille in secessu contubernalis, cum hoc seria, cum hoc iocos miscui.* (Plin. *Ep.* 2.13.5)

---

2. See commentary on § 2 *sub uno contubernio* for both Plinian letters.
3. On this passage see Whitton 2013, 196. Moreover, compare the closing remarks in Plin. *Ep.* 7.20.7 to Tacitus, in which their friendship is said to be enhanced by a number of shared interests and even by their similar reputation; for this passage see the commentary on § 4 *inuicem diligentes*.

273

Unus nos exercuit ludus, magister instituit; una nos laetitia dissoluit, seueritas cohercuit, disciplina formauit. (Sidon. *Ep.* 5.9.3)

And yet, differently from the Plinian letters mentioned (a funding offer and a *commendaticia*), the purpose of Sidon. *Ep.* 5.9 seems to be exclusively that of resuming an already existing epistolary exchange and to suggest that the next generation, that of Sidonius' and Aquilinus' sons, should follow the family tradition.

It has already been pointed out, with regard to previous letters, that Symmachus is wont to write salutations, often very short letters, with the intention of re-establishing or maintaining his network of contacts, but which also have the function, within the letter collection, of illustrating his circle of friends and acquaintances. Symmachus' *Ep.* 8.43 to Callistianus proves to be a useful example of declarations of friendship, since here, like in Sidon. *Ep.* 5.9, the hereditary nature of the bond is invoked in order to strengthen the friendship with the addressee.

Inter cetera parentum decedentium bona amicitiae quoque adfectanda successio est et fortasse studio ualidiore captanda familiaritatis hereditas, quia facultates fortuna praestat, caritas iudicio foederatur. Volo igitur ut inter nos promptius conualescat familiae tuae propagata coniunctio. (Symm. *Ep.* 8.43)

Among the other possessions of our departed fathers, we should also lay claim to the succession of friendship, and perhaps we should appropriate the inheritance of an intimate acquaintance with a greater devotion, since fate lends riches, but affection is established by choice. Therefore it is my wish that the family bond handed down speedily grows strong between us.

It seems also worthy of mention that, like Pliny, Symmachus mentions the hereditariness of friendship as a good reason to stay in touch, in *Ep.* 7.88, a *commendaticia* to Messala.

Amicitiae parentum recte in liberos transferuntur, ut caritas semel inita successoribus eorum uelut hereditario iure proficiat. (Symm. *Ep.* 7.88)

It is befitting that the friendship of fathers is transferred to the sons, so that affection, once engaged, profits those who succeed to it as if by right of inheritance.

Further evidence that the letter is built on recurring themes is also provided by other Sidonian letters; for instance, *Ep.* 5.9 strongly echoes Sidon. *Ep.* 3.1.1, a passage of a letter to Avitus in which Sidonius first recounts their

LETTER 9

shared childhood and upbringing (the same way Sidonius does in *Ep.* 5.9.3) and then refers to friendship as a community of intent and of judgement of character (see *Ep.* 5.9 § 1 and § 4 and the commentaries on those sections). The latter is an idea already expressed in *Ep.* 5.3.2 through the Sallustian motto *idem uelle atque idem nolle, ea demum firma amicitia est.*[4]

Historical context: emperors, generals and usurpers

In *Ep.* 5.9.1 Sidonius relates the negative opinion of Apollinaris, his grandfather, and of Rusticus, the addressee's grandfather, on a number of political personages with whom they coexisted at a time of political turmoil in Gaul. The passing reference to Constantine III, Jovinus, Gerontius and Claudius Postumus Dardanus provides the reader with a glimpse of the political climate through which Apollinaris and Rusticus lived: that of the years of continuous usurpation in the West (407–15).[5]

In the early months of 407, against the regime of Honorius, the soldier Flavius Claudius Constantinus revolted in Britain, crossed the Channel and extended his power to Gaul. Early in 408, the usurper, known as Constantine III, survived the counter-offensive led by the Goth Sarus, under the orders of Honorius' 'generalissimo' Stilicho,[6] and then settled in Arles as Augustus. The usurper rapidly gained recognition in Gaul and, notably, Sidonius' grandfather Apollinaris, who had sided with him, acted as his *praefectus praetorio Galliarum* (408–9). These were crucial years at the imperial court in Ravenna: planning an intervention against Constantine III, Stilicho gathered an army at Pavia; however, the news of the death of Arcadius in the East created a moment of impasse. Stilicho decided not to travel to the eastern imperial court as planned but neither to attack Constantine III;

---

4. *Cat.* 20.4.

5. *Ep.* 5.9.1 *in Constantino incostantiam, in Iouino facilitatem, in Gerontio perfidiam, singula in singulis, omnia in Dardano crimina simul execrarentur.* For a detailed account of events in Gaul between 407 and 416 see Blockley 1998 129–31; Drinkwater 1998; Halsall 2007, 220–4; and, in particular, the analysis by Delaplace 2015, 127–62, who traces a comprehensive picture of the situation in Gaul by comparing it to that in Ravenna and to the contemporary political game of Alaric. For the usurpation years in relation to Sidonius see also Kulikowski 2020, 199–200. All the relevant prosopographical entries are listed in the commentary on *Ep.* 5.9.1.

6. See Zosimus 6.2.3.

following the mutiny of the army at Pavia, Stilicho himself was killed in Ravenna (on 22 August 408).[7]

Meanwhile, Contantine III sent his son (and Caesar) Constans to Spain along with Gerontius, Apollinaris (Sidonius' grandfather), and Rusticus (the addressee Aquilinus' grandfather). Being already *magister officiorum* under Constantine, Rusticus took part in the expedition and was probably named *praefectus praetorio Galliarum* after his friend Apollinaris, in 409.[8] Constans' first expedition to Spain was a success, and so, in late 409, he was once again on his way there, this time as co-Augustus, when he was informed that Gerontius had turned on him and had declared his own son Maximus emperor. Constans therefore turned back to Gaul but was killed in 411 by Gerontius, who then moved against Constantine III. However, at the same time, a contingent from Ravenna was also sent against Constantine III, and many of Gerontius' men sided with the legitimate imperial army; Gerontius hence retreated to Spain, where he committed suicide soon afterward. Defeated and besieged at Arles by Honorius' generals, Contantine III surrendered, handed over his imperial regalia, but despite having had himself ordained as a priest, was treacherously executed in 411 on the orders of Honorius, who thus regained command of south-eastern Gaul.

In 411, in Germania II, a new usurper arose. The Gallo-Roman noble Jovinus was declared emperor and enjoyed the support of both barbarians (Burgundian and Alan warlords in particular)[9] and of the Gallic aristocracy, which was evidently opposed to the reaffirmation of Honorius' power over southern Gaul.[10] The addressee's grandfather, Rusticus, is known to have been one of Jovinus' supporters; moreover, as pointed out by Loyen,[11] Sidonius' grandfather may also have chosen to side with Jovinus after Constantine, given that, in the epitaph Sidonius writes for him, the plural occurs when Apollinaris is said to have been 'a free man under the rule of tyrants' (*liber sub dominantibus tyrannis Ep.* 3.12.5 v.12).[12]

---

7. For a detailed account see in particular Drinkwater 1998, 275–81.

8. On this expedition see the commentary on *Ep.* 5.9.1 *cum in Constantino inconstantiam*.

9. As pointed out by Kulikowski 2020, 200, this allegiance marks the start of a new collaboration between western aristocrats seeking power by siding with warlords outside of imperial hierarchy.

10. See Blockley 1998, 130.

11. Loyen 1970a, 103 n. 39.

12. Van Waarden 2020a, 19 is of the same opinion; note also that the plural could refer to the co-Augusti Constantine III and Constans.

Jovinus' usurpation, however, did not last for long, since the Visigoth Athaulf first declared his allegiance to him and then struck an alliance with Honorius and overthrew Jovinus, who was killed in 413, when on his way to Ravenna. The execution was overseen by Claudius Postumus Dardanus, the praetorian prefect of Gaul and loyal to Honorius. Many of Jovinus' aristocratic supporters were also put to death. Among them, according to Gregory of Tours (*Hist.* 2.9) was Aquilinus' grandfather Rusticus; as the commentary further explains, the possibility that Sidonius' grandfather may have been one of the victims of this purge is debated.[13]

Sidonius' attitude towards his grandfather's political commitment seems worthy of analysis, since in *Ep.* 5.9.1 he does not conceal Apollinaris' support for a usurper; on the contrary, he embraces his decision, which constitutes an important chapter of the family history.[14] And yet, both Apollinaris and Rusticus are said to have had a definite negative opinion of Constantine and Jovinus, despite being in their service; hence, Sidonius seems interested in pointing out that they were fully aware of the shortcomings of their leaders and were disenchanted with the new regimes.

In *Ep.* 5.9.2, the overview of the intertwined family history of Sidonius and the addressee continues with the mention of the generation 'in the middle':[15] that of Sidonius' and Aquilinus' fathers, who are said to have served under Honorius when they were very young (merely *adulescentes*); it ensues that the death of the emperor in 423 constitutes a *terminus ante quem* for their being *tribuni et notarii* (that is, at the beginning of their career) under him. When Honorius died childless, his nephew Valentinian III, aged six, was put on the western throne (425–55), under the regency of his mother, Galla Placidia. In *Ep.* 5.9 the two are also said to have continued their career serving under the new emperor: Aquilinus' father presumably as *uicarius*, while Sidonius' father is known to have been *praefectus praetorio Galliarum*.[16]

---

13. See the commentary below on *Ep.* 5.9.1 *aui nostri* . . .
14. Of this opinion is for instance Harries 1994, 29. Furthermore, it can be argued that Sidonius may not feel the need to condemn or conceal their grandfathers' involvement because, incidentally, having sided with the usurpers and having received positions of power, reflected how influential both their families were.
15. *Ep.* 5.9.2 *aetate* . . . *media*.
16. As explained in the commentary ad loc.

Dating elements

Although *Ep.* 5.9 is characterised by the abundance of autobiographical information, there are no elements which allow one to date the letter *ad annum*. The only chronological evidence, and that is anyway vague, can be deduced from the detail that he is writing at a time 'already driving on the beginnings of old age' (*Ep.* 5.9.4); the melancholy adumbrated by this assertion is an indication that the author feels he is approaching senescence, an impression confirmed by the mention of his son being on the cusp of adulthood, and by the fact that Sidonius is not in Lyon at the time of writing, hence is presumably writing from Clermont, where he is a bishop.[17]

Loyen suggested dating the letter to 476 or 477,[18] while van Waarden recently argued that Sidonius would have felt old age approaching when he reached forty-five (hence between 474 and 477);[19] both seem plausible, although there is no evidence which would allow one to point in the direction of a specific year. Thus, it seems sensible to suggest the text may be dated to a period of time ranging from the start of Sidonius' bishopric to 477. The latter constitutes a *terminus ante quem* since it is in 477 that Books 1–7 were put together for publication.[20]

---

17. Sidonius is often performative when he mentions old age, and he arguably starts 'feeling older' after his appointment as bishop. This passage for instance calls to mind the melancholic seasonal reference in *Ep.* 5.3.3; see the General Introduction for the images of senescence in the *Letters*.
18. Loyen 1970a, 189; a similar date for *Ep.* 5.9 is suggested in *PCBE* 4, s.v. Aquilinus 1, 175 (476/477?) and in *PCBE* 4, s.v. Rusticus 9, 1665 (though without a question mark). Note that the letter is not dated in Anderson 1965; *PLRE* 2, s.v. Aquilinus 3, 125; nor in Mathisen 2020, 82.
19. See van Waarden 2018, 191–2 and 194; for Sidonius' birthdate van Waarden 2020a, 26.
20. See Kelly 2020, 180.

SIDONIUS AQUILINO SUO SALUTEM

1. In meo aere duco, uir omnium uirtutum capacissime, si dignum tu quoque putas, ut quantas habemus amicitiarum causas, tantas habeamus ipsi amicitias. Auitum est quod reposco; testes mihi in praesentiarum aui nostri super hoc negotio Apollinaris et Rusticus aduocabuntur, quos laudabili familiaritate coniunxerat litterarum, dignitatum, periculorum, conscientiarum similitudo, cum in Constantino inconstantiam, in Iouino facilitatem, in Gerontio perfidiam, singula in singulis, omnia in Dardano crimina simul execrarentur.

2. Aetate quae media, patres nostri sub uno contubernio, uixdum a pueritia in totam adulescentiam euecti, principi Honorio tribuni notariique militauere tanta caritate peregrinantes, ut inter eos minima fuerit causa concordiae, quod filii amicorum commemorabantur. In principatu Valentiniani imperatoris unus Galliarum praefuit parti, alter soliditati; sed ita se quodam modo tituli amborum compensatione fraterna ponderauerunt, ut prior fuerit fascium tenore qui erat posterior dignitate.

3. Ventum ad nos, id est uentum est ad nepotes, quos nil decuerit plus cauere, quam ne parentum antiquorumque nostrorum per nos forte uideatur antiquata dilectio. Ad hoc in similem familiaritatem praeter hereditariam praerogatiuam multifaria opportunitate compellimur; aetas utriusque non minus iuncta quam patria; unus nos exercuit ludus, magister instituit; una nos laetitia dissoluit, seueritas cohercuit, disciplina formauit.

4. De cetero, si deus annuit, in annis iam senectutis initia pulsantibus, simus, nisi respuis, animae duae, animus unus, imbuamusque liberos inuicem diligentes idem uelle, nolle, refugere, sectari. Hoc patrum uero iam supra uota, si per Rusticum Apollinaremque proauorum praedicabilium tam reformentur corda quam nomina. Vale.

---

§ 2 aetatequae *L* : aetateque α *MP*
commemorabantur *codd.* : commerebantur *Anderson* : commorabantur *Marolla*
tenore α M[1] *(super lineam) P* : tempore *LM*

§ 4 diligentes *codd.* : diligenter *Wilamowitz*

LETTER 9

SIDONIUS TO HIS DEAR AQUILINUS

1. If you too think it is proper, a man who has the greatest capacity for all virtues, I prize the fact that we have a friendship that is as strong as the many reasons we are friends. What I demand is ancestral; I will, at the present time, call in as witnesses upon this matter our grandfathers Apollinaris and Rusticus, whom a similarity of literary education, offices, dangers and consciousness brought together in precious familiarity; then they would execrate Constantine for his inconstancy, Jovinus for his heedlessness, Gerontius for his treachery, each of these for each of them, but Dardanus for all these faults together.

2. In the generation that is in the middle, our fathers were comrades, barely out of boyhood and becoming young men, they served the emperor Honorius as *tribuni et notarii*, roving with such affection that the fact they were remembered[21] as sons of friends was the least of the reasons for the harmony between them. Under the reign of emperor Valentinian one of them was in charge of a part of Gaul, the other of the entirety of it; yet the honours of both parties were weighted as by fraternal balance in such a way that the one who had been first in holding office was the man who was second in rank.

3. Then it comes to us, that is, it comes to the grandsons, to whom nothing has been more proper than to prevent the love of our fathers and of our grandfathers from perhaps appearing outdated. We are driven to this, to a similar friendship, besides the hereditary prerogative, by manifold favouring circumstances: the ages of both coincide no less than our fatherland, the same school trained us, the same teacher instructed us, the same gladness relaxed us, the same strictness restrained us, the same discipline formed us.

4. As for the rest, if God allows, in the years already driving on the beginnings of old age, if you don't refuse, let us be two souls but one spirit, and let us instruct our sons, who love each other with mutual affection, to desire, refuse, shun or pursue the same things. This bond will indeed exceed the wishes of the fathers, if through Rusticus and Apollinaris the souls as well as the names of their praiseworthy great-grandfathers shall be restored. Farewell.

---

21. Or, if one reads *commorabantur*, 'they were stationed together'.

SIDONIUS: LETTERS BOOK 5, PART 1

Commentary

§ 1

In meo aere duco: While *in meo aere* indicates a tie of friendship already in Cicero (*Fam.* 13.62.1 and 15.14.1) the syntagma *in meo aere duco* previously occurs four times exclusively in Symmachus' letters (as pointed out by Geisler 1887, 366; Gualandri 2020, 307), and mostly in introductory remarks. Given that in *TLL* 1.1075 s.v. *aes* 69–73 (by Bickel) the occurrences in Symmachus and Sidonius are said to be employed only figuratively, *tropice*, the ambiguous meaning in Sidonius' text may be enlightened through the contexts of the Symmachan model which he echoes. In Symm. *Ep.* 1.37.2 to Ausonius, the expression *in meo aere duco* serves as a comment on the addressee's advancement and is therefore translated by Salzman and Roberts 2011, 83 as 'to my profit'; and the same sense may be given to *Ep.* 8.16, where Symmachus comments on the betrothal of Auxentius to Carterius' daughter as being a beneficial event because it strengthens their family ties. It seems that Sidonius' use of the expression may mirror these two occurrences, since he is acknowledging that the friendship benefits him and he can literally 'count it in his prized possessions'. Note that Anderson 1965, 199 translates this passage as 'I consider it an asset', while Loyen 1970a, 188 has 'ce serait pour moi un bien precieux' (but also has a verbatim translation in Loyen 1970a, 237 n. 28). The other two occurrences of the expression in Symmachus do not seem to have the same meaning: in Symm. *Ep.* 3.14 he is 'in debt' of an accommodation to Naucellius; while in *Ep.* 3.43.1, although metaphorically, Symmachus shares the addressee's sense of debt to good fortune (see Pellizzari 1998, 279 and 288).

uir omnium uirtutum capacissime: This expression is not known to occur often; when Ambrose explains the meaning of *Cant.* 7.2 *umbilicus animae*, as being able to 'contain all the virtues', he states it is *omnium uirtutum capax* (*Obit. Valent.* 69); the expression also occurs in *Praef. Bibl.* 8.10 (an explanation of why the *ecclesiasticus* is said to be *panaretos: id est omnium uirtutum capax*). In Sidonius the superlative enhances the affectation of the passage, an impression which is confirmed by the fact that all the other occurrences of *capacissimus* in his corpus do not concern people but places (*Epp.* 3.3.5 *domus*; 5.17.3 *basilica*) and feasts (*Ep.* 4.15.1 *lectisternia*). Note also that the double cretic clausula at *-tum capacissime* occurs without the presence of cursus.

LETTER 9

si dignum tu quoque putas: This expression pertains to epistolary writing since its first occurrence at the beginning of Sen. *Ep.* 20.1 where *si uales et te dignum putas . . . gaudeo* is a variant of *si uales corpore et animo bene est*, as pointed out by Préchac and Noblot 1985, 81 n. 2. Cf. Paul Nol. *Ep.* 4.3, a passage in which Paulinus tells Augustine that *ut in portu salutis, si dignum putas, pariter nauigemus* ('if you think it proper we shall be safe together in the harbour of salvation') and Hier. *Ep.* 90.3. The dactyl iamb clausula (at *tu quoque putas*) is known to be appreciated by Sidonius, as pointed out by Kelly (van Waarden and Kelly 2020, 472).

ut quantas habemus amicitiarum causas, tantas habeamus ipsi amicitias: This declaration of friendship sets the tone of the letter and explains the following mention of their grandfathers as one of the numerous reasons why they should be friends. The sentence ends with a clausula, a cretic tribrach at *-ips(i) amicitias*, with elision.

Auitum est quod reposco: This expression is not known to occur elsewhere. Its meaning is explained by the following sentence, concerning their grand-fathers. For the recurring theme of the hereditary nature of friendship in Pliny and Symmachus, see the introduction to this letter.

testes mihi in praesentiarum: This expression, although inserted in a playful context, evokes the solemnity of judicial language. As pointed out in *TLL* 7.1.673 s.v. *impraesentiarum*, 78–83 (by Rehm), this adverb occurs, with various spellings, from Cato *Agr.* 144.4 on, but is more often attested after Apuleius (where it occurs fourteen times), with numerous occurrences also in Jerome (fifty-seven times), Augustine (thirteen times), Sidonius (seven times) and Mamertus Claudianus (seven times). Cf. Mam. Claud. *Anim.* 2.3, p. 104 *qui ueritati in praesentiarum testificarentur*, the affinity of linguistic choices shared by Sidonius and Mamertus Claudianus has been discussed above.

aui nostri super hoc negotio Apollinaris et Rusticus aduocabuntur: Continuing the judiciary image, Sidonius 'calls in as witnesses' his and Aquilinus' grandfathers. Apollinaris was *praefectus praetorio Galliarum* in 408/9 under Caesar Constans in Spain, and was the first of his family to receive baptism, as can be surmised from the epitaph Sidonius writes for him, preserved in *Ep.* 3.12.5 (vv. 13–16). See also *PLRE* 2 s.v. Apollinaris 1, 113. Decimius Rusticus, already *magister officiorum* under the usurper

Constantine, accompanied Constans in Spain and was probably named *praefectus praetorio Galliarum* after Apollinaris, in 409. In Greg. Tur. *Hist.* 2.9, Rusticus is said to be Constans' prefect, and in *PLRE* 2 s.v. Decimius Rusticus 9, 965 the mention of Rusticus as *praefectus tyrannorum* (Greg. Tur. *Hist.* 2.9) is considered proof he may have served Jovinus as well. Gregory of Tours also relates that Rusticus was among those aristocrats who had been captured and killed by Honorius' commanders in 413. It is doubtful if Apollinaris, unlike his successor in office, managed to survive the purges following the fall of Jovinus. Although Mathisen 2020, 80 believes he did, Harries 1994, 28, Mascoli 2010, 15–16 and van Waarden 2020, 19 argue that he was probably among the victims. Note the cretic rhythm created by the two names Apollinaris and Rusticus, and the cretic spondee at *aduocabuntur*.

laudabili familiaritate: This *iunctura* is not known to have other occurrences; Mathisen's argument (2020, 35) that *familiaritas* and *familiaris* are 'code words' used by Sidonius to indicate intimate friendship commands assent.

litterarum, dignitatum, periculorum, conscientiarum similitudo: The two are said to have shared not only status and upbringing but also the dangers of the turbulent times they lived in, the political choices made and a disenchanted opinion of those they served. The similarity of literary education tellingly precedes that of political careers, Condorelli 2015, 502 observes. *Studiorum ac naturae similitudo* (likeness of literary interests and of nature) is said to be the most distinctive feature of friendship in Cic. *Clu.* 16 (46); see also Cic. *Amic.* 50. In *Ep.* 3.86.2 Symmachus says that he is not surprised that Rufinus and Nicomachus Flavianus are now friends, given the *similitudo* of their virtues; on this letter see Pellizzari 1998, 236–7. The thought that true friends think alike, and so share similar opinions (either good or bad) of others, is interestingly expressed in Sidon. *Ep.* 3.1 to Avitus, a letter mentioned in the introduction and in commentary on § 3 for its similarities with *Ep.* 5.9. After having listed the memories and upbringing shared by Avitus and himself, Sidonius points out they have in common a similarity of judgement which is 'even more powerful and effective in strengthening friendships' (*Ep.* 3.1.1 *quod est ad amicitias ampliandas his ualidius efficaciusque, in singulis quibusque personis uel expetendis aequaliter uel cauendis iudicii parilitate certauimus*); this opinion is expounded in the following paragraph, where Avitus and Sidonius are said to be tied also by *actionum similitudo* (*Ep.* 3.1.2). Compare also *Ep.* 4.4.1 *hic meus frater natalium parilitate, amicus animorum similitudine*. This brief list is opened and closed by clausulae: see the cretic ditrochee at *-iunxerat litterarum* and the paeon I spondee at *-rum similitudo.*

cum in Constantino inconstantiam: Flavius Claudius Constantinus, the usurper sometimes known as Constantine III, ruled from 407 to 411. Proclaimed emperor in 407 by the armies in Britain he was first recognised by Honorius but then, after being besieged in Arles, he surrendered to Honorius' generals in 411 and was killed soon afterwards. See *PLRE* 2 s.v. Constantinus 21, 316 and the introduction to this letter for further context. The mention of Constantine as being 'inconstant' is ascribed by Loyen 1970a, 237 n. 29 to his incongruous attitude towards Sidonius' grandfather Apollinaris, who had been sent to Spain but was later relieved of duty, as is testified exclusively by Zosimus 6.4.4 and 6.13.1, on which see the remarks by Paschoud 1989, 31–2 n. 120. Note that the word-game on Constantine opens a short list of faults of politicians contemporary with Sidonius' and Aquilinus' grandfathers. Although Sidonius is not reluctant to mention Apollinaris' political choice and he feels free 'to acknowledge the period of usurpation as part of his family history' (Harries 1994, 29), he is also keen on showing that their grandfathers did not have a high opinion of these politicians. Similar in tone is also the vague mention of his grandfather Apollinaris as *liber sub dominantibus tyrannis* in the epitaph (*Ep.* 3.12.5 v.12); see the introduction to the letter for further comments. Sidonius is fond of wordplays, in particular those which are etymological or pseudo-etymological, as highlighted by Wolff 2020, 412–13. See e.g. the allusion concerning Seronatus' name being antiphrastic in *Ep.* 2.1.1, and the similar puns in *Ep.* 4.18.5 v. 20 (*perpetuo durent culmina Perpetui*) and *Ep.* 8.11.3 vv. 35–6 (*satis facetum et / solo nomine Rusticum uideto*). Word-games are often found also in Sidonius' poetry, e.g. *Carm.* 9.5–8 (*Felix nomine, mente, honore, forma . . .*); *Carm.* 16.127–8 (*semper mihi Faustus, / semper Honoratus, semper quoque Maximus esto*); *Carm.* 23.154 (*Corneli Tacite, es tacendus ori*); *Carm.* 24.94 (*admitti faciet Probus probatum*). On the detection of wordplays in Sidonius see also Amherdt 2001, 123; 416; Santelia 2012, 142. The syntagma creates a molossus cretic clausula at *-no inconstantiam*; it is not clear whether this is a favoured clausula in Sidonius – see van Waarden and Kelly 2020, 463 n. 3.

in Iouino facilitatem: The usurper Jovinus was proclaimed Augustus in Gaul – see *PLRE* 2, s.v. Iovinus 2, 621. Even though their grandfathers supported him, Sidonius is keen on showing they were aware of Jovinus' flaws; see the introduction to this letter for the political climate of the time. For the specifically negative nuance of the word *facilitas*, which is not signalled in *OLD*, see *TLL* 6.1. 73 s.v. *facilitas* 82 ff. (by Bannier), *cum nota uituperationis fere i.q. neglegentia, credulitas, leuitas.* The word often occurs in Tacitus' negative portraits of rulers: see e.g. the mention of men close to Galba who took advantage of his *facilitas* in *Hist.* 1.12.3; in *Ann.* 11.28.2 the same *facilitas* which had made Claudius easily manipulated by Messalina is turned into an instrument in the hands of her slanderers, and also in *Ann.* 12.61.2 Claudius is said to act *facilitate solita* ('with his usual heedlessness'). See also Suet. *Cl.* 29.2, where the emperor is said to have sentenced to death, *tanta facilitate*, 35 senators and over 300 *equites.* Sidonius employs the word negatively also in *Ep.* 1.11.4, when Paeonius is able to incite the mob against him counting on the *leuis turbae facilitatem.* Note the paeon I spondee clausula created by -*no facilitatem.*

in Gerontio perfidiam: Given that Gerontius was *magister utriusque militiae* under the usurper Constantine (from 407 to 409) but betrayed him and proclaimed as emperor his son Maximus, it seems particularly fitting that he is said to be treacherous, since *perfidia* is often mentioned as a distinctive feature of ruthless military men and of their troops. See in Tac. *Hist.* 3.12.1 the *perfidia ducum* causing concern among Vitellius' supporters; in *Hist.* 4.27.2, Roman soldiers, having been defeated, *non suam ignauiam, sed perfidiam legati culpabant*; in Suet. *Gal.* 3.2, Servius Galba, ancestor of the emperor, is said to have massacred 30,000 Lusitanians through treachery (*perfidia*). On Gerontius, see *PLRE* 2, s.v. Gerontius 5, 508 and the introduction to this letter for broader context.

singula in singulis, omnia in Dardano crimina simul execrarentur: Claudius Postumus Dardanus earns the mention as the worst on the list, since he embodied all the faults of his predecessors. Being loyal to Honorius, he was named *praefectus praetorio Galliarum* in 412–13 and, as such, was responsible for the killing of Jovinus in 413, an action still resented by Sidonius, two generations later. Jerome and Augustine depict their contemporary Dardanus as a fervent Christian, who asked doctrinal questions to both, for which he received two treatises in return (Hier. *Ep.* 129 and Aug. *Ep.* 187); Dardanus is also known to have founded a Christian community near Sisteron, named Theopolis, possibly a homage to Augustine's *ciuitas Dei*, as is testified by *CIL* XII 1524; on Dardanus, see *PLRE* 2, s.v. 346–7 and Mathisen 2020, 89. The paragraph ends with two clausulae: a double cretic at *singula in singulis* (with elision) and a cretic spondee at *execrarentur.*

LETTER 9

§ 2

Aetate quae media: Lütjohann 1887, 84, Anderson 1965, 200 and Loyen 1970a, 188 choose the reading *aetate quae* attested in *L* (although it has never been pointed out that it occurs oddly in the one-word *aetatequae*). *Aetateque* (α*MP*) is not an uninteresting reading, and either solution – the relative with *est* implied or the noun with the enclitic at the beginning of the sentence – seems possible. The expression *media aetas* has occurrences since Plautus, but mostly indicates a stage in life, as in Plaut. *Aul.* 162; Cic. *Cato* 20 (76); Ov. *Fast.* 3.774; Apul. *Met.* 5.16 and in Hier. *Vir. ill.* 53. In Aug. *C. Iul. op. imperf.* 2.187 it indicates a period of time between two laws, while the use of the expression to define a 'middle generation' seems distinctively Sidonian.

patres nostri sub uno contubernio: Just like that of their grandfathers, also the bond of friendship between their fathers constitutes one of the reasons why Sidonius and Aquilinus should be in good terms (see introduction for the hereditary succession of friendly relations). Sidonius' and Aquilinus' fathers are both anonymous, although it seems possible that Sidonius' father could have been named Alcimus, given the names of his daughter Alcima, and of his nephew Alcimus Ecdicius Avitus of Vienne, as is suggested by Mathisen 2020, s.v. Anonymus 8, 134; see also *PLRE* 2, s.v. Anonymus 6, 1220 and see below for the information on his career which can be surmised from this letter. *Ep.* 5.9 constitutes the only source of information on Aquilinus' father, as pointed out in *PLRE* 2, s.v. Anonymus 49, 1227; Mathisen 2020, Anonymus 21, 136. The fathers are said to have been comrades, *sub uno contubernio*, and this expression is not known to have other occurrences, unlike the more common *in contubernio*, for which see *TLL* 4.791 s.v. *contubernium* 80–4 (by Poeschel). The syntagma concerns their serving together, hence Sidonius specifically refers to the military nuance of the word, even though he also states they were close friends, and thus seems to play on the ambiguity of the expression. Note that Sherwin-White 1966, 178 considers the word *contubernalis* to be 'a regular metaphor of literary friendships' in Pliny the Younger's *Letters*, and that according to Gibson and Morello 2012, 140–2 *contubernalis* is an example of 'friendship vocabulary' in Pliny: the term would indicate a peculiar closeness, since *contubernales* (those who are or were daily at one's house) are said to be Pliny's closest or oldest associates, such as Romatius Firmus (*Ep.* 1.19.1), Voconius Romanus (*Epp.* 2.13.5 and 10.4.1), Calvisius Rufus (*Epp.* 1.12.12 and 4.4.1) and Suetonius Tranquillus (*Epp.* 1.24.1 and 10.94.1). *Contubernium* and *contubernalis* rarely occur in Symmachus (in unremarkable contexts), while Sidonius is keen on employing *contubernium* to indicate close friendships. See, for instance, the mention of the *sodalitas contubernii* in *Ep.* 4.6.1, which, according to Amherdt 2001, 197, is used to indicate friendly relations in his youth; see also the figurative use of *contubernium* to indicate a brotherhood *bonorum* in *Ep.* 4.15.1 and *nobilium* in *Ep.* 4.21.6. For other occurrences in Sidonius see Hindermann 2022, 97.

uixdum a pueritia in totam adulescentiam euecti, principi Honorio tribuni notariique militauere: The fathers are said to have been young when they entered the service of Honorius as *tribuni et notarii*: magistrates under the *primicerius* employed as officers, administrative officials, diplomats or jurists of the emperor. See Lengle 1937, 2453–4; note that for their role as *tribuni et notarii* the two are also listed as Anonymus 87 and Anonymus 88 in Teitler 1983, 193–4. The two cretic spondee clausulae, at *-scenti(am) euecti* and at *militauere*, confer rhythm on the passage.

tanta caritate peregrinantes: In Book 5, Sidonius has already mentioned *caritas* as one of the defining features of true friendship, which goes beyond affection; see the commentary on *uera caritas* in *Ep.* 5.3.2. Note the paeon IV spondee clausula at *-te peregrinantes*.

ut inter eos minima fuerit causa concordiae: Note the double cretic clausula at *causa concordiae*.

quod filii amicorum commemorabantur: The fact they were 'known' to be sons of friends was the last of the reasons why they were so close. Anderson 1965, 200 doubted the unanimous manuscript reading *commemorabantur*. In favour of Anderson's suggestion, one could argue that, even though Sidonius employs this verb two times in his corpus (*Epp.* 2.9.10 and 3.13.9) he always refers it to inanimate objects, not to people. Anderson's conjecture, *commerebantur*, seems fitting in terms of rhythm, since it would create a cretic spondee clausula in a passage which is heavily clausulated and is always clausulated at the end of the sentence. And yet, Anderson's conjecture is also problematic, since *commereor* does not have the specific meaning of 'to serve together' suggested by Warmington (Anderson 1965, 201 n. 6) but that of 'to deserve' something bad (and, *latiore sensu, delinquere*) or, more rarely, 'to earn something', as attested in *TLL* 3.1880 s.v. *commereo* 15–62 (by Wulff). It seems possible, therefore, to suggest a different reading:

commorabantur. Its trivialisation in *commemorabantur* with the addition of an extra syllable *-me* would be justifiable as a dittography; furthermore, the meaning of the passage would be that their 'being stationed in the same place' as sons of friends was the last of the reasons to be friends, and the reading *commorabantur* would also be coherent with the previous mention of the two as living *sub uno contubernio*. In terms of rhythm, *commorabantur* (like Anderson's *lectio*) would create a cretic spondee, one of Sidonius' favourite clausulae. However, it should also be pointed out that this verb is not known to occur in Sidonius' corpus.

In principatu Valentiniani imperatoris unus Galliarum praefuit parti, alter soliditati: Sidonius' and Aquilinus' fathers then served under emperor Valentinian III and with a periphrasis – typical of his way of writing – Sidonius informs the reader that Aquilinus' father had administered 'part of Gaul', probably as *uicarius* (Mathisen 2020, s.v. Anonymus 21, 136), while his father had administered 'the entirety of it', being *praefectus praetorio Galliarum*, an appointment which is mentioned in Sidon. *Ep.* 1.3.1 (in a list of prestigious posts held by his ancestors) and, more explicitly, in *Ep.* 8.6.5 *cum pater meus praefectus praetorio Gallicanis tribunalibus praesideret*, when he recalls having been present, in the year 449, at the installation of consul Astyrius at Arles. *Soliditas* as opposed to *pars* occurs exclusively in late Latin, see e.g. Symm. *Ep.* 2.87 and Ambr. *In Psalm.* 118 *Serm.* 14.41.3. Note the cretic spondee at *praefuit parti* and the paeon I spondee at *-ter soliditati*.

sed ita se quodam modo tituli amborum compensatione fraterna ponderauerunt, ut prior fuerit fascium tenore qui erat posterior dignitate: All the manuscripts in Dolveck's α branch (*ACSVat1661*), M^1 and P have *tenore*; while *tempore* is attested in *LM*. Lütjohann 1887, 84, Anderson 1965, 200 and Loyen 1970a, 188 have chosen *tempore* and yet *tenore* is the *lectio difficilior*, and is stemmatically demanded; for this reason it was put in the text. Both *fascium tempore* and *fascium tenore* are not known to have previous occurrences; *fascium tenore*, although discarded by editors, would also be justifiable since the passage would then mean that the one who 'had been first in holding office was the man who was second in rank' (for this post-Augustan meaning of *tenor* see *L&S* s.v.). Again, this would be a particularly studied way of writing that, in a sort of 'fraternal balance', Aquilinus' father received his post (possibly as *uicarius* – see above) before Sidonius' father received his prefecture. The affectedness of the passage is enhanced by the *iunctura compensatio fraterna*, which is not known to have previous occurrences. The ending of this section is also clausulated: note the cretic spondee at *ponderauerunt* and the anapaest ditrochee at *-terior dignitate.*

§ 3

Ventum ad nos, id est uentum est ad nepotes: The family excursus is finished and Sidonius now turns his attention directly to the addressee, with whom he shares not only family ties but also a personal bond, which goes back to their childhood. The section is opened by an anaphora, a figure of speech which also occurs later in this paragraph.

quos nil decuerit plus cauere: Note the anapaest ditrochee at *-cuerit plus cauere.*

quam ne parentum antiquorumque nostrorum per nos forte uideatur antiquata dilectio: Sidonius and Aquilinus are the depositaries of their family bond, hence it is up to them to safeguard and strengthen it. Note that *antiquata dilectio* is a *iunctura* which is not known to occur elsewhere; and that, in this case as well, the studied circumlocution has the effect of conveying simple information with affected prose, as testified also by the polyptota at *antiquorum . . . antiquata* and at *nostrorum . . . nos.* This passage is characterised by heavy clausulation: see the subsequent cretic spondee at *-rumque nostrorum*; an internal clausula (paeon I spondee at *forte uideatur*); and the double cretic at *-quata dilectio.*

Ad hoc in similem familiaritatem praeter hereditariam praerogatiuam multifaria opportunitate compellimur: The three *iuncturae* (*similis familiaritas*; *hereditaria praerogatiua*; *multifaria opportunitas*) are not known to have previous occurrences. The noun *praerogatiua* relates to family ties also in Sidon. *Ep.* 5.1.3 *per agnationis praerogatiuam*; *Ep.* 6.2.3 *paterna praerogatiua*; and, in particular, in *Ep.* 6.7.1, where *praerogatiua domesticae familiaritatis* concerns the relationship between Sidonius' and bishop Fonteius' families. The adjective *multifarius* is attested much later than the adverb *multifariam*; with this meaning it occurs exclusively from Tert. *Adu. Marc.* 1.4 on and is modelled on the Greek πολυποίκιλος; see *TLL* 8.1584 s.v. *multifarius* 4–11 (by Gruber). Note the two clausulae subsidiary to punctuation: the cretic spondee at *praerogatiuam* and the double cretic at *-tate compellimur.*

LETTER 9

aetas utriusque non minus iuncta quam patria: The syntagma is constructed similarly to the list of values their grandfathers shared: the occurrence of *iuncta* mirrors that of *coniunxerat* in § 1. This sentence is also clausulated – see the double cretic at *iuncta quam patria*.

unus nos exercuit ludus . . . disciplina formauit: Sidonius is thus informing the reader that he and Aquilinus are equal in age, that they share childhood memories and have been taught by the same teacher. See the introduction for the similar list of shared memories in Plin. *Ep.* 2.13.5. Compare this passage also with Sidon. *Ep.* 3.1.1 *ipsi hisdem temporibus nati, magistris usi . . .* ('we were born in the same times, we had the same teachers . . .'), where Sidonius reminds the addressee of their long-lasting tie of friendship, which he calls *necessitudo* (see Giannotti 2016, 110–11); for the similarities between this letter and *Ep.* 5.9, see above and the introduction. One can assume that information on childhood or family ties is included for the sake of the reader as a homage to the addressee, given that declarations of friendship of this kind (see e.g. Symm. *Ep.* 8.43 mentioned in the introduction) do not convey any information to the addressees. Mathisen 2005, 8 believes that the *magister* mentioned in this passage is a *magister ludi*, that is, an elementary school teacher, although in this text the mention of *ludus* is independent from that of the teacher; further, it can be argued that Mathisen's identification (2005, 8) of this school teacher with Hoenius, who is named in Sidon. *Carm.* 9.312 as *mihi magister*, commands assent. In terms of style, this passage can be considered as exemplary of Sidonius' fondness for lists; Wolff 2020, 409–10 ascribes similar word accumulations in the *Letters* to the subcategory of *determinatio*: 'a complex succession of groups made up of elements of the same nature and arranged in the same way'. For similar stylistic devices in the first half of the book, see the enumeration of the qualities of Mamertus Claudianus' *De statu animae* in Sidon. *Ep.* 5.2.1, where the use of personification is also comparable to the one in *Ep.* 5.9.3; see also the long lists of faults of the *delatores* in *Ep.* 5.7.1–6. Note that this paragraph, which is opened by the anaphora of *uentum*, ends with the anaphoric repetition of *un*+ nos*; furthermore, the section is highly clausulated, with a cretic spondee at *-sercuit ludus*, a cretic tribrach at *-gister instituit* and a cretic spondee at *-plina formauit*.

§ 4

De cetero: Sidonius is fond of this transitional expression, which has eleven occurrences in his *Letters*, where it often introduces closing remarks; cf. van Waarden 2010, 265.

si deus annuit: For similar customary expressions see the commentary on *Ep.* 5.1.3 *post opem Christi*. The expression occurs in Propertius 1.1.31, where it concerns *Amor* being propitious, *facili . . . annuit aure* (see Fedeli 1980, 84); cf. also Salvianus of Marseille *Gub.* 7.1.2 and Orientius *Comm.* 1.291.

in annis iam senectutis initia pulsantibus: As stated in the introduction, this phrase is useful in terms of dating, given that Sidonius considers himself and Aquilinus to be approaching old age. Although the syntagma is not known to have previous occurrences, see the occurrence of *pulsare* in Hor. *Ep.* 2.2.215–16 where Horace feels no longer young, and he believes it is appropriate for him to dedicate himself to knowledge, instead of poetry, which, on the contrary, is to be practised in youth (see Brink 1982, 411–12; Rudd 1989, 150). The verb is specifically associated with the passing of time, as is signalled in *TLL* 10.2.2610 s.v. *pulso* 35–44 (by Schrickx), in Juvenal 6.192–3 *tu . . . quam sextus et octogesimus annus / pulsat*, when the satirist addresses an old woman saying that 'the eighty-sixth year comes knocking', and Geisler 1887, 366 already draws a comparison between this passage and Sidonius'. Cf. also the similar use of the metaphor of doors to indicate ageing in Ambr. *Obit. Theod.* 15, in which Honorius is said to be 'knocking on the door of adulthood' (*pulsat adulescentiae fores*). Sidonius employs the verb to indicate senescence also in *Carm.* 2.416: the Phoenix, when old age approaches (*pulsante senecta*), gathers cinnamon, which will give new life to its ashes. Note that *-itia pulsantibus*, is a paeon IV cretic.

simus, nisi respuis, animae duae, animus unus: Cf. the occurrence of *similitudo* in §1 ; although this is a recurrent cliché, compare this assertion to Cic. *Amic.* 92 *ut unus quasi animus fiat ex pluribus*, where friendship is said 'to make one soul out of many'. Note the occurrence of *nisi respuis* also in Sidon. *Ep.* 2.4.1, where Sidonius is the bearer of a similar declaration of friendship from Proiectus to the addressee, Sagittarius (or Syagrius).

imbuamusque liberos: the same expression occurs in Val. Max. 6.3 ext. 1 *noluerunt enim ea liberorum suorum animos imbui*, where the Spartans are said to have ordered Archilochus' works to be removed from the city, so that their sons would not be negatively influenced by them; for other occurrences of the verb *imbuere* meaning 'to instruct' in other authors and in Sidonius, see the commentary on Sidon. *Ep.* 5.5.2.

inuicem diligentes: The *lectio tradita* is *diligentes*, but Wilamowitz conjectured *diligenter* (in Lütjohann 1887, 84); however, previous occurrences of *inuicem* with this verb lead to the inference that the transmitted *diligentes* is a fitting reading. In particular, see Plin. *Ep.* 7.20.7 to Tacitus: 'all of this has but one purpose: that we love each other even more ardently (*ut inuicem ardentius diligamus*) since our literary activities, our characters, our reputation and, above all things, the judgement of men tie us together with as many bonds'. Apart from the occurrence of the syntagma, which gives evidence in support of the reading *diligentes*, the context concerning the nature of Pliny's friendship with Tacitus is, in itself, evocative of Sidonius' declaration of friendship to Aquilinus. See also Tert. *Apol.* 39.7, where *uide . . . ut inuicem se diligant* expresses amazement at the philanthropy of good Christians; and, in particular, Sidon. *Ep.* 7.6.1, which begins with the mention of ancient ties of friendship (*uetera iura*) between him and bishop Basilius: *diuque est quod inuicem diligimus ex aequo* ('we have loved one another in equal measure for a long time'). *Inuicem diligentes* is a cretic ditrochee.

idem uelle, nolle, refugere, sectari: A reworking of a passage from Sallust, which Sidonius has already quoted in this book, at *Ep.* 5.3.2 (see the commentary ad loc.); the similarity is also signalled by Savaron 1609, 343 and by Geisler 1887, 366. Among the similar occurrences detected by Savaron, see in particular Min. Fel. 1.3 *eadem uelle uel nolle: crederes unam mentem in duobus fuisse diuisam* ('one would have thought that a single mind had been divided in two'), where the author describes his closeness to Octavius. In a few lines, Sidonius repeatedly conveys the same message: in this paragraph, their being *animae duae, animus unus*; in § 1, the *similitudo* of their grandfathers; and in § 2 the *concordia* of their fathers. This sequence of verbs is closed by a paeon IV spondee clausula at *-fugere, sectari*.

Hoc patrum uero iam supra uota: The passage is here translated in accordance with previous translations by Anderson 1965, 202 ('it would indeed surpass the dearest wishes of their fathers') and by Loyen 1970a, 189 ('un bien qui dépasserait les voeux des parents'). With this meaning, a similar occurrence is in Tac *Ann.* 15.19.2, where the expression *longa patrum uota* concerns 'the longstanding hopes of parents' for their children, as high-lighted in the commentary by Ash 2018, 121. And yet, note that Sidonius may be using a wordplay, since *uota parentis* are a way of indicating one's offspring in a number of texts. See, for instance, the occurrence in Stat. *Silu.* 5.3.146 (on its meaning of 'children', see Gibson 2006, 320 and Liberman 2010, 447); moreover, *uota patrum* indicates 'children' also in Aus. *Ecl.* 19.43 (Green), as explained by Green 1991, 435. Should one give the expression this meaning, Sidonius and the addressee would be their fathers' *uota*; hence a possible double meaning could be that, should his and Aquilinus' sons be on good terms, the familiar bond would surpass *them*, that is, the generation of Sidonius and Aquilinus. Note the cretic spondee clausula at *iam supra uota*.

si per Rusticum Apollinaremque proauorum praedicabilium tam re-formentur corda quam nomina: Aquilinus' and Sidonius' sons have the same names as their great-grandfathers (see the commentary on § 1). Note that the *iunctura paraedicabilis proauus* is not otherwise attested, and that the adjective *praedicabilis* has fewer than twenty occurrences before Sidonius, who employs it also (although with ironic intent) in the description of the parasite in *Ep.* 3.13.3. Rusticus is probably to be identified with the bishop of Lyon who died in 501 (as can be gathered from *CIL* XIII 2395); on him see *PLRE* 2, s.v. Rusticus 5, 964; Mathisen 2020, 119. On Sidonius' son Apollinaris, who followed his father's footsteps, becoming bishop of Clermont in 515, a few months before dying, see *PLRE* 2, s.v. Apollinaris 3, 114; Mathisen 2020, 81 (for his death in 514). Note the cretic spondee at *-pollinaremque*; the cretic tribrach at *praedicabilium*; the internal clausula (a cretic spondee) at *tam reformentur*; and the double cretic clausula at *corda quam nomina*.

LETTER 10

Content

The main theme of the letter is the friendship between two men of culture, Sapaudus and Pragmatius. The complex structure of this text can be summarised as follows:

§ 1   praise of the friendship between the addressee, Sapaudus, and Pragmatius, who was drawn to him out of his love of letters;
§ 2   praise of Pragmatius, who became successful because of his oratorial skills, which led to his marriage with Priscus Valerianus' daughter;
§ 3   praise of Sapaudus' oratorial prowess and list of renowned rhetors he surpassed;
§ 4   the friendship between the two is a beacon of hope amid pervasive literary decline.

The addressee Sapaudus

Sapaudus is praised for his knowledge by both Sidonius and Mamertus Claudianus, whose *Ep.* 2 is addressed to *doctissimo uiro Sapaudo rhetori*.[1] In the same letter, Sapaudus is said to be working as a teacher of rhetoric in Vienne: *Viennensis urbis . . . ciuis et doctor*.[2] There is no element to ascertain whether Sapaudus is also identifiable with a namesake, the addressee of a letter from Leonianus, which is preserved in the collection of Avitus of Vienne (*Ep.* 86); and yet, as advocated by Shanzer and Wood 2002, 279–80, this seems unlikely.[3] Sidonius appears to be in good terms with the addressee, and no

---

1. In Par. lat. 2165, f. 34ᵛ, which is the only witness of this letter (ff. 34ᵛ–35ʳ).
2. Mam. Claud. *Ep.* 2, p. 205.
3. Shanzer and Wood's suggestion that Leonianus may be Avitus' *nom de plume* and that consequently Sapaudus may be a fictitious name is attractive: 'it is possible that Avitus used Sapaudus as a soubriquet for a highly rhetorical friend to whom to send this highly rhetorical letter' (Shanzer and Wood 2002, 279 n. 6).

trace of tension emerges from this friendly letter, as is confirmed by the consistent use of the second person singular throughout the text.[4]

Genre: literary matters and praise of intellectuals

As is argued in the General Introduction, this letter can be ascribed to the category of 'epistles on literary matters', which in this book includes *Ep.* 5.2 to Nymphidius and *Ep.* 5.8 to Secundinus.[5] The common theme of these texts is the praise of friendships between admirable intellectuals – in the case of *Ep.* 5.10, Sapaudus and Pragmatius. Unlike *Epp.* 5.2 and 5.8, in this letter Sidonius seems to be only an observer and an admirer of the close friendship between the two, and is not personally involved as a third member of this close circle.[6]

Therefore, despite the semblance of a congratulatory letter written at the news of their shared brotherhood, *Ep.* 5.10 reveals its nature as a display piece with the aim of praising both Sapaudus and Pragmatius. As will be argued in the following section, in light of the possibility that Mamertus Claudianus may have already read this letter before writing his own letter to Sapaudus, it seems likely that *Ep.* 5.10 circulated independently before being placed in the collection.[7] The considerable length of the digression on Pragmatius (§ 2) in which Sidonius focuses on his social ascent, made possible thanks to his captivating speeches, should therefore be related to the desire to praise both Pragmatius and his father-in-law, Priscus Valerianus, in the collection. As the commentary further explains, Valerianus is himself a friend of Sidonius, who wrote for him *Carm.* 8, a dedicatory poem to accompany the Panegyric of Avitus. In the *carmen* (vv. 5–6), by virtue of his learning, Valerianus is designated as a severe judge of the quality of Sidonius' verses, despite being a friend of his: *dura fronte legit mollis amicitia.*[8]

---

4. The occurrence of the second person plural in the last paragraph coincides with the mention of Sapaudus and Pragmatius together, since Sidonius argues that anyone would wish to be accepted as a 'third member' of their literary circle. Van Waarden 2020b, 431 wrongly lists this letter as an example of the alternating *tu/uos* in the *Letters*; see his *Addenda et Corrigenda* <https://sidonapol.org/companion-add-and-correct>.

5. As is argued in the General Introduction; see also the introductions to *Epp.* 5.2 and 5.8 for Pliny and Symmachus as models.

6. See § 4.

7. See the commentary on *Ep.* 5.7 for a similar inference.

8. Although Sidonius has received popular praise as a poet, and the panegyric has already been read in public, there is a sort of sacredness in sending the work to a trusted *sodalis*

LETTER 10

By praising the appropriateness of the friendship between Sapaudus and Pragmatius, and by fondly mentioning his 'eloquent' friend Priscus Valerianus,[9] Sidonius is describing the literary milieu of which he is a member. Once this letter is put in the perspective of self-presentation of savant Gallic aristocracy, the nature of this – otherwise labyrinthine – text appears more intelligible than it might be at first glance. Moreover, the complexity of the style in which the text is written heightens the impression that Sidonius has dedicated extra care to writing this piece. As is explained in the commentary, the studious choice of rarely attested words and even rarer *iuncturae* which enrich this highly sophisticated text can be considered as further evidence that the letter was conceived as a display piece.[10]

Mamertus Claudianus' letter to Sapaudus

As stated above, Sapaudus also received *Ep.* 2 from Mamertus Claudianus, a letter concerning the praise of the rhetorical knowledge of the addressee, who is depicted as a promising rhetor. Claudianus too, like Sidonius, mourns the end of literary studies and sees the addressee as the last repository of rhetorical knowledge. Aside from the thematic similarities, which will be expounded in the following section, the numerous textual parallels highlighted in the commentary are a clear indication that these letters should be analysed together.

Although the two texts touch upon the same topics, Sidonius and Claudianus' conception of poetics is radically different and, as Alimonti pointed

---

who is supposed to pass honest and stern judgement on the text which is now circulating in written form. As can be surmised from *Carm.* 8.7–10 (*nil totum prodest adiectum laudibus illud / Ulpia quod rutilat porticus aere meo / uel quod adhuc populo simul et plaudente senatu / ad nostrum reboat concaua Roma sophos*) the judgement expressed by Valerianus is far more important than public praise and, ultimately, 'what really matters' to Sidonius. The public acknowledgement he was given, his bronze statue in the Portico of Trajan or even the resounding applauses of the crowd and of the Senate are nothing compared to his opinion (at least for the length of this poem). On the interpretation of these verses see Santelia 2002b, 247–8 and Condorelli 2008, 27.

9. See the commentary on § 2 *socer eloquens* . . .

10. See, for instance, the exquisite Plinian reminiscence opening the letter; the occurrence of the rare word *decoramentum* (§ 2) and of three uncommon *iuncturae* – *dos formae, pulchritudo morum* and *scientiae obtentus* (§ 2), all in paragraph 2, on Pragmatius and on the *litteratus* Priscus Valerianus, which is also the most heavily clausulated. See also the refined expression *Latia eruditio* in § 4.

out,[11] while Sidonius lists a catalogue of both ancient and contemporary rhetors, Claudianus rejects similar less authoritative exempla and is a fierce supporter of traditional models.[12]

> *Tua uero tam clara, tam spectabilis dictio est, ut illi diuisio Palaemonis, grauitas Gallionis, abundantia Delphidii, Agroecii disciplina, fortitudo Alcimi, Adelphii teneritudo, rigor Magni, dulcedo Victorii non modo non superiora sed uix aequiperabilia scribant.* (Sidon. *Ep.* 5.10.3)

> *Naeuius et Plautus tibi ad elegantiam, Cato ad grauitatem, Varro ad peritiam, Gracchus ad acrimoniam, Chrysippus ad disciplinam, Fronto ad pompam, Cicero ad eloquentiam capessendam usui sint.* (Mam. Claud. *Ep.* 2, pp. 205–6)

> Naevius and Plautus are useful for you to obtain elegance, Cato for gravitas, Varro for expertise, Gracchus for sharpness, Crispus for learning, Fronto for splendour, Cicero for eloquence.

Scholars have already highlighted that the same qualities (*grauitas, acrimonia, disciplina* and *pompa*) occur in both contexts;[13] however, there is one aspect which does not seem to have been properly stressed before: Sidonius is not suggesting Sapaudus should emulate these rhetors, as Claudianus does, but, instead, he argues that the addressee has already surpassed them. Therefore, he is not providing Sapaudus with a catalogue of models he should look up to; instead, he is placing him among, and even above, the names listed. It seems likely, anyway, that the mention of less known rhetors as representative of specific oratorical qualities might have irritated Claudianus, who, interestingly, argues that one should avoid altogether reading the *pueriles nugae* of *nouitii* (*Ep.* 2, p. 205).[14] In light of this and of further evidence of verbal similarity throughout Claudianus' letter, which creates an entanglement of Sidonian echoes, Pelttari's recent argument that Claudianus' letter is written as a polemical response to that of Sidonius commands assent.[15]

---

11. Alimonti 1975, 198–9.
12. Some observations on the authors chosen by Claudianus are in Mascoli 2015, 236–8.
13. Alimonti 1975, 201 n. 20; Pelttari 2020, 202.
14. See commentary on § 3 *fortitudo Alcimi*. Claudianus' choice of authors seems influenced by Apuleius *Apol.* 95.5; see Alimonti 1975, 200 n. 19.
15. Pelttari 2020, 191–207 supports his assertion with abundant evidence, which is listed here throughout the commentary: see comments on § 2 *plausibili oratione . . .*; § 3 *ut illi diuisio . . .*; § 4 *quia pauci studia . . .*; § 4 *simul et . . .* Before him, Loyen 1970a, 256 believed Claudianus' letter was written first, followed by Alimonti 1975, 201, who argued that Sidonius was writing in support of Claudianus, with the aim of validating his position.

LETTER 10

The theme of pretended literary decay

In order to address the lament for contemporary literary decline in this letter, it seems useful to point out that this appears to be a topos of letter writing, and to take into consideration a similar observation by one of Sidonius' declared models.[16] In *Ep.* 8.12 to Minicianus, Pliny says that Titinius Capito is about to give a public reading. Pliny, who is enthusiastic about attending, describes Capito as an enlightened intellectual.

> *Colit studia, studiosos amat, fouet, prouehit, multorum qui aliqua componunt portus, sinus, gremium, omnium exemplum, ipsarum denique litterarum iam senescentium reductor ac reformator.* (Plin. *Ep.* 8.12.1)

> He fosters studies and is fond of studious men, whom he supports and advances. To many who engage in writing something, he is a safe harbour, a bosom, a shelter, an example to all. He is indeed a restorer and a reformer of letters which are now in decline.

In the last paragraph of Sidonius' letter (§ 4), the addressee and Pragmatius are pictured as the only hope of survival and renovation of literary studies, to the point that 'if someone after you is favourably inclined to Latin erudition, he shall give thanks to this friendship'. The praise of the two is also followed, like in Pliny, by a wry remark on the state of literary studies. Pliny's *litterae senescentes* seem to be mirrored by Sidonius' remarks on the 'few people who now bring honour to literary studies'. And, one could argue, Pliny's pessimistic remark seems even to be expounded by Mamertus Claudianus in his letter to Sapaudus,[17] when he pictures literary knowledge on the brink of death and about to be entombed (*Ep.* 2, p. 204 *quorum egomet studiorum quasi quandam mortem flebili uelut epitaphio tumularem*) if it were not for Sapaudus, who resuscitated it (*nisi . . . resuscitauisses*).[18]

Sidonius enjoys lamenting the contemporary state of literature, since his letter collection encloses a wide range of similar expressions.[19] Evidence

---

16. By contrast Giannotti 2020, 149, following Schwitter's 2015 arguments, interprets the mentions of literary decay in Sidonius, and in particular that of *Ep.* 8.2, as testimony that the author believed that military defeat was the cause of contemporary cultural decline.

17. Presumably written in response to Sidon. *Ep.* 5.10, as argued below.

18. Compare Claudianus' similar address to Sidonius as a 'restorer of the old eloquence' in the *praefatio* of his *De statu animae*.

19. His concerns are also focused on linguistic decay, for example in *Ep.* 2.10.1 and in *Ep.*

299

is provided for instance by *Ep.* 8.2.1, where, as the commentary further explains, Johannes is represented as a strenuous defender and champion of knowledge, who 'delayed the extinction of literary culture'.[20] Further examples can be drawn from the last two books of Sidonius' correspondence, in particular from *Epp.* 8.6 and 9.7. In *Ep.* 8.6.3, Sidonius argues that anyone, confronted with the words of their ancestors, would appear like a speechless child; he believes that the world is growing old (*per aetatem mundi iam senescenti*) and arts have become fruitless, to the point that little is produced that is worth admiring or remembering.[21] The same scepticism about contemporary literary works emerges in *Ep.* 9.7.2, where Sidonius relates that there is a consensus that *pauca nunc posse similia dictari* ('few things like that can be written nowadays').[22] And yet, Mathisen's note of caution when reading the last two passages discussed above and his caveat not to filter them through the lenses of the modern misconception of late antique 'decay' is in particular worthy of mention.[23] Mathisen's warning can be supported by further evidence if one looks at the contexts in which similar assertions occur. In *Ep.* 8.6 the complaint that few remarkable things are written in the ageing world has the effect of enhancing, through pretended modesty, Sidonius' own literary abilities, since a few lines previously he has reported the enthusiastic judgement of his works made by Flavius Nicetius. The same conclusions can be reached with regard to *Ep.* 9.7, where the lament that 'few things like that can be written nowadays' opens the praise of bishop Remigius' declamations: Sidonius has recently retrieved these works and has eagerly had them copied for himself.

It can be argued, therefore, that deploring the cultural and literary situation of fifth-century Gaul is simply a cliché Sidonius is fond of, one which through contrast enhances the high quality of the literary works mentioned and how learned those who are able to appreciate them are. The same applies, in fact, to Sapaudus and Pragmatius: their being understood by few people, who are able to recognise their value as artists, is further evidence for their exquisite literary taste and, incidentally, it points to how cultivated

---

5.5, specifically in relation to barbarisms; see the introduction to this letter and the commentary on *Ep.* 5.5.3 *barbarus barbarismum.*

20. *Ep.* 8.2.1 *aboleri tu litteras distulisti.*

21. *Ep.* 8.6.3 *parum aliquid hoc tempore in quibuscumque, atque id in paucis, mirandum ac memorabile ostentant.*

22. On the criticism of contemporary literature in *Ep.* 9.7 see Condorelli 2021, 301.

23. Mathisen 1988, 47–8.

the few who do appreciate them are, namely, Sidonius and his peers.[24] As Mathisen points out, despite complaining about the literary decay of his age, Sidonius and other Gallic writers never name a contemporary work which would actually be illustrative of the decline they so often lament.

In light of what has been said on this topos, it may be useful, then, to look again at Pliny's *Ep.* 8.12.1 with different eyes, and to acknowledge that Pliny's mention of contemporary decay can also be considered as literary fiction. Sherwin-White,[25] for instance, suggests comparing this passage to Plin. *Epp.* 1.10, 1.13 and 1.16, in which Pliny pictures contemporary literature as flourishing.[26] It can be argued, therefore, that the image of the ageing literary world in Plin. *Ep.* 8.12.1, far from being a realistic picture, serves the purpose of emphasising, by contrast, the literary prowess of Titinius Capito, and that, similarly, Sidonius and his peers are wont to mention the topos of literary decadence with the aim of stressing their belonging to a cultural elite.

Dating elements

In light of the usual meagre dating elements, one can only suggest a hypothetical time range for when this letter was written. Loyen dates it to the end of 476 or 477, exclusively on the basis of the mention of literary decline in the text.[27] Such a specific date does not seem justifiable, and Alimonti already discards it and notes that the complaint about contemporary literary decadence constitutes a cliché in Sidonius.[28] His suggestion of dating *Ep.* 5.10 and Mam. Claud. *Ep.* 2 to the same years, since the two letters are testimony to an ongoing literary debate between traditionalists and innovators, is deserving of attention.

---

24. Of this opinion is also Mathisen 1988, 49.
25. Sherwin-White 1966, 460
26. See Plin. *Ep.* 1.10.1–2 *si quando urbs nostra liberalibus studiis floruit, nunc maxime floret. Multa claraque exempla sunt;* the similar *incipit* of Plin. *Ep.* 1.13.1 *magnum prouentum poetarum annus hic attulit; toto mense Aprili nullus fere dies quo non recitaret aliquis;* and the praise of the contemporary Pompeius Saturninus in Plin. *Ep.* 1.16.8, where Pliny says that, had Saturninus not been a contemporary, they would have looked for his books and even for his portraits, hence it is only fair to give him the recognition he deserves.
27. Loyen 1970a, 256.
28. Alimonti 1975, 201 n. 20; Gualandri 1979, 27 n. 94.

Furthermore, by virtue of the abundant evidence provided by Pelttari concerning the chronology of the two letters (i.e. that Claudianus' *Ep.* 2 is probably a response to Sidonius' *Ep.* 5.10), one can assume that *Ep.* 5.10 was at least written before the death of Mamertus Claudianus, which is canonically dated to 471.[29] Therefore, dating *Ep.* 5.10 to a time prior to 471 seems reasonable, albeit speculative.

---

29. On which see Loyen 1970b, 218 n. 9; Amherdt 2001, 280; see also the section 'Dating elements' in the introduction to *Ep.* 5.2.

SIDONIUS: LETTERS BOOK 5, PART 1

SIDONIUS SAPAUDO SUO SALUTEM

1. Si quid omnino Pragmatius illustris, hoc inter reliquas animi uirtutes optime facit, quod amore studiorum te singulariter amat, in quo solo uel maxume animum aduertit ueteris peritiae diligentiaeque resedisse uestigia. Equidem non iniuria tibi fautor est; nam debetur ab eo percopiosus litteris honor.

2. Hunc olim perorantem et rhetorica sedilia plausibili oratione frangentem socer eloquens ultro in familiam patriciam adsciuit, licet illi ad hoc, ut sileam de genere uel censu, aetas, uenustas, pudor patrocinarentur. Sed, ut comperi, erubescebat iam etiam tunc uir serius et formae dote placuisse, quippe cui merito ingenii suffecisset adamari. Et uere optimus quisque morum praestantius pulchritudine placet; porro autem praeteruolantia corporis decoramenta currentis aeui profectu defectuque labascunt. Hunc quoque manente sententia Galliis post praefectus Priscus Valerianus consiliis suis tribunalibusque sociauit, iudicium antiquum perseuerantissime tenens, ut cui scientiae obtentu iunxerat subolem, iungeret et dignitatem.

3. Tua uero tam clara, tam spectabilis dictio est, ut illi diuisio Palaemonis, grauitas Gallionis, abundantia Delphidii, Agroecii disciplina, fortitudo Alcimi, Adelphii teneritudo, rigor Magni, dulcedo Victorii non modo non superiora sed uix aequiperabilia scribant. Sane ne uidear tibi sub hoc quasi hyperbolico rhetorum catalogo blanditus quippiam gratificatusque, solam tibi acrimoniam Quintiliani pompamque Palladii comparari non ambigo sed potius adquiesco.

4. Quapropter si quis post uos Latiae fauet eruditioni, huic amicitiae gratias agit et sodalitati uestrae, si quid hominis habet, tertius optat adhiberi. Quamquam, quod est grauius, non sit satis ambitus iste fastidium uobis excitaturus, quia pauci studia nunc honorant, simul et naturali uitio fixum est radicatumque pectoribus humanis, ut qui non intellegunt artes non mirentur artifices. Vale.

§ 2 iam etiam tunc *LMP* : etiam *om.* α

§ 3 aequiperabilia α (equiperabilia *SVat1661*) *MP* : aequiparabilia *L*
scribant *L* : scribantur α *MP*
pompamque *L* : pompam α (*A post correctionem*) *MP*
ambigo α *MP* : ambio *L*

§ 4 sodalitati *A* (*post correctionem*) *Vat1661LMP* : soliditati *CS*

LETTER 10

SIDONIUS TO HIS DEAR SAPAUDUS

1. If there is anything that the honourable Pragmatius does extremely well, it is this among his other personal merits: he loves you exceedingly out of love for literary studies. You are the only one in whom he perceives that traces of the ancient expertise and zeal persist to the highest degree. Certainly it is not without cause that he is your supporter; in fact he owes a great deal of recognition to literary works.

2. Long ago, when he was delivering a speech and shattering the rhetorical benches with a praiseworthy oration, his eloquent father-in-law willingly welcomed him into his patrician family. His age, good looks and modesty, though, were already promoting him for this purpose, not to mention his family and wealth. But, as I have learned, even at that time already, this earnest man was wont to blush for being liked for the appearance he was endowed with, as one for whom being greatly admired for his merits would have been sufficient. And in truth, an excellent man finds favour even more admirably for the excellence of his morals. Besides, the rapidly fleeting ornaments of the body dissolve with the advance and decline of passing years. Later, as prefect of Gaul, Priscus Valerianus associated him with his councils and tribunals, standing determinedly by his former opinion, to such an extent that he also equalised the rank of the man that he had already joined in marriage with his daughter out of regard for his being learned.

3. Your declamation is so clear, so outstanding, that, compared to it, the rhetorical partition of Palaemon, the solemnity of Gallio, the floweriness of Delphidius, the method of Agroecius, the power of Alcimus, the tenderness of Adelphus, the rigour of Magnus, the pleasantness of Victorius, not only do not compose greater orations, but barely even comparable ones. However, so that by this almost hyperbolic enumeration of rhetors I won't seem to you like a flatterer and like someone complaisant, I have no hesitation in comparing you only to the sharpness of Quintilian and to the splendour of Palladius; indeed, I rather assent to it.

4. Therefore, if someone after you is favourably inclined to Latin erudition, he shall give thanks to this friendship and to your companionship, and if he has anything human at all, he'll wish to be accepted as a third in the group. Although, and this is really a shame, this importunity is likely not to be enough to cause your aversion, since there are but few people who now bring honour to literary studies. And, at the same time, it is fixed in human vice and rooted in human souls that those who do not understand the arts do not admire artists. Farewell.

SIDONIUS: LETTERS BOOK 5, PART 1

Commentary

§ 1

Si quid omnino: Among the occurrences of this rare syntagma, see in particular Plin. *Ep.* 4.15.1 *si quid omnino, hoc certe iudicio facio, quod Asinium Rufum singulariter amo* ('if there is anything that I do judiciously, it is certainly that I love Asinius Rufus exceedingly') – see Plin. *Ep.* 4.15.1 also for the occurrence of *singulariter amat* later in § 1. The similarity is also signalled by Geisler 1887, 366 and by Gualandri 2020, 307. It seems likely that Pliny's declaration of friendship could have inspired *Ep.* 5.10.1, since useful comparisons cannot be drawn with other occurrences of *si quid omnino*, which include Apul. *Apol.* 5.2 and Aug. *Conf.* 12.31. Sidonius sometimes employs his favourite rhythms away from the clausulae: the Plinian echo *si quid omnino* is a cretic spondee.

Pragmatius illustris: This letter is the only source of information on Pragmatius, whose career and qualities are listed in the following paragraph. By the fifth century, *illustris* had become the most prestigious of senatorial ranks: an aristocrat first became *clarissimus*, then *spectabilis* and, at the highest level of office holding, he was called *illustris*, a status which entailed greater fiscal and jurisdictional privileges. On senatorial ranks from the fourth century onwards see for instance Jones 1964, vol. I, 528–9 and Chastagnol 1992, 293–6, who also argues (Chastagnol 1996, 52–3) that over the fifth century *illustres* became increasingly younger. The mention of Pragmatius' rank is useful to Sidonius in terms of rhythm, since *-matius illustris* is a paeon IV spondee.

hoc inter reliquas animi uirtutes optime facit: Compare this with Symm. *Ep.* 1.30, where, *inter reliqua uirtutum* ('among his other virtues'), Ausonius is said to be of such an agreeable nature that he is indulgent with minor faults of others.

quod amore studiorum te singulariter amat: Sapaudus' learning was the first quality which had made an impression on Pragmatius. In Cic. *Fam.* 9.8.1, when encouraging Varro to complete *De Lingua Latina*, Cicero argues that he has written the *Academica* featuring a dialogue between them and he could not refrain from declaring how deep a connection they have, through their studies as well as out of affection (*coniunctionem studiorum* *amorisque nostri*). Cf. Plin. *Ep.* 5.21.5, in which the author expresses his fondness for the late Julius Avitus, since he *studiorum amore flagrabat* ('was burning with passion for literary studies'), as well as Plin. *Ep.* 4.28.2 (*studiorum summa reuerentia, summus amor studiosorum*) and the beginning of Sidon. *Ep.* 2.10 (*amo in te quod litteras amas*). For the significance of the occurrence of the Plinian expression *singulariter amo* in this context, see the commentary above on *Si quid omnino*; compare it also with Plin. *Ep.* 1.22.1, when he speaks of Titius Aristo, *quem singulariter et miror et diligo* ('a man I love and admire exceptionally'), and with Plin. *Ep.* 3.5.3 (*a quo singulariter amatus*).

in quo solo uel maxume animum aduertit ueteris peritiae diligentiaeque resedisse uestigia: Sapaudus is first portrayed as the defender of literary studies. Compare this with the similar expression *possis animo aduertere* in Sidon. *Ep.* 1.2.4; further, in *Ep.* 7.8.3 the verb has a slightly different nuance and the expression means 'I concluded', as pointed out by van Waarden 2010, 400. The passage is studiously constructed, as can be inferred from the occurrence of *uetus diligentia*. This *iunctura* is not attested before the third century and it is exclusively known to occur in Solinus 53.30 and, significantly, in Symm. *Ep.* 5.53, where it concerns duties of friendship. Furthermore, the verb *resedeo* in syntagma with *uestigia* is known to occur only twice, both in Christian works (Ambr. *In Psalm.* 118 *Serm.* 22.2; Rufin. *Orig. in Leu.* 8.5). Clausulation marks the beginning (see above) and the end of this first long sentence, since *–disse uestigia* is a double cretic clausula.

Equidem non iniuria tibi fautor est: Pragmatius is Sapaudus' supporter on the basis of their shared literary studies. This is not the first time the term *fautor* occurs in Sidonius, who, for instance, mentions his dedicatees as *fautores*. In Sidon. *Ep.* 1.1.3 (*te inmodicum esse fautorem non studiorum modo uerum etiam studiosorum*), Constantius is said to be a staunch defender of literary studies and of men of letters and, similarly, at the beginning of Book 5 (*Ep.* 5.1.1), Petronius is praised for being *ingenii . . . fautor alieni* (see the commentary ad loc.). In *Ep.* 8.2.1 Johannes is lauded as 'an awakener, defender and champion' of culture (*suscitator, fautor, assertor*) and this praise can be fruitfully compared not only with *Ep.* 5.10 but also with *Mam. Claud. Ep.* 2, as stated in the introduction. Pelttari 2020, 204 highlights how in Mam. Claud. *Ep.* 2, p. 205 the occurrence of *procul iniuria* precedes the praise of Sapaudus, and Pelttari labels it as an 'unconscious echo' of Sidonius' *non iniuria*.

SIDONIUS: LETTERS BOOK 5, PART 1

nam debetur ab eo percopiosus litteris honor: Once again, carefully studied language enriches the paragraph. *Percopiosus* is first attested in Plin. *Ep.* 9.31.1, where it concerns how generous Sardus had been when he had written pages concerning Pliny. Sidonius employs it also in *Ep.* 1.1.4 and, in the adverbial form, in *Ep.* 4.7.3. See Amherdt 2001, 220 and Wolff 2020, 400.

§ 2

Hunc olim perorantem et rhetorica sedilia plausibili oratione frangentem: This remark opens a section which is entirely dedicated to Pragmatius, who is said to have been an able orator in his youth and whose speeches are said to have been vibrant and powerful, to the point that his future father-in-law was captivated by his verve. Geisler 1887, 366, suggests that this passage be compared with Juvenal 7.86 *fregit subsellia uersu*, a verse which describes the reaction at Statius' recitation of his Thebaid. Gualandri 1979, 137–8 argues that *TLL* 6.1250 s.v. *frango* 3–4 (by Bacherler) is wrong in considering the occurrence in Juvenal (and, in consequence, in Sidon. *Ep.* 5.10.2) as metaphorical and is therefore wrong in ascribing it to the meaning of *flectere animum alicuius, mouere*. According to Gualandri, *frango* in both contexts does not indicate simply a consensus, 'ma il fragoroso e concitato applaudire di un pubblico che si agita scompostamente scotendo i sedili'. Similar conclusions are reached by Colton 1995, 362, who believes that in both passages the performances had 'brought down the house with applause' and by Stramaglia 2017, 160–1, who mentions Sidonius' passage as evidence that the seats in Juvenal are 'shattered' because of the enthusiastic jumps of the public. Note that a similar reworking of Juvenal's passage is also in Sidon. *Ep.* 9.14.2. The *iunctura plausibilis oratio* is rare and previously known to occur only in Sen. *Ep.* 59.6 and in Hier. *In Zac.* 2.7. As Gualandri 1979, 138 n. 110 points out, the adjective *plausibilis* is favoured by Sidonius, who employs it with the same meaning of 'something that provokes applause' in *Ep.* 4.1.2 (*panegyrista plausibile*), and with slightly different nuances in *Epp.* 8.10.3 (*amplum plausibilius manifestat ingenium*); 9.13.1 (*sententia . . . plausibilis*); and 9.14.2 (*plausibilibus . . . ulnis*). As Pelttari 2020, 201 points out, Mamertus Claudianus seems to polemically respond to Sidonius' mention of orations 'worthy of applause' when in *Ep.* 2, p. 205 he argues that oratorical strength is 'emasculated' by consensus (*oratoriam fortitudinem plaudentibus concinentiis euirant*). Note that § 2 begins, like § 1, with a cretic spondee at

LETTER 10

-one frangentem. § 2 is the section of the letter which Sidonius appears to put extra care into (because of the rank of Pragmatius and Priscus Valerianus, one could argue): many rarely attested expressions occur in this paragraph, which also appears to be heavily clausulated.

socer eloquens ultro in familiam patriciam adsciuit: Priscus Valerianus, who will later become Pragmatius' father-in-law, was himself an able orator, which is why he valued Pragmatius' eloquence and decided he should join his family. *In familiam adsciscere* is an expression which usually concerns adoption, and in *TLL* 2.765 s.v. *adscisco* 31–2 (by Hey) the Sidonian passage is the only occurrence mentioned with the meaning of joining one's family as a son-in-law. Sidonius' emphasis on the fact that Pragmatius married into a patrician family indicates that he presumably was not originally a patrician, although the following mentions of his *genus* and *census* indicate that nonetheless he was of high birth. Chastagnol 1992, 156 argues that it became easier to access the rank of *patricii* through marriage in particular from the reign of Caracalla on.

licet illi ad hoc, ut sileam de genere uel censu, aetas, uenustas, pudor patrocinarentur: Sidonius' fondness for lists has already been discussed (see e.g. Wolff 2020, 409) and, as argued by Savaron 1609, 345, this passage can be fruitfully compared with Sidon. *Ep.* 2.4.1, where Proiectus is praised for a number of reasons: *illi familiae splendor, probitas morum, patrimonii facultas, iuuentutis alacritas* ('the lustre of his family, the rectitude of his conduct, the wealth of his estates, the liveliness of his youth'). See also the similar occurrence in Ambr. *Ep.* 7.36.23 (*nobilis genere, censu diues*) and in Sidon. *Ep.* 7.2.1 *ut post comperi, plus Massiliensium benignitate prouectus est, quam status sui seu per censum seu per familiam forma pateretur* ('as I discovered afterwards, the generosity of the people of Massilia advanced him further than could be justified by his social position with regard to either his wealth or his origin'); see van Waarden 2010, 145.

Sed, ut comperi: Sidonius employs the syntagma *ut comperi* also in *Epp.* 7.2.1 (see above) and 7.14.10.

erubescebat iam etiam tunc uir serius: On Sidonius' preference for the verb *erubesco* see Hindermann 2022, 288. The sequence *iam etiam tunc*, which is first known to occur in *Laus Pisonis* 35, is rarely attested thereafter in Christian authors, such as, without the interposition of other words,

309

Tert. *Bapt.* 4, Ambr. *Exc. Sat.* 2.118 and Aug. *Ciu.* 16.12. The collation has revealed that *etiam* is omitted not only in *C* but also in all the manuscripts belonging to Dolveck's α branch. The omission itself is not particularly relevant and can be explained as *saut du même au même*, but the fact it is missing in all the branch provides further evidence to confirm Dolveck's stemma (see the General Introduction). Note that Sidonius chooses to call Pragmatius *uir serius*, and this *iunctura* is previously known to occur only in Amm. 26.2.2. On the uncommon choice to characterise a person with the adjective *serius* and for a fruitful comparison with Sozomen (*HE* 6.6.2), see den Boeft et al. 2008, 43. See also the occurrence in Ambr. *In Psalm.* 118 *Serm.* 2.26.2 *ideo uir laudatur serius.*

et formae dote placuisse: Pragmatius is once more remembered for his juvenile handsomeness (see the mention above of his *uenustas*), this time through the rare *iunctura dos formae*, previously known to occur exclusively in Ov. *Met.* 9.716–17, where Ianthe is said to be *laudatissima formae / dote.*

quippe cui merito ingenii suffecisset adamari: The unusual occurrence of the verb *adamo* to indicate affection for a man is further indication of how carefully constructed this letter is. In *TLL* 1.567 s.v. *adamo* 48–50 (by Vollmer) only two passages are listed for this use of the verb, Nep. *Dion* 2.3 (2 is missing in *TLL*) *quem* (*Platonem*) *Dio admiratus est atque adamauit* and Sidon. *Ep.* 5.10, where, incidentally, *-cisset adamari* creates a paeon I spondee. Compare the similar occurrences in Sidon. *Ep.* 2.13.5, where Fulgentius is said to have gained his quaestorship out of his being a *uir litteratus* and *ob ingenii merita*; cf. also *Ep.* 5.1.1 *meritis ingenii proprii*, already mentioned above for the occurrence of *fautor*, and see the commentary ad loc.

Et uere optimus quisque morum praestantius pulchritudine placet: This time Sidonius refers to Pragmatius' inner 'pulchritude'. As argued by Savaron 1609, 345, the idea that inner beauty is preferable to outer appearance is expressed in Avianus *Fab.* 40.11–12 *miremurque magis quos munera mentis adornant, / quam qui corporeis enituere bonis*, a passage which is compared to that of Sidonius also by Ellis 1887, 126. Sidonius himself in *Ep.* 7.14.3–9 stresses the superiority of inner beauty over outer appearance and concludes by saying that he looks at Philagrius with an 'inner eye' (*cordis oculo*). *Pulchritudo morum* is a *iunctura* known to occur previously only in contexts concerning the behaviour of married women. In Ammianus 21.6.4 *corporis morumque pulchritudine pluribus antistante*, the empress Eusebia is said

LETTER 10

to have been superior to other women for her physical and behavioural beauty (see also the description of Hypatius, empress Eusebia's brother, as *uirtutum pulchritudine commendabilis* in Amm. 29.2.16). In Arnobius Junior (a contemporary to Sidonius) *Ad Greg.* 7, the matrona is encouraged to adorn the beauty of her morals (*morum pulchritudinem*) the same way she takes care of her appearance.

porro autem praeteruolantia corporis decoramenta currentis aeui profectu defectuque labascunt: The topos of beauty fading with the passing of time is a common one and, as van Waarden 2018, 196 puts it, although mentions of ageing and death become more and more frequent in Sidonius' correspondence, and he appears to be more reflective, he is also wont to use standard expressions like this one. The verb *praeteruolo* is found in contexts concerning the fleeting nature of time, e.g. in Sen. *Ep.* 108.25 and Aug. *In Psalm.* 38.9. Other occurrences of the verb in Sidonius (*Epp.* 2.12.1 and 5.17.7) do not involve this temporal meaning, for which see *TLL* 10.2.1043 s.v. *praeteruolo* 50–5 (by Mensink). The rarely attested word *decoramentum* heightens the sophistication of the sentence: it is previously attested exclusively in Tert. *Cult. Femin.* 2.12 (*maritales* and *matronales*) and it then makes one appearance in Sidon. *Ep.* 7.9.12, where it concerns the qualities that should determine the choice of the most suitable man for the role of bishop.

Hunc quoque manente sententia Galliis post praefectus Priscus Valerianus consiliis suis tribunalibusque sociauit: Priscus Valerianus was of patrician descent (see above) and related to Eparchius Avitus, as can be gathered from the mention of *purpura celsa* in *Carm.* 8.2, which accompanies the Panegyric of Avitus and is dedicated to Valerianus, expected to be a *destrictus censor*, 'a severe judge' of Sidonius' verses. *Carm.* 8 is addressed to Valerianus as *uir praefectorius*, a thing which leads to the inference that he became *praefectus praetorio Galliarum* before 456, when Avitus was deposed by Ricimer and Majorian; and that, in consequence, *Carm.* 8 was sent to him shortly after the panegyric was declaimed, before Avitus' deposition. On the date of *Carm.* 8 see Kelly 2020, 169; see also the introduction for further context. Moreover, the clause *consiliis suis tribunalibusque sociauit* gives the information that Valerianus chose Pragmatius as his *consiliarius*. On Priscus Valerianus' career see Loyen 1970a, 237–8 n. 33; *PLRE* 2, 1142–3; *PCBE* 4, 1909; Mathisen 2020, 125.

311

iudicium antiquum perseuerantissime tenens: The uncommon superlative of the adverb is first attested in Val. Max. 6.8.1 and, interestingly, in Plin. *Ep.* 4.21.3 *patrem illarum . . . perseuerantissime diligo*; it then has all of his other attestations (ten in total) in Augustine.

ut cui scientiae obtentu iunxerat subolem, iungeret et dignitatem: A further reference to the fact that Pragmatius joined Priscus Valerianus' family by marrying his daughter and that, in doing so, he held office which allowed him to attain the rank of *illustris* (*iungeret et dignitatem*). This passage is carefully constructed, since both the expression *iungo subolem* and the *iunctura scientiae obtentu* do not have previous occurrences. The use of *obtentu* + genitive is post-Augustan and is first attested with the slightly negative meaning of 'under the pretext of', while in later Latin the expression is also used with the meaning of 'by virtue of' or 'out of', as is testified by this passage. Sidonius employs the expression, with different nuances, also in *Carm.* 7.424 (*desidiae obtentu*), *Epp.* 3.2.3 (*dilectionis obtentu*), 4.3.9 (*professionis obtentu*), 7.11.1 (*caritatis obtentu*), 8.6.13 (*tui obtentu*) and 9.3.4 (*dignitatis obtentu*). For the later meaning of the syntagma see *TLL* 9.2.277 s.v. *obtentus* 33–52 (by Lebek); similar conclusions are reached by van Waarden 2010, 555.

§ 3

Tua uero tam clara, tam spectabilis dictio est: After a long digression on Pragmatius and his own family history, Sidonius abruptly changes topic and introduces praise of the addressee, Sapaudus. One could argue that there is a play on the two adjectives and that Sidonius alludes to Sapaudus' rank of *uir spectabilis*, while Pragmatius is a *uir illustris* (see above). With the meaning of 'literary style', *dictio* is often employed by Sidonius; compare his discussion concerning the difference between *dictio sana* and *insana* in *Ep.* 3.14.2, where he argues that the former would feature *scientia*, *pompa* and *proprietas linguae Latinae*, as highlighted by Giannotti 2016, 265. See also the passing remarks on *dictio* in *Ep.* 4.1.1, and the comments on his own style in *Ep.* 8.16.2, which Sidonius believes may be to Constantius' taste, since an experienced reader like himself is likely to appreciate a 'masculine style' rather than a 'spinless' one (*non tantum dictio exossis, tenera, delumbis, quantum uetuscula torosa et quasi mascula placet*). Note that the same letter also ends with further reflection on his literary style, since Sidonius expresses contentment at the thought that it is appreciated by his friends – *Ep.* 8.16.5 *dictio mea, quod mihi sufficit, placet amicis.* For this specific meaning of 'style' see *TLL* 5.1.1007 s.v. *dictio* 15–33 (by Bögel). Although the term often occurs in Symmachus, the author employs it to indicate the letter itself, often called *dictio salutis*, e.g. in Symm. *Epp.* 1.86, 6.37 and 7.22.

ut illi diuisio Palaemonis . . . dulcedo Victorii: The passage is constituted by a succession of elements arranged in the same way (nominative + genitive) typical of Sidonius' way of writing, on which see Amherdt 2001, 111–16; Wolff 2020, 409 and previous remarks on *determinatio* (in the commentary on *Ep.* 5.9.3 *unus nos . . .*). Sidonius' fondness for enumeration has already been discussed in this commentary, cf. the long list of arts composing Mamertus Claudianus' *De statu animae* in Sidon. *Ep.* 5.2.1 (see the commentary ad loc. and the introduction to *Ep.* 5.2 for further comparisons with *Ep.* 4.3.5–7). For a comparison with Mam. Claud. *Ep.* 2, pp. 205–6 and for the possibility that Claudianus was polemically responding to the catalogue of rhetors listed by Sidonius in *Ep.* 5.10.3 see the introduction and in detail Pelttari 2020, 191–207. Most of the list, as noted before in Sidonius, is clausulated: *grauitas Gallionis* is an anapaest ditrochee; *-groecii disciplina* is a cretic ditrochee; *fortitudo Alcimi* is a double cretic (with elision); *-i teneritudo* is a paeon I spondee; *-cedo Victorii* is a double cretic; and *-rabilia scribant* is a paeon I spondee.

diuisio Palaemonis: Quintus Remmius Palaemon was a renowned first-century teacher of grammar, hence the mention of *diuisio* in this context (see the commentary on *Ep.* 5.2.1 *grammatica diuidit*). Palaemon is mentioned by Quintilian (*Inst.* 1.4.20) as a contemporary grammarian and by Juvenal (6.451–5), who states that he 'hates it when a woman holds in her hands his grammar'. See also Juv. 7.215–16, where Palaemon in an exemplary *grammaticus* (similarly to what Sidonius does in this context); although uncommonly high, his wage is said to be reduced because his entourage steals from him. On this passage see Stramaglia 2017, 216–17. Suet. *Gram.* 23.5–6 offers a detailed description of his activity as a school teacher and of his peculiarly high income; for further context see Kaster 1995, 238–41.

grauitas Gallionis: Loyen's identification (1970a, 191 n. 35) of this man with Junius Gallio, a close friend of Seneca the Elder, who adopted his eldest son, seems compelling. Gallio is known to have been an excellent declaimer, as is testified by Seneca *Contr.* 10 *praef.* 13. Seneca the Elder often mentions Gallio's studied remarks on numerous declaimers, poets and orators (e.g. Sen. *Contr.* 2.1.33, 2.5.11, 2.5.13 and 3 *praef.* 2) always calling him *Gallio noster*. Moreover, Quintilian relates that he had written *non pauca* on the subject of rhetoric (see Quint. *Inst.* 3.1.21 and 9.2.91); for further mentions of Gallio see *PIR*[2] I 756. Note that in Anderson 1965, 204 n. 4 Gallio is identified with Marcus Annaeus Novatus, Seneca the Elder's son, who had been adopted by Junius Gallio (thus becoming L. Iunius Gallio); however, there is no strong reason to prefer him to the elder Gallio, given that the latter was a renowned *declamator*, unlike his adoptive son. Compare this passage to the *Frontoniana grauitas* mentioned in Sidonius' praise of Mamertus Claudianus' *De statu animae* (Sidon. *Ep.* 4.3.1); and to Claudianus' own list to Sapaudus in Mam. Claud. *Ep.* 2, p. 206, where *grauitas* is significantly attributed to the more celebrated Cato; see the introduction to this letter.

abundantia Delphidii: With the mention of Delphidius, Sidonius' list moves to a section dedicated to local glories, since Delphidius, Agroecius, Alcimus and Magnus are all mentioned by Ausonius in his *Commemoratio professorum Burdigalensium*. Attius Tiro Delphidius was a known Gallic rhetor, who first taught rhetoric at Bordeaux (Aus. *Prof.* 5.5–12 Green) and then decided to practise as an advocate (Aus. *Prof.* 5.13–18 Green). However, after the fall of Magnentius he resumed his practice as rhetor in Aquitania, as is testified by Aus. *Prof.* 5.33 (Green) and by Hier. *Chron.* s.a. 355; and yet Ammianus (18.1.4) relates that in the year 359 he appeared as an *acerrimus* prosecutor in a trial before Julian. He is also mentioned by Jerome, who writes to his descendant Hedybia that, when Jerome was a young boy, Delphidius had brought prestige to Gaul with his talent as a writer of both prose and verse (Hier. *Ep.* 120 *praef.*, *omnes Gallias prosa uersuque suo inlustrauit ingenio*). On Delphidius see *PLRE* 1, 246; *PCBE* 4, 551–2.

Agroecii disciplina: Censorius Atticus Agricius is also one of the professors active in Bordeaux and praised by Ausonius *Prof.* 14. As pointed out by Green 1991, 349 Agroecius is to be seen as an alternative spelling, which was preferred for instance by the grammarian Agroecius, who was possibly a relative. Green also argues that Jovinus' general Agroetius might have been a son of the rhetor. In Sidonius' letter Agroecius is listed as an example of *disciplina*, a quality which, in Claudianus' letter to Sapaudus (*Ep.* 2, p. 206), is ascribed to the mathematician Chrysippus (cf. also Sidon. *Ep.* 4.3.5 *cum Chrysippo numeros*).

fortitudo Alcimi: Third rhetor of Bordeaux on the list, Latinus Alcimus Alethius is also mentioned by Ausonius in his *Commemoratio*, where he is said (Aus. *Prof.* 2.21–4 Green) to have praised Julian and Flavius Sallustius for their consulship in the year 363. He is also mentioned as a known rhetor by Jerome (*Chron.* s.a. 355) and by Sidonius in *Ep.* 8.11.2. Loyen 1970b, 201 n. 41 identifies him, for no strong reason, with Alethius mentioned in Sidon. *Ep.* 2.7.2. See *PLRE* 1, 39; *PCBE* 4, 106 and Mathisen 2020, 78, who argues that perhaps the rhetor was a distant relative of Sidonius, given his daughter's name, Alcima, and that his nephew was Alcimus Ecdicius Avitus, bishop of Vienne. Note that – although *fortitudo* is not ascribed to any exemplum in particular in Claudianus' letter to Sapaudus – in *Ep.* 2, p. 205 *fortitudo* is mentioned twice. The first occurrence, together with *dulcedo*, concerns praise of Sapaudus' oratorial skills; then *oratoria fortitudo* introduces Claudianus' list of literary models when he asks Sapaudus not to waste time reading *nugae pueriles* which 'unman the oratorical vigour' with an acclaiming claque (*oratoriam fortitudinem plaudentibus concinentiis euirant*). See below also for the antithetical pairing *fortitudo/teneritudo*.

Adelphii teneritudo: While this seems to be the only source of information on a rhetor named Adelphius, the word *teneritudo* occurs in Sidonius' *Ep.* 4.3.4, where it concerns Mamertus Claudianus' style. As pointed out by Gualandri 1979, 79, in *Ep.* 4.3.4 Sidonius describes the stylistic *maturitas* of the friend, which is also interspersed with *teneritudo*. In Sidon. *Ep.* 5.10.3 *fortitudo* and *teneritudo* are contraposed but define two equally valuable oratorical qualities (see Gualandri 1979, 79 n. 13), and the same contraposition can be detected in *Carm.* 14.1, where the tenderness of the epithalamium contrasts with *asperrimas philosophiae et salebrosissimas regulas* ('the harshest and roughest rules of philosophy'); similarly, in *Ep.* 8.11.5 Lampridius is said to be *acer* in his orations, yet *tener* in his poetic compositions.

rigor Magni: In *PLRE* 1, 535 (followed by Mathisen 2020, 106), the mention of Magnus in *Ep.* 5.10.3 is referred to 'Flavius Magnus 10', a rhetor active in Rome who received *Ep.* 70 from Jerome. From an onomastic point of view, this would appear to be the most valid option; however, note that Ausonius dedicates *Prof.* 16 (Green) and *Par.* 3 (Green) to his maternal uncle Aemilius Magnus Arborius. Unlike the previously mentioned rhetors, despite being originally from Bordeaux, he taught in Toulouse. Given the previous examples taken from the *Commemoratio*, the identification with Ausonius' uncle, already suggested by Savaron 1609, 346, may not be an unfair speculation. Ausonius mentions him as *Arborius* in *Par.* 3.2 (Green), but also addresses him as *Magne* in *Prof.* 16.16 (Green): 'an apostrophe using the most expressive of his names', according to Green 1991, 353. Note that the section ends with another antithetic couple, *rigor/dulcedo*, and that *rigor* is also mentioned as the defining characteristic of Persius in a long enumeration of exempla in Sidon. *Carm.* 9.263 *non Persi rigor aut lepos Properti.*

dulcedo Victorii: Loyen's suggestion 1970a, 191 n. 35 to identify this man with Victorius Marcellus, dedicatee of both Quintilian's *Institutio Oratoria* (together with his son) and of Statius' *Siluae* Book 4, seems deserving of attention in light of the following mention of Quintilian himself. In *Inst.* 1 *praef.* 6, Quintilian dedicates the work to Victorius Marcellus. Moreover, Stat. *Silu.* 4.4. (*Epistula ad Victorium Marcellum*) alludes to his role as a young practising orator; see the detailed introduction to Statius' letter by Coleman 1988, 135–8, and, on *Siluae* being a model for Sidonius, see Consolino 2013. By contrast, *PLRE* 1, 1162 (s.v. Victorius 2), Heinzelmann 1982, 713 and Mathisen 2020, 126 believe the mention is to be referred to an otherwise unattested rhetor Victorius, who presumably lived in Bordeaux. See also Pelttari 2020, 196, who lists other possible candidates: Claudius Marius Victor, a fifth-century rhetor active in Marseille (*PLRE* 2, 1160 s.v. Claudius Marius Victor 11) or the Victorius praised for his verses in Sidon. *Ep.* 5.21.1. See above for the mention of *fortitudo* and *dulcedo* as defining elements of Sapaudus' declamation in Mam. Claud. *Ep.* 2.

non modo non superiora sed uix aequiperabilia scribant: Diverging from Lütjohann 1887, 85 and Anderson 1965, 204, Loyen 1970a, 191 once more prefers the odd spelling *aequiparabilia* because it is the reading of *L*; this spelling, however, has its first occurrences in the ninth century. The adjective *aequiperabilis* is known to occur in Plaut. *Curc.* 168, *Trin.* 466 and, significantly, in Apuleius (*Socr.* 3), an important linguistic model for Sidonius, in particular for his use of archaisms. As evidence to substantiate this thesis, note that Gualandri 1979, 173 n. 98 lists *aequiperabilis* as one of the Sidonian archaisms presumably borrowed from Apuleius; and that previous occurrences of *aequiparabilis* are not attested. The reading *scribant* (*L*) is, stemmatically, presumably an emendation, but is preferred to *scribantur* by the three editors and this choice seems correct in light of the meaning of the sentence.

Sane ne uidear tibi sub hoc quasi hyperbolico rhetorum catalogo blanditus quippiam gratificatusque: The adjective *hyperbolicus* is attested only from the fourth century onward, with numerous occurrences in Augustine. Note that it occurs in Sidon. *Ep.* 4.3.4 where Mamertus Claudianus' *eloquium . . . nec per scaturrigines hyperbolicas intumescit* ('is not swollen with hyperbolical gushes'). Cf. also Sidon. *Ep.* 7.2.8; as van Waarden 2010, 183 suggested, the term could be listed as one of Sidonius' Graecisms, and the same applies to the following word, *catalogus*. See *TLL* 6.3.3149 s.v. *hyperbolicus* 65–70 (by Rubenbauer); *TLL* 3.590 s.v. *catalogus* 34 (by Poeschel).

solam tibi acrimoniam Quintiliani: In Mamertus Claudianus' variation of this catalogue, *acrimonia* is the defining quality of Gracchus. As Pelttari 2020, 202 points out, unlike the other rhetorical qualities listed, *acrimonia* is hereafter known to occur only once in Sidonius (*Ep.* 8.6.6) and does not have other occurrences in Mamertus Claudianus.

pompamque Palladii: The reading *pompamque* seems preferable, even if the stemmatic evidence is against it, because it creates a cretic tribrach in a section which is consistently clausulated, while *pompam Palladii* would not create a *clausula*. Geisler 1887, 366 compares this mention with Symm. *Ep.* 1.94, where the rhetorician Palladius is commended to Syagrius and is said to be 'well known to all good men by virtue of his eloquence and erudition'. To Geisler's suggestion, one could add Symm. *Ep.* 1.15.2 (addressed to Ausonius), where Palladius is said to be able to stir the Latin crowd: *diuisionis arte, inuentionum copia, grauitate sensuum, luce uerborum.* For Symmachus' mentions of Palladius in Book 1 see Cameron 2011, 537; Kelly 2015, 206 and 213. Palladius is also mentioned in Symm. *Ep.* 3.50, and may have received Symm. *Ep.* 9.1 (see Callu 2002, 96). Both Callu (1972, 80) and Salzman (Salzman and Roberts 2011, 47–9) believe Symmachus' Palladius (of *Epp.* 1.15, 1.94 and 3.50) to be the same one mentioned in Sidon. *Ep.* 5.10.3, and in light of the rhetorical context of Sidonius' mention, their suggestion seems persuasive. Identifying Palladius with the rhetor in Symmachus makes him identical to Palladius 12 of *PLRE* 1, 660. In contrast, Loyen's 1970a, 191 n. 36 – rather arbitrary – identification of Palladius with the relative mentioned in Rut. Nam. 1.208 (on which see Wolff 2007, 66 n. 95) is not compelling, and nor is Loyen's indication (1960, 187) that the vague mention of the name Petrus in Sidon. *Carm.* 9.308 is to be referred to the same Palladius. In his recent prosopographical entry, Mathisen 2020, 110–11 does not draw a conclusion. As explained by Gualandri 1979, 82 n. 25, the word *pompa* is used here with the technical Ciceronian meaning of *genus demostratiuum* (e.g. Cic. *de Orat.* 2.94) a circumvoluted, jewelled and

317

impactful style which Gualandri calls 'oratoria di parata'; in other Sidonian occurrences the word is employed with a less technical meaning, as in *Carm.* 2.192 or *Ep.* 9.14.6.

comparari non ambigo sed potius adquiesco: The reading *ambigo* is chosen by Anderson and Loyen, in place of *ambio*, attested only in *L* and chosen by Lütjohann. *Ambigo* seems preferable both in terms of meaning, since Sidonius says that he has 'no hesitation in comparing' him to those qualities of Quintilian and Palladius (while the alternative *ambio*, 'I do not seek to . . .', would not be coherent with the following *adquiesco*) and because the syntagma *non ambigo* is first known to occur in Symmachus' *Letters* (*Epp.* 2.46.3, 3.16, 3.32, 7.52 and 9.47), often in closing remarks. Sidonius employs it also in *Ep.* 2.6.2 *[Aruernis] placuisse . . . quod te probasse non ambigo*, when he rejoices because he 'has no doubt' that the Arverni appreciated the same qualities in Menstruanus which Pegasius had praised; moreover, the verb *ambigo* is known to occur more than ten times in his *Letters*, for instance in *Ep.* 4.11.1, where it introduces the eulogy of Mamertus Claudianus (*oculis nostris, ambigo an quempiam deinceps parem conspicaturis*). Anderson 1965, 207 wonders whether *ambigo* and *adquiesco* are legal expressions and suggests that 'Sidonius acquiesces in the verdict (or contention), but that does not mean that he agrees with it', but he is, rather, 'prepared to let it pass'. And yet, a sceptical attitude would not be coherent with the overall praising context; instead, it can be argued that Sidonius' praise is measured, since he compares Sapaudus to known rhetors and to single qualities of the most famous ones, namely Quintilian and Palladius, so that (as he himself points out) no one would accuse him of being overpraising. However, one aspect of Anderson's suggestion is worthy of further reflection in light of the context: the peculiar use of *acquiesco* seems to indicate that Sidonius is embracing a consensus view.

§ 4

Quapropter si quis post uos Latiae fauet eruditioni: This closing section starts with stylistic over-refinement, since the *iunctura Latia eruditio* is not known to have previous occurrences; even the form *Latina eruditio* has previous occurrences only in Eutropius 10.16.3 and Jerome *Ep.* 107.9, when discussing female education. The adjective *Latius* is in itself poetic, post-Augustan and, with the exception of *Ep.* 5.10, Sidonius employs it exclusively in poetry: *Carm.* 5.112 *Latiis fastis*; *Carm.* 7.139 *Latio . . . sanguine*; and *Carm.* 7.513 *Latias . . . arces.*

huic amicitiae gratias agit et sodalitati uestrae: The companionship between Sapaudus and Pragmatius is credited with a key role in the advancement of the literary studies of the time. *Sodalitas* is often used by Sidonius to indicate bonds of intellectual brotherhood, which entailed a deep understanding of one another's literary production, and *sodalitas* is a most appropriate word to define the relationship between Sapaudus and Pragmatius, since the latter was fond of him out of his love for literary studies (see § 1).

si quid hominis habet, tertius optat adhiberi: The rather informal protasis serves the purpose of highlighting that 'literally anyone' would wish to be one of their company. The syntagma *optat adhiberi* in the apodosis seems to be a specifically Symmachan reminiscence: it occurs in Symm. *Epp.* 6.52 and 6.56, both addressed to Flavianus and presumably to his wife (Symmachus' daughter) and both concerning the request that Flavianus join a delegation to Honorius. On the two letters see Marcone 1983, 129–31 and 135–6. Note the paeon I spondee at the end of the sentence.

Quamquam, quod est grauius: The colloquial phrase *quod est grauius* has numerous occurrences since Cicero (e.g. *Caec.* 7 and *S. Rosc.* 115) and Sidonius employs it also in *Ep.* 6.4.2.

non sit satis ambitus iste fastidium uobis excitaturus: Sidonius' pretended pessimism about the literary knowledge of future generations has the effect of further emphasising the culture of Sapaudus and Pragmatius. See Mam. Claud. *Ep.* 2, p. 204, in which Claudianus says the situation is desperate: he would have been ready to entomb (*flebili uelut epitaphio tumularem*) literary studies if it were not for Sapaudus, who was able to revive them (*resuscitauisses*); see the introduction for context. The syntagma *fastidium excitare* seems Sidonian, and occurs also in *Ep.* 8.16.3, when Sidonius tells Constantius that there is almost nothing left in his 'cases and closets' that is worthy of publication, hence he starts contemplating the idea of silencing himself for two reasons: if his writings are well received, the paucity of material will stir the curiosity of an eager reader, while *si refutamur, non excitent multa fastidium* ('if they happen to be dispraised, their being only a few pages long will not excite the reader's aversion').

quia pauci studia nunc honorant: Note the thematic similarity of Plin. *Ep.* 8.12.1, where Titinius Capito is represented as a model and a 'safe harbour' (*portus, sinus, gremium*) to those interested in literature, being himself a renovator of the 'now declining literary studies' (*litterae senescentes*). Pliny's passage has also an echo in Sidon. *Ep.* 4.17.2 to Arbogast, who is pictured as a defender of studies: in him, the traces of 'disappearing literature' can still be found (*uanescentium litterarum remansisse uestigia*). Geisler 1887, 366 suggests a comparison with Plin. *Ep.* 3.18.5 *extincta studia*; note, however, that the letter concerns the specific genre of literary recitals in the presence of friends (which were almost 'extinct' before Pliny decided to revive the practice). On contemporaries not interested in speaking Latin correctly see Sidon. *Ep.* 4.3.1 (on which see Amherdt 2001, 120 and 388) and the passionate praise of Johannes in Sidon. *Ep.* 8.2.1, where the addressee is portrayed like a commander protecting the castaways of an imaginary shipwreck of Latin language. Similar remarks are found in Mam. Claud. *Ep.* 2, p. 204, when Claudianus ascribes the literary decline of his age to lack of diligence rather than to lack of wit: *nostro saeculo non ingenia deesse, sed studia*; to which, a complaint on linguistic decay and corruption through barbarisms follows (see commentary on *Ep.* 5.5.3 *barbarus barbarimum*). In *Ep.* 2, pp. 204–5, Claudianus states that should *multi* become studious, Sapaudus would still stand out, a passage which Pelttari 2020, 203 believes to be responding to Sidonius' mention of *pauci* dedicated to literature. See the introduction for this literary topos.

simul et naturali uitio fixum est radicatumque pectoribus humanis: Pelttari 2020, 201 believes that this sentence is polemically echoed by Mam. Claud. *Ep.* 2, p. 204 where Claudianus argues that the cultural decline of their time is caused by negligence and is not imputable to human nature; Claudianus, in fact, reminds Sapaudus that the nature of humankind is the same that produced someone as great as Cicero. The hendyadic syntagma *fixus et radicatus* is known exclusively in Christian contexts: Ambr. *Inst. uirg.* 1.7 *Christus . . . radicatus et fixus in cordibus nostris*; Rufin. *Orig. in Rom.* 7.9 *fixi et radicati sumus in caritate Dei*; Rufin. *Orig. in Num.* 23.11.1 *non est mens tua fixa et radicata in desideriis terrenorum*.

ut qui non intellegunt artes non mirentur artifices: The letter is closed by this *pointe*, which, however, sounds rather pleonastic. Because of the decline of literary studies, Sapaudus is unlikely to be importuned by youngsters eager to improve their knowledge. It is implicit, therefore, that if a person does not understand the value of arts, he is not going to look up to literary models. See, for a similar syntactic structure, Sidon. *Ep.* 2.2.6 *sicut ornat artem, sic deuenustat artificem,* where Sidonius argues that telling shameful tales honours artistry but is dishonourable for the artist.

Appendix

Corrections to the Apparatus of Lütjohann and Loyen

As stated in the General Introduction, although Lütjohann's apparatus is the only positive apparatus of the works of Sidonius, some corrections are needed, since the collation of Book 5 has highlighted numerous mistakes in the reports of the readings. Here is a list for each manuscript, starting with *P*, the collation of which is particularly flawed in Lütjohann.

P

Dolveck has reached the conclusion that *P* has a far more important place in manuscript tradition than has been argued before. Lütjohann describes it as *satis neglegenter scriptus*;[1] similarly, Mohr states that he has discarded, 'for the benefit of brevity, the *lectiones* in *P* and *F*', and that he makes use of these manuscripts only when *codices meliores* prove to be unhelpful.[2] Loyen too chooses not to use *P* for the *constitutio textus*.[3]

Therefore, Lütjohann's apparatus is the only one that includes the readings of this manuscript; and yet, given that some readings are wrong or wrongly attributed to *P*, it is worth signalling them. Below is a list of readings which in the edition are ascribed to *CFLM* (and which were verified by me)[4]

---

1. Lütjohann 1887, *praef.*, xii.
2. Dolveck 2020, 499 believes the absence of *P* in Mohr's apparatus should be ascribed to it having an excellent text rather than to failings in collation. However, even if *P* may have an excellent text, note that Mohr 1895, *praef.*, iv clarifies that he believes *P* and *F* to be *deteriores* and he intends to use them only when *meliores codices* fail to provide satisfying readings. Hence the lack of consistency regarding their presence in the apparatus.
3. Loyen 1970a, lii.
4. The *lectiones* listed were also checked in said manuscripts, with the exception of *F*, since, given the new stemma, the presence in *F* is subsidiary to that in *P*. Although *F* was checked only for specific problematic *lectiones*, here it is only mentioned when indicated as the sole witness of a reading by Lütjohann.

APPENDIX. CORRECTIONS TO LÜTJOHANN AND LOYEN

whose presence in *P*, however, is not signalled. Therefore, these readings should be read against Lütjohann:[5]

Ep. 5.4 p. 80 line 11: *Simplitio (FP)*;

Ep. 5.7 p. 82 line 1: *Taumasto (CP)*; line 4: *hii (MP)*; line 5: *hii (MP)*; line 9: *hii (FP)*; line 13: *hii (MP)*;

Ep. 5.14 p. 87 line 27: *hebetebantur (L)*, *hẹbetebantur (P)*;

Ep. 5.15 p. 88 line 6: *Ruritio (MP)*;

Ep. 5.17 p. 90 line 20: *Domnitius (CP)*; p. 91 line 2: *distiti (LP)*.

The recognition of Book 5 in *P* gives evidence in favour of Dolveck's proposition that *L*, *M* and *P* belong to the same branch of the family – unlike what can be gathered from both Leo's and Loyen's stemmata[6] – and that *P* is indeed higher than *F*.

More importantly, it seems useful to point out that in Lütjohann's apparatus the following readings are wrongly ascribed to *P*:

Ep. 5.1 p. 78 line 8: *prouintia* ascribed to *CP* is actually a mistake peculiar to *C* (see commentary *ad loc.*);

Ep. 5.7 p. 82 line 23: *letanias* ascribed to *P* instead is *lẹtanias*, as in the signalled *M*;

Ep. 5.7 p. 83 line 13: *falsi* ascribed to *P* is actually *salsi* (a good reading);

---

5. For this reason, for each reading are here given the page and line of Lütjohann's edition, in order to navigate the text more easily. Lütjohann is also inconsistent in listing orthographical variations, and although these are not of major textual significance, for the sake of comprehensiveness it is worth listing his omissions: *Ep.* 5.1 p. 78 line 3: *maximis (CMP)*; line 9: *quanquam (LMP¹)*; line 10: *conditio (CLP)*; *Ep.* 5.2 p. 79 line 12: *exibere (FP)*; line 13: *sacietatem (CMP)*; *Ep.* 5.3 p. 79 line 27: *amicicia (CP)*; p. 80 line 5: *precium (CMP)*, *Ep.* 5.4 p. 80 line 16: *denuncio (CMP)*; *Ep.* 5.5 p. 80 line 21: *quanquam (LMP)*; p. 81 line 5 *negociis (CP)*; line 10 *nichilo (CMP)*; *Ep.* 5.6 p. 81 line 17: *quanquam (LMP)*; line 22: *suspitionis (LP)*; line 24: *michi (CP)*; *Ep.* 5.7 p. 82 line 20: *scolas (C)*; line 23: *lẹtanias (MP)*; line 24: *scithae (CM)*; line 27: *amicicias (CP)*; p. 83 line 3: *discuciantur (CLP)*; line 11: *domicianus (CLMP)* with *M* also not signalled in apparatus; line 14: *nichil (CMP)*; *Ep.* 5.8 p. 83 line 22: *nichil (CMP)*; p. 84 line 2: *nichilo (CMP)*; line 3: *uiciis (CP)*; *Ep.* 5.9 p. 84 line 10: *amiciciarum (CP)*; line 11: *negocio (CP)*; line 22: *dileccio (CP dilectio P¹)*; line 25: *leticia (CP laetitia P¹)*. *Ep.* 5.10 p. 85 line 10: *prestancius (CP)*; line 21: *quanquam (LMP)*; *Ep.* 5.14 p. 88 line 3: *sternatium (FP)*; *Ep.* 5.15, p. 88 line 10: *quanquam (LMP)*; *Ep.* 5.16, p. 88 line 23 *patritius (LMP)*; *Ep.* 5.16, p. 89 line 3: *redibet (CP)*; line 7: *obtima (MP)*; line 12: *quanquam (LMP)*; *Ep.* 5.17, p. 89 line 29: *loquatior (LP)*; *Ep.* 5.17 p. 90 line 21: *pirgum (FP)*; p. 91 line 13: *sentencia (CP)*; line 20: *nunciatum (CLMP)*; *Ep.* 5.18 p. 91 line 27: *tercia (CP)*; line 30: *matheriam (CMP)*; *Ep.* 5.19 p. 92 line 6: *conditione (CLP)*; *Ep.* 5.20 p. 92 line 22: *negocii (CP)*.

6. See the stemma by Friedrich Leo in Lütjohann's edition (1887, xli), which was completed and published after Lütjohann's death; see aso the stemma in Loyen 1970a, liii.

SIDONIUS: LETTERS BOOK 5, PART 1

Ep. 5.10 p. 86 line 4: *edifficacissime* ascribed to *P* is actually *ꝗdifficacissime*;

Ep. 5.19 p. 92 line 4: *uos nosque* ascribed to *P* (and also wrongly to *M* – see below) is actually *nos uosque* as in the other witnesses.

There are numerous readings attested only in *P* and not signalled in Lütjohann's apparatus (although other spellings in other manuscripts are often listed).[7]

C

Lütjohann's collation of *C* is more accurate than that of *P*. In particular, Lütjohann does not list that *Ep.* 5.14 p. 87 line 25, *C* has *sed* instead of *quod* (*cett.*).[8]

L

In the following instances readings in *L* are not listed in Lütjohann's apparatus, although their occurrence in other witnesses is registered:

Ep. 5.10 p. 85 line 2: *inlustris* (which had wrongly been attributed to *C*);

Ep. 5.16 p. 88 line 23: *cogit esse ius* (attributed to *C*[1]);

Ep. 5.19 p. 92 line 13: *ne stringat.*

---

7. Although mainly orthographical variants, they are all listed here for completeness: *Ep.* 5.1 p. 78 line 12 *agnitionis*; *Ep.* 5.2 p. 79 line 7 *arichmetica*; *Ep.* 5.5 p. 81 line 1 *eufoniam*; *Ep.* 5.6 p. 81 line 25 *cauciorem*; *Ep.* 5.7 p. 82 line 7 *ii*; *Ep.* 5.8 p. 83 line 28 *secla*; *Ep.* 5.9 p. 84 line 24 *exercuint*; *Ep.* 5.9 p. 84 line 26 *inicia*; *Ep.* 5.10 p. 85 line 19 *Laciae*; *Ep.* 5.11 p. 85 line 27 *deuintior*; *Ep.* 5.13 p. 87 line 1 *ballenarum*; *Ep.* 5.13 p. 87 line 7 *thrahentes*; *Ep.* 5.16 p. 89 line 1 *obtimus*; *Ep.* 5.16 p. 89 line 13 *exobto*; *Ep.* 5.17 p. 89 line 26 *ampplissimi*; *Ep.* 5.17 p. 89 line 29 *cumueneramus*; *Ep.* 5.17 p. 90 line 16 *ambitiossime*; *Ep.* 5.17 p. 90 line 18 *efflagita*; *Ep.* 5.17 p. 90 line 27 *submoueretur*; *Ep.* 5.17 p. 90 line 28 *cathastropham*; *Ep.* 5.17 p. 91 line 15 *composuit*; *Ep.* 5.17 p. 91 line 18 *faueat*.

8. Among other readings of *C* with orthographical variants, which are missing in Lütjohann but are listed here for the sake of completeness: *Ep.* 5.8 p. 84 line 6: *remminiscendis*; *Ep.* 5.15 p. 88 line 12: *sentenciis*; *Ep.* 5.15 p. 88 line 14: *exhortacio*. The following is also a list of readings wrongly attributed to *C* in the apparatus: *Ep.* 5.1 p. 78 line 7 *accomodatissimum* is actually *acommodatissimum*; *Ep.* 5.10 p. 85 line 2 *inlustris* is actually *illustris*; *Ep.* 5.12 p. 86 line 18 *oculos* is actually *occulos*.

APPENDIX. CORRECTIONS TO LÜTJOHANN AND LOYEN

There are also readings wrongly attributed to *L* in the apparatus:[9]

Ep. 5.7 p. 82 line 2: *tethrarcam* is actually *tetharcam*;
Ep. 5.13 p. 86 line 26: *contractus operam* is actually *contractos operam*;
Ep. 5.14 p. 87 line 19: *caientes* is actually *caienses*;
Ep. 5.17 p. 91 line 3: *ut sedemus* is actually *ut sedimus*;
Ep. 5.17 p. 91 line 17: *fous* is actually *fons.*

M

In the following instances the occurrences in *M* are not listed in Lütjohann's apparatus; the same readings are, however, ascribed to other witnesses:[10]

Ep. 5.1 p. 78 line 7: *accomodatissimum* (wrongly ascribed to *C*) is actually in *M*;
Ep. 5.6 p. 81 line 22: *familiarium* (*LMP*);
Ep. 5.13 p. 87 line 1: *tarmis* (*CMP*);
Ep. 5.17 p. 91 line 2: *distiti* (*LM*).

The following readings are wrongly attributed to *M* in Lütjohann's apparatus:[11]

Ep. 5.14 p. 87 line 23: *ni* should be corrected to *nisi*;
Ep. 5.19 p. 92 line 4: *uos nosque* (and also wrongly to *P* – see above) is actually *nos uosque* (as in *cett.*).

There are also readings only attested in *M*, which are not in the apparatus:

Ep. 5.9 p. 84 line 14: *Geruntio*;
Ep. 5.14 p. 88 line 1: *sumus.*

---

9. Wrongly attributed to *L* are also the following orthographical variants: *Ep.* 5.7 p. 82 line 6: *prouintia* is actually *prouincia* (a good reading); *Ep.* 5.7 p. 82 line 18 *inducias* is actually *indutias* (a good reading); *Ep.* 5.7 p. 83 line 11 *Domicianus* is actually *Domitianus* (a good reading).

10. Less significant orthographical variants are also *Ep.* 5.4 p. 80 line 17 *paciuntur CM*; *Ep.* 5.7 p. 82 line 17 *archariis CMP*[1]; *Ep.* 5.7 p. 83 line 11 *Domicianus CM* (occurrence in *L* is wrong: it is Domitianus – see section on *L*).

11. As before, it is worth listing orthographical variations wrongly attributed to *M*. In *Ep.* 5.14 p. 87 line 21 *quamdam* should be corrected to *quandam* (as in *cett.*); *Ep.* 5.14 p. 87 line 27 *maxume* should be corrected to *maxime* (as in *cett.*); *Ep.* 5.17 p. 90 line 3 *cryptoporticibus* by a hypothetical *M*[2], where my reading is *criptoporticibus*, as in *CP*.

325

Leipzig, UB, Rep. I 48

Dolveck also argues that Leipzig, UB, Rep. I 48 deserves to be collated because of evidence that it was collated by a second hand, contemporary with the manuscript, against a source close to the archetype.[12] In light of Dolveck's suggestion, I collated Book 5 in this witness, but there is no sign of contamination in this book that might be of interest.

The only results worth mentioning concern the notes by a modern hand in the margins, which Dolveck believes may belong to Johann Christoph Wagenseil, the seventeenth-century owner of the manuscript. In *Leip* f. 40^v this hand writes 'lege, halario et, falco' next to the problematic passage of *Ep.* 5.5 *quasi de hilario uetere nouus flacco prorumpas*. Moreover, the modern hand in *Leip* (f. 42^r) underlines the word *fellis* (*Ep.* 5.8.2) and writes in the margin the interesting reading *mellis*;[13] and in *Leip* (f. 44^r) underlines the word *ortuloni* in the text of *Ep.* 5.14 and writes *hortulano* in the margin. After a survey of all the editions, I came to the conclusion that this modern hand was correcting the text of the *Leip* manuscript against Savaron's 1609 edition, which included all three readings listed here; in particular, *halario* was Savaron's own conjecture.[14]

---

12. Dolveck 2020, 503.
13. See commentary ad loc.
14. Savaron 1599, 310.

Bibliography

The abbreviations of journal titles in this bibliography are those of *L'Année philologique*.
All URLs below and in the text were checked and correct at the time of writing (2022).

Adkin, N. (1999) 'Jerome's Vow "Never to Reread the Classics": Some Observations', *REA* 101, 161–7.

Albiani, M. G. (1995) 'La poesia ellenistica ed epigrammatica', in U. Mattioli (ed.), Senectus, *La vecchiaia nel mondo classico*, vol. I, Bologna, 277–360.

Alimonti, T. (1975) 'Apuleio e l'arcaismo in Claudiano Mamerto', in Forma futuri. *Studi in onore del cardinale Michele Pellegrino*, Turin, 189–228.

Amherdt, D. (2001) *Sidoine Apollinaire. Le quatrième livre de la correspondance. Introduction et commentaire*, Bern.

Anderson, W. B. (ed.) (1936) *Sidonius: Poems and Letters*, vol. I, *Poems; Letters Books 1–2*, London.

Anderson, W. B. (ed.) (1965) *Sidonius: Poems and Letters*, vol. 2, *Letters Books 3–9* (finished by W. H. Semple and E. H. Warmington), London.

Anderson, W. S. (ed.) (1993) *P. Ovidii Nasonis Metamorphoses*, Stuttgart.

Ash, R. (ed.) (2018) *Tacitus: Annals, Book XV*, Cambridge.

Baldwin, B. (1981) 'Acclamations in the *Historia Augusta*', *Athenaeum* 59, 138–49.

Baret, E. (ed.) (1878) *Œuvres de Sidoine Apollinaire: Texte latin*, Paris.

Barnes, T. D. (2011) *Constantine: Dynasty, Religion, and Power in the Later Roman Empire*, Chichester.

Bauman, R. A. (1994) 'Tanaquil–Livia and the Death of Augustus', *Historia* 43.2, 177–88.

Bellès, J. (ed.) (1998) *Sidoni Apol·linar: Lletres*, vol. II, *Llibres 4–6*, Barcelona.

Birley, A. R. (1997) 'Marius Maximus: The Consular Biographer', in *ANRW* II.34.3, 2678–757.

Blaise, A. (1975) *Lexicon latinitatis medii aevi praesertim ad res ecclesiasticas investigandas pertinens*, Turnhout.

Blänsdorf, J. (1993) 'Apollinaris Sidonius und die Verwandlung der römischen Satire in der Spätantike', *Philologus* 137.1, 122–31.

— (ed.) (2011) *Fragmenta poetarum Latinorum epicorum et lyricorum, praeter Enni Annales et Ciceronis Germanicique Aratea, post W. Morel et K. Büchner editionem quartam auctam*, Berlin.

Blockley, R. C. (1998) 'The Dynasty of Theodosius', in A. Cameron and P. Garnsey (eds), *The Cambridge Ancient History*, vol. XIII, *The Late Empire, A.D. 337–425*, Cambridge, 111–37.

Bömer, F. (1982) *P. Ovidius Naso, Metamorphosen, Kommentar: Buch XII–XIII*, Heidelberg.

Bonjour, M. and Solignac, A. (1990) 'Sidoine Apollinaire', in *Dict. de Spir.*, vol. XVI, Paris, cols 814–21.

Brink, C. O. (1982) *Horace on Poetry. Epistles Book II: The Letters to Augustus and Florus*, Cambridge.

BIBLIOGRAPHY

Brown, P. M. (1993) *Horace Satires I*, with an introduction, text, translation and commentary, Warminster.

Bruggisser, P. (1993) *Symmaque ou le ritual épistolaire de l'amitié littéraire. Recherches sur le premier livre de la correspondance*, Fribourg.

Cabrol, F., Leclercq, H., et al. (eds) (1923) *Dictionnaire d'archéologie chrétienne et de liturgi*, vol. V, part 2, Paris.

Cain, A. (2009) *The Letters of Jerome: Asceticism, Biblical Exegesis, and the Construction of Christian Authority in Late Antiquity*, Oxford.

Callu, J. P. (ed.) (1972) *Symmaque: Lettres*, texte établi, traduit et commenté, vol. I, *Livres I–II*, Paris.

— (1975) 'Les Constitutions d' Aristote et leur fortune au Bas-Empire (Symm. *Ep.* 3, 11)', *REL* 53, 268–315.

— (ed.) (1982) *Symmaque: Lettres*, texte établi, traduit et commenté, vol. II, *Livres III–V*, Paris.

— (ed.) (1995a) *Symmaque: Lettres*, texte établi, traduit et commenté, vol. III, *Livres VI–VIII*, Paris.

— (1995b) 'À nouveau le savon de Constantin', *Historia* 44.4, 500–2.

— (ed.) (2002) *Symmaque: Lettres*, texte établi, traduit et commenté, vol. IV, *Livres IX–X*, Paris.

— (ed.) (2009) *Symmaque*: texte établi, traduit et commenté, vol. V, *Discours-Rapports*, Paris.

Cameron, A. (2011) *The Last Pagans of Rome*, New York.

— (2015) 'Were Pagans Afraid to Speak their Minds in a Christian World? The Correspondence of Symmachus', in M. R. Salzman, M. Sághy and R. Lizzi Testa (eds), *Pagans and Christians in Late Antique Rome: Conflict, Competition, and Coexistence in the Fourth Century*, Cambridge, 64–111.

Cecconi, G. A. (2002a) *Commento storico al libro II dell'Epistolario di Q. Aurelio Simmaco*, Pisa.

— (2002b) 'L'ipocondria di Simmaco. Critica a un piccolo mito storiografico', in P. Défosse (ed.), *Hommages à Carl Deroux*, vol. II, *Prose et linguistique, Médicine*, Brussels, 466–76.

Charlet, J.-L. (ed.) (2018) *Claudien: Œuvres. Petits poèmes*, Paris.

Chastagnol, A. (1973) 'Le repli sur Arles des services administratifs gaulois en l'an 407 de notre ère', *RH* 249, 23–40.

— (1988) 'Le formulaire de l'épigraphie latine officielle dans l'Antiquité tardive', in A. Donati (ed.), *La terza età dell'epigrafia*, Colloquio Internazionale AIEGL-Borghesi (Bologna 1986), Faenza, 11–65.

— (1992) *Le Sénat romain à l'époque impériale. Recherches sur la composition de l'Assemblée et le statut de ses membres*, Paris.

— (1996) 'La carriera senatoriale nel Basso Impero (dopo Diocleziano)', in S. Roda (ed.), *La parte migliore del genere umano. Aristocrazie, potere e ideologia nell'Occidente tardoantico. Antologia di storia tardoantica. I florilegi (2)*, Turin, 23–57.

Chastagnol, A. and Duval, N. (1974) 'Les survivances du culte impérial dans l'Afrique du Nord à l'époque vandale', in *Mélanges d'histoire ancienne offerts à William Seston*, Paris, 87–118.

Chausson, F. (2002) 'La famille du préfet Ablabius', *Pallas* 60, 205–29.

Chronopoulos, T. (2020) 'Glossing Sidonius in the Middle Ages', in G. Kelly and J. van Waarden (eds), *The Edinburgh Companion to Sidonius Apollinaris*, Edinburgh, 643–64.

Coleman, K. M. (1988) *Statius: Siluae IV*, edited with an English translation and commentary, Oxford.

Colton, R. E. (1995) *Studies of Imitation in Some Latin Authors*, Amsterdam.

BIBLIOGRAPHY

Condorelli, S. (2001a) 'Una particolare accezione di *barbarismus* in Sidonio Apollinare', in U. Criscuolo (ed.), Mnemosynon. *Studi di letteratura e di umanità in memoria di Donato Gagliardi*, Naples, 101–9.

— (2001b) *L'esametro dei* Panegyrici *di Sidonio Apollinare*, Naples.

— (2008) *Il* poeta doctus *nel V secolo d.C. Aspetti della poetica di Sidonio Apollinare*, Naples.

— (2013) 'Gli epigrammi funerari di Sidonio Apollinare', in M. F. Guipponi-Gineste and C. Urlacher-Becht (eds), *La renaissance de l'épigramme dans la latinité tardive, Actes du colloque de Mulhouse, 6–7 octobre 2011*, Paris, 261–82.

— (2015) 'L'inizio della fine: l'epistola IX 1 di Sidonio Apollinare tra *amicitia* ed istanze estetico-letterarie', *BStudLat* 45, 489–511.

— (2020a) 'Metrics in Sidonius', in G. Kelly and J. van Waarden (eds), *The Edinburgh Companion to Sidonius Apollinaris*, Edinburgh, 440–61.

— (2020b) 'Sidonius Scholarship: Twentieth to Twenty-First Centuries', in G. Kelly and J. van Waarden (eds), *The Edinburgh Companion to Sidonius Apollinaris*, Edinburgh, 564–617.

— (2021) 'Sulle perdute *Declamationes* di San Remigio: Sidon. *ep.* 9.7', in M. Manca and M. Venuti (eds), Paulo maiora canamus. *Raccolta di studi per Paolo Mastandrea, Antichistica* 32, 295–309.

Consolino, F. E. (1974) 'Codice retorico e manierismo stilistico nella poetica di Sidonio Apollinare', *ASNP* 3.4, 423–60.

— (1979) *Ascesi e mondanità nella Gallia tardoantica. Studi sulla figura del vescovo nei secoli IV–VI*, Naples.

— (1986) *Claudiano: Elogio di Serena*, Venice.

— (2013) 'Sidonio e le *Silvae*', in P. Galand and S. Laigneau-Fontaine (eds), *La silve: Histoire d'une écriture libérée en Europe, de l'Antiquité au XVIIIe siècle*, Turnhout 213–36.

— (2020) 'Sidonius' Shorter Poems', in G. Kelly and J. van Waarden (eds), *The Edinburgh Companion to Sidonius Apollinaris*, Edinburgh, 341–72.

Conybeare, C. (2000) Paulinus Noster: *Self and Symbols in the Letters of Paulinus of Nola*, Oxford.

Corbeill, A. (2002) 'Ciceronian Invective', in J. M. May (ed.), *Brill's Companion to Cicero. Oratory and Rhetoric*, Leiden, 197–218.

Courtney, E. (2013) *A Commentary on the Satires of Juvenal*, Berkeley.

Cova, P. V. (1966) *La critica letteraria di Plinio il Giovane*, Brescia.

Coville, A. (1928) *Recherches sur l'histoire de Lyon du V siècle au IX siècle: 450–800*, Paris.

Cristante, L. (2005–2006) 'La *praefatio* glossematica di Anth. Lat. 19 R.=6 Sh.B. Una ipotesi di lettura', *Incontri triestini di filologia classica* 5, 235–60.

— (2008) 'La Filologia come Enciclopedia. Il *De Nuptiis Philologiae et Mercurii* di Marziano Capella', *Voces* 19, 51–69.

Cugusi, P. (1983) *Evoluzione e forme dell'epistolografia latina nella tarda Repubblica e nei primi due secoli dell'Impero, con cenni sull'epistolografia preciceroniana*, Rome.

— (1985) *Aspetti letterari dei* Carmina Latina Epigraphica, Bologna.

— (1990) 'Un'epistola recusatoria di Sidonio', *BStudLat* 20, 375–80.

Cupaiuolo, G. (1993) *Tra poesia e politica: Le pasquinate nell'antica Roma*, Naples.

Dahlmann H. (1935) 'M. Terentius Varro 84', *RE* suppl. 6, 1172–277.

d'Alessandro, P. (1997) 'Agostino, Claudiano Mamerto, Cassiodoro e i *Disciplinarum Libri* di Varrone', in E. Degani et al. (eds), ΜΟΥΣΑ *Scritti in onore di Giuseppe Morelli*, Bologna, 357–70.

Dalton, O. M. (1915) *The Letters of Sidonius*, Oxford.

d'Anville (1760) *Notice de l'ancienne Gaule tirée des monumens Romains*, Paris.

BIBLIOGRAPHY

Davidson, I. J. (ed.) (2001) *Ambrose:* De Officiis, edited with an introduction, translation, and commentary, Oxford.

Davis, G. (2011) '*Axones* and *Kurbeis*: A New Answer to an Old Problem', *Historia* 60, 1–35.

de Bruyne, D. (ed.) (1920) *Préfaces de la Bible latine*, Namur.

De Rossi, G. B. (1878) 'Come si possa conciliare il titolo di *flamen perpetuus* con quello di *Christianus*', *Bullettino di Archeologia Cristiana* 3.3, 31–6.

Delaplace, C. (2014) 'Le témoignage de Sidoine Apollinaire: une source historique toujours fiable? À propos de la "conquête de l'Auvergne" par les Wisigoths', in R. Poignault and A. Stoehr-Monjou (eds), *Présence de Sidoine Apollinaire*, Clermont-Ferrand, 19–32.

— (2015) *La fin de l'Empire romain d'Occident. Rome et les Wisigoths de 382 à 531*, Rennes.

den Boeft, J., Drijvers, J. W., den Hengst, D., and Teitler, H. C. (2008) *Philological and Historical Commentary on Ammianus Marcellinus XXVI*, Leiden.

Di Bernardino, A. (1998) 'L'immagine del vescovo attraverso i suoi titoli nel Codice Teodosiano', in É. Rebillard and C. Sotinel (eds), *L'évêque dans la cité du IVe au Ve siècle. Image et autorité*, Rome, 35–48.

Di Marco, M. (1995) *La polemica sull'anima tra <Fausto di Riez> e Claudiano Mamerto*, Rome.

d'Ippolito, F. (1998) *Forme giuridiche di Roma arcaica*, Naples.

Divjak, J. (ed.) (1981) *Sancti Aureli Augustini Opera. Epistolae ex duobus codicibus nuper in lucem prolatae* (CSEL 88), Vienna.

Dolbeau, F. (1984) 'La vie en prose de Saint Marcel, évêque de Die. Histoire du texte et édition critique', *Francia* 11 [1983], 97–130.

Dolveck, F. (2020) 'The Manuscript Tradition of Sidonius', in G. Kelly and J. van Waarden (eds), *The Edinburgh Companion to Sidonius Apollinaris*, Edinburgh, 479–542.

D'Ors, A. (ed.) (2014) *El Código de Eurico. Edición, palingenesia, indices*, Madrid.

Drinkwater, J. F. (1998) 'The Usurpers Constantine III (407–411) and Jovinus (411–413)', *Britannia* 29, 269–98.

Du Cange, C., et al. (1883–1887) *Glossarium mediae et infimae latinitatis*, Niort (1st edtion Paris, 1678).

Dyck, A. R. (ed.) (2013) *Cicero:* Pro Marco Caelio, Cambridge.

Egetenmeyr, V. (2019) '"Barbarians" Transformed: The Construction of Identity in the Epistles of Sidonius Apollinaris', in J. W. Drijvers and N. Lenski (eds), *The Fifth Century: Age of Transformation. Proceedings of the Twelfth Biennial Shifting Frontiers in Late Antiquity Conference*, Bari, 169–81.

— (2021) 'Sidonius Apollinaris's Use of the Term *Barbarus*: An Introduction', in M. Friedrich and J. M. Harland (eds), *Interrogating the 'Germanic': A Category and its Use in Late Antiquity and the Early Middle Ages*, Berlin, 145–65.

Ellis, R. (ed.) (1887) *The Fables of Avianus*, edited with prolegomena, critical apparatus, commentary, excursus and index, Oxford.

Engelbrecht, A. (ed.) (1885) *Claudiani Mamerti Opera* (CSEL 11), Vienna.

— (ed.) (1891) *Fausti Reiensis et Ruricii Opera* (CSEL 21), Vienna.

Escher, K. (2005) *Genèse et évolution du deuxième royaume burgonde (443–534). Les témoins archéologiques*, Oxford.

Faller, O. (ed.) (1968) *Ambrosius, Epistulae et Acta*, tom. I, *Epistularum Libri I–VI* (CSEL 82/1), Vienna.

Fantham, E. (2004) *The Roman World of Cicero's* de Oratore, Oxford.

— (2013) *Cicero's* Pro L. Murena Oratio. *Introduction and Commentary*, Oxford.

Fascione, S. (2016) 'Seronato, Catilina e la *moritura libertas* della Gallia', *Koinonia* 40, 453–62.

— (2018) 'Retorica e realtà: i barbari di Sidonio Apollinare', *InvLuc* 40, 35–44.

— (2019a) *Gli 'altri' al potere: Romani e barbari nella Gallia di Sidonio Apollinare*, Bari.

BIBLIOGRAPHY

— (2019b) 'Simmaco e la difesa della *Romanitas* nell'ottavo libro delle *Epistole* di Sidonio Apollinare', *Koinonia* 43, 363–74.

— (2020) 'Principi identitari e inclusione del "diverso": Sidonio lettore di Simmaco', *BStudLat* 50, 204–11.

Favrod, J. (1997) *Histoire politique du royaume burgonde (443–534)*, Lausanne.

Fedeli, P. (ed.) (1980) *Sesto Properzio. Il primo libro delle Elegie*, introduzione, testo critico e commento, Florence.

— (1998) 'L'epistola commendatizia tra Cicerone e Orazio', *Ciceroniana* 10, 35–53.

—, Dimundo, R. and Ciccarelli, I. (2015) *Properzio: Elegie libro IV*, Nordhausen.

Fernández López, M. C. (1994) *Sidonio Apolinar, humanista de la antigüedad tardía. Su correspondencia*, Murcia.

Fielding, I. (2017) *Transformations of Ovid in Late Antiquity*, Cambridge.

Fo, A. (1999) 'Sidonio nelle mani di Eurico (*Ep.* VIII 9). Spazi della tradizione culturale in un nuovo contesto romanobarbarico', in M. Rotili (ed.), *Memoria del passato, urgenza del futuro. Il mondo romano tra V e VII secolo. Atti delle VI giornate di studio sull'età romanobarbarica* (Benevento, 18–20 giugno 1998), Naples, 17–37.

Fögen, T. (2018) 'Ancient Approaches to Letter-Writing and the Configuration of Communities through Epistles', in P. Ceccarelli, L. Doering, T. Fögen and I. Gildenhard (eds), *Letters and Communities: Studies in the Socio-Political Dimensions of Ancient Epistolography*, Oxford, 44–75.

Foscarini, S. (2019) 'Una pista lessicale nella prosa di Sidonio Apollinare: i grecismi', in S. Condorelli and M. Onorato (eds), Verborum violis multicoloribus: *Studi in onore di Giovanni Cupaiuolo*, Naples, 345–61.

Frederiksen, M. W. (1965) 'The Republican Municipal Laws: Errors and Drafts', *JRS* 55, 183–98.

Freisenbruch, A. (2007) 'Back to Fronto: Doctor and Patient in his Correspondence with an Emperor', in R. Morello and A. D. Morrison (eds), *Ancient Letters: Classical and Late Antique Epistolography*, Oxford, 235–55.

Fromentin, V. and Bertrand, E. (eds) (2008) *Dion Cassius, Histoire Romaine: Livres 45 et 46*, texte établi; traduit et annoté, Paris.

Frye, D. (1990) 'Gundobad, the *Leges Burgundionum* and the Struggle for Sovereignty in Burgundy', *C&M* 41, 199–212.

Furbetta, L. (2013) 'Tra retorica e politica: formazione, ricezione ed esemplarità dell'epistolario di Sidonio Apollinare', in S. Gioanni and P. Cammarosano (eds), *La corrispondenza epistolare in Italia, 2: Forme, stili e funzioni della scrittura epistolare nelle cancellerie italiane (secoli V–XV)*, Trieste, 23–65.

— (2014–2015a) 'Empereurs, rois et délateurs: esquisse d'étude sur la représentation du pouvoir et de ses dégénérescences dans l'oeuvre de Sidoine Apollinaire', *RET* 4, 123–54.

— (2014–2015b) 'Tracce di Ausonio nelle lettere di Sidonio Apollinare (appunti di lettura)', *Incontri di filologia classica* 14, 107–33.

— (2015a) 'L'epitaffio di Sidonio Apollinare in un nuovo testimone manoscritto', *Euphrosyne* 43, 243–54.

— (2015b) 'La lettre de recommandation en Gaule (V^c–VIIe siècles) entre tradition littéraire et innovation', in A. Bérenger and O. Dard (eds), *Gouverner par les lettres, de l'Antiquité à l'époque contemporaine*, Metz, 347–68.

— (2020) 'Sidonius Scholarship: Fifteenth to Nineteenth Centuries', in G. Kelly and J. van Waarden (eds), *The Edinburgh Companion to Sidonius Apollinaris*, Edinburgh, 543–63.

Ganiban, R. T. (2009) 'The Dolus and Glory of Ulysses in Aeneid 2', in R. Ferri et al. (eds), Callida Musa: *Papers on Latin Literature in Honor of R. Elaine Fantham* (MD 61), 57–70.

BIBLIOGRAPHY

Garuti, G. (1979) *Claudiano e la curia dei Visigoti (Bell. Goth.* 481–484), in *Studi di poesia latina in onore di A. Traglia, vol.* II, Rome, 937–49.

Gasti, F. (2017) 'Convertire l'Enciclopedia: Agostino e Varrone', in S. Rocchi and C. Mussini (eds), Imagines Antiquitatis: *Representations, Concepts, Receptions of the Past in Roman Antiquity and the Early Italian Renaissance*, Berlin, 303–18.

Geisler, E. (1887) *Loci similes auctorum Sidonio anteriorum*, in C. Lütjohann (ed.), *Gai Sollii Apollinaris Sidonii epistulae et carmina* (MGH AA 8), Berlin, 351–416.

Giannotti, F. (2016) Sperare Meliora. *Il terzo libro delle* Epistulae *di Sidonio Apollinare*, introduzione, traduzione e commento, Pisa.

— (2020) '*Litteras nosse*: l'*ep*. 8,2 di Sidonio Apollinare e l'importanza della cultura sotto i barbari', *Pan* 9, 143–53.

— (2021) '*Pronus prope o prope patruum*? Nota sul *Propempticon ad libellum* di Sidonio Apollinare (*carm*. 24,84–89)', *BStudLat* 56.1, 169–77.

Gibson, B. (ed.) (2006) *Statius, Silvae 5*, edited with an introduction, translation and commentary, Oxford.

Gibson, R. K. (2011) '<Clarus> Confirmed? Pliny, *Epistles* 1.1 and Sidonius Apollinaris', *CQ* 61.2, 655–9.

— (2012) 'On the Nature of Ancient Letter Collections', *JRS* 102, 56–78.

— (2013a) 'Reading the Letters of Sidonius by the Book', in J. A. van Waarden and G. Kelly (eds), *New Approaches to Sidonius Apollinaris*, Leuven, 196–219.

— (2013b) 'Pliny and the Letters of Sidonius: From Constatius and Clarus to Firminus and Fuscus', *Arethusa* 46.2, 333–55.

— (2020) 'Sidonius' Correspondence', in G. Kelly and J. van Waarden (eds), *The Edinburgh Companion to Sidonius Apollinaris*, Edinburgh, 373–92.

— and Morello, R. (2012) *Reading the Letters of Pliny the Younger: An Introduction*, Cambridge.

Gillett, A. (1999) 'The Accession of Euric', *Francia* 26, 1–40.

Giulietti, I. (2014) *Sidonio Apollinare, difensore della Romanitas.* Epistulae *5, 1–13: Saggio di commento,* PhD diss., University of Macerata.

Godefroy, F. (1881) *Dictionnaire de l'ancienne langue française et des tous ses dialectes: du IX au XV siècle*, vol. I, Paris.

Godefroy, J. (1665) *Codex Theodosianus cum perpetuis commentariis Iacobi Gothofredi*, Lyon.

Green, R. P. H. (ed.) (1991) *The Works of Ausonius*, edited with introduction and commentary, Oxford.

— (2022) *Sidonius Apollinaris: Complete Poems*, translated with introduction and commentary, Liverpool.

Gualandri, I. (1979) Furtiva lectio. *Studi su Sidonio Apollinare*, Milan.

— (2000) 'Figure di barbari in Sidonio Apollinare', in G. Lanata (ed.), *Il tardoantico alle soglie del duemila: diritto, religione, società*, Pisa, 105–29.

— (2020) 'Sidonius' Intertextuality', in G. Kelly and J. van Waarden (eds), *The Edinburgh Companion to Sidonius Apollinaris*, Edinburgh, 279–316.

Guillaumin, J.–Y. (2013) 'Rappel de l'histoire et invitation à l'action dans les Panégyriques de Sidoine Apollinaire', *DHA* suppl. 8, 93–107.

Gustafsson, F. V. (1882) *De Apollinari Sidonio emendando*, Helsinki.

Guy, J.-C. (ed.) (1965) *Jean Cassien, Institutions cénobitiques*, texte latin revu, introduction, traduction et notes (Sources Chrétiennes 109), Paris.

Hadot, I. (1984) *Arts libéraux et philosophie dans la pensée antique*, Paris.

Haenel, G. (ed.) (1857) *Corpus legum ab imperatoribus Romanis ante Iustinianum latarum, quae extra constitutionum codices supersunt,* Leipzig.

Hagendahl, H. (1958) *Latin Fathers and the Classics: A Study on the Apologists, Jerome and Other Christian Writers*, Gothenburg.

BIBLIOGRAPHY

Halsall, G. (2007) *Barbarian Migrations and the Roman West 376–568*, Cambridge.

Hanaghan, M. P. (2019) *Reading Sidonius' Epistles*, Cambridge.

Harries, J. D. (1994) *Sidonius Apollinaris and the Fall of Rome AD 407–485*, Oxford.

— (1996) 'Sidonius Apollinaris and the Frontiers of *Romanitas*', in R. W. Mathisen and H. S. Sivan (eds), *Shifting Frontiers in Late Antiquity*, Aldershot, 31–44.

— (2001) 'Not the Theodosian Code: Euric's Law and Late Fifth-Century Gaul', in R. Mathisen and D. Shanzer (eds), *Society and Culture in Late Antique Gaul: Revisiting the Sources*, Aldershot, 39–51.

— (2014) 'The Empresses' Tale, AD 300–360', in C. Harrison, C. Humfress and I. Sandwell (eds), *Being Christian in Late Antiquity: A Festschrift for Gillian Clark*, Oxford, 197–214.

Heather, P. (2006) *The Fall of the Roman Empire: A New History of Rome and the Barbarians*, New York.

Heinzelmann, M. (1982) 'Gallische Prosopographie 260–527', *Francia* 10, 531–718.

Hernández Lobato, J. (2010a) '*Sterilis Camena*: El *carmen* 9 de Sidonio Apolinar o la muerte de la poesia', *Acme* 63, 97–133.

— (2010b) 'La écfrasis de la Catedral de Lyon como híbrido intersistémico. Sidonio Apolinar y el *Gesamtkunstwerk* tardoantiguo', *AnTard* 18, 297–308.

— (2020) 'Sidonius in the Middle Ages and the Renaissance', in G. Kelly and J. van Waarden (eds), *The Edinburgh Companion to Sidonius Apollinaris*, Edinburgh, 665–85.

Hindermann, J. (2022) *Sidonius Apollinaris' Letters, Book 2*, text, translation and commentary, Edinburgh.

Hodgkin, T. (1880) *Italy and Her Invaders (376–476)*, vol. II, book 3, London.

Horsfall, N. (2013) *Virgil, Aeneid 6: A Commentary*, Berlin.

Huffman, C. A. (1993) *Philolaus of Croton: Pythagorean and Presocratic. A Commentary on the Fragments and Testimonia with Interpretive Essays*, Cambridge.

Hunink, V. (ed.) (1997) *Apuleius of Madauros,* Pro se de magia, vol. I, *Text*, vol. II, *Commentary*, Amsterdam.

Jahn, A. (1874) *Die Geschichte der Burgundionen und Burgundiens bis zum Ende der 1. Dynastie*, Halle.

Janson, T. (1964) *Latin Prose Prefaces: Studies in Literary Conventions*, Stockholm.

John, A. (2018) *Learning and Power: A Cultural History of Education in Late Antique Gaul*, PhD diss., University of Edinburgh.

— (2021) 'Learning Greek in Late Antique Gaul', *CQ* 70.2, 846–64.

Jones, A. H. M. (1964) *The Later Roman Empire 284–602: A Social, Economic and Administrative Survey*, Oxford.

Kaiser, R. (2004) *Die Burgunder*, Stuttgart.

Kampers, G. (2000) 'Caretena – Königin und Asketin. Mosaiksteine zum Bild einer burgundischen Herrscherin', *Francia* 27, 1–32.

Kaser, M. (1955) *Das römische Privatrecht 1. Das altrömische, das vorklassische und klassische Recht*, Munich.

Kaster, R. A. (1988) *Guardians of Language: The Grammarian and Society in Late Antiquity*, Berkeley.

— (ed.) (1995) *C. Suetonius Tranquillus, De grammaticis et rhetoribus*, edited with a translation, introduction, and commentary, Oxford.

— (ed.) (2011) *Macrobius:* Saturnalia, vol. I, *Books 1–2*, edited and translated, Cambridge, MA.

Kaufmann F.-M. (1995) *Studien zu Sidonius Apollinaris*, Frankfurt am Main.

Kay, N. M. (ed.) (1985) *Martial Book XI: A Commentary*, Oxford.

Keats-Rohan, K. S. B. (ed.) (1993) *Ioannis Saresberiensis, Policraticus*, Turnhout.

BIBLIOGRAPHY

Kelly, G. (2008) *Ammianus Marcellinus, the Allusive Historian*, Cambridge.

— (2013) 'Pliny and Symmachus', in B. Gibson and R. Rees (eds), *Pliny the Younger in Late Antiquity, Arethusa* 46.2, 261–87.

— (2015) 'The First Book of Symmachus' Correspondence as a Separate Collection', in P. F. Moretti, R. Ricci, and C. Torre (eds), *Culture and Literature in Latin Late Antiquity: Continuities and Discontinuities*, Turnhout, 197–220.

— (2016) 'Vichy and the Visigoths: Sidonius in Occupied France' (blogpost). <http://research.shca.ed.ac.uk/sidonius/2016/06/29/73>.

— (2018) 'Erasing Victor: Sidonius, Manuscripts, and Prosopography' (blogpost). <http://research.shca.ed.ac.uk/sidonius/2018/02/18/erasing-victor-sidonius-manuscripts-and-prosopography>.

— (2020) 'Dating the Works of Sidonius', in G. Kelly and J. van Waarden (eds), *The Edinburgh Companion to Sidonius Apollinaris*, Edinburgh, 166–94.

— (2021a) 'Surges of Interest' (blogpost).
< https://ausonius.blogspot.com/2021/04/surges-of-interest.html >.

— (2021b) 'Titles and Paratexts in the Collection of Sidonius' Poems', in A. Bruzzone, A. Fo and L. Piacente (eds), *Metamorfosi del classico in età romanobarbarica*, Firenze, 77–97.

— (2021c) 'A Textual and Onomastic Problem in Sidonius' (blogpost). <http://ausonius.blogspot.com/2021/10/a-textual-and-onomastic-problem-in.html>.

Ketelaer, N. and van Leempt, G. (eds) (1473/1474) *Gaii Sollii Apollinaris Sidonii editio princeps*, Utrecht.

Köhler, H. (1995) *Caius Sollius Apollinaris Sidonius: Briefe Buch I*, Einleitung, Text, Übersetzung, Kommentar, Heidelberg.

Kroll, W. (1963) *Die Kultur der ciceronischen Zeit*, vols I and II, Darmstadt.

Kulikowski, M. (2007) 'Marius Maximus in Ammianus and the *Historia Augusta*', *CQ* 57.1, 244–56.

— (2020) 'Sidonius' Political World', G. Kelly and J. van Waarden (eds), *The Edinburgh Companion to Sidonius Apollinaris*, Edinburgh, 197–213.

Laniado, A. (2018) 'L'aristocratie sénatoriale de Constantinople et la préfecture du prétoire d'Orient', in *Constantinople réelle et imaginaire: autour de l'oeuvre de Gilbert Dagron* (*T&MByz* 22.1), Paris, 409–55.

La Penna, A. (1995) 'Gli svaghi letterari della nobiltà gallica nella tarda antichità. Il caso di Sidonio Apollinare', *Maia* 47, 3–34.

Lardet, P. (1993) *L'Apologie de Jérôme contre Rufin: un commentaire*, Leiden.

Leadbetter, W. L. (2009) *Galerius and the Will of Diocletian*, London.

Lengle, J. (1937) 'Tribunus et notarius', *RE* 6, 2453–4.

Lettieri, G. (2013) 'Lattanzio ideologo della svolta costantiniana', in *Costantino I, Enciclopedia costantiniana sulla figura e l'immagine dell'imperatore del cosiddetto editto di Milano 313–2013*, vol. II, Rome 45–57.

Liberman, G. (ed.) (2010) *Stace: Silves. Édition et commentaire critiques*, Paris.

Lilja, S. (1969) 'On the Nature of Pliny's Letters', *Arctos* 6, 61–79.

Löhr, W. (2016) 'Augustine's Correspondence with Pascentius (*Epp.* 238–241) – An Epistolary Power Game?', *RÉAug* 62, 183–222.

Loyen, A. (1943) *Sidoine Apollinaire et l'esprit précieux en Gaule aux derniers jours de l'Empire*, Paris.

— (ed.) (1960) *Sidoine Apollinaire*, vol. I, *Poèmes*, Paris.

— (1963) 'Résistants et collaborateurs en Gaule à l'époque des Grandes Invasions', *BAGB* 22, 437–50.

— (ed.) (1970a) *Sidoine Apollinaire*, vol. II, *Lettres 1–5*, Paris.

— (ed.) (1970b) *Sidoine Apollinaire*, vol. III, *Lettres 6–9*, Paris.

BIBLIOGRAPHY

Luiselli, B. (1992) *Storia culturale dei rapporti tra mondo romano e mondo germanico*, Rome.

Luiselli Fadda, A. M. (1988–1989) 'Cithara barbarica, cythara teutonica, cythara anglica', in A. M. D'Aronco et al., *Studi sulla cultura germanica dei secoli IV–XII in onore di Giulia Mazzuoli Porru*, *RomBarb* 10, Rome, 217–39.

Lütjohann, C. (ed.) (1887) *Gai Sollii Apollinaris Sidonii epistulae et carmina*, MGH AA 8, Berlin.

Malherbe, A. J. (1988) *Ancient Epistolary Theorists*, Atlanta.

Malosse, P.-L. (2004) *Lettres pour toutes circonstances. Les traités épistolaires du Pseudo-Libanios et du Pseudo-Démétrios de Phalère*, Paris.

Manfredi, A. (1994) *I codici latini di Niccolò V*, edizione degli inventari e identificazione dei manoscritti, Vatican City.

Manthe, U. (2002) '*Agnatio*', in H. Cancik, H. Schneider, and M. Landfester, *Der Neue Pauly*, Leiden.

Marasco, G. (1993) 'Costantino e le uccisioni di Crispo e Fausta (326 d.C.)', *RFIC* 121, 297–317.

Marchesi, I. (2008) *The Art of Pliny's Letters: A Poetics of Allusion in the Private Correspondence*, Cambridge.

Marcone, A. (1983) *Commento storico al libro VI dell' Epistolario di Q. Aurelio Simmaco*, Pisa.

— (1987) *Commento storico al libro IV dell' Epistolario di Q. Aurelio Simmaco*, Pisa.

— (1988) 'Due epistolari a confronto: *corpus* pliniano e *corpus* simmachiano', in L. Boffo et al., *Studi di storia e storiografia antiche per Emilio Gabba*, Como, 143–54.

Mari, T. (ed.) (2021) *Consentius'* De barbarismis et metaplasmis, *Critical Edition, Translation, and Commentary*, Oxford.

Marolla, G. (2017) 'Presenza di classici in Girolamo, *epist.* 123 a Geruchia', *VetChr* 57, 127–41.

— (2019) 'Jerome's Two Libraries', in R. Berardi, N. Bruno and L. Fizzarotti (eds), *On the Track of the Books: Scribes, Libraries and Textual Transmission*, Berlin, 91–104.

— (2021a) 'Il trasformismo dell'aristocrazia gallica nelle epistole di Sidonio Apollinare', *eClassica* 6, 59–71.

— (2021b) 'Sidonio Apollinare e il concetto di satira nella tarda antichità', *InvLuc* 43, 129–44.

— (forthcoming a) 'Who Was Sidonius' Correspondent Simplicius? An Identification Problem in the *Letters*', *CQ*.

— (forthcoming b) 'The Names of Sidonius' Addressees and the Manuscript Tradition of the Letters', *Mnemosyne*.

Mascoli, P. (2004) 'Per una ricostruzione del *Fortleben* di Sidonio Apollinare', *InvLuc* 26, 165–83.

— (2010) *Gli Apollinari. Per la storia di una famiglia tardoantica*, Quaderni di *InvLuc* 39, Bari.

— (2015) 'Come estorcere un elogio: una schermaglia epistolare tra Claudiano Mamerto e Sidonio Apollinare', *VetChr* 52, 231–40.

Mathisen, R. W. (1982) 'PLRE II: Suggested *Addenda* and *Corrigenda*', *Historia* 31.3, 364–86.

— (1988) 'The Theme of Literary Decline in Late Roman Gaul', *CPh* 83, 45–52.

— (1993) *Roman Aristocrats in Barbarian Gaul: Strategies for Survival in an Age of Transition*, Austin.

— (1999) *Ruricius of Limoges and Friends. A Collection of Letters from Visigothic Gaul*, Liverpool.

— (2005) 'Bishops, Barbarians, and the "Dark Ages": The Fate of Late Roman Educational Institutions in Late Antique Gaul', in R. Begley and J. Koterski (eds), *Medieval Education*, New York, 3–17.

— (2013a) 'Dating the Letters of Sidonius', in J. A. van Waarden and G. Kelly, *New Approaches to Sidonius Apollinaris*, Leuven, 221–48.

BIBLIOGRAPHY

— (2013b) 'The Council of Turin (398/399) and the Reorganization of Gaul ca. 395/406', *JLA* 6, 264–307.

— (2014) 'La création et l'utilisation de "dossiers" dans les lettres de Sidoine Apollinaire', in R. Poignault and A. Stoehr-Monjou (eds), *Présence de Sidoine Apollinaire*, Clermont-Ferrand, 205–14.

— (2020) 'Sidonius' People', in G. Kelly and J. van Waarden (eds), *The Edinburgh Companion to Sidonius Apollinaris*, Edinburgh, 29–165 [chapter includes 'A Prosopography of Sidonius: Persons Mentioned in the Works of Sidonius (Fourth and Fifth Centuries)', 76–154].

Mayer, R. (ed.) (2001) *Tacitus:* Dialogus de oratoribus, Cambridge.

Mazzoli, G. (2005–2006) 'Sidonio, Orazio e la *lex saturae*', *Incontri triestini di filologia classica* 5, 171–84.

McGeachy, J. A. (1942) *Quintus Aurelius Symmachus and the Senatorial Aristocracy of the West*, Chicago.

McKeown, J. C. (ed.) (1998) *Ovid:* Amores, text, prolegomena and commentary in four volumes, vol. III, *A Commentary on Book Two*, Leeds.

Ménage, G. (1750) *Dictionnaire etymologique de la langue françoise*, nouvelle édition par A.-F. Jault, Paris.

Mendelsohn, C. J. (1907) *Studies in the Word-Play in Plautus*, Philadelphia.

Mercier, C. and Mercier-Rolland, M. (1974) *Le cimitière burgonde de Monnet-la-Ville*, Paris.

Meynis, D. (1872) *Les anciennes églises paroissiales de Lyon*, Lyon.

Micaelli, C. (2014) 'Osservazioni sul *De statu animae* di Claudiano Mamerto', in R. Palla et al. (eds), Clavigero Nostro. *Per Antonio V. Nazzaro*, Pisa, 181–206.

Migne, J.-P. (ed.) (1855) *Ioannis Saresberiensis, Polycraticus* (*PL* 199), Paris, 385–822.

Millar, F. (1967) 'Emperors at Work', *JRS* 57, 9–19.

Mitchell, T. N. (1986) *Cicero:* Verrines II.1, with a translation and commentary, Warminster.

Mohr, P. (ed.) (1895) *Caius Sollius Apollinaris Sidonius*, Leipzig.

Molinier-Arbo, A. (2010) 'Les documents d'archives dans la *Vita Commodi*: degré zéro de l'histoire ou fiction?', *DHA* suppl. 4.1, 87–112.

Mommsen, T. (1965) *Gesammelte Schriften von Theodor Mommsen*, vol. I, Berlin.

Mondin, L. (ed.) (1995) *Decimo Magno Ausonio, Epistole*, introduzione, testo critico e commento, Venice.

Montzamir, P. (2017) 'Du nouveau sur l'épitaphe attribuée à Sidoine Apollinaire', XXXIXe réunion Association pour l'Antiquité Tardive, Jun 2017, Clermont-Ferrand, France. Archive ouverte en Sciences de l'Homme et de la Société (<https://halshs.archives-ouvertes.fr/halshs-02275957/document>).

Moodie, E. K. (2015) *Plautus'* Poenulus: *A Student Commentary*, Ann Arbor.

Morton Braund, S. (ed.) (1996) *Juvenal: Satires Book I*, Cambridge.

Mratschek, S. (2013) 'Creating Identity from the Past: The Construction of History in the Letters of Sidonius', in J. van Waarden and G. Kelly (eds), *New Approaches to Sidonius Apollinaris*, Leuven, 249–71.

— (2017) 'The Letter Collection of Sidonius Apollinaris', in C. Sogno et al., *Late Antique Letter Collections: A Critical Introduction and Reference Guide*, Oakland, 309–36.

— (2020) 'The Silence of the Muses in Sidonius Apollinaris (*Carm.* 12–13, *Ep.* 8.11): Aphasia and the Timelessness of Poetic Inspiration', *JLA* 13, 10–43.

Nisbet, R. G. M. (ed.) (1961) *M. Tulli Ciceronis in L. Calpurnium Pisonem Oratio*, Oxford.

Norton, P. (2007) *Episcopal Elections 250–600: Hierarchy and Popular Will in Late Antiquity*, Oxford.

Oberhelman, S. M. (1988a) 'The *Cursus* in Late Imperial Latin Prose: A Reconsideration of Methodology', *CPh* 83.2, 136–49.

BIBLIOGRAPHY

— (1988b) 'The History and Development of the *Cursus Mixtus* in Latin Literature', *CQ* 38, 228–42.

— and Hall, R. G. (1984) 'A New Statistical Analysis of Accentual Prose Rhythms in Imperial Latin Authors', *CPh* 79.2, 114–30.

Ogilvie, R. M. (1965) *A Commentary on Livy, Books 1–5*, Oxford.

Oldoni, M. (ed.) (1981) *Gregorio di Tours: La storia dei Franchi*, vol. I, Milan.

Olson, S. D. (ed.) (1998) *Aristophanes: Peace*, edited with introduction and commentary, Oxford.

Onorato, M. (2016) *Il castone e la gemma. Sulla tecnica poetica di Sidonio Apollinare*, Naples.

— (2018) 'Un ospite per Apollo: intertestualità interna e codice ausoniano nella metatoria pagina di Sidonio a Lampridio', *BStudLat* 48, 492–523.

— (2020) 'The Poet and the Light: Modulation and Transposition of a Prudentian *Ekphrasis* in Two Poems by Sidonius Apollinaris', in F. Hadjittofi and A. Lefteratou (eds), *The Genres of Late Antique Christian Poetry: Between Modulations and Transpositions*, Berlin, 75–92.

Oost, S. I. (1958) 'The Career of M. Antonius Pallas', *AJPh* 79.2, 113–39.

Palanque, J.-R. (1934) 'La date du transfert de la préfecture des Gaules de Trêves à Arles', *RÉA* 36, 359–65.

— (1973) 'Du nouveau sur la date du transfert de la préfecture des Gaules de Trêves à Arles', *Provence historique* 23, 29–38.

Paschoud, F. (ed.) (1989) *Zosime, Histoire Nouvelle: Livre VI et index* (t. III, 2ᵉ partie), texte établi et traduit, Paris.

— (1999) 'Propos sceptiques et iconoclastes sur Marius Maximus', Historiae Augustae Colloquium Genevense, *Atti dei Convegni sulla Historia Augusta*, Bari, 241–54.

Pellizzari, A. (1998) *Commento storico al libro III dell'Epistolario di Q. Aurelio Simmaco*, Pisa.

Pelttari, A. (2016) 'Sidonius Apollinaris and Horace, *Ars poetica* 14–23', *Philologus* 160.2, 322–36.

— (2017) '*Lector inueniet*: A Commonplace of Late Antiquity', in M. Vinzent (ed.), Studia Patristica XCII, *Papers Presented at the Seventeenth International Conference on Patristic Studies Held in Oxford 2015*, vol. XVIII, Leuven, 215–25.

— (2020) 'The Rhetor Sapaudus and Conflicting Literary Models in Sidonius Apollinaris and Claudianus Mamertus', in A. Di Stefano and M. Onorato (eds), *Lo specchio del modello. Orizzonti intertestuali e Fortleben di Sidonio Apollinare*, Naples, 191–210.

Perutelli, A. (2006) *Ulisse nella cultura romana*, Florence.

Pétré, H. (1948) Caritas. *Étude sur le vocabulaire latin de la charité chrétienne*, Leuven.

Pithou, P. (ed.) (1590) *Epigrammata et poematia vetera*, Paris.

Polara, G. (ed.) (2004) *Optaziano Porfirio: Carmi*, editio altera et augmentata (previous edition 1973), Turin.

Poma, G. (1984) *Tra legislatori e tiranni. Problemi storici e storiografici sull'età delle XII Tavole*, Bologna.

Porena, P. (2007) '"À l'ombre de la pourpre": l'évolution de la préfecture du prétoire entre le IIIᵉ et le IVᵉ siècle', *CCG* 18, 237–62.

— (2014) 'Ancora sulla carriera di Flavius Ablabius, prefetto del pretorio di Costantino', *ZPE* 190, 262–70.

— (2019) '"Rebus Prosopografico": considerazioni sui due Syagri consoli ordinari nel 381 e nel 382', *ZPE* 211, 279–92.

Powell, J. G. F. (ed.) (1988) *Cicero:* Cato maior de senectute, edited with introduction and commentary, Cambridge.

— (2007) 'Invective and the Orator: Ciceronian Theory and Practice', in J. Booth (ed.), *Cicero on the Attack: Invective and Subversion in the Orations and Beyond*, Swansea, 1–23.

BIBLIOGRAPHY

Préchac, F. and Noblot, H. (ed.) (1985) *Sénèque, Lettres à Lucilius*, tome I, *Livres 1–4*, texte établi par F. Préchac, traduit par H. Noblot, 7 ed. rev. et corr. par A. Novara, Paris.

Prévot, F. (1993) 'Deux fragments de l'épitaphe de Sidoine Apollinaire découverts à Clermont-Ferrand', *AnTard* 1, 223–9.

— (1997) 'Sidoine Apollinaire pasteur d'âmes', *AnTard* 5, 223–30.

Pricoco, S. (1965a) 'Sidonio Apollinare tra Claudiano Mamerto e Fausto di Riez e la datazione del "De spiritu sancto"', *Studi su Sidonio Apollinare, Nuovo Didaskaleion* 15, 115–40.

— (1965b) 'Sidonio Apollinare traduttore della *Vita di Apollonio di Tiana*', *Studi su Sidonio Apollinare, Nuovo Didaskaleion* 15, 71–98.

Prost, F. (ed.) (2017) *Quintus Cicéron: Petit manuel de la campagne électorale. Marcus Cicéron: Lettres à son frère Quintus I, 1 et 2.* Texte latin révisé, traduit et commenté, Paris.

Rees, R. (2007) 'Letters of Recommendation and the Rhetoric of Praise', in R. Morello and A. D. Morrison (eds), *Ancient Letters: Classical and Late Antique Epistolography*, Oxford, 149–68.

Reydellet, M. (1981) *La royauté dans la littérature latine de Sidoine Apollinaire à Isidore de Séville*, Rome.

Reynolds, L. D. and Wilson, N. G. (2013) *Scribes and Scholars: A Guide to the Transmission of Greek and Latin Literature*, Oxford (1st edition, 1968).

Ricci, M. L. (ed.) (2001) *Claudiano:* Carmina minora, Bari.

Riese, A. (ed.) (1869) *Anthologia Latina, pars I, Carmina in codicibus scripta, fasc. 1, Libri Salmasiani aliorumque carmina*, Leipzig.

Ritschl, F. (1877) *De M. Terentii Varronis disciplinarum libris commentarius* (Bonn, 1845 = *Opuscula Philologica* III), Leipzig.

Rivière, Y. (2002) *Les délateurs sous l'Empire romain*, Rome.

Roberts, M. (1989) *The Jeweled Style: Poetry and Poetics in Late Antiquity*, Ithaca.

Roda, S. (1981) *Commento storico a libro IX dell'Epistolario di Q. Aurelio Simmaco*, Pisa.

— (1996) 'Polifunzionalità della lettera *commendaticia*: teoria e prassi nell'epistolario simmachiano', in S. Roda (ed.), *La parte migliore del genere umano. Aristocrazie, potere e ideologia nell'Occidente tardoantico. Antologia di storia tardoantica. I florilegi (2)*, Turin, 225–54.

Rose, P. J. (2013) *A Commentary on Augustine's* De cura pro mortuis gerenda: *Rhetoric in Practice*, Leiden.

Rudd, N. (ed.) (1989) *Horace: Epistles Book II and Epistle to the Pisones* ('Ars Poetica'), Cambridge.

Rutledge, S. H. (2001) *Imperial Inquisitions: Prosecutors and Informants from Tiberius to Domitian*, London.

Saitta, B. (2006) *I Burgundi (413–534)*, Rome.

Saller, R. P. (1994) *Patriarchy, Property and Death in the Roman Family*, Cambridge.

Salzman, M. R. and Roberts, M. (2011) *The Letters of Symmachus: Book 1*, translation, general introduction and commentary, Atlanta.

Santelia, S. (2000) 'Sidonio Apollinare e i *bybliopolae*', *InvLuc* 22, 217–39.

— (2002a) *Sidonio Apollinare: Carme 24.* Propempticon ad Libellum, introduzione traduzione e commento, Bari.

— (2002b) 'Quando il poeta parla ai suoi versi: i carmi 8 e 3 di Sidonio Apollinare', *InvLuc* 24, 245–60.

— (2003–2005) 'Storie di libri nella Gallia del V secolo: testimonianze a confronto', *RomBarb* 18, 1–29.

— (2005) *Per amare Eucheria*, Anth. Lat. *386 Shackleton Bailey*, Bari.

— (2007) 'Sidonio Apollinare autore di una epigrafe per la *ecclesia* di Lione: Epist. 2, 10, 4 (Le Blant *ICG* 54)', *VetChr* 44, 305–21.

BIBLIOGRAPHY

— (2012) *Carme 16*: Eucharisticon ad Faustum episcopum, introduzione traduzione e commento, Bari.

— (2016) 'Sidonio Apollinare, *carm*. 23.101–66: una "proposta paideutica"?', *Lexis* 34, 425–44.

— (2019) 'Talia e i Burgundi. Rifrazioni classiche e meccanismi di intertestualità in Sidonio Apollinare, *Carmina*, 12', in O. Cirillo and M. Lentano (eds), *L'esegeta appassionato. Studi in onore di Crescenzo Formicola*, Sesto San Giovanni, 285–307.

— (2021) 'Sidonio Apollinare, carme 9: un *griphus* per il *lector*?', in M. Manca and M. Venuti (eds), Paulo maiora canamus: *Raccolta di studi per Paolo Mastandrea*, Venice, 255–66.

— (forthcoming) *Sidonio Apollinare*, Carmina minora, testo, traduzione e note, con una prefazione di S. Condorelli, Naples.

Santini, C. (2005) '*Tanaquil vel Fortuna*. Una figura femminile nel percorso tra mito, testo e icona', *GIF* 57.2, 189–210.

Savaron, J. (ed.) (1599) *Caii Sollii Apollinaris Sidonii Arvernorum episcopi opera Io. Savaronis multo quam antea castigatius recognovit et librum commentarium adiecit*, Paris.

— (ed.) (1609) *Caii Sollii Apollinaris Sidonii Arvernorum episcopi opera Io. Savaronis II. Editio multis partibus auctior & emendatior; accesserunt indices locupletissimi*, Paris.

Scarpa, L. (ed.) (1988) *Martiani Capellae De nuptiis Philologiae et Mercurii liber VII (Arithmetica)*, introduzione, traduzione e commento, Padova.

Schetter, W. (1964) 'Der gallische Dichter Secundinus', *Philologus* 108, 153–6.

Schievenin, R. (1998) 'Varrone e Marziano Capella', *BStudLat* 28.2, 478–93.

Schiller, H. (1887) *Geschichte der römischen Kaiserzeit*, Gotha.

Schwitter, R. (2015) Umbrosa lux: Obscuritas *in der lateinischen Epistolographie der Spätantike*, Stuttgart.

Scoditti, F. (2009) *Solisti ed esecutori nella cultura musicale romana*, Galatina.

Seeck, O. (1893) 'Ablabius', *RE* 1, 103–4.

— (1897) *Geschichte des Untergangs der antiken Welt*, Berlin.

— (1901) 'Crispus 9', *RE* 4, 1722–4.

— (1909) 'Fausta 3', *RE* 6, 2084–6.

Semple, W. H. (1930) Quaestiones Exegeticae Sidonianae: *Being New Interpretations of Difficult Passages in the Works of Apollinaris Sidonius*, Cambridge.

Shackleton Bailey, D. R. (ed.) (1968) *Cicero's Letters to Atticus 3 and 4*, Cambridge.

— (ed.) (1977) *Cicero*: Epistulae ad Familiares, vol. I, *62–47 B.C.*, Cambridge.

— (ed.) (1980) *Cicero*: Epistulae ad Quintum fratrem et M. Brutum, Cambridge.

— (ed.) (1982) *Anthologia Latina, pars I, Carmina in codicibus scripta, fasc. 1, Libri Salmasiani aliorumque carmina*, Stuttgart.

Shanzer, D. and Wood, I. (2002) *Avitus of Vienne: Letters and Selected Prose*, translated with an introduction and notes, Liverpool.

Sherwin-White, A. N. (1966) *The Letters of Pliny: A Historical and Social Commentary*, Oxford.

Sirmond, J. (ed.) (1614) *C. Sollii Sidonii Arvernorum episcopi opera, Iac. Sirmondi Soc. Iesu presb. cura et studio recognita, notisque illustrata*, Paris.

— (ed.) (1652) *C. Sollii Apollinaris Sidonii Arvernorum episcopi opera, Iac. Sirmondi Soc. Iesu presb. cura et studio recognita, notisque illustrata. Editio secunda, ad eiusdem autographum praelo iampridem paratum diligenter exacta*, Paris.

Smolak, K. (2008) 'Wer sind denn die schon? Barbaren in satirischer Kleindichtung der lateinischen Spätantike (zu Sulpicius Lupercus und Sidonius Apollinaris)', in T. Haye and F. Schnoor (eds), *Epochen der Satire: Traditionslinien einer literarischen Gattung in Antike, Mittelalter und Renaissance*, Hildesheim, 34–54.

— (2011) 'De patronis septipedibus Sidonii Apollinaris', in J.-W. Beck (ed.), *Ad fines imperii Romani anno bismillesimo cladis Varianae*, Leuven, 235–44.

BIBLIOGRAPHY

Sogno, C. (2006) *Q. Aurelius Symmachus: A Political Biography*, Ann Arbor.

— (2017) 'The Letter Collection of Quintus Aurelius Symmachus', in C. Sogno, B. K. Storin, and E. J. Watts (eds), *Late Antique Letter Collections: A Critical Introduction and Reference Guide*, Oakland, 175–89.

Soldevilla, R. M., Castillo A. M., and Valverde, J. F. (2019) *A Prosopography to Martial's Epigrams*, Berlin.

Solignac, A. (1958) 'Doxographies et manuels dans la formation philosophique de saint Augustin', *RecAug* 1, 113–48.

Squillante, M. (2009) 'La biblioteca di Sidonio Apollinare', *Voces* 20, 139–59.

Stein, E. (1995) *Leben und Visionen der Alpais von Cudot (1150–1211)*, Tübingen.

Stevens, C. E. (1933) *Sidonius Apollinaris and His Age*, Oxford.

Stoehr-Monjou, A. (2012) 'Sidoine Apollinaire, *ep.* 5, 8: Constantin le Grand, nouveau Néron', in F. Guillaumont and P. Laurence (eds), *La Présence de l'histoire dans l'épistolaire*, Tours, 239–60.

— (2013) 'Sidonius and Horace: The Art of Memory', in J. van Waarden and G. Kelly (eds), *New Approaches to Sidonius Apollinaris*, Leuven, 133–69.

Stramaglia, A. (2017) *Giovenale, Satire 1, 7, 12, 16. Storia di un poeta*, ristampa corretta della prima edizione del 2008, Bologna.

Stroheker, K. F. (1948) *Der senatorische Adel im spätantiken Gallien*, Tübingen.

Süss, W. (1910) Ethos. *Studien zur älteren griechischen Rhetorik*, Leipzig.

Swift, L. J. (1968) 'Lactantius and the Golden Age', *AJPh* 89.2, 144–56.

Talbert, R. J. A., Bagnall, R. S., et al. (eds) (2000) *Barrington Atlas of the Greek and Roman World*, Princeton.

Tarrant, R. J. (ed.) (2004) *P. Ovidi Nasonis Metamorphoses*, Oxford.

Tatu, L. S. (1887) *Saint Patient, évêque de Lyon, et l'église de Lyon à la fin de la domination romaine dans la province lyonnaise: thèse pour le doctorat*, Lyon.

Teitler, H. C. (1983) Notarii *and* Exceptores*: An Inquiry into Role and Significance of* Notarii *and* Exceptores *in the Imperial and Ecclesiastical Bureaucracy of the Roman Empire (from the Early Principate to circa 450 A.D.)*, Utrecht.

Teske, R. J. (2005) *A Translation for the 21st Century: The Works of Saint Augustine Letters 211–270, 1*–29* (Epistulae 2/4)*, New York.

Thomas, R. F. (ed.) (2011) *Horace: Odes Book IV and Carmen Saeculare*, Cambridge.

Tobler, A. and Lommatzsch, E. (1955) *Altfranzösisches Wörterbuch*, vol. I, Wiesbaden.

Tosi, R. (2018) *Dizionario delle sentenze latine e greche*, terza edizione aggiornata, Milan.

Trapp, M. (2003) *Greek and Latin Letters: An Anthology, with Translation*, Cambridge.

Trisciuoglio, A. (2017) *Studi sul* crimen ambitus *in età imperiale*, Milan.

Trout, D. E. (1999) *Paulinus of Nola: Life, Letters, and Poems*, Berkeley.

Tschernjak, A. (2003) 'Sidonius Apollinaris und die Burgunden', *Hyperboreus* 9, 158–68.

Van Groningen, B. A. (1963) 'ΕΚΔΟΣΙΣ', *Mnemosyne* 16, 1–17.

Van Hoof, L. and Van Nuffelen, P. (eds) (2020) *The Fragmentary Latin Histories of Late Antiquity (AD 300–620)*, edition, translation and commentary, Cambridge.

van Waarden, J. A. (2010) *Writing to Survive: A Commentary on Sidonius Apollinaris, Letters Book 7*, vol. I, *The Episcopal Letters 1–11*, Leuven.

— (2011) 'Sidonio Apollinare poeta e vescovo', *VetChr* 48, 99–113.

— (2013) 'Sidonius in the 21st Century', in J. van Waarden and G. Kelly (eds), *New Approaches to Sidonius Apollinaris*, Leuven, 3–19.

— (2016) *Writing to Survive: A Commentary on Sidonius Apollinaris, Letters Book 7*, vol. II, *The Ascetic Letters 12–18*, Leuven.

— (2018) '"Il tempo invecchia in fretta": la biografia di Sidonio Apollinare nella sua corrispondenza', *InvLuc* 40, 187–98.

BIBLIOGRAPHY

— (2020a) 'Sidonius' Biography in Photo Negative', in G. Kelly and J. van Waarden (eds), *The Edinburgh Companion to Sidonius Apollinaris*, Edinburgh, 13–28.

— (2020b) '"You" and "I" in Sidonius' Correspondence', in G. Kelly and J. van Waarden (eds), *The Edinburgh Companion to Sidonius Apollinaris*, Edinburgh, 418–39.

— and Kelly, G. (2020) 'Prose Rhythm in Sidonius', in G. Kelly and J. van Waarden (eds), *The Edinburgh Companion to Sidonius Apollinaris*, Edinburgh, 462–75.

Vera, D. (1981) *Commento storico alle* Relationes *di Quinto Aurelio Simmaco*, Pisa.

Vessey, M. (2019) 'Sidonius Apollinaris Writes Himself Out: Aut(hol)ograph and Architext in Late Roman Codex Society', in H. Heil (ed.), *Das Christentum im frühen Europa*, Berlin, 117–54.

Vignier, N. (1575) *Rerum Burgundionum Chronicon*, Basilea.

von der Woweren, J. (ed.) (1598) *C. Sollii Sidonii Apollinaris Arvernorum episcopi opera, ex veteribus libris aucta et emendata, notisque Petri Colvii Burgensis illustrata*, Lyon.

von Hartel, W. (ed.) (1999) *Paulini Nolani Opera, pars II, Carmina* (CSEL 30), editio altera supplementis aucta curante M. Kamptner, Vienna.

Walsh, P. G. (2006) *Pliny the Younger: Complete Letters*, a new translation, Oxford.

Whatmough, J. (1970) *The Dialects of Ancient Gaul: Prolegomena and Records of the Dialects*, Cambridge, MA.

Whitton C. (2013) *Pliny the Younger, Epistles Book II*, Cambridge.

Wolff, É. (ed.) (2007) *Rutilius Namatianus: Sur son retour*, nouvelle édition avec la collaboration de S. Lancel pour la traduction et de J. Soler pour l'introduction, Paris.

— (2018) 'Qui était André Loyen, l'éditeur français de Sidoine Apollinaire?', *InvLuc* 40, 211–16.

— (2020) 'Sidonius' Vocabulary, Syntax, and Style', in G. Kelly and J. van Waarden (eds), *The Edinburgh Companion to Sidonius Apollinaris*, Edinburgh, 395–417.

Wood, I. (1990) 'Ethnicity and the Ethnogenesis of the Burgundians', in H. Wolfram and W. Pohl (eds), *Typen der Ethnogenese unter besonderer Berücksichtigung der Bayern*, vol. I, Vienna, 53–69.

— (2016) 'The Legislation of *Magistri Militum*: The Laws of Gundobad and Sigismund', *Clio@Themis* 10, 1–16.

Woods, D. (1998) 'On the Death of the Empress Fausta', *G&R* 45, 70–86.

Wright, W. C. (ed.) (1921) *Philostratus: Lives of the Sophists. Eunapius: Lives of the Philosophers*, Cambridge, MA.

Zecchini, G. (2017) 'Costantino e la morte di Crispo', in V. Neri and B. Girotti (eds), *La storiografia tardoantica. Bilanci e prospettive*, Milan, 127–38.

Index Locorum

Note: 'n.' indicates note

AELIANUS
Varia historia
13.9, 230

ALCAEUS
fr. 374 Voigt, 137

AMBROSE
De excessu fratris Satyri
2.118, 310
De fide
2.2, 233
De institutione uirginis
1.7, 320
De obitu Theodosii
15, 292
De obitu Valentiniani
69, 282
De officiis ministrorum
1.1.4, 104, 118
3.11.70, 62
De paenitentia
2.67, 104, n. 36, 118
Epistulae
2.7.17, 216
7.36.7, 112
7.36.23, 309
Epistulae extra collectionem
3.2, 136
Expositio euangelii sec. Lucam (In Luc.)
7.194, 117
In psalmum 118 sermo
2.26.2, 310
14.41.3, 289
22.2, 307

AMMIANUS MARCELLINUS
Res gestae
14.6.18, 67
14.11.20, 267
15.3.3–11, 239
15.3.3, 240
15.3.4, 240
15.3.5, 240
15.3.9, 240
18.1.4, 314

18.6.2, 230
19.9.2, 222
21.6.4, 310
26.2.2, 310
28.1.5, 222
28.1.15, 222
28.1.23, 172 n. 19, 187
29.2.13, 226
29.2.16, 311
29.3.8, 210
31.2.2, 166
31.12.8, 134

ANTHOLOGIA LATINA
6 SB =19 R, 79 n. 51
387 SB = 391 R, 250

ANTHOLOGIA PALATINA
5.258, 10 n. 40
10.100, 10 n. 40

APOLLONIUS OF RHODES
Argonautica
2.187–93, 228

APONIUS
In canticum canticorum commentarius
8.8, 138
8.17, 138

APULEIUS
Apologia
5.2, 306
74, 185
74.5–6, 191
74.5–7, 211
78.6, 222
94.6, 262
95.5, 160, 298 n. 14
De deo Socratis
3, 316
5, 230
Metamorphoses
1.11, 137
1.14, 137
1.24, 258

INDEX LOCORUM

3.15, 137
4.18, 137
5.16, 287
9.20, 138

ARISTOPHANES
Pax
1189–90, 230

ARNOBIUS
Aduersus nationes
5.1, 181
7.7, 141
7.27, 141

ARNOBIUS JUNIOR
Liber ad Gregoriam in palatio constitutam
7, 311
16, 182
Praedestinatus
1.16, 263
3.13, 183
3.26, 183

ARRIAN
Epicteti dissertationes
4.5.37, 230

AUGUSTINE
Collatio cum Maximino
7, 213
Confessiones
1.14, 160
5.13, 224
12.31, 306
13.23, 141
Contra Faustum Manichaeum
2.2, 157
9.2, 141
Contra Iulianum
2.3.6, 183
2.8.25, 183
4.2, 135
4.90.21–2, 85
Contra Iulianum opus imperfectum
1.137, 262
2.108, 157
2.187, 287
De ciuitate Dei
3.2, 232
5.25, 183
6.2, 71, 84
8.3, 84
16.8, 231
16.12, 310
18.13, 231
De consensu euangelistarum
2.43.91, 198 n. 39

De cura pro mortuis gerenda
3.5, 90
6.8, 183
De doctrina christiana
2.48, 85
3.109, 85
4.3.4, 263
De genesi ad litteram
11.22, 233
De libero arbitrio
2.11, 222
De quantitate animae
28.55, 233
De trinitate
14.7, 86
Enarrationes in Psalmos
38.9, 311
50.24, 111
71.5, 211
76.6, 112
146.11, 222
Epistulae
1*–29*, 7 n. 29
31.2, 221
71.1, 134–5
82, 135
95.9, 213
131, 136
179.1, 56
180.5, 119
187, 286
192.1, 136
217.1, 56
238.1, 91
269, 136
In euangelium Iohannis
108.1, 157
Sermones
20, 112
89.1, 104, 119
138.4, 233
139.2, 62

AUSONIUS
Caesares
1–93, 234
4–5, 234
15–16, 234
Commemoratio professorum Burdigalensium
2.21–4, 315
4.19, 261
5.5–12, 314
5.13–18, 314
5.33, 314
14, 314
15.2, 261
16, 315
16.16, 316

343

INDEX LOCORUM

De herediolo
14, 235
Eclogae
19.43, 294
Ephemeris
1.2, 85
Epistulae
11.5, 261
22.30–1, 180, 237
Mosella
389, 111
Parentalia
praef., 259
3, 315
3.2, 316
Praefationes uariae
2.1–2, 156

AVIANUS
Fabulae
40.11–12, 310

AVITUS OF VIENNE
Epistulae
43, 79 n. 51
86, 295

CAESAR
De bello ciuili
3.3.2, 209

CASSIAN, JOHN
Conlationes
3.19.16, 58
De institutis coenobiorum
4.33, 117

CATO
De agri cultura
144.4, 283
Hist. = *Origines*
81, 110

CATULLUS
Carmina
85, 96 n. 11

CICERO
Brutus
121, 56
Cato maior de senectute
19 (71), 10 n. 40
20 (76), 287
De amicitia
50, 284
92, 292
De domo sua
60, 209

De finibus bonorum et malorum
2.83, 115
De inuentione
1.19.27, 135
De lege agraria
2.12, 139
De natura deorum
2.151, 210
2.158, 210
De officiis
3.93, 62
De oratore
1.5.17, 76
1.6.20, 76
2.94, 317
2.236–7, 189
De re publica
5.3, 164
Epistulae ad Atticum
2.9.1, 209
6.2.2, 186
6.2.3, 186
6.4.1, 182
8.16.1, 260
9.10.10, 134
9.11A.3, 59
12.18.1, 56
15.1A.2, 66
Epistulae ad familiares
8.11.2, 139
9.8.1, 306
13.62.1, 282
15.14.1, 282
15.21.4, 66
16.14.1, 102 n. 29, 120
Epistulae ad Quintum fratrem
1.1, 142, 142 n. 1
2.3.7, 96 n. 13
2.10 (9), 66
2.13.2, 186
In Pisonem
fr. IX N, 189
6.13, 189
In Vatinium
12.30, 189 n. 10, 225
In Verrem
2.1.141, 216
2.2.97, 140
2.2.135, 208, 221
2.4.30, 239
2.4.31, 211, 239
2.4.33, 239
2.4.47, 239
2.5.1, 229
2.5.4, 229
2.5.107, 184
2.5.145, 235

344

INDEX LOCORUM

2.5.146, 157
2.5.149–50, 227
Philippicae
2.80, 260
11.31, 209
Pro Caecina
7, 319
Pro Caelio
37, 140
63, 213
Pro Cluentio
16 (46), 284
36 (102), 215
Pro Fonteio
42, 230
Pro Murena
9.21, 91
Pro S. Roscio Amerino
115, 319
Tusculanae disputationes
3.34.82, 265

CLAUDIAN
Carmina
5.78–84, 225
8.466, 225
26.481–2, 225
Carmina minora
10, 226–7
10.3–4, 226
30.15–16, 237
41.1, 121
41.8, 121
In Rufinum
1.248–9, 157

CLAUDIANUS, MAMERTUS
De statu animae
praef. p. 18, 77 n. 45, 79 n. 52
praef. p. 19, 74, 77 n. 45
praef. p. 20, 57, 74, 77, 77 n. 45, 79, 136, 258
1.1, p. 24, 57, 89
1.3, p. 35, 115
1.12–13, 75
1.15, pp. 59–60, 75, 75 n. 39
1.17–18, 74 n. 37
1.22, p. 81, 76
1.25, p. 88, 75
2.3, p. 104, 283
2.3, p. 108, 75 n. 40, 76, 89
2.7, pp.120–8, 76
2.7, p. 127, 73 n. 35,
2.8, p. 130, 71, 73 n. 34, 84
2.12, p. 149, 76
3.3, p. 158, 89
3.11, p. 173, 85

3.12, p. 176, 137
3.15, p. 184, 60, 75
3.17, p. 188, 88
3.18, p. 189, 58
epilog., p. 191, 78
Epistulae
2, 17, 30, 295, 297, 301–2, 307, 316
2, p. 204, 72, 163, 299, 319–20
2, p. 205, 295 n. 2, 298, 307–8, 313, 315, 320
2, p. 206, 72 n. 33, 298, 313–14

CODEX EURICIANUS
282, 148 n. 31
289, 148 n. 31

CODEX THEODOSIANUS
4.13.1, 223
6.10.3, 222
9.34.1–10, 251
9.34.9, 251 n. 47
9.34.10, 251 n. 48
10.17.3, 117
11.1.34, 223
13.11.4, 117
16.5.30.2, 227

COLUMELLA
De re rustica
7.9.10, 85
8.2.11, 85

CONSENTIUS
De barbarismis et metaplasmis
1.10–20, 151
2.1–10, 151
17.21–18.7, 151

CORNELIUS NEPOS *see* NEPOS, CORNELIUS

CORPUS INSCRIPTIONUM LATINARUM (CIL)
VI 1112, 183
VI 1145, 183
VI 1718, 183
VIII 2241, 183
VIII 7008, 183
VIII 7010, 183
VIII 10205, 183
VIII 10516, 222
VIII 11528, 222
X 7204, 183
XI 3878, 183
XII 1524, 286
XIII 2372 (= *CLE* 1365), 200
XIII 2395, 294

INDEX LOCORUM

CYPRIAN
Ad Quirinum
  3.110, 237
Quod idola dii non sint (dubius)
  4, 141

DIO CASSIUS
  46.18.2, 161
  54.21, 219
  60.19.2, 217
  61.3, 219
  61.34.5, 217
  62.16, 246 n. 22
  67.17.1, 219
  74.2, 236

DIOGENES LAERTIUS
Vitae philosophorum
  8.1.10, 10 n. 40

DIONYSIUS OF HALICARNASSUS
Antiquitates Romanae
  10.51.5, 121
  10.53, 121
  10.57.6, 121

DONATUS
Ars minor
  1, 87
Commentum Terenti
  Hecyra 170, 116

ENNODIUS
Dictiones
  8, 139
Epistulae
  2.12.2, 238
Opusculum
  10.3, 238

EPITAPH OF SIDONIUS (OR OF HIS
  SON)
  vv. 4–7, 147

EPITOME DE CAESARIBUS
  41.11, 267
  41.12, 268

EUNAPIUS
Vitae sophistarum
  6.3.9–13, 266

EURIPIDES
Troades
  283–7, 232

EUTROPIUS
  8.1, 219
  10.6.3, 267
  10.16.3, 318

FAUSTUS OF RIEZ
Epistulae
  12, p. 219, 62

FIRMICUS MATERNUS
Matheseos libri
  3.11.18, 220
  8.7.1, 238

FRONTO
Epistulae ad M. Antoninum imperatorem
  2.14, 230

GAIUS
Digestorum libri
  21.1.18, 85

GELLIUS, AULUS
Noctes Atticae
  1.2.3, 84
  16.15.1, 84

GREGORY OF TOURS
Historia Francorum
  2.9, 277, 284
  2.28, 197

HESIOD
Catalogus mulierum
  fr. 182 M–W, 165
Theogonia
  626–8, 231

HIERONYMUS *see* JEROME

HISTORIA AUGUSTA
Alexander Seuerus
  43.4, 222
Commodus
  18, 235
  19.2, 235
Diadumenus Antoninus
  7.2–4, 246 n. 24
Elagabalus
  35.4–5, 266
Septimius Seuerus
  1.4, 158

HORACE
Ars Poetica
  58–9, 31

346

INDEX LOCORUM

Carmina
  1.37.11–12, 224
  4.3.16, 265
  4.7, 10 n. 40
  4.9.36, 230
Epistulae
  1.7.8, 139
  1.14.38, 233
  2.2.215–16, 292
Saturae (Sermones)
  1.10.41, 137
  1.10.62–3, 263

JEROME
Apologia aduersus libros Rufini
  1.4, 137
  3.6, 262
Chronica
  s.a. 325–6, 267
  s.a. 338, 266
  s.a. 355, 314–15
De uiris illustribus
  53, 287
Epistulae
  8.1, 112
  11.4, 237
  20.2, 86
  22, 7 n. 27
  22.13, 116–17
  22.30, 105, 105 n. 38, 119
  50.5.4, 110
  54, 7 n. 27
  54.9, 231
  60.4, 226
  70, 315
  78.3, 141
  79, 7 n. 27
  90.3, 283
  107.9, 318
  108.19, 237
  120 *praef.*, 314
  123, 7 n. 27
  125.19, 237
  127.8, 112
  129, 286
  130.12, 116
In Ecclesiasten
  1.1, 84
In Ieremiam
  4.1.3, 181
In Isaiam
  9.29.15, 263
In Zachariam
  2.7, 308

JOHN OF SALISBURY
Policraticus
  1.13, 162

JOSEPHUS
Antiquitates Iudaicae
  18.6.6 (182), 219

JULIAN THE APOSTATE
Ceasares
  335–6, 245 n. 15
  336a–b, 267

JUVENAL
  1.15, 160
  1.35, 218–19
  1.36, 218
  1.108–9, 219
  3.213, 226
  6.192–3, 292
  6.451–5, 313
  6.565–71, 237
  7.86, 308
  7.210, 160
  7.215–16, 313
  9.10, 265
  10.244–5, 225
  14.306, 219
  14.329–31, 217
  15.46, 181

LACTANTIUS
Diuinae institutiones
  4.18.6, 198 n. 39
  5.5.1–6, 266
  5.5.13, 266
  5.8.6–9, 266
  7.24.8–11, 266
Epitome diuinarum institutionum
  7.2, 232

LAUS PISONIS
  35, 309

LEX BURGUNDIONUM
  Praef. 146
  Prima Const. 1.2, 163
  Prima Const. 5, 163
  Prima Const. 8, 146
  Prima Const. in fine, 163
  3, 196, 200
  97, 227
  98, 227

LEX ROMANA BURGUNDIONUM
  10.9, 63

LIBANIUS
Epistulae
  1129, 96

347

INDEX LOCORUM

LIVY
Ab Urbe condita
  1.34.7, 236
  1.41.4, 236
  1.58.6, 180
  3.31–3, 121
  3.34.7, 121
  39.37.17, 180

LUCAN
  2.309–10, 182
  7.226–8, 209
  7.272–3, 182

LUCRETIUS
  4.931, 119

MACROBIUS
Saturnalia
  1.16.30, 86
  2.3.5, 161
  7.1.8, 84

MAMERTUS CLAUDIANUS *see*
  CLAUDIANUS, MAMERTUS

MARIUS VICTORINUS
De definitionibus
  l. 6, 62

MARTIAL
Epigrammata
  4.12.1–2, 215
  5.28.7, 230
  7.25.3–4, 261
  8.59.4, 262
  10.51.6, 220
  10.62.10, 160
  11.1, 219
  11.1.5, 219
  12.25.5, 218
  12.28.2, 218
Spectacula
  37 (33), 246 n. 23

MAXIMUS OF TURIN
Sermones
  26.4, 215

MINUCIUS FELIX
Octauius
  1.3, 293

NEPOS, CORNELIUS
Dion
  2.3, 310

OPTATIANUS PORFYRIUS
Carmina (roman num. = acrostic)
  2.II, 267
  3.12, 267
  3.18, 267
  3.VI, 267
  5.28, 267
  7.24, 267
  10.V, 267
  19.32, 267

ORIENTIUS
Commonitorium
  1.291, 292

OVID
Amores
  2.1.17, 137
  3.4.19–20, 231
Ars amatoria
  2.635–6, 137
  3.617–19, 231
Epistulae ex Ponto
  3.2.38, 181
  4.8.83, 225
  4.10.2, 225
Fasti
  3.774, 287
Heroides
  1, 95 n. 10
Ibis
  378, 231
Metamorphoses
  1.625, 231
  2.779, 85
  3.504, 119
  6.568, 225
  8.448, 225
  8.778, 225
  9.716–17, 310
  10.108, 166
  13.69, 114
  13.429–38, 233
  15.199–214, 10 n. 40
Remedia amoris
  594, 181
Tristia
  4.7.17, 231
  5.10.27–8, 182
  5.10.32, 225

PAULI DIACONI EPITOMA FESTI
  85 L, 236

INDEX LOCORUM

PAULINUS OF NOLA
Carmina (ed. Hartel)
  10.192, 237
  10.246, 225
  20.226, 233
Epistulae
  3.1, 111, 115
  4.3, 283

PERSIUS
Saturae
  2.36, 219

PETRONIUS
Satyrica
  44.14, 230

PLAUTUS
Amphitruo
  302, 258
Asinaria
  13, 262
Aulularia
  162, 287
  555, 231
Bacchides
  418, 135
Captiui
  156, 60
  193, 228
  474, 213
Curculio
  147, 137
  153, 137
  168, 316
Poenulus
  587, 215
Pseudolus
  148, 60
Stichus
  230, 230
Trinummus
  425, 228
  466, 316

PLINY THE ELDER
Naturalis historia
  praef. 12, 259
  8.72, 231
  8.194, 236

PLINY THE YOUNGER
Epistulae
  1.1.1, 3
  1.2.6, 89
  1.3, 168 n. 1, 169
  1.9, 168 n. 1, 169

1.10, 301
1.10.1–2, 301 n. 26
1.11.1, 95, 116
1.12.12, 287
1.13, 301
1.13.1, 301 n. 26
1.16, 66, 301
1.16.5, 243, 261
1.16.8, 66 n. 5, 301 n. 26
1.18, 168 n. 1
1.19, 273
1.19.1, 273, 287
1.22.1, 307
1.23, 168 n. 1
1.24.1, 287
2.2, 95
2.2.1, 96 n. 11
2.3.7, 229
2.4.1, 62
2.5.8, 16 n. 55
2.6, 168 n. 1
2.6.6, 142 n. 3
2.7.6, 58
2.13, 273
2.13.5, 273, 287, 291
2.13.5–9, 273
2.17.8, 56
2.19.7, 89
3.4.4–6, 218
3.5.1, 57
3.5.3, 307
3.7, 66
3.13.2, 89, 89 n. 59
3.13.5, 91
3.17, 95
3.18.1, 58
3.18.5, 320
3.19.2, 57
3.21, 66
3.21.1, 261
4.3, 168 n. 1
4.3.4, 243, 261
4.4.1, 287
4.9.7, 180
4.14, 47
4.14.1, 45
4.15.1, 306
4.19.1, 156
4.19.2, 57
4.21.3, 312
4.23, 168 n. 1
4.23.1, 57
4.24, 168 n. 1
4.28.2, 307
5.6.20, 163
5.6.45, 220
5.8, 243

INDEX LOCORUM

5.8.4, 243 n. 9
5.17, 143
5.17.6, 143
5.19.7, 59
5.20.8, 89
5.21.5, 307
6.8.8, 140
6.20.20, 135
6.21.5, 243, 261
6.23.5, 59
6.29, 168 n. 1
6.29.8, 218
6.33.7, 186
6.34, 168 n. 1
7.1.7, 142 n. 3
7.3, 168 n. 1, 169
7.9, 168 n. 1, 169
7.10.2, 186
7.19.5, 218
7.20.7, 273 n. 3, 293
7.26, 168 n. 1
7.27.14, 218
7.28, 168 n. 1
7.29, 219
7.33.4–8, 218
8.4, 66, 67 n. 12
8.6, 219
8.12, 299
8.12.1, 299, 301, 320
8.18.12, 89
8.22, 168 n. 1
8.24, 142, 168 n. 1, 169
9.5, 142, 168 n. 1, 169
9.6, 168 n. 1
9.6.4, 213
9.9, 168 n. 1
9.10.2, 110
9.12, 168 n. 1
9.13, 135
9.13.26, 135
9.17, 168 n. 1
9.21, 168 n. 1, 169
9.24, 168 n. 1
9.29, 168 n. 1
9.30, 168 n. 1
9.31.1, 308
10.3a.2, 58
10.4.1, 287
10.41.1, 58
10.75.2, 62
10.94.1, 287
Panegyricus
52.7, 236
62.2, 61
65.1.4–5, 56
87.1, 58

PLUTARCH
De musica
18.2, 166
Vitae parallelae
Sulla
41.2, 230

PRAEFATIONES IN BIBLIAM LATINAM
8.10, 282

PROPERTIUS
Elegiae
1.1.31, 292
1.16.17–18, 137
3.2.5–6, 165
3.11.2, 215
4.7.15, 85

PRUDENTIUS
Cathemerinon hymnus
6.69, 209

PSEUDO-AUGUSTINE
Sermones
120.1, 138

PSEUDO-DEMETRIUS
Τύποι Ἐπιστολικοί
Praef., 11 n. 43

PSEUDO-LIBANIUS
Ἐπιστολιμαῖοι Χαρακτῆρες
4, 11 n. 43

PSEUDO-QUINTILIAN
Declamationes
12.26, 231

QUINTILIAN
Institutio oratoria
1 *praef.* 6, 316
1.4.20, 313
1.5, 150–1, 163
1.5.7, 150, 152
1.5.9, 150
1.5.10, 150
1.6.38, 157
3.1.21, 314
6 *praef.* 10, 116, 119
9.2.91, 314
10.1.95–6, 73, 84
11.3.143, 160

QUODVULTDEUS (Pseudo-Augustine?)
De quattuor uirtutibus caritatis
6, 116

INDEX LOCORUM

RHETORICA AD HERENNIUM
4.19, 211

RUFINUS
Eusebii historia ecclesiastica translata et continuata
10.18, 181
Origenis commentarius in epistulas ad Romanos hom.
7.9, 320
Origenis commentarius in Leuiticum hom.
8.5, 307
Origenis commentarius in Numeros hom.
6.2, 213
23.11.1, 320

RURICIUS OF LIMOGES
Epistulae
2.26, 29 n. 92

RUTILIUS NAMATIANUS
De reditu suo
1.208, 317
2.49, 226

SALLUST
De coniuratione Catilinae
20.4, 116, 275 n. 4
52.36, 184

SALVIANUS OF MARSEILLE
De gubernatione Dei
7.1.2, 292

SENECA THE ELDER
Controuersiae
2.1.33, 314
2.5.11, 314
2.5.13, 314
3 *praef.* 2, 314
7.8.4, 215
10 *praef.* 13, 313
10.4.9, 110

SENECA THE YOUNGER
De beneficiis
2.29.1, 210
De matrimonio
fr. 79, 236
Epistulae
7.8, 118
15.1, 116
20.1, 283
59.6, 308
76.8, 210
100, 66
108.25, 311
114, 66

119.9, 219
120.19, 219
Naturales quaestiones
1.6.1, 213
4a. *praef.* 15, 217
Oedipus
99–100, 231
Thyestes
605–6, 230

SHEPERD OF HERMAS
Similitudines
9.31, 140

SIDONIUS
Carmina
1.25, 25 n. 77
2, 4, 6
2.106, 141
2.192, 318
2.240–1, 182
2.243–69, 166
2.280–2, 239
2.416, 292
5, 4, 234–5
5.32, 224
5.112, 319
5.153–4, 249 n. 40
5.321–5, 235
5.563, 226
7, 4, 234
7.104–15, 235
7.139, 319
7.219, 226
7.222, 226
7.349, 226
7.424, 312
7.495–9, 255
7.498, 228
7.513, 319
7.550–1, 230
8, 296, 311
8.2, 311
8.5–6, 296
8.7–10, 297 n. 8
9, 46 n. 16
9.5–8, 285
9.9–11, 46
9.14–15, 46
9.263, 316
9.268, 265
9.308, 317
9.312, 291
9.329–31, 79 n. 47
11.133, 36 n. 108
12, 199 n. 46, 250, 250 n. 45
12.4, 158

351

INDEX LOCORUM

12.20–2, 250
13.17–18, 249 n. 40
14.1, 315
15, 64 n. 1
15.200, 64
16, 69 n. 17
16.127–8, 285
18.2, 91
22.3, 91
22.6, 57
22.7, 112
23, 151 n. 44
23.25–7, 260
23.25–8, 246 n. 27
23.71, 255 n. 71
23.154, 285
23.452, 265
23.484, 214
24, 47 n. 19, 144 n. 7, 188
24.3–4, 210
24.37, 144 n. 8
24.39, 236
24.52–74, 93
24.84–9, 126, 189
24.87, 126 n. 13
24.94–5, 128, 285
27, 253

Epistulae
Liber 1
  1.1, 46, 79
  1.1.1, 7 n. 25, 12, 46, 90, 263
  1.1.2, 157
  1.1.3, 78, 307
  1.1.4, 308
  1.2, 248, 254, 262
  1.2.1, 186
  1.2.4, 226, 307
  1.2.5, 254, 254 n. 69
  1.2.9, 262, 265
  1.3.1, 289
  1.4.3, 59
  1.5.1, 57
  1.5.2, 210
  1.5.4, 224
  1.5.8, 102, 117
  1.5.11, 213
  1.6.4, 230
  1.7, 4 n. 14, 99, 189
  1.7.1, 26 n. 84, 99, 99 n. 21
  1.7.3, 99 n. 21, 140, 223
  1.7.4, 43, 144 n. 7, 156–7
  1.7.5, 44 n. 4
  1.7.6, 99
  1.7.8, 229
  1.7.11, 100 n. 24
  1.8.2, 185
  1.9.1, 260

1.9.2, 224
1.9.4, 223
1.9.7, 61
1.9.8, 91
1.10.1, 61, 210
1.11, 56, 247–50, 250 n. 43 and 45
1.11.1, 248 n. 35
1.11.2, 248 n. 36, 265
1.11.3, 249
1.11.4, 138, 286
1.11.6, 222
1.11.7, 248 n. 36
1.11.8, 63
1.11.13, 56, 247 n. 30, 248 n. 37, 251

Liber 2
  2.1, 192, 220
  2.1.1, 285
  2.1.2, 90, 192, 220
  2.1.3, 148 n. 31, 222, 227–8
  2.1.4, 199, 263
  2.2, 10
  2.2.1, 178
  2.2.6, 321
  2.2.7, 91, 140
  2.3.1, 221
  2.4, 48 n. 29, 144 n. 9
  2.4.1, 292, 309
  2.5, 43, 48 n. 27
  2.6.2, 318
  2.7, 48 n. 27
  2.7.2, 315
  2.8.1, 180
  2.8.2, 61, 79
  2.9, 93 n. 5, 125
  2.9.1, 57
  2.9.2, 210
  2.9.3, 125
  2.9.4, 57
  2.9.9, 238, 263
  2.9.10, 288
  2.10, 57, 163, 242, 242 n. 13, 253, 253
    n. 61, 307
  2.10.1, 151, 160, 299 n. 19
  2.10.3, 242, 246, 258, 260
  2.11.2, 221
  2.12.1, 311
  2.13.5, 310
  2.13.8, 113
  2.14, 10
  2.14.1, 56
  2.14.2, 220

Liber 3
  3.1, 115, 284
  3.1.1, 274, 284, 291
  3.1.2, 284
  3.1.4, 119, 167, 220
  3.2, 10

INDEX LOCORUM

3.2.1, 178, 238, 260, 263
3.2.3, 175, 312
3.2.4, 119, 167
3.3, 10, 174, 254
3.3.1, 254
3.3.5, 282
3.3.7, 174 n. 26
3.3.9, 173, 254
3.4, 98, 106, 106 n. 46, 114, 128 n. 22
3.4.1, 106, 172 n. 18, 180, 220
3.4.2, 98, 114, 128 n. 24
3.5, 48 n. 27
3.5.3, 113
3.6.2, 116
3.7, 98, 113, 128 n. 22
3.7.1, 98, 110, 121
3.7.4, 174–5 n. 27, 178
3.9, 48 n. 27
3.10, 48 n. 27
3.10.2, 63
3.11, 94, 124, 127 n. 20, 128–9
3.11.1, 128 n. 26, 129 n. 28
3.11.2, 94, 110, 112, 115, 179
3.12.3, 187
3.12.5, 147 n. 24, 238
3.12.5 v. 12, 276, 285
3.12.5 vv. 13–16, 283
3.13.3, 294
3.13.9, 288
3.13.10, 178, 210
3.13.11, 237–8
3.14.2, 312
Liber 4
4.1, 128
4.1.1, 123 n. 3, 179, 312
4.1.2, 87, 224, 260, 308
4.2.2, 134 (written by Mamertus Claudianus)
4.2.4, 65, 79–80, 134, 136
4.3, 65, 67–8, 70, 70 n. 22, 73, 80, 86, 88
4.3.1, 136, 314, 320
4.3.3, 92
4.3.4, 68, 68 n. 15, 90, 315, 317
4.3.5, 77, 87–8, 313–14
4.3.6, 87–8, 313
4.3.7, 76 n. 41, 88, 313
4.3.8, 77, 88
4.3.9, 117, 312
4.4, 93–4, 124
4.4.1, 113, 284
4.6, 48 n. 27, 93, 100
4.6.1, 288
4.7, 48 n. 29, 124, 130
4.7.1, 221
4.7.2, 186
4.7.3, 112, 308
4.8.1, 186, 221

4.8.4, 113
4.9.3, 57
4.10, 98–9
4.10.1, 128 n. 22
4.10.2, 115
4.11, 43, 65, 70, 70 n. 22
4.11.1, 43 n. 2, 70 n. 21, 84, 318
4.11.2, 65, 260
4.11.5, 222
4.11.6, 61, 74, 80
4.11.7, 80 n. 58, 112, 136
4.12, 93–4, 124, 127 n. 18
4.12.1, 260
4.12.4, 60, 134
4.14, 128 n. 22
4.14.2, 98
4.14.4, 210
4.15.1, 282, 288
4.15.2, 119, 167
4.16.1, 186, 261, 263
4.17, 163
4.17.1, 149, 151
4.17.2, 159, 320
4.17.3, 58
4.18.2, 113
4.18.5, v. 20, 285
4.18.6, 249 n. 39
4.21.4, 158
4.21.6, 288
4.22, 243
4.22.5, 250, 250 n. 44, 268
4.22.6, 183–4, 234
4.24, 48 n. 29
4.24.2, 223
4.24.3, 266
4.24.4, 63
4.24.5, 223
4.24.7, 167
Liber 5
5.1, 8 n. 34, 13–14, 17, 27, 29, 34, 43–63, 48 n. 27, 100 n. 22, 189, 323, 323 n. 5, 324 n. 7–8, 325
5.1.1, 24, 29, 30, 33, 43, 47, 54–9, 167, 258, 307, 310
5.1.2, 29, 33, 35, 43, 47, 52, 54–5, 59–61, 167
5.1.3, 29, 33–4, 43, 54–5, 61–3, 121, 260, 290, 292
5.2, 4, 13–15, 17, 24–5, 29, 34–5, 57, 59, 64–92, 115, 160, 243–4 n. 11–12, 258, 296, 296 n. 5, 302 n. 29, 313, 323 n. 5, 324 n. 7
5.2.1, 23, 26 n. 82, 29, 35, 70 n. 21, 74, 77, 82–9, 291, 313
5.2.2, 23 n. 72, 27, 33 n. 105–6, 35, 82–3, 89–92, 140

INDEX LOCORUM

5.3, 4, 4 n. 14, 9, 11, 13–14, 16–17, 24–6, 26 n. 85, 28 n. 88, 29, 34–5, 44, 44 n. 4, 93–123, 123 n. 3, 127 n. 21, 128–30, 134, 138–9, 141, 168, 170, 170 n. 8–9, 189 n. 7, 209, 243 n. 5, 258, 265, 323 n. 5

5.3.1, 27, 29, 34, 35, 98, 101, 108–15, 127–8 n. 23, 128 n. 23, 138

5.3.2, 29, 30, 34, 35, 101, 108–9, 111, 114–16, 275, 288, 293

5.3.3, 10, 23 n. 72, 34, 35, 98, 101, 103–4, 108–9, 116–19, 278 n. 17

5.3.4, 31, 34–5, 98, 101, 108–9, 114, 119–22, 128 n. 24, 167

5.4, 4 n. 14, 5, 13–14, 16–17, 24–6, 26 n. 85, 29, 34–5, 44 n. 4, 93 n. 2, 94, 97–8 n. 18, 101, 101 n. 28, 123–41, 168, 170, 185, 188 n. 2, 189 n. 8, 239, 258, 323, 323 n. 5, 325 n. 10

5.4.1, 22–3, 27–30, 34–5, 98 n. 18, 110, 128, 128 n. 23, 132–8, 186

5.4.2, 27, 31, 35, 128, 128 n. 24, 132–3, 138–41

5.5, 6 n. 20, 13, 15, 15 n. 53, 24–5, 27, 28 n. 88, 29, 36, 75 n. 40, 92, 142–68, 300 n. 19, 323 n. 5, 324 n. 7, 326

5.5.1, 23 n. 72, 29, 34, 36, 143–4, 150, 154–8, 167

5.5.2, 21, 23, 29, 32, 36, 154–5, 158–63, 164, 293

5.5.3, 31, 56, 89, 145, 154–5, 163–7, 228–9, 300 n. 19, 320

5.5.4, 154–5, 167

5.6, 9–10, 13, 15–17, 24–5, 27, 29, 36, 93–4, 100, 102, 123, 126 n. 15, 127, 142 n. 2, 146 n. 18, 153, 168–88, 195, 198, 201–2, 208–9, 252, 254, 262, 270, 323 n. 5, 324 n. 7, 325

5.6.1, 10, 29, 32, 34, 36, 93 n. 1, 174, 176–82, 188, 188 n. 1, 209, 225

5.6.2, 5, 28–30, 30 n. 93, 171–2, 172 n. 14 and 17, 176–7, 182–87, 191 n. 15, 198, 202, 208–9, 211, 228, 233, 237, 240

5.7, 3 n. 9, 9, 10, 12–13, 16–17, 17 n. 58, 24–7, 28 n. 88, 29, 36, 51, 93–4, 100 n. 22, 102, 123, 126–7, 143, 146 n. 18, 153, 160, 168, 170, 170 n. 10, 171–2, 172 n. 15, 174, 181–2, 185, 188–241, 248 n. 34, 252, 254, 254 n. 65, 262, 269–70, 296 n. 7, 323, 323 n. 5, 324 n. 7, 325, 325 n. 9–10

5.7.1, 5, 25 n. 78, 29, 37, 60, 171, 179, 188 n. 1, 190, 194, 197, 204–5, 208–13, 215, 218, 236, 239, 291

5.7.2, 33 n. 104, 37, 204–5, 213–16, 224, 291

5.7.3, 37–8, 190, 204–5, 216–23, 291

5.7.4, 31, 189 n. 10, 190, 192, 206–7, 224–9, 233, 237, 255 n. 74, 291

5.7.5, 23 n. 72, 30, 190, 206–7, 214, 229–33, 235, 239, 291

5.7.6, 29, 184, 190, 201, 206–7, 216, 233–7, 240, 264, 291

5.7.7, 113, 126 n. 17, 171, 181, 184, 190, 201, 206–8, 211, 216, 228–9, 233, 236–41, 263

5.8, 4, 13–15, 17–18, 24–5, 27, 29, 38, 141, 153, 153 n. 50, 160, 234, 242–71, 296, 296 n. 5, 323 n. 5, 324 n. 7–8

5.8.1, 30, 38, 57, 244, 254, 254 n. 66, 256–60

5.8.2, 21, 23 n. 72, 28–9, 32, 238, 240, 244 n. 10, 246–7 n. 28–9, 249, 256–7, 260–8, 326

5.8.3, 29, 31–2, 33 n. 106, 38, 244, 250, 256–7, 268–71

5.9, 13–14, 18, 24, 28–9, 38, 265, 272–94, 323 n. 5, 324 n. 7, 325

5.9.1, 29, 33 n. 106, 167, 264, 275, 275 n. 5, 276 n. 8, 277, 277 n. 13, 280–7, 291–4

5.9.2, 21, 29, 32, 273 n. 2, 277, 277 n. 15, 280–1, 287–90, 293

5.9.3, 30, 272, 274–5, 280–1, 284, 290–1, 313

5.9.4, 11, 30, 116, 158, 273 n. 3, 275, 278, 280–1, 292–4

5.10, 13, 15, 17, 17 n. 58, 24–5, 27, 30, 33 n. 105–6, 38–9, 51, 72 n. 30, 143, 163, 295–321, 323 n. 5, 324, 324 n. 7–8

5.10.1, 21, 33 n. 105, 39, 44 n. 6, 295, 304–8, 319

5.10.2, 30, 38 n. 111, 39, 295–6, 297 n. 9–10, 298 n. 15, 304–5, 308–12

5.10.3, 30, 34, 39, 295, 298, 298 n. 14–15, 304–5, 312–18

5.10.4, 30, 40, 295–6 n. 6, 297 n. 10, 298 n. 15, 299, 304–5, 318–21

5.11, 13–14, 324 n. 7

5.11.1, 210

5.11.3, 23 n. 72

5.12, 5, 9, 13–14, 324 n. 8

5.12.1, 9 n. 37, 23, 23 n. 72, 139, 186

5.13, 13, 16–17, 92, 192, 220, 324 n. 7, 325

5.13.1, 10, 192, 238

5.13.2, 228

5.13.3, 90

5.14, 5, 9, 13, 15, 227, 323, 323 n. 5, 324–5, 325 n. 11, 326

5.14.2, 21–2

5.14.3, 21

INDEX LOCORUM

5.15, 13–14, 48 n. 28, 60, 323, 323 n. 5, 324 n. 8
5.15.1, 61, 238
5.15.2, 167
5.16, 3, 5, 13–14, 24, 172 n. 17, 323 n. 5, 324, 324 n. 7
5.16.1, 21, 23, 23 n. 72
5.16.2, 185
5.16.3, 21
5.17, 12–13, 15, 17, 247, 253 n. 61, 323, 323 n. 5, 324 n. 7, 325, 325 n. 11
5.17.2, 167
5.17.3, 282
5.17.4, 10, 21, 144 n. 6, 156, 178
5.17.6, 62, 113
5.17.7, 311
5.17.10, 23 n. 72, 60
5.17.11, 91, 247, 264
5.18, 13–14, 323 n. 5
5.19, 13, 15, 323 n. 5, 324–5
5.20, 13, 15–16, 323 n. 5
5.20.1, 23
5.21, 13–14, 17, 92
5.21.1, 316

Liber 6
6.1, 103
6.1.1, 103, 118
6.1.3, 156
6.1.4, 85
6.1.5, 103, 117–18
6.2, 48 n. 27
6.2.2, 113
6.2.3, 290
6.3, 48 n. 27
6.4, 48 n. 27
6.4.1, 221
6.4.2, 186, 208, 221, 319
6.5, 48 n. 27
6.6.2, 167
6.7.1, 290
6.8, 48 n. 28
6.9, 48 n. 27
6.10, 47 n. 23, 48 n. 28
6.10.1, 59, 221
6.11, 48 n. 27
6.12, 172
6.12.3, 171, 171 n. 12, 172, 200, 200 n. 49

Liber 7
7.1.7, 139
7.2.1, 58, 309
7.2.2, 186
7.2.3, 220
7.2.5, 85, 139
7.2.8, 317
7.2.9, 136
7.2.10, 110

7.3.2, 110
7.4, 45, 48 n. 27
7.4.1, 61
7.4.4, 45, 45 n. 12, 94, 115, 124–5 n. 8, 169, 185
7.5.3, 185
7.6.1, 258, 293
7.6.3, 238
7.6.9, 127 n. 20
7.7.2, 211
7.7.6, 135, 220
7.8, 127 n. 20
7.8.3, 307
7.9, 32 n. 101, 46, 127 n. 20
7.9.1, 46–7
7.9.2, 91
7.9.3, 239
7.9.6, 103 n. 33, 118
7.9.9, 85
7.9.11, 265
7.9.12, 311
7.9.19, 226
7.10, 48 n. 27
7.10.1, 175 n. 27, 221
7.10.2, 140
7.11.1, 178, 220, 239, 312
7.11.2, 61
7.12, 100 n. 22
7.12.1, 144 n. 7
7.13.2, 260–1
7.14.1, 58, 136
7.14.3–9, 310
7.14.8, 62
7.14.10, 309
7.17.1, 61, 113
7.17.4, 113
7.18.3, 57
7.18.4, 61, 264

Liber 8
8.1, 43–4, 50, 100 n. 22
8.1.1, 44 n. 5, 152 n. 47
8.2, 299 n. 16
8.2.1, 300, 300 n. 20, 307, 320
8.2.2, 150
8.3, 148
8.3.3, 148
8.4.2, 260
8.6, 300
8.6.1, 57, 116
8.6.3, 300, 300 n. 21
8.6.5, 289
8.6.6, 317
8.6.10, 210
8.6.13, 312
8.8, 144, 144 n. 9, 152 n. 47, 152–3
8.8.1, 145, 156
8.9, 52 n. 42, 198–9 n. 45

INDEX LOCORUM

8.9.1, 178
8.9.4, 52 n. 42
8.10.3, 308
8.11.2, 315
8.11.3, 91, 264
8.11.3 vv. 35–6, 285
8.11.4, 115, 187
8.11.5, 260, 315
8.11.6, 86–7, 265
8.11.7, 238, 261–3
8.13, 48 n. 29
8.13.2, 110
8.13.3, 221
8.13.4, 49
8.15.1, 58
8.16, 44
8.16.2, 312
8.16.3, 319
8.16.5, 167, 313
Liber 9
9.1.3, 79 n. 47, 110
9.1.4, 110
9.3, 69 n. 17, 70 n. 22, 134, 151, 163
9.3.2, 134, 208
9.3.3, 151
9.3.4, 312
9.3.6, 119
9.4.1, 139
9.6, 48 n. 29
9.7, 300, 300 n. 22
9.7.2, 300
9.9, 69 n. 17, 70
9.9.6, 208
9.9.8, 57
9.9.12, 70 n. 21, 84
9.9.14, 87
9.10, 48 n. 28
9.11, 163
9.11.3, 264
9.11.6, 57, 151
9.11.8, 59, 136
9.12, 6
9.12.1–2, 6 n. 22, 263
9.13, 52 n. 42
9.13.1, 308
9.13.2, 260
9.13.4–5, 265
9.14.2, 308
9.14.4, 60, 211, 221
9.14.6, 318
9.15.1, 52 n. 42, 246
9.16, 11
9.16.3, 52 n. 42, 147 n. 26, 167, 185

SILIUS ITALICUS
Punica
13.587–9, 231
13.818–20, 237

SOLINUS
53.30, 307

SOZOMEN
Historia ecclesiastica
6.6.2, 310

STATIUS
Siluae
4.4, 316
5.3.146, 294
Thebais
4.356–60, 165

SUETONIUS
De grammaticis
23.5–6, 313
Vitae Caesarum
Augustus
67, 219
Caligula
47, 158
Claudius
3.2, 134, 235
28.1, 217, 219
29.2, 286
Domitianus
14.2, 246 n. 23
Galba
3.2, 286
6.2, 245 n. 21
Nero
20.1, 158
39.2, 245
Tiberius
59.1, 245 n. 18–20, 266

SYMMACHUS
Epistulae
1.1, 135
1.1.6, 60
1.3.3, 139
1.5.2, 112
1.8, 224
1.10, 120, 141
1.13.1, 96
1.14, 66
1.14.2, 66, 244
1.15, 97 n. 16, 317
1.15.2, 317
1.20.1, 86
1.24, 67
1.30, 306
1.31.1, 261
1.31.2, 184, 233
1.32.3, 160
1.35, 136

INDEX LOCORUM

1.37.2, 282
1.40, 61
1.48, 117
1.59, 134
1.65, 111, 138, 265
1.68, 222
1.78.1, 58
1.86, 185, 313
1.94, 317
1.95.1, 111, 141
2.1, 50
2.1.1, 50
2.6.2, 178
2.12, 198 n. 42
2.18.1, 140
2.18.2, 141
2.25, 169 n. 4
2.35.2, 185
2.46.3, 318
2.48.1, 134
2.49, 112
2.54, 115
2.73, 112
2.75, 222
2.80, 61
2.87, 289
2.89, 136
3.1, 111, 265
3.4, 97 n. 15
3.5.2, 138
3.11, 67 n. 7, 244
3.11.3, 67 n. 8
3.11.4, 67 n. 10
3.12, 67 n. 7, 244
3.12.2, 67 n. 9
3.13, 67 n. 7, 244
3.14, 67 n. 7, 282
3.15, 67 n. 7, 141
3.16, 318
3.18, 97
3.22, 97
3.23, 210
3.26, 111
3.32, 318
3.38, 102, 117
3.43.1, 282
3.50, 317
3.54, 97, 97 n. 16, 134
3.55.2, 186
3.56, 97, 134, 180
3.60, 97
3.69, 169
3.69.1, 184
3.81, 97, 141
3.81.1, 97
3.81.4, 186
3.82, 97

3.82.1, 96, 113
3.83, 97
3.86, 97, 102 n. 29
3.86.2, 124 n. 7, 169–70 n. 6, 184, 284
4.15, 170
4.15.2, 170
4.18.1, 86
4.28.4, 116
4.33, 47
4.33.1, 46
4.42.1, 115
4.54.3, 178
4.58.1, 178
4.59, 97, 112
4.63, 140
4.63.2, 91
5.13, 111
5.25, 119
5.44, 265
5.53, 307
5.55, 90
5.58, 186
5.62, 223
5.70, 186
5.77, 113
5.92, 111, 141, 265
5.97, 178
6.2, 169 n. 4
6.5, 169 n. 4
6.37, 313
6.39, 185
6.52, 319
6.56, 319
7.6, 139
7.14, 220
7.18.3, 57
7.22, 313
7.28, 102, 117
7.52, 318
7.72, 136
7.88, 274
7.99, 111
7.100, 141
7.104.2, 124 n. 7
8.16, 282
8.26, 186
8.29, 124 n. 7
8.43, 274, 291
8.49, 139
8.50, 113
8.51, 140
9.1, 50, 51, 317
9.10, 222
9.10.1, 61
9.13, 67
9.28, 91
9.32, 61

INDEX LOCORUM

9.36, 113
9.47, 318
9.50, 222
9.56, 186
9.59, 61
9.87, 135
9.112, 157
9.129, 169 n. 4
Orationes
2.29, 263
4.7, 237
Relationes ad principes
3.15, 228
9.3, 209

TACITUS
Agricola
34, 211
Annales
1.2.1, 215
1.33, 241
1.69, 241
2.30.3, 235
2.75, 241
3.4, 241
11.3.2, 235
11.28.2, 286
11.30, 217
11.33–5, 217
11.37–8, 217
12.53, 219
12.61.2, 286
12.67, 235
13.23, 134
14.64, 268
15.25, 209
15.19.2, 293
16.28, 218
16.29.1, 218
16.33.2, 218
Dialogus de oratoribus
8.2–3, 218
12.6, 84
Historiae
1.5, 236
1.12.3, 286
1.38, 236
2.31, 236
2.57, 217
2.95, 218
3.12.1, 286
3.67, 225
4.7.3, 218
4.27.2, 286
4.50, 218

TERENCE
Hecyra
226, 135

TERTULLIAN
Aduersus Hermogenem
13, 135
Aduersus Marcionem
1.4, 290
Apologeticum
39.7, 293
De baptismo
4, 310
De carnis resurrectione
62, 213
De corona militis
1, 230
De cultu feminarum
2.12, 311
Scorpiace
12, 111

TIBULLUS
Elegiae
2.6.12, 137
3.2.17–18, 224

ULPIAN
Liber singularis regularum
11.4, 157

VALERIUS MAXIMUS
Facta et dicta memorabilia
6.3 ext. 1, 292
6.8.1, 312

VARRO
Res rusticae
2.2.7, 238

VERGIL
Aeneis
1.347–50, 233
2.7, 232
2.57–198, 232
2.90, 232
2.152, 232
2.164, 232
2.195, 232
2.270, 180
2.762, 232
3.19–68, 233
4.402–3, 76
4.542, 232
6.815, 235
8.244, 119
9.308, 224
11.381, 76

INDEX LOCORUM

Georgica
    1.502, 232
    2.378–9, 233
    4.83, 76

VITA SANCTI MARCELLI
    9.1–2, 200, 237

VITRUVIUS
De architectura
    3.1.3, 58

VULGATA
Canticum Canticorum
    5.6, 138
    7.2, 282
Deuteronomium
    21.11–13, 70 n. 22

Esther
    3.9, 222
Euangelium secundum Iohannem
    1.4.18, 111
Euangelium secundum Lucam
    6.4, 76
Euangelium secundum Matthaeum
    7.3, 76
    21.12–19, 104, 119
    24.20, 76
Prouerbia
    6.6, 76

ZOSIMUS
    2.29.2, 267–8
    2.40.3, 266
    6.2.3, 275 n. 6
    6.4.4, 285
    6.13.1, 285

INDEX NOMINUM ANTIQUORUM

Only the most relevant passages in which the ancient persons are mentioned in the text are indexed here. For further mentions of individuals marked with an asterisk (*) see the Index Locorum.

Ablabius (cos. 331), 244, 251–2, 256, 263–6
Achilles, mythological hero, 160
Adelphius, rhetor, 39, 298, 304–5, 315
Aeneas, mythological hero, 180, 224, 232
Aeschines, orator, 68, 87
Agrippina the Elder, 201–2, 206–7, 241
Agrippina the Younger, empress, 219, 235
Agrippinus, priest, 113
Agroecius (or Agricius), Censorius Atticus, rhetor, 39, 298, 304–5, 314
Alamanni, 263
Alaric I, leader of the Visigoths (d. 410), 183, 225
Alcima, daughter of Sidonius, 287, 315
Alcimus (?), father of Sidonius, 272, 277, 280–1, 287
Alcimus, rhetor, 39, 298, 304–5, 314–15
Alypius, addressee of Paulinus of Nola and Therasia, 115
*Ambrose, bishop of Milan, 7 n. 26, 28, 91, 104–5, 118, 136, 145, 216
Amphion, mythological figure, 154–5, 164–5
Ancus Marcius, fourth king of Rome (conventionally 640–617 BC), 206–7, 235
Anthemiolus, son of emperor Anthemius, 105–6
Anthemius, emperor (467–72), 4–6, 44, 105–6, 114, 189 n. 7, 199
Antias, Valerius, historian, 181
Antiope, mythological figure, 164
Antonia minor, 219
Antoninus, Arrius, poet, 261
Aper, addressee of Sidonius, 5, 9, 15
Apollinaris, cousin of Sidonius, 93–4, 97–101, 123–9, 168–71, 191, 202, 209, 239
Apollinaris, grandfather of Sidonius, 275–7, 285
Apollinaris, son of Sidonius, 147, 272, 274, 280–1, 294
*Apuleius, poet, 28, 30, 189–91, 283
Aquilinus, addressee of Sidonius, 272–7, 290–3
Araneola, wife of Polemius, 64

Arbogast, *comes ciuitatis Treuirorum*, 149–51
Arcadius, emperor of the East (383–408), 275
Archilochus, poet, 293
Archimedes, mathematician, 87
Archytas of Tarentum, philosopher, 76
Argus, mythological figure, 206–7, 231
Aristo, Titius, friend of Pliny the Younger, 307
Arpinas *see* Cicero
Arrius Antoninus *see* Antoninus, Arrius
Arvandus, *Praefectus praetorio Galliarum* (464–8), 4–5, 26, 43–4, 99–100, 110, 128–30, 170, 188–9, 223, 229
Arverni, 173, 178, 211, 318
Asiaticus, freedman of Vitellius, 204–5, 216–17
Astyrius (cos. 449), 289
Athaulf, king of the Visigoths (411–15), 277
*Augustine of Hippo, 7, 56–8, 71, 73, 75 n. 38, 91, 104–5, 119, 134, 136, 160, 221, 283, 286, 312, 317
Augustus (Octavian), emperor (27 BC – 14 CE) 215–16, 219, 245 n. 15
Aurelianus, Lucius Domitius, emperor (270–5), 183
*Ausonius, poet, 28, 46 n. 16, 66–7, 86, 96–7, 136, 180–1, 184, 233–4, 237, 244–5, 261, 282, 306, 314–17
Auxanius, friend of Sidonius, 99, 113
Auxentius, acquaintance of Symmachus, 282
Avienus, Gennadius (cos. 450), 223
Avitus, addressee and relative of Sidonius (cousin?), 115, 274, 284
*Avitus, bishop of Vienne, 79 n. 51, 287, 295
Avitus, Eparchius, emperor (455–6) and Sidonius' father-in-law, 3–4, 228, 234, 255, 296, 311
Avitus, Julius, addressee of Pliny the Younger, 307
Avitus, Lollianus, proconsul, friend of Apuleius, 160, 262

Bacchae, 181
Baebius Macer *see* Macer, Baebius

INDEX NOMINUM ANTIQUORUM

Basilius, bishop of Aix, 293
Basilius, Fl. Caecina Decius (cos. 463), 223
Bauto, Flavius (cos. 385), addressee of
    Symmachus, 170
Briareus of the Hekatoncheires, mythological
    figure, 206–7, 231
Britons, 211
Burgundian queen (*anonyma* wife of
    Chilperic I), 170–3, 181, 184, 199–202,
    237–8, 241
Burgundians, 2, 5, 9, 24–7, 44, 94, 105–6,
    126, 142–3, 145–9, 153, 158–9, 164–75,
    180, 191–203, 212, 220, 227–9, 234–41,
    248, 250, 254, 269–70
Burgundio, addressee of Sidonius, 211

*Caesar, Julius, 59, 182
Caligula (Gaius), emperor (37–41), 158,
    206–7, 235
Callistianus, addressee of Symmachus, 274
Calminius, addressee of Sidonius, 5, 9, 13, 139
Calpurnia, informant of Narcissus, 217
Calpurnia Hispulla *see* Hispulla, Calpurnia
Calpurnius Piso *see* Piso, Calpurnius
Calvisius Rufus *see* Rufus, Calvisius
Camenae (muses), 70–3, 86
Caninius, friend of Pliny the Younger, 66
Capito, Octavius Titinius, friend of Pliny the
    Younger, 299, 301, 320
Caracalla, emperor (188–217), 309
Caretena, Burgundian queen, 25, 200–1
Carterius, addressee of Symmachus, 282
Carus, Mettius, *delator*, 204–5, 216–18
Catena, informant, 240
Catilina, Lucius Sergius, 116, 192 n. 19
Cato of Utica, 182, 184
*Cato the Censor, 298, 314
Catullinus, friend of Sidonius 158, 249–50
Celsinus Titianus *see* Titianus, Celsinus
Cerialis, addressee of Pliny the Younger, 89
Chilperic I, *magister utriusque militiae per Gallias*
    (473/4) and king of the Burgundians, 25,
    94, 146, 169 n. 3, 171–3, 176–7, 182–7,
    194–202, 208–9, 228, 233–41
Chilperic II, nephew of Chilperic I, 194–200
Chrysippus, philosopher, 68, 87, 298, 314
Cibyratae, Verre's henchmen, 184, 190,
    206–7, 211, 229, 239–40
*Cicero, Marcus Tullius (cos. 63 bc), orator,
    10, 25 n. 79, 28, 48, 66, 71–2, 76, 84,
    116, 142, 145, 159–62, 189–90, 208–10,
    229, 239–40, 298
*Claudianus, Claudius, poet, 121, 225–6
*Claudianus, Mamertus, philosopher, 4–5,
    14–15, 17, 24, 30, 34, 43, 57–9, 64–92,
    112, 134, 184, 283, 295–9, 302, 308,
    313–15, 317, 319–20

Claudius, emperor (41–54), 206–7, 216–17,
    219, 235, 286
Cleomenes, appointed commander under
    Verres, 184
Cleopatra, informant of Narcissus, 217
Cleopatra, queen of Egypt, 224
Clodia, 140
Commodus, emperor (180–92), 235–6, 246
*Consentius, grammarian, 150–2
Constans, Caesar (408–9/10), son of
    Constantine III, 276, 283–4
Constantine I, emperor (306–37), 183, 223,
    240, 243–6, 249, 251–2, 256–7, 263–4,
    266–8
Constantine III, usurper (407–11), 264,
    275–7, 280–1, 283–6
Constantius, addressee of Sidonius, 10, 44,
    46, 78, 175, 178, 238, 242–3, 307, 312,
    319
Constantius II, emperor (324–61), son of
    Constantine I, 201, 239–40, 252, 266
Crispus, Caesar (316–26), son of emperor
    Constantine I, 240, 243, 251–2, 257–8,
    267–8

Dardanus, Claudius Postumus, 275, 277,
    280–1, 286
Deiotarus, tetrarch of Galatia, 209
Delphidius, rhetor 39, 298, 304–5, 314
Demosthenes, orator, 68, 87
Desideratus, addressee of Sidonius, 79, 180
Diocletian, emperor (284–305), 194, 266
Domitian, emperor (81–96), 206–7, 216,
    218–19, 234–6, 246
Domnicius, friend of Sidonius, 113
Donidius, addressee of Sidonius, 113, 125

Ecdicius, brother-in-law of Sidonius, 5, 10,
    14, 24, 173–5, 185, 199, 254
Egyptians, 181, 209
Elagabalus, emperor (218–22), 266
Eriphius, addressee of Sidonius, 13, 113, 144
    n. 6
Euclid, mathematician, 68, 87
Eulalia, cousin of Sidonius 101, 123 n. 3,
    128–9
*Eunapius of Sardis, historian, 268
Euphrates of Tyre, philosopher, 68, 88
Euric, king of the Visigoths (466/7–84), 4, 5,
    9, 44, 105, 114, 146 n. 23, 148, 173, 189
    n.7, 192, 198–9 n. 45, 255
Euryalus and Nisus, mythological heroes, 224
Eusebia, empress, 310–11
Eusebius, friend of Symmachus, 141

Fabius Iustus *see* Iustus, Lucius Fabius
Fannia, daughter of Thrasea Paetus, 218

361

INDEX NOMINUM ANTIQUORUM

Fausta, empress, 240, 243, 251–2, 255–6, 267–8

Faustinus, old friend of Sidonius, 113

*Faustus, bishop of Riez, 4, 57, 62, 69–70, 75, 84, 87, 89, 134, 151, 208

Felix, Magnus *praefectus praetorio Galliarum* (469), 46, 79 n. 47, 98–101, 106–7, 110, 113–15, 121, 127–9, 180, 285

Ferreolus, Tonantius *praefectus praetorio Galliarum* (451/3), 43, 93 n. 5, 99–100 n. 22, 125, 144, 156–7, 189, 210, 236

Filimatia, friend of Sidonius, 79, 180

Firmus, Romatius, addressee of Pliny the Younger, 273, 287

Flavianus, Nicomachus addressee of Symmachus, 115, 124 n. 7, 134, 136, 140, 169, 185, 198 n. 42, 284, 319

Fonteius, bishop of Vaison, 45, 115, 124–5 n. 8, 290

*Fronto, M. Cornelius, 16, 48 n. 26, 298, 314

Fulgentius, praised by Sidonius, 310

Fundanius, Gaius, author of palliatae, 137

Gaius *see* Caligula

Galba, emperor (68–9), 206–7, 235–6, 245, 286

Galba, Servius (cos. 144 BC), 286

Galla Placidia *see* Placidia

Gallio, (Junius?), rhetor, 39, 298, 304–5, 313–14

Gelasius, addressee, 52 n. 42, 246

Germanicus, general, 158–9, 201–2, 206–8, 236, 239, 241

Gerontius, *magister miltum* and *comes* of Constantine III (407–9), 275–6, 280–1, 286

Geruchia, addressee of Jerome, 7 n. 27

Getae *see* Goths

Glycerius, Western emperor (473–4), 269

Godigisel, son of Gundioc, 196–7

Godomar, son of Gundioc, 196–7

Goths, 175, 180–1, 183, 211, 220, 225, 228, 241, 255, 270

Gracchus, Gaius, 298, 317

Graecus (bishop), addressee of Sidonius, 139, 211

Gregorius, addressee of Symmachus, 97

*Gregory of Tours, 194, 197, 284

Gundahar (or Gundicar), king of Burgundians, 194 n. 24, 196

Gundioc, king of Burgundians, 146, 158, 195–7

Gundobad, king of Burgundians, 146–7, 196–7, 200–1, 252

Harpies, 206–7, 228

Hector, mythological figure, 180

Helpidius, addressee of Symmachus, 141

Helvidius Priscus *see* Priscus, Helvidius

Hephaestio, addressee of Symmachus, 140

Herennius Rufinus *see* Rufinus, Herennius

Herennius Senecio *see* Senecio, Herennius

Herod Antipas, tetrarch of Galilee (4 BC–AD 39), 197–8

Heronius, addressee of Sidonius, 61

Hesperius, addressee of Sidonius, 57, 151, 242

Hesperius, Decimius Hilarianus, son of Ausonius, addressee of Symmachus, 58

Hieronymus *see* Jerome

Hippo of Metapontum, philosopher, 76

Hispulla, Calpurnia, addressee of Pliny the Younger, 57, 156

Hoenius, Sidonius' teacher, 291

Honorius, emperor of the West (393–423), 183, 251 n. 48, 275–7, 280–1, 283, 284–6, 288, 292, 319

*Horace, 10 n. 40, 31, 57, 112, 230, 249, 249 n. 39, 265

Hormidac, *dux*, 182

Hortensius Hortalus, Quintus, orator, 68, 87, 229

Huns, 166, 228

Hypatius, empress Eusebia's brother (cos. 359), 311

Iulianus, Rusticus, addressee of Symmachus, 97 n. 15, 111, 138

Iustus, Lucius Fabius, addressee of Pliny the Younger, 95

*Jerome of Stridon, 7, 28, 57, 75–6, 105, 134–5, 137–8, 262, 267, 283, 286, 314–15, 318

Jesus, 104–5, 245 n. 15

Johannes, *grammaticus,* 300, 307, 320

Jovinus, usurper (411–13), 275–7, 280–1, 284–6, 314

Julian of Aeclanum, engaged in a literary controversy with Augustine, 262

*Julian the Apostate, emperor (Caesar 355–61, Augustus 361–3), 172, 187, 245, 267, 314–15

Julius Avitus *see* Avitus, Julius

Julius Servianus *see* Servianus, Julius

Jupiter, 266 (*see also* Zeus)

*Juvenal, satirist, 28, 189–90, 217, 308

*Lactantius, 68, 88, 266

Lampridius, rhetor and poet, 52 n. 42, 86–7, 178, 187, 198, 262, 265, 315

Laomedon, mythical king of Troy, 206–7, 232

Leo I, emperor of the East (457–74), 269

Leo of Narbonne, addressee of Sidonius, 6, 148, 183, 234

INDEX NOMINUM ANTIQUORUM

Leonianus (Avitus of Vienne's *nom de plume?*), 295

Licinius, freedman of Augustus, 204–5, 216–17, 219

*Livy, historian, 67, 120, 145, 202, 236–7

Lollianus Avitus *see* Avitus, Lollianus

Lucontius, addressee of Sidonius, 113

Lucretia, legendary heroine, 180, 237

*Lucretius, 66

Lupus, bishop, 57, 103, 118, 151–2, 156, 208

Lusitanians, 286

Macer, Baebius, addressee of Pliny the Younger, 57

*Macrobius, 160–1

Magnus, rhetor (either Flavius Magnus or Aemilius Magnus Arborius), 39, 298, 304–5, 315–16

Magnus Felix *see* Felix, Magnus

Majorian (or Maiorianus), emperor (457–61), 4, 56, 234, 247–51, 311

Mamertus Claudianus *see* Claudianus, Mamertus

Manicheans, followers of the Manichean religion, 135, 224

Marcella, addressee of Jerome, 7, 112

*Marcellus, saint 200, 201

Marcellus, Titus Clodius Eprius, cos. suff. (62 and 74), 216–18

Marinianus, addressee of Symmachus, 111

Marius Maximus, biographer, 235–6

*Martial, 66, 160, 217–20, 261, 265

Massa, slanderer, 38, 204–5, 216–19

Maximilianus, addressee of Symmachus, 140

Maximus, priest (addressee of Sidonius), 266

Maximus, usurper (son of Gerontius), 276, 286

*Maximus of Turin, 182

Menstruanus, friend of Sidonius, 318

Mercurius, informant, 240

Messala, addressee of Symmachus, 274

Messalina, empress, 217, 286

Minicianus, addressee of Pliny the Younger, 299

Narcissus, freedman under Claudius, 204–5, 216–17, 219

Naucellius, Iulius (or Iunius), addressee of Symmachus, 67, 141, 244, 282

Neoterius, addressee of Symmachus, 265

Nepos, Julius, emperor (474–5, d. 480), 5, 9, 94, 148, 168, 172, 174, 185–6, 199, 202, 209

Nero, emperor (54–68), 158, 206–7, 216, 218–19, 235, 245–6, 251, 255–6, 266–8

Nicetius, Flavius, panegyrist, 300

Nicomachus Flavianus *see* Flavianus, Nicomachus

Numa Pompilius, second king of Rome (conventionally 715–673 BC), 164

Nymphidius, addressee of Sidonius, 24, 64, 79, 82–3, 90, 244 n. 11, 296

Oceanus, addressee of Augustine, 119

Octavia, Claudia, wife of Nero, 267–8

Oedipus, mythological figure, 231

Olympus, musician, 166

Oresius, addressee of Sidonius, 263

Orpheus, mythological figure, 68, 88

Otho, emperor (69), 206–7, 235–6

*Ovid, 112, 181, 225, 231, 249

Paeonius, *praefectus praetorio Galliarum* (456/7), 138, 247–8, 251, 286

Paetus, Thrasea, senator, 218

Palaemon, Quintus Remmius, teacher of grammar, 39, 298, 304–5, 312–14

Palladius, rhetor, 40, 304–5, 317–18

Pallas, Marcus Antonius, freedman, 38, 204–5, 216–17, 219

Papianilla, wife of Sidonius, 3, 5, 14, 24, 144 n. 8, 185

Papianilla, wife of Tonantius Ferreolus, 144, 144 n. 8, 236

Parthenius, freedman under Nero, 204–5, 216–17, 219

Pastor, addressee of Sidonius, 13, 16

Patiens, bishop of Lyon, 171 n. 12, 172, 200

Paulinus, addressee of Pliny the Younger, 95

*Paulinus of Nola, 7, 53 n. 46, 115, 180–1, 213, 225, 237, 283

Pegasius, addressee of Sidonius, 318

Pelagians, followers of Pelagius, 56, 135, 181

*Persius, satirist, 316

Petreius, addressee of Sidonius (and nephew of Mamertus Claudianus), 43, 65

Petronius, addressee of Sidonius, 8 n. 34, 24, 43–5, 47–8, 50–6, 58, 63, 99, 100 n. 22, 152 n. 47

Petronius Secundus *see* Secundus, Petronius

Petrus, mentioned by Sidonius, 317

Petrus Chrysologus, 182

Phaedra, mythological figure, 267

Phalaris, tyrant of Syracuse, 190, 206–7, 234–5

Philagrius, addressee of Sidonius, 62, 310

Piso, Calpurnius, writer, 143

Placidia, Galla, Augusta, 277

Plato, 70, 73 n. 35, 76

*Plautus, 30, 60, 91, 215, 228, 230, 262, 298

*Pliny the Elder, 57, 67

INDEX NOMINUM ANTIQUORUM

*Pliny the Younger, 7, 12–13, 15–16, 27–8, 45–9, 66–7, 79, 142–3, 168, 243, 272–4, 299, 301

Polemius, *praefectus praetorio Galliarum* (husband of Araneola), 64, 98–100, 128 n. 22

Polydorus, mythological figure, son of Priamus, 232–3

Polymestor, Thracian king, 206–7, 232–3

Pompeius Saturninus *see* Saturninus, Pompeius

Pompey, 59

Pomponius Bassus, addressee of Pliny the Younger, 57

Poppaea Sabina, wife of emperor Nero, 246

Porus, Indian king, 93

Pragmatius, *illustris*, 38, 44 n. 6, 295–7, 299–300, 304–12, 319

Priamus, mythical king of Troy, 232–3

Priscus, Helvidius, praetor, 218

Priscus, (L. Iavolenus?), addressee of Pliny the Younger, 273

Priscus Valerianus *see* Valerianus, Priscus

Proba, Anicia Faltonia, addressee of Augustine, 136

Probinus, addressee of a letter in verse by Claudius Claudianus, 121

Probus, addressee of Symmachus, 134

Probus, brother of Magnus Felix, 87, 101, 128–9, 179, 285

Procne, mythological figure, 225

Proiectus, friend of Sidonius, 292, 309

*Propertius, poet, 316

Protadius, addressee of Symmachus, 45–6, 86

Pudens, addressee of Sidonius, 13, 15

Pygmalion, brother of Dido, 206–7, 232–3

Pythagoras, 10 n. 40, 88

Quadratus, addressee of Pliny the Younger, 135

*Quintilian, rhetor 28, 73, 150–1, 304–5, 317–18

Quintus Tullius Cicero, brother of Cicero, 182

Remigius, bishop of Reims, 300

Richomeres, addressee of Symmachus, 97, 134, 169, 180, 184

Romanus, Vergilius, author, 261

Romanus, Voconius, friend of Pliny the Younger, 273, 287

Romatius Firmus, *see* Firmus, Romatius

Rufinus, Flavius, *praefectus praetorio Orientis* (392–5), addressee of Symmachus, criticised by Claudian, 97, 102 n. 29, 157, 169, 184, 225, 284

Rufinus, Herennius, accuser of Apuleius, 185, 190–1, 211

*Rufinus of Aquileia, writer and translator, 137, 181, 262

Rufus, Calvisius, friend of Pliny the Younger, 287

*Ruricius, bishop of Limoges, 29, 261

Rusticus, Decimius, grandfather of Aquilinus, 272, 275–7, 278 n. 18, 280–1, 283–4, 294

Rusticus, son of Aquilinus, 272, 274, 280–1, 294

Rusticus Iulianus *see* Iulianus, Rusticus

Sabinianus, presbyter, 263

Sagittarius *see* Syagrius

*Sallust (C. Sallustius Crispus), 107–8, 116, 275, 298

Sallustius, addressee of Symmachus, 90

Sallustius, Flavius (cos. 363), 315

Sapaudus (rhetor), addressee of Sidonius, 15, 24, 38, 72, 163, 295–300, 304–7, 312, 314–16, 318–20

Sarmatians, 181

Saturn, 245 n. 18, 256–7, 266

Saturninus, Pompeius, author and friend of Pliny the Younger, 66, 261, 301 n. 26

Scythians, 182, 206–7, 227, 255 n. 74

Secundinus (poet), addressee of Sidonius, 4, 15, 24, 57, 141, 153, 242–4, 246–9, 253–60, 263–4, 268–71, 296

Secundus, Petronius, politician under Nerva, 219

*Seneca, 66, 91, 245

Senecio, Herennius, writer and stoic, 218

Seronatus, *uicarius VII prouinciarum* (469?/472?), 10, 16, 90, 192–3, 199, 220, 225, 227–8, 285

Servianus, Julius, addressee of Pliny the Younger, 95

Servius Tullius, sixth king of Rome (conventionally 578–535 BC), 236–7

Sigismund, king of Burgundians, 146–7

Simplicius, (probably a relative and) addressee of Sidonius, 25, 31, 44, 93–4, 97–102, 115, 123–33, 135, 137–41, 168–70, 179, 185, 188 n. 2, 239

Sinon, mythological figure, 206–7, 231–2

Socrates, 68, 87

Solon, Athenian statesman, 120–1, 145, 153 n. 49, 154–5, 164–5

Sphinx 206–7, 231

Spurinna, Vestricius, friend of Pliny the Younger, 143

*Statius, poet 57, 79, 308, 316

Stilicho, general, 225, 275–6

*Suetonius Tranquillus, biographer, 216, 234, 245, 287

Syagrius, addressee of Sidonius, 15, 24, 142–50, 152–67

INDEX NOMINUM ANTIQUORUM

Syagrius, Flavius (cos. 381), addressee of
  Symmachus, 111, 156, 317
Syagrius, Flavius Afranius (cos. 382), 142,
  144, 156–7
Sychaeus, mythical figure, husband of Dido,
  233
*Symmachus, Q. Aurelius (cos. 391), 7,
  12–16, 24 n. 74, 27–8, 45–51, 66–7, 96–8,
  102, 110–13, 129–30, 134–6, 138–41,
  169–70, 185–6, 193, 233–4, 243–4, 258,
  263, 265, 274, 282

*Tacitus, P. Cornelius, historian, 28, 189–90,
  216–19, 235–7, 241
Tanaquil, wife of Tarquinius Priscus, 180–1,
  201–2, 206–7, 236–7, 241
Tarquinius Priscus (Lucumo) fifth king of
  Rome (conventionally 616–579 BC), 201,
  206–8, 236, 239, 241
Tarquinius Superbus, seventh king of Rome
  (534–510 BC), 206–7, 235
Tetrarch see Chilperic I
Thalassus, friend of Symmachus, 186–7
Thales of Miletus, astronomer, 88
Thaumastus, cousin of Sidonius, 43–4,
  93–4, 99–100, 123–7, 168, 170, 173–4,
  176–7, 179–81, 188–9, 193, 204–5, 209,
  211–12
Thaumastus, uncle of Sidonius, 99–100, 126
Theoderic I, king of the Visigoths (418–51),
  226, 255
Theoderic II, king of the Visigoths (453–
  66/7), 3–4, 226, 228, 248, 254–5, 259
Theodosius I, emperor (379–95), 97, 112,
  136
Theodosius II, emperor (402–50), 183
Theophrastus, philosopher, 84
Therasia of Nola, wife of Paulinus, 181, 237
Thrasea Paetus see Paetus, Thrasea
Tiberius, emperor (14–37), 206–7, 219, 235,
  241, 245, 266
Timarchides, Verres' freedman, 208, 221
Titans, mythological figures, 231
Titianus, Celsinus, brother of Symmachus,
  111
Titinius Capito see Capito, Octavius Titinius
Titius Aristo see Aristo, Titius
Tonantius Ferreolus see Ferreolus, Tonantius

Trajan, emperor (98–117), 56, 58, 62, 235,
  297 n. 8
Tullius Hostilius, third king of Rome
  (conventionally 672–641 BC), 235
Tyrannopolitani, people of Lyon, 31–2, 234,
  242, 248, 253–4, 256–7, 264, 269–70

Ulysses (Odysseus), 95 n. 10, 114, 207, 232

Valentinian I, emperor (364–75), 172, 187,
  210, 263
Valentinian III, emperor (424–55), 277,
  280–1, 289
Valerianus, Priscus, *praefectus praetorio Galliarum*
  (before 456), 38, 295–7, 304–5, 309,
  311–12
Valerius Antias see Antias, Valerius
*Varro, Marcus Terentius, antiquarian, 57,
  70–3, 84, 238, 298, 306
Vatinius, Publius, tribune, 161, 225
*Vergil, poet, 76, 154–5, 159–60, 232, 255
Vergilius Romanus see Romanus, Vergilius
Verres, governor of Sicily, 157, 184, 190, 208,
  211, 221, 229, 235, 239–40
Vespasian, emperor (69–79), 218, 234
Vestricius Spurinna see Spurinna, Vestricius
Victor, Claudius Marius, rhetor, 316
Victorius, poet, 14, 17
Victorius (Marcellus?), rhetor, 39, 298, 304–5,
  316
Vincentius, *magister militum* (469), 99
Vindicius, letter bearer, 43, 45, 47, 53–5,
  59–60, 63
Visigoths, 2, 4–5, 9, 27, 94, 106, 124, 145–6,
  148, 158–9, 174–5, 178, 189 n. 7, 193,
  199, 203, 225, 254
Vitalis, layman of Carthage, addressee of
  Augustine, 56
Vitalis, possibly *prafectus annonae*, addressee of
  Symmachus, 139
Vitellius, emperor (69), 206–7, 216–18, 225,
  235–6, 286
*Vitruvius, 58, 77, 88
Voconius Romanus see Romanus, Voconius
Volusianus, bishop of Tours, 113

Zethus, mythological figure, 68, 88
Zeus (*see also* Jupiter), 164, 231

365